EXPERT SYSTEMS

Principles and Programming

PWS-KENT Series in Computer Science

Borse, FORTRAN 77 for Engineers

Borse, FORTRAN 77 and Numerical Methods
for Engineers

Brand, Problem Solving with Pascal

Brainerd, FORTRAN 77 Fundamentals and Style

Firebaugh, Artificial Intelligence

Giarratano and Riley, Expert Systems

Goldberg, PASCAL

Hennefeld, Using BASIC: An Introduction to
Computer Programming, Third Edition

Hennefeld, Using Microsoft and IBM BASIC:
An Introduction to Computer Programming

Hennefeld, Using Turbo PASCAL: 3.0, 4.0, and 5.0

Kapps and Stafford, Assembly Language
for the PDP-11: RT-RSX-UNIX, Second Edition

Korsh, Data Structures, Algorithms, and Program Style

Korsh and Garrett, Data Structures, Algorithms,
and Program Style Using C

Lane and Mooney, A Practical Approach to Operating Systems

Lane, Data Communications Software Design

Payne, Advanced Structured BASIC: File Processing
with the IBM-PC

Payne, Structured Basic for the IBM-PC
with Business Applications

Pollack, Structured FORTRAN 77 (HP)

Popkin, Advanced Structured COBOL, Second Edition

Popkin, Comprehensive Structured COBOL,
Third Edition

Popkin, Introductory Structured COBOL Programming,
Second Edition

Radford and Haigh, Turbo PASCAL for the IBM-PC

Riley, A Second Course in Turbo PASCAL

Riley, Data Abstraction and Structure:
An Introduction To CS II

Riley, Programming Using Turbo PASCAL

Riley, Using MODULA-2

Riley, Using PASCAL: An Introduction to CS I

Rojiani, Programming in BASIC

Rood, Logic and Structured Design for Computer Programmers

Runnion, Structured Programming in Assembly Language

Skvarcius, Problem Solving Using PASCAL:
Algorithm Development and Programming Concepts

Smith, Design and Analysis of Algorithms

Weinman, FORTRAN for Scientists and Engineers

Weinman, VAX FORTRAN

Worthington, C Programming

EXPERT SYSTEMS

Principles and Programming

Joseph Giarratano, Ph.D

University of Houston - Clear Lake

Gary Riley

NASA - Johnson Space Center

PWS-KENT Publishing Company
Boston

PWS-KENT
Publishing Company

20 Park Plaza
Boston, Massachusetts 02116

PWS-KENT Publishing Company is a division of Wadsworth, Inc.

Library of Congress Cataloging-in-Publication Data

Giarratano, Joseph C.
    Expert systems : principles and programming / Joseph C.
  Giarratano, Gary Riley.
        p.   cm.
    Includes index.
    ISBN 0-87835-335-6
    1. Expert systems (Computer science) 2. CLIPS (Computer program
  language) 3. Rule-based programming. I. Riley, Gary, 1962-
  II. Title.
  QA76.76.E95G53 1989
  006.3--dc19   88-23393
                                                             CIP

Printed in the United States of America
10 9 8 7 6 5

DEDICATION

To my family Jane, Jenna, Melissa, and Anthony (JCG).

To my parents (GDR).

CONTENTS

PREFACE

Expert systems have experienced tremendous growth and popularity since their commercial introduction in the early 1980's. Today, expert systems are used in business, science, engineering, manufacturing, and many other fields.

This book is meant to educate students about expert systems theory and programming. The material is written at the upper–division / graduate level suitable for majors in computer science, computer information systems, engineering, and other fields who are interested in expert systems. New terminology is shown in boldface and immediately explained. Numerous examples and references help clarify the meaning of the text and provide guidance for supplementary reading.

Expert Systems: Principles and Programming is divided into two parts: theory in Chapters 1–6, and programming in expert systems in Chapters 7–12. The first part comprises the theory behind expert systems and how expert systems fits into the scope of computer science.

While a previous course in Artificial Intelligence (AI) is helpful, this book provides a self–contained introduction to AI topics that are appropriate for expert systems. The first part of the book covers the logic, probability, data structures, AI, and other topics that form the theory of expert systems.

We have tried to explain the theory behind expert systems so that a student may make an informed decision regarding the appropriate use of expert system technology. The important point we emphasize is that like any other tool, expert systems have advantages and disadvantages. The theory also explains how expert systems relate to other programming methods such as conventional programming. Another reason for discussing theory is that the student can read current research papers in expert systems. Because expert systems draw from so many diverse fields, it is difficult for a beginner to just start reading papers with comprehension.

The second part of this book is an introduction to the CLIPS expert system tool. This part is a practical introduction to expert system programming that serves to reinforce and clarify the theoretical concepts developed in the first part. Students learn the practical problems associated with expert system development using CLIPS, a modern, powerful expert system tool. A complete executable copy of CLIPS is included in this book.

CLIPS was developed by NASA at the Artificial Intelligence Section of the Johnson Space Center. Today, CLIPS is used for real–world projects in government, business, and industry. It is available on virtually every type of computer including IBM PC and clones, VAX, HP, Sun, Macintosh, and Cray. Code developed in CLIPS runs very fast and is very portable. CLIPS is available from COSMIC for a nominal fee which includes the entire 25K lines of C source code in which CLIPS is written. As with the theory part of the book, the programming part can be understood by students with some programing experience in a high-level language.

Some expert systems courses have a term project associated with them. A project is an excellent way to develop skills in expert systems. Students usually complete small expert systems of 50–150 rules in a semester project of their choice. A few projects that have been done by students using CLIPS include automobile diagnosis, taxi scheduling, personnel scheduling, computer network management, weather forecasting, stock market prediction, consumer buying advice, and diet advice.

The suggested plan for a one–semester course is as follows.

1) Cover Chapter 1 to provide a quick introduction to expert systems. In particular, assign Problems 1, 2, and 3.

2) Cover Chapters 7–10 to introduce the syntax of CLIPS. It is helpful for students to recode Problem 2 of Chapter 1 to contrast the expert system approach with the language they originally used in Chapter 1. This contrast is very useful in pointing out the differences between a rule–based language such as CLIPS, and LISP, PROLOG, or whatever the original language used for Problem 2.

3) Chapters 11 and 12 may be covered for a stronger programming emphasis in the course. Chapter 11 on efficiency in rule-based languages is not essential to an introductory course. It may be discussed if there is interest in building large expert systems or where efficiency is important. Chapter 12 presents a collection of topics that illustrates interesting problems solved using CLIPS.

Alternatively, after Chapter 10, the instructor may return to the theory section. If students have a strong background in logic and PROLOG, most of Chapters 2 and 3 may be skipped. Students who have had a LISP–based introductory AI course or none at all will benefit from Chapters 2 and 3 if a strong emphasis on logic and the fundamental theory of expert systems is desired. If students have a strong background in probability and statistics, the material in Chapter 4 up to Section 4.11 can be skipped.

4) Sections 4.11 to the end of Chapter 4, and Chapter 5 discusses advanced topics in expert systems concerning methods of dealing with uncertainty. These topics include probabilistic inference, Certainty Factors, Dempster–Shafer theory, and fuzzy theory. Students will gain an understanding of these methods in sufficient detail so that they can read current papers in the field and start doing research, if desired.

5) Chapter 6 discusses the software engineering of expert systems, and is meant for those students planning to work on large expert systems. It is not necessary to discuss this chapter before assigning term projects, In fact, it would be best to cover this chapter last so that the student can appreciate all the factors that go into building a quality expert system.

A manual with solutions to the odd numbered problems, and another manual of the tables and figures of the books suitable for viewgraphs is available from the publisher.

ACKNOWLEDGEMENTS

In writing this book, a number of people have made very helpful comments. These include: Chris Culbert, Dan Bochsler, Tim Dawn, Ted Leibfried, Jack Aldridge, Bob Lea, Chet Lund, Andre de Korvin, Arlan DeKock, Marjorie Schlaikjer, and the anonymous reviewers. We also appreciate the excellent cooperation and facilities of the Desktop Publishing Center in the AV Center at the University of Houston–Clear Lake.

FOREWORD

When AI was born in the mid-fifties, its primary concerns were centered on game playing, planning, and problem solving. In the environment of that era, it would have been very difficult to predict that three decades later the most important application areas of AI would be centered on knowledge engineering and, more particularly, on expert systems.

Expert systems as we know them today have their roots in the pioneering work of Feigenbaum, Lederberg, Shortliffe, and Buchanan at Stanford University in the late sixties and early seventies. What is remarkable about this work—and MYCIN in particular—is that it still serves as a paradigm for much of the current activity in expert and, more generally, knowledge-based systems.

During the past few years, demonstrable successes of expert systems in specialized application areas such as medical diagnosis and computer system configuration have led to an explosion of interest in a much wider variety of applications ranging from battle plan management and optimal routing to fault diagnosis, optimal portfolio selection, and the assessment of credit worthiness of loan applicants.

The mushrooming of applications has generated two distinct needs: (a) the development of a better understanding of how to deal with the key problems of knowledge representation, inference, and uncertainty management; and (b) the development of expert system shells and/or programming languages which minimize the effort needed for constructing a knowledge representation system and an inference engine for a particular application.

The book written by Joseph Giarratano and Gary Riley is the only book at this juncture which addresses both of these needs. Its first part deals authoritatively with the basic issues underlying the representation of knowledge, logical inference, and the management of uncertainty. In this part, particularly worthy of note are the chapters on reasoning under uncertainty which present a wealth of information on the basic approaches which are in use today. Included in these chapters are insightful descriptions of the techniques employing classical probability theory, certainty factors *a la* MYCIN and PROSPECTOR, the Dempster-Shafer theory, and fuzzy logic. No other text offers such a wide coverage.

The second part presents a detailed account of CLIPS, an expert system programming language written in C which is intended to serve as a versatile tool for the development and implementation of expert systems. CLIPS is related to OPS5 and ART, and has a capability for inference under uncertainty.

In combination, the two parts provide an up-to-date and comprehensive account of the principles of expert systems and their practice. To write a book of this kind is clearly a difficult task and the reader has to be prepared to invest a substantial amount of effort to assimilate the wealth of information presented by the authors. As one of the most sophisticated and most important areas of AI, the theory and practice of expert systems contains many complex and as yet not fully understood problems. Joseph Giarratano and Gary Riley deserve the thanks of all of us for undertaking a difficult task and making an important contribution to a better understanding of the fundamentals of expert systems and their application to real-world problems.

Lotfi A. Zadeh
Berkeley, CA.
January, 1989

Automate, emigrate, or evaporate are the options that face our country today. The best choice is to automate in order to be competitive with the rest of the world in manufacturing and to accomplish our goals in space exploration. The key to automation and our future lies in the effective application of the computer science field called artificial intelligence (AI). AI, which can be thought of as the emulation of human intelligence through computer software and hardware, permits us to put many years of thought into each decision. For example, AI technology has already reduced the time to solve problems requiring extensive mathematical analysis from years to minutes. The transition of AI technology from the research lab to everyday use has been made possible by tremendous advances in computer hardware technology which have produced economical, yet powerful, processors and high density memory. While such hardware is necessary, it is not sufficient. The evolution of powerful and productive AI software tools from the research world to the scientific, engineering, and business environments has been slow and frustrating until recently.

To solve the problems of moving AI technology from the research world to practical applications, the Artificial Intelligence Section at NASA/Johnson Space Center developed an expert system tool written in, and fully integrated with, the "C" language: the C Language Integrated Production System (CLIPS). CLIPS was designed specifically to provide high portability, low cost, and easy integration with existing or conventional software systems.

CLIPS is also designed to interface with other languages such as FORTRAN and Ada. The Ada compatibility issues have been addressed in two ways. First, the current release version of CLIPS, although written entirely in C, can be used as a black-box in most Ada environments which support full multilanguage integration. An Ada interface package has been written for the DEC VMS Ada compiler and successfully demonstrated. Second, an Ada version of CLIPS is currently under development. The intent is to make the Ada CLIPS 100% syntax compatible with the C version of CLIPS so that previously developed systems can be easily ported to the Ada version. This product is scheduled for release in the summer of 1989.

The Congress has charged NASA with the task of stimulating the widest possible use of its new technology in the national interest. NASA seeks to meet that responsibility through its Technology Utilization Program, whose aim is to broaden and accelerate the technology transfer process. This will repay with interest to the nation a substantial dividend on the national investment in aerospace research in the form of new products, new businesses, and new jobs. The program is designed to serve as a channel linking NASA technology with those who might be able to apply it productively.

NASA's mechanism for making software technology available to the private sector is the Computer Management Software and Information Center (COSMIC™). Located at the University of Georgia, COSMIC gets a continual flow of government developed software and identifies those programs that can be adapted to secondary usage. The

Center's library contains more than 1,400 programs for such tasks as structural analysis, design of fluid systems, electronic circuit design, chemical analyses, determination of building energy requirements, and a variety of other functions including artificial intelligence. COSMIC customers can purchase a program for a fraction of its original cost and get a return that is many times the investment.

The Artificial Intelligence Section at the Johnson Space Center is very pleased to participate in this process by placing the CLIPS language in COSMIC for use by the nation in enhancing productivity, competitiveness, and education. As has been the case since time immemorial, "necessity is the mother of invention" produced the CLIPS language. As this book documents, CLIPS provides a rich and productive development environment for rule-based systems.

The authors of this book have worked with CLIPS since its beginning. Gary Riley has done most of the programming of CLIPS and Joseph Giarratano wrote the official CLIPS tutorial distributed with CLIPS by COSMIC. Their knowledge and experience is amply demonstrated in this book. In addition, the CLIPS development team of NASA received the prestigious National Aeronautics and Space Act Award for Scientific and Technical Contributions. These awards by the Administrator of NASA are for scientific and technical contributions which have significant value in the conduct of aeronautical and space activities.

Although CLIPS is but one of the first steps, it is an important step in the evolution of a technology that may be the most important advance in the history of mankind. CLIPS and other AI tools will help restore this nation's competitiveness in the international arena.

Robert T. (Bob) Savely
Head, Artificial Intelligence Section
Lyndon B. Johnson Space Center
National Aeronautics and Space Administration

EXPERT SYSTEMS

Principles and Programming

CHAPTER 1 INTRODUCTION TO EXPERT SYSTEMS

1.1 INTRODUCTION

This chapter is a broad introduction to expert systems. The fundamental principles of expert systems are introduced. The advantages and disadvantages of expert systems are discussed and the appropriate areas of application for expert systems are described. The relationship of expert systems to other methods of programming are discussed.

1.2 WHAT IS AN EXPERT SYSTEM

The first step in solving any problem is defining the problem area or **domain** to be solved. This consideration is just as true in artificial intelligence (AI) as in conventional programming. However, because of the mystique formerly associated with AI, there is a lingering tendency to still believe the old adage "It's an AI problem if it hasn't been solved yet". This type of mind-set may have been popular in the 1970's when AI was entirely in a research stage. However, today there are many real-world problems that are being solved by AI and many commercial applications of AI.

Although general solutions to classic AI problems such as natural language translation, speech understanding, and vision have not been found, restricting the problem domain may still produce a useful solution. For example, it is not difficult to build simple natural language systems if the input is restricted to sentences of the form: noun, verb, and object. Currently, systems of this type work very well in providing a user-friendly interface to many software products such as database systems and spreadsheets. In fact, the parsers associated with popular computer text-adventure games today exhibit an amazing degree of ability in understanding natural language.

As Figure 1-1 shows, AI has many areas of interest. The area of **expert systems** is a very successful approximate solution to the classic AI problem of programming intelligence. Professor Edward Feigenbaum of Stanford University, an early pioneer of expert systems technology, has defined an expert system as "... an intelligent computer program that uses knowledge and inference procedures to solve problems that are difficult enough to require significant human expertise for their solution." (Feigenbaum 82). That is, an expert system is a computer system which **emulates** the decision-making ability of a human expert. The term emulate means that the expert system is intended to act in all respects like a human expert. An emulation is much stronger than a simulation which is only required to act like the real thing in some respects.

Although a general purpose problem solver still eludes us, expert systems function very well in their restricted domains. As proof of their success, you need only observe the many applications of expert systems today in business, medicine, science, and engineering as well as all the books, journals, conferences and products devoted to expert systems.

Artificial Intelligence

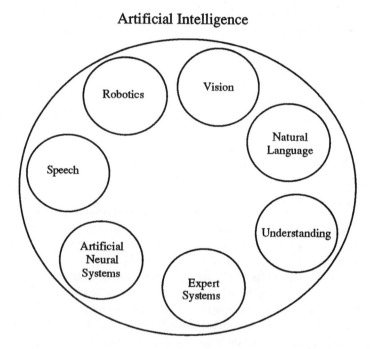

Figure 1-1
Some Areas of Artificial Intelligence

Expert systems is a branch of AI that makes extensive use of specialized knowledge to solve problems at the level of a human **expert**. An expert is a person who has **expertise** in a certain area. That is, the expert has knowledge or special skills that are not known or available to most people. An expert can solve problems that most people cannot solve at all or solve them much more efficiently (but not as cheaply). When expert systems were first developed in the 1970's, they contained expert knowledge exclusively. However, the term expert system is often applied today to any system which uses expert system technology. This expert system technology may include special expert system languages, programs, and hardware designed to aid in the development and execution of expert systems.

The knowledge in expert systems may be either expertise, or knowledge which is generally available from books, magazines, and knowledgeable persons. The terms expert system, **knowledge-based system** or **knowledge-based expert system** are often used synonymously. Most people use expert system simply because it's shorter, even though there may be no expertise in their expert system, only general knowledge.

Figure 1-2 illustrates the basic concept of a knowledge-based expert system. The user supplies facts or other information to the expert system and receives expert advice or **expertise** in response. Internally, the expert system consists of two main components. The knowledge-base contains the knowledge with which the **inference engine** draws conclusions. These conclusions are the expert system's responses to the user's queries for expertise.

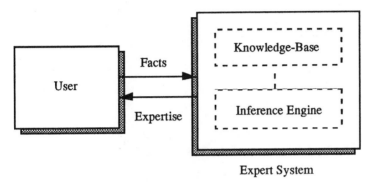

Figure 1-2
Basic Concept of an Expert System Function

Useful knowledge-based systems also have been designed to act as an intelligent assistant to a human expert. These intelligent assistants are designed with expert systems technology because of the development advantages. As more knowledge is added to the intelligent assistant, it acts more like an expert. Developing an intelligent assistant may be a useful milestone in producing a complete expert system. In addition, it may free up more of the expert's time by speeding up the solution of problems.

An expert's knowledge is specific to one **problem domain** as opposed to knowledge about general problem-solving techniques. A problem domain is the special problem area such as medicine, finance, science or engineering and so forth that an expert can solve problems in very well. Expert systems, like human experts, are generally designed to be experts in one problem domain. For example, you would not normally expect a chess expert to have expert knowledge about medicine. Expertise in one problem domain does not automatically carry over to another.

The expert's knowledge about solving specific problems is called the **knowledge domain** of the expert. For example, a medical expert system designed to diagnose infectious diseases will have a great deal of knowledge about certain symptoms caused by infectious diseases. In this case the knowledge domain is medicine and consists of knowledge about diseases, symptoms, and treatments. Figure 1-3 illustrates the relationship between the problem and knowledge domain. Notice that this knowledge domain is entirely included within the problem domain. The portion outside the knowledge domain symbolizes an area in which there is not knowledge about all the problems.

One expert system usually does not have knowledge about other branches of medicine such as surgery or pediatrics. Although its knowledge of infectious disease is equivalent to a human expert, the expert system would not know anything about other knowledge domains unless it was programmed with that domain knowledge.

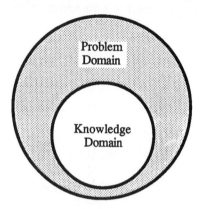

Figure 1-3
A Possible Problem and Knowledge Domain Relationship

In the knowledge domain that it knows about, the expert system reasons or makes inferences in the same way that a human expert would infer the solution of a problem. That is, given some facts, a conclusion that follows is inferred. For example, if your spouse hasn't spoken to you in a month, you may infer that he or she had nothing worthwhile to say. However, this is only one of several possible inferences.

As with any new technology, we still have a lot to learn about expert systems. Table 1-1 summarizes the differing views of the participants in a technology. In this table, the technologist may be an engineer or software designer and the technology may be hardware or software. In solving any problem, these are questions that need to be answered or the technology will not be successfully used. Like any other tool, expert systems have appropriate and inappropriate applications. As our experience with expert systems grows, we will discover what these applications are.

Person	Question
Manager	What can I use it for?
Technologist	How can I best implement it?
Researcher	How can I extend it?
Consumer	How will it help me? Is it worth the trouble and expense? How reliable is it?

Table 1-1
Differing Views of Technology

1.3 ADVANTAGES OF EXPERT SYSTEMS

Expert systems have a number of attractive features.

- *Increased Availability.* Expertise is available on any suitable computer hardware. In a very real sense, an expert system is the mass production of expertise.
- *Reduced cost.* The cost of providing expertise per user is greatly lowered.
- *Reduced Danger.* Expert systems can be used in environments that might be hazardous for a human.
- *Permanence.* The expertise is permanent. Unlike human experts who may retire, quit or die, the expert system's knowledge will last indefinitely.
- *Multiple expertise.* The knowledge of multiple experts can be made available to work simultaneously and continuously on a problem at any time of day or night. The level of expertise combined from several experts may exceed that of a single human expert (Harmon 85).
- *Increased reliability.* Expert systems increase confidence that the correct decision was made by providing a second opinion to a human expert or break a tie in case of disagreements by multiple human experts. Of course, this method probably won't work if the expert system was programmed by one of the experts. The expert system should always agree with the expert, unless a mistake was made by the expert. However, this may happen if the human expert is tired or under stress. *or the expert system has a bug*
- *Explanation.* The expert system can explicitly explain in detail the reasoning that led to a conclusion. A human may be too tired, unwilling or unable to do this all the time. This increases the confidence that the correct decision is made.
- *Fast response.* Fast or real-time response may be necessary for some applications. Depending on the software and hardware used, an expert system may respond faster and be more available than a human expert. Some emergency situations may require responses faster than a human and so a real-time expert system is a good choice (Hugh 88) (Ennis 86).
- *Steady, unemotional, and complete response at all times*. This may be very important in real-time and emergency situations when a human expert may not operate at peak efficiency because of stress or fatigue.
- *Intelligent tutor.* The expert system may act as an intelligent tutor by letting the student run sample programs and explaining the system's reasoning.
- *Intelligent Database.* Expert systems can be used to access a database in an intelligent manner (Kerschberg 86) (Schur 88).

The process of developing an expert system has an indirect benefit also since the knowledge of human experts must be put into an explicit form for entering in the computer. Because the knowledge is then explicitly known instead of being implicit in the expert's mind, it can be examined for correctness, consistency and completeness. The knowledge may then have to be adjusted or re-examined which improves the quality of the knowledge.

1.4   GENERAL CONCEPTS OF EXPERT SYSTEMS

The knowledge of an expert system may be represented in a number of ways. One common method of representing knowledge is in the form of IF THEN type **rules**, such as

```
IF the light is red THEN stop
```

Although this is a trivial example, many significant expert systems have been built by expressing the knowledge of experts in rules. In fact, the knowledge-based approach to developing expert systems has completely supplanted the early AI approach of the 1950's and 1960's which tried to use sophisticated reasoning techniques with no reliance on knowledge.

Today, a wide range of knowledge-based expert systems have been built. Large systems containing thousands of rules, such as the XCON/R1 system of Digital Equipment Corporation, know much more than any single human expert on how to configure computer systems (McDermott 84). Many small systems for specialized tasks have also been constructed with several hundred rules. These small systems may not operate at the level of an expert but are designed to take advantage of expert systems technology to perform knowledge-intensive tasks. For these small systems, the knowledge may be in books, journals, or other publicly available documentation.

In contrast, a classic expert system embodies unwritten knowledge that must be extracted from an expert by extensive interviews with a **knowledge engineer** over a long period of time. The process of building an expert system is called **knowledge engineering** and is done by a knowledge engineer (Michie 73). Knowledge engineering refers to the acquisition of knowledge from a human expert or other source and its coding in the expert system.

The general stages in the development of an expert system are illustrated in Figure 1-4. The knowledge engineer first establishes a dialog with the human expert in order to elicit the expert's knowledge. This stage is analogous to a system designer in conventional programming discussing the system requirements with a client for whom the program will be constructed. The knowledge engineer then codes the knowledge explicitly in the knowledge-base. The expert then evaluates the expert system and gives a critique to the knowledge engineer. This process iterates until the system's performance is judged to be satisfactory by the expert.

The expression **knowledge-based system** is a better term for the application of knowledge-based technology since it may be used for the creation of either expert systems or knowledge-based systems. However, like the term artificial intelligence, it is common practice today to use the term expert systems when referring to both expert systems and knowledge-based systems, even when the knowledge is not at the level of a human expert.

Expert systems are generally designed very differently from conventional programs because the problems usually have no algorithmic solution and rely on inferences to achieve a reasonable solution. Note that a reasonable solution is about the best we can expect if no algorithm is available to help us achieve the optimum solution. Since the expert system relies on inference, it must be able to explain its reasoning so that its reasoning can be checked. An **explanation facility** is an integral part of sophisticated expert systems. In fact, elaborate explanation facilities may be designed to allow the user to explore multiple lines of "What if..." type questions, called **hypothetical reasoning** and even translate natural language into rules.

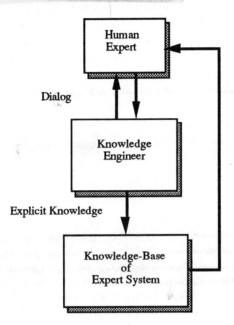

Figure 1-4
Development of an Expert System

Some expert systems even allow the system to learn rules by example, through **rule induction**, in which the system creates rules from tables of data. Formalizing the knowledge of experts into rules is not simple, especially when the expert's knowledge has never been systematically explored. There may be inconsistencies, ambiguities, duplications or other problems with the expert's knowledge that are not apparent until attempts are made to formally represent the knowledge in an expert system.

Human experts also know the extent of their knowledge and qualify their advice as the problem reaches their **limits of ignorance**. A human expert also knows when to "break the rules". Unless expert systems are explicitly designed to deal with uncertainty, they will make recommendations with the same confidence even if the data they are dealing with is inaccurate or incomplete. An expert systems advice, like a human expert's, should degrade gracefully at the boundaries of ignorance instead of abruptly.

A practical limitation of many expert systems today is lack of **causal knowledge**. That is, the expert systems do not really have an understanding of the underlying causes and effects in a system. It is much easier to program expert systems with **shallow knowledge** based on empirical and heuristic knowledge than **deep knowledge** based on the basic structure, function, and behavior of objects. For example, it is much easier to program an expert system to prescribe an aspirin for a person's headache than program all the underlying biochemical, physiological, anatomical and neurological knowledge about the human body. The programming of a causal model of the human body would be an enormous task and even if successful, the response time of the system would probably be extremely slow because of all the information that the system would have to process.

One type of shallow knowledge is **heuristic knowledge**, where the term heuristic comes from the Greek and means to discover. Heuristics are not guaranteed to succeed in the same way that an algorithm is a guaranteed solution to a problem. Instead, heuristics are rules of thumb or empirical knowledge gained from experience which may aid in the solution but are not guaranteed to work. However, in many fields such as medicine and engineering, heuristics play an essential role in some types of problem solving. Even if an exact solution is known, it may be impractical to use because of cost or time constraints. Heuristics can provide valuable shortcuts that can reduce time and cost.

Another problem with expert systems today is that their expertise is limited to the knowledge domain that the systems know about. Typical expert systems cannot generalize their knowledge by using **analogy** to reason about new situations that the way people can. Although rule induction helps, only limited types of knowledge can be put into an expert system this way. The customary way of building an expert system by having the knowledge engineer repeat the cycle of interviewing the expert, constructing a prototype, testing, interviewing, and so on is a very time consuming and labor intensive task. In fact, this problem of transferring human knowledge into an expert system is so major that it is called the **knowledge acquisition bottleneck**. This is a descriptive term because the knowledge acquisition bottleneck constricts the building of an expert system like an ordinary bottleneck constricts fluid flow into a bottle.

In spite of their present limitations, expert systems have been very successful in dealing with real-world problems that conventional programming methodologies have been unable to solve, especially those dealing with uncertain or incomplete information. The important point is to be aware of the advantages and limitations of this new technology so that it can be appropriately utilized.

1.5 CHARACTERISTICS OF AN EXPERT SYSTEM

An expert system is usually designed to have the following general characteristics.

- *High performance.* The system must be capable of responding at a level of competency equal to or better than an expert in the field. That is, the quality of the advice given by the system must be very high.
- *Adequate response time.* The system must also perform in a reasonable time, comparable to or better than the time required by an expert to reach a decision. An expert system that takes a year to reach a decision compared to an expert's time of one hour would not be too useful. The **time constraints** placed on the performance of an expert system may be especially severe in the case of real-time systems, when a response must be made within a certain time interval.
- *Good reliability.* The expert system must be reliable and not prone to crashes or else it will not be used.
- *Understandable.* The system should be able to explain the steps of its reasoning while executing so that it is understandable. Rather than being just a "black box" that produces a miraculous answer, the system should have an explanation capability in the same way that human experts can explain their reasoning. This feature is very important for several reasons.

One reason is that human life and property may depend on the answers of the expert system. Because of the great potential for harm, an expert system must be able to justify its conclusions in the same way a human expert can explain why a certain conclusion was reached. Thus, an explanation facility provides an understandable check of the reasoning for humans.

A second reason for having an explanation facility occurs in the development phase of an expert system to confirm that the knowledge has been correctly acquired and is being correctly used by the system. This is very important in debugging since the knowledge may be incorrectly entered due to typos or be incorrect due to misunderstandings between the knowledge engineer and the expert. A good explanation facility allows the expert and knowledge engineer to verify the correctness of the knowledge. Also, because of the way that typical expert systems are constructed, it is very difficult to read a significant program listing and understand its operation.

An additional source of error may be unforeseen interactions in the expert system, which may be detected by running test cases with known reasoning that the system should follow. As we will discuss in more detail later, multiple rules may apply to a given situation about which the system is reasoning. The flow of execution is not sequential in an expert system so that you cannot just read its code line by line and understand how the system operates. That is, the order in which rules have been entered in the system is not necessarily the order in which they will be executed. The expert system acts much like a parallel program in which the rules are independent knowledge processors.

- *Flexibility.* Because of the large amount of knowledge that an expert system may have, it is important to have an efficient mechanism for adding, changing, and deleting knowledge. One reason for the popularity of rule-based systems is the efficient and modular storage capability of rules.

Depending on the system, an explanation facility may be simple or elaborate. A simple explanation facility in a rule-based system may simply list all the facts that made the latest rule execute. More elaborate systems may do the following.

- *List all the reasons for and against a particular hypothesis.* A hypothesis is a goal which is to be proved such as "The patient has a tetanus infection" in a medical diagnostic expert system. In a real problem, there may be multiple hypotheses, just as a patient may have several diseases at once. A hypothesis can also be viewed as a fact whose truth is in doubt and must be proved.
- *List all the hypotheses that may explain the observed evidence.*
- *Explain all the consequences of a hypothesis.* For example, assuming that the patient does have tetanus, there should also be evidence of fever as the infection runs its course. If this symptom is then observed, it adds credibility that the hypothesis is true. If the symptom is not observed, it reduces the credibility of the hypothesis.
- *Give a **prognosis** or prediction of what will occur if the hypothesis is true.*
- *Justify the questions that the program asks of the user for further information.* These questions may be used to direct the line of reasoning to likely diagnostic paths. In most real problems, it is too expensive or take too long to explore all possibilities, and some way must be provided to guide the search for the correct solution. For example, consider the cost, time and effect of administering all possible medical tests to a patient complaining of a sore throat.
- *Justify the knowledge of the program.* For example, if the program claims that the hypothesis "The patient has a tetanus infection" is true, the user could ask for an explanation. The program might justify this conclusion on the basis of a rule which says that if the patient has a positive blood test for tetanus, the patient has tetanus. Now the user could ask the program to justify this rule. The program could respond by stating that a positive blood test for a disease is proof of the disease.

In this case, the program is actually quoting a **metarule**, which is knowledge about rules. The prefix meta means above or beyond. Some programs such as Meta-DENDRAL have been explicitly created to infer new rules (Buchanan 78). A hypothesis is justified by knowledge and the knowledge is justified by a **warrant** that it is correct. A warrant is essentially a meta-explanation that explains the expert systems explanation of its reasoning.

Knowledge can easily grow **incrementally** in a rule-based system. That is, the knowledge base can grow little by little as rules are added so that the performance and correctness of the system can be continually checked. If the rules are properly designed, the interactions between rules will be minimized or eliminated to protect against unforeseen effects. The incremental growth of knowledge facilitates **rapid prototyping** so that the knowledge engineer can quickly show the expert a working prototype of the expert system. This is an important feature because it maintains the expert's and management's interest in the project. Rapid prototyping also quickly exposes any gaps, inconsistencies or errors in the expert's knowledge or the system so that corrections can immediately be made.

1.6 THE DEVELOPMENT OF EXPERT SYSTEMS TECHNOLOGY

AI has many branches concerned with speech, vision, robotics, natural language understanding, and learning and expert systems. The roots of expert systems lie in many disciplines. In particular, one of the major roots of expert systems is the area of human information processing, called **cognitive science**. Cognition is the study of how humans process information. In other words, cognition is the study of how people think, especially when solving problems.

The study of cognition is very important if we want to make computers emulate human experts. Often, experts can't explain how they solve problems—the solution just comes to them. If the expert can't explain how a problem is solved, it's not possible to encode the knowledge in an expert system based on explicit knowledge. In this case, the only possibility is programs that learn by themselves to emulate the expert. These are programs based on induction and artificial neural systems, to be discussed later.

Human Problem-Solving and Productions

The development of expert systems technology draws on a wide background. Table 1-2 is a brief summary of some important developments that have converged in modern expert systems. Whenever possible, the starting dates of projects are used. Many projects extend over many years. These developments are covered in more detail in this chapter and others. The best single reference for all the early systems is the three-volume *Handbook of Artificial Intelligence* (Feigenbaum 81).

In the late 1950's and 1960's, a number of programs were written with the goal of general problem solving. The most famous of these was the **General Problem Solver** created by Newell and Simon and described in a series of papers culminating in their monumental 920-page work on cognition, *Human Problem Solving* (Newell 72).

One of the most significant results demonstrated by Newell and Simon was that much of human problem solving or **cognition** could be expressed by IF THEN type **production rules**. For example, IF it looks like it's going to rain THEN carry an umbrella, or IF your spouse is in a bad mood THEN don't appear happy. A rule corresponds to a small, modular collection of knowledge called a **chunk**. The chunks are organized in a loose arrangement with links to related chunks of knowledge. One theory is that all human memory is organized in chunks. An example of a rule representing a chunk of knowledge is

Year	Events
1943	Post production rules; McCulloch and Pitts Neuron Model
1954	Markov Algorithm for controlling rule execution
1956	Dartmouth Conference; Logic Theorist; Heuristic Search; "AI" term coined
1957	Perceptron invented by Rosenblatt; GPS (General Problem Solver) started (Newell, Shaw and Simon)
1958	LISP AI language (McCarthy)
1962	Rosenblatt's *Principles of Neurodynamics* on Perceptions
1965	Resolution Method of automatic theorem proving (Robinson) Fuzzy Logic for reasoning about fuzzy objects (Zadeh) Work begun on DENDRAL, the first expert system (Feigenbaum, Buchanan, et.al.)
1968	Semantic nets, associative memory model (Quillian)
1969	MACSYMA math expert system (Martin and Moses)
1970	Work begins on PROLOG (Colmerauer, Roussell, *et. al.*)
1971	HEARSAY I for speech recognition *Human Problem Solving* popularizes rules (Newell and Simon)
1973	MYCIN expert system for medical diagnosis(Shortliffe, *et. al.*) leading to GUIDON, intelligent tutoring (Clancey) and TEIRESIAS, explanation facility concept (Davis) and EMYCIN, first shell (Van Melle, Shortliffe and Buchanan) HEARSAY II, blackboard model of multiple cooperating experts
1975	Frames, knowledge representation (Minsky)
1976	AM (Artificial Mathematician) creative discovery of math concepts (Lenat) Dempster-Shafer Theory of Evidence for reasoning under uncertainty Work begun on PROSPECTOR expert system for mineral exploration (Duda, Hart, *et. al.*)
1977	OPS expert system shell (Forgy), used in XCON/R1
1978	Work started on XCON/R1 (McDermott, DEC) to configure DEC computer systems Meta-DENDRAL, metarules and rule induction (Buchanan)
1979	Rete Algorithm for fast pattern matching (Forgy) Commercialization of AI begins Inference Corp. formed (releases ART expert system tool in 1985)
1980	Symbolics, LMI founded to manufacture LISP machines
1982	SMP math expert system; Hopfield Neural Net; Japanese Fifth Generation Project to develop intelligent computers
1983	KEE expert system tool (IntelliCorp)
1985	CLIPS expert system tool (NASA)

Table 1-2
Some Important Events in the History of Expert Systems

```
IF the car doesn't run and
   the fuel gauge reads empty
THEN fill the gas tank
```

Newell and Simon popularized the use of rules to represent human knowledge and showed how reasoning could be done with rules. Cognitive psychologists have used rules as a model to explain human information processing. The basic idea is that sensory input provides stimuli to the brain. The stimuli trigger the appropriate rules of **long-term memory** which produce the appropriate response. Long-term memory is where our knowledge is stored. For example, we all have rules such as

```
IF there is flame THEN there is a fire
IF there is smoke THEN there may be a fire
IF there is a siren THEN there may be a fire
```

Notice that the last two rules are not expressed with complete certainty. The fire may be out, but there may still be smoke in the air. Likewise, a siren does not prove that there is a fire since it may be a false alarm. The stimuli of seeing flames, smelling smoke, and hearing a siren will trigger these and similar types of rules.

Long-term memory consists of many rules having the simple IF THEN structure. In fact, a Grand Master chess expert may know 50,000 or more chunks of knowledge about chess patterns. In contrast to the long-term memory, the **short-term memory** is used for the temporary storage of knowledge during problem solving. Although long-term memory can hold hundreds of thousands or more chunks, the capacity of working memory is surprisingly small—4 to 7 chunks. As a simple example of this, try visualizing some numbers in your mind. Most people can only see 4 to 7 numbers at once. Of course we can memorize many more than 4 to 7 numbers. However, those numbers are kept in long-term memory.

One theory proposes that short-term memory represents the number of chunks that simultaneously can be active and considers human problem-solving as a spreading of these activated chunks in the mind. Eventually, a chunk may be activated with such intensity that a conscious thought is generated and you say to yourself, "Hmm.. something's burning."

The other element necessary for human-problem solving is a **cognitive processor.** The cognitive processor tries to find the rules that will be **activated** by the appropriate stimuli. Not just any rule will do. For example, you wouldn't want to fill your gas tank every time you heard a siren. Only a rule which matched the stimuli would be activated. If there are multiple rules that are activated at once, the cognitive processor must perform a conflict resolution to decide which rule has highest priority. The rule with highest priority will be executed. for example, if both of the following rules are activated

```
IF there is a fire THEN leave
IF my clothes are burning THEN put out the fire
```

then the actions of one rule will be executed before the other. The **inference engine** of modern expert systems corresponds to the cognitive processor.

The Newell and Simon model of human problem-solving in terms of long-term memory (rules), short-term memory (working memory), and a cognitive processor (inference engine) is the basis of modern rule-based expert systems.

Rules like these are a type of **production system**. Rule-based production systems are a popular method of implementing expert systems today. The individual rules that comprise a production system are the **production rules**. In designing an expert system, an important factor is the amount of knowledge or **granularity** of the rules. Too little granularity makes it difficult to understand a rule without reference to other rules. Too much granularity makes the expert system difficult to modify since several chunks of knowledge are intermingled in one rule.

Until the mid-sixties, a major quest of AI was to produce intelligent systems that relied little on domain knowledge and greatly on powerful methods of reasoning. Even the name General Problem Solver illustrates the concentration on machines that were not designed for one specific domain but were intended to solve many types of problems. Although the methods of reasoning used by general problem solvers were very powerful, the machines were eternal beginners. When presented with a new domain, they had to discover everything from first principles and were not as good as human experts who relied on domain knowledge for high performance.

An example of the power of knowledge is playing chess. The best chess players are humans despite the fact that computers are much faster than people in doing calculations. Studies have shown (Chase 73) that human expert chess players do not have super powers of reasoning but instead rely on knowledge of chesspiece patterns built up over years of play. As mentioned previously, one estimate places an expert chess player's knowledge at about 50,000 patterns. Humans are very good at recognizing patterns such as pieces on a chessboard. Instead of trying to reason ahead ten or twenty possible moves for every piece as a computer might, the human analyzes the game in terms of patterns that reveal long-term threats while remaining alert for short-term surprise moves.

While domain knowledge is very powerful, it is generally limited to the domain. For example, a person who becomes an expert chess player does not automatically become an expert at solving math problems or even a checkers expert. While some knowledge may carry over to another domain, such as careful planning of moves, this is a skill rather than genuine expertise.

By the early seventies, it became apparent that domain knowledge was the key to building machine problem-solvers that could function at the level of human experts. Although methods of reasoning are important, studies have shown that experts do not primarily rely on reasoning for problem-solving. In fact, reasoning may play a minor role in an expert's problem solving. Instead, experts rely on a vast knowledge of heuristics and experience that they have built up over the years. If an expert cannot solve a problem based on expertise, then it is necessary for the expert to reason from first principles and theory (or more likely ask another expert). The reasoning ability of an expert is generally no better than that of an average person in dealing with a totally unfamiliar situation. The early attempts at building powerful problem-solvers based only on reasoning have shown that a problem-solver is crippled if it must rely solely on reasoning.

The insight that domain knowledge was the key to building real-world problem solvers led to the success of expert systems. The successful expert systems today are thus knowledge-based expert systems rather than general problem solvers. In addition, the same technology that led to the development of expert systems has also led to the development of knowledge-based systems that do not necessarily contain human expertise.

While expertise is considered knowledge that is specialized and known only to a few, knowledge is generally found in books, periodicals and other widely available resources. For example, the knowledge of how to solve a quadratic equation or perform integration and differentiation is widely available. Knowledge-based computer programs such as MACSYMA and SMP are available to perform automatically these and many other mathematical operations on either numeric or symbolic operands. Other knowledge-based programs may perform process control of manufacturing plants. Today the terms **knowledge-based programming** and expert systems are often used synonymously. In fact, expert systems is now considered an alternative programming model or **paradigm** to conventional algorithmic programming.

The Rise of Knowledge-based Systems

With the acceptance of the knowledge-based paradigm in the 1970's, a number of successful prototype expert systems were created. These systems could interpret mass spectrograms to identify chemical constituents (DENDRAL), diagnose illness (MYCIN), analyze geologic data for oil (DIPMETER) and minerals (PROSPECTOR), and configure computer systems (XCON/R1). The news that PROSPECTOR had discovered a mineral deposit worth $100 million dollars and that XCON/R1 was saving Digital Equipment Corporation (DEC) millions of dollars a year triggered a sensational interest in the new expert systems technology by 1980. The branch of AI that had started off in the 1950's as a study of human information processing had now grown to achieve commercial success by the development of practical programs for real-world use.

The MYCIN expert system was very important for several reasons. First, it demonstrated that AI could be used for practical real-world problems. Second, MYCIN was the testbed of new concepts such as the explanation facility, automatic acquisition of knowledge, and intelligent tutoring that are found in a number of expert systems today. The third reason that MYCIN was important is that it demonstrated the feasibility of the expert system **shell**.

Previous expert systems such as DENDRAL were one–of–a–kind systems in which the knowledge–base was intermingled with the software that applied the knowl-edge, the inference engine. MYCIN explicitly separated the knowledge–base from the inference engine. This was extremely important to the development of expert system technology since it meant that the essential core of the expert system could be reused.

That is, a new expert system could be built much more rapidly than a DENDRAL-type system by emptying out the old knowledge and putting in knowledge about the new domain. The part of MYCIN that dealt with inference and explanation, the shell, could then be refilled with knowledge about the new system. The shell produced by removing the medical knowledge of MYCIN was called EMYCIN (Essential or Empty MYCIN).

By the late seventies, the three concepts that are basic to most expert systems today had converged, as shown in Figure 1-5. These concepts are rules, the shell, and knowledge.

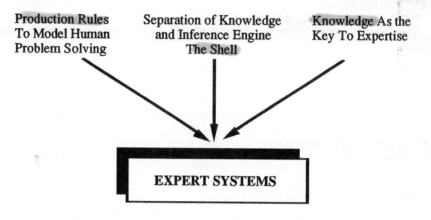

Figure 1-5
Convergence Of Three Important Factors To Create
The Modern Rule-based Expert System

By 1980 new companies started to bring expert systems out of the university laboratory and produce commercial products. Powerful new software for expert system development was introduced such as the Automated Reasoning Tool (ART) by the Inference Corp., the Knowledge Engineering Tool (KEE) by IntelliCorp, and Rulemaster by Radian Corp. In addition, specialized new hardware was developed to run the software with greater speed than ever before. Companies such as Symbolics and LMI introduced computers referred to as LISP machines because they were designed for LISP, the underlying base language of the expert systems development software. In LISP machines, the native assembly language, operating system, and all other fundamental code were done in LISP.

CLIPS

Unfortunately, this high technology also commanded a high price. While a single-user LISP machine was much more powerful and productive than a general purpose machine running LISP, the single-user machine and a single-user software license cost a total of $100,000. Establishing an AI lab with a half-dozen programmers could easily cost a half-million dollars.

These objections were overcome in the mid-80's by the introduction of powerful development software such as CLIPS by NASA. CLIPS is written in C for speed and portability, and also uses a powerful pattern matching called the Rete Algorithm. CLIPS is free to Government users and Government contractors. The cost to other users is $312 (as of 1988) which includes the complete 25,000 lines of CLIPS source code.

Any C compiler that supports the standard Kernigan and Richie C language can be used to install CLIPS. CLIPS has been installed on the IBM PC and compatibles, VAX, Hewlett-Packard, Sun, Cray and many other makes of computers. A version for the Macintosh is also available that supports the full Macintosh interface with pull-down windows and mouse support. The speed of CLIPS on a 80386 or 68020 microcomputer is compatible with the state-of-the-art LISP-based development software and LISP machines.

1.7 EXPERT SYSTEMS APPLICATIONS AND DOMAINS

Conventional computer programs are used to solve many types of problems. Generally, these problems have algorithmic solutions that lend themselves well to conventional programs and programming languages such as FORTRAN, Pascal, Ada, and so on. In many application areas such as business and engineering, numeric calculations are of primary importance. By contrast, expert systems are primarily designed for symbolic reasoning.

While languages such as LISP and PROLOG are also used for symbolic manipulation, they are more general purpose than expert system shells. This does not mean that it is not possible to build expert systems in LISP and PROLOG. In fact, many expert systems have been built with PROLOG and LISP. PROLOG especially has a number of advantages for diagnostic systems because of its built-in backward chaining. Rather, it is more convenient and efficient to build large expert systems with shells and utility programs specifically designed for expert system building. Instead of "re-inventing the wheel" every time a new expert system is to be built, it is more efficient to use specialized tools designed for expert system building than general purpose tools.

Applications of Expert Systems

Expert systems have been applied to virtually every field of knowledge. Some have been designed as research tools while others fulfill important business and industrial functions. One example of an expert system in routine business use is the XCON system of Digital Equipment Corp. (DEC). The XCON system (originally called R1) was developed in conjunction with John McDermott of Carnegie-Mellon University. XCON is an expert configuring system for DEC computer systems (McDermott 84).

The **configuration** of a computer system means that when a customer places an order, all the right parts—software, hardware, and documentation—are supplied. For large systems, the customer's system is set up or configured at the factory and tested to insure that it meets the customer's requirements. Unlike the purchase of a TV set or a home computer, there are many options and interconnections possible with a large computer system. In putting together a large system, it's not enough to just ship the requested number of CPU's, disk drives, terminals and so forth. The proper interconnections and cabling must also be supplied and the system checked to verify that it is working correctly.

The XCON system is probably one of the most successful expert systems in routine use and saves DEC millions of dollars a year, reduces time to configure an order, and improves the accuracy of an order. XCON can configure an average order in about two minutes, which is fifteen times faster than a human. Also, while the humans configured orders correctly 70% of the time, XCON has an accuracy of 98%. These are important concerns since configuring a complex computer system at the factory involves considerable effort. It is very expensive to configure a system partially and then find out the system cannot meet the customer's requirements or that other components are needed and shipment will be delayed until the parts arrive.

Hundreds of expert systems have been built and reported in computer journals, books, and conferences. This probably represents only the tip of the iceberg since many companies and military organizations will not report their systems because of proprietary or secret knowledge contained in the systems. Based on the systems described in the open literature, certain broad classes of expert systems applications can be discerned, as shown in Table 1-3.

Class	General Area
Configuration	Assemble proper components of a system in the proper way.
Diagnosis	Infer underlying problems based on observed evidence.
Instruction	Intelligent teaching so that a student can ask *Why*, *How* and *What If* type questions just as if a human was teaching.
Interpretation	Explain observed data.
Monitoring	Compares observed data to expected data to judge performance.
Planning	Devise actions to yield a desired outcome.
Prognosis	Predict the outcome of a given situation.
Remedy	Prescribe treatment for a problem.
Control	Regulate a process. May require interpretation, diagnosis, monitoring, planning, prognosis, and remedies.

Table 1-3
Broad Classes of Expert Systems

Examples of some expert systems are shown in Tables 1-4 through 1-9 (Waterman 86), and in the Historical Bibliography at the end of the chapter .

Name	Chemistry
CRYSALIS	Interpret a protein's 3-D structure
DENDRAL	Interpret molecular structure
TQMSTUNE	Remedy Triple Quadruple Mass Spectrometer (keep it tuned)
CLONER	Design new biological molecules
MOLGEN	Design gene-cloning experiments
SECS	Design complex organic molecules
SPEX	Plan molecular biology experiments

Table 1-4
Chemistry Expert Systems

Name	Electronics
ACE	Diagnosis telephone network faults
IN-ATE	Diagnosis oscilloscope faults
NDS	Diagnose national communication net
EURISKO	Design 3-D microelectronics
PALLADIO	Design and test new VLSI circuits
REDESIGN	Redesign digital circuits to new
CADHELP	Instruct for computer aided design
SOPHIE	Instruct circuit fault diagnosis

Table 1-5
Electronics Expert Systems

Name	Medicine
PUFF	Diagnosis lung disease
VM	Monitors intensive-care patients
ABEL	Diagnosis acid-base/electrolytes
AI/COAG	Diagnosis blood disease
AI/RHEUM	Diagnosis rheumatoid disease
CADUCEUS	Diagnosis internal medicine disease
ANNA	Monitor digitalis therapy
BLUE BOX	Diagnosis/remedy depression
MYCIN	Diagnosis/remedy bacterial infections
ONCOCIN	Remedy/manage chemotherapy patients
ATTENDING	Instruct in anesthetic management
GUIDON	Instruct in bacterial infections

Table 1-6
Medical Expert Systems

Name	Engineering
REACTOR	Diagnosis/remedy reactor accidents
DELTA	Diagnosis/remedy GE locomotives
STEAMER	Instruct operation - steam powerplant

Table 1-7
Engineering Expert Systems

Name	Geology
DIPMETER	Interpret dipmeter logs
LITHO	Interpret oil well log data
MUD	Diagnosis/remedy drilling problems
PROSPECTOR	Interpret geologic data for minerals

Table 1-8
Geology Expert Systems

Name	Computer Systems
PTRANS	Prognosis for managing DEC computers
BDS	Diagnosis bad parts in switching net
XCON	Configure DEC computer systems
XSEL	Configure DEC computer sales order
XSITE	Configure customer site for DEC computers
YES/MVS	Monitor/control IBM MVS operating system
TIMM	Diagnosis DEC computers

Table 1-9
Computer Expert Systems

Appropriate Domains for Expert Systems

Before starting to build an expert system, it is essential to decide if an expert system is the appropriate paradigm. For example, one concern is whether an expert system should be used instead of an alternative paradigm such as conventional programming. The appropriate domain for an expert system depends on a number of factors.

• *Can the problem be solved effectively by conventional programming?* If the answer is yes, then an expert system is not the best choice. For example, consider the problem of diagnosing some equipment. If all the symptoms for all malfunctions are known in advance, then a simple table lookup or decision tree of the fault is adequate. Expert systems are best suited for situations in which there is no efficient algorithmic solution. Such cases are called **ill-structured problems** and reasoning may offer the only hope of a good solution.

As an example of an ill-structured problem, consider the case of a person who is thinking about travel and visits a travel agent. While most people have a destination and plans, there are exceptions. Table 1-10 lists some characteristics of an ill-structured problem as indicated by the person's responses to the travel agent's questions.

Travel Agent's Questions	Responses
Can I help you?	I'm thinking about going somewhere
Where do you want to go?	I'm not sure where to go
Any particular destination?	I just like to travel; destination's not important
How much can you afford?	I don't have enough money to go
Can you get some money?	I don't know how to get the money
When do you want to go?	I must go soon

Table 1-10
An Example of an Ill-structured Problem

Although this is probably an extreme case, it does illustrate the basic concept of an ill-structured problem. As you can see, an ill-structured problem would not lend itself well to an algorithmic solution because there are so many possibilities.

In dealing with ill-structured problems, there is a danger in that the expert system design may accidentally mirror an algorithmic solution. That is, the development of the expert system may unknowingly discover an algorithmic solution. A clue that this has happened occurs if a solution is found that requires a rigid **control structure**. That is, the rules are forced to execute in a certain sequence by the knowledge engineer explicitly setting the priorities of many rules. Forcing a rigid control structure on the expert system cancels a major advantage of expert system technology, which is dealing with unexpected input that does not follow a predetermined pattern (Parrello 88). That is, expert systems react opportunistically to their input, whatever it is. Conventional programs generally expect input to follow a certain sequence. An expert system with a lot of control often indicates a disguised algorithm and may be a good candidate for recoding as a conventional program.

- *Is the domain well-bounded?* It is very important to have well-defined limits on what the expert system is expected to know and what its capabilities should be. For example, suppose you wanted to create an expert system to diagnose headaches. Certainly medical knowledge of a physician would be put in the knowledge-base. However, for a deep understanding of headaches, you might also put in knowledge about neurochemistry, then its parent area of biochemistry, then chemistry, molecular biophysics, and so forth perhaps down to subnuclear physics. Other domains such as biofeedback, psychology, psychiatry, physiology, exercise, yoga, and stress management may also have pertinent knowledge about headaches. The point of all this is—when do you stop adding domains? The more domains, the more complex the expert system becomes.

In particular, the task of coordinating all the expertise becomes a major task. In the real world, we know from experience how difficult it is to have coordinated teams of experts working on problems, especially when they come up with conflicting recommendations. If we knew how to program well the coordination of expertise, then we could try programming an expert system to have the knowledge of multiple experts. Attempts have been made to coordinate multiple expert systems in the HEARSAY II and HEARSAY III systems. However, it is a complex task that should be viewed more as research rather than producing a deliverable expert system product.

- *Is there a need and a desire for an expert system?* Although it's great experience to build an expert system, it's rather pointless if no one is willing to use it. If there already are many human experts, it's difficult to justify an expert system based on the reason of scarce human expertise. Also, if the experts or users don't want the system, it will not be accepted even if there is a need for it.

Management especially must be willing to support the system. This is even more critical for expert systems than conventional programs because expert systems is a new technology. This means that there are few experienced people and more uncertainty about what can be accomplished. However, the area of expert systems deserves more support because it attempts to solve the problems that cannot be done by conventional programming. The risks are greater but so are the rewards.

- *Is there at least one human expert who is willing to cooperate?* There must be an expert who is willing, and preferably enthusiastic, about the project. Not all experts are willing to have their knowledge examined for faults and then put into a computer. Even if there are multiple experts willing to cooperate in the development, it might be wise to limit the number of experts involved in development. Different experts may have different ways of solving a problem, such as requesting different diagnostic tests. Sometimes, they may even reach different conclusions. Trying to code multiple methods of problem-solving in one knowledge-base may create internal conflicts and incompatibilities.

- *Can the expert explain the knowledge so that it is understandable by the knowledge engineer?* Even if the expert is willing to cooperate, there may be difficulty in expressing the knowledge in explicit terms. As a simple example of this difficulty, can you explain in words how you move a finger? Although you could say it's done by contracting a muscle in the finger, the next question is—how do you contract a finger muscle? The other difficulty in communication between expert and knowledge engineer is that the knowledge engineer doesn't know the technical terms of the expert. This problem is particularly acute with medical terminology. It may take a year or longer for the knowledge engineer to even understand what the expert is talking about, let alone translate that knowledge into explicit computer code.

• *Is the problem-solving knowledge mainly heuristic and uncertain?* Expert systems *are* appropriate when the expert's knowledge is largely heuristic and uncertain. That is, the knowledge may be based on experience, called **experiential knowledge**, and the expert may have to try various approaches in case one doesn't work. In other words, the expert's knowledge may be a trial-and-error approach, rather than one based on logic and algorithms. However, the expert can still solve the problem faster than someone else who is not an expert. This is a good application for expert systems. If the problem can be solved simply by logic and algorithms, it is best solved by a conventional program.

1.8 LANGUAGES, SHELLS AND TOOLS

A fundamental decision in defining a problem is deciding how best to model it. Sometimes experience is available to aid in choosing the best paradigm. For example, experience suggests that a payroll is best done using conventional procedural programming. Experience also suggests that it is preferable to use a commercial package, if available, rather than writing one from scratch. A general guide to selecting a paradigm is to consider the most traditional one first—conventional programming. The reason for doing this is because of the vast amount of experience we have with conventional programming and the wide variety of commercial packages available. If a problem cannot be effectively done by conventional programming, then turn to non-conventional paradigms such as AI.

Although expert systems is a branch of AI, there are specialized languages for expert systems that are quite different from the commonly used AI languages such as LISP and PROLOG. While many others have been developed, such as IPL-II, SAIL, CONNIVER, KRL and Smalltalk, few are widely used except for research (Scown 85).

An expert system language is a higher order language than languages like LISP or C because it is easier to do certain things, but there is also a smaller range of problems that can be addressed. That is, the specialized nature of expert system languages makes them very suitable for writing expert systems but not for general purpose programming. In many situations, it is even necessary to exit temporarily from an expert system language to perform a function in a procedural language.

The primary functional difference between expert system languages and procedural languages is the focus of representation. Procedural languages focus on providing flexible and robust techniques to represent data. For example, data structures such as arrays, records, linked lists, stacks, queues, and trees are easily created and manipulated. Modern languages such as Modula-2 and Ada are designed to aid in **data abstraction** by providing structures for encapsulation such as modules and packages. This provides a level of abstraction which is then implemented by methods such as operators and control statements to yield a program. The data and methods to manipulate the data are tightly interwoven. In contrast, expert system languages focus on providing flexible and robust ways to represent knowledge. The expert system paradigm allows two levels of abstraction: data abstraction and **knowledge abstraction**. Expert system languages specifically separate the data from the methods of manipulating the data. An example of this separation is that of facts (data abstraction) and rules (knowledge abstraction) in a rule-based expert system language.

This difference in focus also leads to a difference in program design methodology. Because of the tight interweaving of data and knowledge in procedural languages, programmers must carefully describe the sequence of execution. However, the explicit separation of data from knowledge in expert system languages requires considerably less rigid control of execution sequence. Typically, an entirely separate piece of code, the inference engine, is used to apply the knowledge to the data. This separation of knowledge and data allows a higher degree of parallelism and modularity.

In choosing a language, a basic question should be whether the problem is knowledge or intelligence intensive. Expert systems rely on a great deal of specialized knowledge or expertise to solve a problem, while AI emphasizes a problem solving approach. Expert systems often rely on a pattern matching within a restricted knowledge domain to guide their execution while AI generally concentrates on searching paradigms in less restricted domains.

The customary way of defining the need for an expert system program is to decide if you want to program the expertise of a human expert. If such an expert exists and will cooperate, then an expert system approach may be successful.

The road to selecting an expert system language is paved with confusion. A few years ago the choice of an expert system language was fairly straightforward. There were only about a half-dozen languages available, and they were generally free or cost a nominal amount from the universities where they were developed.

However, with the explosive commercial growth in the expert systems field since the 1970's, the selection of a language is no longer so simple. Today there are dozens of languages available ranging in price up to $75,000. While it is still possible to obtain some of the older languages such as OPS5 free or at a nominal cost from the universities where they were developed, there is a price to pay in terms of efficiency, lack of modern features and support.

Besides the confusing choice of the many languages available today, the terminology used to describe the languages is confusing. Some vendors refer to their products as "tools," while others refer to "shells" and still others talk about "integrated environments". For clarity in this book, the terms will be defined as follows:

- **language**: A translator of commands written in a specific syntax. An expert system language will also provide an inference engine to execute the statements of the language. Depending on the implementation, the inference engine may provide forward chaining, backward chaining, or both. Under this language definition, LISP is not an expert system language while PROLOG is. However, it is possible to write an expert system language using LISP, and write AI in PROLOG. For that matter you can even write an expert system or AI language in assembly language. Questions of development time, convenience, maintainability, efficiency and speed determine what language software is written in.

- **tool**: A language plus associated utility programs to facilitate the development, debugging, and delivery of application programs. Utility programs may include text and graphics editors, debuggers, file management, and even code generators. Cross assemblers may also be provided to port the developed code to different hardware. For example, an expert system may be developed on a Digital Equipment Corp. VAX and then cross-assembled to run on a Motorola 68000. Some tools may even allow the use of different paradigms such as forward and backward chaining in one application.

In some cases, a tool may be integrated with all its utility programs in one environment to present a common interface to the user. This approach minimizes the need for the user to leave the environment to perform a task. For example, a simple tool may not provide facilities for file management and so a user would have to exit the tool to give operating system commands. An integrated environment allows easy exchange of data between utility programs in the environment. Some tools do not even require the user to write any code. Instead, the tool allows a user to enter knowledge by examples from tables or spreadsheets and generate the appropriate code itself.

• **shell**: A special purpose tool designed for certain types of applications in which the user must only supply the knowledge base. The classic example of this is the EMYCIN (empty MYCIN) shell. This shell was made by removing the medical knowledge base of the MYCIN expert system.

MYCIN was designed as a backward chaining system to diagnose disease. By simply removing the medical knowledge, EMYCIN was made which could be used as a shell to contain knowledge about other kinds of consultative systems which use backward chaining. The EMYCIN shell demonstrated the reusability of the essential MYCIN software such as the inference engine and user interface. This was a very important step in the development of modern expert system technology because it meant that an expert system would not have to be built from scratch for each new application.

There are many ways of characterizing expert systems such as representation of knowledge, forward or backward chaining, support of uncertainty, hypothetical reasoning, explanation facilities and so forth. Unless a person has built a number of expert systems, it is difficult to appreciate all of these features, especially those found in the more expensive tools. The best way to learn expert systems technology is to develop a number of systems with an easy-to-learn language and then invest in a more sophisticated tool if you need its features.

1.9 ELEMENTS OF AN EXPERT SYSTEM

The elements of a typical expert system are shown in Figure 1-6. In a rule-based system, the knowledge base contains the domain knowledge needed to solve problems coded in the form of rules. While rules are a popular paradigm for representing knowledge, other types of expert systems use different representations, as discussed in Chapter 2.

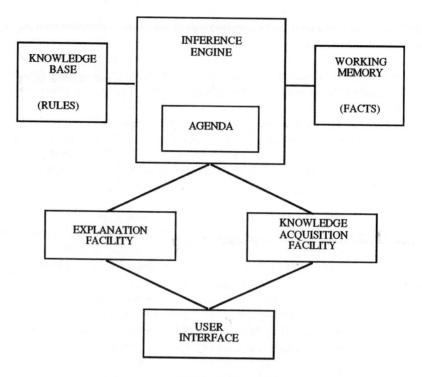

Figure 1-6
Structure of a Rule-Based Expert System

An expert system consists of the following components:

- **user interface** - the mechanism by which the user and the expert system communicate.
- **explanation facility** - explains the reasoning of the system to a user.
- **working memory** - a **global database** of facts used by the rules.
- **inference engine** -makes inferences by deciding which rules are satisfied by facts, prioritizes the satisfied rules, and executes the rule with the highest priority.
- **agenda** - a prioritized list of rules created by the inference engine, whose patterns are satisfied by facts in working memory.
- **knowledge acquisition facility** - an automatic way for the user to enter knowledge in the system rather than by having the knowledge engineer explicitly code the knowledge.

The knowledge acquisition facility is an an optional feature on many systems. In some expert system tools like KEE and First Class, the tool can learn by rule induction through examples and automatically generate rules. However, the examples are generally from tabular or spreadsheet type data better suited to decision trees. General rules constructed by a knowledge engineer can be much more complex than the simple rules from rule induction.

Depending on the implementation of the system, the user interface may be a simple text-oriented display or a sophisticated high-resolution, bit-mapped display. This high-resolution display is commonly used to simulate a control panel with dials and displays.

The knowledge base is also called the **production memory** in a rule-based expert system. As a very simple example, consider the problem of deciding to cross a street. The productions for the two rules are as follows, where the arrows mean that the system will perform the actions on the right of the arrow if the conditions on the left are true.

```
the light is red → stop
the light is green → go
```

The production rules can be expressed in an equivalent pseudocode IF THEN format as:

```
Rule: Red_light
IF
        the light is red
THEN
        stop

Rule: Green_light
IF
        the light is green
THEN
        go
```

Each rule is identified by a name. Following the name is the IF part of the rule. The section of the rule between the IF and THEN part of the rule is called by various names such as the **antecedent, conditional part, pattern part** or **left-hand-side (LHS)**. The individual condition

```
the light is green
```

is called a **conditional element** or a **pattern**.

Some examples of rules from real systems are:

```
MYCIN system for diagnosis of meningitis and
bacteremia (bacterial infections)
IF
     The site of the culture is blood, and
```

```
        The identity of the organism is not known with
            certainty, and
        The stain of the organism is gramneg, and
        The morphology of the organism is rod, and
        The patient has been seriously burned
THEN
        There is weakly suggestive evidence (.4) that the
            identity of the organism is pseudomonas


XCON/R1 for configuring DEC VAX computer systems
IF
        The current context is assigning devices to
            Unibus modules and
        There is an unassigned dual-port disk drive and
        The type of controller it requires is known and
        There are two such controllers, neither of which
            has any devices assigned to it, and
        The number of devices that these controllers can
            support is known
THEN
        Assign the disk drive to each of the controllers,
            and
        Note that the two controllers have been
            associated and that each supports one drive
```

In a rule-based system, the inference engine determines which rule antecedents, if any, are satisfied by the facts. Two general methods of inferencing are commonly used: **forward chaining** and **backward chaining** as the problem solving strategies of expert systems. Other methods used for more specific needs may include means-ends analysis, problem reduction, backtracking, plan-generate-test, hierarchical planning and the least commitment principle, and constraint handling.

Forward chaining is reasoning from facts to the conclusions resulting from those facts. For example, if you see that it is raining before leaving home (the fact), then you should take an umbrella (the conclusion).

Backward chaining involves reasoning in reverse from a hypothesis, a potential conclusion to be proved, to the facts which support the hypothesis. For example, if you have not looked outside and someone enters with wet shoes and an umbrella, your hypothesis is that it is raining. In order to support this hypothesis, you could ask the person if it was raining. If the response is yes, then the hypothesis is proven true and becomes a fact. As mentioned before, a hypothesis can be viewed as a fact whose truth is in doubt and needs to be established. The hypothesis can then be interpreted as a goal to be proven.

Depending on the design, an inference engine will do either forward or backward chaining. For example, OPS5 and CLIPS are designed for forward chaining while EMYCIN performs backward chaining. Some types of inference engines, such as ART and KEE, offer both. The choice of inference engine depends on the type of problem. Diagnostic problems are better solved with backward chaining while prognosis, monitoring and control are better done by forward chaining.

The working memory may contain facts regarding the current status of the traffic light such as "the light is green" or "the light is red". Either or both of these facts may be in working memory at the same time. If the traffic light is working normally, only one fact will be in memory. However, it is possible that both facts may be in working memory if there is a malfunction in the light. Notice the difference between the knowledge base and working memory. Facts do not interact with one another. The fact "the light is green" has no effect on the fact "the light is red". Instead, our knowledge of traffic lights says that if both facts are simultaneously present, then there is a malfunction in the light.

If there is a fact "the light is green" in working memory, the inference engine will notice that this fact satisfies the conditional part of the green light rule and put this rule on the agenda. If a rule has multiple patterns, then all of its patterns must be simultaneously satisfied for the rule to be placed on the agenda. Some patterns may even be satisfied by specifying the absence of certain facts in working memory.

A rule whose patterns are all satisfied is said to be **activated** or **instantiated**. Multiple activated rules may be on the agenda at the same time. In this case, the inference engine must select one rule for **firing**. The term firing comes from Neurophysiology, the study of the nervous system. An individual nerve cell or **neuron** emits an electrical signal when stimulated. No amount of further stimulation can cause the neuron to fire again for a short time period. This phenomenon is called refraction. Rule-based expert systems are built using refraction in order to prevent trivial loops. That is, if the green light rule kept firing on the same fact over and over again, the expert system would never accomplish any useful work.

Various methods have been invented to provide refraction. In one type of expert system language called OPS5, each fact is given a unique identifier called a **timetag** when it is entered in working memory. After a rule has fired on a fact, the inference engine will not fire on that fact again because its time stamp has been used.

Following the THEN part of a rule is a list of **actions** to be executed when the rule fires. This part of the rule is known as the **consequent** or **right-hand side** **(RHS)**. When the red light rule fires, it's action "stop" is executed. Likewise, when the green light rule fires, it's action is "go". Specific actions usually include the addition or removal of facts from working memory or printing results. The format of these actions depends on the syntax of the expert system language. For example, in OPS5, ART, and CLIPS, the action to add a new fact called "stop" to working memory would be (assert stop). Because of their LISP ancestry, these languages were designed to require parentheses around patterns and actions.

The inference engine operates in **cycles**. Various names have been given to describe the cycle such as **recognize-act cycle**, **select-execute cycle**,

situation-response cycle, and **situation-action cycle**. By any name for a cycle, the inference engine will repeatedly execute a group of tasks until certain criteria cause execution to cease. The tasks of a cycle for OPS5, a typical expert system shell, are shown in the following pseudocode as **conflict resolution, act, match,** and **check for halt**.

> WHILE not done
> > **Conflict Resolution:** If there are activations, then select the one with highest priority else done.
> > **Act:** Sequentially perform the actions on the RHS of the selected activation. Those which change working memory have immediate effect in this cycle. Remove the activation which has just fired from the agenda.
> > **Match:** Update the agenda by checking if the LHS of any rules are satisfied. If so activate them. Remove activations if the LHS of their rules are not satisfied any more.
> > **Check for Halt:** If a halt action is performed or break command given, then done.
> END-WHILE
> **Accept a new user command**

Multiple rules may be activated and put on the agenda during one cycle. Also, activations will be left on the agenda from previous cycles unless they are deactivated because their LHS is no longer satisfied. Thus the number of activations on the agenda will vary as execution proceeds. Depending on the program, an activation may always be on the agenda but never selected for firing. Likewise some rules may never become activated. In these cases, the purpose of these rules should be re-examined because the rules are either unnecessary or their patterns were not correctly designed.

The inference engine executes the actions of the highest priority activation on the agenda, then the next highest priority activation and so on until no activations are left. Various priority schemes have been designed into expert system shells. Generally, all shells let the knowledge engineer define the priority of rules.

Agenda conflicts occur when different activations have the same priority and the inference engine must decide on one rule to fire. Different shells have different ways of dealing with this problem. In the original Newell and Simon paradigm, those rules entered first in the system had the highest default priority (Newell 72a). In OPS5, rules with more complex patterns have a higher priority. In ART and CLIPS, rules have the same default priority unless assigned different ones by the knowledge engineer.

At this time, control is returned to the **top-level** command interpreter for the user to give further instructions to the expert system shell. The top-level is the default mode in which the user communicates with the expert system and is indicated by the task "Accept a new user command". It is the top-level which accepts the new command.

The top-level is the user interface to the shell while an expert system application is under development. More sophisticated user interfaces are usually designed for the expert system to facilitate its operation. For example, the expert system may have a user interface for control of a manufacturing plant that shows a block diagram of the plant with a high resolution, bit-mapped color display. Warnings and status messages may appear in flashing colors with simulated dials and gauges. In fact, more effort may go into the design and implementation of the user interface than in the expert system knowledge base, especially in a prototype. Depending on the capabilities of the expert system shell, the user interface may be implemented by rules or in another language called by the expert system.

An explanation facility will allow the user to ask how the system came to a certain conclusion and why certain information is needed. The question of how the system came to a certain conclusion is easy to answer in a rule-based system since a history of the activated rules and contents of working memory can be maintained in a stack. Sophisticated explanation facilities may allow the user to ask "What If" type questions to explore alternate reasoning paths through hypothetical reasoning.

1.10   PRODUCTION SYSTEMS

One of the most popular type of expert system today is the rule-based system. Rules are popular for a number of reasons.

- *Modular nature.* This makes it easy to encapsulate knowledge and expand the expert system by incremental development.
- *Explanation facilities.* It is easy to build explanation facilities with rules since the antecedents of a rule specify exactly what is necessary to activate the rule. By keeping track of which rules have fired, an explanation facility can present the chain of reasoning that led to a certain conclusion.
- *Similarity to the human cognitive process.* Based on the work of Newell and Simon, rules appear to be a natural way of modeling how humans solve problems. The simple IF THEN representation of rules make it easy to explain to experts the structure of the knowledge that you are trying to elicit from them. Other advantages of rules are described in (Hayes-Roth 85).

Rules are a type of production whose origins go back to the 1940's. Because of the importance of rule-based systems, it is worthwhile to examine the development of the rule concept. This will give you a better idea of why rule-based systems are so useful for expert systems.

Post Production Systems

Production systems were first used in symbolic logic by Post (Post 43) who originated the name. He proved the important and amazing result that any system of mathematics or logic could be written as a certain type of production rule system. This result established the great capability of production rules for representing major classes of knowledge rather than being limited to a few types. Under the term **rewrite rules,** they are also used in linguistics as a way of defining the grammar of a language. Computer languages are commonly defined using the Backus-Naur Form (BNF) of production rules.

The basic idea of Post was that any mathematical or logic system is simply a set of rules specifying how to change one string of symbols into another set of symbols. That is, given an input string, the antecedent, a production rule could produce a new string, the consequent. This idea is also valid with programs and expert systems where the initial string of symbols is the input data and the output string is some transformation of the input.

As a very simple case, if the input string is "patient has fever" the output string might be "take an aspirin". Note that there is no meaning attached to these strings. That is, the manipulations of the strings is based on syntax and not any semantics or understanding of what a fever, aspirin, and patient represent. A human knows what these strings in terms of the real-world mean but a Post production system is just a way of transforming one string into another. A production rule for this example could be

```
Antecedent → Consequent
person has fever → take aspirin
```

where the arrow indicates the transformation of one string into another. We can interpret this rule in terms of the more familiar IF THEN notation as

```
IF person has fever THEN take aspirin
```

The production rules can also have multiple antecedents. For example,

```
person has fever AND
    fever is greater than 102 → see doctor
```

Note that the special connective AND is not part of the string. The AND indicates that the rule has multiple antecedents.

A Post production system consists of a group of production rules, such as the following (where the numbers in parentheses are for our discussion).

```
(1)    car won't start → check battery
(2)    car won't start → check gas
(3)    check battery AND battery bad → replace battery
(4)    check gas AND no gas → fill gas tank
```

If there is a string "car won't start", the rules (1) and (2) may be used to generate the strings "check battery" and "check gas". However, there is no control mechanism that applies both these rules to the string. Only one rule may be applied, both or none. If there is another string "battery bad" and a string "check battery", then rule (3) may be applied to generate the string "replace battery".

There is no special significance to the order in which rules are written. The rules of our example could also have been written in the following order and it would still be the same system.

```
(4)    check gas AND no gas → fill gas tank
(2)    car won't start → check gas
(1)    car won't start → check battery
(3)    check battery AND battery bad → replace battery
```

Although Post production rules were useful in laying part of the foundation of expert systems, they are not adequate for writing practical programs. The basic limitation of Post production rules for programming is lack of a **control strategy** to guide the application of the rules. A Post system permits the rules to be applied on the strings in any manner because there is no specification given on how the rules should be applied.

As an analogy, suppose you go to the library to find a certain book on expert systems. At the library, you start randomly looking at books on the shelves for the one you want. If the library is fairly large, it will take a very long time to find the book you need. Even if you find the section of books on expert systems, your next random choice could take you to an entirely different section, such as French cooking. The situation becomes even worse if you need material from the first book to help you determine the second book that you need to find. A random search for the second book will also take a long time.

Markov Algorithms

The next advance in applying production rules was made by Markov, who specified a control structure for production systems (Markov 54). A **Markov algorithm** is an ordered group of productions which are applied in order of priority to an input string. If the highest priority rule is not applicable, then the next one is applied and so forth. The Markov algorithm terminates if either (1) the last production is not applicable to a string or (2) a production that ends with a period is applied.

Markov algorithms can also be applied to substrings of a string, starting from the left. For example, the production system consisting of the single rule

```
AB → HIJ
```

when applied to the input string GABKAB produces the new string GHIJKAB. Since the production now applies to the new string, the final result is GHIJKHIJ.

The special character ∧ represents the **null string** of no characters. For example, the production

    A → ∧

deletes all occurrences of the character A in a string.

Other special symbols represent any single character and are indicated by lower-case letters a, b, c, and so forth. These symbols represent single-character variables and are an important part of modern expert system languages. For example, the rule

    AxB → BxA

will reverse the characters A and B.

The Greek letters α, β, and so forth are used for special punctuation of strings. The Greek letters are used because they are distinct from the alphabet of ordinary letters.

An example of a Markov algorithm that moves the first letter of an input string to the end is shown following (Elson 73). The rules are ordered in terms of highest priority (1), next highest (2) and so forth. The rules are prioritized in the order that they are entered.

    (1) $\alpha xy \rightarrow y\alpha x$
    (2) $\alpha \rightarrow \wedge$.
    (3) $\wedge \rightarrow \alpha$

For the input string ABC, the execution trace is shown in Table 1-11.

Rule	Success or Failure	String
1	F	ABC
2	F	ABC
3	S	αABC
1	S	BαAC
1	S	BCαA
1	F	BCαA
2	S	BCA

Table 1-11
Execution Trace of a Markov Algorithm

Notice that the α symbol acts analogously to a temporary variable in a conventional programming language. However, instead of holding a value, the α is used as a place holder to mark the progression of changes in the input string. Once its job is done, the α is eliminated by rule 2. The program then ends when rule 2 is applied since there is a period after rule 2.

The Rete Algorithm

Notice that there is a definite control strategy to Markov algorithms with higher priority rules ordered first. As long as the highest priority rule applies, it is used. If not, the Markov algorithm tries lower priority ones. Although the Markov algorithm can be used as the basis of an expert system, it is very inefficient for systems with many rules. The problem of efficiency becomes of major importance if we want to create expert systems for real problems containing hundreds or thousands of rules. No matter how good everything else is about a system, if a user has to wait a long time for a response, the system will not be used. What we really need is an algorithm that knows about all the rules and can apply any rule without having to try each rule sequentially.

A solution to this problem is the **Rete Algorithm** developed by Charles L. Forgy at Carnegie-Mellon University in 1979 for his Ph.D thesis on the OPS (Official Production System at Carnegie-Mellon) expert system shell. The Rete Algorithm is a very fast pattern-matcher that obtains its speed by storing information about the rules in a network. Instead of having to match facts against every rule on every recognize-act cycle, the Rete algorithm only looks for changes in matches on every cycle.This greatly speeds up the matching of facts to antecedents since the static data that doesn't change from cycle to cycle can be ignored. This topic will be discussed further in the chapters on CLIPS. Fast pattern matching algorithms such as the Rete completed the foundation for the practical application of expert systems. Figure 1-7 summarizes the foundations of modern rule-based expert system technologies.

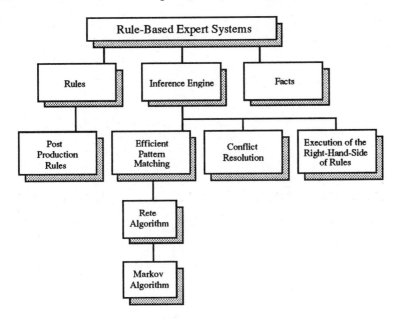

Figure 1-7
Foundations of Modern Rule-based Expert Systems

Different versions of the OPS language and shell have been developed such as OPS2, OPS4, and OPS5. A newer commercial version developed by Forgy is OPS83, a very fast shell. However, OPS83 has a significantly different syntax from the OPS5 style and is partly procedural for faster execution.

1.11 PROCEDURAL PARADIGMS

Programming paradigms can be classified as procedural and nonprocedural. Figure 1-8 shows a **taxonomy** or classification of the procedural paradigms in terms of languages. Figure 1-9 shows a taxonomy for nonprocedural paradigms. These figures illustrate the relationship of expert systems to other paradigms. These figures should be considered only as a general guide and not as strict definitions. Some of the paradigms and languages have characteristics that may place them in more than one class. For example, some people consider functional programming a procedural paradigm while others refer to it as declarative (Ghezzi 87a).

Figure 1-8
Procedural Languages

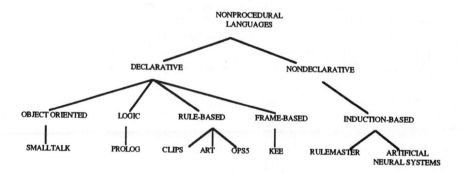

Figure 1-9
Nonprocedural Languages

An **algorithm** is a method of solving a problem in a finite number of steps. The implementation of an algorithm in a program is a **procedural program**. The terms **algorithmic programming**, *procedural programming*, and *conventional programming* are often used synonymously to mean non-AI type programs. A common conception of a procedural program is that it proceeds sequentially, statement by statement, unless a branch instruction is encountered. Another often used synonym for procedural program is **sequential** program. However, the term sequential programming implies too much constraint since all modern programming languages support recursion and so programs may not be strictly sequential.

The distinguishing feature of the procedural paradigm is that the programmer must specify exactly *how* a problem solution must be coded. Even code generators must produce procedural code. In a sense, the use of code generators is **nonprocedural** programming because it removes most or all of the procedural code writing from the programmer. The goal of non-procedural programming is to have the programmer specify *what* the goal is and let the system determine how to accomplish it.

Imperative Programming

The terms **imperative** and **statement-oriented** are used synonymously. Languages such as FORTRAN, Ada, Pascal, Modula-2, COBOL, and BASIC all have the dominant characteristic that statements are imperatives or commands to the computer telling it what to do. Imperative languages developed as a way of freeing the programmer from coding assembly language in the von Neumann architecture. Consequently, imperative languages offer great support to variables, assignment operations, and repetition. These are all low-level operations that modern languages attempt to hide by providing features such as recursion, procedures, modules, packages and so forth. Imperative languages are also characterized by their emphasis on rigid control structure and their associated **top-down** program designs.

A serious problem with all languages is the difficulty of proving the correctness of programs. From the AI standpoint, another serious problem is that imperative languages are not very efficient symbol manipulators. Because the imperative language architecture was molded to fit the von Neumann computer architecture, we have languages that can support number-crunching very well but not symbolic manipulation. However, imperative languages such as C and Ada have been used as the underlying base language to write expert system shells. These languages and the shells built from them run more efficiently and quickly on common general purpose computers than the early shells built using LISP.

Because of their sequential nature, imperative languages are not very efficient for directly implementing expert systems, especially rule-based ones. As an illustration of this problem, consider the problem of encoding the information of a real-world problem with hundreds or thousands of rules. For example, the XCON system used by Digital Equipment Corporation (DEC) to configure computer systems currently has about 7000 rules in its knowledge base. Early unsuccessful attempts were made to code this program in FORTRAN and BASIC before settling on the successful expert systems approach. The direct way of coding this knowledge in an imperative language would require 7000 IF THEN statements or a very, very long CASE. This style of coding would present major efficiency problems since all 7000 rules need to be searched for matching patterns on every recognize-act cycle. Note that the inference engine and its recognize-act cycle would also have to be coded in the imperative language.

The efficiency of the program could be improved if rules were ordered so that those most likely to be executed were put at the beginning. However, this would require considerable tuning of the system and would change as new rules are added, or old ones deleted and modified. A better method for improving efficiency would be to build a tree of the rule patterns to reduce search time in determining which rules should be activated. Rather than making the programmer manually construct the tree, it should preferably be built automatically by the computer based on the pattern and action syntax of the IF THEN rules. It would also be helpful to have an IF THEN syntax that was more conducive to representing knowledge and had powerful pattern matching tests. This requires the development of a parser to analyze input structure and an interpreter or compiler to execute the new IF THEN syntax.

When all of these techniques for improving efficiency are implemented, the result is a dedicated expert system. If the inference engine, parser and interpreter are removed to provide easy development of other expert systems, they comprise an expert system shell. Of course, instead of doing all of this development from scratch, today it is much easier just to use an existing shell which is documented and extensively tested.

Functional Programming

The nature of **functional programming**, as exemplified by languages such as LISP and APL, is very different from statement-oriented languages with their heavy reliance on elaborate control structures and top-down design. The fundamental idea of functional programming is to combine simple functions to yield more powerful functions. This is essentially a **bottom-up** design in contrast to the common top-down designs of imperative languages.

Functional programming is centered around **functions**. Mathematically, a function is an **association** or rule that maps members of one set, the **domain**, into another set, the **codomain**. An example of a function definition is

```
cube(x) ≡ x*x*x, where x is a real number and
cube is a function with real values
```

The three parts of the function definition are:

(1) the association, $x*x*x$
(2) the domain, real numbers
(3) codomain, real numbers

of the cube function. The symbol ≡ means "is equivalent to" or "is defined as". The following notation is a shorthand way of writing that the cube mapping is from the domain of real numbers, symbolized as $\Re$, to the codomain of real numbers.

```
cube:R → R
```

A general notation for a function f that maps from a domain S to a domain T is $f{:}S{\rightarrow}T$ (Gersting 82). The **range** of the function f is the set of all **images** $f(s)$ where s is an element of S. For the case of the cube function, the images of s are $s*s*s$ and the range is the set of all real numbers. The range and codomain are the same for the cube function. However, this may not be true for other functions such as the square function, x*x, with domain and codomain of real numbers. Since the range of the square function is only non-negative real numbers, the range and codomain are not the same.

Using set notation, the range of a function can be written as

```
R ≡ {f(s) | s ∈ S}
```

The **curly braces** { } denote a **set**. The **bar**, |, is read as "where". The above statement can be read that the range R is equivalent to the set of values $f(s)$ where every element s is in the set S. The association is a set of ordered pairs (s,t), where $s \in S$, $t \in T$, and $t{=}f(s)$. Every member of S must have one and only one element of T associated with it. However, multiple t values may be associated with a single s. As a simple example, every positive number n has two square roots, $\pm \sqrt{n}$.

Functions may also be defined recursively as in

```
factorial(n) ≡ n*factorial(n-1)
   where n is an integer and
   factorial is an integer function
```

Recursive functions are commonly used in functional languages such as LISP.

Mathematical concepts and expressions are **referentially transparent** because the meaning of the whole is completely determined from its parts. No synergism is involved between the parts. As an example, consider the functional expression $x+(2*x)$. The result is obviously $3*x$. Both $x+(2*x)$ and $3*x$ give the same results no matter what values are substituted for x. Even other functions can be substituted for x and the result is the same. For example, let $h(y)$ be some arbitrary function. Then $h(y) + (2 * h(y))$ would still be equivalent to $3*h(y)$.

Now consider the following assignment statement in an imperative computer language such as Pascal.

```
sum := f(x) + x
```

If the parameter x is passed by reference and its value is changed in the function call, $f(x)$, what value will be used for x? Depending on how the compiler is written, the value of x might be the original value if it was saved on a stack, or the new value if x was not saved. Another source of confusion occurs if the one compiler evaluates expressions right-to-left while another evaluates left-to-right. In this case, $f(x)+x$ would not evaluate the same as $x+f(x)$ on different compilers even if the same language was used. Other side-effects may occur due to global variables. Thus, unlike mathematical functions, program functions are not referentially transparent.

Functional programming languages were created to be referentially transparent. Five parts make up a functional language:

- **data objects** for the language functions to operate on
- **primitive functions** to operate on the data objects
- **functional forms** to synthesize new functions from other functions
- **application operations** on functions that returns a value and
- **naming procedures** to identify new functions.

Functional languages are generally implemented as interpreters for ease of construction and immediate user response.

In LISP (LISt Processing), data objects are **symbolic expressions** (S-expressions) that are either **lists** or **atoms**, while in **APL** (A Programming Language) the objects are arrays. Examples of lists are

```
(milk eggs cheese)
(shopping (groceries (milk eggs cheese) clothes
(pants)))
()
```

Lists are always enclosed in matching parentheses with spaces separating the elements. The elements of lists can be atoms, such as milk, eggs, and cheese, or embedded lists such as (milk eggs cheese) and (pants). Lists can be split up but atoms cannot. The **empty list**, (), contains no elements and is called **nil**.

There must be some primitive functions provided by the language as a basis for building more complex functions. In the original version of LISP, created by John McCarthy in 1960, there were few primitives, as shown in Table 1-12. Primitives CAR, CDR, CPR, and CTR are acronyms named after the specific hardware registers in the first machine to run LISP. CPR and CTR are now obsolete but the acronyms of the others have remained. Also shown are the **predicates** of LISP. Predicates are special functions that return values representing true and false.

The original version of LISP was called pure LISP because it was purely functional. However, it was also not very efficient for writing programs. Non-functional additions have been made to LISP to increase the efficiency of writing programs. For example, SET acts as the assignment operator, while LET and PROG can be used to create local variables and execute a sequence of S-expressions. Although these act like functions, they are not functional in the original mathematical sense.

Function	Predicates
QUOTE	ATOM
CAR	EQ
CDR	NULL
CPR	
CTR	
CONS	
EVAL	
COND	
LAMBDA	
DEFINE	
LABEL	

Table 1-12
Original LISP Primitives and Functions

Since its creation, LISP has been the leading AI language in the United States. Many of the original expert system shells were written in LISP because it is so easy to experiment with LISP. However, conventional computers do not execute LISP very efficiently and execute the shells built using LISP even worse. In order to circumvent this problem, several companies offer machines specifically designed to execute LISP code. These LISP machines use it completely, even as their assembly language. However, the LISP machines cost considerably more than conventional machines and are for single users.

This problem of high cost has an impact on both the development and the **delivery problem**. It is not enough just to develop a great program if it cannot be delivered for use because of high cost. A good development workstation is not necessarily a good delivery vehicle due to speed, power, size, weight, environmental or cost constraints. Some applications may even require that the final code be placed in ROM for reasons of cost and nonvolatility. Putting code into ROM can be a problem with some AI and expert systems tools that require special hardware to run. It's better to consider this possibility in advance rather than have to recode a program later.

An additional problem is that of embedding AI with conventional programming languages such as C, Ada, Pascal and FORTRAN. For example, certain applications which require extensive number-crunching are best done in conventional languages rather than in LISP, or expert systems languages written in LISP or PROLOG.

Unless special provisions are made, expert systems which are written in LISP are generally difficult to embed in anything other than LISP programs. One major consideration in selecting an AI language should be the language in which the tool is written. For reasons of portability, efficiency, and speed, many expert systems tools are now being written in or converted to C. This also eliminates the problem of requiring expensive special hardware for LISP-based applications.

1.12   NONPROCEDURAL PARADIGMS

Nonprocedural paradigms do not depend on the programmer giving exact details for how a problem is to be solved. This is the opposite of the procedural paradigms which specify *how* a function or statement sequence computes. In nonprocedural paradigms, the emphasis is on specifying *what* is to be accomplished and letting the system determine how to accomplish it.

Declarative Programming

The **declarative paradigm** separates the **goal** from the methods used to achieve the goal. The user specifies the goal while the underlying mechanism of the implementation tries to satisfy the goal. A number of paradigms and associated programming languages have been created to implement the declarative model.

Object-oriented Programming

The **object-oriented** paradigm is another case of a paradigm which can be considered partly imperative and partly declarative. The term object-oriented today is used in two different ways. The expression **object-oriented design** is growing in popularity as a programming methodology in imperative programming languages such as Ada and Modula-2. The basic idea is to design a program by considering the data used in the program as objects and then implementing operations on those objects. This is the opposite of top-down design which proceeds by stepwise refinement of a program's control structure. In fact, object-oriented design is essentially what used to be called bottom-up design. Unfortunately, the term bottom-up never sounded quite as impressive as object-oriented.

As an example of object-oriented design, consider the task of writing a program to manage a charge account with an interactive menu (Riley 87). The important data objects are current balance, amount of charge, and amount of payment. Various operations can be defined to act on the data objects. These operations would be add charge, make payment, and add monthly interest. Once all data objects, operations and the menu interface are defined, coding can begin. This object-oriented design methodology is well-suited to a program that has a weak control structure. It would not be as suitable in a program that requires a strong control structure such as a payroll application. For the payroll case there is a definite sequence of steps to follow.

1.   Obtain time-card data
2.   Account for sick-leave and vacation time
3.   Multiply hours worked X rate of pay

4. Multiply overtime hours X overtime rate
5. Add bonus or sales commissions, if applicable
6. Subtract deductions for taxes, insurance, dues and retirement
7. Issue paycheck

Object-oriented design requires no special language features. It can be done in FORTRAN, BASIC, C and so on. Languages such as Ada and Modula-2 support object-oriented design because these languages have features to encapsulate data in modules and packages.

The term **object-oriented programming** was originally used for languages such as Smalltalk, which was specifically designed for objects. The term is now often used to mean programming of an object-oriented design even in a language which has no true object support.

Smalltalk has features to support objects built into the language. In fact, Smalltalk has a programming environment entirely built using objects. Smalltalk is descended from SIMULA 67, a language developed for simulation. SIMULA 67 introduced the concept of **class** which led to the concept of information hiding in modules. A class is essentially a type which is a template that defines the structure of data. In fact, the concept of type in Pascal and Modula-2 came from class. An **instance** of a class is a data object that can be manipulated. The term instance has carried over to expert systems where it denotes a fact that matches a pattern. Likewise, a rule is said to be instantiated if its LHS is satisfied. The terms activated and instantiated in rule-based systems are synonymous.

Another significant concept that came from SIMULA 67 is **inheritance**. In SIMULA 67, a **subclass** could be defined to inherit the properties of classes. For example, one class may be defined to consist of objects that can be used in a stack and another class defined to be complex numbers. Now a subclass can be easily defined as objects that are complex numbers used in a stack. That is, these objects have inherited properties from both classes above them, called **superclasses**. The concept of inheritance can be extended to organize objects in a hierarchy where objects can inherit from their classes, which can inherit from their classes, and so on. Inheritance is very useful since objects can inherit properties from their classes without the programmer having to specify every property. Many expert systems tools today such as ART and KEE allow inheritance because it is a very powerful tool in constructing large groups of facts.

Logic Programming

One of the first AI applications of computers was in proving logic theorems with the Logic Theorist program of Newell and Simon. This program was first reported at the Dartmouth Conference on AI in 1956 and caused a sensation because electronic computers previously had been used only for numeric calculations. Now a computer was actually reasoning the proofs of mathematical theorems, which had been a task that only mathematicians were thought capable of doing.

In the Logic Theorist and its successor, the General Problem Solver (GPS), Newell and Simon concentrated on trying to implement powerful algorithms that could solve any problem. While the Logic Theorist was meant only for mathematical theorem proving, GPS was designed to solve any kind of logic problem, including games and puzzles such as chess, Tower of Hanoi, Missionaries and Cannibals, and cryptarithmetic. An example of their famous cryptarithmetic (secret arithmetic) puzzle is

```
    DONALD
+   GERALD
    ROBERT
```

and it is known that D=5. The object is to figure out the arithmetic values of the other letters in the range 0-9.

GPS was the first problem solving program to clearly separate the problem solving knowledge from the domain knowledge. This paradigm of explicitly separating the problem-solving knowledge from the domain knowledge is now used as the basis of expert systems. In expert systems today, the inference engine decides what knowledge should be used and how it should be applied.

Efforts continued to improve mechanical theorem proving. By the early 1970's, it had been discovered that computation is a special case of mechanical, logical deduction (Kowalski 1985). When backward chaining was applied to sentences of the form "conclusion if conditions", it was powerful enough for significant theorem proving. The conditions can be thought of as representing patterns to be matched as in production rules discussed earlier. Sentences expressed in this form are called Horn clauses after Alfred Horn, who first investigated them. In 1972, the language PROLOG was created by Kowalski, Colmerauer and Roussel to implement logic programming by backward chaining using Horn clauses.

Backward chaining can be used both to express the knowledge in a declarative representation and also control the reasoning process. Typically, backward chaining proceeds by defining smaller **subgoals** that must be satisfied if the initial goal is to be satisfied. These subgoals are then further broken down into smaller subgoals and so forth.

An example of declarative knowledge is the following classic example.

```
    All men are mortal
    Socrates is a man
```

can be expressed in the Horn clauses

```
    someone is mortal
        if someone is a man
    Socrates is a man
        if (in all cases)
```

For the sentence about Socrates, the if condition is true in all cases. In other words, the knowledge about Socrates does not require any pattern to match. Contrast this with the mortal case in which someone must be a man for the pattern of the if condition to be satisfied.

Notice that a Horn clause can be interpreted as a procedure that tells how to satisfy a goal. That is, to determine if someone is mortal, it is necessary to determine if someone is a man. As a slightly more complex example,

```
A car needs gas, oil and inflated tires to run
```

can be expressed in a Horn clause as

```
x is a car and runs
   if x has gas and
   if x has oil and
   if x has inflated tires
```

Notice how the problem of determining if a car will run has been reduced to three simpler subproblems or subgoals. Now suppose there is some additional declarative knowledge as follows.

```
The fuel gauge shows not-empty if a car has gas
The dipstick shows not-empty if a car has oil
The air pressure gauge shows at least 20 if a car has
inflated tires
The fuel gauge shows not-empty
The dipstick reads empty
The air pressure gauge shows at least 15
```

These can be translated into the following Horn clauses.

```
x has gas
   if the fuel gauge shows not-empty
x has oil
   if the dipstick shows not-empty
x has inflated tires
   if the air pressure gauge shows at least 20
Fuel gauge is not empty
   if (in all cases)
Dipstick reads empty
Air pressure is at least 15
   if (in all cases)
```

From these clauses, a mechanical theorem prover can prove that the car will not run because there is no oil and insufficient air pressure.

One of the advantages of backward chaining systems is that execution can proceed in parallel. That is, if multiple processors were available they could work on satisfying subgoals simultaneously. This parallel operation can greatly speed up the execution of programs and is one of the reasons that the Japanese chose PROLOG as the programming language for their Fifth Generation Computer project (Moto-Oka 1982). This is an ambitious project to develop the next generation of computers for the 1990's with capabilities far surpassing current models. These machines were to be programmed with declarative techniques, but this approach has run into difficulties. The Fifth Generation project was announced by the Japanese in 1981 with a budget of $850 million dollars. The twenty-six initial goals of the project included natural language translation of Japanese to English and vice-versa, problem-solving and inferencing a thousand times faster than current machines, ability to read handwritten text, understand pictures, intelligent access of huge databases, and to converse in natural language.

PROLOG is more than just a language. At a minimum, PROLOG is a shell since it requires

- an interpreter or inference engine
- a database (facts and rules)
- a form of pattern matching called **unification**
- a **backtracking** mechanism to pursue alternate subgoals if a search to satisfy a goal is unsuccessful

More elaborate versions of PROLOG such as TurboPROLOG from Borland are tools because of all the enhancements provided.

As an example of backward chaining, suppose you can pay for the oil to make the car run if you have cash or a credit card. One subgoal is checked to see if you have cash. If there is no fact that you do have cash, the backtracking mechanism will then explore the other subgoal to see if you have a credit card. If you have a credit card, the goal of paying for oil can be satisfied. Notice that the absence of a fact to prove a goal is just as effective, although perhaps less efficient, than a negative fact such as "Dipstick reads empty." Either negative facts or missing facts can cause a goal to be unsatisfied.

If the backtracking and pattern matching mechanisms are not needed by the problem, then the programmer must work around them or code in a different language. One of the advantages of logic programming is executable specifications. That is, specifying the requirements of a problem by Horn clauses produces an executable program. This is very different from conventional programming in which the requirements document does not look at all like the final executable code. Newer imperative languages such as Ada attempt to circumvent this problem by offering the capability of using Ada itself as the program description language (PDL). The PDL can be used as a skeleton on which to build the rest of the program. If the PDL does not work right, then neither will the program.

Unlike production rule systems, the order in which subgoals, facts and rules are entered in a PROLOG program has significant effects. Efficiency and therefore speed are affected by the way that PROLOG searches its database. However, there are programs that execute correctly if subgoals, facts, and rules are entered one way but go into an infinite loop or have a run-time error if the order changes (Ghezzi 87b).

Expert Systems

Expert systems can be considered declarative programming because the programmer does not specify how a program is to achieve its goal at the level of an algorithm. For example, in a rule-based expert system, any of the rules may become activated and put on the agenda if its LHS matches the facts. The order that the rules were entered does not affect which rules are activated. Thus, the program statement order does not specify a rigid control flow. Other types of expert systems are based **frames**, discussed in chapter 2, and **inference nets** discussed in chapter 4.

There are a number of differences between expert systems and conventional programs. Table 1-13 lists some typical differences.

Characteristic	Conventional Program	Expert System
Control by ...	Statement order	Inference engine
Control and data	Implicit integration	Explicit separation
Control Strength	Strong	Weak
Solution by ...	Algorithm	Rules and inference
Solution search	Small or none	Large
Problem solving	Algorithm is correct	Rules
Input	Assumed correct	Incomplete, incorrect
Unexpected input	Difficult to deal with	Very responsive
Output	Always correct	Varies with problem
Explanation	None	Usually
Applications	Numeric, file, and text	Symbolic reasoning
Execution	Generally sequential	Opportunistic rules
Program design	Structured design	Little or no structure
Modifiability	Difficult	Reasonable
Expansion	Done in major jumps	Incremental

Table 1-13
Some Typical Differences between Conventional Programs and Expert Systems

Expert systems are often designed to deal with uncertainty because reasoning is one of the best tools that we have discovered for dealing with uncertainty. The uncertainty may arise in the input data to the expert system and even the knowledge-base itself. At first this may seem surprising to people used to conventional programming. However, much of human knowledge is heuristic, which means that it may only work correctly part of the time. In addition, the input data may be incorrect, incomplete, inconsistent and have other errors. Algorithmic solutions are not capable of dealing with situations like this because an algorithm guarantees the solution of a problem in a finite series of steps.

Depending on the input data and the knowledge-base, an expert system may come up with the correct answer, a good answer, a bad answer or no answer at all. While this may seem shocking at first, the alternative is no answer all the time. Again, the important thing to keep in mind is that a good expert system will perform no worse than the best problem-solver for problems like this—a human expert—and may do better. If we knew an efficient algorithmic method that was better than an expert system, we would use it. The important thing is to use the best, and perhaps only, tool for the job.

Nondeclarative Programming

Nondeclarative paradigms are becoming popular. These new paradigms are being increasingly used for a wide variety of applications. They can be used in stand-alone applications or in conjunction with other paradigms.

Induction-based Programming

An application of AI that is attracting interest is **induction-based** programming. In this paradigm, the program learns by example. One application to which this paradigm has been applied is database access. Instead of the user having to type in the specific values for one or more fields for a search, it is only necessary to select one or more appropriate example fields with those characteristics. The database program infers the characteristics of the data and searches the database for a match.

Expert system tools such as 1st-Class and KDS offer induction-learning by which they accept examples and case studies and automatically generate rules.

1.13   ARTIFICIAL NEURAL SYSTEMS

A new development in programming paradigms arose in the 1980's called **artificial neural systems (ANS)**, based on how the brain processes information. This paradigm is sometimes called **connectionism** because it models solutions to problems by training simulated neurons connected in a network. Many researchers are investigating neural nets. The nets hold great potential as the front-end of expert systems that require massive amounts of input from sensors as well as real-time response.

The Traveling Salesman Problem

ANS has had remarkable success in providing real-time response to complex pattern recognition problems. In one case, a neural net running on an ordinary microcomputer obtained a very good solution to the Traveling Salesman problem in 0.1 seconds compared to the optimum solution that required an hour of CPU time on a mainframe (Port 86). The Traveling Salesman problem is important because it is the classic problem faced in optimizing the routing of signals in a telecommunications system. Optimizing routing is important in minimizing the travel time, and thus efficiency and speed.

The basic Traveling Salesman problem is to compute the shortest route through a given list of cities. Table 1-14 shows the possible routes for one to four cities. Notice that the number of routes is proportional to the factorial of the number of cities minus one, $(N-1)!$.

Number of Cities	Routes
1	1
2	1–2-1
3	1–2–3-1
	1–3–2-1
4	1–2–3–4-1
	1–2–4–3-1
	1–3–2–4-1
	1–3–4–2-1
	1–4–2–3-1
	1–4–3–2-1

Table 1-14
Traveling Salesman Problem Routes

While there are $9! = 362880$ routes for ten cities, there are $29! = 8.8E30$ possible routes for thirty cities. The Traveling Salesman problem is a classic example of **combinatorial explosion** because the number of possible routes increases so rapidly that there are no practical solutions for realistic numbers of cities. If it takes 1 hour of a mainframe CPU time to solve for thirty cities, it will take 30 hours for thirty-one cities and 330 hours for thirty-two cities. These are actually very small numbers when compared to the thousands of telecommunications switches and cities that are used in routing of data packets and real items.

A neural net can solve the ten-city case just as fast as the thirty-city case while a conventional computer takes much longer. For the ten-city case, the neural net came up with one of the two best routes and for the thirty-city case, it came up with one of the best 100,000,000 routes. This is more impressive if it is realized that this route is in the top 1E-22 of the best solutions. Although neural nets may not always give the optimum answer, they can provide a best guess in real-time. In many cases, a 99.999999999999999 % correct answer in one millisecond is better than a 100 % correct answer in thirty hours.

Elements of an ANS

An ANS is basically an analog computer that uses simple processing elements connected in a highly parallel manner. The processing elements perform very simple Boolean or arithmetic functions on their inputs. The key to the functioning of an ANS is the **weights** associated with each element. It is the weights which represent the information stored in the system.

A typical artificial neuron is shown in Figure 1-10. The neuron may have multiple inputs but only one output. The human brain contains about 10^{10} neurons and one neuron may have thousands of connections to another. The input signals to the neuron are multiplied by the weights and are summed to yield the total neuron input, I. The weights can be represented as a matrix and identified by subscripts.

$$I \equiv \text{Neuron Input}_i = \sum_j W_{ij} \, I_j$$

$$\text{Neuron Output} = \frac{1}{1 + e^{-(I - \theta)}}$$

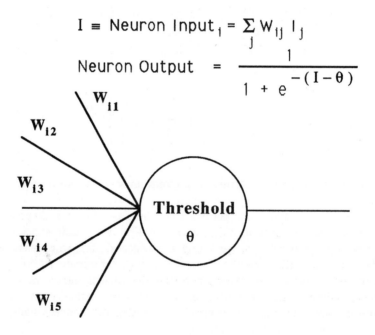

Figure 1-10
A Neuron Processing Element

The neuron output is often taken as a **sigmoid function** of the input. The sigmoid is representative of real neurons which approach limits for very small and very large inputs. The sigmoid is called an **activation function,** and a commonly used function is $(1+e^{-x})^{-1}$. Each neuron also has an associated **threshold value,** θ, which is subtracted from the total input I. Figure 1-11 shows an ANS which can compute the **exclusive-OR (XOR)** of its inputs using a technique called **back-propagation.**

The XOR gives a true output only when its inputs are not all true or not all false. The number of nodes in the hidden layer will vary depending on the application and design.

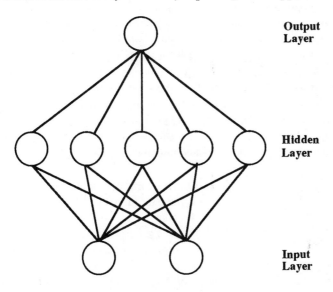

Figure 1-11
A Back-propagation Net

Neural nets are not programmed in the conventional sense. There are about thirteen known neural net learning algorithms, such as **counter-propagation** and back-propagation, to train nets. The programmer "programs" the net by simply supplying the input and corresponding output data. The net learns by automatically adjusting weights in the network which connect the neurons. The weights and the threshold values of neurons determine the propagation of data through the net and so its correct response to the training data. Training the net to the correct responses may take hours or days depending on the number of patterns that the net must learn, the hardware, and software. However, once the learning is accomplished, the net responds very quickly.

If software simulation is not fast enough, ANS can be fabricated in chips for real-time response. Once the network has been trained and the weights determined, a chip can be constructed. AT&T and other companies are fabricating experimental neural net chips containing hundreds of neurons. In the next few years, it is very likely that chips will be fabricated containing thousands of neurons.

Characteristics of ANS

ANS architecture is very different from a conventional computer architecture. In a conventional computer, it is possible to correlate discrete information with memory cells. For example, a Social Security number could be stored as ASCII code in a contiguous group of memory cells. By examining the contents of this contiguous group, the Social Security number could be directly reconstructed. This reconstruction is possible because there is a one-to-one relationship between each character of the Social Security number and the memory cell that contains the ASCII code of that character.

ANS are modeled after current brain theories in which information is represented by the weights. However, there is no direct correlation between a specific weight and a specific item of stored information. This distributed representation of information is similar to that of a hologram in which the lines of the hologram act as a diffraction grating to reconstruct the stored image when laser light is passed through.

A neural net is a good choice when there is much empirical data and no algorithm exists which provides sufficient accuracy and speed. ANS offers several advantages compared to the storage of conventional computers.

- *Storage is very **fault tolerant**.* Portions of the net can be removed and there is only a degradation in quality of the stored data. This occurs because the information is stored in a distributed manner.

- *The quality of the stored image degrades gracefully in proportion to the amount of net removed.* There is no catastrophic loss of information. The storage and quality features are also characteristic of holograms.

- *Data is naturally stored in the form of **associative memory**.* An associative memory is one in which partial data is sufficient to recall of the complete stored information. This contrasts with conventional memory in which data is recalled by specifying the address of the data to be recalled. A partial or noisy input may still elicit the complete original information.

- *Nets can extrapolate and interpolate from their stored information.* Training teaches a net to look for significant features or relationships in the data. Afterwards, the net can extrapolate to suggest relationships on new data. In one experiment (Hinton 86), a neural net was trained on the family relationships of twenty-four hypothetical people. Afterwards, the net could also answer correctly relationships about which it had not been trained.

- *Nets have **plasticity**.* Even if a number of neurons are removed, the net can be retrained to its original skill level if enough neurons remain. This is also a characteristic of the brain in which portions can be destroyed and the original skill levels can be relearned in time.

These characteristics make ANS very attractive for robot spacecraft, oil field equipment, underwater devices, process control and other applications that need to function a long time in a hostile environment without repair. Besides the issue of reliability, ANS offer the potential of low maintenance cost because of plasticity. Even if hardware repair can be done, it will probably be more cost-effective to reprogram the neural net than replace it.

ANS are generally not well-suited for applications that require number-crunching or an optimum solution. Also, if a practical algorithmic solution exists, an ANS is not a good choice.

Developments in ANS Technology

The origins of ANS started with the mathematical modeling of neurons by McCulloch and Pitts in 1943 (McCulloch 43). An explanation of learning by neurons was given by Hebb in 1949 (Hebb 49). In Hebbian learning, a neuron's efficiency in triggering another neuron increases with **firing**. The term firing means that a neuron emits an electrochemical impulse which can stimulate other neurons connected to it. There is evidence that the conductivity of connections between neurons at their connections, called **synapses**, increases with firing. In ANS, the weight of connections between neurons is changed to simulate the changing conductance of natural neurons.

In 1961, Rosenblatt published an influential book dealing with a new type of artificial neuron system he had been investigating called a **perceptron** (Rosenblatt 61). The perceptron was a remarkable device that showed capabilities for learning and pattern recognition. It basically consisted of two layers of neurons and a simple learning algorithm. The weights had to be manually set in contrast to modern ANS that set the weights themselves based on training. Many researchers entered the field of ANS and began studying perceptrons during the 1960's.

The early perceptron era came to an end in 1969 when Minsky and Papert published a book called *Perceptrons* that showed the theoretical limitations of perceptrons as a general computing machine (Minsky 69). They pointed out a deficiency of the perceptron in being able to compute only 14 of the 16 basic logic functions, which means that a Perceptron is not a general purpose computing device. In particular, they proved a perceptron could not recognize the exclusive-OR. Although they had not seriously investigated multiple layer ANS, they gave the pessimistic view that multiple layers would probably not be able to solve the XOR problem. Government funding of ANS research ceased in favor of the symbolic approach to AI using languages such as LISP and algorithms. New methods of representing symbolic AI information by frames, invented by Minsky, became popular during the 1970's. Further work on perceptrons has continued with new types able to overcome Minsky's objections (Reece 87). Because of their simplicity, perceptrons and other ANS are easy to construct with modern integrated circuit technology.

ANS research continued on a small scale in the 1970's. However, the field finally entered a renaissance starting with the work of Hopfield in 1982 (Hopfield 82). He put ANS on a firm theoretical foundation with the two-layer Hopfield Net and demonstrated how ANS could solve a wide variety of problems. The general structure of a Hopfield Net is shown in Figure 1-12. In particular, he showed how an ANS could solve the Traveling Salesman Problem in constant time as compared to the combinatorial explosion encountered by conventional algorithmic solutions. An electronic circuit form of an ANS could solve the Traveling Salesman Problem in 1 μ second. Other combinatorial optimization problems can easily be done by ANS such as the four-color map, the Euclidean-match (Hopfield 86b), and the transposition code (Tank 85).

An ANS that can easily solve the XOR problem is the **back-propagation** net, also known as the **generalized delta rule** (Rumelhart 86). The back-propagation net is commonly implemented as a three-layer net, although additional layers can be specified. The layers between the input and output layers are called **hidden layers** because only the input and output layers are visible to the external world. An important theoretical result from mathematics, the Kolmogorov Theorem, can be interpreted as proving that a three-layer network with n inputs and 2n + 1 neurons in the hidden layer can map any continuous function (Hecht-Nielsen 86).

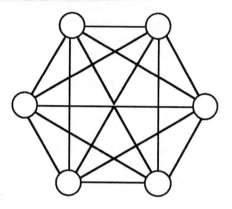

Figure 1-12
A Hopfield Artificial Neural Net

Applications of ANS Technology

A significant example of learning by back-propagation was demonstrated by a neural net that learned correct pronunciation of words from text (Sejnowski 86). The ANS was trained by correcting its output using a Digital Equipment Corp. text to speech device called DECTalk. It required twenty years of linguistic research to devise rules for correct pronunciation used by DECTalk. The ANS taught itself equivalent pronunciation skills overnight by simply listening to the correct pronunciation of speech from text. No linguistic skills were programmed into the ANS.

Investigations of the ANS are under way for recognition of radar targets by electronic and optical computers (Farhat 86). New implementations of neural nets using optical components promise optical computers with speeds millions of times faster than electronic ones. Optical implementation of ANS is attractive because of the inherent parallelism of light. That is, light rays do not interfere with one another as they travel. Huge numbers of photons can easily be generated and manipulated by optical components such as mirrors, lenses, high-speed programmable spatial light modulators, arrays of optical bistable devices that can function as optical neurons, and diffraction gratings. Optical computers designed as ANS appear to be complementary to one another.

Commercial Developments in ANS

A number of new companies and existing firms have been organized to develop ANS technology and products. Nestor markets an ANS product called NestorWriter that can recognize handwritten input and convert it to text using a PC. Other companies such as TRW, SAIC, HNC, Synaptics, Neural Tech, Revelations Research and Texas Instruments market a variety of ANS simulators and hardware accelerator boards to speed up learning. One of the best bargains for getting started in neural computing is volume 3 of Rumelhart's books on Parallel Distributed Processing available from the MIT Press. The book describes a half-dozen ANS simulators and also includes a diskette with software for an IBM PC compatible machine for $27.50. By purchasing a 386 accelerator card for an IBM XT or compatible, a person can have a very powerful system for ANS at low cost.

1.14 CONNECTIONIST EXPERT SYSTEMS AND INDUCTIVE LEARNING

It is possible to build expert systems using ANS. In one system, the ANS is the knowledge-base constructed by training examples from medicine for disease (Gallant 88). In this system, the expert system tries to classify a disease from its symptoms into one of the known diseases that the system has been trained on. An inference engine called MACIE (Matrix Controlled Inference Engine) was designed that uses the ANS knowledge-base. The system uses forward chaining to make inferences and backward chaining to query the user for any additional data needed to produce a solution. Although an ANS by itself cannot explain why its weights are set to certain values, MACIE can interpret the ANS and generate IF THEN rules to explain its knowledge.

An ANS expert system such as this uses **inductive learning**. That is, the system **induces** the information in its knowledge-base by example. Induction is the process of inferring the general case from the specific. Besides ANS, there are a number of commercially available expert systems shells that explicitly generate rules from examples. The goal of inductive learning is to reduce or eliminate the knowledge acquisition bottleneck. By placing the burden of knowledge acquisition on the expert system, the development time may be reduced and the reliability may be increased if the system induces rules that were not known by a human.

1.15 SUMMARY

In this chapter we have reviewed the problems and developments which have led to expert systems. These problems that expert systems are used for are generally not solvable by conventional programs because they lack a known or efficient algorithm. Since expert systems are knowledge-based, they can be effectively used for real-world problems that are ill-structured and difficult to solve by other means.

The advantages and disadvantages of expert systems were also discussed in the context of selecting an appropriate problem domain for an expert system application. Criteria for selecting appropriate applications were given.

The essentials of an expert system shell were discussed with reference to rule-based expert systems. The basic recognize-act inference engine cycle was described and illustrated by a simple rule example. Finally, the relationship of expert systems to other programming paradigms was described in terms of the appropriate domain of each paradigm. The important point of all this is the concept that expert systems should be viewed as another programming tool that is suitable for some applications and unsuitable for others. Later chapters will describe the features and suitability of expert systems in much more detail.

PROBLEMS

1-1.   Identify a person other than yourself who is considered an expert or very knowledgeable. Interview this expert and discuss how well this person's expertise would be modeled by an expert system in terms of each criterion in the section "Advantages of Expert Systems."

1-2.   a)   Write ten nontrivial rules expressing the expert of problem 1's knowledge.

b)   Write a program that will give your expert's advice. Include test results to show that each of the ten rules gives the correct advice. For ease of programming, you may allow the user to provide input from a menu.

1-3.   a)   In Newell and Simon's book, *Human Problem Solving*, they mention the 9-Dot Problem. Given 9 dots arranged as follows, how can you draw four lines through all the dots without (a) lifting your pencil from the paper and (b) crossing any dot? (Hint: you can extend the line past the dots)

> •   •   •
> •   •   •
> •   •   •

b)   Explain your reasoning (if any) in finding the solution and whether an expert system or some other type of program would be a good paradigm to solve this type of problem.

1-4.   Write a program that can solve cryptarithmetic problems. Show the result for the following problem, where D=5.

```
    DONALD
 +  GERALD
    ROBERT
```

1-5.   Write a set of production rules to extinguish five different types of fire such as oil, chemical and so forth, given the type of fire.

1-6.
a) Write a set of production rules to diagnose three types of poison based on symptoms.
b) Modify the program so that it will also recommend a treatment once the poison has been identified.

1-7.   Write a report on three different applications of expert systems that were not discussed in this chapter. Include a copy of your sources of information.

1-8.   Give ten heuristic IF THEN type rules that save you time.

1-9.   Give ten IF THEN type heuristic rules for buying a used car.

1-10.   Give ten IF THEN type heuristic rules for planning your class schedule.

1-11.   Give ten IF THEN type heuristic rules for buying a motorcycle.

1-12.   Give ten IF THEN type heuristic rules for buying a three-wheeled vehicle.

1-13.   Give ten IF THEN type heuristic rules for excuses for a late assignment.

1-14.   Write a report on XCON, XSEL and all the other expert systems for sales and manufacturing used by Digital Equipment Corp. In particular, discuss how all the expert systems cooperate to work together. Use the two most recent articles for reference and include a copy of the articles with your report.

1-15.   Answer the following questions about one of the classic expert systems referenced in the Historical Bibliography by looking up at least three appropriate papers or other references. Include a copy of all references with your answers.

a) What were the purposes in developing it?
b) How successful was it for research purposes?
c) Was it ever commercially successful or put into routine use?
d) What other expert systems, if any, were an outgrowth of it?
e) What new concepts did it develop?

Bibliography

(Buchanan 78). Bruce G. Buchanan and Edward A. Feigenbaum, "Dendral and Meta-Dendral: Their Applications Dimension," *Artificial Intelligence*, **11**, (1), pp. 5-24, 1978.

(Chase 73). W. G. Chase and Herbert A. Simon, "The Mind's Eye in Chess," *Visual Information Processing*, ed. W. G. Chase, Academic Press, 1973.

(Elson 73). Mark Elson, *Concepts of Programming Languages*, Science Research Associates, p. 290, 1973.

(Ennis 86). R. L. Ennis *et al.*, "A Continuous Real-time Expert System for Computer Operations," *IBM J. Res. Develop.*, **30**, (1), pp. 14-28, 1986.

(Farhat 86). N.H. Farhat, *et al.*, "Optical Analog of Two-Dimensional Neural Networks and Their Application in Recognition of Radar Targets," *Proceedings of the Neural Networks for Computing Meeting*, Snowbird, UT, pp. 146-152, 1986.

(Feigenbaum 81). Edward A. Feigenbaum, *Handbook of Artificial Intelligence*, Heuris Tech Press/William Kaufman, Inc., 1981-2.

(Feigenbaum 82). Edward A. Feigenbaum, "Knowledge Engineering in the 1980's," Dept. of Computer Science, Stanford University, Stanford CA, 1982.

(Forgy 82). Charles Forgy, "Rete: A Fast Algorithm for the Many Pattern/Many Object Pattern Match Problem,"*Artificial Intelligence*, **19**, pp. 17-37, 1982.

(Gallant 88). Stephen L. Gallant, "Connectionist Expert Systems," *Comm. of the ACM*, **31**, (2), pp. 152-169, Feb. 1988.

(Gersting 82). Judith L. Gersting, *Mathematical Structures for Computer Science*, W. L. Freeman and Co., pp. 64-67, 1982.

(Ghezzi 87a). Carlo Ghezzi and Mehdi Jazayeri, *Programming Language Concepts*, John Wiley and Sons, Inc., p. 293, 1987.

(Ghezzi 87b). *op. cit.*, pp. 304-306.

(Harmon 85). Paul Harmon and David King, *Expert Systems*, John Wiley, p. 21, 1985.

(Hayes-Roth 85). Frederick Hayes-Roth, "Rule-based Systems," *Communications of the ACM*, **28**, (9), pp. 921-932, Sept. 1985.

(Hebb 49). D. O. Hebb, *Organization of Behavior*, John Wiley, 1949.

(Hecht-Nielsen 87). Robert Hecht-Nielsen, "Kolmogorov's Mapping Neural Network Existence Theorem," *Proceedings of the First International Conference on Networks*, **III**, pp.11-14, June1987.

(Hinton 86). Geoffrey E. Hinton, "Learning Distributed Representations of Concepts," *Proceedings 8th Annual Conference of the Cognitive Science Society*, Lawrence Erlbaum Assoc., Hillsdale, NJ, 1986.

(Hopfield 82). J. J. Hopfield, "Neural Networks and Physical Systems with Emergent Collective Computational Abilities," Proceedings of the National Academy of Sciences, USA, **79**, (8), pp. 2554-2558, 1982.

(Hopfield 86a). John J. Hopfield and David W. Tank, "Computing with Neural Circuits: A Model," *Science*, **233**, pp. 625-633, 1986.

(Hopfield 86b). John J. Hopfield and David W. Tank, *Disordered Systems and Biological Organization*, Springer-Verlag, 1986.

(Hugh 88). Dafydd Ab Hugh, "The Future of Flying," *AI Expert*, pp. 66-69, Jan. 1988.

(Kerschberg 86). Larry Kerschberg, ed., *Expert Database Systems: Proceedings from the First International Workshop*, Benjamin/Cummings Publishing Co., 1986.

(Kowalski 1985). Robert Kowalski, "Logic Programming," *Byte*, p. 161, August 1985.

(Markov 54). A. A. Markov, *A Theory of Algorithms*, National Academy of Sciences, USSR, (in English) 1954.

(McCulloch 43). Warren S. McCulloch and Walter Pitts, "A Logical Calculus of the Ideas Immanent in Nervous Activity," *Bulletin of Mathematical Biophysics*, **5**, pp. 115-137, 1943.

(McDermott 84). John McDermott and Judith Bachant, "R1 Revisited: Four Years in the Trenches," *AI Magazine*, **V**, (3), pp. 21-32, Fall 1984.

(Michie 73). D. Michie, "Knowledge Engineering," *Cybernetics*, **2**, pp. 197-200, 1973.

(Minsky 69). *Perceptrons-An Introduction to Computational Geometry*, MIT Press, 1969. Note: a second edition was published in 1988 containing some handwritten corrections and an additional chapter criticizing the modern ANS algorithms such as back-propagation.

(Moto-Oka 1982) Moto-Oka, T., ed., *Fifth Generation Computer Systems*, Elsevier, 1982.

(Newell 72). Allen Newell and Herbert A. Simon, *Human Problem Solving*, Prentice-Hall, 1972.

(Newell 72a) *op. cit.* p. 33.

(Parrello 88). Bruce Parrello, "Car Wars: The (Almost) Birth of an Expert System," *AI Expert*, pp. 60-64, Jan. 1988.

(Post 43). Emil L. Post, "Formal Reductions of the General Combinatorial Decision Problem," *American Journal Of Mathematics*, **65**, pp. 197-215, 1943.

(Reece 87). Peter Reece, "Perceptrons & Neural Nets," *AI Expert*, pp. 50-57, Jan. 1987. Note: this article includes a listing in BASIC for a perceptron

(Riley 87). David D. Riley, *Data Abstraction and Structures*, boyd & fraser, pp. 305-349, 1987.

(Rosenblatt 61). F. Rosenblatt, *Principles of Neurodynamics*, Sparten Books, 1961.

(Rummelhart 86). David E. Rumelhart, James L. McClelland et al., "Learning Internal Representations by Error Propagation," *Parallel Distributed Processing*, **1**, The MIT Press, 1986.

(Schur 88). Stephen Schur, "The Intelligent Data Base," *AI Expert*, pp. 26-34, Jan. 1988.

(Scown 85). Susan B. Scown, *The Artificial Intelligence Experience: An Introduction*, Digital Equipment Corp., p. 78, 1985.

(Sejnowski 86). Terence J. Sejnowski and Charles R. Rosenberg, "NETtalk: A Parallel Network that Learns to Read Aloud," *Technical Report JHU/EECS-86/01*, John Hopkins University, 1986.

(Tank 85). David W. Tank and John J. Hopfield, *IEEE Circuits Systems*, **CAS-33**, p. 533, 1985.

(Waldrop 87). M. Mitchell Waldrop, *Man-Made Minds*, Walker and Co., p. 35, 1987.

(Waterman 86). Donald A. Waterman, *A Guide to Expert Systems*, Addison-Wesley Publishing Co., pp. 41-48, 1986.

A BRIEF HISTORICAL BIBLIOGRAPHY
OF EXPERT SYSTEMS

AGE   *Knowledge Engineering Assistance*
Nii, H.P. and Aiello, N., "AGE (Attempt to Generalize): A Knowledge-based Program for Building Knowledge-based Programs," *IJCAI*, pp. 645-655, 1979.

AL/X   *Expert System Shell Based on MYCIN and PROSPECTOR*
Reiter, J., "AL/X: An Expert System Using Plausible Inference," Intelligent Terminals, Ltd., Oxford, 1980.

CASNET   *Management of Glaucoma Treatment*
Weiss, S. *et al.*, "A Model-based Method for Computer-aided Medical Decision Making. *Artificial Intelligence*, **11**, pp. 145-172, 1978.

CENTAUR   *Analyze Pulmonary (Lung) Tests*
Aikins, J.S., "Prototypes and Production Rules: An Approach to Knowledge Representation for Hypothesis Formation," *IJCAI* , pp. 1-3, 1979.

CRYSALIS   *Uses X-ray Data to Determine Protein Structure*
Englemore, R. and Terry, A., "Structure and Function of the CRYSALIS System," *IJCAI*, pp. 250-256, 1979.

DENDRAL   *Identify Organic Compounds from Mass Spectrometer Data*
Buchanan, B.G. and Feigenbaum, E.A, "DENDRAL and Meta-DENDRAL: Their Applications Dimension," *Artificial Intelligence*, **11**, pp. 5-24, 1978.

EMYCIN   *Expert System Shell Developed from MYCIN*
Van Melle, W., "A Domain-independent Production Rule System for Consultation Programs," *IJCAI*, pp. 923-925, 1979.

GUIDON   *Intelligent Tutor for EMYCIN-Based Systems*
Clancey, W.J., "Dialogue Management for Rule-based Tutorials," *IJCAI*, pp. 155-161, 1979.

INTERNIST   *Diagnose Internal Medicine Problems*
Pople, H.E., Myers, J.D. and Miller, R.A., "DIALOG: A Model of Diagnostic Logic for Internal Medicine", *IJCAI* , pp. 848-855, 1975.

MACSYMA   *Solves Math Problems of Algebra, Trigonometry and Calculus*
Genesereth, M.R., "The Role of Plans in Automated Consultation," *IJCAI*, pp. 311-319, 1979.

META-DENDRAL   *Induces Rules of Molecular Structure from Mass*
                    Spectrometer Data
Buchanan, B.G. and Mitchell, T., "Model-directed Learning of Production Rules,"
    Waterman, D.A. and Hayes-Roth, F. (eds) *Pattern Directed Inference Systems*,
    Academic Press, pp. 297-312, 1978.

MOLGEN   *Plan Experiments on Molecular Genetics*
Marin, N., *et al.*, "Knowledge-based Management for Experiment Planning in
    Molecular Genetics," *IJCAI*, pp. 882-887, 1977.

MYCIN   *Diagnosis and Treatment of Meningitis and Certain Other Blood*
             Diseases.
Davis, R., Buchanan, B.G. and Shortliffe, E.H., "Production Systems as a
    Representation for a Knowledge-based Consultation Program," *Artificial
    Intelligence*, **8**, (1), pp. 15-45, 1977.

PROSPECTOR *Identification of Minerals, and Selection of Drilling Sites*
Duda, R., Gaschnig, J. and Hart, P., "Model Design in the PROSPECTOR Consultant
    System for Mineral Exploration," D. Michie, ed., *Expert Systems in the
    Micro-Electronic Age*, Edinburgh University Press, pp. 153-167, 1979.

PUFF   *Analyze Pulmonary (Lung) Tests*
Kunz, J.C. et al., "A Physiological Rule-based System for Interpreting Pulmonary
    Function Test Rules," *Heuristic Programming Memo HPP-78-19*, Stanford U.

XCON/R1   *Configure VAX Computer Systems*
John. McDermott and Judith Bachant, "R1 Revisited: Four Years in the Trenches," *AI
    Magazine*, **V**, (3), pp. 21-32, Fall 1984.

SACON   *Structural Engineering*
Bennett, J.S. and Engelmore, R.S., "SACON: A Knowledge-based Consultant for
    Structural Analysis," *IJCAI*, pp. 47-49, 1979.

SU/X   *Signal Interpretation*
Nii, H.P. and Feigenbaum, E.A., "Rule-based Understanding of Signals," Waterman,
    D.A. and Hayes-Roth, F. (eds.) *Pattern Directed Inference Systems*, Academic
    Press, pp. 483-501, 1978.

TEIRESIAS   *Knowledge Acquisition Program Developed for MYCIN*
Davis, R., "Interactive Transfer of Expertise: Acquisition of New Inference Rules,"
    Artificial Intelligence, **12**, (2), pp. 121-158, 1979.

CHAPTER 2 THE REPRESENTATION OF KNOWLEDGE

2.1 INTRODUCTION

In this chapter, we will discuss some of the commonly used representations of knowledge for expert systems. Knowledge representation is of major importance in expert systems for two reasons. First, expert system shells are designed for a certain type of knowledge representation such as rules or logic. Second, the way in which an expert system represents knowledge affects the development, efficiency, speed, and maintenance of the system. In the next chapter, we will discuss how inferences are made.

2.2 THE MEANING OF KNOWLEDGE

Knowledge, like love, is one of those words that everyone knows the meaning of, yet finds it hard to define. Like love, knowledge has many meanings. Other words such as data, facts and information are often used synonymously with knowledge.

The study of knowledge is **epistemology** (Angeles 81). It is concerned with the nature, structure, and origins of knowledge. Figure 2-1 illustrates some of the categories of epistemology. Besides the philosophical kinds of knowledge expressed by Aristotle, Plato, Descartes, Hume, Kant and others, there are two special types called **a priori** and **a posteriori**. The term *a priori* comes from the Latin and means "that which precedes". *A priori* knowledge comes before and is independent of knowledge from the senses. As an example, the statements "everything has a cause" and "all triangles in the plane have 180 degrees" are examples of *a priori* knowledge. *A priori* knowledge is considered to be universally true and cannot be denied without contradiction. Logic statements, mathematical laws and the knowledge possessed by teenagers are examples of *a priori* knowledge.

The opposite of *a priori* knowledge is knowledge derived from the senses, *a posteriori* knowledge. The truth or falsity of *a posteriori* knowledge can be verified using sense experience, as in the statement "the light is green". However, since sensory experience may not always be reliable, *a posteriori* knowledge can be denied on the basis of new knowledge without the necessity of contradictions. For example, if you see someone with brown eyes, you would believe that their eyes were brown. However, if you later saw that person removing brown contact lenses to reveal blue eyes, your knowledge would have to be revised.

Knowledge can be further classified into **procedural knowledge, declarative knowledge**, and **tacit knowledge**. The procedural and declarative knowledge types correspond to the procedural and declarative paradigms discussed in Chapter 1.

Procedural knowledge is often referred to as knowing how to do something. An example of procedural knowledge is knowing how to boil a pot of water. Declarative knowledge refers to knowing that something is true or false. It is concerned with knowledge expressed in the form of declarative statements such as "Don't put your fingers in a pot of boiling water."

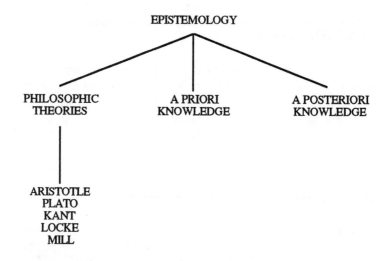

Figure 2-1
Some Categories of Epistemology

Tacit knowledge is sometimes called **unconscious knowledge** because it cannot be expressed by language. An example is knowing how to move your hand. On a gross scale, you might say that you move your hand by tightening or relaxing certain muscles and tendons. But at the next lower level, how do you know how to tighten or relax the muscles and tendons? Other examples are walking or riding a bicycle. In computer systems, ANS is related to tacit knowledge because normally the neural net cannot directly explain its knowledge, but may be able to if given an appropriate program (see Section 1.14).

Knowledge is of primary importance in expert systems. In fact, an analogy to Wirth's classic expression

```
Algorithms + Data Structures = Programs
```

for expert systems is

```
Knowledge + Inference = Expert Systems
```

As used in this book, knowledge is part of a hierarchy, illustrated in Figure 2-2. At the bottom is noise, consisting of items that are of no interest and which obscure data. The next higher level is data, which are items of potential interest. Processed data are information which is of interest. Next is knowledge, which represents very specialized information. In Chapter 1, knowledge in rule-based expert systems was defined as the rules that were activated by facts to produce new facts or conclusions. This process of inferencing is the second essential part of an expert system. The term inferencing is generally used for mechanical systems such as expert systems. Reasoning is generally used for human thinking.

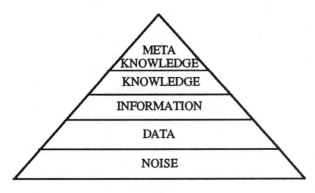

Figure 2-2
The Hierarchy of Knowledge

The term facts can mean data or information. Depending on how they are written, expert systems may draw inferences using data or information. Expert systems may also (1) separate data from noise, (2) transform data into information or (3) transform information into knowledge.

As an example of these concepts, consider the following sequence of 24 numbers.

```
137178766832525156430015
```

Without knowledge, this entire sequence may appear to be noise. However, if it is known that this sequence is meaningful, then the sequence is data. Determining what is data and what is noise is like the old saying about gardening "A weed is anything that grows that isn't what you want".

Certain knowledge may exist to transform data into information. For example, the following algorithm processes the data to yield information.

```
Group the numbers by two's.
Ignore any two-digit numbers less than 32.
Substitute the ASCII characters for the two-digit
numbers.
```

Application of this algorithm to the previous 24 numbers yields the information

```
GOLD 438+
```

Now knowledge can be applied to this information. For example, there may be a rule

```
IF gold is less than 500
   and the price is rising (+)
THEN
   buy gold
```

Although not explicitly shown in the figure, expertise is a specialized type of knowledge that experts have. Expertise is not commonly found in public sources of information such as books and papers. Instead, expertise is the implicit knowledge of the expert that must be extracted and made explicit so that it can be encoded in an expert system. Above knowledge is **metaknowledge** where one meaning of the prefix **meta** means "above." Metaknowledge is knowledge about knowledge and expertise. An expert system may be designed with knowledge about several different domains. Metaknowledge would specify which knowledge-base was applicable.

For example, an expert system could have knowledge-bases about car repair of 1988 Chevrolets, 1985 Fords and 1989 Cadillacs. Depending on what car needed repair, the appropriate knowledge-base would be used. It would be inefficient of memory and speed to have all of the knowledge-bases in memory at once. In addition, there could be conflicts as the expert system tries to decide the applicable rules from all knowledge-bases at once. Metaknowledge may also be used within one domain to decide what group of rules in the domain are most applicable.

In a philosophical sense, **wisdom** is the peak of all knowledge. Wisdom is the metaknowledge of determining the best goals of life and how to obtain them. A rule of wisdom might be

```
IF I have enough money to keep my spouse happy
THEN retire and enjoy life
```

However, due to the extreme scarcity of wisdom in the world, we shall restrict ourselves to knowledge-based systems and leave wisdom-based systems to philosophical engineering.

2.3   PRODUCTIONS

A number of different knowledge representation techniques have been devised. These include rules, semantic nets, frames, scripts, knowledge-representation languages such as KL-1 (Woods 83) and KRYPTON (Brachman 83), conceptual graphs (Sowa 84), and others (Brachman 80). As described in Chapter 1, production rules are very commonly used as the knowledge-base in expert systems since their advantages greatly outweigh their disadvantages.

One formal notation for defining productions is Backus-Naur form (BNF) (McGettrick 80). This notation is a **metalanguage** for defining the **syntax** of a language. Syntax defines the form, while **semantics** refers to meaning. A metalanguage is a language for describing languages. The prefix meta means above, and so a metalanguage is above normal language.

There are many types of languages such as natural languages, logic languages, mathematics, and computer languages. The BNF notation for a simple English language rule that a sentence consists of a noun and a verb followed by a period is the following production rule.

```
<sentence> ::= <subject> <verb> <end-mark>
```

where the **angle brackets, <>**, and ::= are symbols of the metalanguage and not of the language being specified. The symbol "::=" means "is defined as" and is the BNF equivalent of the arrow,→ , used in Chapter 1 with production rules. In order to avoid confusion with the Pascal assignment operator, :=, we will use the arrow.

The terms within angle brackets are called **nonterminal** symbols or simply non-terminals. A nonterminal is a variable in that it represents another term. The other term may be a nonterminal or a **terminal**. A terminal cannot be replaced by anything else and so is a constant.

The nonterminal <sentence> is special because it is the one **start symbol** from which the other symbols are defined. In the definition of programming languages, the start symbol is usually named <program>. The production rule

```
<sentence> → <subject> <verb> <end-mark>
```

states that a sentence is composed of a subject followed by a verb, followed by an end-mark. The following rules complete the nonterminals by specifying their possible terminals. The **bar** means "or" in the metalanguage.

```
<subject> → I | You | We
<verb> → left | came
<end-mark> → . | ? | !
```

All possible sentences in the language, the productions, can be produced by successively replacing each nonterminal by its right-hand-side non-terminals or terminals until all non-terminals are eliminated. The following are some productions.

```
I left.
I left?
I left!
You left.
You left?
You left!
We left.
We left?
```

```
We left!
```

A set of terminals is called a **string** of the language. If the string can be derived from the start symbol by replacing nonterminals by their definition rules, then the string is called a valid **sentence**. For example "We", "WeWe", and "leftcamecame" are all valid strings of the language, but are not valid sentences.

A **grammar** is a complete set of production rules which defines a language unambiguously. While the previous rules do define a grammar, it is a very restricted one because there are so few possible productions. For example, a more elaborate grammar could also include direct objects, as in the productions

```
<sentence>  → <subject> <verb> <object> <end-mark>
<object>  → home | work | school
```

Although this is a valid grammar, it is too simple for practical use. A more practical grammar is the following where the end-mark has been left out for simplicity.

```
<sentence>  → <subject phrase> <verb> <object phrase>
<subject phrase>  → <determiner> <noun>
<object phrase>  → <determiner> <adjective> <noun>
<determiner>  → a | an | the | this | these | those
<noun>  → man | eater
<verb>  → is | was
<adjective>  → dessert | heavy
```

The <determiner> is used to indicate a specific item. Using this grammar, sentences such as

```
the man was a dessert eater
an eater was the heavy man
```

can be generated.

A **parse tree** or **derivation tree** is a graphic representation of a sentence decomposed into all the terminals and nonterminals used to derive the sentence. Figure 2-3 shows the parse tree for the sentence "the man was a heavy eater". However, the string "man was a heavy eater" is not a valid sentence because it lacks the determiner in the subject phrase. A compiler creates a parse tree when it tries to determine if statements in a program conform to the valid syntax of a language.

The tree in Figure 2-3 shows that the sentence "the man was a heavy eater" can be derived from the start symbol by applying appropriate productions. The steps in this process are shown following, where the **double arrow, =>**, means apply the productions shown.

```
<sentence> => <subject phrase> <verb> <object phrase>
<subject phrase> => <determiner> <noun>
<determiner> => the
<noun> => man
<verb> => was
<object phrase> => <determiner> <adjective> <noun>
<determiner> => a
<adjective> => heavy
<noun> => eater
```

An alternative way of using productions is to generate valid sentences by substituting all the appropriate terminals for nonterminals, as discussed previously. Of course, not all productions, such as "the man was the dessert", may make much sense.

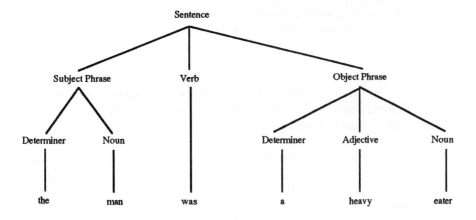

Figure 2-3
Parse Tree of a Sentence

2.4 SEMANTIC NETS

A **semantic network**, or net, is a classic AI representation technique used for propositional information (Stillings 87). A semantic net is sometimes called a **propositional net**. As discussed before, a proposition is a statement that is either true or false, such as "all dogs are mammals" and "a triangle has three sides". Propositions are a form of declarative knowledge because they state facts. In mathematical terms, a semantic net is a labeled, directed graph. A proposition is always true or false and is called **atomic** because its truth value cannot be further divided. Here the term atomic is used in the classical sense of an indivisible object. In contrast, the fuzzy propositions discussed in Chapter 5 need only be usually true or false.

Semantic nets were first developed for AI as a way of representing human memory and language understanding (Quillian 68). Quillian used semantic nets to analyze the meanings of words in sentences. Since then, semantic nets have been applied to many problems involving knowledge representation.

The structure of a semantic net is shown graphically in terms of **nodes** and the **arcs** connecting them. Nodes are often referred to as objects and the arcs as **links** or **edges**. The links of a semantic net are used to express relationships. Nodes are generally used to represent physical objects, concepts, or situations. Figure 2-4 (a) shows a net in which the links indicate an airline's routes between cities. Nodes are circles and links are the lines connecting nodes. The arrows show the directions in which planes can fly, hence the term *directed graph*. For this airline, its planes can only fly *from* New York to Chicago directly, and not *vice versa*. In Figure 2-4 (b), the links show the relationship between members of a family.

Relationships are of primary importance in semantic nets because they provide the basic structure for organizing knowledge. Without relationships, knowledge is simply a collection of unrelated facts. With relationships, knowledge is a cohesive structure about which other knowledge can be inferred. For example, in Figure 2-4 (b), it can be inferred that Ann and Bill are the grandparents of John even though there is no explicit link labeled "grandfather-of".

Semantic nets are sometimes referred to as **associative nets** because nodes are associated or related to others. In fact, Quillian's original work modelled human memory as an associative net in which concepts were the nodes and links formed the connections between concepts. According to this model, as one concept node is stimulated by reading words in a sentence, its links to other nodes are activated in a spreading pattern. If another node receives sufficient activations, the concept would be forced up into the conscious mind. For example, although you know thousands of words, you are only thinking of the specific words in this sentence as you read it.

Certain types of relationships have proven very useful in a wide variety of knowledge representations. Rather than defining new relationships for different problems, it is customary to use these customary types. The use of common types makes it easier for different people to understand an unfamiliar net.

Two types of commonly used links are **IS-A** and **A-KIND-OF**, which are sometimes written as **ISA** and **AKO** (Winston 84). Figure 2-5 is an example of a semantic net using these links. In this figure, the IS-A means "is an instance of" and refers to a specific member of a class. A **class** is related to the mathematical concept of a set in that it refers to a group of objects. While a set can have elements of any type, the objects in a class have some relation to one another. For example, it is possible to define a set consisting of

{ 3, eggs, blue, tires, art }

However, members of this set have no common relationship. In contrast, the class consisting of planes, trains, and automobiles are related because they are all types of transportation.

The link AKO is used here to relate one class to another. The AKO is not used to relate a specific individual because that is the function of IS-A. The AKO relates an individual class to a parent class of classes of which the individual is a child class.

(a) A General Net

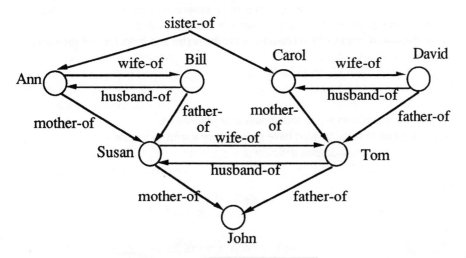

(b) A Semantic Net

Figure 2-4
Two Types of Nets

From another viewpoint, the AKO relates **generic** nodes to generic nodes while the IS-A relates an instance or **individual** to a generic class. In Figure 2-5 notice that the more general classes are at the top and more specific classes at the bottom. The more general class that an AKO arrow points to is called a **superclass**. If a superclass has an AKO pointing to another node, then it is also a class of the superclass the AKO points to. Another way of expressing this is that an AKO points from a **subclass** to a class. The link **ARE** is sometimes used for AKO where ARE is read as the ordinary word "are".

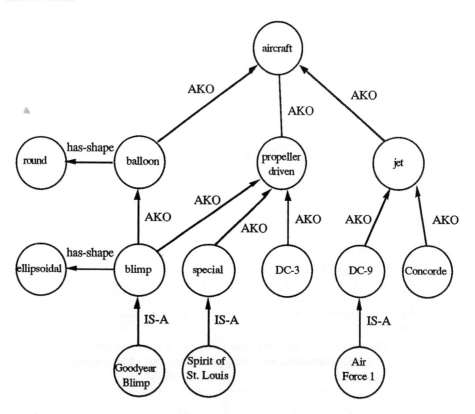

Figure 2-5
A Semantic Net with IS-A and A-Kind-Of (AKO) Links

The objects in a class have one or more **attributes** in common. Each attribute has a **value**. The combination of attribute and value is a **property**. For example, a blimp has attributes of size, weight, shape, color and so forth. The value of the shape attribute is ellipsoidal. In other words, a blimp has the property of an ellipsoidal shape. Other links may also be found in semantic nets. Like ISA, the **IS** link defines a value. For example, if the President is in a DC-9, then Air Force 1 IS a DC-9. The **CAUSE** link expresses causal knowledge. Hot air CAUSES a balloon to rise.

Since the Goodyear Blimp is a blimp and blimps have ellipsoidal shape, it follows that the Goodyear Blimp is ellipsoidal. The duplication of one node's characteristics by a descendent is called **inheritance**. Unless there is more specific evidence to the contrary, it is assumed that all members of a class will inherit all the properties of their superclasses. For example, balloons have a round shape. However, since the blimp class has a link pointing to the ellipsoidal shape, this takes precedence. Inheritance is a very useful tool in knowledge representation because it eliminates the necessity of repeating common characteristics. Links and inheritance provide a very efficient means of knowledge representation since many complex relationships can be shown with a few nodes and links.

2.5   OBJECT-ATTRIBUTE-VALUE TRIPLES

One problem with using semantic nets is that there is no standard definition of link names. For example, some books use IS-A for both generic and individual relations (Barr 81) (Staugaard 87). The IS-A is then used in the sense of the ordinary words "is a" and is also used for AKO. In the expert system tool ART, the IS-A relates two classes of objects while INSTANCE-OF relates an individual to a class.

Another common link is HAS-A which relates a class to a subclass. The HAS-A points opposite to the AKO and is often used to relate an object to a part of the object. For example,

```
car HAS-A engine
car HAS-A tires
car IS-A ford
```

More specifically, the IS-A relates a value to an attribute while a HAS-A relates an object to an attribute.

The three items of object, attribute, and value occur so frequently that it is possible to build a simplified semantic net using just them. An **object-attribute-value triple** (OAV), or **triplet** , can be used to characterize all the knowledge in a semantic net and was used in the expert system MYCIN for diagnosing infectious diseases. The OAV triple representation is convenient for listing knowledge in the form of a table and thus translating the table into computer code by rule induction. An example of an OAV triple table is shown in Table 2-1.

Object	Attribute	Value
apple	color	red
apple	type	mcintosh
apple	quantity	100
grapes	color	red
grapes	type	seedless
grapes	quantity	500

Table 2-1
An OAV Table

OAV triples are especially useful for representing facts, and the patterns to match the facts in the antecedent of a rule. The semantic net for such a system consists of nodes for objects, attributes, and values connected by HAS-A and IS-A links. If only a single object is to be represented and inheritance is not required, then an even simpler representation called **attribute-value pairs**, or simply **AV**, may suffice.

2.6 PROLOG AND SEMANTIC NETS

Semantic nets are easy to translate into PROLOG. For example

```
is_a(goodyear_blimp,blimp).
is_a(spirit_of_st_louis,special).
has_shape(blimp,ellipsoidal).
has_shape(balloon,round).
```

are PROLOG statements that express some of the relationships in the semantic net of Figure 2-5. A period marks the end of a statement.

Essentials of PROLOG

Each of the statements above is a PROLOG **predicate expression**, or simply predicate, because it is based on predicate logic. However, PROLOG is not a true predicate logic language because it is a computer language with executable statements. In PROLOG, a predicate expression consists of the predicate name, such as is_a, followed by zero or more arguments enclosed in parentheses and separated by commas. Some examples of PROLOG predicates and comments in parentheses follow.

```
color(red).                 (red is a color)
father_of(tom,john).        (tom is the father of john)
mother_of(susan,john).      (susan is the mother of john)
parents(tom,susan,john).    (tom and susan are the
                             parents of john)
```

Predicates with two arguments are more easily understood if you consider the predicate name following the first argument. The meaning of predicates with more than two arguments must be explicitly stated, as the parents predicate illustrates. Another difficulty is that semantic nets are primarily useful for representing binary relationships since a drawn line has only two ends, of course. It's not possible to draw the parents predicate as a single directed edge since there are three arguments. The idea of drawing tom and susan together in one parents node and john at the other leads to a new complication. It is then impossible to use the parents node for other binary relationships such as mother-of since it would also involve tom.

Predicates can also be expressed with relations such as the IS-A and HAS-A.

```
is_a(red,color).
has_a(john,father).
has_a(john,mother).
has_a(john,parents).
```

Notice that the has_a predicates do not express the same meaning as previously because john's father, mother, and parents are not explicitly named. In order to name them, some additional predicates must be added.

```
is_a(tom,father).
is_a(susan,mother).
is_a(tom,parent).
is_a(susan,parent).
```

Even these additional predicates do not express the same meaning as the original predicates. For example, we know that John has a father and that Tom is a father, but this does not provide the information that Tom is the father of John.

All of the preceding statements actually describe facts in PROLOG. Programs in PROLOG consist of facts and rules in the general form of **goals** shown following.

$$p :- p_1, p_2, \ldots p_N.$$

where p is called the rule's head and the p_i are the **subgoals**. Normally, this expression is a Horn clause which states that the head goal, p, is satisfied if and only if all of the subgoals are satisfied. The exception is when the special predicate for failure is used. A failure predicate is convenient because it's not easy to prove negation in classical logic and PROLOG is based on classical logic. Negation is viewed as the failure to find a proof and this can be a very long and involved process if there are many potential matches. The **cut** and special failure predicate makes the negation process more efficient by reducing the searching for a proof.

The commas separating the subgoals represent a logical AND. The symbol, :-, is interpreted as an IF. If only the head exists and there is no right-hand side, as in

```
p.
```

then the head is considered true. This is why predicates such as the following are considered facts and thus must be true.

```
color(red).
has_a(john,father).
```

Another way of thinking about facts is that a fact is an unconditional conclusion that does not depend on anything else and so the IF, :- , is not necessary. In contrast,

PROLOG rules require the IF because they are conditional conclusions whose truth depends on one or more conditions. As an example, the parent rules are as follows.

```
parent(X,Y) :- father(X,Y).
parent(X,Y) :- mother(X,Y).
```

which mean that X is the parent of Y if X is the father of Y or if X is the mother of Y. Likewise, a grandparent can be defined as

```
grandparent(X,Y) :- parent(X,Z),parent(Z,Y).
```

and ancestor can be defined as

```
(1) ancestor(X,Y) :- parent(X,Y).
(2) ancestor(X,Y) :- ancestor(X,Z),ancestor(Z,Y).
```

where (1) and (2) are used for identification purposes in this book.

Searching in PROLOG

A system for executing PROLOG statements is generally an interpreter, although some systems can generate compiled code. The general form of a PROLOG system is shown in Figure 2-6. The user interacts with PROLOG by entering predicate queries and receiving answers. The **predicate database** contains the rule and fact predicates that have been entered and so forms the knowledge-base. The interpreter tries to determine if a query predicate that the user enters is in the database. The answer returned is yes if it is in the database or no if it is not. If the query is a rule, the interpreter will try to satisfy the subgoals by conducting a **depth-first search** as shown in Figure 2-7. For contrast, a **breadth-first search** is also shown although this is not the normal mode of PROLOG.

In a depth-first search, the search goes down as far as possible and then back up. In PROLOG, the search also goes from left to right. A breadth-first search proceeds one level at a time before descending to the next lower level.

As an example of goal searching in PROLOG, consider the ancestor rules defined as (1) and (2). Assume the following facts are now input.

```
(3) parent(ann,mary).
(4) parent(ann,susan).
(5) parent(mary,bob).
(6) parent(susan,john).
```

Now suppose PROLOG is queried to determine if ann is the ancestor of susan

```
:-ancestor(ann,susan).
```

where the absence of a head indicates a **query**, which is a condition to be proved by PROLOG. Facts, rules, and queries are the three types of Horn clauses of PROLOG. A condition can be proved if it is the conclusion of an instance of a clause. Of course, the clause itself must be provable and this is done by proving the conditions of the clause.

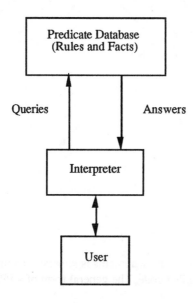

Figure 2-6
General Organization of a PROLOG System

On receipt of this input, PROLOG will start searching for a statement whose head matches the input pattern of ancestor(ann,susan). This is called **pattern matching** just like the pattern matching to facts in the antecedent of a production rule. The search starts from the first statement that was entered (1), the **top**, to the last statement (6), the **bottom**. There is a possible match with the first ancestor rule (1). The variable X matches ann and the variable Y matches susan. Since the head matches, PROLOG will now try to match the body of (1), yielding the subgoal parent(ann,susan). PROLOG now tries to match this subgoal against clauses and eventually matches with the fact (4) parent(ann,susan). There are no more goals to match and PROLOG answers "yes" because the original query is true.

As another example, suppose the query is

```
:-ancestor(ann, john).
```

The first ancestor rule (1) matches and X is set to ann while Y is set to john. PROLOG now tries to match the body of (1), parent(ann,john) with every parent statement. None match and so the body of (1) cannot be true. Since the body of (1) is not true, the head cannot be true.

(a) Depth-first Search

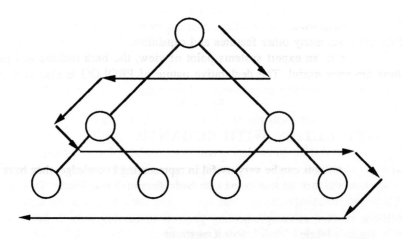

(b) Breadth-first Search

Figure 2-7
Depth-first and Breadth-first Searches for an Arbitrary Tree

Since (1) cannot be true, PROLOG then tries the second ancestor statement (2). X
is set to ann and Y is set to john. PROLOG tries to prove the head of (2) is true by
proving the subgoals of (2) are both true. That is, ancestor(ann,Z) and ancestor(Z,john)
must be proven true. PROLOG tries to match the subgoals in a left to right manner
starting with ancestor(ann,Z). Starting from the top, this first matches statement (1)
and so PROLOG tries to prove the body of (1), parent(ann,Z). Starting to search from

the top again this body first matches statement (3) and so PROLOG sets Z to mary. Now PROLOG tries to match the second subgoal of (2) as ancestor(mary,john). This matches (1) and so PROLOG tries to satisfy its body, parent(mary,john). However there is no parent(mary,john) in the statements (3) - (6) and so this search fails.

PROLOG then reconsiders its guess that Z should be mary. Since this choice did not work, it tries to find another value that will work. Another possibility arises from (4) by setting Z to susan. This technique of going back to try a different search path when one path fails is backtracking, and is often used for problem solving.

With the choice of Z as susan, PROLOG attempts to prove ancestor(susan,john) is true. By (1), the body parent(susan,john) must be proven true. Indeed, the fact (3) does match and so the query

```
:-ancestor(ann,john)
```

is proven true since its conditions have been proven true.

Notice that the control structure of PROLOG is of the Markov Algorithm type where searching for pattern matching is normally determined by the order that the Horn clause are entered. This contrasts with rule-based expert systems which normally follow the Post paradigm in which the order that rules are entered does not the search.

PROLOG has many other features and capabilities not mentioned in this brief introduction. From an expert systems point of view, the backtracking and pattern matching are very useful. The declarative nature of PROLOG is also very useful because a program specification is an executable program.

2.7 DIFFICULTIES WITH SEMANTIC NETS

Although semantic nets can be very useful in representing knowledge, they have limitations such as the lack of link name standards discussed previously. This makes it difficult to understand what the net is really designed for and whether it was designed in a consistent manner. A complementary problem to naming links is the naming of nodes. If a node is labeled "chair", does it represent

a specific chair
the class of all chairs
the concept of a chair
the person who is the chair of a meeting

or some other meaning? For a semantic net to represent **definitive knowledge**, that is, knowledge that can be defined, the link and node names must be rigorously defined. Of course, the same problems may occur in programming languages.

Another problem is the combinatorial explosion of searching nodes, especially if the response to a query is negative. That is, for a query to produce a negative result, many or all of the links in a net may have to be searched. As shown in the traveling salesman problem in Chapter 1, the number of links is the factorial of the number of nodes minus one if they are all connected. Although not all representations will require this degree of connectivity, the possibility of a combinatorial explosion exists.

Semantic nets were originally proposed as a model of human associative memory in which one node has links to others and information retrieval occurs due to a spreading activation of nodes. However, other mechanisms must also be available to the human brain since it does not take a long time for a human to answer the query—Is there a football team on Pluto? There are about 10^{10} neurons in the human brain and about 10^{15} links. If all knowledge were represented by a semantic net, it would take a very, very long time to answer negative queries like the football question because of all the searching involved with 10^{15} links.

Semantic nets are logically inadequate because they cannot define knowledge in the way that logic can. A logic representation can specify a certain chair, some chairs, all chairs, no chairs and so forth as will be discussed later in this chapter. Another problem is that semantic nets are heuristically inadequate because there is no way to embed heuristic information in the net on how to efficiently search the net. A **heuristic** is a rule of thumb which may help in finding a solution but is not guaranteed as an algorithm is guaranteed to find a solution. Heuristics are very important in AI because typical AI problems are so hard that an algorithmic solution does not exist or is too inefficient for practical use. The only standard control strategy built into a net that might help is inheritance but not all problems may have this structure.

A number of approaches have been tried to correct the inherent problems of semantic nets. Logic enhancements have been made, and heuristic enhancements have been tried by attaching procedures to nodes. The procedures will be executed when the node becomes activated. However, the resulting systems gained little in capability at the expense of the natural expressiveness of semantic nets. The conclusion of all this effort is that like any tool, semantic nets should be used for those things they do best, showing binary relationships, and not be distorted into a universal tool.

2.8   SCHEMATA

A semantic net is an example of a **shallow knowledge structure**. The shallowness occurs because all the knowledge in the semantic net is contained in the links and nodes. The term knowledge structure is analogous to a data structure in that it represents an ordered collection of knowledge rather than just data. A **deep** knowledge structure has causal knowledge that explains why something occurs. For example, it is possible to build a medical expert system with shallow knowledge as follows.

```
IF a person has a fever
   THEN take an aspirin
```

But these systems do not know the fundamental biochemistry of the body and why aspirin decreases fever. The rule could have been defined as

```
IF a person has a pink monkey
THEN take a refrigerator
```

In other words, the expert system's knowledge is shallow because it is based on syntax and not semantics, where any two words could be substituted for X and Y in the following rule

```
IF a person has a (X)
THEN take a (Y)
```

Note that (X) and (Y) are not variables in this rule, but represent any two words. Doctors have causal knowledge because they have taken many courses and have experience treating ill people. If a treatment is not working right, doctors can reason about it to find an alternative. In other words, an expert knows when to break the rules.

Many types of real world knowledge cannot be represented by the simple structure of a semantic net. More complex structures are needed to better represent complex knowledge structures. In AI, the term schema (plural **schemas** or **schematas**) is used to describe a more complex knowledge structure than the semantic net. The term schema comes from psychology where it refers to the continual organizing of knowledge or responses by a creature due to stimuli. That is, as creatures learn the causal relationship between a cause and its outcome, they will try to repeat the cause if pleasurable or avoid the cause if painful.

For example, the acts of eating and drinking are pleasurable **sensorimotor** schematas that involve coordinating information from the senses with the required motor (muscle) movements to eat and drink. A person does not have to think about this tacit knowledge to know to do these acts, and it is very difficult to explain exactly how it is done down to the level of controlling muscles. An even more difficult schema to explain is how to ride a bicycle. Try explaining a sense of balance!

Another type of schema is the **concept schema** by which we represent concepts. For example, everyone has the concept of animal. If most people were asked to explain what an animal is, they would probably describe it in terms of something that has four legs, and fur. Of course, the concept of animal differs depending on whether the person grew up on a farm, in a city, near a river and so forth. However, we all have **stereotypes** in our minds of concepts. While the term stereotype may have a derogatory meaning in casual language, in AI it means a typical example. Thus a stereotype of an animal might be something like a dog to many people.

A conceptual schema is an abstraction in which specific objects are classified by their general properties. For example, if you see a small red, round-like object with a green stem under a sign that says Artificial Fruit, you will probably recognize it as an artificial apple. The object has the properties of applehood that you associate with the conceptual schema of apple, except for being a real apple of course.

The conceptual schema of a real apple will include general properties of apples such as sizes, colors, tastes, uses, and so forth. The schema will not include details of exactly where the apple was picked, the truck by which it was transported to the supermarket, the name of the person who put it on the shelf and so forth. These details are not important to the properties that comprise your abstract concept of an apple. Also, note that a person who is blind may have a very different concept schema of an apple in which texture is most important.

By focusing on the general properties of an object, it is easier to reason about them without becoming distracted by irrelevant details. Customarily, schemas have internal structure to their nodes while semantic nets do not. The label of a semantic net is all the knowledge about the node. A semantic net is like a data structure in computer science in which the search key is also the data stored in the node. A schema is like a data structure in which nodes contain records. Each record may contain data, records or pointers to other nodes.

2.9   FRAMES

One type of schema that has been used in many AI applications is the **frame** (Minsky 75). Another type of schema is the **script**, which is essentially a time-ordered sequence of frames (Schank 77). Proposed as a method for understanding vision, natural language and other areas, frames provide a convenient structure for representing objects that are typical to a given situation such as stereotypes. In particular, frames are useful for simulating commonsense knowledge, which is a very difficult area for computers to master. While semantic nets are basically a two dimensional representation of knowledge, frames add a third dimension by allowing nodes to have structures. These structures can be simple values or other frames.

The basic characteristic of a frame is that it represents related knowledge about a narrow subject which has much default knowledge. A frame system would be a good choice for describing a mechanical device such as an automobile. Components of the car such as the engine, body, brakes and so forth would be related to give an overall view of their relationships. Further detail about the components could be obtained by examining the structure of the frames. Although individual brands of cars will vary, most cars have common characteristics such as wheels, engine, body, transmission and so forth. The frame contrasts with the semantic net which is generally used for broad knowledge representation.

Just as with semantic nets, there are no standards for defining frame-based systems. A number of special purpose languages have been designed for frames, such as FRL, SRL, KRL, KEE, HP-RL and frame enhancement features to LISP such as LOOPS and FLAVORS (Finin 86).

A frame is analogous to a record structure in a high-level language such as Pascal or an atom with its property list in LISP. Corresponding to the fields and values of a record are the **slots** and slot **fillers** of a frame. A frame is basically a group of slots and fillers that define a stereotypical object. An example of a frame for a car is shown in Figure 2-8. In OAV terms, the car is the object, the slot name corresponds to the attribute, while the filler is the value.

Slots	Fillers
manufacturer	General Motors
model	Chevrolet Caprice
year	1979
transmission	automatic
engine	gasoline
tires	4
color	blue

Figure 2-8
A Car Frame

Most frames are not as simple as that of Figure 2-8. The utility of frames lies in hierarchical frame systems and inheritance. By using frames in the filler slots and inheritance, very powerful knowledge representation systems can be built. In particular, frame-based expert systems are very useful for representing causal knowledge because their information is organized by cause and effect. By contrast, rule-based expert systems generally rely on unorganized knowledge that is not causal.

Some frame-based tools such as KEE, allow a wide range of items to be stored in slots. Frame slots may hold rules, graphics, comments, debugging information, questions for users, hypotheses concerning a situation or other frames.

Frames are generally designed to represent either generic or specific knowledge. Figure 2-9 illustrates a generic frame for the concept of human property.

Slots	Fillers
name	property
specialization_of	a_kind_of object
types	(car, boat, house) if-added: Procedure ADD_PROPERTY
owner	default: government if-needed: Procedure FIND_OWNER
location	(home, work, mobile)
status	(missing, poor, good)
under_warranty	(yes,no)

Figure 2-9
A Generic Frame for Property

The fillers may be values such as property in the name slot, or a range of values as in the types slot. The slots may also contain procedures attached to the slots, called **procedural attachments**. These are generally of three types. The **if-needed** type are procedures to be executed when a filler value is needed but none are initially present or the **default** value is not suitable. Defaults are of primary importance in frames because they model some aspects of the brain. Defaults correspond to the expectations of a situation that we build up based on experience. When we encounter a new situation, the closest frame is modified to help us adjust to the situation. People do not start from scratch in every new situation. Instead, the defaults or other fillers are modified. Defaults are often used to represent commonsense knowledge. That is, commonsense knowledge can be considered to be the knowledge that is generally known that we use when no more situation specific knowledge is available.

The **if-added** type is run for procedures to be executed when a value is to be added to a slot. In the types slot, the if-added procedure executes a procedure called ADD-PROPERTY to add a new type of property, if necessary. For example, this procedure would be run for jewelry, TV, stereo and so forth since the types slot does not contain these values.

An **if-removal** type is run whenever a value is to be removed from a slot. This type of procedure would be run if a value was obsolete.

Slot fillers may also contain relations, as in the specialization_of slots. The a-kind-of and is-a relations are used in Figures 2-9, 2-10, and 2-11 to show how these frames are hierarchically related. The frames of Figures 2-9 and 2-10 are generic frames while that of Figure 2-11 is a specific frame because it is an instance of the car frame. We have adopted the convention here that a-kind-of relations are generic and is-a relations are specific.

Slots	Fillers
name	car
specialization_of	a-kind-of property
types	(sedan, sports, convertible)
manufacturer	(GM, Ford, Chrysler)
location	mobile
wheels	4
transmission	(manual, automatic)
engine	(gasoline, diesel)

Figure 2-10
Car Frame—A Generic Subframe of Property

Frame systems are designed so that more generic frames are at the top of the hierarchy. It is assumed that frames can be customized for specific cases by modifying the default cases and creating more specific frames. Frames attempt to model real world objects by using generic knowledge for the majority of an object's attributes and specific knowledge for special cases. For example, we commonly think of birds as creatures that can fly. Yet certain types of birds such as penguins and ostriches cannot fly. These types represent more specific classes of birds and their characteristics would be found lower in a frame hierarchy than birds like canaries or robins. In other words, the top of the bird frame hierarchy specifies things which are more true of all birds while the lower levels reflect the fuzzy boundaries between real world objects. The object which has all of the typical characteristics is called a **prototype**, which literally means the first type.

Slots	Fillers
name	John's car
specialization_of	is_a car
manufacturer	GM
owner	John Doe
transmission	automatic
engine	gasoline
status	good
under_warranty	yes

Figure 2-11
An Instance of a Car Frame

Frames may also be classified by their application. A **situational frame** contains knowledge about what to expect in a given situation, such as a birthday party. An **action frame** contains slots that specify the actions to be performed in a given situation. That is, the fillers are procedures to perform some actions, such as removing a defective part from a conveyer belt. An action frame represents procedural knowledge. The combination of situational and action frames can be used to describe cause-and-effect relationships in the form of **causal knowledge frames**.

Very sophisticated frame systems have been built for a variety of tasks. Two of the most impressive systems that have demonstrated the power of frames can creatively discover mathematical concepts (Lenat 77) and describe mathematical understanding in domains like linear algebra (Rissland 78). In these systems, the slots were used as generators of tasks such as questions to answer. The AM system of Lenat would make conjectures of interesting new concepts and explore them.

2.10   DIFFICULTIES WITH FRAMES

Frames were originally conceived as a paradigm for representing stereotyped knowledge. The important characteristic of a stereotype is that it have well-defined features so that many of its slots have default values. Mathematical concepts are good examples of stereotypes well-suited to frames. The frame paradigm has an intuitive appeal because their organized representation of knowledge is generally easier to understand than logic, or production systems with many rules (Jackson 86).

However, major problems have appeared in frame systems that allow unrestrained alteration or cancellation of slots (Brachman 85). The classic example of this problem is illustrated with a frame describing elephants in Figure 2-12.

name	elephant
specialization_of	a-kind-of mammal
color	grey
legs	4
trunk	a cylinder

Figure 2-12
Elephant Frame

At first sight, the elephant frame seems like a reasonable, generic description of elephants. However, suppose there exists a specific, three-legged elephant called Clyde. This instance of an elephant may have lost a leg due to an accident or simply lied about losing a leg to get his name in a book. The significant thing is that the elephant frame claims that an elephant has four legs, not three. Thus we cannot consider the elephant frame to be a definition of an elephant.

Of course, the frame could be modified to allow three-legged or two-legged or one-legged or even legless elephants as exceptions. However, this does not provide a very good definition. Additional problems may arise with the other slots. Suppose Clyde gets a bad case of jaundice and his skin turns yellow. Is he then not an elephant?

An alternative to viewing a frame as a definition is to consider it as describing a typical elephant. However, this leads to other problems because of inheritance. Notice that the elephant frame says that an elephant is a-kind-of mammal. Since we are interpreting frames as typical, then our frame system says that a typical elephant is a typical mammal. Although an elephant is a mammal, it is probably not a typical mammal. On the basis of quantity, people, cows, sheep or rats are probably more representative of typical mammals.

Most frame systems do not provide a way of defining unalterable slots. Since any slot can be changed, the properties that a frame inherits can be altered or cancelled anywhere in the hierarchy. This means that every frame is really a primitive frame because there is no guarantee that properties are common. Each frame makes up its own rules and so each frame is a primitive. Nothing is really certain in such an unrestrained system, and so it is impossible to make universal statements such as defining an elephant. Also, from simpler definitions such as elephant, it is impossible to reliably build composite objects such as elephant-with-three-legs.

The same types of problems apply to semantic nets with inheritance. If the properties of any node can be changed, then nothing is certain.

2.11 LOGIC AND SETS

In addition to rules, frames, and semantic nets, knowledge can also be represented by the symbols of **logic**, which is the study of the rules of exact reasoning. An important part of reasoning is inferring conclusions from premises. The application of computers to perform reasoning has resulted in **logic programming** and the development of logic-based languages such as PROLOG. Logic is also of primary importance in expert systems in which the inference engine reasons from facts to conclusions. In fact, a descriptive term for logic programming and expert systems is **automated reasoning systems**.

The earliest formal logic was developed by the Greek philosopher Aristotle in the fourth century B.C. Aristotelian logic is based on the **syllogism** of which he invented 14 types and 5 more were invented in medieval times. Syllogisms have two **premises** and one **conclusion** which is inferred from the premises. Shown following is the classic example of a syllogism.

```
Premise:      All men are mortal
Premise:      Socrates is a man
Conclusion:   Socrates is mortal
```

In a syllogism, the **premises** provide the evidence from which the conclusion must necessarily follow. A syllogism is a way of representing knowledge. Another way of representing knowledge is in the form of a **Venn diagram**, as shown in Figure 2-13.

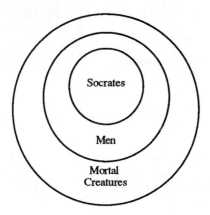

Figure 2-13
Venn Diagram

The outer circle represents all mortal creatures. The inner circle representing men is drawn entirely within the mortal circle to indicate that all men are mortal. Since Socrates is a man, the circle representing him is drawn entirely within the men.

Strictly speaking, the circle representing Socrates should be a point since a circle implies a class. For readability, we'll use circles for all. The conclusion that Socrates is mortal is a consequence of the fact that his circle is within that of mortal creatures and so he must be mortal.

In mathematical terms, a circle of the Venn diagram represents a set, which is a collection of objects. The objects within a set are called its **elements**. Some examples of sets are

```
A = {1,3,5}
B = {1,2,3,4,5}
C = {0,2,4,...}
D = {...,-4,-2,0,2,4,...}
E = {airplanes,balloons,blimps,jets}
F = {airplanes,balloons}
```

where the dots, ..., called ellipses, indicate the terms continued on indefinitely.

The Greek symbol epsilon, $\in$, indicates an element is a member of a set. For example, $1 \in A$, means that the number 1 is an element of the set A defined previously. If an element is not a member of a set, the symbol $\notin$ is used, as in $2 \notin A$.

If two arbitrary sets, such as X and Y, are defined such that every element in X is an element of Y, then X is a **subset** of Y and is written in the mathematical form $X \subset Y$ or $Y \supset X$. From the definition of a subset, it follows that every set is a subset of itself. A subset which is not the set itself is called a **proper subset**. For example, the set X defined previously is a proper subset of Y. In discussing sets, it is useful to consider the sets under discussions as subsets of a **universal set**. The universal set changes as the topic of discussion change. Figure 2-14 illustrates a subset formed as the **intersection** of two sets in the universe of all cars. In discussing numbers, the universe would be all numbers. The universe is drawn as a rectangle surrounding its subsets. Universal sets are not used just for convenience. The indiscriminate use of conditions to define sets can result in logical paradoxes.

If we let A be the set of all blue cars, B the set of all cars with manual transmission and C be the set of all blue cars with manual transmission, we can write

$$C = A \cap B$$

where the symbol $\cap$ represents the intersection of sets. Another way of writing this is in terms of elements x as follows

$$C = \{x \in \mathcal{U} \mid (x \in A) \land (x \in B)\}$$

where

$\mathcal{U}$ represents the universe set.

$\mid$ is read as "such that". A colon, :, is sometimes used instead of $\mid$.

∧ is the **logical AND**.

The expression for C is read that C consists of those elements x in the universe such that x is an element of A and x is an element of B. The logical AND comes from Boolean algebra. An expression consisting of two operands connected by the logical AND operator is true if and only if both operands are true. If A and B have no elements in common, then A ∩ B = Ø where the Greek letter phi, Ø, represents the **empty set** or **null set** { }, which has no elements. Sometimes the Greek letter lambda, Λ, is used for the null set. Other notations for the universe set are sometimes the numeral 1 and the numeral 0 for the null set. Although the null set has no elements, it is still a set. An analogy is a restaurant with a set of customers. If nobody comes, the set of customers is empty.

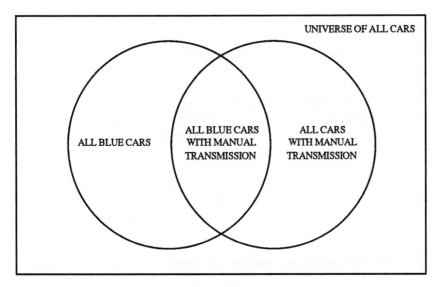

Figure 2-14
Intersecting Sets

Another set operation is **union** which is the set of all elements in either A or B. This is represented as

$$A \cup B = \{x \in \mathcal{U} \mid (x \in A) \vee (x \in B)\}$$

where

∪ is the set operator for **union**
∨ is the **logical OR** operator.

The **complement** of set A is the set of all elements not in A.

$$A' = \{x \in \mathcal{U} \mid \sim (x \in A)\}$$

where

the prime, ´, means complement of a set
the tilde, ~, is the **logical NOT** operator

The Venn diagrams for these basic operations are shown in Figure 2-15.

(a) INTERSECTION OF SETS

(b) UNION OF SETS

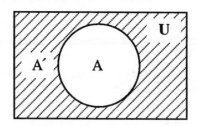

(c) COMPLEMENT OF A SET

Figure 2-15
Basic Set Operations

2.12 PROPOSITIONAL LOGIC

The oldest and one of the simplest types of **formal logic** is the syllogism. The term *formal* means that the logic is concerned with the form of logical statements rather than their meaning. In other words, formal logic is concerned with the syntax of statements rather than their semantics. Although the term formal logic may sound intimidating, it is no more difficult than algebra. In fact, algebra is really a formal logic of numbers. For example, suppose you were asked to solve the following problem. A school has 25 computers with a total of 60 memory boards. Some of the computers have two memory boards while others have four. How many computers of each type are there? The solution can be written algebraically as follows.

```
25 = X + Y
60 = 2X + 4Y
```

which can easily be solved for X=20 and Y=5.

Now consider this problem. There are 25 animals in a barnyard with a total of 60 legs. Some of the animals have two legs while others have four. How many animals of each type are there? As you can see, the same algebraic equations apply whether we are talking about computers, animals or anything. In the same way that algebraic equations let us concentrate on the mathematical manipulation of symbols without regard to what they represent, formal logic lets us concentrate on the reasoning without becoming confused by what objects we are reasoning about.

As an example of formal logic, consider the syllogism with the nonsense words squeeg and moof.

```
Premise:      All squeegs are moofs
Premise:      John is a squeeg
Conclusion:   John is a moof
```

Although the words squeeg and moof are nonsense and have no meaning, the *form* of this argument is still correct. That is, the argument is **valid** no matter what words are used because the syllogism has a valid form. In fact any syllogism of the form

```
Premise:      All X are Y
Premise:      Z is a X
Conclusion:   Z is a Y
```

is valid no matter what is substituted for X, Y, and Z. This example illustrates that meanings do not matter in formal logic. Only the form or appearance is important. This concept of separating the form from the meaning or semantics is what makes logic such a powerful tool. By separating the form from the semantics, the validity of an argument can be considered objectively, without prejudice caused by the semantics.

An analogy to formal logic is algebra, in which the correctness of expressions such as $X + X = 2X$ holds whether X is an integer, apples, airplanes, or anything.

Aristotelian syllogisms were the foundations of logic until 1847, when the English mathematician George Boole published the first book describing **symbolic logic**. Although Leibnitz had developed his own version of symbolic logic in the 17th Century, it never achieved general use. One of the new concepts that Boole proposed was a modification of the Aristotelian view that the subject have existence, called **existential import**. According to the classic Aristotelian view, a proposition such as "All mermaids swim well" could not be used as a premise or conclusion because mermaids don't exist. The Boolean view, now called the modern view, is to relax this restriction. The importance of the modern view is that empty classes can now be reasoned about. For example, a proposition such as "All disks that fail are cheap" could not be used in an Aristotelian syllogism unless there was at least one disk that had failed.

Another contribution of Boole was the definition of a set of **axioms** consisting of symbols to represent objects and classes, and algebraic operations to manipulate the symbols. Axioms are the fundamental definitions from which logical systems such as mathematics and logic itself are built. Using only the axioms, theorems can be constructed. A theorem is a statement that can be proved by showing how it is derived from the axioms. Between 1910 to 1913, Whitehead and Russell published their monumental 2000-page, three-volume work *Principia Mathematica* which showed a formal logic as the basis of mathematics. This was hailed as a great milestone because it appeared to put mathematics on a firm foundation rather than appealing to intuition by totally eliminating the meaning of arithmetic and instead concentrating on forms and their manipulation. Because of this, mathematics has been described as a collection of meaningless marks on paper. However, in 1931 Gödel proved that formal systems based on axioms could not be always proved internally consistent, and so free from contradictions.

Propositional logic, sometimes called **propositional calculus**, is a symbolic logic for manipulating propositions. In particular, propositional logic deals with the manipulation of **logical variables** which represent propositions. Although most people think of calculus in terms of the calculus invented by Newton and Leibnitz, the word has a more general meaning. It comes from the Latin word calculus and means a little stone used for calculations. The general meaning of calculus is a special system for manipulating symbols. Other terms used for propositional logic is the **statement calculus** or the **sentential calculus**. Sentences are generally classified as one of four types, as illustrated in Table 2-2.

Propositional logic is concerned with the subset of declarative sentences which can be classified as either true or false. A sentence whose truth value can be determined is called a **statement** or **proposition**. A statement is also called a **closed sentence** because its truth value is not open to question. The sentence "This statement is false" cannot be classified as either true or false. It is an example of a paradox known as the Liar's Paradox. The sentence "Spinach tastes wonderful" has an uncertain truth value because it is true for some people and not true for others. A sentence such as "A square has four equal sides" has a definite truth value of true, while the sentence "George Washington was the second president" has a truth value of false. The sentence "He is tall" is called an **open sentence** because it contains a variable "He". Truth values cannot be assigned to open sentences until we know the specific person or instance referred to by the variable. Another difficulty with this sentence is the meaning of the word "tall". What's tall to some people is not tall to others. While this ambiguity of "tall" cannot be handled in the propositional or predicate calculus, it can be easily dealt with in fuzzy logic, described in Chapter 5.

Type	Example
Imperative	Do what I tell you!
Interrogative	What is that?
Exclamatory	That's great!
Declarative	A square has four equal sides.

Table 2-2
Types of Sentences

A **compound statement** is formed by using logical connectives on individual statements. The common logical connectives are shown in Table 2-3.

Connective	Meaning
$\wedge$	AND; **conjunction**
$\vee$	OR; **disjunction**
$\sim$	NOT; **negation**
$\rightarrow$	if...then; **conditional**
$\leftrightarrow$	if and only if; **biconditional**

Table 2-3
Some Logical Connectives

Strictly speaking, the negation is not a connective because it is a unary operation that applies to the one operand following, so it doesn't really connect anything. The negation has higher precedence than the other operators and so it is not necessary to put parentheses around it. That is, a statement like $\sim p \wedge q$ means the same as $(\sim p) \wedge q$.

The conditional is analogous to the arrow of production rules in that it is expressed as an if...then form. For example

```
if it is raining then carry an umbrella
```

can be put in the form

```
p → q
```

where

```
p = it is raining
q = carry an umbrella
```

Sometimes the $\supset$ is used for $\rightarrow$. Another term for the conditional is **material implication**.

The biconditional, $p \leftrightarrow q$, is equivalent to

```
(p → q) ∧ (q → p)
```

and is true only when p and q have the same truth values. That is, p$\leftrightarrow$q is true only when p and q are both true or when they are both false. The biconditional has the following meanings:.

```
p if and only if q
q if and only if p
if p then q, and if q then p
```

A **tautology** is a compound statement that is always true, whether its individual statements are true or false. A **contradiction** is a compound statement which is always false. A **contingent** statement is one which is neither a tautology nor a contradiction. Tautologies and contradictions are called analytically true and analytically false respectively, because their truth value can be determined by their form alone. For example, the truth table of $p \vee \sim p$ shows it is a tautology, while $p \wedge \sim p$ is a contradiction.

If a conditional is also a tautology, then it is called an **implication** and has the symbol $\Rightarrow$ in place of $\rightarrow$. A biconditional that is also a tautology is called a **logical equivalence** or **material equivalence** and symbolized by either $\Leftrightarrow$ or $\equiv$. Two statements that are logically equivalent always have the same truth values. For example, $p \equiv \sim\sim p$.

Unfortunately, this is not the only possible definition for implication, since there are 16 possible truth tables for two variables that can take on true and false values. In fact, one paper has reviewed eleven different definitions of the implication operator used in expert systems (Whalen 85).

The conditional does not mean exactly the same as the IF...THEN in a procedural language or a rule-based expert system. In procedural and expert systems, the IF...THEN means to execute the actions following the THEN if the conditions of the IF are true. In logic, the conditional is defined by its truth table. Its meaning can be translated into natural language in a number of ways. For example, if

```
p → q
```

where p and q are any statements, this can be translated as

```
p implies q
if p then q
p, only if q
p is sufficient for q
q if p
q is necessary for p
```

As an example, let p represent "you are 21 or older" and q represent "you can vote". The conditional p → q can mean

```
you are 21 or older implies you can vote
if you are 21 or older then you can vote
you are 21 or older, only if you can vote
you are 21 or older is sufficient for you can vote
you can vote if you are 21 or older
you can vote is necessary for you are 21 or older
```

In some cases above, a change of grammar is necessary to make these grammatically correct English sentences. The last example says if q does not occur, then neither will p. If is expressed in correct grammar as "Being able to vote requires you to be 21 or older".

Values for the binary logical connectives are shown in Table 2-4.

p	q	$p \wedge q$	$p \vee q$	$p \rightarrow q$	$p \leftrightarrow q$
T	T	T	T	T	T
T	F	F	T	F	F
F	T	F	T	T	F
F	F	F	F	T	T

Table 2-4
Truth Table of the Binary Logical Connectives

These are binary connectives because they require two operands. The negation connective, ~, is a unary operator on the one operand that follows it, as shown in Table 2-5.

p	$\sim p$
T	F
F	T

Table 2-5
Truth Table of Negation

A set of logical connectives is **adequate** if every truth function can be represented using only the connectives from the adequate set. Examples of adequate sets are { ∼, ∧, ∨ }, { ∼, ∧ }, {∼, ∨ } and { ∼, → }.

A single element set is called a **singleton**. There are two adequate singleton sets. These are the NOT-OR (**NOR**) and the NOT-AND (**NAND**). The NOR set is { ↓ } and the NAND set is { | }. The " | " operator is called a **stroke** or **alternative denial**. It is used to deny that both p and q are true. That is, p I q affirms that at least one of the statements p or q is true. The **joint denial operator**, "↓", denies that either p or q is true. That is, p ↓ q affirms that both p and q are false.

2.13 THE FIRST ORDER PREDICATE LOGIC

Although propositional logic is useful, it does have limitations. The major problem is that propositional logic can only deal with complete statements. That is, it cannot examine the internal structure of a statement. Propositional logic cannot even prove the validity of a syllogism such as

```
All humans are mortal
All women are humans
Therefore, all women are mortal
```

In order to analyze more general cases, the **predicate logic** was developed. Its simplest form is the **first order** predicate logic and is the basis of logic programming languages such as PROLOG. In this section, we will use the term predicate logic to refer to first order predicate logic. Propositional logic is a subset of predicate logic.

Predicate logic is concerned with the internal structure of sentences. In particular, it is concerned with the use of special words called **quantifiers**, such as "all", "some" and "no". These words are very important because they explicitly quantify other words and so make sentences more exact. All the quantifiers are concerned with "how many"and so permit a wider scope of expression than propositional logic.

2.14 THE UNIVERSAL QUANTIFIER

A universally quantified sentence has the same truth value for all replacements in the same domain. The **universal quantifier** is represented by the symbol ∀ followed by one or more arguments for the **domain variable**. The symbol ∀ is interpreted as "for every" or "for all". For example, in the domain of numbers

$$(\forall x) \quad (x + x = 2x)$$

states that for every x (where x is a number), the sentence x + x = 2x is true. If we represent this sentence by the symbol p, then it can be expressed even more briefly as

```
(∀ x)  (p)
```

As another example, let p represent the sentence "all dogs are animals", as in

```
(∀ x)  (p)  ≡ (∀ x)  (if x is a dog → x is a animal)
```

The opposite statement is "no dogs are animals" and is written as

```
(∀ x)  (if x is a dog → ~x is a animal)
```

It may also be read as

```
Every dog is not an animal
All dogs are not animals
```

As another example, all triangles are polygons is written as follows.

```
(∀ x)  (x is a triangle → x is a polygon)
```

and is read "for all x, if x is a triangle, then x is a polygon". A shorter way of writing logic statements involving predicates is using **predicate functions** to describe the properties of the subject. The above logic statement can also be written

```
(∀ x)  (triangle(x) → polygon(x))
```

Predicate functions are usually written in a briefer notation using capital letters to represent the predicates. For example, let T=triangle and P=polygon. Then the triangle statement can be written even more briefly as

```
(∀ x)  (T(x) → P(x))    or    (∀ y)  (T(y) → P(y))
```

Note that any variables could be used in place of the dummy variables x and y. As another example, let H be the predicate function for human and M be the function for mortal. Then the statement that all humans are mortal can be written as

```
(∀ x)  (H(x) → M(x))
```

and is read that for all x, if x is human, then x is mortal. This predicate logic sentence can also be represented as a semantic net as shown in Figure 2-16. It can also be expressed in terms of rules as

```
IF x is human
THEN x is mortal
```

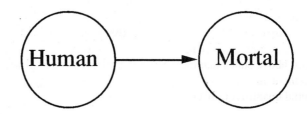

Figure 2-16
Semantic Net Representation of a Predicate Logic Statement

The universal quantifier can also be interpreted as a conjunction of predicates about instances. As mentioned earlier, an instance is a particular case. For example, a dog named Sparkler is a particular instance of the class of dogs and could be written as

```
Dog(Sparkler)
```

where Dog is the predicate function and Sparkler is an instance.

A predicate logic sentence such as

$$(\forall x) \quad P(x)$$

can be interpreted in terms of instances a_i as

$$P(a_1) \quad \wedge \quad P(a_2) \quad \wedge \quad P(a_3) \quad \wedge \ \ldots \ P(a_N)$$

where the dots indicate that the predicates extend on to all members of the class. This statement says that the predicate applies to all instances of the class.

Multiple quantifiers can be used. For example, the commutative law of addition for numbers requires two quantifiers, as in

$$(\forall x) \quad (\forall y) \quad (x + y = y + x)$$

which states that "for every x and for every y, the sum of x and y equals the sum of y and x".

2.15   THE EXISTENTIAL QUANTIFIER

Another type of quantifier is the **existential quantifier**. An existential quantifier describes a statement as being true for at least one member of the domain. This is a restricted form of the universal quantifier which states that a statement is true for all members of the domain. The existential quantifier is written as $\exists$ followed by one or more arguments. For example

```
(∃ x) (x · x = 1)
(∃ x) (elephant(x) ∧ name(Clyde))
```

The first sentence above states that there is some x whose product with itself equals 1. The second statement says there is some elephant with the name Clyde.

The existential quantifier may be read in a number of ways, such as

```
there exists
at least one
for some
there is one
some
```

As another example,

```
(∀ x) (elephant(x) → four-legged(x))
```

says that all elephants are four-legged. However, the statement that some elephants are three-legged is written with the logical AND and existential quantifier as follows.

```
(∃ x) (elephant(x) ∧ three-legged(x))
```

Just as the universal quantifier can be expressed as a conjunction, the existential quantifier can be expressed as a disjunction of instances, a_i.

```
P(a₁) ∨ P(a₂) ∨ P(a₃) ∨ ...P(aₙ)
```

Quantified statements and their negations are shown in Table 2-6 for the example in which P represents "elephants are mammals". The numbers in parentheses are just to identify the examples for the following discussion.

Example	Meaning
(1 a) (∀ x) (P)	All elephants are mammals.
(1 b) (∃ x) (~P)	Some elephants are not mammals.
(2 a) (∃ x) (P)	Some elephants are mammals.
(2 b) (∀ x) (~P)	No elephants are mammals.

Table 2-6
Examples of Negated Quantifiers

Examples (1 a) and (1 b) are negations of each other and so are (2 a) and (2 b). Notice that the negation of a universally quantified statement of (1 a) is an existentially quantified statement of the negation of P as shown by (1 b). Likewise, the negation of an existentially quantified statement of (2 a) is the universally quantified statement of the negation of P as shown by (2 b).

2.16   QUANTIFIERS AND SETS

Quantifiers may be used to define sets over a universe, $\mathcal{U}$, as shown in Table 2-7.

Set Expression	Logical Equivalent
$A = B$	$\forall x\,(x \in A \leftrightarrow x \in B)$
$A \subseteq B$	$\forall x\,(x \in A \rightarrow x \in B)$
$A \cap B$	$\forall x\,(x \in A \wedge x \in B)$
$A \cup B$	$\forall x\,(x \in A \vee x \in B)$
A'	$\forall x\,(x \in \mathcal{U} \mid \sim(x \in A))$
$\mathcal{U}$ (Universe)	T (True)
$\emptyset$ (empty set)	F (False)

Table 2-7
Some Set Expressions and Their Logical Equivalents

The relation that A is a proper subset of B, written as $A \subset B$ means that while all elements in A are in B, there is at least one element in B which is not in A. Letting E represent elephants, and M representing mammals, the set relation

```
E ⊂ M
```

states that all elephants are mammals, but not all mammals are elephants. Letting G=gray and F=four-legged, all gray, four-legged elephants are mammals is written

```
(E ∩ G ∩ F) ⊂ M
```

Using the following definitions, some examples of quantified sentences are shown.

```
E=elephants
R=reptiles
G=gray
F=four-legged
D=dogs
M=mammals


No elephants are reptiles
E ∩ R = Ø
Some elephants are gray
```

```
E ∩ G ≠ Ø
No elephants are grey
E ∩ G = Ø
Some elephants are not gray
E ∩ G´ ≠ Ø
All elephants are gray and four-legged
E ⊂ (G ∩ F)
All elephants and dogs are mammals
(E ∪ D) ⊂ M
Some elephants are four-legged and are gray
(E ∩ F ∩ G) ≠ Ø
```

As another analogy of sets and logic forms, de Morgan's laws are shown following in Table 2-8. where the equivalence symbol, ≡, the (biconditional) means that the statement on the left has the same truth value as the statement on the right. That is, the statements are equivalent.

Set	*Logic*
$(A \cap B)' \equiv A' \cup B'$	$\sim(p \wedge q) \equiv \sim p \vee \sim q$
$(A \cup B)' \equiv A' \cap B'$	$\sim(p \vee q) \equiv \sim p \wedge \sim q$

Table 2-8
Set and Logic Forms of De Morgan's Laws

2.17 LIMITATIONS OF PREDICATE LOGIC

Although predicate logic is very useful in many types of situations, there are many types of statements that cannot even be expressed in predicate logic using the universal and existential quantifiers (Rescher 64). For example, the following statement cannot be expressed in predicate logic.

```
Most of the class received A's
```

In this statement, the quantifier *Most* means more than half.

The *Most* quantifier cannot be expressed in terms of the universal and existential quantifiers. To implement *Most*, a logic must provide some predicates for counting, as in fuzzy logic described in Chapter 5. Another limitation of predicate logic is expressing things that are sometimes, but not always true. This problem can also be solved by fuzzy logic. However, introducing counting also introduces more complications into the logic system and makes it more like mathematics.

2.18 SUMMARY

In this chapter, we have reviewed the elements of the theory of knowledge and some techniques for representing knowledge. Knowledge representation is of major importance in expert systems. Knowledge can be classified by a number of ways such as *a priori*, *a posteriori*, procedural, declarative and tacit. Production rules, semantic nets, schemata, frames and logic are common methods by which knowledge is represented in expert systems. Each of these paradigms has advantages and disadvantages. Before designing an expert system, you should decide which is the best paradigm for the problem to be solved. Rather than trying to use one tool for all problems, pick the best tool for the problem.

PROBLEMS

2-1.   Draw a semantic net for computers using AKO and IS-A links. Consider the classes of microcomputer, minicomputer, mainframe, supercomputer, computing system, dedicated, general purpose, board-level, computer-on-a-chip, single processor and multi-processor. Include specific instances.

2-2.   Draw a semantic net for computer communications using AKO and IS-A links. Consider the classes of local area net, wide area net, token ring, star, centralized, decentralized, distributed, modems, telecommunications, bulletin boards and electronic mail. Include specific instances.

2-3.   Draw a frame system for the building in which you are attending classes. Consider offices, classrooms, laboratories and so forth. Include instances with filled slots for one type of each frame such as office and classroom.

2-4.   Draw an action frame system telling what to do in case of hardware failure for your computer system. Consider disk crash, power supply, CPU and memory problems.

2-5.   Draw the Venn diagram and write the set expression for

a)   exclusive-OR of two sets A and B consists of all elements that are in one, but not both sets. The exclusive-OR is also called the **symmetric set difference** and is symbolized by the "/". For example

    {1,2} / {2,3} = {1,3}

b)   **set difference** of two sets, symbolized by "–", consists of all the elements in the first set that are not also in the second. For example

```
{1,2} - {2,3} = {1}
```

where {1,2} is the first set and {2,3} is the second.

2-6.   Write the truth tables and determine which of the following are tautologies, contradictions or **contingent statements**, which are neither. For (a) and (b), first express the statements with logic symbols and connectives.

   a)   If I pass this course and make an 'A' then
        I pass this course or I make an 'A'.
   b)   If I pass this course then I make an 'A'
        and
        I pass this course and I do not make an 'A'.
   c) $((A \wedge \sim B \rightarrow (C \wedge \sim C)) \rightarrow (A \rightarrow B)$
   d) $(A \rightarrow B) \wedge (\sim B \vee C) \wedge (A \wedge \sim C)$
   e) $A \rightarrow \sim B$

2-7.   Two sentences are logically equivalent if and only if they have the same truth value. Thus if A and B are any statements, the biconditional statement, $A \leftrightarrow B$, or the equivalence, $A \equiv B$, will be true in every case, giving a tautology. Determine if the two sentences below are logically equivalent by writing them using logical symbols and determining if the truth table of their biconditional is a tautology.

```
If you eat a banana split, then you cannot eat a pie.
If you eat a pie, then you cannot eat a banana split.
```

2-8.   Write the logical equivalent corresponding to set difference and symmetric set difference.

2-9.   Show that the following are identities for any sets A, B, and C and Ø as the null set.

   a) $(A \cup B) \equiv (B \cup A)$
   b) $(A \cup B) \cup C \equiv A \cup (B \cup C)$
   c) $A \cup \emptyset \equiv A$
   d) $A \cap B \equiv B \cap A$
   e) $A \cap A' \equiv \emptyset$

2-10.   Write the following in quantified form

   a)   All dogs are mammals.

    b)   No dog is an elephant.

    c)   Some programs have bugs.

    d)   None of my programs have bugs.

    e)   All of your programs have bugs.

2-11.   The **power set**, $\mathcal{P}(S)$, of a set S is the set of all elements which are subsets of S. $\mathcal{P}(S)$ will always have at least the null set, $\emptyset$, and S as members.

    a)   Find the power set of A = {2, 4, 6}.

    b)   For a set with N elements, how many elements does the power set have?

2-12.   a)   Write the truth table for the following:

Meaning	Definition
either p or q	$(p \lor q) \land \sim(p \land q)$
neither p nor q	$\sim(p \lor q)$
p unless q	$\sim q \to p$
p because q	$(p \land q) \land (q \to p)$
no p is q	$p \to \sim q$

    b)   Show that $(p \lor q) \land \sim(p \land q) \equiv p \land q$

2-13.   a)   Write the NOR and NAND truth tables.

    b)   Prove that $\{ \downarrow \}$ and $\{ \mid \}$ are adequate sets by expressing $\sim$, $\land$, and $\lor$ in terms of $\downarrow$ and then in terms of $\mid$ by constructing truth tables to show the logical equivalences as follows.

$$\sim\sim p \equiv p$$
$$(p \land q) \equiv (p \downarrow p) \downarrow (q \downarrow q)$$
$$\sim p \equiv p \mid p$$
$$(p \lor q) \equiv (p \mid p) \mid (q \mid q)$$

    c)   Since $p \to q \equiv \sim(p \land \sim q)$, express $p \to q$ in terms of $\downarrow$.

    d)   What is the advantage and disadvantage of using adequate singleton sets in terms of (i) notation and (ii) construction of chips for electronic circuits.

2-14.   What are the advantages and disadvantages of designing an expert system with knowledge about several domains?

BIBLIOGRAPHY

(Angeles 81). Peter A. Angeles, *Dictionary of Philosophy*, Barnes & Noble Books, 1981.

(Barr 81). Arron Barr and Edward A. Feigenbaum, editors, *The Handbook of Artificial Intelligence, Volume 1*, William Kaufmann, Inc., 1981.

(Brachman 80). R.J. Brachman and B. C. Smith, eds., *SIGART Newsletter, Special Issue on Knowledge Representation*, **70**, Feb. 1980.

(Brachman 83). R.J. Brachman, R. E. Fikes, and H. L. Levesque, "KRYPTON: A Functional Approach to Knowledge Representation," *IEEE Computer*, **16**, p. 67, 1983.

(Brachman 85). Ronald J. Brachman, "I Lied about the Trees," *AI Magazine*, Vol. 6, (3), pp. 80-93, Fall 1985.

(Finin 86). Tim Finin, "Understanding Frame Languages, Part I," *AI Expert*, pp. 44-50, Nov. 1986.

(Jackson 86). Peter Jackson, *Introduction to Expert Systems*, Addison-Wesley, 1986.

(Lenat 77). Doug B. Lenat, "Automated Theory Formation in Mathematics," *Proceedings of the Fifth International Joint Conference on Artificial Intelligence*, 1977.

(McGettrick 80). Andrew D. McGettrick, *The Definitions of Programming Languages*, Cambridge University Press, 1980.

(Minsky 75). Marvin Minsky, "A Framework for Representing Knowledge," in *The Psychology of Computer Vision*, ed. Patrick Winston, McGraw-Hill, pp. 211-217, 1975.

(Quillian 68). M.R. Quillian, "Semantic Memory," *Semantic Information Processing*, ed. by Marvin Minsky, The MIT Press, pp. 227-270, 1968.

(Rissland 78). E.L. Rissland, "Understanding Understanding Mathematics," *Cognitive Science*, **2**, pp. 361-383, 1978.

(Schank 77). Roger C. Shank and R.P. Abelson, *Scripts, Plans, Goals, and Understanding*, pub. by Lawrence Erlbaum, 1977.

(Sowa 84). J.F. Sowa, *Conceptual Structures: Information Processing in Mind and Machine*, Addison-Wesley, 1984.

(Staugaard 87). Andrew C. Staugaard, Jr., *Robotics and AI: An introduction to Applied Machine Intelligence*, Prentice-Hall, 1987.

(Stillings 87). Neil A. Stillings et al., *Cognitive Science: An Introduction*, The MIT Press, 1987.

(Whalen 85). Thomas Whalen and Brian Schott, "Alternative Logics for Approximate Reasoning in Expert Systems: A Comparative Study," *Int. J. Man-Machine Studies*, **22**, pp. 327-346, 1985.

(Winston 84). Patrick Henry Winston, *Artificial Intelligence*, second edition, Addison-Wesley, 1984.

(Woods 83). W.A. Woods, "What's Important About Knowledge Representation?" *IEEE Computer*, **16**, p. 22, 1983.

CHAPTER 3 METHODS OF INFERENCE

3.1 INTRODUCTION

In this chapter, we will discuss various methods of reasoning or inference. This topic is particularly important in expert systems because reasoning is the common technique by which expert systems solve problems. Expert systems are commonly used when an inadequate algorithm or no algorithmic solution exists and reasoning offers the only possibility of a solution.

3.2 TREES, LATTICES, AND GRAPHS

A **tree** is a hierarchical data structure consisting of **nodes** which store information or knowledge and **branches** which connect the nodes. Branches are sometimes called **links** or **edges** and nodes sometimes called **vertices**. Figure 3-1 shows a general binary tree which has 0, 1, or 2 branches per node. In an **oriented tree**, the **root node** is the highest node in the **hierarchy** and the **leaves** are the lowest. A tree can be considered a special type of semantic net in which every node except the root has exactly one **parent** and zero or more **child** nodes. For the usual type of binary tree, there are a maximum of two children per node, and the left and right child nodes are distinguished.

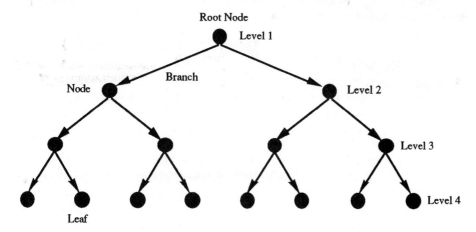

Figure 3-1
Binary Tree

If a node has more than one parent it is in a network. In Figure 3-1, notice that there is only one sequence of edges or **path** from the root to any node since it is not possible to move against an arrow. In oriented trees, the arrows all point downward.

Trees are a special case of a general mathematical structure called a **graph**. The terms network or simply net are often used synonymously with graph when describing a particular example of a graph such as a telephone network. A graph can have zero or more links between nodes and no distinction between parents and children. A simple example of a graph is a map where the cities are the nodes and the links are the roads. The links may have arrows or directions associated with them and a **weight** to characterize some aspect of the link. An analogy is one-way streets with weight limits on how much trucks can carry through the streets. The weights in a graph can be any type of information. If the graph represents an airline route, the weights can be miles between cities, cost of flying, fuel consumption and so forth.

An artificial neural system is another example of a graph with cycles since during training there is feedback of information from one layer of the net to another which modifies the weights. A simple graph has no links which come immediately back on the node itself, as shown in Figure 3-2 (a). A **circuit** or **cycle** is a path through a graph which begins and ends on the same node, as does the path ABCA in Figure 3-2 (a). An **acyclic** graph has no cycles. A **connected graph** has links to all its nodes. A graph with directed links, called a **digraph** and a **self-loop** is shown in Fig. 3-2 (c). A directed acyclic graph is a **lattice**, and an example is shown in Figure 3-2 (d). A tree with only a single path from the root to its one leaf is a **degenerate tree**. The degenerate binary trees of three nodes are shown in Figure 3-2 (e). Generally in a tree, the arrows are *not* explicitly shown because they are assumed pointing down.

Trees and lattices are useful for classifying objects because of their hierarchical nature with parents above children. An example is a family tree which shows the relationships and ancestry of related people. Another application of trees and lattices is making decisions and these are called **decision trees** or **decision lattices**. We will use the term **structure** to refer to both trees and lattices. A decision structure is both a knowledge representation scheme and a method of reasoning about its knowledge. An example of a decision tree for classifying animals is shown in Figure 3-3. This example is for the classic game of guessing an animal. The nodes contain questions, the branches "yes" or "no" responses to the questions and the leaves contain the guess of what the animal is.

A small portion of a decision tree to classify raspberries is shown in Figure 3-4. Unlike Computer Science trees, classification trees may be drawn with the root down. Not shown is the root which has a branch to the "Leaves Simple" node and another branch to the "Leaves Compound" node. The decision process starts at the bottom by identifying gross features, such as whether the leaves are simple or compound. More specific details requiring closer observation are used as we travel up the tree. That is, larger sets of alternatives are examined first and then the decision process starts narrowing down the possibilities to smaller sets. This is a good way of organizing the decisions in terms of the time and effort to carry out more detailed observations.

If the decisions are binary, then a binary decision tree is easy to construct and very efficient. Every question goes down one level in the tree. One question can decide one of two possible answers. Two questions can decide one of four possible answers. Three questions can decide one of eight possible answers and so on. If a binary tree is constructed such that all the leaves are answers and all the nodes leading down are questions, there can be a maximum of 2^N answers for N questions. For example, 10 questions can classify one of 1,024 animals while 20 questions can classify one of 1,048,576 possible answers.

Another useful feature of decision trees is that they can be made **self-learning**. If the guess is wrong, a procedure can be called to query the user for a new, correct classification question and the answers to the "yes" and "no" responses. A new node, branches and leaves can then be dynamically created and added to the tree. In the original Animals program written in BASIC, knowledge was stored in DATA statements. When the user taught the program a new animal, automatic learning took place as the program generated new DATA statements containing information about the new animal. In Pascal and other languages with pointer capability, the animal knowledge can be stored in trees. Using the expert system shell OPS5, new rules can be built automatically as the program learns new knowledge. This **automated knowledge acquisition** is very useful since it can circumvent the knowledge acquisition bottleneck described in Chapter 1.

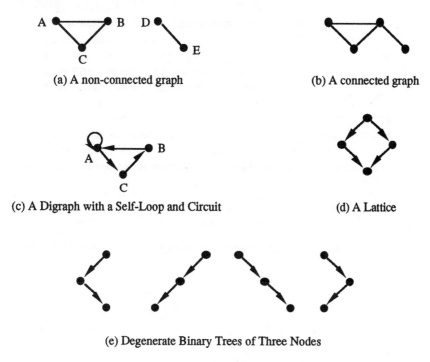

(a) A non-connected graph

(b) A connected graph

(c) A Digraph with a Self-Loop and Circuit

(d) A Lattice

(e) Degenerate Binary Trees of Three Nodes

Figure 3-2

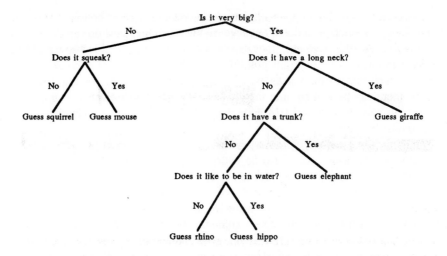

Figure 3-3
Decision Tree Showing Knowledge About Animals

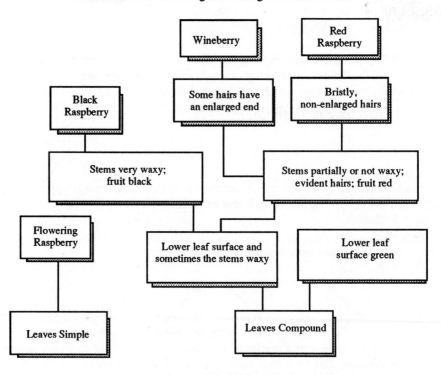

Figure 3-4
Portion of a Decision Tree for Species of Raspberries

Decision structures can be mechanically translated into production rules. This can easily be done by a breadth-first searching of the structure and generating IF...THEN rules at every node. For example, the decision tree of Figure 3-3 could be translated into rules as follows

```
IF QUESTION = "IS IT VERY BIG?" AND RESPONSE = "NO"
   THEN  QUESTION := "DOES IT SQUEAK?"

IF QUESTION = "IS IT VERY BIG?" AND RESPONSE = "YES"
   THEN  QUESTION := "DOES IT HAVE A LONG NECK?"
```

and so forth for the other nodes. A leaf node would generate an ANSWER response rather than a question. Appropriate procedures would also query the user for input and construct new nodes if wrong.

Although decision structures are very powerful classification tools, they are limited because they cannot deal with variables as an expert system can. Expert systems are general purpose tools rather than simply classifiers.

3.3 STATE AND PROBLEM SPACES

Graphs can be applied to many practical problems. A very useful method of describing the behavior of an object is to define a graph called the **state space**. A state is a collection of characteristics which can be used to define the status or **state** of an object. The state space is the set of states showing the **transitions** between states that the object can experience. A transition takes an object from one state to another.

Examples of State Spaces

As a simple example of state spaces, consider the purchase a soft drink from a machine. As you put coins into the machine, it makes a transition from one state to another. Figure 3-5 illustrates the state space assuming that only quarters and nickels are available and 55¢ is required for a drink. Adding other coins such as dimes and fifty-cent pieces makes the diagram more complicated and is not shown.

The start and success states are drawn as double circles to make them easier to identify. The states are shown as circles and the possible transitions to other states are drawn as arrows. Notice that this diagram is a weighted digraph, where the weights are the possible coins that can be input to the machine in every state.

This diagram is also called a **finite state machine** diagram because it describes the finite number of states of a machine. The term machine is used in a very general sense. The machine can be a real object, an algorithm, a concept and so forth. Associated with every state are the actions that drive it to another state. At any time, the machine can be in only one state. As the machine accepts input to a state, it progresses from that state to another. If the correct inputs are given, the machine will progress from the start to the success or final state. If a state is not designed to accept a certain input, the machine will become hung up in that state. For example, the soft drink machine has no provision to accept dimes. If someone puts a dime in the machine, the response is undefined. A good design will include the possibility of invalid inputs from every state and provide for transitions to an error state. The error state is designed to give appropriate error messages and take whatever action is necessary.

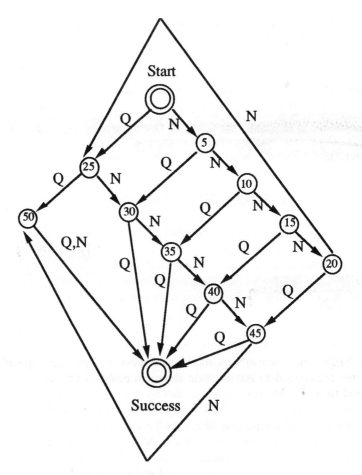

Figure 3-5
State Diagram for a Soft Drink Vending Machine
Accepting Quarters (Q) and Nickels (N)

Finite state machines are often used in compilers and other programs to determine the validity of an input. For example, Figure 3-6 shows part of a finite state machine to test input strings for validity. Characters of the input are examined one at a time.

Only the character strings WHILE, WRITE and BEGIN will be accepted. Arrows are shown from the BEGIN state for successful input, and also for erroneous input going to the error state. For efficiency, some states such as the one pointed to by "L" and "T" are used for testing both WHILE and WRITE.

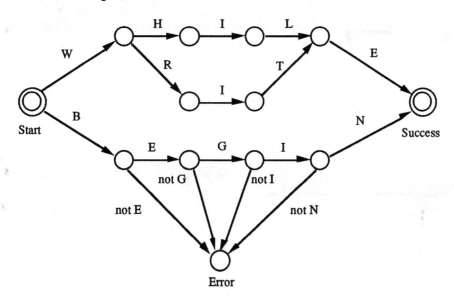

Figure 3-6
Part of a Finite State Machine for Determining
Valid Strings WHILE, WRITE, and BEGIN.
Only Some of the Error State Transitions are Shown

State diagrams are also useful in describing the solution of problems. In these kinds of applications, we can think of the state space as a **problem space** where the some states correspond to intermediate stages in problem solving and some states correspond to answers. In a problem space, there may be multiple success states corresponding to possible solutions. Finding the solution to a problem in a problem space involves finding a valid path from start (problem statement) to success (answer). The animal decision tree can be viewed as a problem space where the yes/no responses to questions determine the state transition.

Another example of a problem space occurs in the classic Monkey and Bananas problem shown in Figure 3-7. The problem is to give instructions to a monkey telling how to retrieve some bananas hanging from the ceiling. The bananas are out of reach. Inside the room is a couch and a ladder. The initial starting configuration is typically with the monkey on the couch. Instructions might be

```
jump off couch
move to ladder
```

```
move ladder under bananas' position
climb ladder
grab bananas
```

The instructions will vary depending on the initial configuration of monkey, couch and ladder. Since there are a number of initial start states, the special double circles for the start is not shown. For example, another possible starting state is with the monkey on the couch under the bananas. The monkey will then have to push the couch out of the way before moving the ladder under the bananas. In the simplest starting state, the monkey is already on the ladder under the bananas.

Although this problem seems obvious to a human, it involves a considerable amount of reasoning. A practical application of reasoning system like this is giving instructions to a robot concerning the solution of a task. Rather than assuming that all objects in the environment are fixed in place, a general solution is a reasoning system which can deal with a variety of situations. A rule-based solution to the Monkeys and Bananas problem is distributed with the CLIPS disks.

Another useful application of graphs is exploring paths to find a problem's solution. Figure 3-8 (a) shows a simple net for the Traveling Salesman problem. In this example, assume the problem is to find a complete path from node A which visits all other nodes. As usual in the Traveling Salesman problem, no node can be visited twice. Figure 3-8 (b) shows all the possible paths starting from node A in the form of a tree. The correct paths ABDCA and ACDBA are shown as thick lines in this graph.

Depending on the search algorithm, the exploration of paths to find the correct one may involve a considerable amount of backtracking. For example, the path ABA may be first searched unsuccessfully, and then backtracked to B. From B, the paths CA, CB, CDB, and CDC will be unsuccessfully searched. Next the path BDB will be unsuccessfully searched until the first correct path ABDCA is found.

Ill-structured Problem Spaces

A useful application of state spaces is in characterizing ill-structured problems (Pople 82). In Chapter 1, an ill-structured problem was defined to have uncertainties associated with it. These uncertainties can be specified more precisely by a problem space. As an example of an ill-structured problem, let's consider again the case of a person who is thinking about traveling and visits a travel agent, as discussed in Chapter 1. Table 3-1 lists some characteristics of this ill-structured problem as a problem space, indicated by the person's responses to the travel agent's questions.

If you compare Table 3-1 to Table 1-10 listed in Chapter 1, you'll see that the concept of a problem space lets us specify more precisely the characteristics of an ill-structured problem. It is essential to characterize these parameters precisely to determine if a solution is feasible and if so, what is needed for a solution. A problem is not necessarily ill-structured just because it has one, some, or even all of these characteristics since much depends on the severity. For example, all theorem proving problems have an infinite number of potential solutions, but this does not make theorem proving an ill-structured problem.

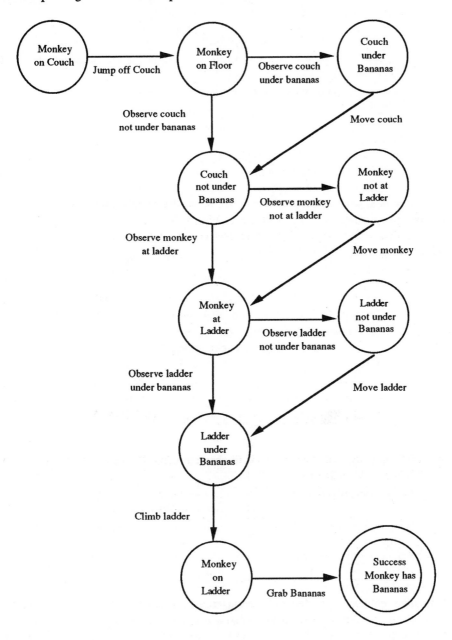

Figure 3-7
The State Space for the Monkey and Bananas Problem

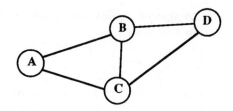

(a) Graph of a Traveling Salesman Problem

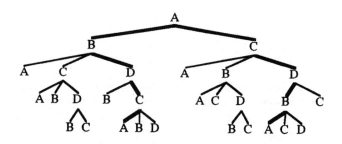

(b) Search Paths (optimal path shown by thick edges)

Figure 3-8
A Traveling Salesman Problem

As you can see from this table, there are many uncertainties and yet human beings such as travel agents cope with them everyday. While not all cases may be as bad as this, it indicates why an algorithmic solution would be very difficult.

Characteristic	Response
Goal not explicit	I'm thinking about going somewhere
Problem space unbounded	I'm not sure where to go
Problem states not discrete	I just like to travel; the destination is not important
Intermediate states difficult to achieve	I don't have enough money to go
State operators unknown	I don't know how to get the money
Time constraint	I must go soon

Table 3-1
Example of An Ill-structured Problem for Travel

A well-formed problem is one in which we know the explicit problem, goal, and operators that can be applied to go from one state to another. A well-formed problem is

deterministic because when an operator is applied to a state, we are sure of the next state. The problem space is bounded and the states are discrete. This means that there are a finite number of states and each state is well-defined.

In the travel problem, the states are unbounded because there are infinitely many possible destinations that a traveler might go to. An analogous situation occurs with an analog meter which may indicate an infinite number of possible readings. If we consider each reading of the meter to be a state, then there are an infinite number of states and they are not well-defined because they correspond to real numbers. Since there are an infinite number of real numbers between any two real numbers, the states are not discrete because the next state differs only infinitesimally. In contrast, the readings of a digital meter are bounded and discrete.

3.4 AND-OR TREES AND GOALS

Many types of expert systems use backward chaining to find solutions to problems. PROLOG is a good example of a backward chaining system which tries to solve a problem by breaking it up into smaller subproblems and solving them. Solving a problem is considered by optimists as a goal to be achieved. In order to accomplish a goal, zero or more subgoals may need to be accomplished.

One type of tree or lattice that is useful in representing backward chaining problems is the AND-OR tree. Figure 3-9 shows a simple example of an AND-OR lattice to solve the goal of obtaining a college degree. To accomplish this goal, you can either attend a college in person or through correspondence courses. With correspondence courses, work can be performed either by mailing assignments or electronically using a home computer and modem.

In order to satisfy requirements for the degree, three subgoals must be accomplished: (1) apply for admittance, (2) take courses and (3) apply to graduate. Notice that there is an arc through the edges from the Satisfy Requirements goal to these three subgoals. The arc through the edges indicate that Satisfy Requirements is an AND-node that can only be satisfied if all three of its subgoals are satisfied. Goals without the arc such as Mail, Computer and Modem, and In Person are OR-nodes in which accomplishing any of these subgoals satisfies its parent goal of Get a College Degree.

This diagram is a lattice because the Satisfy Requirements subgoal has three parent nodes: (1) Mail, (2) Computer and Modem, and (3) In Person. Notice that it would be possible to draw this diagram as a tree by simply duplicating the subgoal Satisfy Requirements and its subtree of goals for the Mail, Computer and Modem, and In Person goals. However, since the Satisfy Requirements is the same for each of its parents, there is no real advantage and it uses more paper to draw the tree.

As another simple example, Figure 3-10 shows an AND-OR tree for the problem of getting to work by different possible ways. For completeness, this could also be converted into a lattice. For example, an edge could be added from the node Drive to Train Station to the Car node and from Walk to Train Station to the Walk node. Figure 3-11 shows an AND-exclusive OR type lattice.

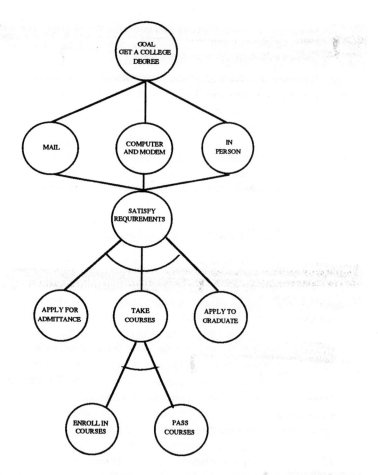

Figure 3-9
AND-OR Lattice Showing How to Obtain a College Degree

Another way of describing problem solutions is an AND-OR-NOT lattice which uses logic gate symbols instead of the AND-OR tree type notation. The logic gate symbols for AND, OR and NOT are shown in Figure 3-12. These gates implement the truth tables for AND, OR and NOT discussed in Chapter 2. Figure 3-13 shows Figure 3-9 implemented with AND and OR gates.

AND-OR trees and decision trees have the same basic advantages and disadvantages. The main advantage of AND-OR-NOT lattices is their potential implementation in hardware for fast processing speeds. These lattices can be custom designed for fabrication as integrated circuits. In practice, one type of logic gate such as the NOT-AND or NAND is used for reasons of manufacturing economy rather than separate AND, OR and NOT gates. From logic, it can be proved that any logic function can be implemented by a NAND gate. An integrated circuit with one type of device is cheaper to manufacture than one with multiple types of logic gates.

A chip using forward chaining can compute the answer very quickly as a function of its inputs since processing proceeds in parallel. Chips like this can be used for real-time monitoring of sensor data and make an appropriate response depending on the inputs. The main disadvantage is that like other decision structures, a chip designed for logic cannot handle situations it was not designed for. However, an ANS implemented on a chip can handle unexpected inputs.

3.5 DEDUCTIVE LOGIC AND SYLLOGISMS

In Chapter 2, we discussed the representation of knowledge by logic. Now you will see how inferences are made to derive new knowledge or information. In the remainder of this chapter, we will discuss different methods of inference. Figure 3-14 is an overview of the methods of inference. A brief summary is the following.

* *Deduction.* Logical reasoning in which conclusions must follow from their premises
* *Induction.* Inference from the specific case to the general.
* *Intuition.* No proven theory. The answer just appears, possibly by unconsciously recognizing an underlying pattern. Expert systems do not implement this type of inference yet. ANS may hold promise for this type of inference since they can extrapolate from their training rather than just provide a conditioned response or interpolation. That is, a neural net will always give its best guess for a solution.
* *Heuristics.* Rules of thumb based on experience.
* *Generate and Test.* Trial and error. Often used with planning for efficiency.
* *Abduction.* Reasoning back from a true conclusion to the premises that may have caused the conclusion.
* *Default.* In the absence of specific knowledge, assume general or common knowledge by default.
* *Autoepistemic.* Self-knowledge
* *Nonmonotonic.* Previous knowledge may be incorrect when new evidence is obtained.
* *Analogy.* Inferring a conclusion based on the similarities to another situation.

Although not explicitly shown in Figure 3-14, **commonsense knowledge** may be a combination of any of these types. Commonsense reasoning is the type that people use in ordinary situations, and is very difficult for computers. The application of fuzzy logic to commonsense reasoning is discussed in Chapter 5.

One of the most often used methods of drawing inferences is **deductive logic**, which has been used since ancient times to determine the validity of an **argument**. Although people commonly use the word argument to describe an angry "exchange of views," it has a very different meaning in logic. A logical argument is a group of statements in which the last is claimed to be justified on the basis of the previous ones in the **chain of reasoning.** One type of logical argument is the syllogism, which was briefly discussed in Chapter 2. As an example of a syllogism

Premise:	Anyone who can program is intelligent
Premise:	John can program
Conclusion:	Therefore, John is intelligent

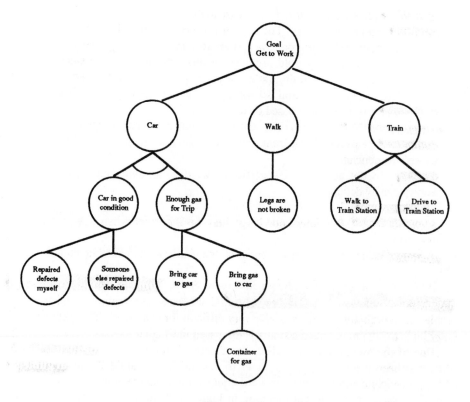

Figure 3-10
A Simple AND-OR Tree Showing Methods of Getting to Work

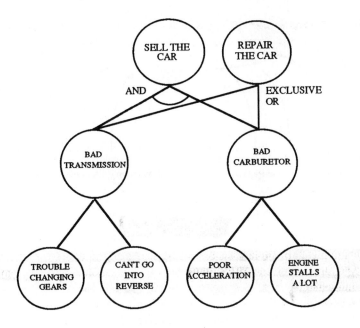

Figure 3-11
AND-OR Lattice for Car Selling/Repair Decision

Figure 3-12
AND, OR, and NOT Logic Gate Symbols

Figure 3-13
AND-OR Logic Gate Representation for Figure 3-9

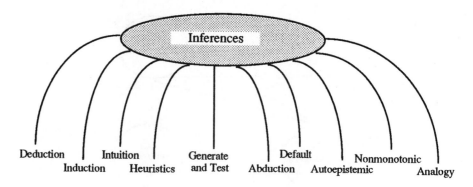

Figure 3-14
Types of Inference

In an argument, the premises are used as evidence to support the conclusions. The premises are also called the **antecedent** and the conclusion is called the **consequent**. The essential characteristic of deductive logic is that the true conclusion *must* follow from true premises. A line is customarily drawn to separate the premises from the conclusion, as shown above, so that it is not necessary to explicitly label the premises and conclusion.

The argument could have been written more briefly as

```
Anyone who can program is intelligent
John can program
∴ John is intelligent
```

where the three dots, ∴, mean "therefore."

Let's take a closer look at syllogistic logic now. The main advantage of studying syllogisms is that it is a simple, well-understood branch of logic that can be completely proven. Also, syllogisms are often useful since they can be expressed in terms of IF THEN rules. For example, the previous syllogism can be rephrased as

```
IF   Anyone who can program is intelligent and
     John can program
THEN John is intelligent
```

In general, a syllogism is any valid deductive argument having two premises and a conclusion. The classic syllogism is a special type called a **categorical syllogism**. The premises and conclusions are defined as categorical statements of the following four forms, as shown in Table 3-2.

Note that in logic, the term schema specifies the logical form of the statement. This also illustrates another use of the word schema, which is different from its AI use discussed in Chapter 2. In logic, the word schema is used to show the essential form of an argument. Schemata may also specify the logical form of an entire syllogism as in

```
All M is P
All S is M
∴ All S is P
```

Form	Schema	Meaning
A	All S is P	universal affirmative
E	No S is P	universal negative
I	Some S is P	particular affirmative
O	Some S is not P	particular negative

Table 3-2
Categorical Statements

 The subject of the conclusion, S, is called the **minor term** while the predicate of the conclusion, P, is called the **major term**. The premise containing the major term is called the **major premise** and the premise containing the minor term is called the **minor premise**. For example

```
Major Premise:      All M is P
Minor Premise:      All S is M
Conclusion:   All S is P
```

is a syllogism said to be in **standard form,** with its major and minor premises identified. The **subject** is the object that is being described while the **predicate** describes some property of the subject. For example, in the statement

```
All microcomputers are computers
```

the subject is "microcomputers" and the predicate is "computers." In the statement

```
All microcomputers with 8 megabytes
are computers with a lot of memory
```

the subject is "microcomputers with 8 megabytes" and the predicate is "computers with a lot of memory."
     The forms of the categorical statements have been identified since ancient times by the letters A, E, I and O. The A and I indicate affirmative and are thought to come from the first two vowels of the Latin word "affirmo" (I affirm), while E and O come from "nego" (I negate). The A and I forms are said to be **affirmative in quality** by affirming that the subjects are included in the predicate class. The E and O forms are **negative in quality** because the subjects are excluded from the predicate class.
     The verb "is" is called the **copula** from the Latin which means to connect. The copula connects the two parts of the statement . In the standard categorical syllogism, the copula is the present tense form of the verb "to be." So another version is

```
All S are P
```

The third term of the syllogism, M, is called the **middle term** and is common to both premises. The middle term is essential because a syllogism is defined such that the conclusion cannot be inferred from either of the premises alone. So the argument

```
All A is B
All B is C
∴ All A is B
```

is not a valid syllogism since it follows from the first premise alone.

The **quantity** or **quantifier**, describes the portion of the class included. The quantifiers "All" and "No" are **universal** because they refer to entire classes. The quantifier "Some" is called **particular** because it refers to just part of the class.

The **mood** of a syllogism is defined by the three letters that give the form of the major premise, minor premise and conclusion, respectively. For example, the syllogism

```
All M is P
All S is M
∴ All S is P
```

is an AAA mood.

There are four possible patterns of arranging the S, P, and M terms as shown in Table 3-3. Each pattern is called a **figure** with the number of the figure specifying its type.

	Figure 1	*Figure 2*	*Figure 3*	*Figure 4*
Major Premise	M P	P M	M P	P M
Minor Premise	S M	S M	M S	M S

Table 3-3
Patterns of Categorical Statements

So the previous example is completely described as an AAA-1 syllogism type. Just because an argument has a syllogistic form does not mean that it is a valid syllogism. Consider the AEE-1 syllogism form:

```
All M is P
No S is M
∴ No S is P
```

is not a valid syllogism as can be seen from the example

```
All microcomputers are computers
No mainframe is a microcomputer
∴ No mainframe is a computer
```

Rather than trying to think up examples to prove the validity of syllogistic arguments, there is a **decision procedure** which can be used. A decision procedure is a method of proving validity. A decision procedure is some general mechanical method or algorithm by which the process of determining validity can be automated. While there are decision procedures for syllogistic logic and propositional logic, Church showed in 1936 that there is none for predicate logic. Instead, people must apply creativity to generate proofs.

The decision procedure for propositions is simply constructing a truth table and examining it for tautology. The decision procedure for syllogisms can be done using Venn diagrams with three overlapping circles representing S, P, and M as shown in Figure 3-15 (a). For the syllogism form AEE-1:

```
All M is P
No S is M
∴ No S is P
```

the major premise is illustrated in Figure 3-15 (b). The lined section of M indicates that there are no elements in that portion. In (c), the minor premise is included by lining its portion with no elements. From (c), it can be seen that the conclusion of AEE-1 is false since there are some S in P.

As another example, consider EAE-1:

```
No M is P
All S is M
∴ No S is P
```

This is valid as can be seen from Figure 3-16 (c).

Venn diagrams that involve "Some" quantifiers are a little more difficult to draw. The general rules for drawing categorical syllogisms under the Boolean view that there may be no members in the A and E statements are:

1. If a class is empty, it is shaded.
2. Universal statements, A and E, are always drawn before particular ones.
3. If a class has at least one member, mark it with an *.
4. If a statement does not specify in which of two adjacent classes an object exists, place an * on the line between the classes.
5. If an area has been shaded, no * can be put in it.

As an example,

```
Some computers are laptops
All laptops are transportable
∴ Some transportables are computers
```

which can be put in IAI-4 type

```
Some P are M
All M are S
∴ Some S are P
```

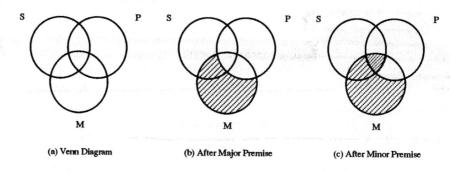

(a) Venn Diagram   (b) After Major Premise   (c) After Minor Premise

Figure 3-15
Decision Procedure for Syllogism AEE-1

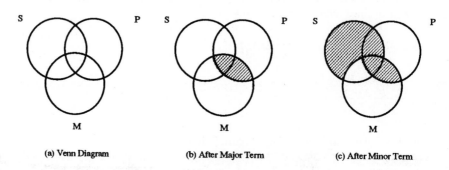

(a) Venn Diagram   (b) After Major Term   (c) After Minor Term

Figure 3-16
Decision Procedure for Syllogism EAE-1

Following the rules 2 and 1 for Venn diagrams, we start with the universal statement for the minor premise and shade it as shown in Figure 3-17 (a). Next rule 3 is applied to the particular major premise and a * is drawn as shown in Figure 3-17 (b). Since the conclusion "Some transportables are computers" is shown in the diagram, it follows that the argument IAI-4 is a valid syllogism.

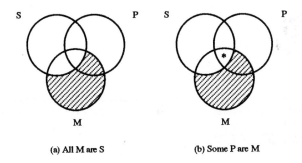

(a) All M are S   (b) Some P are M

Figure 3-17
Syllogism of IAI-4 Type

3.6 RULES OF INFERENCE

Although Venn diagrams are a decision procedure for syllogisms, the diagrams are inconvenient for more complex arguments because the diagrams become more difficult to read. However, there is a more fundamental problem with syllogisms because they address only a small portion of the possible logical statements. In particular, categorical syllogisms only address categorical statements of the A, E, I and O form.

Propositional logic offers another means of describing arguments. In fact, we often use propositional logic without realizing it. For example, consider the following propositional argument.

```
If there is power, the computer will work
There is power
∴ The computer will work
```

This argument can be expressed in a formal way by using letters to represent the propositions as follows.

```
A = There is power
B = The computer will work
```

and so the argument can be written as

```
A → B
A
∴ B
```

Arguments like this occur often. A general schema for representing arguments of this type is

$$p \rightarrow q$$
$$\underline{p}$$
$$\therefore q$$

where p and q are logical variables which can represent any statements. The use of logical variables in propositional logic allows more complex types of statements than the four syllogistic forms A, E, I, and O. Inference schema of this propositional form is called by a variety of names: **direct reasoning, modus ponens, law of detachment** and **assuming the antecedent**.

Notice that this example can also be expressed in the syllogistic form

```
All computers with power will work
This computer has power
This computer will work
```

which demonstrates that *modus ponens* is really a special case of syllogistic logic. *Modus ponens* is important because it forms the basis of rule-based expert systems. The compound proposition, $p \rightarrow q$, corresponds to the rule while the p corresponds to the pattern that must match the antecedent for the rule to be satisfied. However, as discussed in Chapter 2, the conditional $p \rightarrow q$ is not exactly equivalent to a rule because the conditional is a logical definition defined by a truth table and there are many possible definitions of the conditional.

Generally we will follow the convention of logic theory of using capital letters such as A, B, C... to represent constant propositions such as "There is power." Small letters such as p, q, r... will represent logical variables, which can stand for different constant propositions. Note that this convention is opposite to that of PROLOG which uses capital letters for variables.

This *modus ponens* schema could also have been written with differently named logical variables as

$$r \rightarrow s$$
$$\underline{r}$$
$$\therefore s$$

and the schema would still mean the same.

Another notation for this schema is

$$r, \; r \rightarrow s; \; \therefore s$$

where the comma is used to separate one premise from another and the semicolon indicates the end of the premises. Although so far we have only looked at arguments with two premises, a more general form of an argument is

$$P_1, \; P_2, \; \ldots \; P_N; \; \therefore C$$

where the capital letters P_i represent premises such as r, r $\rightarrow$ s and C is the conclusion. Notice how this resembles the goal satisfaction statement of PROLOG discussed in Chapter 2.

```
p :- p₁, p₂, ... pₙ.
```

The goal, p, is satisfied if all the subgoals p_1, p_2, ... p_N are satisfied. An analogous argument for production rules can be written in the general form

$$C_1 \wedge C_2 \wedge \ldots C_N \rightarrow A$$

which means that if each condition, C_i, of a rule is satisfied, then the action A of the rule is done. As discussed previously, a logical statement of the form above is strictly not equivalent to a rule because the logical definition of the conditional is not the same as a production rule. However, this logical form is a useful intuitive aid in thinking about rules.

The notation of the logic operators AND and OR have different forms in PROLOG compared to the usual $\wedge$ and $\vee$. The comma between subgoals in PROLOG means a conjunction, $\wedge$, while the disjunction, $\vee$, is indicated with a semicolon. For example,

```
p :- p₁; p₂.
```

means that p is satisfied if p_1 or p_2 is satisfied. Conjunctions and disjunctions can be mixed. For example,

```
p :- p₁, p₂; p₃, p₄.
```

is the same as the two PROLOG statements

```
p :- p₁, p₂.
p :- p₃, p₄.
```

In general, if the premises and conclusion are all schemata, the argument

$$P_1, P_2, \ldots P_N; \therefore C$$

is a formally valid deductive argument if and only if

$$P_1 \wedge P_2 \wedge \ldots P_N \rightarrow C$$

is a tautology. As an example

$$(p \wedge q) \rightarrow p$$

is a tautology because it is true for any values, T or F, of p and q. You can verify this by constructing the truth table.

The argument of *modus ponens*,

$$p \rightarrow q$$
$$\underline{p}$$
$$\therefore q$$

is valid because it can be expressed as a tautology.

$$(p \rightarrow q) \wedge p \rightarrow q$$

Note that we are assuming that the arrow has lower precedence than conjunction and disjunction. This saves writing additional parentheses such as

$$((p \rightarrow q) \wedge p) \rightarrow q$$

The truth table for *modus ponens* is shown in Table 3-4. It is a tautology since the values of the argument, shown in the rightmost column, are all true no matter what the values of its premises. Notice that in the third, fourth, and fifth columns, the truth values are written under certain operators such as the $\rightarrow$ and $\wedge$. These are called the **main connectives** because they connect the two main parts of a compound proposition.

p	q	$p \rightarrow q$	$(p \rightarrow q) \wedge p$	$(p \rightarrow q) \wedge p \rightarrow q$
T	T	T	T	T
T	F	F	F	T
F	T	T	F	T
F	F	T	F	T

Table 3-4
Truth Table for *Modus Ponens*

Although this method of determining valid arguments works, it does require checking every row of the truth table. The number of rows is 2^N where N is the number of premises and so the rows increase very rapidly with the number of premises. For example, five premises would require 32 rows to be checked while ten premises require 1024 rows. A shorter method of determining a valid argument is to consider only those rows of the truth table in which the premises are all true. The equivalent definition of a valid argument states that it is valid if and only if the conclusion is true for each of these rows. That is, the conclusion is tautologically implied by the premises. For *modus ponens*, the $p \rightarrow q$ premise and p premise are both true only in the first row, and so is the conclusion. Hence, *modus ponens* is a valid argument. If there were any other row in which the premises were all true and the conclusion false, then the argument would be invalid.

The shorter way of expressing the truth table for *modus ponens* is shown in Table 3-5, where all the rows are explicitly shown. In practice, only those rows which have true premises such as the first row need be considered.

		Premises		Conclusion
p	*q*	$p \rightarrow q$	*p*	*q*
T	T	T	T	T
T	F	F	T	F
F	T	T	F	T
F	F	T	F	F

Table 3-5
Alternate Short-form Truth Table for *Modus Ponens*

The truth table for *modus ponens* shows that it is valid because the first row has true premises and a true conclusion, and there are no other rows which have true premises and a false conclusion.

Arguments can be deceptive. To show this, first consider the following valid example of *modus ponens*.

```
If there are no bugs, then the program compiles
There are no bugs
∴ The program compiles.
```

Compare this with the following argument that somewhat resembles *modus ponens*.

```
If there are no bugs, then the program compiles
The program compiles
∴ There are no bugs
```

Is this a valid argument? The schema for arguments of this type is

$$p \rightarrow q$$
$$\underline{q}$$
$$\therefore p$$

and its short-form truth table is shown in Table 3-6.

Notice that this argument is not valid. Although the first row does show that the conclusion is true if all the premises are true, the third row shows that if the premises are true, the conclusion is false. Thus this argument fails the if and only if criteria of a valid argument. Although many programmers wish arguments like this were true, logic (and experience) proves it a **fallacy** or invalid argument. This particular fallacious argument is called the **fallacy of the converse.**

		Premises		Conclusion
p	q	$p \rightarrow q$	q	p
T	T	T	T	T
T	F	F	F	T
F	T	T	T	F
F	F	T	F	F

Table 3-6
Short-form Truth Table of $p \rightarrow q$, q; $\therefore$ p

As another example, the argument schema

$$p \rightarrow q$$
$$\sim q$$
$$\therefore \sim p$$

is valid since Table 3-7 shows the conclusion is true only when the premises are true.

		Premises		Conclusion
p	q	$p \rightarrow q$	$\sim q$	$\sim p$
T	T	T	F	F
T	F	F	T	F
F	T	T	F	T
F	F	T	T	T

Table 3-7
Short-form Truth Table of $p \rightarrow q$, ~q; $\therefore$ ~p

This particular schema is called by a variety of names: **indirect reasoning, modus tollens,** and **law of contraposition.**

   Modus ponens and *modus tollens* are **rules of inference**, sometimes called **laws of inference.** Table 3-8 shows some of the laws of inference.

   The Latin name *modus* means "way" while *ponere* means "assert" and *tollere* means to "deny." The real name of the *modus* rules and their literal meanings are shown in Table 3-9. *Modus ponens* and *modus tollens* are short for the first two types (Stebbing 50). The Rule of Inference numbers correspond to those in Table 3-8.

Law of Inference	Schemata	
1. Law of Detachment	$p \rightarrow q$ $\underline{p \quad\quad}$ $\therefore q$	
2. Law of the Contrapositive	$\underline{p \rightarrow q \quad}$ $\therefore \sim q \rightarrow \sim p$	
3. Law of Modus Tollens	$p \rightarrow q$ $\underline{\sim q \quad}$ $\therefore \sim p$	
4. Chain Rule (Law of the Syllogism)	$p \rightarrow q$ $\underline{q \rightarrow r \quad}$ $\therefore p \rightarrow r$	
5. Law of Disjunctive Inference	$p \vee q$ $\underline{\sim p \quad}$ $\therefore q$	$p \vee q$ $\underline{\sim q \quad}$ $\therefore p$
6. Law of the Double Negation	$\underline{\sim(\sim p)}$ $\therefore p$	
7. De Morgan's Law	$\underline{\sim(p \wedge q) \quad}$ $\therefore \sim p \vee \sim q$	$\underline{\sim(p \vee q) \quad}$ $\therefore \sim p \wedge \sim q$
8. Law of Simplification	$\underline{p \wedge q}$ $\therefore p$	$\underline{p \wedge q}$ $\therefore q$
9. Law of Conjunction	p $\underline{q \quad\quad}$ $\therefore p \wedge q$	
10. Law of Disjunctive Addition	$\underline{p \quad\quad}$ $\therefore p \vee q$	
11. Law of Conjunctive Argument	$\sim(p \wedge q)$ $\underline{p \quad\quad}$ $\therefore \sim q$	$\sim(p \wedge q)$ $\underline{q \quad}$ $\therefore \sim p$

Table 3-8
Some Rules of Inference for Propositional Logic

Rule of Inference Number	Name	Meaning "mood which by..."
1	modus ponendo ponens	affirming, affirms
3	modus tollendo tollens	denying, denies
5	modus tollendo ponens	denying, affirms
11	modus ponendo tollens	affirming, denies

Table 3-9
The Modus Meanings

The rules of inference can be applied to arguments with more than two premises. For example, consider the following argument:

```
Chip prices rise only if the yen rises.
The yen rises only if the dollar falls and
    if the dollar falls then the yen rises.
Since chip prices have risen,
    the dollar must have fallen.
```

Let the propositions be defined as follows.

```
C = chip prices rise
Y = yen rises
D = dollar falls
```

Recall from Section 2.12 that one of the meanings of the conditional is "p, only if q." A proposition such as "The yen rises only if the dollar falls" has this meaning and so is represented as $C \rightarrow Y$. The entire argument has the following form.

```
C → Y
(Y → D) ∧ (D → Y)
C
∴ D
```

The second premise has an interesting form which can be further reduced by using a variant of the conditional. The conditional $p \rightarrow q$ has several which are the **converse, inverse,** and **contrapositive.** These are listed with the conditional, for completeness, in Table 3-10.

conditional	$p \rightarrow q$
converse	$q \rightarrow p$
inverse	$\sim p \rightarrow \sim q$
contrapositive	$\sim q \rightarrow \sim p$

Table 3-10
The Conditional and Its Variants

As usual, it is assumed that the negation operator has a higher priority than the other logical operators and so no parentheses are used around ~p and ~q.

If the conditional $p \rightarrow q$ and its converse $q \rightarrow p$ are both true, then p and q are equivalent. That is $p \rightarrow q \wedge q \rightarrow p$ is equivalent to the biconditional $p \leftrightarrow q$ or equivalence $p \equiv q$. In other words, p and q always take the same truth values. If p is T then q is true and if p is F then q is F. The argument becomes

```
(1) C → Y
(2) Y ≡ D
(3) C
∴ D
```

where numbers are now used to identify the premises. Since Y and D are equivalent from (2), we can substitute D for Y in (1) to yield

```
(4) C → D
```

where (4) is an inference made on the basis of (1) and (2). Premises (3) and (4) and the conclusion are:

```
(4) C → D
(3) C
∴ D
```

which can be recognized as a schema of *modus ponens*. Hence the argument is valid.

The substitution of one variable that is equivalent to another is a rule of inference called the **rule of substitution**. The rules of *modus ponens* and substitution are two basic rules of deductive logic.

A formal logic proof is usually written by numbering the premises, conclusion and inferences as shown following

```
1. C → Y
2. (Y → D) ∧ (D → Y)
3. C                    / ∴ D
4. Y ≡ D                2 Equivalence
5. C → D                1 Substitution
6. D                    3,5 Modus Ponens
```

Lines 1, 2 and 3 are the premises and conclusion while 4, 5 and 6 are the inferences obtained. The right-hand column lists the rule of inference and line numbers used to justify the inference.

3.7 LIMITATIONS OF PROPOSITIONAL LOGIC

Consider our familiar classic argument.

```
All men are mortal
Socrates is a man
Therefore, Socrates is mortal
```

We know that this is a valid argument since it is a valid syllogism. Can we prove it valid using propositional logic? To answer this question, let's first write the argument as a schema.

```
p = All men are mortal
q = Socrates is a man
r = Socrates is mortal
```

and so the argument schema is

```
p
q
∴ r
```

Notice that there are no logical connectives in the premises or conclusions and so each premise and each conclusion must have a different logical variable. Also, propositional logic has no provision for quantifiers and so there is no way to represent the quantifier "all" in the first premise. The only representation of this argument in propositional logic is thus the schema above of three independent variables.

To determine if this is a valid argument, consider the truth table of three independent variables for all possible combinations of T and F shown in Table 3-11.

p	q	r
T	T	T
T	T	F
T	F	T
T	F	F
F	T	T
F	T	F
F	F	T
F	F	F

Table 3-11
Truth Table for the Schema p, q; ∴ r

The second row of this truth table shows the argument to be invalid because the premises are true while the conclusion is false.

The invalidity of this argument should *not* be interpreted as meaning the conclusion is incorrect. Any person would recognize this as a correct argument. The invalidity simply means that *the argument cannot be proven under propositional logic.* The argument can be proven valid if we examine the internal structure of the premises. For example, we would have to attribute some meaning to "all" and recognize "men" as the plural of "man". However, syllogisms and the propositional calculus do not allow the internal structure of propositions to be examined. This limitation is overcome by predicate logic and this argument is a valid argument under predicate logic. In fact, all of syllogistic logic is a valid subset of first order predicate logic and can be proven valid under it.

The only valid syllogistic form of the proposition is

```
If Socrates is a man, then Socrates is mortal.
Socrates is a man.
Therefore, Socrates is mortal.
```

Let

```
p = Socrates is a man
q = Socrates is mortal
```

The argument becomes

$$p \rightarrow q$$
$$\underline{p}$$
$$\therefore q$$

which is a valid syllogistic form of *modus ponens*.

As another example, consider the following classic argument.

```
All horses are animals
Therefore, the head of a horse is the head of an
animal
```

We know that this argument is correct and yet it cannot be proved under propositional logic, although it can be proven under predicate logic (see problem 3-12)

3.8 FIRST ORDER PREDICATE LOGIC

Syllogistic logic can be completely described by predicate logic. Table 3-12 shows the four categorical statements and their representation in predicate logic.

Type	Schema	Predicate Representation
A	All S is P	$(\forall x)\ (S(x) \rightarrow P(x))$
E	No S is P	$(\forall x)\ (S(x) \rightarrow {\sim}P(x))$
I	Some S is P	$(\exists x)\ (S(x) \wedge P(x))$
O	Some S is not P	$(\exists x)\ (S(x) \wedge {\sim}P(x))$

Table 3-12
Representation of the Four Categorical Syllogisms using Predicate Logic

In addition to the rules of inference previously discussed, predicate logic has rules that deal with quantifiers.

The Rule of Universal Instantiation essentially states that an individual may be substituted for a universal. For example if ϕ is any proposition or **propositional function**

```
(∀ x) φ(x)
∴ φ(a)
```

is a valid inference, where *a* is an instance. That is, *a* refers to a specific individual while x is a variable that ranges over all individuals. For example, this can be used to prove that Socrates is human,

```
(∀ x) H(x)
∴ H(Socrates)
```

where H(x) is the propositional function that says x is a human. The above states that for every x, that x is human, and so by inference Socrates is human.

Other examples of the Rule of Universal Instantiation are:

```
(∀ x) A(x)
∴ A(c)
```

```
(∀ y) (B(y) ∨ C(b))
∴ B(a) ∨ C(b)
```

```
(∀ x) [A(x) ∧ (∃ x) (B(x) ∨ C(y))]
∴ A(b) ∧ (∃ x) (B(x) ∨ C(y))
```

In the first example, the instance *c* is substituted for x. In the second example, notice that the instance *a* is substituted for *y* but not for *b* since b is not included in the **scope** of the quantifier. That is, a quantifier such as $\forall$ x applies only to x variables. The variables such as x and y used with quantifiers are called **bound** while the others are called **free**. In the third example, the quantifier x has as its scope only A(x). That is, $\forall$ x does not apply to the existential quantifier $\exists$ x and its scope over B(x) $\vee$ C(y). The convention of nested quantifiers such as this is that the scope ends when a new quantifier is used, even if it uses the same variable such as x.

The formal proof of the syllogism

```
All men are mortal
Socrates is a man
∴ Socrates is mortal
```

is shown following, where H=man, M=mortal, and s=Socrates.

```
1. (∀ x) (H(x) → M(x))
2. H(s)                    /∴ M(s)
3. H(s) → M(s)             1 Universal Instantiation
4. M(s)                    2,3 Modus Ponens
```

3.9 LOGIC SYSTEMS

A logic system is a collection of objects such as rules, axioms, statements and so forth organized in a consistent manner. The logic system has several goals.

The first goal is to specify the forms of arguments. Since logical arguments are meaningless in a semantic sense, a valid form is essential if the validity of the argument is to be determined. Thus, one important function of a logic system is to determine the **well-formed formulas (wffs)** that are used in arguments. Only wffs can be used in logic arguments. For example, in syllogistic logic,

```
All S is P
```

could be a wff, but

```
All
All is S P
Is S all
```

are not wffs. Although the symbols of the alphabet are meaningless, the sequence of symbols that make up the wff are meaningful.

The second goal of a logic system is to indicate the rules of inference that are valid. The third goal of a logic system is to extend itself by discovering new rules of inference and so extend the range of arguments that can be proven. By extending the range of arguments, new wffs called **theorems** can be proven by a logic argument.

When a logic system is well developed, it can be used to determine the validity of arguments in a way that is analogous to calculations in systems such as arithmetic, geometry, calculus, physics and engineering. Logic systems have been developed such as the Sentential or Propositional Calculus, the Predicate Calculus and so forth. Each system relies on formal definitions of its **axioms** or **postulates**, which are the fundamental definitions of the system. From these axioms, people (and sometimes computer programs such as AM), try to determine what can be proven. Anyone who has studied Euclidian geometry in high school is familiar with axioms and the derivation of geometric theorems. Just as geometric theorems can be derived from geometric axioms, so can logic theorems be derived from logic axioms.

An axiom is simply a fact or **assertion** that cannot be proven from within the system. Sometimes we accept certain axioms because they make "sense" by appealing to commonsense or observation. Other axioms, such as "parallel lines meet at infinity," do not make intuitive sense because they appear to contradict Euclid's axiom of parallel lines as never meeting. However, this axiom about parallel lines meeting at infinity is just as reasonable from a purely logical viewpoint as Euclid's and is the basis of one type of non-Euclidian geometry.

A formal system requires the following.

1. An alphabet of symbols.
2. A set of finite strings of these symbols, the wffs.
3. Axioms, the definitions of the system.
4. Rules of inference, which enable a wff, A, to be deduced as the conclusion of a finite set, Γ, of other wffs where Γ= {A₁, A₂ ... Aₙ}. These wffs must be axioms or other theorems of the logic system. For example, a propositional logic system can be defined using only *modus ponens* to derive new theorems.

If the argument

$$A_1, \quad A_2, \quad \ldots \quad A_N; \quad \therefore \quad A$$

is valid, then A is said to be a **theorem** of the formal logic system and is written with the symbol ⊢. For example, Γ ⊢ A, means that A is a theorem of the set of wffs, Γ. A more explicit schema of a proof that A is a theorem is the following.

$$A_1, \quad A_2, \quad \ldots \quad A_N \vdash A$$

The symbol ⊢, which indicates that the following wff is a theorem, is not a symbol of the system. Instead, ⊢ is a **metasymbol** because it is used to describe the system itself. An analogy is a computer language such as Pascal. Although programs can be specified using Pascal's syntax, there is no syntax in Pascal for indicating a valid program.

A rule of inference in a formal system specifies exactly how new assertions, the theorems, can be obtained from axioms and previously derived theorems. An example of a theorem is our syllogism about Socrates, written in predicate logic form

$$(\forall\ x)\ (H(x)\ \rightarrow M(x))\,,\ H(s)\ \vdash M(s)$$

where H is the predicate function for man and M is the predicate function for mortal. Since M(s) can be proven from its axioms on the left, it is a theorem of these axioms. However, note that M(Zeus) would not be a theorem since Zeus, the Greek god, is not a man, and there is no alternative way of showing M(Zeus).

If a theorem is a tautology, it follows that Γ is the null set since the wff is always true and so does not depend on any other axioms or theorems. A theorem which is a tautology is written with the symbol ⊨, as in ⊨ A. For example, if A ≡ p ∨ ~p, then

$$\vDash\ p \vee \sim p$$

states that p ∨ ~p is a theorem which is a tautology. Notice that whatever values are assigned to p, either T or F, the theorem p ∨ ~p is always true. An assignment of truth values is an **interpretation** of a wff. A **model** is an interpretation in which the wff is true. For example, a model of p → q is p = T and q = T. A wff is called **consistent** or **satisfiable** if there is an interpretation that makes it true, and **inconsistent** or **unsatisfiable** if the wff is false in *all* interpretations. An example of an inconsistent wff is p ∧ ~p.

A wff is **valid** if it is true in all interpretations, else it is **invalid**. For example, the wff p ∨ ~p is valid, while p → q is an invalid wff since it is not true for p = T and q = F. A wff is **proved** if it can be shown to be valid. All propositional wffs can be proved by the truth table method since there is only a finite number of interpretations for wffs and so the propositional calculus is **decidable**. However, the predicate calculus is not decidable since there is no general method of proof like truth tables for all predicate calculus wffs.

One example of a valid predicate calculus wff that can be proved, is that for any predicate B

$$(\exists\ x)\ B(x)\ \rightarrow\ \sim\ [(\forall\ x)\ \sim\ B(x)]$$

which shows how the existential quantifier can be replaced by the universal quantifier. This predicate calculus wff is therefore a theorem.

There is a big difference between an expression like ⊢ A and ⊨ B. The A is a theorem and so can be proven from the axioms by the rules of inference. The B is a wff and there may be no known proof to show its derivation. While propositional logic is decidable, predicate logic is not. That is, there is no mechanical procedure or algorithm for finding the proof of a predicate logic theorem in a finite number of steps. In fact, there is a theoretical proof that there is no decision procedure for predicate logic. However, there are decision procedures for subsets of predicate logic like syllogisms and propositional logic. Sometimes, predicate logic is referred to as **semidecidable** because of this.

As a very simple example of a complete formal system, define

Alphabet : The single symbol "1"
Axiom : The string "1" (which happens to be the same as the symbol 1)
Rule of Inference : If any string $ is a theorem, then so is the string $11. This rule can be written as a Post production rule,

    $ → $11.
      If $ = 1 then this rule gives $11 = 111.
      If $ = 111 then the rule gives $11 = 11111 and in general
          1, 111, 11111, 1111111, ...

The strings above are the theorems of this formal system (Minsky 67).

Although strings like 11111 do not look like the types of theorems we are used to seeing, they are perfectly valid logic theorems. These particular theorems also have a semantic meaning because they are the odd numbers expressed in a **unary number system** of the single symbol 1. Just as the binary number system has only the alphabet symbols 0 and 1, the unary number system has only the single symbol 1. Numbers in the unary and decimal system are expressed as

Unary	Decimal
1	1
11	2
111	3
1111	4
11111	5

and so forth.

Notice that because of our rule of inference and axiom, the strings 11, 1111, and so forth cannot be expressed in our formal system. That is, 11 and 1111 are certainly strings from our formal alphabet, but they are not theorems or wffs because they cannot be proven using only the rule of inference and the axiom. This formal system allows only the derivation of the odd numbers, not the even numbers. The axiom "11" must be added in order to be able to derive the even numbers.

Another property of a formal system is **completeness**. A set of axioms is **complete** if every wff can either be proved or **refuted**. The term refute means to prove some assertion is false. In a complete system, every logically valid wff is a theorem. However, since predicate logic is not decidable, coming up with a proof depends on our luck and cleverness. Of course, another possibility is writing a computer program that will try to derive proofs and let it grind away.

A further desirable property of a logical system is that it be **sound**. A sound system means that every theorem is a logically valid wff. In other words, a sound system will not allow a conclusion to be inferred that is not a logical consequence of its premises. No invalid arguments will be inferred as valid.

There are different **orders** of logic. A **first order** language is defined so that the quantifiers operate on objects that are variables such as $\forall x$. A **second order** language would have additional features such as two kinds of variables and quantifiers. In addition to the ordering variables and quantifiers, the second-order logic can have quantifiers which range over function and predicate symbols. An example of second order logic is the **equality axiom**, which states that two objects are equal if all predicates of them are equal. If P is any predicate of one argument, then

$$x = y \equiv (\forall P) [P(x) \leftrightarrow P(y)]$$

is a statement of the equality axiom using a second order quantifier, $\forall P$, which ranges over all predicates.

3.10 RESOLUTION

The very powerful **resolution** rule of inference introduced by Robinson in 1965 is commonly implemented in theorem proving AI programs (Robinson 65). In fact, resolution is the primary rule of inference in PROLOG. Instead of many different inference rules of limited applicability such as *modus ponens*, *modus tollens*, merging, chaining and so forth, PROLOG uses the one general purpose inference rule of resolution. This application of resolution makes automatic theorem provers such as PROLOG practical tools for solving problems. Instead of having to try different rules of inference and hoping one succeeds, the single rule of resolution can be applied. This approach can greatly reduce the search space.

As a way of introducing resolution, let's first consider the syllogism about Socrates expressed in PROLOG as follows, where comments are shown with a % sign

```
mortal(X) :- man(X).     % All men are mortal
man(socrates).           % Socrates is a man
:- mortal(socrates).     % Query - is Socrates mortal?
yes                      % PROLOG answers yes
```

PROLOG uses a **quantifier-free** notation. Notice that the universal quantifier, $\forall$, is implied in the statement that all men are mortal.

PROLOG is based on first-order predicate logic. However it also has a number of extensions to make it easier for programming applications. These special programming features violate pure predicate logic and are called **extralogical features**: input/output, cut (which alters the search space) and assert/retract (to alter truth values without any logical justification).

Before resolution can be applied, the wff must be in a **normal** or standard form. The three main types of normal forms are **conjunctive normal form**, clausal form, and its Horn clause subset. The basic idea of normal form is to express wffs in a standard form that uses only the $\wedge$, $\vee$, and possibly $\sim$. The resolution method is then applied to normal form wffs in which all other connectives and quantifiers have been eliminated. This conversion to normal form is necessary because resolution is an operation on pairs of disjuncts which produces new disjuncts, which simplifies the wff.

The following illustrates a wff in conjunctive normal form, which is defined as the conjunction of disjunctions which are **literals**.

$$(P_1 \vee P_2 \vee \ldots) \wedge (Q_1 \vee Q_2 \vee \ldots) \wedge \ldots (Z_1 \vee Z_2 \vee \ldots)$$

Terms such as P_i must be literals, which mean that they contain no logical connectives such as the conditional and biconditional, or quantifiers. A literal is an atomic formula or a negated atomic formula. For example, the following wff

$$(A \vee B) \wedge (\sim B \vee C)$$

is in conjunctive normal form. The terms within parentheses are clauses.

$$A \lor B \text{ and } {\sim}B \lor C$$

As will be shown later, any predicate logic wff, which includes propositional logic as a special case, can be written as clauses. The full **clausal form** can express any predicate logic formula but may not be as natural or readable for a person (Kowalski 79). The syntax of PROLOG is the Horn clause subset which makes mechanical theorem proving by PROLOG much easier and efficient to implement than standard predicate logic notation or full clausal form. As mentioned in Chapter 1, PROLOG allows only one head. A full clausal form expression is generally written in a special form called Kowalski clausal form

$$A_1, A_2, \ldots A_N \rightarrow B_1, B_2, \ldots B_M$$

which is interpreted that if all the subgoals A_1, A_2, ... A_N are true, then one or more of B_1 or B_2 ... or B_M are true also. Note that sometimes the direction of the arrow is reversed in this notation. This clause written in standard predicate notation is

$$A_1 \land A_2 \ldots A_N \rightarrow B_1 \lor B_2 \ldots B_M$$

This can be expressed in **disjunctive form** as the disjunction of literals using the equivalence

$$p \rightarrow q \equiv {\sim}p \lor q$$

so

$$A_1 \land A_2 \ldots A_N \rightarrow B_1 \lor B_2 \ldots B_M$$
$$\equiv {\sim}(A_1 \land A_2 \ldots A_N) \lor (B_1 \lor B_2 \ldots B_M)$$
$$\equiv {\sim}A_1 \lor {\sim}A_2 \ldots {\sim}A_N \lor B_1 \lor B_2 \ldots B_M$$

where de Morgan's law

$${\sim}(p \land q) \equiv {\sim}p \lor {\sim}q$$

is used to simplify the last expression.

As discussed in Chapter 1, PROLOG uses a restricted type of clausal form, the Horn clause, in which only one head is allowed

$$A_1, A_2, \ldots A_N \rightarrow B$$

which is written in PROLOG syntax as

```
B  :-  A₁, A₂, ...  Aₙ
```

 The problem with trying to prove a theorem directly is the difficulty of deducing it using only the rules of inference and axioms of the system. It may take a very long time to derive a theorem or we may not be clever enough to derive it at all. To prove a theorem is true, the classical method of **reductio ad absurdum** or method of contradiction, is used. In this method, we try to prove the negated wff is a theorem. If a contradiction results, then the original non-negated wff is a theorem.

 The basic goal of resolution is to infer a new clause, the **resolvent**, from two other clauses called **parent clauses**. The resolvent will be have fewer terms than the parents. By continuing the process of resolution, eventually a contradiction will be obtained or the process is terminated because no progress is being made. A simple example of resolution is shown in the following argument.

$$A \lor B$$
$$\underline{A \lor {\sim}B}$$
$$\therefore A$$

One way of seeing how the conclusion follows is by writing the premises as

$$(A \lor B) \land (A \lor {\sim}B)$$

One of the Axioms of Distribution is

$$p \lor (q \land r) \equiv (p \lor q) \land (p \lor r)$$

Applying this to the premises gives

$$(A \lor B) \land (A \lor {\sim}B) \equiv A \lor (B \land {\sim}B) \equiv A$$

where the last step follows since $(B \land {\sim}B)$ is always false. This follows from the Law of the Excluded Middle which states that something cannot be both true and false. In fuzzy logic discussed in Chapter 5, we'll see that this law does not hold. Another way of writing this uses the term **nil** or **null**, which means empty, nothing or false. For example, a nil pointer in Pascal points to nothing, while the Law of Excluded Middle states $(B \land {\sim}B) \equiv$ nil.

 The example of resolution shows how the parent clauses $(A \lor B)$ and $(A \lor {\sim}B)$ can be simplified into the resolvent A. Table 3-13 summarizes some basic parent clauses and their resolvents in clause notation, where the comma separating clauses means $\land$.

Parent Clauses	Resolvent	Meaning
$p \rightarrow q, p$ or $\sim p \vee q, p$	q	Modus Ponens
$p \rightarrow q, q \rightarrow r$ or $\sim p \vee q, \sim q \vee r$	$p \rightarrow r$ or $\sim p \vee r$	Chaining or Hypothetical Syllogism
$\sim p \vee q, p \vee q$	q	Merging
$\sim p \vee \sim q, p \vee q$	$\sim p \vee p$ or $\sim q \vee q$	TRUE (a tautology)
$\sim p, p$	nil	FALSE (a contradiction)

Table 3-13
Clauses and Resolvents

3.11   RESOLUTION SYSTEMS AND DEDUCTION

Given wffs $A_1, A_2, \ldots A_N$ and a logical conclusion or theorem C, we know

$$A_1, A_2, \ldots A_N \vdash C$$

is equivalent to stating

$$(1) \quad A_1 \wedge A_2 \ldots A_N \rightarrow C \equiv \sim(A_1 \wedge A_2 \ldots A_N) \vee C$$
$$\equiv \sim A_1 \vee \sim A_2 \ldots \sim A_N \vee C$$

is valid. Suppose we take the negation as follows

$$\sim [A_1 \wedge A_2 \ldots A_N \rightarrow C]$$

Now

$$p \rightarrow q \equiv \sim p \vee q$$

and so the above becomes

$$\sim [A_1 \wedge A_2 \ldots A_N \rightarrow C] \equiv \sim [\sim(A_1 \wedge A_2 \ldots A_N) \vee C]$$

From de Morgan's laws

$$\sim(p \vee q) \equiv \sim p \wedge \sim q$$

and so the above becomes

$$(2) \quad \sim[A_1 \wedge A_2 \ldots A_N \to C] \equiv [\sim\sim (A_1 \wedge A_2 \ldots A_N) \wedge \sim C]$$
$$\equiv A_1 \wedge A_2 \ldots A_N \wedge \sim C$$

Now if (1) is valid, then its negation (2) must be invalid. In other words, if (1) is a tautology then (2) must be a contradiction. Formulas (1) and (2) represent two equivalent ways of proving that a formula C is a theorem. Formula (1) can be used to prove a theorem by checking to see if it is true in all cases. Equivalently, formula (2) can be used to prove a theorem by showing (2) leads to a contradiction.

As mentioned in the previous section, proving a theorem by showing its negation leads to a contradiction is proof by *reductio ad absurdum*. The primary part of this type of proof is the **refutation**. To refute something means to prove it false. Resolution is a sound rule of inference that is also **refutation complete** because the empty clause will always be the eventual result if there is a contradiction in the set of clauses. Essentially, this means that **resolution refutation** will terminate in a finite number of steps if there is a contradiction. Although resolution refutation can't tell us how to *produce* a theorem, it will definitely tell us if a wff *is* a theorem.

As a simple example of proof by resolution refutation, consider the argument

$$A \to B$$
$$B \to C$$
$$\underline{C \to D}$$
$$\therefore A \to D$$

To prove that the conclusion $A \to D$ is a theorem by resolution refutation, first convert it to disjunctive form using the equivalence

$$p \to q \equiv \sim p \vee q$$

So

$$A \to D \equiv \sim A \vee D$$

and its negation is

$$\sim (\sim A \vee D) \equiv A \wedge \sim D$$

The conjunction of the disjunctive forms of the premises and the negated conclusion gives the conjunctive normal form suitable for resolution refutation.

$$(\sim A \vee B) \wedge (\sim B \vee C) \wedge (\sim C \vee D) \wedge A \wedge \sim D$$

The resolution method can now be applied to the premises and conclusion. Figure 3-18 shows a method of representing resolution refutation in the form of a **resolution refutation tree** diagram, where clauses on the same level are resolved. The root, which is the final resolvent, is nil as can be verified from the last row of Table 3-13 for ~p, p, and so the original conclusion A → D is a theorem.

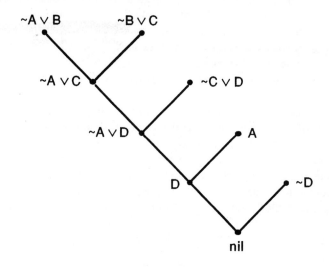

Figure 3-18
Resolution Refutation Tree

3.12   SHALLOW AND CAUSAL REASONING

Resolution systems and production rule systems are two popular paradigms for proving theorems. Although most people think of a theorem in the mathematical sense, we have seen that a theorem is actually the conclusion of a valid logical argument. Now consider an expert system which uses an inference chain. In general, a longer chain represents more causal or deep knowledge, while shallow reasoning commonly uses a single rule or a few inferences. Besides the length of the inference chain, the quality of knowledge in the rules is also a major factor in determining deep and shallow reasoning. Sometimes another definition of shallow knowledge is used, called **experiential knowledge**, which is knowledge based on experience.

The conclusion of an inference chain is a theorem because it is proven by the chain of inference, as demonstrated by the previous example.

A → B, B → C, C → D ⊢ A → D

In fact, expert systems which use an inference chain to establish a conclusion are really using theorems. This result is very important because otherwise we could not use expert systems for causal inference. Instead, expert systems would be restricted to shallow inferences of single rules with no chaining.

Let's look at some rules now in order to better contrast shallow and deep reasoning. As a first example, consider the following rule, where the number in parentheses is for identification purposes only.

```
(1)  IF a car has
        a good battery
        good sparkplugs
        gas
        good tires
     THEN the car can move
```

This is a perfectly good rule which could be used in an expert system.

One of the important features of an expert system is the explanation facility, as discussed in Chapter 1. Rule based expert systems make it easy for the system to explain its reasoning. In this case, if the user asked why the car can move, the expert system could respond by listing its conditional elements:

```
a good battery
good sparkplugs
gas
good tires
```

This is an elementary type of explanation facility since the system only lists the conditional elements of the rule. More sophisticated explanation facilities can be designed to list previous rules which have fired and resulted in the current rule firing. Other explanation facilities may allow the user to ask "What if" type questions to explore alternative reasoning paths.

This rule is also an example of **shallow reasoning**. That is, there is little or no understanding of cause and effect in shallow reasoning because there is little or no inference chain. The previous rule is essentially a heuristic in which all the knowledge is contained in the rule. The rule becomes activated when its conditional elements are satisfied and not because there is any understanding by the expert system of what function the conditional elements perform. In shallow reasoning, there is little or no **causal chain** of cause and effect from one rule to another. In the simplest case, the cause and effect are contained in one with no relationship to any other rule. If you think of rules in terms of the chunks of knowledge discussed in Chapter 1, shallow reasoning makes no connections between chunks and so is like a simple reflex reaction.

The advantage of shallow reasoning compared to causal reasoning is the ease of programming. Easier programming means the development time is shorter, the program is smaller, faster and costs less to develop.

Frame and semantic nets are two useful models for causal or **deep reasoning**. The term *deep* is often used synonymously for causal reasoning to imply a deep understanding of the subject. However, a deep understanding implies that besides understanding the causal chain by which a process occurs, you also understand the process in an abstract sense.

One classic expert system using frames and having a causal understanding is the Steamer system built by the US Navy to teach the operation of ship propulsion plants (Hollan 84). A deep expert system is the LISP Tutor which is designed to act as an intelligent tutor for teaching students LISP (Reiser 85).

We can add simple causal reasoning to our rule by defining additional rules such as

```
(2)   IF the battery is good
      THEN there is electricity

(3)   IF there is electricity
         and the sparkplugs are good
      THEN the sparkplugs will fire

(4)   IF the sparkplugs fire
         and there is gas
      THEN the engine will run

(5)   IF the engine runs
         and there are good tires
      THEN the car will move
```

Notice that with causal reasoning, the explanation facility can give a good explanation of what each car component does since each element is specified by a rule. Such a causal system also makes it easier to write a diagnostic system to determine what effect a bad component will have. Causal reasoning may be used for an arbitrary refinement of the operation of a system limited by the speed of execution, memory size and increasing development cost.

Causal reasoning can be used to construct a **model** of the real system that behaves in all respects like the real system. Such a model can be used for simulation to explore hypothetical reasoning of the "What if" type of queries. However, causal models are neither always necessary nor desirable. For example, the MUD system serves as a consultant to drilling fluid or mud engineers (Kahn 85). Drilling fluid, called mud because of its resemblance to mud, is an important aid in drilling for a number of reasons, such as cooling and lubrication of the bit. MUD diagnoses problems with the mud and suggests treatments.

A causal system would not be of much use because the drilling engineer cannot normally observe the causal chain of events occurring far below the ground. Instead, the engineer can only observe the symptoms on the surface and not the unobservable intermediate events of potential diagnostic significance.

The situation is very different in medicine where physicians have a wide range of diagnostic tests that can be used to verify intermediate events. For example, if a person complains of feeling ill, the physician can check for fever. If there is a fever, there may be an infection and so a blood test may be done. If the blood test reveals a tetanus infection, the physician may check the person for recent cuts due to a rusty object. In contrast, if the drilling fluid becomes salty, the drilling engineer may suspect the drill has gone through a salt dome. However, there is no simple way to check this since it's not possible to go into the hole, and a seismic test is expensive and not always reliable. Because drilling engineers cannot normally test intermediate hypotheses the way that physicians can, they do not approach diagnostic problems the way that physicians do, and MUD reflects this approach.

Another reason for not using causal reasoning in MUD is that there are a limited number of diagnostic possibilities and symptoms. Most of the relevant tests used by MUD are conducted routinely and input in advance. There is little advantage in an interactive query session with an engineer to explore alternate diagnostic paths if the system knows all the relevant tests and diagnostic paths. If there were many possible diagnostic paths to follow with verifiable intermediate hypothesis, there would be an advantage to causal knowledge because the engineer could work with the system to prune the search to likely paths.

Because of the increased requirements for causal reasoning, it may become necessary to combine certain rules into a shallow reasoning one. The resolution method with refutation can be used to prove that a single rule is a true conclusion of multiple rules. The single rule is the theorem that will be proved by resolution.

As an example, suppose we want to prove that rule (1) is a logical conclusion of rules (2) – (5). Using the following propositional definitions, the rules can be expressed as follows.

```
B = battery is good      C = car will move
E = there is electricity F = sparkplugs will fire
G = there is gas         R = engine will run
S = sparkplugs are good  T = there are good tires
```

$$(1) \quad B \wedge S \wedge G \wedge T \rightarrow C$$
$$(2) \quad B \rightarrow E$$
$$(3) \quad E \wedge S \rightarrow F$$
$$(4) \quad F \wedge G \rightarrow R$$
$$(5) \quad R \wedge T \rightarrow C$$

The first step in applying resolution refutation is to negate the conclusion or goal rule.

$$(1') \quad \sim(B \wedge S \wedge G \wedge T \rightarrow C) = \sim[\sim(B \wedge S \wedge G \wedge T) \vee C]$$
$$= \sim[\sim B \vee \sim S \vee \sim G \vee \sim T \vee C]$$

Now each of the other rules is expressed in disjunctive form using equivalences such as

$$p \rightarrow q \equiv \sim p \lor q \text{ and } \sim (p \land q) \equiv \sim p \lor \sim q.$$

to yield the following new versions of (2) - (5).

(2') $\sim$B $\lor$ E
(3') $\sim$(E $\land$ S) $\lor$ F = $\sim$E $\lor$ $\sim$S $\lor$ F
(4') $\sim$(F $\land$ G) $\lor$ R = $\sim$F $\lor$ $\sim$G $\lor$ R
(5') $\sim$(R $\land$ T) $\lor$ C = $\sim$R $\lor$ $\sim$T $\lor$ C

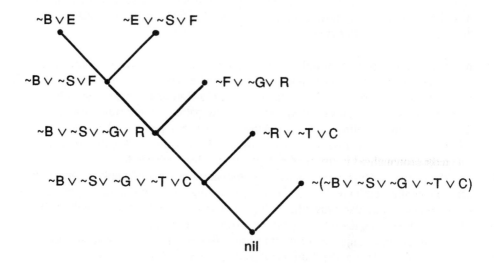

Figure 3-19
Resolution Refutation Tree for the Car Example

As described in the previous section, a convenient way of representing the successive resolvents of (1') - (5') is with a resolution refutation tree, as shown in Figure 3-19. Starting at the top of the tree, the clauses are represented as nodes which are resolved to produce the resolvent below. For example

~B $\lor$ E and ~E $\lor$ ~S $\lor$ F

are resolved to infer

~B $\lor$ ~S $\lor$ F

which is then resolved with

~F $\lor$ ~G $\lor$ R

to infer

~B ∨ ~S ∨ ~G ∨ R

and so forth. For simplicity in drawing, the last resolvents are implied rather than drawing in every single one.

Since the root of the tree is nil, this is a contradiction. By refutation, the original conclusion

B ∧ S ∧ G ∧ T → C

is a theorem since its negation leads to a contradiction. Thus rule (1) does logically follow from rules (2) - (5).

3.13 RESOLUTION AND FIRST ORDER PREDICATE LOGIC

The resolution method is also used with the first order predicate logic. In fact, it is the primary inference mechanism of PROLOG. However, before resolution can be applied, a wff must be put in clausal form. As an example,

```
Some programmers hate all failures
No programmer hates any success
∴ No failure is a success
```

Define the following predicates.

```
P(x) = x is a programmer
F(x) = x is a failure
S(x) = x is a success
H(x,y) = x hates y
```

The premises and negated conclusion are written as

```
(1)  (∃ x) [P(x) ∧ (∀ y) (F(y) → H(x,y))]
(2)  (∀ x) [P(x) → (∀ y) (S(y) → ~H(x,y))]
(3)  ~(∀ y) (F(y) → ~S(y))
```

where the conclusion has been negated in preparation for resolution.

Conversion to Clausal Form

The following nine steps are an algorithm to convert first order predicate wffs to clausal form. This procedure is illustrated using wff (1) from the previous page.

1. Eliminate conditionals, $\rightarrow$, using the equivalence

$$p \rightarrow q \equiv \sim p \lor q$$

so the wff(1) becomes

$$(\exists\ x)\ \ [P(x)\ \land\ (\forall\ y)\ \ (\sim F(y)\ \lor\ H(x,y))]$$

2. Wherever possible, eliminate negations or reduce the scope of negation to one atom. Use the equivalences shown in Appendix A such as

$$\sim\sim p \equiv p$$
$$\sim(p \land q)\ \equiv\ \sim p \lor \sim q$$
$$\sim(\exists\ x)\ P(x)\ \equiv\ (\forall\ x)\ \sim P(x)$$
$$\sim(\forall\ x)\ P(x)\ \equiv\ (\exists\ x)\ \sim P(x)$$

3. Standardize variables within a wff so that the bound or dummy variables of each quantifier have unique names. Note that the variable names of a quantifier are dummy. That is,

$$(\forall\ x)\ P(x)\ \equiv\ (\forall\ y)\ P(y)\ \equiv\ (\forall\ z)\ P(z)$$

and so the standardized form of

$$(\exists\ x)\ \sim P(x)\ \lor\ (\forall\ x)\ P(x)$$

is

$$(\exists\ x)\ \sim P(x)\ \lor\ (\forall\ y)\ P(y)$$

4. Eliminate existential quantifiers, $\exists$, by using **Skolem functions,** named after the Norwegian logician Thoralf Skolem. Consider the wff

$$(\exists\ x)\ L(x)$$

where L(x) is defined as the predicate which is true if x is < 0. This wff can be replaced by

$$L(a)$$

where *a* is a constant such as -1 that makes L(a) true. The *a* is called a Skolem constant which is a special case of the Skolem function. For the case in which there is a universal quantifier in front of an existential one

$$(\forall\ x)\ (\exists\ y)\ L(x,y)$$

where L(x,y) is true if the integer *x* is less than the integer *y*. This wff means that for every integer *x* there is an integer *y* which is greater than *x*. Notice that the formula does not tell how to compute *y* given a value for *x*. Assume a function *f(x)* exists which produces a *y* greater than *x*. So the above wff becomes Skolemized as

$$(\forall\ x)\ L(x,f(x))$$

The Skolem function of an existential variable within the scope of a universal quantifier is a function of all the quantifiers on the left. For example,

$$(\exists\ u)\ (\forall\ v)\ (\forall\ w)\ (\exists\ x)\ (\forall\ y)\ (\exists\ z)\ P(u,v,w,x,y,z)$$

is Skolemized as

$$(\forall\ v)\ (\forall\ w)\ (\forall\ y)\ P(a,v,w,f(v,w),y,g(v,w,y))$$

where *a* is some constant and the second Skolem function, *g*, must be different from the first function, *f*. Our example wff becomes

$$P(a)\ \wedge\ (\forall\ y)\ (\sim F(y)\ \vee\ H(a,y))$$

5. Convert the wff to **prenex form** which is a sequence of quantifiers, Q, followed by a **matrix** M. In general, the quantifiers can be either $\forall$ or $\exists$. However, in this case, step 4 has already eliminated all existential quantifiers and so the Q can only be $\forall$. Also, since each $\forall$ has its own dummy variable, all the $\forall$ can be moved to the left of the wff and the scope of each $\forall$ can be the entire wff.

Our example becomes

$$(\forall\ y)\ [P(a)\ \wedge\ (\sim F(y)\ \vee\ H(a,y)]$$

where the matrix is the term in brackets.

6. Convert the matrix to conjunctive normal form, which is a conjunctive of clauses. Each clause is a disjunction. Our example is already in conjunctive normal form where one clause is P(a) and the other is ($\sim$F(y) $\vee$ H(a,y)). If necessary, the following distributive rule can be used as necessary to put the matrix in conjunctive normal form.

$$p\ \vee\ (q\ \wedge\ r)\ \equiv\ (p\ \vee\ q)\ \wedge\ (p\ \vee\ r)$$

7. Drop the universal quantifiers as unnecessary since all the variables in a wff at this stage must be bound. The wff is now the matrix. Our example wff becomes

```
P(a) ∧ (~F(y) ∨ H(a,y))
```

8. Eliminate the ∧ signs by writing the wff as a set of clauses. Our example is

```
{ P(a), ~F(y) ∨ H(a,y) }
```

which is usually written without the braces as the clauses

```
P(a)
~F(y) ∨ H(a,y)
```

9. Rename variables in clauses, if necessary, so that the same variable name is only used in one clause. For example, if we had the clauses

```
P(x) ∧ Q(x) ∨ L(x,y)
~P(x) ∨ Q(y)
~Q(z) ∨ L(z,y)
```

these could be renamed as

```
P(x1) ∧ Q(x1) ∨ L(x1,y1)
~P(x2) ∨ Q(y2)
~Q(z) ∨ L(z,y3)
```

If we carry out the procedure to convert to clausal form the second premise and the negated conclusion of our example, we finally obtain the clauses

```
(1a)  P(a)
(1b)  ~F(y) ∨ H(a,y)
(2a)  ~P(x) ∨ ~S(y) ∨ ~H(x,y)
(3a)  F(b)
(3b)  S(b)
```

where the numbers refer to the original premises and negated conclusion. Thus, premises (1) and (3) are converted to two clauses with suffixes (a) and (b), while premise (2) is converted to the single clause (2a).

Unification and Rules

Once the wffs have been converted to clausal form, it is usually necessary to find appropriate **substitution instances** for the variables. That is, clauses such as

```
~F(y)  ∨  H(a,y)
F(b)
```

cannot be resolved on the predicate *F* until the arguments of *F* match. The process of finding substitutions for variables to make arguments match is called **unification**.

Unification is one feature that distinguishes expert systems from simple decision trees. Without unification, the conditional elements of rules could only match constants. This means that a specific rule would have to be written for every possible fact. For example, suppose someone wanted to sound a fire alarm if a sensor indicated smoke. If there are N sensors, you would need a rule for each sensor as follows.

```
IF sensor 1 indicates smoke THEN sound fire alarm 1
IF sensor 2 indicates smoke THEN sound fire alarm 2
...
IF sensor N indicates smoke THEN sound fire alarm N
```

However, with unification, a variable called ?N can be used for the sensor identifier so that one rule can be written as follows.

```
IF sensor ?N indicates smoke THEN sound fire alarm ?N
```

When two complementary literals are unified, they can be eliminated by resolution. For the two preceding clauses, the substitution of *y* by *b* gives

```
~F(b)  ∨  H(a,b)
F(b)
```

The predicate *F* has now been unified and can be resolved into

```
H(a,b)
```

A substitution is defined as the simultaneous replacement of variables by terms different from the variables. The terms may be constants, variables or functions. The substitution of terms for variables is indicated by the set

$$\{ \ t_1/v_1, \ t_2/v_2 \ ... \ t_N/v_N \ \}$$

If θ is such a set and A an argument, then Aθ is defined as the substitution instance of A. For example, if

```
θ = { a/x, f(y)/y, x/z }
A = P(x) ∨ Q(y) ∨ R(z)
```

then

$$A\theta \;=\; P(a) \;\vee\; Q(f(y)) \;\vee\; R(x)$$

Notice that the substitution is simultaneous, so that we get R(x) and not R(a).
Suppose there are two clauses C_1 and C_2 defined as

```
C₁  =  ~P(x)
C₂  =  P(f(x))
```

One possible unification of P is

```
C₁'  =  C₁ { f(x)/x }  =  ~P(f(x))
```

Another possible unification for P is the two substitutions using the constant *a*

```
C₁''  =  C₁ { f(a)/x }  =  ~P(f(a))
C₂'   =  C₂ { a/x }  =  P(f(a))
```

Notice that P(f(x)) is more general than P(f(a)) since there are infinitely many instances of P(f(x)) that can be produced by substituting a constant for x. A clause like C_1 is called the **most general clause**.

In general, a substitution θ is called a **unifier** for a set of clauses { A_1, A_2, ... A_n } if and only if $A_1\theta = A_2\theta = ... A_n\theta$. A set which has a unifier is called **unifiable**. The **most general unifier (mgu)** is that from which all the other unifiers are instances. This can be expressed more formally by stating that θ is the most general unifier if and only if for each unifier, α, of a set, there is a substitution β such that

$$\alpha \;=\; \theta\beta$$

where $\theta\beta$ is the compound substitution created by first applying θ and then β. The **Unification Algorithm** is a method of finding the most general unifier for a finite unifiable set of arguments (Chang 73, Nilsson 80).

For our example with clauses (1a) - (3b), the results of substitution and unification are shown in the resolution refutation tree of Figure 3-20. Since the root is nil, the negated conclusion is false and so the conclusion is valid that "No failure is a success."

The examples used so far are very simple and their resolution is very straightforward, although tedious for a human. However, in many other situations the resolution process may lead to a dead end and so backtracking is necessary to try alternative clauses for resolution. Although resolution is very powerful and is the basis of PROLOG, it may be inefficient for some problems. One of the problems with resolution is that it has no efficient built-in search strategy and so the programmer must supply heuristics, such as the PROLOG cut, for efficient searching.

A number of modified versions of resolution have been investigated. such as **unit preference, input resolution, linear resolution** and **set of support** (Amble 87). The main advantage of resolution is that it is a single powerful technique that is adequate for many cases. This makes it easier to build a mechanical system such as PROLOG than systems which attempt to implement many different rules of inference. Another advantage of resolution is that when successful, resolution automatically provides a proof by showing the sequence of steps to a nil.

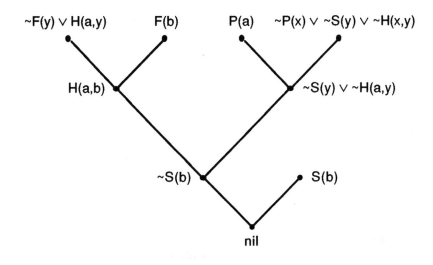

Figure 3-20
Resolution Refutation Tree to Prove No Failure is a Success

3.14 FORWARD AND BACKWARD CHAINING

A group of multiple inferences that connect a problem with its solution is called a **chain**. A chain that is searched or traversed from a problem to its solution is called a forward chain. Another way of describing forward chaining is reasoning from facts to the conclusions which follow from the facts. A chain that is traversed from a hypothesis back to the facts which support the hypothesis is a backward chain. Another way of describing a backward chain is in terms of a goal which can be accomplished by satisfying subgoals. As this shows, the terminology used to describe forward and backward chaining depends on the problem being discussed.

Chaining can be easily expressed in terms of inference. For example, suppose we have rules of the *modus ponens* type

$$p \rightarrow q$$
$$\underline{p}$$
$$\therefore \quad q$$

that form a chain of inference, such as the following.

```
elephant(x)  →  mammal(x)
mammal(x)  →  animal(x)
```

These rules may be used in a causal chain of forward inference which deduces that Clyde is an animal given that Clyde is an elephant. The inference chain is illustrated in Figure 3-21. Notice that the same diagram also illustrates backward chaining.

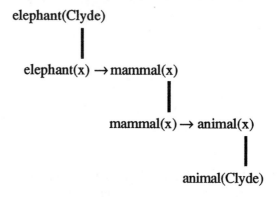

Figure 3-21
Causal Forward Chain

In Figure 3-21, the causal chain is represented by the sequence of bars, I, connecting the consequent of one rule to the antecedent of the next. A bar also indicates the unification of variables to facts. For example, the variable x in the predicate elephant(x) must first be unified with the fact elephant(Clyde) before the elephant rule can be applied. The causal chain is really a sequence of implications and unifications, as shown in Figure 3-22.

Figure 3-22
Explicit Causal Chain

Backward chaining is the reverse process. That is, suppose we want to prove the hypothesis animal(Clyde). The central problem of backward chaining is to find a chain linking the evidence to the hypothesis. The fact elephant(Clyde) is called the **evidence** in backward chaining to indicate that it is used to support the hypothesis, like the way that evidence in a court is used to prove the guilt of the defendant.

As a simple example of forward and backward chaining, suppose you are driving and suddenly see a police car with flashing lights and siren. By forward chaining, you may infer that the police want you or someone else to stop. That is, the initial facts support two possible conclusions. If the police car pulls up right in back of you or the police wave at you, a further inference is that they want you rather than someone else. Adopting this as a working hypotheses, you can apply backward chaining to reason why.

Some possible intermediate hypotheses are littering, speeding, malfunctioning equipment and driving a stolen vehicle. Now you examine the evidence to support these intermediate hypotheses. Was it the beer bottle that you threw out the window, going 100 in a 30 miles per hour speed zone, the broken tail-lights or the license plates identifying the stolen car you're driving? In this case, each piece of evidence supports an intermediate hypothesis and so they are all true. Any or all of these intermediate hypotheses are possible reasons to prove the working hypothesis that the police want you.

It's helpful to visualize forward and backward chaining in terms of a path through a problem space in which the intermediate states correspond to intermediate hypotheses under backward chaining or intermediate conclusions under forward chaining. Table 3-14 summarizes some of the common characteristics of forward and backward chaining. Note that the characteristics in this table are meant only as a guide. It is certainly possible to do diagnosis in a forward chaining system and planning in a backward chaining one. In particular, explanation is facilitated in backward chaining because the system can easily explain exactly what goal it is trying to satisfy. In forward chaining, explanation is not so easily facilitated because the subgoals are not explicitly known until they are discovered.

Forward Chaining	*Backward Chaining*
Planning, monitoring, control	Diagnosis
Present to future	Present to past
Antecedent to consequent	Consequent to antecedent
Data driven, bottom-up reasoning	Goal driven, top-down reasoning
Work forward to find what solutions follow from the facts	Work backward to find facts that support the hypothesis
Breadth-first search facilitated	Depth-first search facilitated
Antecedents determine search	Consequents determine search
Explanation not facilitated	Explanation facilitated

Table 3-14
Some Characteristics of Forward and Backward Chaining

Figure 3-23 illustrates the basic concept of forward chaining in a rule-based system. Rules are triggered by the facts which satisfy their antecedent or left-hand-sides

(LHS). For example, the rule R_1 must be satisfied by facts B and C for it to be activated. However, only fact C is present and so R_1 is not activated. Rule R_2 is activated by facts C and D which are present and so R_2 produces the intermediate fact H. Other satisfied rules are R_3, R_6, R_7, R_8, and R_9. The execution of rules R_8 and R_9 produce the conclusions of the forward chaining process. These conclusions may be other facts, output and so forth.

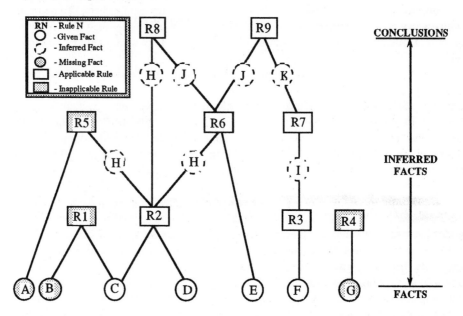

Figure 3-23
Forward Chaining

Forward chaining is called **bottom-up reasoning** because it reasons from the low-level evidence, facts, to the top-level conclusions that are based on the facts. Bottom-up reasoning in an expert system is analogous to bottom-up conventional programming that was discussed in Chapter 1. Facts are the elementary units of the knowledge-based paradigm since they cannot be decomposed into any smaller units that have meaning. For example, the fact "duck" has definite meanings as a noun and as a verb. However, if it is decomposed any further, the result is the letters d, u, c, and k which have no special meaning. In conventional programs, the basic units of meaning are data.

By custom, higher-level constructs that are composed of lower-level ones are put at the top. So reasoning from the higher-level constructs such as hypotheses down to the lower-level facts which may support the hypotheses is called **top-down reasoning** or backward chaining. Figure 3-24 illustrates the concept of backward chaining. In order to prove or disprove hypotheses H, at least one of the intermediate hypotheses H_1, H_2, or H_3 must be proven. Notice that this diagram is drawn as an AND-OR tree to indicate that in some cases such as H_2, all its lower-level hypotheses must be present to support H_2. In other cases, such as the top-level hypotheses, H, only one lower-level hypotheses is necessary. In backward chaining, the system will commonly elicit evidence from the user to aid in proving or disproving hypotheses. This contrasts with a forward chaining system in which all the relevant facts are usually known in advance.

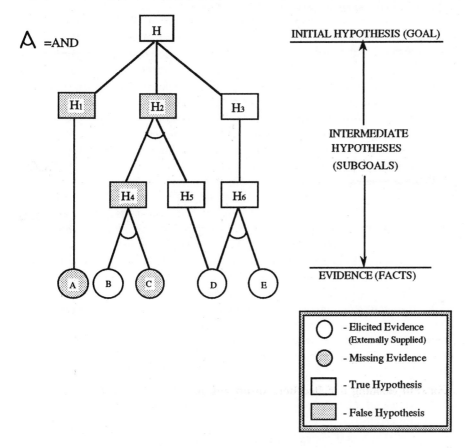

Figure 3-24
Backward Chaining

If you look back at Figure 3-4 in Section 3.2, you will see that the decision net is organized very well for backward chaining. The top-level hypotheses are the different types of raspberries such as flowering raspberry, black raspberry, wineberry, and red raspberry. The evidence to support these hypotheses is lower down. The rules to identify a raspberry can be easily written. For example,

```
IF the leaves are simple THEN flowering raspberry
```

One important aspect of eliciting evidence is asking the right questions. The right questions are those which improve the efficiency in determining the correct answer. One obvious requirement for this is that the expert system should only ask questions that deal with the hypotheses that it is trying to prove. While there may be hundreds or thousands of questions that the system could ask about, there is a cost in time and money to obtain the evidence to answer the questions. Also, accumulating certain types of evidence such as medical test results may be uncomfortable and possibly hazardous to the patient (in fact, it's difficult to think of a pleasurable medical test).

Ideally, the expert system should also allow the user to volunteer evidence even if the system has not asked for it. Allowing the user to volunteer evidence speeds up the backward chaining process and makes the system more convenient for the user. The volunteered evidence may let the system skip some links in the causal chain or pursue a completely new approach. The disadvantage is that more complex programming of the expert system is involved since the system may not follow a chain link by link.

Good applications for forward and backward chaining are shown in Figure 3-25. For simplicity, these diagrams are drawn as trees instead of a general network. A good application for forward chaining occurs if the tree is wide and not very deep. This is because forward chaining facilitates a breadth-first search. That is, forward chaining is good if the search for conclusions proceeds level by level. In contrast, backward chaining facilitates a depth-first search. A good tree for depth-first search is narrow and deep.

Notice that the structure of the rules determines the search for a solution. That is, the activation of a rule depends on the patterns that the rule is designed to match. The patterns on the LHS determines whether a rule can become activated by facts. The actions on the RHS determines the facts that are asserted and deleted and so affect other rules. An analogous situation exists for backward chaining except that hypotheses are used instead of rules. Of course, an intermediate hypotheses may be simply a rule that is matched on its consequent instead of its antecedent.

As a very simple example, consider the following IF THEN type rules.

```
IF  A  THEN  B
IF  B  THEN  C
IF  C  THEN  D
```

If fact A is given and the inference engine is designed to match facts against antecedents, then the intermediate facts B and C will be asserted and conclusion D. This process corresponds to forward chaining.

In contrast, if the fact (actually hypotheses) D is asserted and the inference engine matches facts against consequents, the result corresponds to backward chaining. In systems designed for backward chaining, such as PROLOG, the backward chaining mechanism includes a number of features such as automatic backtracking to facilitate backward chaining.

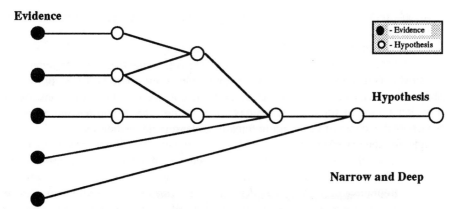

Evidence

Hypothesis

Narrow and Deep

(a) Good Application of Backward Chaining

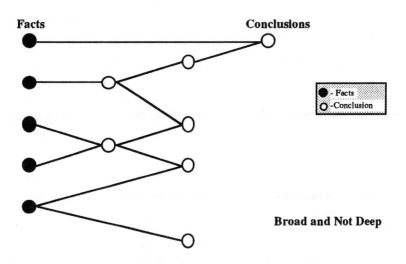

Facts

Conclusions

Broad and Not Deep

(b) Good Application of Forward Chaining

Figure 3-25
Forward and Backward Chaining

Backward chaining can be accomplished in a forward chaining system and vice-versa by redesign of the rules. For example, the previous rules for forward chaining can be rewritten as

```
IF  D  THEN  C
IF  C  THEN  B
IF  B  THEN  A
```

Now C and B are considered as subgoals or intermediate hypotheses that must be satisfied to satisfy the hypotheses D. The evidence A is the fact that indicates the end of the generation of subgoals. If there is a fact A, then D is supported and considered true under this chain of backward inference. If there is no A, then the hypotheses D is unsupported and considered false.

One difficulty with this approach is efficiency. A backwards chaining system facilitates depth-first search while a forward chaining system facilitates breadth-first search. Although you can write a backward chaining application in a forward chaining system and vice-versa, the system will not be as efficient in its search for a solution. The second difficulty is a conceptual one. The knowledge elicited from the expert will have to be altered to meet the demands of the inference engine. For example, a forward chaining inference engine matches the antecedent of rules while a backward chaining one matches the consequent. That is, if the expert's knowledge is naturally backward chaining, it will have to be totally restructured to cast it in a forward chaining mode and vice-versa.

3.15 OTHER METHODS OF INFERENCE

A number of other types of inference are sometimes used with expert systems. While these methods are not as general purpose as deduction, they are very useful.

Analogy

Besides deduction and induction, another powerful inference method is **analogy**. The basic idea of reasoning by analogy is to try and relate old situations as a guide to new ones. All living creatures are very good at applying analogical reasoning in their lives, which is essential because of the tremendous number of new situations that are encountered in the real world. Rather than treating every new situation as unique, it's often helpful to try and see the similarities of the new situation to old ones that we know how to deal with. Analogical reasoning is related to induction. While induction makes inferences from the specific to the general of the same situation, analogy tries to make inferences from situations that are not the same. Analogy cannot make formal proofs like deduction. Instead, analogy is a heuristic reasoning tool that may sometimes work.

An example of reasoning by analogy is medical diagnosis. When you see a doctor because of a medical problem, the doctor will elicit information from you and note the symptoms of the problem. If your symptoms are identical or strongly similar to those of other people with Problem X, the doctor may infer by analogy that you have Problem X. Of course, backward chaining may also be used.

Notice that this diagnosis is not a deduction, because you are unique. Just because someone else with the problem shows certain symptoms doesn't mean that you will exhibit the same symptoms. Instead, the doctor assumes that your symptoms make you analogous to a person with the same symptoms and known problem. This initial diagnosis is a hypothesis that medical tests may either prove or disprove. It's important to have an initial working hypothesis because it narrows down the thousands of potential problems. It would be prohibitively expensive and time-consuming to just start giving you every possible test without an initial hypothesis.

As an example of the utility of reasoning by analogy, suppose two people play a game called the 15 Game (Fischler 87). They take turns in picking a number from 1 to 9 with the constraint that the same number cannot be used twice. The first person whose numbers add up to 15 wins. Although at first this seems like a strange game which requires some thinking, an analogy can make it very easy to play.

Consider the tic-tac-toe board below with values assigned to each cell as shown.

6	1	8
7	5	3
2	9	4

This is a **magic square** because the sum of the values in the rows, columns, and diagonals is a constant. The tic-tac-toe board with the magic square values can be considered an analogy to the 15 Game. Playing the 15 Game is now very easy if you think in terms of tic-tac-toe and then translate the winning strategy to the 15 Game.

This particular magic square is called the **standard square** of **order** 3. The term order refers to the number of rows or columns of a square. There is only one unique square of order 3. Other magic squares can be created by rotating or reflecting the standard square. Another way to construct magic squares is by adding the same constant to each cell. Knowing this information allows us to deduce the winning strategies for the 24 Game where the numbers must be selected from the set

    {2, 3, 4, 5, 6, 7, 8, 9, 10}

or the 33 Game using the set

    {3, 4, 5, 6, 7, 8, 9, 10, 11}

We can now use induction to infer the winning strategy for the 15 + 9N Game, where N is any natural number 1, 2, 3, ... by thinking of the game as analogous to a tic-tac-toe board which is analogous to a magic square of values

    {1+N, 2+N, 3+N, 4+N, 5+N, 6+N, 7+N, 8+N, 9+N}

Using the analogy of the order 3 square for games of three moves, by induction we can infer that magic squares of higher order can be used for games involving more than three moves. For example, the magic square of order 4

16	3	2	13
5	10	11	8
9	6	7	12
4	15	14	1

allows you to play the winning strategy of the four move—34 Game by thinking of it in terms of tic-tac-toe. In contrast to the one standard order 3 square, there are 880 standard squares of order 4, which allows considerably more games (Smith 84).

Reasoning by analogy is an important part of commonsense reasoning, which is very difficult for computers (and children). Other applications of analogy have been to learning (Carbonell 82).

Generate-and-Test

Another method of inference is the classic AI strategy of **generate-and-test**, sometimes called generation and test, which involves the generation of a likely solution and then testing it to see if the proposed solution meets all the requirements. If the solution is satisfactory, then quit, else generate a new solution, test again and so forth. This method was used in the first expert system, DENDRAL, conceived in 1965, to aid in identifying organic molecular structures (Buchanan 78). Data from an unknown sample are supplied by a mass spectrometer and input to DENDRAL which generates all the potential molecular structures which could produce the unknown spectrogram. DENDRAL then tests the most likely candidate molecules by simulating their mass spectrogram and comparing it to the original unknown. Another program which uses generate-and-test is the AM (Artificial Mathematician) program to infer new mathematical concepts (Lenat 82).

In order to reduce the enormous number of potential solutions, generate-and-test is normally used with a planning program to limit the likely potential solutions for generation. This variation is called **plan-generate-test** and is used for efficiency in many systems. For example, the medical diagnosis expert system MYCIN also has the capability of planning a therapeutic drug treatment after a patient's disease has been diagnosed (Chancey 85). A **plan** is essentially finding chains of rules or inferences that connect a problem with a solution, or goal, with the evidence to support it. Planning is most efficiently done by simultaneously searching forward from the facts and back from the goal.

The MYCIN planner first creates a prioritized list of therapeutic drugs to which the patient is sensitive. In order to reduce undesirable drug interactions, it's best to limit the number of drugs that a patient receives, even if the patient is thought to be suffering from several different infections. The generator takes the prioritized list from the planner and generates sublists of one or two drugs if possible. These sublists are then tested for efficacy against the infections, patient's allergies, and other considerations before a decision is made to administer them to the patient.

Generate-and-test can also be considered the basic inference paradigm of rules. If the conditional elements of a rule are satisfied, it generates some actions such as new facts. The inference engine tests these facts against the conditional elements of rules in the knowledge-base. Those rules which are satisfied are put on the agenda and the top priority rule generates its actions, which are then tested and so forth. Thus generate-and-test produces an inference chain which may lead to the correct solution.

Abduction

Inference by **abduction** is another method that is commonly used in diagnostic problem-solving.The schema of abduction resembles *modus ponens*, but is actually very different as shown in Table 3-15.

Abduction	Modus ponens
$p \rightarrow q$	$p \rightarrow q$
q	p
$\therefore p$	$\therefore q$

Table 3-15
Comparison of Abduction and Modus Ponens

Abduction is another name for a fallacious argument that we discussed in Section 3.6 as the Fallacy of the Converse. Although abduction is not a valid deductive argument, it is a useful method of inference and has been used in expert systems. Like analogy, which also is not a valid deductive argument, abduction may be useful as a heuristic rule of inference. That is, when we have no deductive method of inference, abduction may prove useful but is not guaranteed to work. Analogy, generate and test, and abduction are all methods that are not deductive and are not guaranteed to work all the time. From true premises, these methods cannot prove true conclusions. However, these techniques are very useful in reducing the search space by generating reasonable hypotheses which can then be used with deduction.

Abduction is sometimes referred to as reasoning from observed facts to the best explanation (Reggia 85). As an example of abduction, consider the following.

```
IF x is an elephant THEN x is an animal
IF x is an animal THEN x is a mammal
```

If we know that Clyde is a mammal, can we conclude that Clyde is an elephant?

The answer to this question depends on whether we are talking about the real world or our expert system. In the real world, we could not make this conclusion with any degree of certainty. Clyde could be a dog, cat, cow or any other kind of animal that was a mammal but not an elephant. In fact, considering how many species of animals there are, the probability of Clyde being an elephant is rather low without knowing any more information about Clyde.

However, in an expert system with only the preceding rules, we could say by abduction with 100% certainty that if Clyde is a mammal, then Clyde is an elephant. This inference follows from a **closed world assumption** in which we have assumed that nothing else exists outside the closed world of our expert system. Anything that cannot be proven is assumed false in a closed world. Under the closed world assumption, all the possibilities are known. Since the expert system consists of only these two rules and only an elephant can be a mammal, then if Clyde is a mammal, he must be an elephant.

Suppose we add a third rule, as follows.

```
IF x is a dog THEN X is an animal
```

We can still operate our expert system under the closed world assumption. However, now we cannot conclude with 100% certainty that Clyde is an elephant. All we can be sure of is that Clyde is either an elephant or a dog.

In order to decide between the two, more information is needed. For example, if there is another rule

```
IF x is a dog THEN x barks
```

and evidence that Clyde barks, the rules can be revised as follows.

```
(1)  IF x is an animal THEN x is a mammal
(2)  IF x barks THEN x is an animal
(3)  IF x is a dog THEN x barks
(4)  IF x is an elephant THEN x is an animal
```

Now a backward chain of abductive inference using rules (1), (2) and (3) can be made to show that Clyde must be a dog.

A backward chain of abduction is not the same as the customary meaning of backward chaining. The term *backward chaining* means that we are trying to prove a hypothesis by looking for evidence to support it. Backward chaining would be used in trying to prove that Clyde is a mammal. Of course, for our small system, there are no other possibilities. However, other classifications could be added for reptiles, birds, and so forth.

If it's known that Clyde is a mammal, abduction could be used to determine if Clyde is an elephant or a dog. Forward chaining would be used if it is known that Clyde is an elephant and we wanted to know if he is a mammal. As you can see, the choice of inference method depends on what is to be determined. Since forward chaining is deductive, only its conclusions are always guaranteed valid. Table 3-16 summarizes the purpose of each of the three inference techniques.

Inference	Start	Purpose
Forward chaining	Facts	Conclusions that must follow
Backward chaining	Uncertain conclusion	Facts to support the conclusion
Abduction	True conclusion	Facts which may follow

Table 3-16
Summary of the Purpose of Forward chaining,
Backward chaining, and Abduction

A number of AI and expert systems have used frame-based abduction for diagnostic problem-solving (Basili 85) (Miller 82) (Pople 82) (Reggia 83). In these systems, the knowledge-base contains **causal associations** between disorders and symptoms. Inferences are made using generate-and-test of hypotheses for the disorders.

Nonmonotonic Reasoning

Normally, the addition of new axioms to a logic system means that more theorems can be proven since there are more axioms from which theorems can be derived. This property of increasing theorems with increasing axioms is is known as **monotonicity** and systems such as deductive logic are called **monotonic systems**.

However, a problem can occur if a newly introduced axiom partially or completely contradicts a previous axiom. In this case, the theorems that had been proven may no longer be valid. Thus, in a **nonmonotonic system**, the theorems do not necessarily increase as the number of axioms increase.

The concept of nonmonotonicity has an important application to expert systems. As new facts are generated, which is analogous to theorems being proved, a monotonic expert system would keep building up facts. A major problem can occur if one or more facts becomes false because a monotonic system cannot deal with changes in the truth of axioms and theorems. As a very simple example, suppose there is a fact that asserts the time. As soon as time changes by one second, the old fact is no longer valid. A monotonic system would not be capable of dealing with this situation. As another example, suppose a fact was asserted by an aircraft identification system that a target was hostile. Later, new evidence proves the target is friendly. In a monotonic system, the original identification of hostile could not be changed. A nonmonotonic system allows the retraction of facts.

As another application, suppose you wanted to write an explanation facility for an expert system that would allow a user to go back to previous inferences and explore alternate inference paths of *What If* type questions. All inferences made after the desired previous one must be retracted from the system. Besides facts, rules may also have been excised from the system and so must be put back in the knowledge base for nonmonotonicity. Further complications arise in systems such as OPS5 in which rules can be created automatically on the right-hand-side of rules during execution. For nonmonotonicity, any inferred rules made after the previous desired inference would have to be excised from the system. Keeping track of all inferences made can consume a lot of memory and significantly slow down the system.

In order to provide for nonmonotonicity, it is necessary to attach a justification or dependency to each fact and rule that explains the reason for belief in it. If a nonmonotonic decision is made, then the inference engine can examine the justification of each fact and rule to see if it is still believed, and also to possibly restore excised rules and retracted facts that are believed again.

The problem of justifying facts was first pointed out in the **frame problem**, which is not the same concept as the frames discussed in Chapter 2 (McCarthy 69). The frame problem is a descriptive term named after the problem of identifying what has or has not changed in a movie frame. Motion pictures are photographed as a succession of still pictures called frames. When played back at 24 frames per second or faster, the human eye cannot distinguish the individual frames and so the illusion of motion results. An AI frame problem is to recognize changes in an environment over time. As an example, consider the Monkey and Bananas Problem discussed in Chapter 2. Suppose the monkey must step on a red box to reach the bananas and so the action is "push red box under bananas." Now the frame problem is—How do we know the box is still red after the action? Pushing the box should not change the environment. However, other actions such as "Paint the box blue" will change the environment. In some expert system tools, an environment is called a **world** and consists of a set of related facts (Filman 88). An expert system may keep track of multiple worlds to do hypothetical reasoning simultaneously. The problem of maintaining the correctness or truth of a system is called **truth maintenance** (Doyle 79). Truth maintenance or a variation called **assumption-based truth maintenance** is essential for keeping each world pure by retracting unjustified facts (de Kleer 86).

As a simple example of nonmonotonic reasoning, let's consider the classic example of Tweety the bird. In the absence of any other information, we would therefore assume that since Tweety is a bird, then Tweety can fly. This is an example of **default reasoning**, much like the defaults used in frame slots. Default reasoning can be considered as a rule which makes inferences about rules, a **metarule** which states

```
IF X is not known for certain, and
   there is no evidence contradicting X
THEN tentatively conclude Y
```

Metarules are discussed more extensively in the next section.

In our case the metarule has the more specific form

```
X is the rule "All birds can fly," and
   fact "Tweety is a bird"
Y is the inference "Tweety can fly"
```

In terms of production rules, this can be expressed as a rule in our knowledge-base which says

```
IF X is a bird THEN X can fly
```

and the fact that exists in working memory

```
Tweety is a bird
```

Unifying the fact with the antecedent of the rule gives the inference that Tweety can fly.

Now comes the problem. Suppose an additional fact is added to working memory which says that Tweety is a penguin. We know that penguins cannot fly and so the inference that Tweety can fly is incorrect. Of course, there must be a rule in the system which also states this knowledge or else the fact will be ignored.

In order to maintain the correctness of our system, the incorrect inference must be removed. However, this may not be sufficient if other inferences were based on the incorrect inference. That is, other rules may have used the incorrect inference as evidence to draw additional inferences and so on. This is a problem of truth maintenance. The inference that Tweety can fly was a **plausible inference** that is based on default reasoning. The term *plausible* means not impossible, and will be discussed further in Chapter 4.

One way of allowing for nonmonotonic inference is by defining a sentential operator M, which can be informally defined as "is consistent" (McDermott 82). For example

$$(\forall x) \ [Bird(x) \ \wedge \ M(Can\_fly(x)) \rightarrow \ Can\_fly(x)]$$

which can be stated as "For every x, if x is a bird and it is consistent that a bird can fly, then x can fly." A more informal way of stating this is "Most birds can fly." The term "is consistent" means that there are no contradictions with other knowledge. However, this interpretation has been criticized as really stating that the only birds which cannot fly are those which have been inferred not capable of flying (Moore 85). This is an example of **autoepistemic reasoning**, which literally means reasoning about your own knowledge. Both default and autoepistemic reasoning are used in **commonsense reasoning**, which humans generally do quite well but is very difficult for computers.

Autoepistemic reasoning is reasoning about your own knowledge as distinct from knowledge in general. Generally, you can do this very well because you know the limits of your knowledge. For example, suppose a total stranger came up and stated you were their spouse. You would immediately know (unless you had amnesia) that you were not their spouse because you had no knowledge of that stranger. The general metarule of autoepistemic reasoning is

```
IF I have no knowledge of X
THEN X is false
```

Notice how autoepistemic reasoning relies on the closed world assumption. Any fact that is not known is assumed false. In autoepistemic reasoning, the closed world is your self-knowledge.

Autoepistemic and default reasoning are both nonmonotonic. However, the reasons are different. Default reasoning is nonmonotonic because it is **defeasible**. The term defeasible means that any inferences are tentative and may have to be withdrawn as new information becomes available. However, pure autoepistemic reasoning is not defeasible because of the closed world assumption that declares all true knowledge is already known to you. For example, since married people know who is their spouse (unless they want to forget), a married person would not accept that a total stranger was their spouse if they were told that. Because most people recognize that they have imperfect memories, they do not adhere to pure autoepistemic reasoning. Of course, computers do not have this problem.

Autoepistemic reasoning is nonmonotonic because the meaning of an autoepistemic statement is **context-sensitive**. The term *context-sensitive* means that the meaning changes with the context. As a simple example of context-sensitivity, consider how the word "read" is pronounced in the two sentences

```
I have read the book
I will read the book
```

The pronunciation of "read" is context sensitive.

Now consider a system consisting of the following two axioms.

```
(∀ x) [Bird(x) ∧ M(Can_fly(x))→ Can_fly(x)]
Bird(Tweety)
```

In this logic system, Can_fly(Tweety) is a theorem derived by unification of Tweety with the variable x and implication.

Now suppose a new axiom is added which states that Tweety cannot fly and thus contradicts the previously derived theorem.

```
~Can_fly(Tweety)
```

The M-operator must change its operation on its argument because now M(Can_fly(Tweety)) is not consistent with the new axiom. In this new context of three axioms, the M-operator would not give a TRUE result for Can_fly(Tweety) because it conflicts with the new axiom. The returned value by the M-operator must be FALSE in this new context, and so the conjunction is FALSE. Thus, there is no implication to produce the theorem Can_fly(Tweety) and no conflict.

One way of implementing this by rules is as follows.

```
IF x is a bird AND x is typical
THEN x can fly
```

```
IF x is a bird AND x is nontypical
THEN x cannot fly

Tweety is a bird
Tweety is nontypical
```

Notice that this system does not invalidate the conclusion Can_fly(Tweety), but rather prevents the incorrect rule from firing at all. This is a much more efficient method of of truth maintenance than if we had one rule and the special axiom ~Can_fly(Tweety). Now we have a more general system that can easily handle other nonflying birds such as ostriches without our having to continually add new inferences, which is what the system is supposed to do.

3.16 METAKNOWLEDGE

The Meta-DENDRAL program uses induction to infer new rules of chemical structure. Meta-DENDRAL is an attempt to overcome the knowledge-bottleneck of trying to extract molecular structural rules from human experts. Meta-DENDRAL has been very successful, rediscovering known rules and inferring new ones.

As an example, the following metarule is taken from the TEIRESIAS knowledge acquisition program for MYCIN, the expert system to diagnose blood infections and meningitis (Feigenbaum 79).

```
METARULE 2
IF
The patient is a compromised host, and
There are rules which mention in their premise
    pseudomonas, and
There are rules which mention in their premise
    klebsiellas
THEN
There is suggestive evidence (.4) that the former
    should be done before the latter
```

The number .4 in the action of the rule is a degree of certainty and will be discussed in a later chapter.

TEIRESIAS acquires knowledge interactively from an expert. If a wrong diagnosis has been made by MYCIN, then TEIRESIAS will lead the expert back through the chain of incorrect reasoning until the expert states where the incorrect reasoning started. While going back through the reasoning chain, TEIRESIAS will also interact with the expert to modify incorrect rules or acquire new rules.

Knowledge about new rules is not immediately put into MYCIN. Instead, TEIRESIAS checks to see if the new rule is compatible with similar rules. For example, if the new rule describes how an infection enters the body and other accepted rules have a conditional element stating the portal of entry to the body, then the new rule should also. If the new rule does not state the portal of entry, then TEIRESIAS will query the user about this discrepancy. TEIRESIAS has a **rule model** pattern of similar rules that it knows about, and tries to fit the new rule into its rule model. In other words, the rule model is the knowledge that TEIRESIAS has about its knowledge. An analogous situation for a human would occur if you went to a car dealer to buy a new car and the dealer tried to sell you a car with three wheels.

The metaknowledge of TEIRESIAS is of two types. The METARULE 2 described previously is a control strategy which tells how rules are to be applied. In contrast, the rule model type of metaknowledge determines if the new rule is in the appropriate form to be entered in the knowledge-base. In a rule-based expert system, determining if the new rule is in the correct form is **verification** of the rule. Determining that a chain of correct inferences leads to the correct answer is called **validation**. Validation and verification are so interdependent that the acronym **V&V** is commonly used to refer to both. A more colloquial definition of the terms from software engineering is (Boehm 84)

```
Verification:   "Am I building the product right?"
Validation:     "Am I building the right product?"
```

V&V will be discussed in more detail in a later chapter.

3.17 SUMMARY

In this chapter, the commonly used methods of inferencing for expert systems have been discussed. Inferencing is particularly important in expert systems because it is the technique by which expert systems solve problems. The application of trees, graphs and lattices to the representation of knowledge was discussed. The advantages of these structures to inferences were illustrated.

Deductive logic was covered starting with simple syllogistic logic. Next, the propositional and first-order predicate logic was discussed. Truth tables and rules of inference were described as ways of proving theorems and statements. The characteristics of logical systems such as completeness, soundness, and decidability were mentioned.

The resolution method of proving theorems was discussed for propositional logic and first-order predicate logic. The nine steps involved in converting a well-formed formula to clausal form were illustrated by an example. Skolemization, the prenex-normal form, and unification were all discussed in the context of converting a wff to clausal form.

Another powerful method of inferences, analogy, was discussed. Although not widely used in expert systems because of the difficulty in implementing it, analogy is often used by people and should be considered in the design of expert systems.

Generate-and-test was also discussed with an example of its use in MYCIN. The application of metaknowledge in TEIRESAS was described and its relationship to verification and validation of expert systems.

PROBLEMS

3-1.   Write a decision tree program that is self-learning. Teach it the animal knowledge of Figure 3-3.

3-2.   Write a program that will automatically translate the knowledge stored in a binary decision tree into IF...THEN type rules. Test it with the animal decision tree of problem 3-1.

3-3   Draw a semantic net containing the raspberries knowledge of Figure 3-4.

3-4.   Draw the state diagram showing a solution to the classic problem of the farmer, fox, goat and cabbage. In this problem a farmer, fox, goat and cabbage are on one bank of a river. A boat must be used to transport them to the other side. However, the boat can only be used to hold two at a time (and only the farmer can row). If the fox is left with the goat and the farmer is not present, then the fox will eat the goat. If the goat is left alone with the cabbage, the goat will eat it.

3-5.   Draw a state diagram for a well-structured travel problem having

a)   three methods of payment: cash, check, or charge
b)   traveler's interests: sun, snow
c)   four possible destinations depending on the traveler's interests and money
d)   three types of transportation

Write IF THEN rules to advise a traveler where to go depending on money and interests. Pick real destinations and find the costs to get there from your location.

3-6.   Determine whether the following are valid or invalid arguments

a) $p \rightarrow q, \sim q \rightarrow r, r; \therefore p$
b) $\sim p \vee q, p \rightarrow (r \wedge s), s \rightarrow q; \therefore q \vee r$
c) $p \rightarrow (q \rightarrow r), q; \therefore p \rightarrow r$

3-7.   Using the Venn diagram decision procedure, determine if the following are valid or invalid syllogisms.

a)   AEE-4
b)   AOO-1

    c) OAO-3
    d) AAI-1
    e) OAI-2

3-8.   Prove whether the following are fallacies or rules of inference. Give an example of each.

    a) Complex Constructive Dilemma

$$p \rightarrow q$$
$$r \rightarrow s$$
$$\underline{p \lor r}$$
$$\therefore q \lor s$$

    b) Complex Destructive Dilemma

$$p \rightarrow q$$
$$r \rightarrow s$$
$$\underline{\sim q \lor \sim s}$$
$$\therefore \sim p \lor \sim r$$

    c) Simple Destructive Dilemma

$$p \rightarrow q$$
$$p \rightarrow r$$
$$\underline{\sim q \lor \sim r}$$
$$\therefore \sim p$$

    d) Inverse

$$p \rightarrow q$$
$$\underline{\sim p}$$
$$\therefore \sim q$$

3-9.   Draw the conclusion from the following premises, taken from Lewis Carroll, author of the famous *Alice's Adventures in Wonderland*.

    a) All the dated letters in this room are written on blue paper.
    b) None of them are in black ink, except those that are written in the third person.
    c) I have not filed any of them that I can read.
    d) None of them, that are written on one sheet, are undated.
    e) All of them, that are not crossed, are in black ink.
    f) All of them, written by Brown, begin with "Dear Sir,"

g) All of them, written on blue paper, are filed.
h) None of them, written on more than one sheet, are crossed.
i) None of them, that begin with "Dear Sir," are written in the third person.

Hint: Use the law of contrapositives and define

A = beginning with "Dear Sir"	B = crossed	C = dated
D = filed	E = in black ink	F=in third person
G = letters that I can read	H = on blue paper	I = on one sheet
J = written by Brown		

3-10.   Give a formal proof using predicate logic for the syllogism

```
No software is guaranteed
All programs are software
∴ No programs are guaranteed
```

3-11.   Use the following to write quantified first order predicate logic formulas.

```
P(x) = x is a programmer
S(x) = x is smart
L(x,y) = x loves y
```

   a) All programmers are smart.
   b) Some programmers are smart.
   c) No programmers are smart.
   d) Someone is not a programmer.
   e) Not everyone is a programmer.
   f) Everyone is not a programmer.
   g) Everyone is a programmer.
   h) Some programmers are not smart.
   i) There are programmers.
   j) Everyone loves someone.

Hint: Use Appendix B.

3-12.   Consider the predicate logic argument:

```
A horse is an animal
```

Therefore, the head of a horse is the head of an animal. Define

```
H(x,y) = x is the head of y
A(x) = x is an animal
```

```
S(x) = x is a horse
```

The premise and conclusion are

```
(∀ x) (S(x) → A(x))
(∀ x) {[(∃ y) (S(y) ∧ H(x,y))] →
        [(∃ z) (A(x) ∧ H(x,z))]}
```

Prove the conclusion using resolution refutation. Show all nine steps in clausal conversion for the conclusion.

3-13.   a) Obtain information from your bank or savings & loan on the criteria for obtaining a car loan. Write a backward chaining system of rules to determine if an applicant should get a car loan. Be as specific as possible.

        b) Obtain information on qualifying for a home mortgage. Give the modifications of your car loan program to handle home loans as well as car loans.

        c) Obtain information on qualifying for a business loan. Give the modifications to the car-mortgage program to handle business loans as well.

3-14.   Write a production system of causal rules to simulate the operation of the carburetor of your car. You may obtain this information from the repair guide for your car. Be as detailed as possible.

3-15.   Using the repair guide for your car, write a production system that can diagnose and remedy carburetor problems for your car given symptoms of problems.

3-16.   If the conclusion is false and you wanted to determine the facts which followed, would you use abduction or another method of inference? Explain.

3-17.   Write IF THEN rules to identify raspberries using the portion of the decision tree shown in Figure 3-4

3-18.   A parent and two children are on the left bank of a river and wish to cross to the right side. The parent weighs 200 lb and each child weighs 100 lb. One boat is available with a capacity of 200 lb. At least one person is required to row the boat. Draw the decision tree showing showing all the possibilities for them crossing the river and indicate the successful path through the tree so that they all cross. Assume the following operators in labeling your tree.

```
SL-Single child crosses from left to right
SR-Single child crosses from right to left
BL-Both children cross from left to right
```

BR—Both children cross from right to left
PL—Parent crosses from left to right
PR—Parent crosses from right to left

3-19. a) Draw a logic diagram version of the AND-exclusive-OR car decision of Figure 3-11. Note that you will have to implement the exclusive-OR using standard AND, OR, and NOT elements.

   b) Write forward chaining IF THEN rules to determine which hypothesis to follow, i.e., sell or repair.

BIBLIOGRAPHY

(Amble 87). Tore Amble, *Logic Programming and Knowledge Engineering*, Addison-Wesley, 1987, pp. 41-42.

(Basili 85). V. Basili and C. Ramsey, "ARROWSMITH-P: A Prototype Expert System for Software Engineering Management," in *Proc. Expert Systems in Government Symposium*, ed. K. Karna, 1985.

(Boehm 84). Barry W. Boehm, "Verifying and Validating Software Requirements and Design Specifications," *IEEE Software J.*, Jan. 1984.

(Buchanan 78). Bruce G. Buchanan and Edward A. Feigenbaum, "Dendral and Meta-Dendral: Their Applications Dimension," *Artificial Intelligence*, **11**, (1), pp. 5-24, 1978.

(Carbonell 82). James G. Carbonell, "Learning by Analogy: Formulating and Generalizing Plans from Past Experience," in *Machine Learning*, ed. R. S. Michalski, J. G. Carbonell and T. M. Mitchell, Palo Alto, CA: Tioga Pub. Co., 1982.

(Chancey 85). William J, Chancey, "Details of the Revised Therapy Algorithm," in *Rule-based Expert Systems*, ed. Bruce G. Buchanan and Edward H. Shortliffe, pp. 133-146, 1985.

(Chang 73). Chin-Liang Chang and Richard Char-Tung Lee, *Symbolic Logic and Mathematical Theorem Proving*, Academic Press, p. 77, 1973.

(de Kleer 86). J. de Kleer, "An Assumption-based Truth Maintenance System," *Artif. Intell.*, **28**, (2), pp. 127-162, Jan. 1986.

(Doyle 79). J. Doyle, "A Truth Maintenance System," *Artificial Intelligence*, **12**, (3), pp. 231-272, 1979.

(Feigenbaum 79). Edward A. Feigenbaum, "Themes and Case Studies of Knowledge Engineering," *Expert Systems in the Micro-Electronic Age*, ed. Donald Michie, pp. 3-25, 1979.

(Filman 88). Robert E. Filman, "Reasoning With Worlds and Truth Maintenance in a Knowledge-Based Programming Environment," *C. ACM*, **31**, (4), pp. 382-401, April 1988.

(Fischler 87). Martin A. Fischler and Oscar Firschein, *The Eye, the Brain, and the Computer*, Addison-Wesley, p. 65, 1987.

(Hollan 84). James D. Hollan *et al.*, "Steamer: An Interactive Inspectable Simulation-based Training System," *AI Magazine*, **5**, (2), pp. 15-27, Summer 1984

(Kahn 85). Gary Kahn, "On When Diagnostic Systems Want To Do Without Causal Knowledge," in *Advances in Artificial Intelligence*, ed. T. O'Shea, Elsevier Science Publishers, pp. 41-50, 1985.

(Kowalski 79). Robert Kowalski, "Algorithm = Logic + Control," *Comm. ACM*, **22**, (7), pp. 424-436, 1979.

(Lenat 82). Douglas B. Lenat, "AM: An Artificial Intelligence Approach to Discovery in Mathematics as Heuristic Search," in *Knowledge-based Systems in Artificial Intelligence*, ed. R. Davis and D. B. Lenat, McGraw-Hill, 1982.

(McCarthy 69). J. McCarthy and P. Hayes, " Some Philosophical Problems from the Standpoint of Artificial Intelligence," in *Machine Intelligence*, **4**, ed. B. Meltzer and D. Michie, Edinburgh Univ. Press, pp. 463-502, 1969.

(McDermott 82). D. McDermott, "Nonmonotonic Logic II: Nonmonotonic Modal Theories," *J. ACM*, **29** (1), pp. 33-57, 1982.

(Miller 82). R. Miller, H. Pople, and J. Myers, "INTERNIST-1, An Experimental Computer-based Diagnostic Consultant for General Internal Medicine," *New England J. of Medicine*, **307**, pp. 468-476, 1982.

(Minsky 67). Marvin Minsky, *Computation: Finite and Infinite Machines*, Prentice-Hall, p. 228, 1967.

(Moore 85). Robert C. Moore, "Semantical Considerations on Nonmonotonic Logic," *Artificial Intelligence*, **25**, pp. 75-95, 1985.

(Nilsson 80). Nils J. Nilsson, *Principles of Artificial Intelligence,* Tioga Publishing Co., pp. 142-143, 1980.

(Pople 82). H. Pople, "Heuristic Methods for Imposing Structure on Ill-structured Problems: The Structure of Medical Diagnostics," ed. P. Szolovits, *Artificial Intelligence in Medicine*, pp. 119-190, 1982.

(Reggia 83). J. Reggia, D. Nau, and P. Wang, "Diagnostic Expert Systems Based on a Set Covering Model," *Int. J. of Man-Machine Studies*, pp. 437-460, 1983.

(Reggia 85). J. Reggia, "Abductive Inference," in *Proc. of Expert Systems in Government Symposium*, ed. K. Karna, *IEEE Press*, pp. 484-489, 1985

(Reiser 85). B.J. Reiser *et al.*, "Dynamic Student Modelling in an Intelligent Tutor for LISP Programming," *IJCAI*, pp. 8-14, 1985

(Rescher 64). Nicholas Rescher, *Introduction to Logic*, St. Martin's Press, pp. 258-259, 1964.

(Robinson 65). J.A. Robinson, "A Machine-Oriented Logic Based on the Resolution Principle," *J. ACM*, **12**, (1), pp. 23-41, Jan. 1986.

(Smith 84). Karl J. Smith, *The Nature of Mathematics*, 4th Ed., Brooks/Cole Publishing Co., p. 12, 1984.

(Stebbing 50). L.S. Stebbing, *A Modern Introduction to Logic*, Methuen & Co. Ltd., 7th Ed., pp. 104-105, 1950.

CHAPTER 4 REASONING UNDER UNCERTAINTY

4.1 INTRODUCTION

In this chapter, various methods of reasoning under **uncertainty** will be discussed. This topic is very important in expert systems since many expert system applications involve uncertain information.

4.2 UNCERTAINTY

Uncertainty can be considered as the lack of adequate information to make a decision. Uncertainty is a problem because it may prevent us from making the best decision and may even cause a bad decision. In medicine, uncertainty may prevent the best treatment for a patient or contribute to an incorrect therapy. In business, uncertainty may mean financial loss instead of profit.

A number of theories have been devised to deal with uncertainty. These include classical probability, Bayesian probability, Hartley theory based on classical sets (Hartley 1928), Shannon theory based on probability (Shannon 1948), Dempster-Shafer theory (Shafer 1976), and Zadeh's fuzzy theory (Zadeh 1965). In particular, the Shannon theory has proven very popular for telecommunications and also has been applied to many diverse areas such as biology, psychology, music and physics.

All living creatures are experts at dealing with uncertainty or they could not survive in the real world. In particular, human beings are used to uncertainty about traffic, weather, job, school and so forth. After awhile, we all become experts at driving under various traffic conditions, what to do in case of a cold, easy classes to take and many other things. Dealing with uncertainty requires reasoning under uncertainty.

The deductive method of reasoning described in Chapter 3 is called **exact reasoning** because it deals with exact facts and the exact conclusions that follow from those facts. Recall that in a deductive argument, the conclusion must follow from the premises. When uncertain facts are involved, the number of possible conclusions may greatly increase increases the difficulty of finding the best conclusion.

Unfortunately, determining the "best" conclusion may not be easy. A number of different methods have been proposed for dealing with uncertainty to aid in picking the best conclusion. It is the responsibility of the expert systems designer to pick the most appropriate method depending on the application. While there are expert system tools that incorporate mechanisms for reasoning under uncertainty, they are generally not flexible in allowing other methods to be used.

While there are many expert systems applications which can be done with exact reasoning, many others require **inexact reasoning** involving uncertain facts, rules or both. Classic examples of successful expert systems which deal with uncertainty are MYCIN for medical diagnosis and PROSPECTOR for mineral exploration.

In the MYCIN and PROSPECTOR systems, conclusions are arrived at even when all the evidence to conclusively prove the conclusion is not known. Although it is possible to arrive at a more reliable conclusion by performing more tests, there are problems with the increasing time and cost of performing the tests. These constraints of time and money are particularly important in the case of medical treatment. Delaying treatment for more tests adds considerable cost while in the meantime, the patient may die. In the case of mineral exploration, the costs of additional tests is also a significant factor. It may be more cost effective to start drilling when you are 95% certain of success than spend hundreds of thousands of dollars to be 98% certain.

4.3 TYPES OF ERRORS

Many different types of **errors** can contributes to uncertainty. Different theories of uncertainty attempt to resolve some or all of these errors to provide the most reliable inference. Figure 4-1 illustrates a simplified classification scheme for errors.

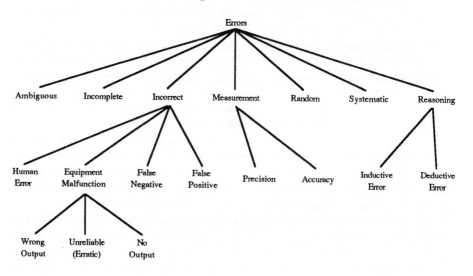

Figure 4-1
Types of Errors

This figure should strictly be drawn as a lattice since there may be interconnections between many of the different types of errors. For example, human error could be linked to ambiguity, measurement, reasoning and so on.

Table 4-1 gives examples of these errors.

The first type of error shown is **ambiguity** in which something may be interpreted in more than one way.

The second type of error is **incompleteness** where some information is missing.

A third type of error is **incorrectness** in which the information is wrong. Possible causes of incorrectness are human error, such as the accidental misreading of a dial or data, lying or misinformation, and malfunctioning equipment.

Example	Error	Reason
Turn the valve off	Ambiguous	What valve?
Turn valve-1	Incomplete	Which way?
Turn valve-1 off	Incorrect	Correct is on
Valve is stuck	False positive	Valve is not stuck
Valve is not stuck	False negative	Valve is stuck
Turn valve-1 to 5	Imprecise	Correct is 5.4
Turn valve-1 to 5.4	Inaccurate	Correct is 9.2
Turn valve-1 to 5.4 or 6 or 0	Unreliable	Equipment error
Valve-1 setting is 5.4 or 5.5 or 5.1	Random Error	Statistical Fluctuation
Valve-1 setting is 7.5	Systematic Error	Miscalibration
Valve-1 is not stuck because its never been stuck before	Invalid Induction	Valve is stuck
Output is normal and so valve-1 is in good condition	Invalid deduction	Valve is stuck in open position

Table 4-1
Examples of Common Types of Errors

A **hypothesis** is an assumption to be tested. The **null hypothesis** is the assumption initially made, such as "The valve is stuck." One type of incorrect information is called **false positive** which means accepting a hypothesis when it is not true. Likewise a **false negative** means rejecting a hypothesis when it is true. Thus if the valve is really not stuck, then accepting the hypothesis that it is stuck is a false positive. In statistics, this is called a **Type I error**. Likewise, if the valve is really stuck and the hypothesis "The valve is stuck" is rejected, this is a false negative or **Type II error**.

The next two types of error shown in Table 4-1 are **errors of measurement**. These are errors of **precision** and **accuracy**. Although these terms are sometimes used synonymously, they are very different. Consider two rulers, one of which is graduated in millimeters and the other is graduated in centimeters. Obviously, the millimeter ruler is more precise than the centimeter one. However, suppose the graduations of the millimeter ruler were incorrectly made. In that case, the millimeter ruler is inaccurate and its measurements cannot be trusted unless a correction factor is known. Thus accuracy corresponds to the truth while precision corresponds to how well the truth is known. For the two rulers, the millimeter ruler measures precision ten times more precisely than the centimeter one.

Another type of error is **unreliability**. If the measuring equipment supplying the facts is unreliable, the data is **erratic**. An erratic reading is one that is not constant but fluctuates. Sometimes it may be correct and sometimes not.

A reading that fluctuates may be caused by the basic random nature of the system being studied, such as the decay of radioactive atoms. Because the cause of the decay is a quantum mechanics phenomenon, the rate of decay fluctuates randomly about a mean value. The random fluctuations about the mean constitute a **random error** and lead to uncertainty of the mean. Other types of random error may be caused by Brownian motion, electronic noise due to thermal effects and so forth. However, erratic readings may also be caused by a loose connection.

A **systematic error** is one which is not random but instead introduced because of some bias. For example, the miscalibration of a ruler so that its graduations are smaller than normal gives a systematic error that indicates readings are higher than normal.

4.4 ERRORS AND INDUCTION

The next type of error is an **invalid induction**. "The valve is not stuck because it's never been stuck before." The process of **induction** is the opposite of deduction. While deduction proceeds from the general to the specific, as in

```
All men are mortal
Socrates is a man
```

to deduce the specific conclusion

```
Socrates is mortal
```

Induction tries to generalize from the specific to the general, as in

```
My disk drive has never crashed
∵ It will never crash
```

where the symbol ∵ stands for the inductive "therefore" in contrast to the deductive ∴ "therefore."

Except for mathematical induction, inductive arguments can never be proven correct. Instead, inductive arguments can only provide some degree of confidence that the conclusion is correct. We would not have much confidence in the preceding inductive argument. The following is a stronger argument.

```
The fire alarm goes off
∵ There is a fire
```

An even stronger argument is

```
The fire alarm goes off
I smell smoke
∵ There is a fire
```

Although this is a strong argument, it is not proof that there is a fire. The smoke could be coming from hamburgers cooking on a grill and the fire alarm could have been set off accidentally. Proof of a fire is the following:

```
The fire alarm goes off
I smell smoke
My clothes are burning
∴ There is a fire
```

Notice that this is a deductive argument because you can see the flames.

Expert systems may consist of deductive and inductive rules, where the inductive rules are of a heuristic nature. Induction has also been applied to the automatic generation of rules, as you will see in a later chapter on knowledge acquisition.

Besides uncertainty with facts, the rules of an expert system may have uncertainty if they are based on heuristics. A heuristic is commonly called a rule of thumb because it is based on experience. Sometimes experience is a good guide. However, it may not be applicable to 100% of the cases since experience is heuristic. For example, you would expect that everyone who jumps off a 50-story building would be killed. However, people can jump off a 50-story building and not be killed—if they wear a parachute.

One of the interesting characteristics of human experts is that they reason well under uncertainty. Even if there is a great deal of uncertainty, experts can usually make good judgements, or they won't be considered experts for long.

Another characteristic is that experts can easily revise their opinions if it turns out that some of the original facts were wrong. This is nonmonotonic reasoning, as discussed in Chapter 3. It is more difficult to program expert systems to backtrack their reasoning process because all the intermediate facts need to be saved and a history kept of rule firings. Human experts appear to revise their reasoning with little effort.

Besides inductive errors, there may also be deductive errors or fallacies, as described in Chapter 3. As an example of a fallacious schema discussed in Chapter 3

```
p → q
q
∴ p
```

For example

```
If the valve is in good condition,
    then the output is normal
The output is normal
∴ The valve is in good condition
```

is a fallacious argument. The valve may be stuck in the open condition so that the output is normal. However, if it is necessary to close the valve, the problem will show up. This can be very serious if the valve needs to be closed quickly as in the case of an emergency shutdown of a nuclear reactor.

In contrast to the previous errors we have discussed, inductive and deductive errors are errors of reasoning. These types of errors lead to the incorrect formulation of rules.

Generally, humans do not seem to process uncertain information in the best way (Hink 87). Even experts are not immune to making mistakes, especially under uncertainty. This can be a major problem in knowledge acquisition when the expert's knowledge must be quantified in rules. Inconsistencies, inaccuracy and all the other possible errors of uncertainty may show up. Experts will then have to correct their knowledge, which can delay the completion of the expert system.

4.5   CLASSICAL PROBABILITY

An old but still very important tool in AI problem solving is **probability** (Farley 1983). Probability is a quantitative way of dealing with uncertainty which originated in the 17th Century when some French gamblers asked help from the leading mathematicians such as Pascal, Fermat and others. Gambling had become very popular and since large amounts of money were involved, gamblers wanted methods to aid in calculating the odds of winning.

The theory of **classical probability** was first proposed by Pascal and Fermat in 1654 (Parratt 61). Since then much work has been done of probability and several new branches developed. Many applications of probability have been shown to science, engineering, business, economics and virtually every other field.

The Definition of Classical Probability

Classical probability is also called *a priori* **probability** because it deals with ideal games or systems. As discussed in Chapter 2, the term *a priori* means, "before," that is, without regard to the real world. A priori probability considers games such as dice, cards, coins or whatever, as ideal systems that do not become worn out.

Ideal systems do not exhibit the real world characteristics of wear-and-tear because then they would not have precisely reproducible characteristics. That is, a real die (plural dice) may exhibit a bias towards some particular numbers after one side becomes worn down after numerous throws. Likewise, depending on the manufacture, a real die may exhibit a preference towards higher numbers because more pips (small colored holes) are drilled in higher numbers. This bias was determined by analyzing data from

1,000,000 throws of a real die; in which a new die was used every 20,000 throws to avoid bias caused by uneven wearing of the faces. The fraction of times different numbers came up is shown in Table 4-2 (Shafer 76).

Number	1	2	3	4	5	6
Fraction	.155	.159	.164	.169	.174	.179

Table 4-2
Results of 1,000,000 Throws of a Die

In an ideal system, all numbers occur equally which makes analysis much easier.
The fundamental formula of classical probability is defined as the probability

$$P = \frac{W}{N}$$

where W is the number of wins and N is the number of equally possible **events**, which are the possible outcomes of an experiment or **trial**. For example, if you throw a die once, there are six possible events from this single trial. The die may come to rest with its top showing either a 1, 2, 3, 4, 5 or 6. Under classical probability, it is assumed that any of these six events is equally possible and so the probability of rolling a 1, P(1), is

$$P(1) = \frac{1}{6}$$

Likewise

$$P(2) = \frac{1}{6}$$

and so forth.
The probability of losing, Q, is

$$Q = \frac{N - W}{N} = 1 - P$$

The fundamental formula for P is an *a priori* definition because the probability is calculated *before* the game is played. The term *a priori* means "that which precedes" or "before the event" when discussing probabilities. An *a priori* probability assumes that all possible events are known and that each event is equally likely to happened.
For example, in rolling a die, the possible spots on each face are known as 1, 2, 3, 4, 5, and 6. Also, if the die is **fair**, not loaded, then each side is equally likely to come up. Likewise, in a fair deck of cards, all 52 cards are known and equally likely to be

drawn under a fair shuffle. The probability of any one face of the die coming up is 1/6 and for any card is 1/52.

When repeated trials give exactly the same result, the system is **deterministic**. If it is not deterministic, it is **nondeterministic** or random. In some types of expert system shells, nondeterminism is used to prevent bias in rule firings. When the patterns of multiple rules are satisfied and there is no explicit preference as to which rule should be executed, the inference engine makes an arbitrary choice of the rule to be executed. This prevents a bias in which one rule, say the first one entered, is fired.

Sample Spaces

The result of a trial is a **sample point** and the set of all possible sample points define a **sample space**. For example, if a single die is rolled, any one of the sample points 1, 2, 3, 4, 5 or 6 can occur. Figure 4-2 (a) shows the sample space for the roll of a single die. The sample space is the set { 1, 2, 3, 4, 5, 6 }.

An **event** is a subset of the sample space. For example, the event { 1 } occurs if the die comes up with a 1. A **simple event** has only one element and a **compound event** has more than one, as shown in Figure 4-2.

(a) Sample Space for a Single Die   (b) A Simple {5} and Compound Event {3,6}

Figure 4-2
Sample Space and Events

A graphical way of determining the sample space is constructing an **event tree**. As a simple example, suppose there are two computers which either work, W, or don't work, D. Figure 4-3 shows the event tree while Table 4-3 shows a table form of the sample space. Note that the compound events are listed in the order { computer1, computer2 }. The sample space is { WW, WD, DW, DD }.

This type of event tree is a binary tree since only binary probabilities are involved. That is, either the computer works or it doesn't. Many other cases have this type of tree. For example, the toss of coins leads to a binary event tree since there are only two possible outcomes for every throw.

Probability and statistics are fields that make extensive use of each other's theories. Statistics is concerned with collecting and analyzing data about **populations,** a set from which samples are drawn. One goal of statistics is to make inferences about the parent population from which the sample population is drawn. A typical example of statistical inference is to infer what proportion of registered voters will be in favor of a certain candidate being elected based on a telephone poll of sample registered voters.

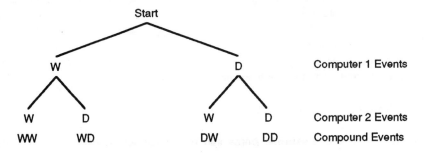

Figure 4-3
Event Tree for Compound Event

| | | Computer 2 | |
		W	D
Computer 1	W	WW	WD
	D	DW	DD

Table 4-3
Sample Space of Binary Events

One application of probability theory is to deduce whether the sample of voters is really representative of all voters, or whether it may be biased in favor of a certain party. Although this example relates to real objects, people, other populations such as the possible number of coin tosses is conceptual or hypothetical. Every coin toss is a sample of the hypothetical population of all coin tosses.

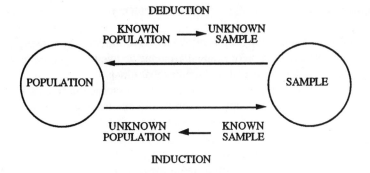

Figure 4-4
Deductive and Inductive Reasoning About Populations and Samples

Deduction and induction are the basis of reasoning about populations as shown in Figure 4-4. Given a known population, deduction lets us make inferences about the unknown sample. Correspondingly, given a known sample, induction lets us make inferences about the unknown population.

Theory of Probability

A formal theory of probability can made using three axioms:

$$axiom\ 1:\quad 0 \leq P(E) \leq 1$$

This axiom defines the range of probability to be the real numbers from 0 to 1. Negative probabilities are not allowed. **A certain event** is assigned probability 1 and an **impossible event** assigned probability 0.

$$axiom\ 2:\quad \sum_i P(E_1) = 1$$

This axiom states that the sum of all events which do not affect each other, called **mutually exclusive events**, is 1. Mutually exclusive events have no sample point in common. For example, a computer cannot be both working correctly and not working correctly at the same time.

As a corollary of this axiom

$$P(E) + P(E') = 1$$

where E' is the complement of event E. This corollary means that the probability of an event occurring plus the probability of it not occurring is 1. That is, the occurrence and nonoccurrence of an event is a mutually exclusive and complete sample space.

$$axiom\ 3:\quad P(E_1 \cup E_2) = P(E_1) + P(E_2)$$

where E_1 and E_2 are mutually exclusive events. This axiom means that if E_1 and E_2 cannot both occur simultaneously (mutually exclusive events) then the probability of one or the other occurring is the sum of their probabilities.

From these axioms, theorems can be deduced concerning the calculation of probabilities under other situations, such as nonmutually exclusive events, as we shall see later. While these axioms form the basis for a theory of probability, notice that they *do not specify the basic probabilities P(E)*. Since the basic probabilities of events are determined by other methods such as *a priori*.

These axioms put probability on a sound theoretical basis. In fact, the axiomatic theory is also called the **objective theory of probability.** These particular axioms were devised by Kolmogorov. An equivalent theory using axioms of conditional probability was created by Renyi (Lindley 65).

4.6   EXPERIMENTAL AND SUBJECTIVE PROBABILITIES

Other than ideal games with equal likelihood, classical probability cannot answer questions like what is the probability of your disk drive crashing tomorrow or what is the life expectancy of a 25 year old male.

In contrast to the *a priori* approach, **experimental probability** defines the probability of an event, P(E), as the limit of a frequency distribution

$$P(E) = \lim_{N \to \infty} \frac{f(E)}{N}$$

where f(E) is the frequency of outcomes of an event for N observed total outcomes. This type of probability is also called *a posteriori* probability, which means "after the event." Another term for *a posteriori* is the **posterior probability**. The idea of *a posteriori* is to measure the frequency that an event occurs for a large number of trials and from this induce the experimental probability.

For example, to determine the experimental probability of your disk drive crashing, you could take a poll of other people with your type of drive. The results of a hypothetical poll are shown in Table 4-4.

Total Percent Crashed	Hours Used
10	100
25	250
50	500
75	750
99	1000

Table 4-4
Hypothetical Time for a Disk Drive to Crash

If your drive has been used 750 hours, then you could induce that there is a 75% probability of it crashing tomorrow. Notice that this 75% figure is an induction rather than a deduction. Unlike an ideal game, your disk drive is not exactly the same as others. There may be differences in the materials used, quality control, environmental conditions and use that affect the drive and its longevity. It is much easier to produce simple devices such as dice or cards with much finer tolerances than a complex piece of equipment like a disk drive.

Another type of experimental probability can be induced from mortality tables used by life insurance companies that show the probability of a person dying as a function of age and sex. Calculating the odds of *your* mortality based on these tables is an induction since you are unique. An analogous situation holds for house insurance. Unless your house burns down a lot so that the individual experimental probability can be calculated, the experimental probabilities used will be based on similar types of houses.

Another type of probability is **subjective probability**. Suppose you were asked the probability that automobiles using superconducting electric motors would cost $10,000 by the year 2000. Since there is no data on the cost of these cars, there is no way to extrapolate the costs to see if $10,000 is a reasonable figure.

You could guess that optical drives would follow the same cost/time curves of magnetic drives, but the technologies are very different.

Subjective probability deals with events that are not reproducible and have no historical basis on which to extrapolate, such as drilling an oil well at a new site. However, a subjective probability by an expert is better than no estimate at all and is usually very accurate (or the expert won't be an expert for long) (Sioshansi 1983).

A subjective probability is actually a belief or opinion expressed as a probability rather than a probability based on axioms or empirical measurement. Beliefs and opinions of an expert play important roles in expert systems, as we shall see in this chapter. Table 4-5 summarizes the different types of probabilities that we have discussed.

Names	Formula	Characteristics
a priori (classical, theoretical, mathematical, symmetric equiprobable equal-likelihood)	$P(E) = \dfrac{W}{N}$ where W is the number of outcomes of event E for a total of N possible outcomes	Repeatable events Equally likely outcomes Exact math form known Not based on experiment All possible events and outcomes known

a posteriori
 	
(experimental, empirical, scientific, relative frequency, statistical)
 	
$P(E) \approx \dfrac{f(E)}{N}$
	$P(E) = \lim_{N \to \infty} \dfrac{f(E)}{N}$
	
	where f(E) is the frequency, f, that event, E, is observed for N total outcomes
		Repeatable events
		   based on experiments
		Approximated by a finite
		   number of experiments
		Exact math form unknown

subjective
 	
(personal)
	See Section 4.12	Nonrepeatable events
		Exact math form unknown
		Relative frequency
		   method not possible
		Based on expert's experience
		   judgement, opinion, or
		   belief

Table 4-5
Types of Probabilities

4.7 COMPOUND PROBABILITIES

The probabilities of compound events can be computed from their sample spaces. As a very simple example, consider the probability of rolling a die such that the outcome is an even number and a number divisible by 3. This can be expressed in terms of a Venn diagram for the sets

```
A = { 2, 4, 6 }    B = { 3, 6 }
```

in the sample space of the die as shown in Figure 4-5.

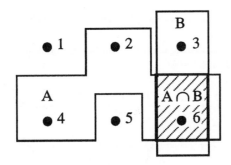

Figure 4-5
Compound Probability of Rolling a Single Die
to Give an Even Number and a Number Divisible by 3

Notice that the intersection of the sets A and B is

```
A ∩ B = { 6 }
```

The compound probability of rolling an even number and a number divisible by 3 is

$$P(A \cap B) = \frac{n(A \cap B)}{n(S)} = \frac{1}{6}$$

where n is the number of elements in the sets and S is the sample space.

Events that do not affect each other in any way are called **independent events**. For two independent events A and B, the probability is simply the product of the individual probabilities. Events A and B are said to be **pairwise independent**.

```
P(A ∩ B) = P(A) P(B)
```

Two events are called **stochastically independent events** if and only if the above formula is true. The term **stochastic** comes from the Greek and means "guess." It is commonly used as a synonym for probability, random or chance. Thus, a stochastic experiment has a random outcome in contrast to the nonrandom outcome of a deterministic experiment.

For three events, you might assume that independence is

$$P(A \cap B \cap C) = P(A) \; P(B) \; P(C)$$

Unfortunately, life and probability are not that simple. The formula for the **mutual independence** of N events requires that 2^N equations be satisfied. This requirement is summarized by the following equation, where the asterisks mean that every combination of an event and its complement must be satisfied.

$$P(A^*_1 \cap A^*_2 \; \ldots \; \cap A^*_N) = P(A^*_1) \; P(A^*_2) \; \ldots \; P(A^*_N)$$

For three events, the above equation for mutual independence requires that *all* the following equations all be satisfied.

$$P(A \cap B \cap C) = P(A) \; P(B) \; P(C)$$
$$P(A \cap B \cap C') = P(A) \; P(B) \; P(C')$$
$$P(A \cap B' \cap C) = P(A) \; P(B') \; P(C)$$
$$P(A \cap B' \cap C') = P(A) \; P(B') \; P(C')$$
$$P(A' \cap B \cap C) = P(A') \; P(B) \; P(C)$$
$$P(A' \cap B \cap C') = P(A') \; P(B) \; P(C')$$
$$P(A' \cap B' \cap C) = P(A') \; P(B') \; P(C)$$
$$P(A' \cap B' \cap C') = P(A') \; P(B') \; P(C')$$

The pairwise independence of every two events is not enough to guarantee mutual independence, as shown in Problem 4-6.

For our die, the events of an even number and a number divisible by three definitely affect each other and so is *not* a stochastic experiment. The probability of an even number on one die and a number divisible by three on another *is* stochastic,

$$P(A \cap B) = P(A) \; P(B) = \frac{3}{6} \cdot \frac{2}{6} = \frac{1}{6}$$

Now let's consider the case of the union of events, $P(A \cup B)$. Define *n* as a function which returns the number of elements of a set. If we add the number of elements in A to those in B, and divide by the total elements in the sample space n(S),

$$(1) \quad P(A \cup B) = \frac{n(A) + n(B)}{n(S)} = P(A) + P(B) \quad \text{incomplete see \#}$$

then the result will be too big if the sets overlap. If you look at Figure 4-5, applying this formula gives

$$P(A \cup B) = \frac{3 + 2}{6} = \frac{5}{6}$$

but you can easily see that there are only four elements in the union since

$$A \cup B = \{\ 2,\ 3,\ 4,\ 6\ \}$$

The problem is that just adding n(A) to n(B) is counting the set intersection { 6 } twice since it belongs to both A and B.

The correct formula simply requires subtracting the extra probability of set intersection

$$(2)\ \ P(A \cup B) = P(A) + P(B) - P(A \cap B)$$

which for our die reduces to

$$P(A \cup B) = \frac{3}{6} + \frac{2}{6} - \frac{1}{6} = \frac{4}{6} = \frac{2}{3}$$

Formula (1) holds when the sets are disjoint and so have no elements in common. It is a special case of formula (2), which is called the **Additive Law**. The Additive Law can also be derived as a theorem using the three axioms of probability discussed earlier. The Additive Law for three events is

$$\begin{aligned} P(A \cup B \cup C) = &\ P(A) + P(B) + P(C) \\ &- P(A \cap B) - P(A \cap C) - P(B \cap C) \\ &+ P(A \cap B \cap C) \end{aligned}$$

Other laws for neither A nor B and the exclusive-OR of A and B can also be derived from the axioms. The value of these laws for compound probabilities is that (1) experiments do not have to be made for each possible combination of probabilities and (2) the individual elements of large sample spaces do not have to be counted.

4.8 CONDITIONAL PROBABILITIES

Events that are not mutually exclusive influence one another. Knowing that one event has occurred may cause us to revise the probability that another event will occur.

Multiplicative Law

The probability of an event A, given that event B occurred, is called a **conditional probability** and indicated by $P(A \mid B)$. The conditional probability is defined as

$$P(A \mid B) = \frac{P(A \cap B)}{P(B)} \text{ for } P(B) \neq 0$$

The probability P(B) is the *a priori* or prior probability before any information is known. When used in association with a conditional probability, the prior probability is sometimes called the **unconditional probability** or an **absolute probability**.

This definition of conditional probability can be intuitively explained if you look at the example of Figure 4-6, which is a sample space of eight events. From Figure 4-6, the probabilities can be calculated as the ratios of the number of events, n(A) or n(B), to the total number in the sample space n(S). That is,

$$P(A) = \frac{n(A)}{n(S)} = \frac{4}{8}$$

$$P(B) = \frac{n(B)}{n(S)} = \frac{6}{8}$$

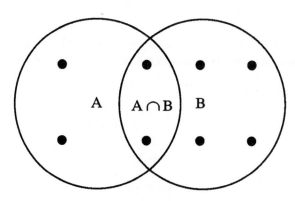

Figure 4-6
Sample Space of Two Intersecting Events

If we know that event B has occurred, the reduced sample space is just that of B.

$$n(S) = 6$$

Since B occurred, only the events in A that are associated with B are considered.

$$P(A \mid B) = \frac{n(A \cap B)}{n(B)} = \frac{2}{6}$$

To express the result in terms of probabilities, just divide the numerator and denominator of the above by n(S),

$$P(A \mid B) = \frac{\dfrac{n(A \cap B)}{n(S)}}{\dfrac{n(B)}{n(S)}}$$

$$= \frac{P(A \cap B)}{P(B)} \qquad \text{for } P(B) \neq 0$$

The **Multiplicative Law** of probability for two events is then defined as

$$P(A \cap B) = P(A \mid B) \; P(B)$$

which is equivalent to the following.

$$P(A \cap B) = P(B \mid A) \; P(A)$$

The Multiplicative Law for three events is the following.

$$P(A \cap B \cap C) = P(A \mid B \cap C) \; P(B \mid C) \; P(C)$$

and the **Generalized Multiplicative Law** is

$$P(A_1 \cap A_2 \cap \ldots \cap A_N) = P(A_1 \mid A_2 \cap \ldots \cap A_N) \; \cdot$$
$$P(A_2 \mid A_3 \cap \ldots \cap A_N) \; \cdot$$
$$\ldots \; P(A_{N-1} \mid A_N) \; P(A_N)$$

As an example of probabilities, Table 4-6 shows hypothetical probabilities of a disk crash using a Brand X drive within one year.

		Brand X	Not Brand X'	Total of Rows
Crash	C	0.6	0.1	0.7
No crash	C'	0.2	0.1	0.3
Total of Columns		0.8	0.2	1.0

Table 4-6
Hypothetical Probabilities of a Disk Crash Within One Year

The probabilities of 0.6, 0.1, 0.2 and 0.1 inside the middle region in the table are called **interior probabilities** and represent the intersections of events. The sum of the rows and columns are displayed as *Totals*, and are called **marginal probabilities** because they lie on the margin of the table.

Tables 4-7 and 4-8 show the set and probability meanings in more detail. Figure 4-7 shows the Venn diagram of the sample space intersection. From Table 4-8, you can see that the sum of total row probabilities and total column probabilities is 1.

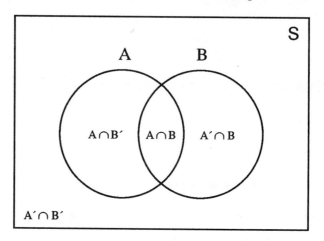

Figure 4-7
The Sample Space Interpretation of Two Sets

	X	X′	Total of Rows
C	C ∩ X	C ∩ X′	C = (C ∩ X) ∪ (C ∩ X′)
C′	C′ ∩ X	C′ ∩ X′	C′ = (C′ ∩ X) ∪ (C′ ∩ X′)
Total of Columns	X = (C′ ∩ X) ∪ (C ∩ X)	X′ = (C′ ∩ X′) ∪ (C ∩ X′)	S (Sample Space)

Table 4-7
Set Interpretation

	X	X′	Total of Rows
C	P(C ∩ X)	P(C ∩ X′)	P(C)
C′	P(C′ ∩ X)	P(C′ ∩ X′)	P(C′)
Total of Columns	P(X)	P(X′)	1.0

Table 4-8
Probability Interpretation of Two Sets

Using Table 4-8, the probabilities of all events can be calculated. Some probabilities are:

(1) The probability of a crash for both Brand X and not Brand X (the sample space) is

P(C) = 0.7

(2) The probability of no crash for the sample space is

P(C') = 0.3

(3) The probability of using Brand X is

P(X) = 0.8

(4) The probability of not using Brand X is

P(X') = 0.2

(5) The probability of a crash and using Brand X is

P(C ∩ X) = 0.6

(6) The probability of a crash, given that Brand X is used, is

$$P(C \mid X) = \frac{P(C \cap X)}{P(X)} = \frac{0.6}{0.8} = 0.75$$

(7) The probability of a crash, given that Brand X is not used, is

$$P(C \mid X') = \frac{P(C \cap X')}{P(X')} = \frac{0.1}{0.2} = 0.50$$

Probabilities (5) and (6) may appear to have similar meanings when you read their descriptions. However (5) is simply the intersection of two events, while (6) is a conditional probability. The meaning of the intersection, (5), is the following.

```
If a disk drive is picked randomly, then 0.6 of the
time it will be Brand X and have crashed.
```

In other words, we are just picking samples from the population of disk drives. Some of those drives are Brand X and have crashed (0.6), some are not Brand X and have crashed (0.1), some are Brand X and have not crashed (0.2), and some are not Brand X and have not crashed (0.1).

In contrast, the meaning of the conditional probability (6) is very different.

```
If a Brand X drive is picked, then 0.75 of the time
it will have crashed.
```

Notice that in the conditional probability, we are picking those items (Brand X) of interest to us and considering them as the new sample space.

If any of the following equations is true, then events A and B are **independent**.

$$P(A \mid B) = P(A) \text{ or}$$
$$P(B \mid A) = P(B) \text{ or}$$
$$P(A \cap B) = P(A) \; P(B)$$

If any one of these equations are true, then so are the others.

Bayes' Theorem

The conditional probability, $P(A \mid B)$, states the probability of event A given that event B occurred. The inverse problem is to find the **inverse probability** which states the probability of an earlier event given that a later one occurred. This type of probability occurs often, as in the case of medical or equipment diagnosis where symptoms appear and the problem is to find the most likely cause. The solution to this problem is **Bayes' Theorem**, also sometimes called Bayes' Formula, Bayes' Rule or Bayes' Law, named after the 18th Century British clergyman and mathematician, Thomas Bayes.

As an example of Bayes' theorem, let's see how it applies to the disk drive crashes. From the conditional probability (6), there is a 75% probability a Brand X drive will crash within one year, while based on (7), the probability of a non-Brand X drive crash within one year is 50%. The inverse question is, suppose you have a drive and don't know its brand, what is the probability that if it crashes, it is Brand X? Non-Brand X?

A situation like this, in which you don't really know the drive, occurs all the time since computer manufacturers seldom make their own drives. Instead many buy drives from an original equipment manufacturer (OEM) and repackage the drives to sell under their own label. Depending on what OEM offers the lowest cost, the drive may vary from year to year with only the computer manufacturers label remaining the same.

Given that a drive crashed, the probability of it being Brand X can be stated using conditional probability and the results (1), (5).

$$P(X \mid C) = \frac{P(C \cap X)}{P(C)} = \frac{0.6}{0.7} = \frac{6}{7}$$

Alternatively, using the Multiplicative Law on the numerator, and (1), (3), (6)

$$P(X \mid C) = \frac{P(C \mid X) \; P(X)}{P(C)} = \frac{(0.75)(0.8)}{0.7} = \frac{0.6}{0.7} = \frac{6}{7}$$

The probability $P(X \mid C)$ is the **inverse** or *a posteriori* probability, which states that if the drive crashed, it was Brand X. Figure 4-8 shows a decision tree for the disk crashes. The square symbol indicates an **act** or decision, and the circle indicates an **event** or occurrence. The prior probabilities are those before the experiments of measuring crashes. The posterior or inverse probabilities are those determined after the completion of the experiments. The posterior probabilities allow us to revise the prior probabilities to obtain more accurate results.

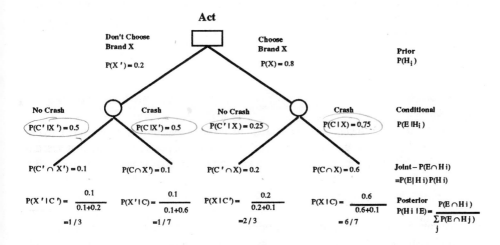

Figure 4-8
Decision Tree for the Disk Crashes

The general form of Bayes' Theorem can be written in terms of events, E, and hypotheses (assumptions), H, in the following alternative forms.

$$P(H_i \mid E) = \frac{P(E \cap H_i)}{\sum_j P(E \cap H_j)}$$

$$= \frac{P(E \mid H_i)\, P(H_i)}{\sum_j P(E \mid H_j)\, P(H_j)}$$

$$= \frac{P(E \mid H_i)\, P(H_i)}{P(E)}$$

4.9 HYPOTHETICAL REASONING AND BACKWARD INDUCTION

Bayes' Theorem is commonly used for decision tree analysis of business and the social sciences. The method of **Bayesian decision making** is also used in the

PROSPECTOR expert system to decide favorable sites for mineral exploration. PROSPECTOR has achieved a great deal of fame as the first expert system to discover a valuable molybdenum deposit worth $100,000,000.

As an example of Bayesian decision making under uncertainty, let's look at the problem of oil exploration. Initially, the prospector must decide what the chances are of finding oil. If there is no evidence either for or against oil, the prospector may assign the subjective prior probabilities for oil, O, of

$$P(O) = P(O') = 0.5$$

With no evidence, an assignment of probabilities that are equally weighted between possible outcomes is said to be made **in desperation**. The term *in desperation* does not mean that the prospector is (necessarily) in desperate need. It is a technical term for the unbiased prior assignment of probabilities. The prospector believes that there is better than a 50-50 chance of finding oil, and assumes the following.

$$P(O) = 0.6 \quad P(O') = 0.4$$

A very important tool in oil and mineral exploration is the **seismic survey**. In this technique, dynamite or machinery creates sound pulses which travel through the earth. The sound waves are detected by microphones at various locations. By observing the arrival time of pulses and distortion of the sound waveform, it is possible to determine geologic structures and the possibility of oil and minerals. Unfortunately seismic tests are not 100% accurate. The sound waves may be affected by some types of geologic structures so the test reports the presence of oil when there really is none (false positive). Likewise, the test may report the absence of oil when there really is oil (false negative). Assume that the past history of the seismic test has given the following conditional probabilities, where + means a positive outcome and - is a negative outcome. Note that these are conditional probabilities because the cause (oil or no oil) must have occurred before the effect (test result). A posterior probability would be from an effect (test result) back to the cause (oil or no oil). Generally, a conditional probability is forward in time while a posterior probability is backward in time.

$$P(+ \mid O) = 0.8 \qquad P(- \mid O) = 0.2 \text{ (false } -)$$
$$P(+ \mid O') = 0.1 \text{ (false } +) \quad P(- \mid O') = 0.9$$

Using the prior and conditional probabilities, we can construct the initial probability tree as shown in Figure 4-9. Also shown are the joint probabilities, which are calculated from the prior and conditional probabilities.

The Addition Law is then used to calculate the total probability of a + and a - test.

$$P(+) = P(+ \cap O) + P(+ \cap O') = 0.48 + 0.04 = 0.52$$
$$P(-) = P(- \cap O) + P(- \cap O') = 0.12 + 0.36 = 0.48$$

Figure 4-9
Initial Probability Tree for Oil Exploration

Figure 4-10
Revised Probability Tree for Oil Exploration

The P(+) and P(-) are unconditional probabilities that can now be used to calculate the posterior probabilities at the site, as shown in Figure 4-10. For example, the P(O' | -) is the posterior probability for no oil at the site based on a negative test. The joint probabilities are then computed. Notice that the joint probabilities of Figure 4-10 are the same as in Figure 4-9. The revision of probabilities is necessary to give good results when experimental information, such as the seismic test results, occurs after the initial probability estimates (or guess).

Figure 4-11 shows the initial Bayesian decision tree using the data from Figure 4-10. The **payoffs** at the bottom of the tree are positive if money is made and negative if money is lost. The assumed amounts are shown in Table 4-9.

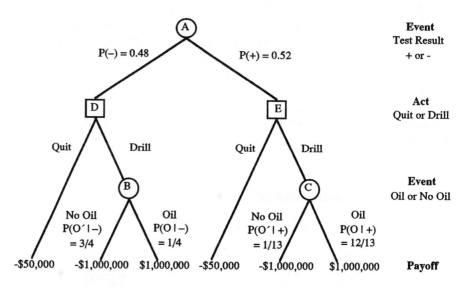

Figure 4-11
Initial Bayesian Decision Tree for Oil Exploration

Oil lease, if successful	$1,250,000
Drilling expense	-$200,000
Seismic survey	-$50,000

Table 4-9
Payoff Table for the Oil Exploration Problem

Thus, if oil is found, the payoff is $1,250,000 - $200,000 - $50,000 = $1,000,000 while a decision to quit after the seismic test result gives a payoff of -$50,000.

In order for the prospector to make the best decision, the **expected payoff** must be calculated at event node A. The expected payoff is the amount the prospector can make by following the best course of action. To compute the expected payoff at the start, A, we must work backwards from the leaves. In probability theory, this process is called **backward induction**. That is, in order to achieve the expected payoff or goal that we want, we must reason backwards to find the causes that will lead us to the goal.

The expected payoff from an event node is the sum of the payoffs times the probabilities leading to the payoffs.

```
Expected payoff at node C
$846,153 = ($1,000,000) (12/13) - ($1,000,000) (1/13)

Expected payoff at node B
-$500,000 = ($1,000,000) (1/4) - ($1,000,000) (3/4)
```

At the action node E, we must decide between an expected payoff of -$50,000 by quitting or $846,153 by drilling. Since $846,153 is greater than -$50,000, we will induce that this is the better action and write it over node E. The path to quitting will be **pruned** or **poisoned** by breaking it with a "=" symbol to indicate this path will not be followed, as in Figure 4-12. Likewise at action node D, the best choice between a payoff of -$50,000 and a payoff of -$500,000 is -$50,000 and so this is written at D.

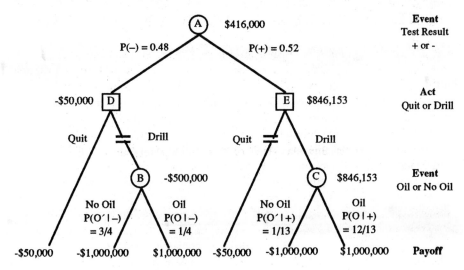

Figure 4-12
Complete Bayesian Decision Tree for Oil Exploration
Using Backward Induction

Finally, the expected payoff at the beginning is computed as follows.

```
Expected payoff at node A
$416,000 = ($846,153) (0.52) - ($50,000) (0.48)
```

and this value is written at node A. No path can be pruned at node A because we have already decided to do the seismic test. To decide on a seismic test, the decision tree would have to be extended backward before node A. Notice that in backward induction, we are reasoning back in time so that our actions in the future will be optimum.

The decision tree is an example of hypothetical reasoning or "What if" type situations. By exploring alternate paths of action, we can prune paths that do not lead to optimal payoffs. Some types of expert system tools such as ART from the Inference Corp, have elaborate mechanisms for hypothetical reasoning and poisoning.

The decision tree of Figure 4-12 shows the optimal strategy for the prospector. If the seismic test is positive, the site should be drilled. If the seismic test is negative, the site should be abandoned. Although this is a very simple example of Bayesian decision making, it does illustrate the type of reasoning involved in dealing with uncertainty. In more complex cases, such as deciding to use a seismic test, the decision trees may grow much larger (Lapin 78).

4.10   TEMPORAL REASONING AND MARKOV CHAINS

Reasoning about events that depend on time is called **temporal reasoning** and is something that humans do fairly easily. However, it is difficult to formalize **temporal events** so that a computer can make temporal inferences. Yet expert systems that reason about temporal events such as aircraft traffic control could be very useful. Expert systems that reason over time have been developed in medicine. These include the VM system (Fagan 1979) for ventilator management of patients on a respirator, to help them breathe. Other systems are CASNET for eye glaucoma treatment (Weiss 78) and the digitalis therapy advisor for heart patients (Gorry 78).

Except for VM, the other medical systems mentioned above have a much easier problem of temporal reasoning compared to an aircraft control system that must operate in **real time**. Most expert systems cannot operate in real time because of the inference engine design and large amounts of processing required. An expert system that does a lot of temporal reasoning to explore multiple hypotheses in real time is very difficult to build. Different temporal logics have been developed based on different axioms (Turner 84). Different theories are based on the way that certain questions are answered. Does time have a first and last moment? Is time continuous or discrete? Is there only one past but many possible futures?

Depending on how these questions are answered, many different logics can be developed (McDermott 82) (Allen 81). Temporal logic is also useful in conventional programs, such as in the synthesis and the synchronization of processes in concurrent programs (Manna and Wolper 84).

Another approach to temporal reasoning is with probabilities. We can think of a system moving from one state to another as evolving over time. The system can be anything that is probabilistic such as stocks, voters, weather, business, disease, equipment, genetics and so forth. The system's progression through a sequence of status is called a **stochastic process** if it is probabilistic.

It is convenient to represent a stochastic process in the form of a transition matrix. For the simple case of two states, S_1 and S_2, the transition matrix is

$$
\begin{array}{c}
\text{Future} \\[4pt]
\begin{array}{cc} S_1 & S_2 \end{array} \\[2pt]
\text{Present} \quad
\begin{array}{c} S_1 \\ S_2 \end{array}
\left[\begin{array}{cc} P_{11} & P_{12} \\ P_{21} & P_{22} \end{array} \right]
\end{array}
$$

where P_{mn} is the probability of a transition from state m to state n.

As an example, assume that 10% of all people who now use Brand X drives will buy another Brand X drive when needed. Also, 60% of the people who don't use Brand X now will buy Brand X when they need a new drive (the only good thing about Brand X is their advertising). Over a long period of time, how many people will use Brand X?

The transition matrix, T, is

$$
\begin{array}{c}
\begin{array}{cc} X & X' \end{array} \\[2pt]
T = \begin{array}{c} X \\ X' \end{array}
\left[\begin{array}{cc} 0.1 & 0.9 \\ 0.6 & 0.4 \end{array} \right]
\end{array}
$$

where the sum of each row must add up to 1. A vector whose components are not negative and add up to 1 is called a **probability vector**. Each row of T is a probability vector. One way of interpreting the transition matrix is in terms of a state diagram as shown in Figure 4-13. Notice that there is a 0.1 probability of remaining in state X, a 0.4 probability of remaining in state X', a 0.9 probability of going from X to X', and a 0.6 probability of going from X' to X.

Figure 4-13
State Diagram Interpretation of a Transition Matrix

Suppose initially that 80% of the people use Brand X. Figure 4-14 (a) shows a probability tree for a few state transitions, where the states are labeled by state number and drive owned. Notice how the tree is starting to grow. If there were ten transitions, the tree would have $2^{10} = 1024$ branches. An alternate way of drawing the tree as a lattice is shown in Figure 4-14 (b). The advantage of the lattice representation is that it doesn't need so many links connecting the states.

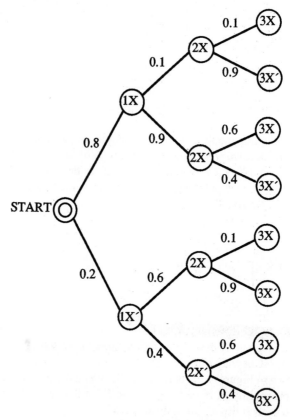

(a) Tree Diagram of States

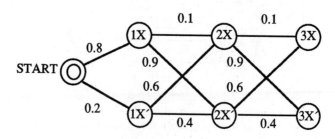

(b) Lattice Diagram of States
Figure 4-14
Tree and Lattice Diagrams of States Evolving Over Time

The probability of the system being in a certain state can be represented as a row matrix called the **state matrix**.

$$S = [\; P_1 \quad P_2 \quad \ldots \quad P_N \;]$$

where $P_1 + P_2 + \ldots + P_N = 1$

Initially with 80% of the people owning Brand X, the state matrix is

$$S_1 = [\; 0.8 \quad 0.2 \;]$$

As time goes on, these numbers will change depending on what drive people buy.

In order to calculate the number of people in state 2 having Brand X and not Brand X, just multiply the state matrix times the transition matrix using the ordinary laws of matrix multiplication

$$S_2 = S_1 \; T$$

which gives

$$S_2 = [\; 0.8 \quad 0.2 \;] \begin{bmatrix} 0.1 & 0.9 \\ 0.6 & 0.4 \end{bmatrix}$$

$$= [\; (0.8)(0.1)+(0.2)(0.6) \quad (0.8)(0.9)+(0.2)(0.4) \;]$$

$$= [\; 0.2 \quad 0.8 \;]$$

Multiplying this second state by the transition matrix gives

$$S_3 = S_2 \; T$$

$$= [\; 0.2 \quad 0.8 \;] \begin{bmatrix} 0.1 & 0.9 \\ 0.6 & 0.4 \end{bmatrix}$$

$$S_3 = [\; 0.5 \quad 0.5 \;]$$

Multiplying this third state by the transition matrix gives

$$S_4 = S_3 \; T$$

$$= [\; 0.5 \quad 0.5 \;] \begin{bmatrix} 0.1 & 0.9 \\ 0.6 & 0.4 \end{bmatrix}$$

$$S_4 = [\ 0.35 \quad 0.65\ ]$$

The next states are

$$S_5 = [\ 0.425 \quad 0.575\ ]$$

$$S_6 = [\ 0.3875 \quad 0.6125\ ]$$

$$S_7 = [\ 0.40625 \quad 0.59375\ ]$$

$$S_8 = [\ 0.396875 \quad 0.602125\ ]$$

Notice that the states are converging on

$$[\ 0.4 \quad 0.6\ ]$$

which is called a **steady-state matrix**. The system is said to be in equilibrium when it is in the steady-state since it does not change. It's interesting that the steady-state values do not depend on the initial state. If any initial probability vector had been used, the steady-state values would be the same.

A probability vector S is a steady-state matrix for the transition matrix T if

$$(1) \quad S = S\ T$$

If T is a **regular transition matrix**, which has some power with only positive elements, then a unique steady-state S exists (Kemeny 59). The fact that the transition matrix elements are positive means that at some time, it is possible to be in any state no matter what the initial state had been. That is, every state is potentially accessible.

A **Markov chain process** is defined as having the following characteristics.

(1) Having a finite number of possible states.
(2) The process can be in one and only one state at a time.
(3) The process moves or **steps** successively from one state to another over time.
(4) The probability of a move depends only on the immediately preceding state.

For example, given a finite set of states {A,B,C,D,E,F,G,H,I}, then if the next state that the process goes to after H is I, the conditional probability is the following.

$$P(I \mid H) = P(I \mid H \cap G \cap F \cap E \cap D \cap C \cap B \cap A)$$

Notice how the lattice diagram of Figure 4-14 (b) resembles a chain.

The disk drive case is a Markov chain process and the steady-state matrix can be found by applying equation (1). Assume some arbitrary vector S with components X and Y and apply equation (1) as follows.

$$[\ X \quad Y \ ] \begin{bmatrix} 0.1 & 0.9 \\ 0.6 & 0.4 \end{bmatrix} = [\ X \quad Y \ ]$$

Multiplying the left side and setting its elements equal to the corresponding elements on the right hand side gives

```
0.1 X + 0.6 Y = X
0.9 X + 0.4 Y = Y
```

which is a dependent system of equations. Solving for X in terms of Y gives

$$X = \frac{0.6}{0.9} Y = \frac{2}{3} Y$$

To completely solve for X and Y, we'll make use of the fact that the sum of the probabilities equals 1. That is

```
X + Y = 1
```

and so

$$X = 1 - Y = \frac{2}{3} Y$$

and therefore

$$X = \frac{2}{5} \qquad Y = \frac{3}{5}$$

so the steady-state matrix is

```
[ 0.4   0.6 ]
```

which is what our trial values were indeed converging to.

4.11 THE ODDS OF BELIEF

So far we have been concerned with probabilities as measures of repeatable events of ideal systems. However, humans are experts at calculating the probabilities of many nonrepeatable events such as medical diagnosis and mineral exploration where each patient and site are unique. In order to make expert systems in areas like this, we must expand the scope of events to deal with propositions, which are statements that are true or false. For example, an event may be

```
"The patient is covered with red spots"
```

and the proposition is

```
"The patient has measles"
```

Given that A is a proposition, the conditional probability

```
P(A | B)
```

is not necessarily a probability in the classical sense if the events and propositions cannot be repeated or have a mathematical basis. Instead, P(A | B) can be interpreted as the **degree of belief** that A is true, given B.

If $P(A \mid B) = 1$, then we believe that A is certainly true. If $P(A \mid B) = 0$, then we believe A is certainly false while other values, $0 < P(A \mid B) < 1$, mean that we are not entirely sure that A is true or false. From statistics, the term **hypothesis** is used for some proposition whose truth or falseness is not known for sure on the basis of some **evidence**. The conditional probability is then referred to as the **likelihood**, as in P(H | E), which expresses the likelihood of a hypothesis, H, based on some evidence, E.

Although P(H | E) has the form of a conditional probability, it actually means something different—the likelihood or degree of belief. Probability refers to repeatable events, while likelihood refers to our degree of belief in non-repeatable events. Since expert systems are models of human experts, P(H | E) is generally the expert's degree of belief that some hypothesis is true given some evidence, E. Of course, if the events are repeatable, then P(H | E) is simply the probability.

If we agree that P(H | E) means the likelihood or degree of belief, then what does a value such as 50% or 95% mean? For example, suppose you are 95% sure that your car will start the next time it's started. One way of interpreting this likelihood is in terms of the **odds** of a bet. The odds on A against B given some event C is

$$\text{odds} = \frac{P(A \mid C)}{P(B \mid C)}$$

If B = A´

$$\text{odds} = \frac{P(A \mid C)}{P(A´ \mid C)} = \frac{P(A \mid C)}{1 - P(A \mid C)}$$

defining

$$P = P(A \mid C)$$

gives

$$odds = \frac{P}{1 - P} \quad \text{and} \quad P = \frac{odds}{1 + odds}$$

In terms of gambling odds, we can interpret P as wins and 1 - P as losses, so

$$odds = \frac{wins}{losses}$$

Knowing the odds allows the probability or likelihood to be calculated and vice versa.

The likelihood of P = 95% is thus equivalent to

$$odds = \frac{.95}{1 - .95} = 19 \text{ to } 1$$

that you believe the car will start. That is, you should be **indifferent** to a bet of odds at 19 to 1 that the car will start. If someone offers a $1 bet that the car won't start, you will pay $19 if it doesn't start. Whenever a degree of belief is stated as a probability, you can interpret it in terms of a bet at equivalent odds. In other words, you should be indifferent to the real situation with its degree of belief or the equivalent odds of a bet.

Probabilities are generally used with deductive problems in which a number of different events, E_i, may occur given the same hypothesis. For example, given that a die rolls an even number, there are three possible events

```
P(2 | even)
P(4 | even)
P(6 | even)
```

In probability, we are generally interested in $P(E_i \mid H)$ where E_i are the possible events from a common hypothesis. In statistics and inductive reasoning, we know the event that has occurred and want to find the likelihood of the hypothesis that can cause E, which is $P(E \mid H_i)$. Probability is naturally forward chaining or deductive while likelihood is backward chaining and inductive. Although we use the same symbolism, $P(X \mid Y)$, for probability and likelihood, the applications are different. Normally we refer to the likelihood of a hypothesis or the probability of an event.

One theory that has been developed using degrees of belief is **personal probability** (Savage 54). In personal probability, **states** are the possible hypotheses and the **consequences** are the results of actions based on the beliefs.

4.12   SUFFICIENCY AND NECESSITY

Bayes' Theorem is

$$(1) \quad P(H \mid E) = \frac{P(E \mid H) \, P(H)}{P(E)}$$

and for the negation of H becomes

$$(2) \quad P(H' \mid E) = \frac{P(E \mid H') \, P(H')}{P(E)}$$

Dividing (1) by (2) gives

$$(3) \quad \frac{P(H \mid E)}{P(H' \mid E)} = \frac{P(E \mid H) \, P(H)}{P(E \mid H') \, P(H')}$$

Defining the prior odds on H as

$$O(H) = \frac{P(H)}{P(H')}$$

and the posterior odds as

$$O(H \mid E) = \frac{P(H \mid E)}{P(H' \mid E)}$$

and finally defining the **likelihood ratio**

$$(4) \quad LS = \frac{P(E \mid H)}{P(E \mid H')}$$

then (3) becomes

$$(5) \quad O(H \mid E) = LS \; O(H)$$

Equation (5) is known as the **odds-likelihood form** of Bayes' Theorem. It is a more convenient form of Bayes' Theorem to work with than equation (1).

The factor LS is also called the **likelihood of sufficiency** because if $LS = \infty$, then the evidence E is logically sufficient for concluding that H is true. If E is logically sufficient for concluding H, then $P(H \mid E) = 1$ and $P(H \mid E') = 0$. Equation (5) can be used to solve for LS as follows.

$$(6) \quad LS = \frac{O(H \mid E)}{O(H)} = \frac{\dfrac{P(H \mid E)}{P(H' \mid E)}}{\dfrac{P(H)}{P(H')}}$$

Now P(H) / P(H') is some constant, C, and so equation (6) becomes

$$LS = \frac{\dfrac{1}{0}}{C} = \infty$$

Equation (4) also shows in this case that H is sufficient for E. Table 4-10 summarizes the meaning of other values of LS.

The likelihood of necessity, LN, is defined similarly to LS as

$$(7) \quad LN = \frac{O(H \mid E')}{O(H)} = \frac{P(E' \mid H)}{P(E' \mid H')} = \frac{\dfrac{P(H \mid E')}{P(H' \mid E')}}{\dfrac{P(H)}{P(H')}}$$

and

$$(8) \quad O(H \mid E') = LN \; O(H)$$

If LN = 0, then P(H | E') = 0. This means that H must be false when E' is true. In other words if E is not present, then H is false, which means that E is necessary for H.

LS	Effect on Hypothesis
0	H is false when E is true or E' is necessary for concluding H
small $(0 < LS \ll 1)$	E is unfavorable for concluding H
1	E has no effect on belief of H
large $(1 \ll LS)$	E is favorable for concluding H
∞	E is logically sufficient for H or Observing E means H must be true

Table 4-10
Relationship Between Likelihood Ratio, Hypothesis, and Evidence

LN	Effect on Hypothesis
0	H is false when E is absent or E is necessary for H
small (0 < LN << 1)	Absence of E is unfavorable for concluding H
1	Absence of E has no effect on H
large (1 << LN)	Absence of E is favorable for H
∞	Absence of E is logically sufficient for H

Table 4-11
Relationship Between Likelihood of Necessity, Hypothesis, and Evidence

Table 4-11 shows the relationship between LN, E, and H. Notice that it is the same as Table 4-10 with "evidence" replaced by "absence of evidence."

The likelihood values LS and LN must be provided by a human expert in order to compute the posterior odds. The form of equations (5) and (8) is simple for people to understand. The LS factor shows how much the prior odds are changed when the evidence is present. The LN factor shows how much the prior odds are changed when the evidence is absent. These forms make it easier for a human expert to then specify the LS and LN factors.

As an example, in the PROSPECTOR expert system, there is a rule which specifies how evidence of a certain mineral supports a hypothesis.

```
IF there are quartz-sulfide veinlets
THEN there is a favorable alteration
     for the potassic zone
```

This particular intermediate hypothesis provides support for other hypotheses leading to the top-level hypothesis that copper is present. The LS and LN values for this rule are

```
LS = 300
LN = 0.2
```

which means that observation of quartz-sulfide veinlets is very favorable while not observing the veinlets is mildly unfavorable. If LN were << 1, then the absence of quartz-sulfide veinlets would strongly suggest the hypothesis is false. An example is the rule

```
IF glassy limonite
THEN best mineralization favorability
```

with

```
LS = 1000000
LN = 0.01
```

4.13 UNCERTAINTY IN INFERENCE CHAINS

Uncertainty may be present in rules, evidence used by the rules, or both. In this section, you will see some real-world problems of uncertainty and how probability provides an answer.

Expert Inconsistency

From equation (4) of the preceding section,

```
if LS > 1 then P(E | H') < P(E | H)
```

Subtracting each side from 1 reverses the inequality

```
1 - P(E | H') > 1 - P(E | H)
```

Since $P(E' \mid H) = 1 - P(E \mid H)$, and $P(E' \mid H') = 1 - P(E \mid H')$, then (7) becomes

$$LN = \frac{1 - P(E \mid H)}{1 - P(E \mid H')} < 1$$

The constraints on the values of LS and LN are summarized as the following.

```
Case 1: LS > 1 and LN < 1
```

From equations (4) and (7), the other cases are

```
Case 2: LS < 1 and LN > 1
```

```
Case 3: LS = LN = 1
```

Although these three cases are mathematically rigorous constraints on the values of LS and LN, they don't always work out in the real world. For the expert system PROSPECTOR used for mineral exploration, it was not uncommon for experts to specify an LS > 1 and LN = 1, which is not one of these three cases. That is, the expert is saying that the observation of evidence is important but the absence of the evidence is unimportant.

This last case shows that the likelihood theory based on Bayesian probability theory is incomplete for the mineral exploration problem. That is, the Bayesian likelihood theory is only an approximation to a theory that can also deal with the case that LS > 1 and LN = 1. For domains in which expert's opinions satisfy one of the first three cases, the Bayesian likelihood theory is satisfactory.

Uncertain Evidence

In the real world we are seldom absolutely sure of anything except death and taxes. Although so far we have concentrated on uncertain hypotheses, the more general and realistic situation is uncertain hypotheses *and* uncertain evidence.

For the general case, assume that the degree of belief in the **complete evidence**, E, is dependent on the **partial evidence**, e, by

```
P (E | e)
```

The complete evidence is the total evidence which represents all possible evidence and hypotheses which comprises E. The partial evidence, e, is the portion of E that we know. If we do know all the evidence, then E = e and

```
P (E | e) = P (E)
```

where P(E) is the prior likelihood of the evidence E. The likelihood P(E | e) is our belief in E given our imperfect knowledge, e, of the complete evidence E.

As an example, suppose that people in your neighborhood who started drilling for oil in their kitchens have become rich. You may consider a hypothesis and evidence

```
H = I'm going to get rich
E = there is oil under my kitchen
```

as expressed in the rule

```
IF there is oil under my kitchen
THEN I'm going to get rich              P (H | E) = 1
```

At this initial stage, you do not know for certain that there is oil under your kitchen. Conclusive evidence would be drilling a test well, but this is rather expensive. So you consider the partial evidence, e, in support of E as follows.

- Other people in the neighborhood have struck it rich.
- There is some black substance always seeping up around the kitchen stove (which your spouse has blamed on your cooking and cleaning until now).
- A stranger came to the door and offered $20,000,000 for your house because she said that she liked the view.

Based on this partial evidence, you may decide that the likelihood of oil under your kitchen is rather high, $P(E \mid e) = 0.98$.

In a probabilistic or likelihood type of inference chain, if H depends on E and E is based on some partial evidence e, then $P(H \mid e)$ is the likelihood that H depends on e. By the rule for conditional probability

$$P(H \mid e) = \frac{P(H \cap e)}{P(e)}$$

Figure 4-15 illustrates how H can be considered to be made up of E and e. So the above becomes

$$P(H \mid e) = \frac{P(H \cap E \cap e) + P(H \cap E' \cap e)}{P(e)}$$

Using the rule of conditional probability gives

$$P(H \mid e) = \frac{P(H \cap E \mid e) \, P(e) + P(H \cap E' \mid e) \, P(e)}{P(e)}$$

$$(1) \quad P(H \mid e) = P(H \cap E \mid e) + P(H \cap E' \mid e)$$

Another way of expressing (1) follows since

$$P(H \cap E \mid e) = \frac{P(H \cap E \cap e)}{P(e)}$$

$$(2) \quad P(H \cap E \mid e) = \frac{P(H \mid E \cap e) \, P(E \cap e)}{P(e)}$$

and since

$$P(E \mid e) = \frac{P(E \cap e)}{P(e)}$$

then (2) becomes

$$P(H \cap E \mid e) = P(H \mid E \cap e) \, P(E \mid e)$$

Likewise

$$P(H \cap E' \mid e) = P(H \mid E' \cap e) \, P(E' \mid e)$$

and (1) becomes

$$(3) \quad P(H \mid e) = P(H \mid E \cap e) \ P(E \mid e) \ +$$
$$P(H \mid E' \cap e) \ P(E' \mid e)$$

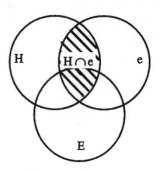

$$H \cap e = H \cap E \cap e + H \cap E' \cap e$$

Figure 4-15
The Intersection of H and e

Normally, we do not know the probabilities $P(H \mid E \cap e)$ and $P(H \mid E' \cap e)$. However, if we assume these can be approximated by $P(H \mid E)$ and $P(H \mid E')$, then (3) simplifies to

$$(4) \quad P(H \mid e) = P(H \mid E) \ P(E \mid e)$$
$$+ \ P(H \mid E') \ P(E' \mid e)$$

Equation (4) is essentially a linear interpolation of $P(H \mid e)$ vs. $P(E \mid e)$. The endpoints are

$$(i) \quad E \text{ is true and so } P(H \mid e) = P(H \mid E).$$
$$(ii) \quad E \text{ is false and so } P(H \mid e) = P(H \mid E').$$

The problem with equation (4) shows up when $P(E \mid e)$ equals the prior probability $P(E)$. If the system obeys pure Bayesian probability, then

$$(5) \quad P(H \mid e) = P(H \mid E) \ P(E) \ + \ P(H \mid E') \ P(E')$$
$$(6) \quad P(H \mid e) = P(H)$$

which is correct.

However, in the real world, experience has shown that human experts give subjective probabilities that are almost certain to be inconsistent. For example, if the expert uses the inconsistent case of LS > 1 and LN = 1, then

$$O(H \mid E') = LN \ O(H) = O(H)$$

and since

$$O = \frac{P}{1 - P}$$

then

(7) $P(H \mid E') = P(H)$

Using (7) in (5) gives

$P(H \mid e) = P(H \mid E) \ P(E) + P(H) \ P(E')$

$= P(H \mid E) \ P(E) + P(H) \ (1 - P(E))$

(8) $P(H \mid e) = P(H) + P(H \mid E) \ P(E) - P(H) \ P(E)$

Now

$O(H \mid E) = LS \ O(H)$

If LS = 1 then

$O(H \mid E) = O(H)$
$P(H \mid E) = P(H)$

Since the human expert has specified LS > 1, then P(H | E) > P(H) and so the term

$P(H \mid E) \ P(E) - P(H) \ P(E)$

in equation (8) will be > 0, where 0 is the lower bound when LS = 1. Hence from (8)

$P(H \mid e) > P(H)$

when LS > 1 and LN = 1

This contradicts the fact that P(H | e) should equal P(H) when P(E | e) = P(E). Since P(H | e) > P(H), the probability is greater than it should be and may become magnified further as the inference from one rule is used by another in an inference chain.

Correcting Uncertainty

One way of correcting this problem is to assume that P(H | e) is a piecewise linear function (Duda 76). This is an *ad hoc* assumption that worked well with PROSPECTOR but is not based on traditional probability theory. The function is chosen linear for simplicity in calculations.

The function matches the constraints at the three circled points in Figure 4-16. The formula for P(H | e) is calculated using linear interpolation as follows.

$$
P(H \mid e) =
\begin{cases}
P(H \mid E') + \dfrac{P(H) - P(H \mid E')}{P(E)} \; P(E \mid e) \\[4pt]
\qquad \text{for } 0 \le P(E \mid e) < P(E) \\[10pt]
P(H) + \dfrac{P(H \mid E) - P(H)}{1 - P(E)} \; [P(E \mid e) - P(E)] \\[4pt]
\qquad \text{for } P(E) \le P(E \mid e) \le 1
\end{cases}
$$

Using this formula, the inconsistent case discussed before of LS > 1 and LN = 1, can be satisfied. Now the value of P(H | e) remains the same if P(E | e) < P(E), and increases if P(E | e) ≥ P(E). The reason for choosing this piecewise rather than a single straight line, is to ensure that when P(E | e) = P(E), then P(H | e) = P(H).

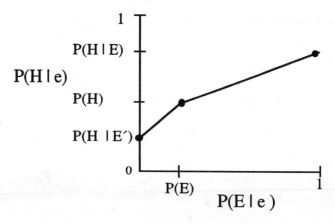

Figure 4-16
Piecewise Linear Interpolation Function for Partial Evidence in PROSPECTOR

4.14 THE COMBINATION OF EVIDENCE

The simplest type of rule is of the form

```
IF E THEN H
```

where E is a single piece of known evidence from which we can conclude that H is true. Unfortunately, not all rules may be this simple so compensation for uncertainty is necessary.

Classifications of Uncertain Evidence

More complex situations arise if there is uncertainty about the rule. This uncertainty can be expressed as a probability or likelihood depending on whether we are dealing with reproducible events or subjective probabilities. For simplicity, we'll use the term probability for uncertainties.

The different situations can be classified on whether the evidence is certain or uncertain and whether there is **simple evidence** or **compound evidence**. Simple evidence consists of a single piece of evidence such as

```
IF the transmission is bad
THEN repair the car
```

while compound evidence consists of multiple pieces of evidence usually linked by AND connections, as in

```
IF the transmission is bad AND
   the carburetor is bad
THEN sell the car
```

or expressed formally

```
IF E₁ and E₂ then H
```

We may assign a probability to this rule such as $P(H \mid E_1 \cap E_2) = 0.80$ which means we are 80% sure the car should be sold on the basis of this evidence.

A further refinement of the evidence is determining its probability. For example, the probability of the transmission being bad may depend on two symptoms.

(a) Transmission fluid is leaking
(b) The car won't go into reverse

These observations lead to a probability of the transmission evidence. For example, on the basis of symptoms (a) and (b), we may decide

```
P(E | e) = 0.95

where E = transmission is bad
      e = symptoms (a) and (b) above
```

Now let's examine in more detail the probabilities associated with the different situations.

Situation 1: One piece of known evidence concludes H

This is the simplest case with rules of the form

```
IF E THEN H
```

Before any evidence is known, the prior probability of H is P(H). After the evidence is known the probability of H changes by Bayes' Theorem

$$P(H \mid E) = \frac{P(H \cap E)}{P(E)} = \frac{P(H \cap E)}{P(E \cap H) + P(E \cap H')}$$

$$P(H \mid E) = \frac{P(H \mid E) \; P(H)}{P(E \mid H) \; P(H) + P(E \mid H') \; P(H')}$$

where P(E) is the probability of observing E.

Situation 2: Two pieces of known evidence conclude H

This is a more complex case than situation 1 and corresponds to rules of the form

```
IF E₁ and E₂ then H
```

After E_1 and E_2 are observed, the probability of H change from the prior P(H) to

$$P(H \mid E_1 \cap E_2) = \frac{P(H \cap E_1 \cap E_2)}{P(E_1 \cap E_2)}$$

$$= \frac{P(H \cap E_1 \cap E_2)}{P(E_1 \cap E_2 \cap H) + P(E_1 \cap E_2 \cap H')}$$

(1) $P(H \mid E_1 \cap E_2)$

$$= \frac{P(E_1 \cap E_2 \mid H)}{P(E_1 \cap E_2 \mid H) \; P(H) + P(E_1 \cap E_2 \mid H') \; P(H')}$$

This formula cannot be reduced further unless a simplifying assumption is made. If the evidence E_1 and E_2 are assumed conditionally independent of each other, then

```
P(E₁ ∩ E₂ | H)  = P(E₁ | H) P(E₂ | H)
P(E₁ ∩ E₂ | H´) = P(E₁ | H´) P(E₂ | H´)
```

and so (see problem 4-12 for conditional independence)

```
(2) P(H | E₁ ∩ E₂)
```

$$= \frac{P(E_1 \mid H) \; P(E_2 \mid H)}{P(E_1 \mid H) \; P(E_2 \mid H) + O(H´) \; P(E_1 \mid H´) \; P(E_2 \mid H´)}$$

Equation (2) is a major simplification of equation (1) since the probabilities are now all expressed in terms of the individual probabilities rather than the joint ones such as $P(E_1 \cap E_2 | H´)$. There are problems with this assumption of conditional independence that will be discussed later.

While (2) is a simplification, it still does require knowledge of the prior probabilities $P(E_1)$ and $P(E_2)$. It's usually difficult for experts to state prior probabilities because they don't reason that way. For example, if a person goes to see a doctor, the doctor does not assume that the person has a cold *a priori*, because that is the most common disease and so its probability is highest.

The major problem in assigning prior probabilities is the difficulty of determining them for likelihoods. For probabilities involving reproducible events such as throwing dice, it's easy to acquire the probabilities by empirical or theoretical studies. However, when dealing with events such as finding a major mineral deposit, it's impossible to determine the prior likelihoods exactly. For example, what's the prior likelihood that your house sits on land with a major gold deposit under it? Is it 0.0000001, 0.00000001, or some other number? These are unique situations in which the prior probabilities cannot be determined.

Situation 3: N pieces of uncertain evidence conclude H

This is the general case of uncertainty in the evidence and in the rule which depends on the evidence. As the number of pieces of evidence increases, it becomes impossible to determine all the joint and prior probabilities or likelihoods. Different approximations have been used to account for the general case of N pieces of evidence.

Combining Evidence by Fuzzy Logic

Conjunction of Evidence

Suppose a rule

```
IF E THEN H
```

has E as the conjunction of evidence, as in

```
IF E₁ AND E₂ AND ... Eₙ THEN H
```

All the E_i must be true with some probability for the antecedent to be true. In the general case, each piece of evidence is based on partial evidence e. The probability of the evidence is

$$P(E \mid e) = P(E_1 \cap E_2 \cap \ldots E_N \mid e)$$

$$= \frac{P(E_1 \cap E_2 \cap \ldots E_N \cap e)}{P(e)}$$

If the evidence, E_i, are all conditionally independent, then the joint probability becomes the product of the individual probabilities. This follows from the Generalized Multiplicative Law. As an example, for two pieces of evidence

$$P(E_1 \cap E_2 \mid e) = \frac{P(E_1 \cap E_2 \cap e)}{P(e)}$$

$$= \frac{P(E_2 \mid E_1 \cap e) \; P(E_1 \mid e) \; P(e)}{P(e)}$$

Using the assumption of independence,

$$P(E_2 \mid e) = P(E_2 \mid E_1 \cap e)$$

because the evidence E_1 does not contribute any knowledge toward E_2. So

$$P(E_2 \cap E_1 \mid e) = P(E_2 \mid e) \; P(E_1 \mid e)$$

and in general

$$P(E_1 \cap E_2 \cap \ldots E_N \mid e) = \prod_{i=1}^{N} P(E_i \mid e)$$

Although this formula is correct in a theoretical sense, there are two difficulties in applying it to real-world problems. First, the individual $P(E_i \mid e)$ are usually not independent in the real world. Second, the multiplication of many factors leads to a product that is generally far too small for $P(E \mid e)$.

An approximate solution to this problem is use of **fuzzy logic** to calculate $P(E \mid e)$ as follows.

```
P(E | e) = min [P(Ei | e)]
```

where the **min function** returns the minimum value of all the $P(E_i \mid e)$. In the PROSPECTOR system, this formula was satisfactory. Once $P(E \mid e)$ is determined, it can be used with the piecewise linear formula for $P(H \mid e)$.

The main problem with the fuzzy logic formula is that it makes $P(E \mid e)$ insensitive to any $P(E_i \mid e)$ except the minimum. This means that even if all the other probabilities increase and the minimum remains the same, no change in $P(E \mid e)$ will be effected. That is, the minimum $P(E_i \mid e)$ blocks other probability changes from propagating through the inference chain. An advantage of the fuzzy logic formula is that it is computationally simple.

Disjunction Of Evidence

If the rule is a disjunction of evidence

```
IF E₁ OR E₂ OR ... Eɴ THEN H
```

then it can be shown (see Problem 4-13) that assuming independence of the evidence gives

$$P(E \mid e) = 1 - \prod_{i=1}^{N} [1 - P(E_i \mid e)]$$

The problem with this formula is that the calculated probability is much too high. The formula used by PROSPECTOR as an alternative to this is based on fuzzy logic.

```
P(E | e) = max [P(Ei | e)]
```

where the **max function** returns the maximum $P(E_i \mid e)$.

Logical Combination of Evidence

If the antecedent is a logical combination of evidence, then the fuzzy logic and negation rules can be used to combine evidence. For example,

```
IF E₁ AND (E₂ OR E₃´) THEN H
```

then

```
E = E₁ AND (E₂ OR E₃´)
E = min {P (E₁ | e), max [P (E₂ | e), 1 - P (E₃ | e)]}
```

Although these formulas from fuzzy logic have been successfully used by a number of systems, other functions for combining evidence may be defined. For example, the following is an alternative to the max function of disjunction (Quinlan 86)

$$P (E_1 \cup E_2 \mid H) = min [1, P (E_1 \mid H) + P (E_2 \mid H)]$$

Effective Likelihoods

For the general case, multiple rules with uncertain evidence and inconsistent prior probabilities may conclude a specific hypothesis. Assuming conditional independence of the evidence and all the E_i contributing to H are true, then

$$O (H \mid E_1 \cap E_2 \cap \ldots E_N) = \left[\prod_{i=1}^{N} LS_i \right] O (H)$$

where LS_i is defined as

$$LS_i = \frac{P (E_i \mid H)}{P (E_i \mid H´)}$$

and a similar formula holds if all the evidence contributing to H is false.

$$O (H \mid E_1´ \cap E_2´ \cap \ldots E_N´) = \left[\prod_{i=1}^{N} LN_i \right] O (H)$$

where

$$LN_i = \frac{P (E_i´ \mid H)}{P (E_i´ \mid H´)}$$

In the general case of inconsistent prior probabilities and uncertain evidence, the **effective likelihood ratio**, LE, is defined as

$$LE_i = \frac{O (H \mid e_i)}{O (H)}$$

where e_i is the i'th partial evidence contributing to H. The updating of H based on uncertain and inconsistent evidence is analogous to the previous case

$$O(H \mid e_1 \cap e_2 \cap \ldots e_N) = \left[\prod_{i=1}^{N} LE_i \right] O(H)$$

For an expert system using uncertain evidence and inconsistent prior probabilities, this formula can be used in the following way.

a) Store the prior odds of each rule and the LE from each contribution to the rule.
b) Whenever $P(E_i \mid e_i)$ is updated, compute the new LE_i and posterior odds.

Difficulties with Conditional Independence

Although the assumption of conditional independence is useful in simplifying the Bayes' Theorem, there are a number of problems. The assumption is mainly useful in the initial phases of building up an expert system, when the general behavior of the system is more important than correct numerical results. Initially, a knowledge engineer may be more interested in developing correct inference chains than the correct numbers. That is, in some system, intermediate hypothesis 10 should be activated by evidence 23 and 34. Hypothesis 10 and evidence 8 should then activate hypotheses 52 and 96. Hypothesis 15 should *not* be activated by evidence 23 and 24, and so on.

As shown by equation (2) of this section, under conditional independence only five probabilities are required to compute $P(H \mid E_1 \cap E_2)$. These are

$$P(E_1 \mid H), \ P(E_2 \mid H), \ P(E_1 \mid H'), \ P(E_2 \mid H'), \ P(H)$$

The other probability $P(H')$ needed to compute $O(H')$ is not independent of the others since

$$P(H') = 1 - P(H)$$

Another formula for $P(H \mid E_1 \cap E_2)$ is shown in problem 4-12 (b). This formula involves four other probabilities

$$P(H \mid E_1), \ P(H \mid E_2), \ P(H' \mid E_1), \ P(H' \mid E_2)$$

Thus, there are a total of nine probabilities that can be used to calculate $P(H \mid E_1 \cap E_2)$ but only five are really needed to be specified. Given the five, the other four can be calculated.

This constraint on the number of independent probabilities becomes a real problem as the expert system matures. Once the inference chains function correctly, the knowledge engineer must ensure that the correct numbers are output. Because of the conditional independence assumption, the knowledge engineer does not have complete freedom to tune all nine probabilities by adjusting their values to yield the desired results.

The conditional independence assumption fixes the joint probability $P(E_1 \cap E_2)$ since

$$P(E_1 \cap E_2) =$$

$$P(E_1) P(E_2) \left[\frac{P(H \mid E_1) P(H \mid E_2)}{P(H)} + \frac{P(H' \mid E_1) P(H' \mid E_2)}{P(H')} \right]$$

This means that the prior probabilities $P(E_1)$, $P(E_2)$, and $P(H)$ now constrain $P(E_1 \cap E_2)$. This runs contrary to the knowledge of the human expert who may know $P(E_1)$, $P(E_2)$, and $P(E_1 \cap E_2)$ separately. Conditional independence thus restricts applying all the human expert's knowledge.

Although the assumption of conditional independence appears reasonable, it does depend on the real situation being modeled by the expert system and so may not hold in all cases. One paper went beyond this, and claimed that the conditional independence is usually false (Szolovits 78). Another paper claimed that conditional independence implies strict independence and this proves that the evidence is irrelevant to updating hypotheses (Pednault 81)! However, this claim has been disproved by another paper (Glymour 85).

Another method of applying subjective Bayesian probabilities shows how the assumption of conditional independence can be weakened so that the strict independence is no longer implied (Pearl 82).

4.15   INFERENCE NETS

Up to this point, the examples of forward and backward chaining that you have seen have been very small, consisting of a few rules. For real-world problems, the number of inferences required to support a hypothesis or reach a conclusion are much larger. In addition, many or all of these inferences are made under uncertainty of the evidence and rules themselves. Probabilistic reasoning and Bayes' Theorem have been used successfully in real-world systems such as this.

An inference net is a good architecture for expert systems that rely on a taxonomy of knowledge. A taxonomy is a classification and is commonly used in the natural sciences such as geology and biology. You have already seen a simple taxonomy in the figure classifying the different kinds of blackberries in the Chapter 2 problems.

A taxonomy is useful for two purposes. It helps to organize knowledge about a subject by classifying objects and showing their relationships to other objects. Important features such as inheritance of properties are made clear by taxonomies.

A second reason that taxonomies are useful is that they can guide the search for proof of a hypothesis, such as "there is copper ore at this site." This aids in proving or disproving hypotheses is very important in areas such as mineral exploration since there is rarely any direct evidence of valuable ore at the surface. Before deciding to invest the time and money for drilling, a geologist tries to gather evidence to support this hypothesis.

PROSPECTOR

The classic expert system that uses probabilistic reasoning is PROSPECTOR (Duda 79). PROSPECTOR is designed to aid exploration geologists in determining whether a site is favorable for ore deposits of certain types. The basic idea of PROSPECTOR is to encode the expert economic geologists' knowledge of different ore **models** in the PROSPECTOR expert system. A geologic model is a group of evidence and hypotheses that support a certain type of mineral being present at a site. Besides aiding in identifying minerals, PROSPECTOR could also recommend the best location to drill on the site. As more models are created, the capabilities of PROSPECTOR increase.

The data for each model is organized as an **inference net**. Figure 4-17 summarizes the types of nets discussed so far and shows a very simple inference net in (d). Inference net nodes can represent evidence to support other nodes which represent the hypotheses such as the type of mineral present. In 1983, there were 22 mineral models in PROSPECTOR of which a few are summarized in Table 4-12.

Model Name	Model Description	Number of Nodes	Number Askable	Number of Rules
PCD	Porphyry Copper	200	97	135
RFU	Roll-front Uranium	185	147	169
SPB	Sandstone-hosted Lead	35	21	32

Table 4-12
Some PROSPECTOR Models

In Table 4-12, the number of nodes is the total number in the model. The number of **askable nodes** are those which ask questions of the user to obtain observable evidence. The number of rules in the table are probabilistic inference rules. As you can see, there is much uncertainty in the models, and probability is important in supporting hypotheses.

Inference Networks

Each model for PROSPECTOR is encoded as a network of connections or relations between evidence and hypotheses. Thus, an inference net is a type of semantic net. Observable facts, such as the type of rock formations obtained from field exploration, comprise the evidence to support the intermediate hypotheses. Groups of intermediate hypotheses are used to support the **top-level hypothesis**, which is what we want to prove. If it's not important to distinguish between evidence and hypotheses, the term

assertion is used for either one. A small portion of the inference net for the top-level hypothesis of the porphyry copper model is shown in Figure 4-18.

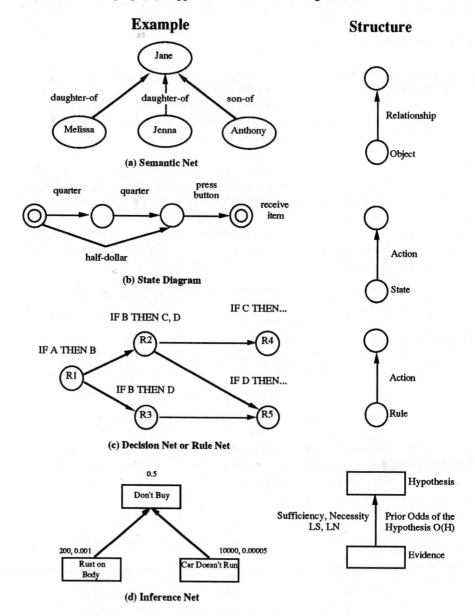

Figure 4-17
Some Types of Networks

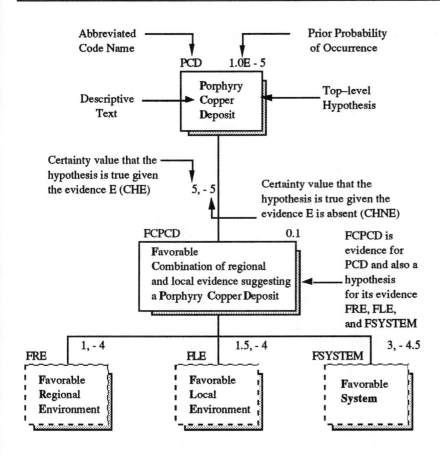

Abbreviated Code Name

Prior Probability of Occurrence

PCD   1.0E - 5

Porphyry Copper Deposit

Descriptive Text

Top–level Hypothesis

Certainty value that the hypothesis is true given the evidence E (CHE)

5, - 5

Certainty value that the hypothesis is true given the evidence E is absent (CHNE)

FCPCD   0.1

Favorable Combination of regional and local evidence suggesting a Porphyry Copper Deposit

FCPCD is evidence for PCD and also a hypothesis for its evidence FRE, FLE, and FSYSTEM

FRE   1, - 4

Favorable Regional Environment

FLE   1.5, - 4

Favorable Local Environment

FSYSTEM   3, - 4.5

Favorable System

Dashed boxes indicate the node contains other nodes (ar is defined elsewhere)

Figure 4-18
The Top-level Porphyry Copper Hypothesis of PROSPECTOR
Expressed Using Certainty Factors

The **certainty factors** CHE and CHNE are used in PROSPECTOR because experience has shown that experts find it difficult to specify posterior probabilities or likelihood ratios. Similar experiences were found in the MYCIN system for diagnosing blood disease, where physicians did not like to specify probabilities, and certainty factors were used. As in MYCIN, certainty factors are ranked on an 11-point scale from -5 to +5 where -5 means "definitely not" and +5 means "definitely yes."

PROSPECTOR is not a pure probabilistic system because it uses fuzzy logic and certainty factors for combining evidence. Certainty factors and fuzzy logic will be discussed in more detail in Chapter 5.

Figure 4-18 shows the FRE node expanded in more detail.

Figure 4-19
A Small Part of the PROSPECTOR Inference Net for Porphyry Copper

This particular diagram has two numbers above nodes which are the likelihood ratio, LS, and necessity measure, LN, separated by commas. For example the LS, LN values for the node labeled RCIB at the left bottom is 20,1. The acronym of each node stands for its description, such as RCIB for "the region contains intrusive breccias." Also shown at the top of each node is the single number of the prior probability, such as 0.001 for RCIB.

Inference Relations

Evidence supporting or disproving a hypothesis is directed up the inference net. For example, RCS, RCAD, RCIB, RCVP, and SMIRA all support or disprove the intermediate hypothesis SMIR. The intermediate hypothesis SMIR is also evidence for its hypothesis HYPE, which is evidence for FLE and so on.

Evidence can be combined in two general ways to yield the relationships desired by the geologist in the definition of the model.

- **logical combinations** such as by AND and OR nodes. As mentioned in the previous section, fuzzy logic can be used to calculate the result at these logical nodes.

- **weighted combinations** using the likelihood ratios, LS, and necessity ratios, LN. The posterior odds are calculated from

$$O(H \mid E) = LS \; O(H)$$

when the evidence E is known true and

$$O(H \mid E) = LN \; O(H)$$

when E is known to be false. If E is not known for certain, then P(H | E) can be calculated by linear interpolation, as discussed in the previous section.

The term weighted combination arises because of the general case in which multiple pieces of evidence contribute to a hypothesis. As shown in the previous section

$$O(H \mid E_1 \cap E_2 \cap \ldots E_N) = \left[\prod_{i=1}^{N} LS_i \right] O(H)$$

The log of this is

$$\log O(H \mid E_1 \cap E_2 \cap \ldots E_N) = \log O(H) + \sum_{i=1}^{N} \log LS_i$$

which can be interpreted as each LS_i casting $\log LS_i$ "votes" for the hypothesis. Each $\log LS_i$ is a weight that affects the hypothesis.

Although PROSPECTOR is sometimes called a rule-based system because weighted combinations correspond to rules such as

```
IF E₁ AND E₂ AND ... Eₙ THEN H
```

it is not as flexible as a true production system based on rules. One limitation is lack of a full mechanism to bind variables. PROSPECTOR is a custom-designed system which emphasizes efficiency and control for geological applications rather than the generality of a production system.

The weighted combinations are also an example of **plausible relations**. The term plausible means that there is some evidence for belief. PROSPECTOR is an example of a system which uses plausible inference for or against a hypothesis. The plausible inferences of PROSPECTOR is based on Bayesian probabilities with the LS and LN values supplied by human experts.

Plausible and other different degrees of belief are illustrated in the fuzzy graph of Figure 4-20. The terms have the following general meanings as shown in Table 4-13.

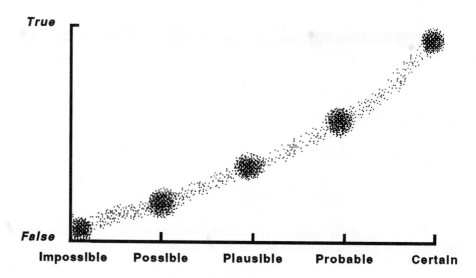

Degrees of Belief

Figure 4-20
Relative Meaning of Some Terms Used to Describe Evidence

Term	Evidence Relative to Hypothesis
impossible	definitely known against
possible	not definitely disproved
plausible	some evidence exists
probable	some evidence for
certain	definitely known supporting

Table 4-13
Some Terms Used With Evidence

The graph of Figure 4-20 is purposely drawn fuzzy to illustrate the vague nature of these terms and the vagueness in progression from one to another. In Figure 4-20, notice how our belief in a hypothesis increases from "impossible" to "certain." A **certain belief** means that the belief is true while an **impossible belief** means that it is false. There is no uncertainty involved with certain and impossible beliefs. These beliefs are equivalent to logical true and logical false. The term **certain evidence** is sometimes used in an ambiguous way. Certain evidence is logically true or false. That is, there is no uncertainty associated with certain evidence. This means that certain evidence corresponds to either certain belief (logically true) or an impossible belief (logically false).

A **possible belief** means that no matter how remote, the hypothesis cannot be ruled out. For example, before scientific analysis of the Moon's surface, it was possible, but very, very, very remote, for the Moon to be made of green cheese. This possibility existed because no definite proof was available.

A **plausible belief** means that more than a possibility exists. The term *plausible* is often used in legal cases to mean reasonable, but without hard evidence to back up the belief. Thus, even before scientific studies, it was not plausible that the moon was made of green cheese.

A **probable belief** means that there is some evidence favoring the hypothesis but not enough to definitely prove it.

Without field evidence, such as observation of RCIB, the relations in Figure 4-19 for a particular site are merely plausible. As evidence accumulates, the plausible relations may become *probable* and then *definite*.

A third type of relation in inference nets is **contexts**, which block the propagation of information until it is appropriate. The use of contexts enables or disables portions of the inference net until certain portions are known present, absent or unknown. One purpose of contexts is to avoid having the system ask the user for questions about some evidence until it is established that the evidence is needed.

The basic idea of contexts is to control the order in which assertions are pursued by the system. Contexts state a required condition that must be proven before an assertion can be used. Contexts are indicated by a dashed arrow with a certainty range under it as in the case of FMGS and PT. The PT node is blocked unless there is evidence with certainty values in the range 0 to +5 that there are fine to medium grain sizes of **porphyritic** rocks. Porphyritic rocks are igneous rocks whose **texture** or appearance consists of small crystals embedded within the rock holding it, the **matrix**. Igneous rocks are those formed by the solidification of molten rock called magma from deep within the earth. Certain types of igneous rocks that extend above ground called **intrusive breccias**, are evidence of mineral formations such as porphyry copper.

Thus, porphyry copper consists of small copper crystals embedded within a rock matrix that holds the crystals. Porphyry copper is the most commonly occurring form of copper. Unless there are at least small crystals present of fine to medium grain size, it's not worth asking about porphyritic texture and so the expert system should be intelligent enough not to ask this question. An expert system that asks unnecessary questions is inefficient and will quickly annoy the user.

The certainty range of 0 to +5 for the context means that the PT node will not be pursued unless the user indicates absence of evidence corresponding to a certainty factor of 0 or some positive amount ranging up to +5 for definitely present.

All three methods of combining or permitting evidence are really relations between nodes. They all specify how a change in the probability of one assertion affects others.

Inference Net Architecture

Formally, an **inference net** can be defined as a directed, acyclic graph in which the nodes are assertions and the arcs are measures of uncertainty such as LS and LN. Figure 4-21 (a), (b), and (c) could be used as valid inference net architectures because they have no cycles. Note that in the inference tree, the arrows point toward the hypothesis in contrast to the arrows pointing away from the root in a data structure tree. As described in Chapter 3, in an acyclic graph, there is no way to return to the starting point by following the arrows. In (d) there is a cycle involving four nodes. The reason for prohibiting cycles is to prevent circular reasoning in establishing a hypothesis. A valid exception in rule-based systems is to establish a loop by having two rules trigger each other until a terminating condition is satisfied.

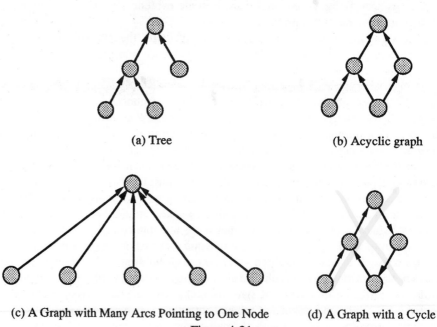

(a) Tree   (b) Acyclic graph

(c) A Graph with Many Arcs Pointing to One Node   (d) A Graph with a Cycle

Figure 4-21

Some Types of Graphs

Figure 4-21 (c) is an undesirable type of graph for an inference net. The problem is that when many pieces of evidence contribute to a single hypothesis, there is a greater chance of undesirable interactions between the evidence. It's generally better to restructure this type into a more tree-like structure with intermediate hypotheses.

The PROSPECTOR inference net is also a **partitioned semantic net** to group portions of the net into meaningful units. Partitioned semantic nets were developed by Hendrix to allow power of predicate calculus such as quantification, implication, negation, disjunction, and conjunction (Hendrix 79). Recall from Chapter 2 that ordinary semantic nets are really designed for expressing descriptive knowledge through relations. While frames are better for causal knowledge, they are difficult to use in expressing logical relationships.

The basic idea of a partitioned semantic net is to group sets of nodes and arcs in abstract **spaces** which define the scope of their relationships. A familiar analogy to a space is the scope of a module or package in a structured language. For example, the Figure 4-18 FRE node can be considered a space with structure shown in Figure 4-19.

The power of semantic nets comes in modeling statements. In fact, Hendrix first developed them for expressing natural language in his Ph.D. dissertation. Statements are like the propositions of evidence and hypotheses that make up the nodes of inference nets. As a simple example of a partitioned semantic net for a statement, consider "there is a computer with a color screen." Notice that this is an existential statement because of the "there is" quantifier.

Figure 4-22 shows the partitioned semantic net expression of this statement using three spaces. SPACE-1 consists of some general related concepts about computers. SPACE-2 consists of the particular computer we are talking about, which has been given the identifier COMPUTER-1. SPACE-3 consists of the specific relation COMPONENTS-OF-1 which has its object the specific COLOR-SCREEN-1 that we are concerned about. Each arc labeled *element* shows that one state is an element of another. The arc labeled *entity* shows which specific computer is the entity with the specific color screen.

The advantage of a partitioned semantic net is shown by a portion of a PROSPECTOR rule for STIR using FMGS evidence as shown in Figure 4-23. The rule can be stated as "If there is an entity named E-1 whose cardinality is ABUNDANT and is composed of INTRUSIVE ROCKS then the consequent is the rule of Suggestive Texture of Igneous Rocks." Note that the diagram has been simplified by not including the requirement that the antecedent also have a fine to medium grain size.

Notice that in Figure 4-23, one partitioned semantic net makes up the antecedent of the rule and one net makes up the consequent. Although the consequent of this rule is trivial, other rules will have a more complex structure (Duda 78). The advantage of the partitioned semantic nets is that the system can infer relationships between nodes that are indirectly linked. Thus the knowledge of the system is deeper than shallow knowledge.

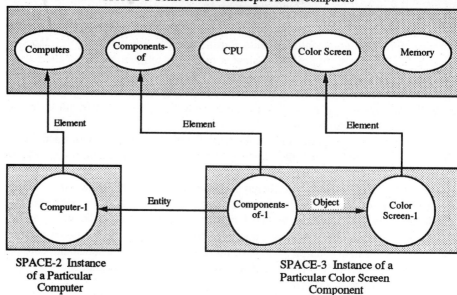

Figure 4-22
A Simple Partitioned Semantic Net About a Computer

4.16 THE PROPAGATION OF PROBABILITIES

Inference nets such as PROSPECTOR have a **static knowledge structure.** That is, the nodes and connections between them are fixed in order to retain the relationships between nodes in the knowledge structure. This contrasts with a rule-based system in which rules whose patterns match facts are put on the agenda, conflict resolution is performed, and then the top priority rule is executed. Thus a common rule-based system is **a dynamic knowledge structure** because there are no fixed connections between rules as there are between nodes in an inference net.

While the structure of an inference net is static, the probabilities associated with each hypothesis node change as evidence is obtained. In fact, this change of probabilities is the *only* thing that does change in an inference net. The basic characteristic of an inference net is the change of probabilities from their prior probabilities to posterior probabilities as evidence is accumulated. This change of probabilities moves upwards to ultimately support or disprove a top-level hypothesis such as the existence of porphyritic copper, PCDA.

Let's examine some of the stages in the propagation of probabilities for PCDA on the basis of some evidence. This will serve as an explicit example of many of the formulas that you have seen. Referring to Figure 4-19, we will follow the propagation of probabilities from the evidence node "the Region Contains Intrusive Breccias," with acronym RCIB.

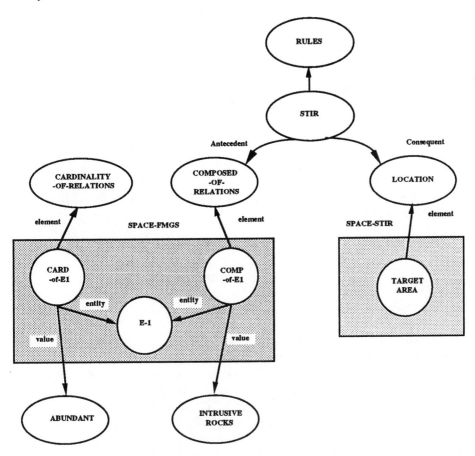

Figure 4-23
Simplified Portion of the PROSPECTOR Partitioned
Semantic Net for the STIR Rule Using FMGS Evidence

If the user says that intrusive breccias are certainly present, then

```
P(E | e) = P(RCIB | e) = 1
```

From Figure 4-19, notice that the LN values for the other evidence of SMIR are all 1. That is, if the user makes no comment about evidence for stocks, dikes and volcanic plugs, these make no contribution to SMIR and so can be ignored in the propagation of probabilities.

The reason all this evidence can be ignored comes from the formula for compound evidence discussed in Section 4.14

$$O(H \mid e) = \left[\prod_{i=1}^{N} L_i \right] O(H)$$

where the $L_i = LS_i$ for all evidence that is known true and $L_i = LN_i$ is used for known false evidence. If there is no evidence known, then $P(E_i \mid e)$ reduces to the prior odds of the evidence, $P(E_i)$ and so $P(H \mid E_i)$ reduces to the prior odds $P(H)$. Thus

$$L_i = \frac{O(H \mid e_i)}{O(H)} = \frac{O(H)}{O(H)} = 1$$

and these L_i make no contribution to $O(H \mid E)$. For example, when only RCIB is known true, the odds of SMIR are

$$O(H \mid E) = LS_{RCVP} \; LS_{RCAD} \; LS_{RCS} \; LS_{SMIRA} \; LS_{RCIB}$$

$$= 1 \cdot 1 \cdot 1 \cdot 1 \cdot 20$$

$$O(SMIR \mid RCIB) = 20$$

Another interesting feature of the SMIR evidence is the OR node called SMIRA. Notice that all the evidence for SMIR also goes to SMIRA. If there is any evidence contributing to SMIR such as RCS, RCAD, RCIB, or RCVP, then the OR node of SMIRA contributes nothing to SMIR since LS for SMIRA is 1. However, if there is no evidence of RCS, RCAD, RCIB, and RCVP, then the LN value of 0.0002 of SMIRA makes the probability of SMIR essentially zero. Basically, this means that while the absence of one or more of the evidences for SMIR is unimportant (LS = 1), the absence of all evidence is very important in ruling out SMIR.

The addition of OR nodes, AND nodes, LS and LN values lets the model designer manipulate the way in which evidence affects a hypothesis. However, in some complex cases, the addition of many OR and AND nodes to suit the evidence requirements will obscure the inference net so that it is difficult for a person to understand. The addition of these extra nodes also requires more testing of the model.

From Figure 4-19, LS = 20 for intrusive breccias, RCIB, and $P(SMIR) = 0.03$. Since

$$odds = O = \frac{P}{1 - P}$$

then the prior odds of SMIR are

$$O(SMIR) = \frac{0.03}{1 - 0.03} = 0.0309$$

If the evidence E is certain, then the posterior odds are

$$O(H \mid E) = LS\ O(H)$$

$$O(SMIR \mid RCIB) = 20 \cdot 0.0309 = 0.618$$

and the posterior probability is calculated from the fundamental odds formula.

$$P = \frac{O}{1 + O}$$

$$P(H \mid E) = \frac{O(H \mid E)}{1 + O(H \mid E)}$$

$$P(H \mid E) = \frac{0.618}{1 + 0.618} = 0.382$$

and so the posterior probability of SMIR given certain evidence of RCIB is

$$P(SMIR \mid RCIB) = 0.382$$

The HYPE prior odds are

$$O(HYPE) = \frac{0.01}{1 - 0.01} = 0.0101$$

At this point it would be tempting to use

$$O(H \mid E) = LS\ O(H)$$

$$O(HYPE \mid SMIR) = LS_{SMIR}\ O(SMIR)$$

$$= 300 \cdot \frac{0.0101}{1 + 0.0101} = 3.00$$

as the odds of HYPE due to SMIR, but it would be wrong. The formula

$$O(H \mid E) = LS\ O(H)$$

is true when the evidence E is certain. This formula expresses the change in the hypothesis' probability assuming that the evidence is certain. However, SMIR is not known for certain. In fact, the probability of SMIR given certain intrusive breccias is

```
P(SMIR | RCIB) = 0.382
```

which means that the likelihood of our belief is 38.2% that SMIR is true.

What we really need is the probability of the HYPE hypothesis based on the uncertain evidence of SMIR which is P(HYPE | RCIB). One way of calculating this uses the formula for P(H | e) discussed in Section 4.14 as

$$
P(H \mid e) = \begin{cases} P(H \mid E') + \dfrac{P(H) - P(H \mid E')}{P(E)} \, P(E \mid e') \\[2pt] \qquad \text{for } 0 \le P(E \mid e) < P(E) \\[10pt] P(H) + \dfrac{P(H \mid E) - P(H)}{1 - P(E)} \, [P(E \mid e) - P(E)] \\[2pt] \qquad \text{for } P(E) \le P(E \mid e) \le 1 \end{cases}
$$

where the uncertainty in the SMIR evidence is

```
P(E | e) = P(SMIR | RCIB) = 0.382
```

and the probability we want is

```
P(H | e) = P(HYPE | SMIR)
```

where all we know is

$$
P(H \mid E) = \frac{O(H \mid E)}{1 + O(H \mid E)} = \frac{3.00}{1 + 3.00} = 0.75
$$

and the prior odds from Figure 4-19 are

```
P(H) = P(HYPE) = 0.01

P(E) = P(SMIR) = 0.03
```

Since P(E | e) > P(E), we will use the formula for P(E) ≤ P(E | e) ≤ 1 to compute P(H | E) as follows.

$$
P(H \mid e) = 0.01 + \frac{(0.75 - 0.01)\ (0.382 - 0.03)}{1 - 0.03}
$$

```
P(HYPE | RCIB) = 0.279
```

which is the posterior probability of HYPE.

This propagation of probabilities continues up the inference net. Now the probability P(HYPE | RCIB) is the uncertain evidence of FLE. The posterior probability P(FLE | RCIB) is calculated using the same formula with values adjusted for FLE.

$$P(E) = P(HYPE) = 0.01$$

$$P(E \mid e) = P(HYPE \mid RCIB) = 0.279$$

$$P(H) = P(FLE) = 0.005$$

$$O(H \mid E) = O(FLE \mid HYPE) = LS_{HYPE} \; O(FLE)$$

$$= 200 \cdot 0.005 = 1$$

$$P(H \mid E) = P(FLE \mid HYPE) = O/(1 + O) = 1/(1 + 1) = 0.5$$

$$P(H \mid e) = P(FLE \mid RCIB)$$

$$= 0.005 + \frac{(0.5 - 0.005) \; (0.279 - 0.01)}{1 - 0.01}$$

$$P(FLE \mid RCIB) = 0.140$$

4.17 SUMMARY

In this chapter we started by discussing the basic concepts of reasoning under uncertainty and the possible types of errors caused by uncertainty. The elements of classical probability theory was reviewed. The differences between classical theory and other theories of probability such as experimental and subjective probabilities was discussed. Methods of combining probabilities and Bayes' Theorem was covered. The relationship of belief to probability and the meaning of likelihood was described. The classic expert system PROSPECTOR was analyzed to illustrate how these concepts of probability were used in a real system. The PROSPECTOR system was also used to introduce inference nets and partitioned semantic nets.

PROBLEMS

4-1.   a)   Using only the three axioms of probability, prove the Additive Law of probability.

$$P(A \cup B) = P(A) + P(B) - P(A \cap B)$$

Hint: Any event $X \cup Y$ can be written in the form $X \cup (X' \cap Y)$ where X and $X' \cap Y$ are mutually exclusive. Also, write B as the union of two mutually exclusive sets.

b) Given two computers which either work correctly or do not, what is the probability using the Additive Law that at least one works correctly.

4-2.   Given events A and B that may overlap, derive the probability in terms of sets using the axioms of probability for

a)   neither A nor B
b)   either A or B, not both (exclusive OR)

4-3. /   Three bins contain some good and defective components as follows

Bin	Good	Bad
1	8	2
2	3	1
3	2	2

Over a long period of time, 20% of components are drawn from bin 1, 30% from bin 2 and 50% from bin 3.

a)   Draw a probability tree.
b)   If a defective part is drawn, what are the probabilities it came out of each bin? Write the probability table showing the outcomes, prior, conditional, joint and posterior probabilities.

4-4   A person is considering the purchase of a disk drive and is trying to decide among three brands. The following table shows the person's preferences and probability of crashes within one year. (preferences are a function of cost, speed, capacity and reliability).

Brand	Probability of Choosing	Probability of a Crash
X	0.3	0.1
Y	0.5	0.3
Z	0.2	0.6

a)   Make up a probability table showing outcomes, prior, conditional, joint and posterior probabilities.
b)   What is the probability of each disk crashing within one year?

c) What is the probability of any drive crashing within one year?
d) For a crash within one year, what is the probability of Brand X, Y or Z?

4-5.   A screening test is a low cost way of checking large groups of people for a disease. A more costly but accurate test shows that 1% of all people have the disease. The screening test indicates the disease (test positive) in 90% of those who have it, and in 20% of those who do not have the disease (false positive).

a) Make a table showing the outcomes, prior, conditional, joint and posterior probabilities.
b) What % of people who test positive don't have the disease (false +).
c) What % of people who test negative do have the disease (false −).

4-6.   To show that pairwise independence does not necessarily mean mutual independence, define the following events for the toss of two dice.

A = even first die
B = even second die
C = even sum

a) Draw the sample space of the two dice. Draw A, B, and A ∩ B.
b) Write the elements of A ∩ B, C, A ∩ C, and B ∩ C.
c) What is P(C)?
d) Show the pairwise independence

```
P (A ∩ B)  =  P (A)  P (B)
P (A ∩ C)  =  P (A)  P (C)
P (B ∩ C)  =  P (B)  P (C)
```

e) Show

$$P (A \cap B \cap C) = P (A \cap B) \neq P (A \cap B) \ P (C)$$

which proves that pairwise independence does not mean mutual independence.

4-7.   For mutually exclusive sets A and B

a) What is P(A ∣ B′) expressed in terms of A and B? (not expressed in terms of A and B′)
b) What is the numeric value of P(A′ ∣ B)?
c) What is the numeric value of P(A ∣ B)?
d) What is P(A′ ∣ B′) expressed in terms of A and B? (not expressed in terms of A′ and B′)

e)   What is

(i) $P(A \mid B) + P(A' \mid B)$
(ii) $P(A \mid B') + P(A' \mid B')$

4-8.   a)   Prove that

$$P(A \cap B \cap C) = P(A \mid B \cap C) \; P(B \mid C) \; P(C).$$

b)   Prove that

$$P(A \cap B \mid C) = P(A \mid B \cap C) \; P(B \mid C).$$

4-9.   A disk drive may malfunction with either fault F_1 or F_2, but not both. The possible symptoms are

```
A = { bad writes, bad reads }

B = { bad reads }
```

and F_2 is three times as likely to occur as F_1. For this type of drive

```
P(A | F₁) = 0.4       P(B | F₁) = 0.6

P(A | F₂) = 0.2       P(B | F₂) = 0.8
```

What are the probabilities of a disk drive with fault F_1? F_2?

4-10.   Given the transition matrix for switching brands of disk drives in a year

Next Year

		X	Y	Z
	X	.5	.5	0
This Year	Y	.25	.5	.25
	Z	0	.5	.5

a)   Assuming that initially 50% of the people use drive X, 25% use drive Y, and 25% use drive Z, what percent will be using each drive in 1, 2, and 3 years?

b)   Determine the steady state matrix.

4-11.　a)　Given N people selected at random, what is the probability that no two have the same birthday?

　b)　What is the probability for 30 people?

4-12.　Under conditional independence of E_1 and E_2, show that for a rule involving the conjunction of known evidence

```
IF  E₁  AND  E₂  THEN  H
```

that

　a)

$$P(H \mid E_1 \cap E_2) =$$

$$\frac{P(E_1 \mid H) \ P(E_2 \mid H)}{P(E_1 \mid H) \ P(E_2 \mid H) + O(H') \ P(E_1 \mid H') \ P(E_2 \mid H')}$$

　b)

$$P(H \mid E_1 \cap E_2) =$$

$$\frac{P(H \mid E_1) \ P(H \mid E_2)}{P(H \mid E_1) \ P(H \mid E_2) + O(H) \ P(H' \mid E_1) \ P(H' \mid E_2)}$$

4-13.　Given a rule with a disjunction of evidence

```
IF  E₁  OR  E₂  OR  ...  Eₙ  THEN  H
```

show that on the basis of probability theory and assuming conditional independence of the evidence

$$P(E \mid e) = 1 - \prod_{i=1}^{N} (1 - P(E_i \mid e))$$

where E is the evidence and e is the relevant observations toward E.

4-14.　Given the following evidence as the antecedent of

```
IF  E  THEN  H
```

write the fuzzy logic expressions for $P(E \mid e)$.

　a)　$E = E_1 \text{ OR } (E_2 \text{ AND } E_3')$
　b)　$E = (E_1 \text{ AND } E_2) \text{ OR } (E_3 \text{ AND } E_4)$
　c)　$E = (E_1' \text{ AND } E_2') \text{ OR } E_3$

d) $E = E_1' \text{ AND } (E_2' \text{ OR } E_3)$

e) $E = E_1' \text{ OR } (E_2 \text{ AND } E_3)$

4-15.   For the inference net of porphyritic copper, assume RCS is known true and RCAD is known false. What is the updated probability of FRE?

BIBLIOGRAPHY

(Allen 81). J. F. Allen, "An Internal-based Representation of Temporal Knowledge," *Proc. 7th IJCAI*, pp. 221-226, 1981.

(Copi 73). Irving M. Copi, *Symbolic Logic*, 4th Ed., Macmillan Pub. Co., pp. 127-128, 1973.

(Duda 76). Richard O. Duda, Peter E. Hart and Nils J. Nilsson, "Subjective Bayesian Methods for Rule-based Inference Systems," *National Computer Conference* (AFIPS Conference Proceedings vol. 45), pp. 1075-1082, 1976.

(Duda 78). Richard O. Duda, et. al. "Semantic Network Representations in Rule-based Inference Systems," in *Pattern-directed Inference Systems*, ed. by D. A. Waterman and Frederick Hayes-Roth, Academic Press, pp. 203-221, 1978.

(Duda 84). Richard O. Duda and Rene´ Reboh, "AI and Decision Making: The PROSPECTOR Experience," *Artificial Intelligence for Business*, ed. Walter Reitman, Ablex Pub. Corp, p. 136, 1984.

(Duda 79). Richard Duda, Hohn Gaschnig and Peter Hart, "Model Design in the PROSPECTOR Consultant System for Mineral Exploration," in *Expert Systems in the Micro-electronic Age*, ed. Donald Michie, Edinburgh University Press, pp. 153-167, 1979.

(Fagan 79). L. M. Fagan, J. C. Kunz, E. A. Feigenbaum and J. J. Osborn, "Representation of Dynamic Clinical Knowledge: Measurement Interpretation in the Intensive Care Unit," *Proc. 6th IJCAI*, pp. 260-262, 1979.

(Farley 83). Arthur M. Farley, "A Probabilistic Model for Uncertain Problem Solving," *IEEE Transactions on Systems, Man, and Cybernetics*, **SMC-13**, (4), pp. 568-579, July/August 1983.

(Glymour 85). Clark Glymour, "Independence Assumptions and Bayesian Updating," *Artificial Intelligence*, **25**, pp. 95-99, 1985.

(Gorry 78). G. A. Gorry, H. Silverman, and S. G. Pauker, "Capturing Clinical Expertise: A Computer Program That Considers Clinical Responses to Digitalis," *Amer. J. Med.*, **64**, pp. 452-460, 1978.

(Hartley 28). R. V. L. Hartley, "Transmission of Information," *The Bell System Technical Journal*, **7**, pp. 535-563, 1928.

(Hendrix 79). Gary Hendrix, "Encoding Knowledge in Partitioned Networks" in *Associative Networks*, ed. by N. Findler, Academic Press, pp. 51-92, 1979.

(Hink 87). Robert F. Hink and David L. Woods, "How Humans Process Uncertain Knowledge: An Introduction for Knowledge Engineers," *AI Magazine*, **8**, (3), pp. 41-53, Fall 1987.

(Jackson 86). Peter Jackson, *Introduction to Expert Systems*, Addison-Wesley, p. 79, 1986.

(Kemeny 59). John G. Kemeny *et al.*, *Finite Mathematical Structures*, Prentice-Hall, p. 399, 1959.

(Lapin 78). Lawrence Lapin, *Statistics for Modern Business Decisions*, 2nd Ed., Harcourt Brace Jovanovich, p. 704, 1978.

(Lindley 65). D. V. Lindley, *Introduction to Probability and Statistics from a Bayesian Viewpoint, Part 1, Probability*, Cambridge University Press, p. xi, 1965.

(Manna and Wolper 84). Z. Manna and P. Wolper, "Synthesis of Communicating Processes from Temporal Logic," *ACM Trans. on Programming Languages and Systems*, **6**, (1), pp. 68-93, 1984.

(McDermott 82). D. McDermott, "A Temporal Logic for Reasoning About Plans and Actions," *Cognitive Science*, **6**, pp. 101-155, 1982.

(Parrat 61). Lyman G. Parratt, *Probability and Experimental Errors in Science*, John Wiley, p. 6, 1986.

(Pearl 82). Judea Pearl, "Reverend Bayes on Inference Engines: A Distributed Hierarchical Approach," *Proceedings AAAI*, **2**, pp. 133-136, 1982.

(Pednault 81). E.D. P. Pednault, S.W. Zucker and L.V. Muresan, "On the Independence Assumption Underlying Subjective Bayesian Inference," *Artificial Intelligence*, **16**, pp. 213-222, 1981.

(Quinlan 86). J. Ross Quinlan, "INFERNO: A Cautious Approach to Uncertain Inference," in *Expert Systems*, ed. Phillip Klahr and Donald Waterman, pp. 350-390, 1986.

(Rauch 84). Herbert E. Rauch, "Probability Concepts for an Expert System Used for Data Fusion," *The AI Magazine*, pp. 55-60, 1984.

(Rescher 64). Nicholas Rescher, *Introduction to Logic*, St. Martin's Press, pp. 258-259, 1964.

(Savage 54). L. J. Savage, *The Foundations of Statistics*, John Wiley, 1954.

(Shafer 76). Glenn Shafer, *A Mathematical Theory of Evidence,* Princeton University Press, p. 10, 1976.

(Shannon 48). Claude Shannon, "The Mathematical Theory of Communication," *The Bell System Technical Journal*, **27**, pp. 379-423; 623-656, 1948.

(Sioshansi 83). F. Perry Sioshansi, "Subjective Evaluation Using Expert Judgement: An Application," *IEEE Transactions on Systems, Man, and Cybernetics*, **SMC-13**, (3), pp. 391-397, May/June 1983.

(Stebbing 50). L.S. Stebbing, *A Modern Introduction to Logic*, Methuen & Co. Ltd., London, 7th Ed., pp. 104-105, 1950.

(Szolovits 78). P. S. Szolovits and S. G. Pauker, "Categorical and Probabilistic Reasoning in Medical Diagnosis," *Artificial Intelligence*, **11**, pp. 115-144, 1978.

(Turner 84). Raymond Turner, *Logics for Artificial Intelligence*, chapter 6, pub. by Ellis Horwood, Ltd., 1984.

(Weiss 78). S. Weiss, C. Kulikowski, S. Amarel, and A. Safir, "A Model-Based Method for Computer-Aided Medical Decision Making," *Artificial Intelligence* **11**, pp. 145-172, 1978.

(Zadeh 65). Lotfi A. Zadeh, "Fuzzy Sets," *Information and Control*, **8**, pp. 338-353. June 1965

CHAPTER 5 INEXACT REASONING

5.1 INTRODUCTION

This chapter continues the discussion of reasoning under uncertainty began in Chapter 4. The main paradigm for reasoning under uncertainty in Chapter 4 was probabilistic reasoning and Bayes' Theorem. In this chapter we shall examine several other approaches to dealing with uncertainty.

Probability theory can be considered as a theory of **reproducible uncertainty**. As described in Chapter 4, probability was originally developed for ideal games of chance in which the same experiment could be reproduced indefinitely. While the subjective probability theory described in Chapter 4 has been successfully used with PROSPECTOR, there are many other applications that are better served by other theories. These alternative theories were specifically developed to deal with human belief rather than the classic frequency interpretation of probability. All these theories are examples of **inexact reasoning** in which the antecedent, the conclusion, and even the meaning of the rule itself is uncertain to some extent.

5.2 UNCERTAINTY AND RULES

This section provides an overview of rules and uncertainty. Later sections will cover specific methods of dealing with uncertainty in rules.

Sources of Uncertainty in Rules

Figure 5-1 illustrates a high-level view of uncertainty in rule-based systems. This uncertainty may come from the individual rules, conflict resolution, and incompatibilities among the consequents of rules. The goal of the knowledge engineer is to minimize or eliminate these uncertainties, if possible.

Minimizing the uncertainties of individual rules is part of the verification of the rule. As mentioned in Section 3.15, verification is concerned with the correctness of the system's building blocks. For a rule-based system, the building blocks are the rules.

Just because the individual rules are correct doesn't mean the system will give a correct answer. Due to incompatibilities among rules, the inference chains may not be correct and so validation is necessary. For a rule-based system, part of validation is minimizing uncertainty in the inference chains. Verification can be viewed as minimizing the local uncertainties while validation minimizes the global uncertainty of the entire expert system. As a rough analogy to civil engineering, verification would ask if a bridge is being built properly in terms of good materials and assembly. Validation would ask if the bridge can handle the required traffic load and most important—is the bridge being built at the right location? Both verification and validation are necessary to insure a quality expert system, as discussed further in Chapter 6.

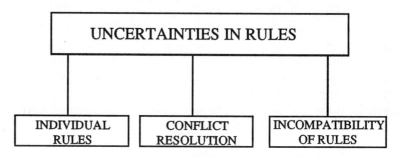

Figure 5-1
Major Uncertainties in a Rule-based Expert System

The top-level view of uncertainties in individual rules of Figure 5-1 is expanded in more detail in Figure 5-2. Besides the possible errors involved in the creation of rules, as described in Section 4.3, there are uncertainties associated with assignment of likelihood values. For probabilistic reasoning as described in Chapter 4, these uncertainties are with the sufficiency, LS, and necessity, LN, values. Since the LS and LN values are based on estimates from humans, there is uncertainty with them. There is also an uncertainty with the likelihood of the consequent. For probabilistic reasoning, this was written as P(H I E) for certain evidence and P(H I e) for uncertain evidence.

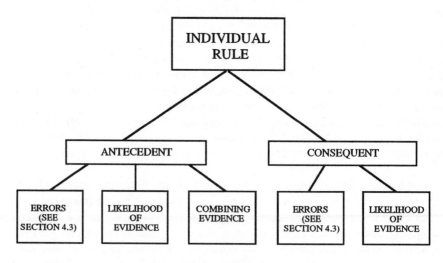

Figure 5-2
Uncertainties in Individual Rules

Another source of uncertainty is the combining of the evidence. Should the evidence be combined

as E_1 AND E_2 AND E_3

or as E_1 AND E_2 OR E_3

or as E_1 AND NOT E_2 OR E_3

or some other possible way of logical combination using AND, OR, and NOT?

Lack of Theory

As mentioned in Chapter 4, the *ad hoc* introduction of formulas such as fuzzy logic to a probabilistic system introduces a problem. The expert system does not then have a sound theoretical foundation based on classical probability, and so represents an *ad hoc* method that works for a limited case. The danger of *ad hoc* methods is that there is no complete theory to guide the application or warn of inappropriate situations.

Another example of an *ad hoc* method that you have seen is the use of LS and LN factors with inference networks. Theoretically, an inference net with N nodes is a probabilistic system with an event space of N possible events. Thus, there are 2^N possible probabilities. In practice for real world situations, few of these probabilities are known. Rather than trying to enumerate all the probabilities, the LS and LN factors are used for significant (we hope) arcs between nodes. Use of LS and LN values for significant arcs greatly reduces the complexity of the net.

However, the LS and LN shortcut also has the detrimental effect that there is no theoretical guarantee that the sum of the conditional probabilities for each hypothesis in the net will be unity. This may not matter much to the user if the goal is simply to obtain a relative ranking of all the hypotheses in the net. For example, the user interested in the porphyry copper hypothesis may well be satisfied to know that the node indicating a favorable likelihood of copper is greatest, even if it is not 1. However, the absolute probability is important also. Even though the copper hypothesis is ranked number 1, is it worth drilling if the probability of finding copper is very low, say 0.00000001?

Rule Interactions

Another source of uncertainty is conflict resolution of uncertainty. If the knowledge engineer specifies the **explicit priority** of rules, there is a potential source of error since the priority may not be optimum or correct. Other problems with conflict resolution occur because of the **implicit priority** of rules.

Conflict resolution is part of a major source of uncertainty caused by the interactions between rules. The interaction of rules depends on conflict resolution, and the

compatibility of rules as shown in Figure 5-3. The compatibility of rules has uncertainty from five major causes.

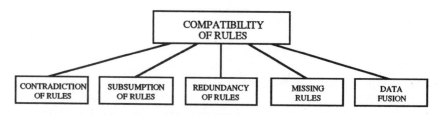

Figure 5-3
Uncertainty Associated with the Compatibilities of Rules

One cause of uncertainty is the potential **contradiction of rules**. Rules may fire with contradictory consequents. This may happen if the antecedents are not specified properly. As a very simple example, assume two rules in the knowledge-base

```
(1)  IF there is a fire THEN put water on it

(2)  IF there is a fire THEN don't put water on it
```

Rule (1) is applicable for ordinary fires such as wood fires. Rule (2) is applicable for oil or grease fires. The problem is that the antecedents are not specified precisely enough for the type of fire. If a fact exists "there is a fire," then both rules will be executed with contradictory consequents and a resulting increase in uncertainty.

A second source of uncertainty is **subsumption of rules**. One rule is subsumed by another if a portion of its antecedent is a subset of another rule. For example, suppose there are two rules that both have the same conclusion.

```
(3)  IF E₁ THEN H

(4)  IF E₁ AND E₂ THEN H
```

If only E_1 is present, then there is no problem since only rule (3) will be activated. However if both E_1 and E_2 exist, then both rules (3) and (4) will be activated and conflict resolution on them is necessary.

Conflict Resolution

There is uncertainty in conflict resolution regarding priority for firing. This uncertainty depends on a number of factors as illustrated in Figure 5-4.

The first factor is the shell or tool used. In OPS5, a rule with more specific patterns has a higher priority. The **specificity** of an OPS5 rule depends on the number of patterns and the internal complexity of each pattern. For example, a pattern

```
(blimp ellipsoidal)
```

is more specific than a pattern

```
(blimp)
```

For our two rules, rule (4) is more specific because it has two patterns in its antecedent and thus has a higher implicit priority. In an OPS5 system, rule (4) is executed first.

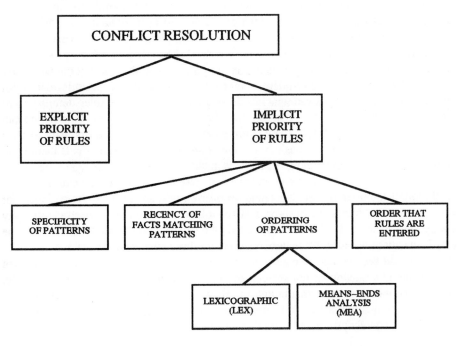

Figure 5-4
Uncertainty Associated with Conflict Resolution

However, there are other complications in OPS5. Besides the specificity, there is also the consideration of **recency of facts**. Whenever a fact is entered in the working memory, it receives a unique **timetag** indicating when it was entered. Thus, a rule with the pattern

```
(5) IF E₃ THEN H
```

would have a higher priority than rule (3) if fact E_3 was entered after E_1.

The ordering of patterns within a rule also makes a difference. OPS5 allows two different **control strategies** called **lexicographic (LEX)** and **means ends**

analysis (MEA). These strategies determine how the inference engine interprets rule patterns. A control strategy is selected by entering a strategy command to the expert system interpreter. Under LEX, pattern order makes no difference, except possibly in efficiency. Thus, the following two rules are essentially the same under LEX.

```
IF E₁ AND E₂ THEN H

IF E₂ AND E₁ THEN H
```

MEA is the strategy used by Newell and Simon's General Problem Solver discussed in Chapter 1. The basic idea of MEA is to keep reducing the difference between starting and success states. In the OPS5 implementation of MEA, the first pattern is very important because it acts to control the pattern matching process. The purpose of MEA is to help the system keep executing a certain task without becoming distracted by very recent facts that have entered working memory. MEA prioritizes rules on the basis of the first pattern which follows the IF. If one of the rules dominates the others on the basis of the first pattern, then that rule is selected. This domination can be by specificity or recency. If there is more than one dominant rule first pattern, then MEA orders the rules on the basis of the remaining patterns. Eventually, if there is no dominant rule, an arbitrary choice of a rule is made.

The order that rules are entered in the expert system may also be a factor in conflict resolution. If the inference engine cannot prioritize rules, an arbitrary choice should be made. However, unless the designers of the inference engine have been careful, the choice may be deterministic in a sense because it depends on the entry of the rule. This may come about because the designers of the inference engine used a stack or queue to store rules on the agenda. For an arbitrary choice of equally prioritized rules, there really should be a random choice from the stack or queue. Instead, the designers may simply take the easy way out and pop the stack or take the next rule from the queue. This selection method is easy but introduces a known artifact into the system because the choice of equally prioritized rules is not arbitrary.

Subsumption and Uncertainty

The problem of subsumption becomes more uncertain if there are likelihoods associated with the rules, as in

```
(6) IF E₁ THEN H with LS₁

(7) IF E₁ AND E₂ THEN H with LS₂
```

For example, consider the following rules.

```
IF the starter motor doesn't work
THEN check the battery with LS₁ = 5
```

```
IF the starter motor doesn't work AND
    the lights don't work
THEN check the battery with LS₂ = 10
```

where LS_2 is greater than LS_1 because of more evidence supporting the conclusion.

From Chapter 4, the posterior odds formula

$$(8) \quad O(H \mid E) = \left[\prod_{i=1}^{N} LS_i \right] O(H)$$

means that the product is $5 \cdot 10 = 50$, if both E_1 and E_2 are observed.

However (8) was really meant to describe rules whose evidence combines independently. The antecedents of (6) and (7) are not really independent because they share evidence E_1 in common. Thus, E_1 AND E_2 subsume E_1 because E_1 alone is a special case of E_1 AND E_2. The product of the likelihood ratios LS_1 and LS_2 is thus erroneously high because the antecedents are not independent. A solution is to replace LS_2 by the ratio LS_2 / LS_1 so that when both E_1 and E_2 exist, the correct product LS_2 is computed. It may be hard to detect subsumption manually in a large knowledge-base.

A third cause of uncertainty is **redundant rules** which have the same consequent and evidence. Generally these are accidentally entered by the knowledge engineer or accidentally occur when a rule is modified by pattern deletion. For example,

```
IF E₁ AND E₂ THEN H

IF E₂ AND E₁ AND E₃ THEN H
```

are redundant rules if E_3 is deleted since the antecedents are the same pattern. Deciding which reduntant rule to delete is not necessarily simple. One redundant rule may lead to greater system efficiency if a rare pattern is listed first. The inference engine may not need to check the second pattern for a match if the first pattern fails to match. A further complication arises in expert system shells such as OPS5, in which the order of activation depends on the user-selected control strategy. Like the case of subsumption, redundant rules also give an erroneously high product of the likelihood ratio.

The fourth cause of uncertainty in rule consequents arises from **missing rules**, which occurs if the human expert forgets or is unaware of a rule such as

```
IF E₄ THEN H
```

If evidence E_4 is ignored, then H is not concluded with the strength it deserves. One advantage of an inference network such as PROSPECTOR is the explicit nature of the network which makes it easy to identify hypotheses that are impossible or difficult to achieve. If there are missing rules, the inference net may imply the need for these rules.

The fifth cause of uncertainty occurs because of problems with **data fusion**. This term refers to the uncertainty associated with fusing data from different types of information. For example, in making a diagnosis, a physician may consider evidence from widely different sources such as a physical exam, lab tests, patient history, socioeconomic environment, mental and emotional states, family and job problems, and so forth. These are all different types of evidence that must be fused to support a final hypothesis. The fusion of this evidence from so many different sources is much more difficult than evidence in one domain such as geology.

Likewise a business decision may depend on the market for goods, economic conditions, foreign trade, takeover attempts, company politics, personal problems, unions, and many other factors. As with the medical problem, it is very difficult to assign likelihood ratios to all these factors and determine a reasonable combining function.

5.3   CERTAINTY FACTORS

Another method of dealing with uncertainty uses **certainty factors**, originally developed for the MYCIN expert system.

Difficulties with the Bayesian Method

Like the geological problem addressed by PROSPECTOR, medical diagnosis is almost always subject to uncertainty. The major difference is that there are a limited number of geologic hypotheses about minerals since there are only 92 natural elements. Possible disease hypotheses are much greater because there are many more micro-organisms.

While Bayes' Theorem is useful in medicine, its accurate use depends on knowing many probabilities. For example, Bayes' Theorem may be used to determine the probability of a specific disease given certain symptoms as

$$P(D_i \mid E) = \frac{P(E \mid D_i)\, P(D_i)}{P(E)} = \frac{P(E \mid D_i)\, P(D_i)}{\sum\limits_{j} P(E \mid D_j)\, P(D_j)}$$

where the sum over j extends to all diseases, and

D_i is the i'th disease,

E is the evidence,

P(E) is the prior probability of the patient having the disease before any evidence is known,

$P(E \mid D_i)$ is the conditional probability that the patient will exhibit evidence E given that disease D_i is present.

It is usually impossible to determine consistent and complete values for all these probabilities for the general population.

In practice, evidence tends to accumulate piece by piece. This accumulation costs considerable time and expense, especially when medical tests are involved. These factors of time, cost and potential risk to the patient of the test usually limit the number of tests performed to a minimum required for a good diagnosis (and malpractice protection).

A convenient form of Bayes' Theorem which expresses the accumulation of incremental evidence like this is (see Problem 5-1)

$$P(D_i \mid E) = \frac{P(E_2 \mid D_i \cap E_1) \; P(D_i \mid E_1)}{\sum_j P(E_2 \mid D_j \cap E_1) \; P(D_j \mid E_1)}$$

where E_2 is the new evidence added to the existing body of evidence, E_1, to yield the new evidence

$$E = E_1 \cap E_2$$

Although this formula is exact, all these probabilities are not generally known. Also, the situation grows much worse as more pieces of evidence accumulate and so more probabilities are required.

Belief and Disbelief

Besides the problem of amassing all the conditional probabilities for the Bayesian method, another major problem that appeared with medical experts was the relationship of belief and disbelief. At first sight, this may appear trivial since obviously disbelief is simply the opposite of belief. In fact, the theory of probability states that

$$P(H) + P(H') = 1$$

and so

$$P(H) = 1 - P(H')$$

For the case of a posterior hypothesis that relies on evidence, E

$$(1) \quad P(H \mid E) = 1 - P(H' \mid E)$$

However, when the MYCIN knowledge engineers began interviewing medical experts, they found that physicians were extremely reluctant to state their knowledge in the form of equation (1).

For example, consider a MYCIN rule such as the following (Shortliffe 85).

```
IF 1) The stain of the organism is gram positive, and
   2) The morphology of the organism is coccus, and
   3) The growth conformation of the organism is
```

```
          chains
     THEN There is suggestive evidence (0.7) that the
          identity of the organism is streptococcus
```

In simple terms, this rule says that if a bacterial organism becomes colored when treated with Gram's stain and resembles chains of spheres, then there is a 70% likelihood that it is a type named streptococcus. This can be written in terms of posterior probability as

$$(2) \quad P(H \mid E_1 \cap E_2 \cap E_3) = 0.7$$

where the E_i correspond to the three patterns of the antecedent.

The MYCIN knowledge engineers found that while an expert would agree to equation (2), they became uneasy and refused to agree with the probabilistic result

$$(3) \quad P(H' \mid E_1 \cap E_2 \cap E_3) = 1 - 0.7 = 0.3$$

This reluctance by the expert to agree to equation (3) illustrates again that these numbers such as 0.7 and 0.3 are likelihoods of belief, not probabilities.

In order to fully appreciate this problem of inconsistent belief and disbelief, consider the following example. Suppose this is your last course required for a degree. Assume your grade-point-average (GPA) has not been too good and you need an 'A' in this course to bring up your GPA. The following formula may express your belief in the likelihood of graduation.

```
     (4) P(graduating | 'A' in this course) = 0.70
```

Notice that this likelihood is not 100%. The reason it's not 100% is that a final audit of your courses and grades must be made by the school. There could be problems due to a number of reasons that would still prevent your graduation such as the following.

1) School catalog changes so that not all your courses counted toward the degree.
2) You forgot to take a required course.
3) Rejection of transfer courses.
4) Rejection of some elective courses you took.
5) Tuition and library fines that you owe and were hoping would be forgotten.
6) Your GPA was lower than you thought and an 'A' still won't raise it up.
7) "They" are out to get you.

Assuming that you agree with (4) (or perhaps your own value for the likelihood) then by equation (1)

```
     (5) P(not graduating | 'A' in this course) = 0.30
```

Although equation (5) is correct from a probabilistic viewpoint, it somehow seems intuitively wrong. It's just not right that if you really work hard and get an 'A' in this course, then there is a 30% chance that you won't graduate. Equation (5) should make you as uneasy as the medical expert who believes

$$P(H \mid E_1 \cap E_2 \cap E_3) = 0.70$$

but won't believe the probabilistic consequence

$$P(H' \mid E_1 \cap E_2 \cap E_3) = 0.30$$

The fundamental problem is that while $P(H \mid E)$ implies a cause and effect relationship between E and H, there may be no cause and effect relationship between E and H'. Yet the equation

$$P(H \mid E) = 1 - P(H' \mid E)$$

implies a cause and effect relationship between E and H' if there is a cause and effect between E and H.

These problems with the theory of probability led Shortliffe to investigate other ways of representing uncertainty. The method that he used with MYCIN was based on **certainty factors** derived from Carnap's theory of confirmation (Carnap 1950). Carnap distinguished two types of probability.

One type of probability is ordinary probability associated with the frequency of reproducible events. The second type is called **epistemic probability** or the **degree of confirmation** because it confirms a hypothesis based on some evidence. This second type is another example of the degree of likelihood of a belief.

Measures of Belief and Disbelief

In MYCIN, the degree of confirmation was originally defined as the certainty factor, which is the difference between belief and disbelief.

$$CF(H,E) = MB(H,E) - MD(H,E)$$

where

CF is the certainty factor in the hypothesis H due to evidence E
MB is the **measure of increased belief** in H due to E
MD is the **measure of increased disbelief** in H due to E

The certainty factor is a way of combining belief and disbelief into a single number.

Combining the measures of belief and disbelief into a single number has two uses. First, the certainty factor can be used to rank hypotheses in order of importance. For example, if a patient has certain symptoms which suggest several possible diseases, then the disease with the highest CF would be the one that is first investigated by ordering tests.

The measures of belief and disbelief were defined in terms of probabilities by

$$
\text{MB(H,E)} = \begin{cases} 1 & \text{if } \text{P(H)} = 1 \\ \dfrac{\max[\text{P(H | E)}, \text{P(H)}] - \text{P(H)}}{\max[1,0] - \text{P(H)}} & \text{otherwise} \end{cases}
$$

$$
\text{MD(H,E)} = \begin{cases} 1 & \text{if } \text{P(H)} = 0 \\ \dfrac{\min[\text{P(H | E)}, \text{P(H)}] - \text{P(H)}}{\min[1,0] - \text{P(H)}} & \text{otherwise} \end{cases}
$$

Now max[1,0] is always 1 and min [1,0] is always 0. The reason for writing 1 and 0 in terms of max and min is to show the formal symmetry between MB and MD. The equations for MB and MD differ only in the replacement of max by min and vice versa.

According to these definitions, some characteristics are shown in Table 5-1.

Characteristics	*Values*
Ranges	$0 \le MB \le 1$ $0 \le MD \le 1$ $-1 \le CF \le 1$
Certain True Hypothesis $P(H \mid E) = 1$	MB $=1$ MD $= 0$ CF $=1$
Certain False Hypothesis $P(H' \mid E) = 1$	MB $= 0$ MD $=1$ CF $= -1$
Lack of Evidence $P(H \mid E) = P(H)$	MB $= 0$ MD $= 0$ CF $= 0$

Table 5-1
Some Characteristics of MB, MD, and CF

The certainty factor, CF, indicates the net belief in a hypothesis based on some evidence. A positive CF means the evidence supports the hypothesis since MB > MD. A CF = 1 means that the evidence definitely proves the hypothesis. A CF = 0 means one of two possibilities. First, a CF = MB - MD = 0 could mean that both MB and

MD are 0. That is, there is no evidence. The second possibility is that MB = MD and both are nonzero. The result is that the belief is cancelled out by the disbelief.

A negative CF means that the evidence favors the negation of the hypothesis since MB < MD. Another way of stating this is that there is more reason to disbelieve a hypothesis than to believe it. For example, a CF = -70% means that the disbelief is 70% greater than the belief. A CF = 70% means that the belief is 70% greater than the disbelief. Notice that with certainty factors, there are no constraints on the individual values of MB and MD. Only the difference is important. For example

```
CF = 0.70 = 0.70 - 0
          = 0.80 - 0.10
```

and so forth.

Certainty factors allow an expert to express a belief without committing a value to the disbelief. As shown in Problem 5-2,

```
CF (H,E) + CF (H´,E) = 0
```

which means that if evidence confirms a hypothesis by some value CF(H | E), the confirmation of the negation of the hypothesis is not 1 - CF(H | E) which would be expected under probability theory. That is,

```
CF (H,E) + CF (H´,E) ≠ 1
```

The fact that CF(H | E) + CF(H´ | E) = 0 means that evidence supporting a hypothesis reduces support to the negation of the hypothesis by an equal amount so that the sum is always 0.

For the example of the student graduating if an 'A' is given in the course

```
CF (H,E) = 0.70      CF (H´,E) = -0.70
```

which means

```
(6) I am 70% certain that I will graduate if I get an
    'A' in this course.

(7) I am -70% certain that I will not graduate if I
    get an 'A' in this course.
```

Notice that the -70% comes about because certainty factors are defined on the interval

```
-1 ≤ CF (H,E) ≤ +1
```

where 0 means no evidence. So certainty values greater than 0 favor the hypothesis while certainty factors less than 0 favor the negation of the hypothesis. Statements (6) and (7) are equivalent using certainty factors analogous to the fact that "yes = not no." The above CF values might be elicited by asking

```
How much do you believe that getting an 'A' will help
you graduate?
```

if the evidence is to confirm the hypothesis or

```
How much do you disbelieve that getting an 'A' will
help you graduate?
```

An answer of 70% to each question will set CF(H I E) = 0.70 and CF(H´ I E) = -0.70. In MYCIN, rather than asking certainties on a percentage scale, the experts were asked to give certainty on a scale of 1 to 10, where 10 was definite. The user could answer UNK for unknown evidence corresponding to CF = 0.

Calculating with Certainty Factors

Although the original definition of CF was

```
CF = MB - MD
```

there were difficulties with this definition because one piece of disconfirming evidence could control the confirmation of many other pieces of evidence. For example, ten pieces of evidence might produce a MB = 0.999 and one disconfirming piece with MD = 0.799 could then give

```
CF = 0.999 - 0.799 = 0.200
```

In MYCIN, a rule's antecedent CF must be > 0.2 for the antecedent to be considered true and activate the rule. This **threshold value** of 0.2 was not done as a fundamental axiom of CF theory, but rather as an *ad hoc* way of minimizing the activation of rules which only weakly suggest a hypothesis. Without a threshold, many rules may be activated of little or no value and greatly reduce the system's efficiency.

The definition of CF was changed in MYCIN in 1977 to be

$$CF = \frac{MB - MD}{1 - \min(MB, MD)}$$

to soften the effects of a single piece of disconfirming evidence on many confirming pieces of evidence. Under this definition with MB = 0.999, MD = 0.799

$$CF = \frac{0.999 - 0.799}{1 - \min(0.999, 0.799)} = \frac{0.200}{1 - 0.799} = 0.995$$

which is very different from the previous definition that gave 0.999 - 0.799 = 0.200 and so did not activate a rule since it was not greater than 0.2. Now the 0.995 will cause the rule to be activated.

The MYCIN methods for combining evidence in the antecedent of a rule are shown in Table 5-2. Notice that these are the same as the PROSPECTOR rules based on fuzzy logic.

Evidence, E	Antecedent Certainty
E_1 AND E_2	$\min[CF(H,E_1), CF(H,E_2)]$
E_1 OR E_2	$\max[CF(H,E_1), CF(H,E_2)]$
NOT E	$- CF(H,E)$

Table 5-2
MYCIN Rules for Combining Antecedent Evidence of Elementary Expressions

For example, given a logical expression for combining evidence such as

$$E = (E_1 \text{ AND } E_2 \text{ AND } E_3) \text{ OR } (E_4 \text{ AND NOT } E_5)$$

the evidence E would be computed as

$$E = \max[\min(E_1, E_2, E_3), \min(E_4, -E_5)]$$

For values

$$E_1 = 0.9 \quad E_2 = 0.8 \quad E_3 = 0.3$$
$$E_4 = -0.5 \quad E_5 = -0.4$$

the result is

$$E = \max[\min(0.9, 0.8, 0.3), \min(-0.5, -(-0.4)]$$
$$= \max[0.3, -0.5]$$
$$= 0.3$$

The fundamental formula for the CF of a rule

$$\text{IF E THEN H}$$

is given by the formula

$$(8) \quad CF(H, e) = CF(E, e) \ CF(H, E)$$

where

CF(E,e) is the certainty factor of the evidence E making up the antecedent of the rule base on uncertain evidence *e*.

CF(H,E) is the certainty factor of the hypothesis assuming that the evidence is known with certainty, when CF(E,e) = 1.

CF(H,e) is the certainty factor of the hypothesis based on uncertain evidence *e*.

Thus, if all the evidence in the antecedent is known with certainty, the formula for the certainty factor of the hypothesis is

$$CF(H, e) = CF(H, E)$$

since CF(E,e) = 1.

As an example of these certainty factors, consider the CF for the streptococcus rule discussed before,

```
IF 1) The stain of the organism is gram positive, and
   2) The morphology of the organism is coccus, and
   3) The growth conformation of the organism is
      chains
THEN There is suggestive evidence (0.7) that the
     identity of the organism is streptococcus
```

where the certainty factor of the hypothesis under certain evidence is

$$CF(H, E) = CF(H, E_1 \cap E_2 \cap E_3) = 0.7$$

and is also called the **attenuation factor**.

The attenuation factor is based on the assumption that all the evidence—E_1, E_2 and E_3—is known with certainty. That is,

$$CF(E_1, e) = CF(E_2, e) = CF(E_3, e) = 1$$

where *e* is the observed evidence that leads to the conclusion that the E_i are known with certainty. These CF values are analogous to the conditional probabilities of the evidence of PROSPECTOR, $P(E \mid e)$. The attenuation factor expresses the degree of certainty of the hypothesis given certain evidence.

Just as with PROSPECTOR, a complication occurs if all the evidence is not known with certainty. With PROSPECTOR, the interpolation formula $P(H \mid e)$ was used for uncertain evidence. In the case of MYCIN, the fundamental formula (8) must be used to determine the resulting CF value since $CF(H, E_1 \cap E_2 \cap E_3) = 0.7$ is no longer valid for uncertain evidence.

For example, assuming

```
CF (E₁, e)  = 0.5
CF (E₂, e)  = 0.6
CF (E₃, e)  = 0.3
```

then

```
CF (E, e)  = CF (E₁ ∩ E₂ ∩ E₃, e)
           = min [CF (E₁, e), CF (E₂, e), CF (E₃, e) ]
           = min [0.5, 0.6, 0.3]
           = 0.3
```

Since the CF of the antecedent, CF(E,e) > 0.2, the antecedent is considered true and so the rule is activated. The certainty factor of the conclusion is

```
CF (H, e)  = CF (E, e)  CF (H, E)
           = 0.3 · 0.7
           = 0.21
```

Suppose another rule also concludes the same hypothesis, but with a different certainty factor. The certainty factors of rules concluding the same hypothesis is calculated from the **combining function** for certainty factors defined as

$$(9) \quad CF_{COMBINE}(CF_1, CF_2) = \begin{cases} CF_1 + CF_2 \ (1 - CF_1) & \text{both} > 0 \\[2mm] \dfrac{CF_1 + CF_2}{1 - \min(|CF_1|, |CF_2|)} & \text{one} < 0 \\[2mm] CF_1 + CF_2 \ (1 + CF_1) & \text{both} < 0 \end{cases}$$

where the formula for $CF_{COMBINE}$ used depends on whether the individual certainty factors are positive or negative. The combining function for more than two certainty factors is applied incrementally. That is, the $CF_{COMBINE}$ is calculated for two CF values, and then the $CF_{COMBINE}$ is combined using formula (9) with the third CF value, and so forth. Figure 5-5 summarizes the calculations with certainty factors for two rules based on uncertain evidence and concluding the same hypothesis. Note that this is *not* an AND/OR tree because $CF_{COMBINE}$ has nothing to do with AND and OR goals.

In our example, if another rule concludes streptococcus with certainty factor $CF_2 = 0.5$, then the combined certainty using the first formula of (9) is

```
CF_COMBINE (0.21, 0.5)  = 0.21 + 0.5 (1 - 0.21) = 0.605
```

Suppose a third rule also has the same conclusion, but with a $CF_3 = -0.4$. Then the second formula of (9) is used to give

$$CF_{COMBINE}(0.605, -0.4) = \frac{0.605 - 0.4}{1 - \min(|0.605|, |-0.4|)}$$

$$= \frac{0.205}{1 - 0.4}$$

$$= 0.34$$

The $CF_{COMBINE}$ formula preserves the commutativity of evidence. That is

$$CF_{COMBINE}(X, Y) = CF_{COMBINE}(Y, X)$$

and so the order in which evidence is received does not affect the result.

Rather than storing separate MB and MD values for each hypothesis, MYCIN stored the current $CF_{COMBINE}$ with each hypothesis and combined it with new evidence as it became available.

$$CF_{COMBINE}(CF_1, CF_2) = \begin{cases} CF_1 + CF_2(1 - CF_1) & \text{both} > 0 \\\\ \dfrac{CF_1 + CF_2}{1 - \min(|CF_1|, |CF_2|)} & \text{one} < 0 \\\\ CF_1 + CF_2(1 + CF_1) & \text{both} < 0 \end{cases}$$

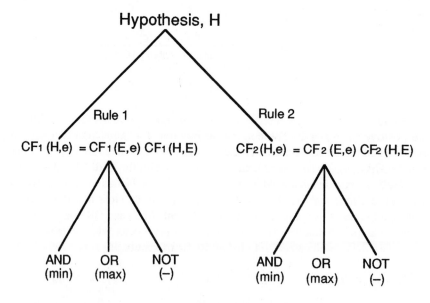

Figure 5-5
Calculating the Combined Certainty Factor of Two Rules
with the Same Hypothesis Based on Uncertain Evidence

Difficulties with Certainty Factors

Although MYCIN was very successful in diagnosis, there were difficulties with the theoretical foundations of certainty factors. While certainty factors had some basis in both probability theory and confirmation theory, the CF were also partly *ad hoc*. The major advantage of CF was the simple computations by which uncertainty could be propagated in the system. The CF were also easy to understand and clearly separated belief from disbelief.

However, there were problems with CF. One problem was that the CF values could be the opposite of conditional probabilities. For example, if

$$P(H_1) \quad = 0.8 \quad P(H_2) \quad = 0.2$$
$$P(H_1 \mid E) = 0.9 \quad P(H_2 \mid E) = 0.8$$

then

$$CF(H_1, E) = 0.5 \text{ and } CF(H_2, E) = 0.75$$

Since one purpose of CF is to rank hypotheses in terms of likely diagnosis, it is a contradiction for a disease to have a higher conditional probability $P(H \mid E)$ and yet have a lower certainty factor, $CF(H,E)$.

The second major problem with CF is that in general

$$P(H \mid e) \neq P(H \mid i) \, P(i \mid e)$$

where *i* is some intermediate hypothesis based on evidence *e*, and yet the certainty factor of two rules in an inference chain is calculated as independent probabilities by

$$CF(H, e) = CF(H, i) \, CF(i, e)$$

The above formula is only true in the special case that the statistical population with property H is contained in the population with property *i*, and that is contained in the population with property *e* (Adams 85). The success of MYCIN in spite of these problems is probably due to the short inference chains and simple hypotheses. There could be real problems in applying certainty factors to other domains that did not have short inference chains and simple hypotheses. In fact, Adams demonstrated that the theory of certainty factors is really an approximation to standard probability theory.

5.4 DEMPSTER-SHAFER THEORY

In this section, we will discuss a method of inexact reasoning called the **Dempster-Shafer theory** or Shafer-Dempster theory. It is based on work done originally by Dempster, who attempted to model uncertainty by a range of probabilities rather than as a single probabilistic number (Dempster 67). Shafer extended and refined Dempster's work in a book published in 1976 called *A Mathematical Theory of Evidence* (Shafer 76). A further extension called **evidential reasoning** deals with information that is expected to be uncertain, imprecise and occasionally inaccurate (Garvey 81) (Lowrance 82). The Dempster-Shafer theory has a good theoretical foundation. Certainty Factors can be shown to be a special case of Dempster-Shafer theory, which puts Certainty Factors on a theoretical rather than an *ad hoc* basis (Gordon 85).

Frames of Discernment

The Dempster-Shafer theory assumes that there is a fixed set of mutually exclusive and exhaustive elements called the **environment** and symbolized by the Greek letter Θ.

$$\Theta = \{\theta_1,\ \theta_2,\ \ldots\theta_N\}$$

The environment is another term for the universe of discourse in set theory. That is, the environment is the set of objects that are of interest to us. Some examples of environments might be

```
Θ = {airliner, bomber, fighter}
Θ = {red, green, blue, orange, yellow}
Θ = {barn, grass, person, cow, car}
```

Notice that the elements are all mutually exclusive. For example, an airliner is not a bomber or a fighter; red is not green; grass is not a cow and so forth. Assume that all possible elements of the universe are in the set and so the set is exhaustive. For simplicity in our discussion, assume also that Θ is a finite set. However, work has been done on Dempster-Shafer environments whose elements are continuous variables such as time, distance, velocity, and so forth (Strat 84).

One way of thinking about Θ is in terms of questions and answers. Suppose

```
Θ = {airliner, bomber, fighter}
```

and the question is, "What are the military aircraft?". The answer is the subset of Θ

```
{θ₂, θ₃} = {bomber, fighter}
```

Likewise, the question, "What are the civilian aircraft?" is the set

```
{θ₁} = {airliner}
```

which is called a **singleton set** because it has only one element.

Each subset of Θ can be interpreted as a possible answer to a question. Since the elements are mutually exclusive and the environment is exhaustive, there can be only one correct answer subset to a question. Of course, not all possible questions may be meaningful nor interesting to ask. However, the important point to realize is that the subsets of the environment are all possible valid answers in this universe of discourse. Each subset can be considered an implied proposition such as

```
The correct answer is {θ₁, θ₂, θ₃}
The correct answer is {θ₁, θ₂}
```

and so on for all subsets, where "The correct answer is," is implied with the subset.

All the possible subsets of the aircraft environment are shown in Figure 5-6, with lines drawn to indicate the relationship of sets. The abbreviations A,B,F are used for airliner, bomber, and fighter. This diagram is drawn as a hierarchical lattice with Θ at the top and the null set $\emptyset = \{\}$ at the bottom. Usually, the null set is not explicitly shown because it always corresponds to the false answer. That is, $\emptyset$ always corresponds to the one proposition

```
The correct answer is none
```

Notice that the figure is a lattice and not a tree because the subset nodes may have more than one parent. The lattice is hierarchical because it is drawn from larger sets to smaller sets. For example, one path from Θ to $\emptyset$ expresses the hierarchical relation of subsets connecting parent to child, such as

```
∅ ⊂ {A} ⊂ {A,B} ⊂ {A,B,F}
```

As discussed in Section 2.10, a relationship between two sets X and Y, such as

```
X ⊆ Y
```

means that all elements of X are elements of Y and is written more formally

```
X ⊆ Y = {x | x ∈ X → x ∈ Y}
```

This states that if x is an element of set X then this implies x is also an element of set Y. If $X \subseteq Y$, but $X \neq Y$, there is at least one element of Y that is not an element of X and X is called a *proper subset* of Y, and is written

```
X ⊂ Y
```

An environment is called a **frame of discernment** when its elements may be interpreted as possible answers, and only one answer is correct. The term *discern* means that it's possible to distinguish the one correct answer from all the other possible answers to a question. If the answer is not in the frame, then the frame must be enlarged to accommodate the additional knowledge of elements θ_{N+1}, θ_{N+2} and so forth. One correct answer requires that the set be exhaustive and that the subsets are disjoint.

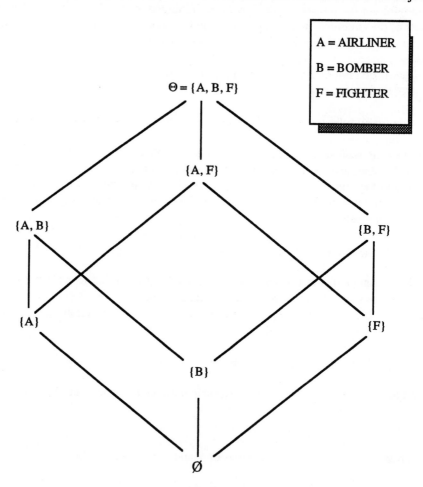

Figure 5-6
All Subsets of the Aircraft Environment

A set of size N has exactly 2^N subsets, including itself, and these subsets define the power set (see Problem 2-11), written as $\mathcal{P}(\Theta)$. Thus, for the aircraft environment

$$\mathcal{P}(\Theta) = \{\emptyset, \{A\}, \{B\}, \{F\}, \{A, B\}, \{A, F\}, \{B, F\}, \{A, B, F\}\}$$

The power set of the frame of discernment has as its elements all answers to the possible questions of the environment. This means there is a one-to-one correspondence between $P(\Theta)$ and the answers to all possible questions of the environment.

Mass Functions and Ignorance

In Bayesian theory, the posterior probability changes as evidence is acquired. Likewise in Dempster-Shafer theory, the belief in evidence may vary. It's customary in Dempster-Shafer theory to think about the *degree of belief in evidence* as analogous to the **mass** of a physical object. That is, the mass of evidence supports a belief. The **evidence measure**, symbolized by the letter m, is analogous to the amount of mass. Another term for mass is the **basic probability assignment (bpa)** or sometimes simply **basic assignment**, because of an analogy in the form of the equations describing probability densities and mass. However, because of potential confusion with probability theory, we shall not use these terms and simply refer to *mass*. The reason for the analogy with an object of mass is to consider belief as a quantity that can move around, be split up, and combined. It may be helpful to think of the object as composed of clay so that pieces of it can be removed and stuck together again.

A fundamental difference between Dempster-Shafer theory and probability theory is the treatment of **ignorance**. As discussed in Chapter 4, probability theory must distribute an equal amount of probability even in ignorance. For example if you have no prior knowledge, then you must assume the probability P of each possibility is

$$P = \frac{1}{N}$$

where N is the number of possibilities. As mentioned in Chapter 4, this assignment of P is made *in desperation*, or using a more impressive-sounding term, by using the **principle of indifference**.

The extreme case of applying the principle of indifference occurs when there are only two possibilities, such as oil or no oil, symbolized by H and H´. In cases like this, P = 50% even when there is no knowledge at all since probability theory says that

$$P(H) + P(H´) = 1$$

That is, anything which does not support *must* refute, since ignorance is not allowed.

This can lead to some ridiculous consequences if applied without thinking. For example, either there is or is not oil under your house. By the principle of indifference, if you have *absolutely no other knowledge*, there is a 50% probability of having oil under your house. If you think about it, a 50% chance of oil is very impressive and offers a better chance at getting rich quick than any legal investment. Since there is a 50% chance of oil, should you immediately withdraw all your savings, hire a drilling rig and start drilling in the kitchen?

Following this same line of reasoning, application of the principle of indifference and probability theory says there is a 50% chance of

```
diamonds
a pirate's treasure
fur coats
green cheese
your next homework assignment
```

and anything else you can think of under your house. (In fact, you can probably become rich by just going on TV and telling everyone how *they* can become rich by sending in $9.95 for your book on probability theory. This is also the best reason for never cleaning. If you don't know what's there, it could be anything and so there's a 50% chance of getting rich by discovering something valuable.)

Even if the principle of indifference is not used, the constraint

```
P(H) + P(H´) = 1
```

forces the assignment of probability to the negation of the hypothesis even if there is no evidence for this. As discussed in Section 5.3, this is not a good assumption with many types of belief such as medical knowledge. However, probability theory requires that evidence which does not support a hypothesis must refute it.

The Dempster-Shafer theory does not force belief to be assigned to ignorance or refutation of a hypothesis. Instead the mass is assigned only to those subsets of the environment to which you wish to assign belief. Any belief that is not assigned to a specific subset is considered **no belief** or **nonbelief** and just associated with the environment Θ. Belief that refutes a hypothesis is disbelief, which is *not* nonbelief.

For example, suppose that a sensor such as an Identification Friend or Foe (IFF) obtains no response from the transponder of an aircraft (Bogler 87). An IFF is a radio transmitter/receiver that transmits a radio message to an aircraft. If the aircraft is friendly, its transponder should respond by sending back its identification code. Aircraft that do not respond are assumed hostile by default. An aircraft may not respond to IFF for a variety of reasons such as

- Malfunction in the IFF
- Malfunction in the aircraft transponder
- No IFF on the aircraft
- Jamming of the IFF signal
- Orders to maintain radio silence

Assume that the failure of IFF to elicit a response indicates a belief in the evidence of 0.7 that the target aircraft is hostile, where hostile aircraft are only considered to be bombers and fighters. Thus, the mass assignment is to the subset {B,F}, and

$$m_1(\{B,F\}) = 0.7$$

where m_1 refers to this first IFF sensor evidence.

The rest of the belief is left with the environment, Θ, as nonbelief.

$$m_1(\Theta) = 1 - 0.7 = 0.3$$

Every set in the power set of the environment which has a mass greater than 0 is a **focal element**. The term *focal element* is used because a set X such that m(X) > 0 is a power set element in which the available evidence is focused or concentrated.

The Dempster-Shafer theory has a major difference with probability theory which would assume that

$$P(hostile) = 0.7$$

$$P(non-hostile) = 1 - 0.7 = 0.3$$

In probability theory, if the belief in hostile is 0.7 then the disbelief in hostile must be 0.3. Instead, the 0.3 in Dempster-Shafer theory is held as nonbelief in the environment by $m(\Theta)$. This means *neither belief nor disbelief* in the evidence to a degree of 0.3. We believe that the target is hostile to a degree of 0.7 and are reserving judgement of 0.3 in disbelief, and the additional belief in hostile. It's very important to realize that the assignment of 0.3 to the environment Θ does not assign *any* value to the proper subsets of Θ even though these subsets include the hostile subsets {B,F}, {B}, and {F}.

Going back to the student example of the last section,

$$m(getting an 'A' and graduating) = 0.7$$

would not automatically mean

$$m(getting an 'A' and not graduating) = 0.3$$

unless both of these were assigned values.

A mass has considerably more freedom than probabilities, as Table 5-3 shows.

Dempster-Shafer Theory	Probability Theory
$m(\Theta)$ does not have to be 1	$\sum_i P_i = 1$
If $X \subseteq Y$, it is not necessary that $m(X) \le m(Y)$	$P(X) \le P(Y)$
No required relationship between $m(X)$ and $m(X')$	$P(X) + P(X') = 1$

Table 5-3
Comparison of Dempster-Shafer Mass with Probability Theory

Every mass can formally be expressed as a function that maps each element of the power set into a real number in the interval 0 to 1. This simply means that the belief in a subset may take any values from 0 to 1. This mapping is formally stated

$$m: \; \mathcal{P}(\Theta) \; \rightarrow \; [0,1]$$

By convention, the mass of the empty set is usually defined as zero.

$$m(\emptyset) \; = \; 0$$

and the sum of all the masses for every subset, X, of the power set is 1.

$$\sum_{X \, \in \, \mathcal{P}(\Theta)} m(X) \; = \; 1$$

For example, in the aircraft environment

$$\sum_{X \, \in \, \mathcal{P}(\Theta)} m(X) \; = \; m(\{B,F\}) \; + \; m(\Theta) = \; 0.7 \; + \; 0.3 \; = \; 1$$

Combining Evidence

Now let's look at the case in which additional evidence becomes available. We would like to combine all the evidence to produce a better estimate of belief in the evidence. To show how this is done, let's first look at an example that is a special case of the general formula for combining evidence.

Suppose that a second type of sensor identifies the target as a bomber with a belief in the evidence of 0.9. The masses of evidence from the sensors are now the following.

$$m_1(\{B,F\}) \; = \; 0.7 \qquad m_1(\Theta) \; = \; 0.3$$

$$m_2(\{B\}) \quad \; = \; 0.9 \qquad m_2(\Theta) \; = \; 0.1$$

where m_1 and m_2 refer to the first and second types of sensors.

This evidence can be combined using the following special form of **Dempster's Rule of Combination**, to yield the **combined mass**,

$$m_1 \; \oplus \; m_2(Z) \; = \; \sum_{X \, \cap \, Y \, = \, Z} m_1(X) \; m_2(Y)$$

where the sum extends over all elements whose intersection $X \cap Y = Z$. The $\oplus$ **operator** denotes the **orthogonal sum** or **direct sum** which is defined by summing the mass product intersections on the right-hand side of the rule. Dempster's rule combines masses to produce a new mass that represents a **consensus** of the original, possibly conflicting evidence. The new mass is a *consensus* because it tends to favor agreement rather than disagreement by only including masses in the set intersections. The set intersections represent common elements of evidence. An important point is that the rule should be used to combine evidence having *independent errors*, which is *not* the same as independently gathered evidence.

Table 5-4 shows the masses and product intersections for the aircraft environment arranged in a table. Each set intersection is followed by its numeric mass product.

	$m_2(\{B\}) = 0.9$	$m_2(\Theta) = 0.1$
$m_1(\{B,F\}) = 0.7$	{B} 0.63	{B,F} 0.07
$m_1(\Theta) = 0.3$	{B} 0.27	Θ 0.03

Table 5-4
Confirming Evidence

The entries in the table are calculated by cross-multiplying mass products of rows and columns as follows, where T_{ij} denotes the i'th row and j'th column of the table.

$T_{11}\ (\{B\})\ =\ m_1\ (\{B,F\})\ m_2\ (\{B\})\ =\ (0.7)\ (0.9)\ =\ 0.63$

$T_{21}\ (\{B\})\ =\ m_1\ (\Theta)\ m_2\ (\{B\})\ =\ (0.3)\ (0.9)\ =\ 0.27$

$T_{12}\ (\{B,F\})\ =\ m_1\ (\{B,F\})\ m_2\ (\Theta)\ =\ (0.7)\ (0.1)\ =\ 0.07$

$T_{22}\ (\Theta)\ =\ m_1\ (\Theta)\ m_2\ (\Theta)\ =\ (0.3)\ (0.1)\ =\ 0.03$

Once the individual mass products have been calculated as shown above, then according to Dempster's Rule the products over the common set intersections are added

$m_3\ (\{B\})\ =\ m_1\ \oplus\ m_2\ (\{B\})\ =\ 0.63\ +\ 0.27\ =\ 0.90$ bomber
$m_3\ (\{B,F\})\ =\ m_1\ \oplus\ m_2\ (\{B,F\})\ =\ 0.07$ bomber or fighter
$m_3\ (\Theta)\ =\ m_1\ \oplus\ m_2\ (\Theta)\ =\ 0.03$ nonbelief

The $m_3(\{B\})$ represents the belief that the target is a bomber and *only* a bomber. However, $m_3(\{B,F\})$ and $m_3(\Theta)$ imply additional information. Since their sets include a bomber, it's plausible that their orthogonal sums may contribute to a belief in the bomber. So their $0.07 + 0.03 = 0.1$ may be added to the belief of 0.90 in the bomber set to yield the maximum belief that it could be a bomber—the plausible belief. Instead of restricting belief to a single value, there is a **range of belief** in the evidence. The belief ranges from a minimum 0.9 that is known for the bomber, to the maximum plausible $0.90 + 0.1 = 1$ that it *might* be a bomber. The true belief is assumed somewhere in the range 0.9 to 1.

In evidential reasoning, the evidence is said to induce an **evidential interval**. The **lower bound** is called the **support (Spt)** in evidential reasoning and **Bel** in Dempster-Shafer theory. The **upper bound** is called the **plausibility (Pls)**. For this example, the evidential interval is [0.90,1], the lower bound is 0.90 and the upper bound is 1. The support is the *minimum belief* based on the evidence, while the plausibility is the *maximum belief* we are willing to give. In general, the ranges of Bel and Pls are $0 \le$ Bel $\le$ Pls ≤ 1. In Dempster-Shafer theory, the lower and upper bounds are sometimes called the lower and upper probabilities, based on Dempster's original paper (Dempster 67). Table 5-5 shows some common evidential intervals (Wesley 86).

Evidential Interval		*Meaning*
[1,1]		Completely true
[0,0]		Completely false
[0,1]		Completely ignorant
[Bel,1]	where 0 < Bel < 1 here	Tends to support
[0,Pls]	where 0 < Pls < 1 here	Tends to refute
[Bel,Pls]	where 0 < Bel $\le$ Pls < 1 here	Tends to both support and refute

Table 5-5
Some Common Evidential Intervals

The support or **belief function, Bel**, is the *total belief* of a set and *all* its subsets. Bel is all the mass that supports a set, and is defined in terms of the mass.

$$\text{Bel}(X) \;=\; \sum_{Y \subseteq X} m(Y)$$

As an example, in the aircraft environment for the first sensor

$$\begin{aligned}
\text{Bel}_1(\{B,F\}) &= m_1(\{B,F\}) + m_1(\{B\}) + m_1(\{F\}) \\
&= 0.7 + 0 + 0 = 0.7
\end{aligned}$$

The Bel function is sometimes called the **belief measure** or simply belief. However, note that the belief function is very different from the mass, which is the belief in the evidence assigned to a *single* set. For example, suppose that you own a Ford and hear that the police are looking for a Ford that was used as the getaway car in a bank robbery. There is a big difference between hearing that the police looking for *a* Ford, and hearing that the police are looking for *your* Ford. Mass is the belief in a set and *not* any of its subsets, while a belief function applies to a set and *all* its subsets. Bel is the *total belief* and so is more global than the *local belief* of mass. Because of the interrelationship of mass and Bel, Dempster-Shafer theory is also called a theory of belief functions. In a general sense, Dempster's rule can then be interpreted as a way of combining belief functions. The mass and belief function are related by

$$m(X) = \sum_{Y \subseteq X} (-1)^{|X - Y|} Bel(Y)$$

where $|X - Y|$ is the **cardinality** of the set,

$$X - Y = \{x \mid x \in X \text{ and } x \notin Y\}$$

That is, $|X - Y|$ is the number of elements in the set $X - Y$.

Since belief functions are defined in terms of masses, the combination of two belief functions also can be expressed in terms of orthogonal sums of the masses of a set and all its subsets. For example,

$$Bel_1 \oplus Bel_2(\{B\}) = m_1 \oplus m_2(\{B\}) + m_1 \oplus m_2(\emptyset)$$
$$= 0.90 + 0 = 0.90$$

Normally, the null set mass is not written since it's usually defined to be zero. The total belief for the bomber-fighter subset {B,F}, has more subsets than the above.

$$Bel_1 \oplus Bel_2(\{B,F\})$$
$$= m_1 \oplus m_2(\{B,F\}) + m_1 \oplus m_2(\{B\}) + m_1 \oplus m_2(\{F\})$$
$$= 0.07 + 0.90 + 0 = 0.97$$

The terms for {B} and {F} are included because they are subsets of {B,F}. From Figure 5-6, you can see that {B,F} has subsets {B} and {F}. Since no mass was given {F}, then $m(\{F\}) = 0$ and so it does not contribute anything to the sum. In fact, $m(\{F\})$ and the other masses of value zero never entered into Table 5-4 at all since the result of any cross products with them would be zero. If masses had been assigned to every subset of {A,B,F} except the null set, which is zero, then Table 5-4 would be a $(2^3 - 1)(2^3 - 1) = 7 \cdot 7 = 49$-cell table.

The combined belief function for Θ based on all evidence is the following.

$$Bel_1 \oplus Bel_2(\Theta) = m_1 \oplus m_2(\Theta) + m_1 \oplus m_2(\{B,F\}) + m_1 \oplus m_2(\{B\})$$
$$= 0.03 + 0.07 + 0.90 = 1$$

Actually, $Bel(\Theta) = 1$ in all cases since the sum of masses must always equal 1. The combination of evidence just *redistributes* the masses in different subsets.

The evidential interval of a set S, EI(S), may be defined in terms of the belief.

$$EI(S) = [Bel(S), 1 - Bel(S')]$$

If $S = \{B\}$, then $S' = \{A,F\}$ and

```
Bel({A,F})  =  m₁ ⊕ m₂({A,F})  +
                m₁ ⊕ m₂({A})  +
                m₁ ⊕ m₂({F})
            =  0 + 0 + 0 = 0
```

since these are not focal elements and the mass is zero for nonfocal elements. Thus, the evidential interval for {B} is the following.

```
EI({B})  =  [0.90,1 - 0]
         =  [0.90,1]
```

Likewise, if S = {B,F}, then S´ = {A} and

```
Bel({A})  =  0
```

since {A} is not a focal element. Also

```
Bel({B,F})  =  Bel₁ ⊕ Bel₂({B,F}) = 0.97
EI({B,F})   =  [0.97,1 - 0] = [0.97,1]
EI({A})     =  [0,1]
```

where the evidential interval [0, 1] reflects our *total ignorance* of {A}.

The evidential interval of [total belief, plausibility] can be expressed,

[evidence for support, evidence for support + ignorance]

Under probability theory, this interval is the single point,

[evidence for support, evidence for support]

since ignorance is not allowed. That is, evidence which does not support, must refute. The plausibility is defined as the degree to which the evidence fails to refute X.

$$Pls(X) = 1 - Bel(X´) = 1 - \sum_{Y \subseteq X´} m(X´)$$

The plausible belief, Pls, stretches belief to the absolute maximum in which the unassigned belief $m(\Theta)$ may possibly contribute to the belief. While the $m(\Theta)$ could be a bomber, fighter, or airliner, under the assumption of plausibility it is assumed to contribute belief to one of its subsets. Since {B} is a subset of Θ, it is plausible that the 0.3 belief of $m_1(\Theta)$ might be assigned to a bomber. Recall from Section 4.15 that a plausible belief is a little stronger than a possible belief, but not necessarily a belief supported by strong evidence. Another point is that Θ isn't the only type of set that stretches the belief of any set X. Any set that intersects X and its complement does it.

The **dubiety (Dbt)** or **doubt** represents the degree to which X is disbelieved or refuted. The **ignorance (Igr)** is the degree to which the mass supports X and X'. These are defined as follows.

```
Dbt = Bel(X´) = 1 - Pls(X)
```

```
Igr(X) = Pls(X) - Bel(X)
```

The Normalization of Belief

Suppose a third sensor now reports conflicting evidence of an airliner

```
m₃({A}) = 0.95    m(Θ) = 0.05
```

Table 5-6 shows how the cross products are calculated.

	$m_1 \oplus m_2(\{B\})$ 0.90	$m_1 \oplus m_2(\{B,F\})$ 0.07	$m_1 \oplus m_2(\Theta)$ 0.03
$m_3(\{A\}) = 0.95$ $m(\Theta) = 0.05$	Ø 0.855 {B} 0.045	Ø 0.0665 {B,F} 0.0035	Ø 0.0285 Θ 0.0015

Table 5-6
Combining Additional Evidence, m_3

The null set, Ø, occurs because {A} and {B} have no elements in common and neither does {A} and {B,F}. Thus

```
m₁ ⊕ m₂ ⊕ m₃({A})   = 0.0285
m₁ ⊕ m₂ ⊕ m₃({B})   = 0.045
m₁ ⊕ m₂ ⊕ m₃({B,F}) = 0.0035
m₁ ⊕ m₂ ⊕ m₃(Θ)     = 0.0015
m₁ ⊕ m₂ ⊕ m₃(Ø)     = 0  (by definition of the null set)
```

Note that for this example, the sum of all the masses is less than 1

$$\sum m_1 \oplus m_2 \oplus m_3(X) = .0285 + .045 + .0035 + .0015$$
$$= .0785$$

where the sum ranges over all focal elements. However, a sum of 1 is required since the combined evidence, $m_1 \oplus m_2 \oplus m_3$, is a valid mass and the sum over all focal elements must be 1. The fact that the sum is less than 1 presents a problem.

The solution to this problem is a **normalization** of the focal elements by dividing each focal element by

$$1 - \kappa$$

where κ is defined for any sets X and Y as

$$\kappa = \sum_{X \cap Y = \emptyset} m_1(X) \; m_2(Y)$$

In our example,

$$\kappa = 0.855 + 0.0665 = 0.9215$$

and so

$$1 - \kappa = 1 - 0.9215 = 0.0785$$

Dividing each $m_1 \oplus m_2 \oplus m_3$ focal element by $1 - \kappa$ gives the normalized values

$$
\begin{aligned}
m_1 \oplus m_2 \oplus m_3\{A\} &= 0.363 \\
m_1 \oplus m_2 \oplus m_3\{B\} &= 0.573 \\
m_1 \oplus m_2 \oplus m_3\{B, F\} &= 0.045 \\
m_1 \oplus m_2 \oplus m_3(\Theta) &= 0.019
\end{aligned}
$$

Notice that the one evidence of {A} has considerably eroded the belief in {B}, as would be expected.

The total normalized belief in {B} is now

$$Bel(\{B\}) = m_1 \oplus m_2(\{B\}) = 0.573$$

$$
\begin{aligned}
Bel(\{B\}') &= Bel(\{A, F\}) \\
&= m_1 \oplus m_2 \oplus m_3(\{A, F\}) + \\
&\quad\; m_1 \oplus m_2 \oplus m_3(\{A\}) + \\
&\quad\; m_1 \oplus m_2 \oplus m_3(\{F\}) \\
&= 0 + 0.363 + 0 = 0.363
\end{aligned}
$$

and so the evidential interval is now

$$
\begin{aligned}
EI(\{B\}) &= [Bel(\{B\}), 1 - Bel(\{B\}')] \\
&= [0.573, 1 - 0.363] \\
&= [0.573, 0.637]
\end{aligned}
$$

Notice that the support and plausibility of {B} has been greatly reduced by the conflicting evidence of {A}.

The general form of Dempster's Rule of Combination is,

$$m_1 \oplus m_2(Z) = \frac{\displaystyle\sum_{X \cap Y = Z} m_1(X) \ m_2(Y)}{1 - \kappa}$$

where κ is defined again for convenience. No orthogonal sum is defined if $\kappa = 1$.

$$\kappa = \sum_{X \cap Y = \emptyset} m_1(X) \ m_2(Y)$$

κ indicates the amount of **evidential conflict**. $\kappa = 0$ for completely compatibility, and is 1 for complete contradiction. Values of $0 < \kappa < 1$ show partial compatibility.

Moving Masses and Sets

The moving mass analogy is helpful in understanding support and plausibility. The main concepts are the following.

- The support is the mass assigned to a set and all its subsets.
- Mass of a set can move freely into its subsets.
- Mass in a set cannot move into its supersets.
- Moving mass from a set into its subset can only contribute to the plausibility of the subset, not its support.
- Mass in the environment, Θ, can move into *any* subset since Θ is outside all.

In Figure 5-7 (a), all the mass is assumed inside set X and so

```
m(X)  = 1
```

which means that the support of X is 1. The plausibility of X is also 1 because all the mass is in X and there is no superset which can contribute mass. Thus

```
EI(X)  = [1,1]
```

If $m(X) = 0.5$ then $EI(X) = [0.5, 0.5]$ and in general, if $m(X) = a$, where *a* is any constant, then $EI(X) = [a,a]$.

In Figure 5-7 (b), assume that $m(X) = 0.6$ and $m(Y) = 0.4$, which are also their supports. The plausibility of X is 0.6 since the mass of Y cannot move to X. However, the mass of X can move inside Y since Y is a subset of X and so the plausibility of Y is $0.4 + 0.6 = 1$. Thus, the evidential intervals for X and Y are the following.

```
EI({X}) = [0.6,0.6]
EI({Y}) = [0.4,1]
```

Figures 5-7 (c) and (d) are used in Problem 5-4.

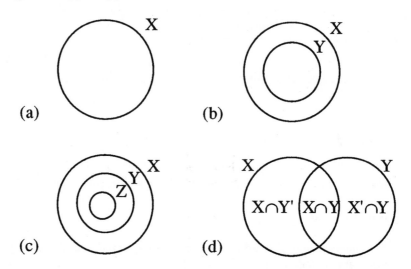

Figure 5-7
Sets Illustrating Support and Plausibility

Difficulty with the Dempster-Shafer Theory

One difficulty with the Dempster-Shafer theory occurs with normalization and may lead to results which are contrary to our expectations (Zadeh 84a). The problem with normalization is that it ignores the belief that the object being considered does not exist.

An example quoted by Zadeh is the belief by two doctors, A and B, in a patient's illness. The beliefs in the patient's problem are as follows.

```
m_A(meningitis)  = 0.99
m_A(brain tumor) = 0.01
m_B(concussion)  = 0.99
m_B(brain tumor) = 0.01
```

Notice that both doctors think there is a very low chance, 0.01, of a brain tumor but greatly disagree on the major problem. The Dempster rule of combination gives a combined belief of 1 in the brain tumor. This result is very unexpected and against our intuition since both doctors had agreed the brain tumor was very improbable. The same result of 1 for brain tumor would occur no matter what the other probabilities were.

5.5   APPROXIMATE REASONING

In this section we will discuss a theory of uncertainty based on **fuzzy logic**. Fuzzy logic is primarily concerned with quantifying and reasoning using natural language in which many words have ambiguous meanings, such as: *tall, hot, dangerous, a little, very much*, and so on. Fuzzy logic is a development from the basic theory of fuzzy sets which was first stated in Lotfi Zadeh's 1965 paper (Zadeh 65). Since then, the theory has been extended and applied to many fields, as shown in Table 5-7 (Maiers 85). The Maiers paper also includes 450 references to these areas. Another book on fuzzy theory contains over 3000 references (Kandel 82).

```
Control Algorithms
Medical Diagnosis
Decision Making
Economics
Engineering
Environmental
Literature
Operations Research
Pattern Recognition
Psychology
Reliability
Security
Science
```

Table 5-7
Some Applications Of Fuzzy Theory

Fuzzy Sets and Natural Language

The traditional way of representing which objects are members of a set is in terms of a **characteristic function**, sometimes called a **discrimination function**. If an object is an element of a set, then its characteristic function is 1. If an object is not an element of a set, then its characteristic function is 0. This definition is summarized by the following characteristic function.

$$\mu_A(x) = \begin{cases} 1 & \text{if } x \text{ is an element of set A} \\ 0 & \text{if } x \text{ is not an element of set A} \end{cases}$$

where the objects x are elements of some universe X.

The characteristic function can also be defined in terms of a functional mapping (see Section 1.10, Subsection *Functional Programming*)

$$\mu_A(x) : X \rightarrow \{0,1\}$$

which states that the characteristic function maps a universal set X to the set consisting of 0 and 1. This definition simply expresses the classical concept that an object is either in a set or not in a set. Sets to which this applies are called **crisp sets** in contrast to fuzzy sets. This type of thinking dates from the Aristotelian view of **bivalent logic** or **two-valued logic** in which true and false are the only possibilities.

The problem with this bivalent logic is that we live in an analog, not a digital world. In the real world, things are generally not in one state or another. It is only in conventional computer architecture using digital logic that bivalent logic holds. The development of analog theories of computation such as artificial neural systems and fuzzy theory more accurately represents the real world.

In fuzzy sets, an object may belong partially to a set. The degree of membership in a fuzzy set is measured by a generalization of the characteristic function called the **membership function** or **compatibility function** defined as

$$\mu_A(x) \; : \; X \to [0,1]$$

Although this definition looks superficially like the definition of the characteristic function, it is actually very different. The characteristic function maps all elements of X into one of exactly two elements: 0 or 1. In contrast, the membership function maps X into the codomain of real numbers defined in the **interval** from 0 to 1 inclusive and symbolized by [0,1]. That is, the membership function is a real number

$$0 \le \mu_A \le 1$$

where 0 means no membership and 1 means full membership in the set. A particular value of the membership function, such as 0.5, is called a **grade of membership**.

Although it may seem strange at first to talk about an element being only partially in a set, it is actually more natural than the classical two-valued sets. Although many people wish it were, the real world is not just yes or no, black or white, right or wrong, on or off. Just as there are many shades of gray, not just black and white, so too there are many different gradations of meaning in the real world. Only debts and computer source code must be exact.

Using the membership function, real world situations can be described. As a very simple example, consider cloudy days. A crisp set description requires an arbitrary decision as to what constitutes a cloudy day. Is a cloudy day one with a few clouds, many clouds, totally overcast, partially overcast, or some other definition? Is a rainy day one with 1" of precipitation, 2", 3", or is it a certain rate of precipitation?

Fuzzy sets and concepts are commonly used in natural language, such as the following.

```
"John is tall"
"The weather is hot"
"Turn the dial a little higher"
"Most tests are hard"
```

```
"If the dough is much too thick, add a lot of water"
```

where the words in italics refer to fuzzy sets and quantifiers. All these fuzzy sets and quantifiers can be represented and operated on in fuzzy theory. In particular, the "most" quantifier that was pointed out as a major limitation of predicate logic in Section 2.16, can be handled in fuzzy logic, as you will see shortly.

In natural language, the terms *vague* and *fuzzy* are sometimes used synonymously. However, there is a major difference between the terms in the context of fuzzy theory. A **fuzzy proposition** contains words such as *tall* which is the identifier of a fuzzy set TALL. Here we shall follow the convention of using all capitals to label fuzzy sets such as this. In contrast to a classic proposition such as, "John is exactly five feet tall," which represents a proposition which is either true or false, a fuzzy proposition may have degrees of truth. For example, the fuzzy proposition "John is tall," may be true to some degree: *A Little True, Somewhat True, Fairly True, Very True*, and so on. A fuzzy truth value is called a **fuzzy qualifier**, and may be used as a fuzzy set or to modify a fuzzy set. Unlike crisp propositions which are not allowed to have quantifiers, fuzzy propositions may have **fuzzy quantifiers**, such as *Most, Many, Usually*, and so on, with no distinction between statements and propositions as in the classical case.

The term "vague" is used in the sense of incomplete information. For example, "John is somewhere" is vague if it does not provide sufficient information for a decision. A fuzzy proposition such as "He is tall" may also be vague if we do not know who the pronoun refers to. There are also degrees of vagueness. A proposition, "John is tall" is less vague than "He is tall" but is still vague if we do not know which John.

Many fuzzy words are used in natural language, such as those shown in Table 5-8. The meaning of these words can be defined in terms of fuzzy sets, as you'll see shortly. Compound terms, such as those shown in Table 5-9, can also be defined and manipulated in fuzzy theory.

While it's difficult to think of an object as only being partially in a set, another way is to consider the membership functions as representing the degree to which an object has some attribute. This concept of degree of attribute is expressed by the alternate meaning of the membership function as a compatibility function. The term compatibility means how well one object conforms to some attribute and is really better for describing fuzzy sets. However, the term membership function is most commonly used in the literature and so we will use it. In thinking about fuzzy sets, you may find it helpful to consider fuzzy elements as an object-attribute-value triplet as described in Chapter 2. For crisp sets, there is only the object-attribute since it is assumed the value is either 0 or 1. That is, in crisp sets, an element is either in a set or not in a set. For fuzzy sets, the value may be anywhere in the range from 0 to 1.

To illustrate the concept of fuzzy sets, consider the previous example.

```
"John is tall"
```

If the person is an adult, one possible membership function is shown in Figure 5-8.

low
medium
high
very
not
more or less
little
several
few
many
more
most
about
approximately
sort of
a great deal

Table 5-8
Some Fuzzy Terms of Natural Language

very low
more or less low
approximately low
not low
not very low
not more or less low
medium to sort of high
higher than slightly low
low to sort of medium
most high

Table 5-9
Compound Fuzzy Natural Language Terms

If a person is an adult, then anyone about 7 feet and taller is considered to have a membership function of 1.0. Anyone less than 5 feet is not considered to be in the fuzzy set TALL and so the membership function is 0. Between 5 and 7 feet, the membership function is monotonically increasing with height.

This particular membership function is only one of many possible functions. The membership functions will be very different for the average person, basketball players, jockeys, and so on. For example, a five-foot tall jockey is considered tall to some degree for a jockey even though the membership function for a five-foot tall person in Figure 5-8 is 0.

Depending on the application, a membership function may be constructed from one person's opinions or from a group of people. In an expert system, the membership function will be constructed from the expert's opinion that is being modeled by the system. Although the opinion of tallness is not likely to be modeled in an expert system, many other opinions may be modeled. Some examples might be credit risk for a loan, hostile intent of an unknown aircraft, quality of a product, suitability of a candidate for a job, and so on. Notice that opinions like these are not simple yes-or-no ones. Although it's possible to establish threshold values for a yes or no decision, there is a real question as to the validity of a crisp threshold. For example, should a person be turned down for a mortgage loan because his or her income is $29,999.99 and the threshold is $30,000.00?

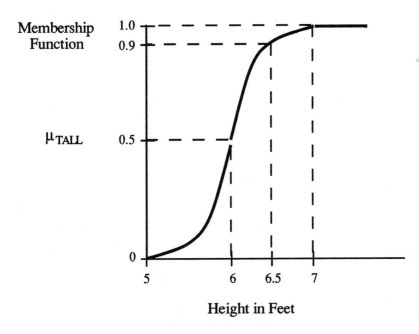

Figure 5-8
A Membership Function for the Fuzzy Set TALL

Intuitively, the membership function for a group of people also may be thought of in terms of an opinion poll. Suppose a group of off-the-street people was asked to specify a minimum value for the word *tall*. No one would probably say that someone under 5 feet is tall. Likewise everyone would probably say someone 7 feet and over is tall. In between 5 feet and 7 feet, the percentage of people agreeing as to what constitutes *tall* is analogous to the membership function curve shown in Figure 5-8. As the value for tall increases from 5 to 6 feet, more and more people might agree that someone is tall. For this particular membership function, the **crossover point** for tall is 6 feet. A crossover point is where $\mu = 0.5$. In terms of our opinion analogy, 50% of the people would agree that someone 6 feet and over is tall. At 6.5 feet, the percentage of people agreeing is 90%. From 7 feet up, everyone agrees on tallness and so the membership function is flat at 1.

It's important to realize that although this example is given in terms of an opinion poll of a group, the membership function is really *not* a frequency distribution. As we discussed in Chapter 4, probabilities are used for repeatable observations of the same or identical objects. Although each person in the group might give a repeatable opinion when asked the question again, the opinions are likelihoods because they express a personal belief.

The **S-function** is a mathematical function that is often used in fuzzy sets as a membership function. It is defined as follows.

$$S(x;\ \alpha,\beta,\gamma) = \begin{cases} 0 & \text{for } x \leq \alpha \\[2mm] 2\left(\dfrac{x-\alpha}{\gamma-\alpha}\right)^2 & \text{for } \alpha \leq x \leq \beta \\[2mm] 1-2\left(\dfrac{x-\gamma}{\gamma-\alpha}\right)^2 & \text{for } \beta \leq x \leq \gamma \\[2mm] 1 & \text{for } x \geq \gamma \end{cases}$$

A plot of the S-function is shown in Figure 5-9.

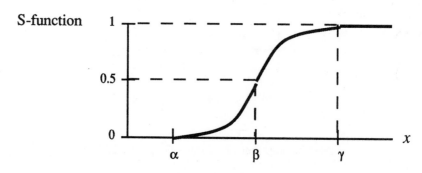

Figure 5-9
The S-function

The S-function can be a valuable tool in defining fuzzy functions such as the word tall. Rather that maintaining a table of data defining the membership function, all the data may be compactly represented by a formula. In this definition, α, β, and γ are parameters which may be adjusted to fit the desired membership data. Depending on the given membership data, it may be possible to give an exact fit for some values of α, β, and γ, or the fit may be only approximate. Of course, the membership function may simply be defined as an S-function with no reference to any tabular data. Other functions such as triangular ones may also be defined depending on the application.

The S-function is flat at a value of 0 for $x \leq \alpha$ and at 1 for $x \geq \gamma$. In between α and γ, the S-function is a quadratic function of x. As you can see from Figure 5-9, the β parameter corresponds to the crossover point of 0.5 and is $(\alpha + \gamma) / 2$. For the TALL membership function of Figure 5-8, the S-function is the following

$$(1) \quad S(x; \ 5, \ 6, \ 7) = \begin{cases} 0 & \text{for } x \leq 5 \\[2em] 2 \left(\dfrac{x - 5}{7 - 5} \right)^2 = \dfrac{(x - 5)^2}{2} & \\[1em] & \text{for } 5 \leq x \leq 6 \\[2em] 1 - 2 \left(\dfrac{x - 7}{7 - 5} \right)^2 = 1 - \dfrac{(x - 7)^2}{2} & \\[1em] & \text{for } 6 \leq x \leq 7 \\[2em] 1 & \text{for } x \geq 7 \end{cases}$$

A membership function for the fuzzy proposition "X is close to γ" is shown in Figure 5-10. For example, this membership function could represent all numbers close to a specified value γ, as in "X is close to 6", where X could be defined as {5.9,6,6.1}. The membership function may be expressed as

$$\mu_{CLOSE}(x) = \frac{1}{1 + \left(\dfrac{x - \gamma}{\beta} \right)^2}$$

with crossover points

$$x = \gamma \pm \beta$$

The parameter β is the **half-width** of the curve at the crossover point, as shown in Figure 5-10. Larger values of β correspond to a wider curve and smaller values correspond to a more narrow curve. A larger β means that numbers must be more close to γ to have a significantly large membership value. Notice that in this definition, the membership function only goes to zero at infinity.

A function that also gives a similar curve, but does go to zero at specified points is the following.

$$\Pi(x; \ \beta, \ \gamma) = \begin{cases} S(x; \ \gamma - \beta, \ \gamma - \beta/2, \ \gamma) & \text{for } x \leq \gamma \\[1em] 1 - S(x; \ \gamma, \ \gamma + \beta/2, \gamma + \beta) & \text{for } x \geq \gamma \end{cases}$$

This **∏-function** is plotted in Figure 5-11. Notice that the β parameter is now the **bandwidth** or **total width** at the crossover points. The ∏-function goes to zero at the points

$$x = \gamma \pm \beta$$

while the crossover points are at

$$x = \gamma \pm \frac{\beta}{2}$$

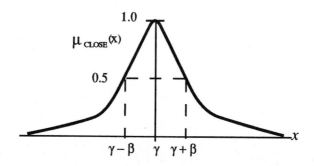

Figure 5-10
A Membership Function for the Fuzzy Proposition "X is close to γ"

Instead of a continuous function, the membership function can be a finite set of elements. For example, in the universe of heights defined as

$$\mathcal{U} = \{5, 5.5, 6, 6.5, 7, 7.5, 8\}$$

a fuzzy subset can be defined for a finite set of elements for TALL as follows.

$$TALL = \{0/5, .125/5.5, .5/6, .875/6.5, 1/7, 1/7.5, 1/8\}$$

In this fuzzy set, the symbol "/" separates the membership grades from the numbers corresponding to the heights. Note that the "/" does not mean division in customary fuzzy set notation. The fuzzy set elements for which $\mu(x) > 0$ make up the **support** of the fuzzy set. For TALL, the support is all the elements except 0/5.

A finite fuzzy subset of N elements is represented in standard fuzzy notation as the union of fuzzy singletons μ_i/x_i, where the "+" signs are Boolean notation for union.

$$(2) \quad F = \mu_1/x_1 + \mu_2/x_2 + \ldots \mu_N/x_N$$

$$F = \sum_{i=1}^{N} \mu_i / x_i$$

$$F = \bigcup_{i=1}^{N} \mu_i / x_i$$

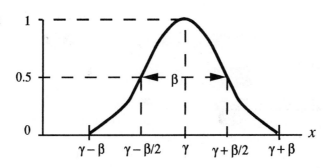

Π-function

Figure 5-11
The Π-function

In some papers, the "/" symbol is not written and so F can be written in the forms

$$(3) \quad F = \mu_1 x_1 + \mu_2 x_2 + \ldots \mu_n x_N$$

$$F = \sum_{i=1}^{N} \mu_i x_i$$

$$F = \bigcup_{i=1}^{N} \mu_i x_i$$

Both equations (2) and (3) represent finite fuzzy subsets of N elements. Equation (3) is useful for writing fuzzy sets in a compact symbolic form. However, the forms of equation (3) are difficult for people to read when numbers are involved , such as in

$$F = .127 + .385$$

Without the "/" separator, it is impossible to tell if the membership grades are .1 and .3, or .12 and .38, or something else. This is why the notation

$$F = .1/27 + .38/5$$

is better when dealing with numbers.

The **support** of a fuzzy set, F, is a subset of the universe set, X, defined as

$$\text{support}(F) = \{x \mid x \in X \text{ and } \mu_F(x) > 0 \}$$

The support set is usually written with the abbreviation **supp**, as in

$$\text{supp}(F)$$

for compactness. The advantage of the support is that a fuzzy set F can be written as

$$F = \{ \mu_F(x)/x \mid x \in \text{supp}(F) \}$$

which means that only those fuzzy elements whose membership function is greater than zero contribute to F. Thus, the TALL set can be written without the 0/5 element since this element is not in the support set.

$$\text{TALL} = \{.125/5.5, .5/6, .875/6.5, 1/7, 1/7.5, 1/8\}$$

Although there is only a small savings of one element, the reduction in elements can be significant for fuzzy sets with many elements of membership zero.

A related concept to the support is α–**cuts**. The α-cut of a set is a nonfuzzy set of the universe whose elements have a membership function greater than or equal to some value α.

$$F_\alpha = \{ x \mid \mu_F(x) \geq \alpha \} \qquad \text{for } 0 < \alpha \leq 1$$

Some α-cuts of the TALL set are

$$\text{TALL}_{0.1} = \{ 5.5, 6, 6.5, 7, 7.5, 8 \}$$

$$\text{TALL}_{0.5} = \{ 6, 6.5, 7, 7.5, 8 \}$$

$$\text{TALL}_{0.8} = \{ 6.5, 7, 7.5, 8 \}$$

$$\text{TALL}_1 = \{ 7, 7.5, 8 \}$$

Notice that the α-cuts of a set are subsets of the support. The values of α can be chosen arbitrarily but are usually picked to select desired subsets of the universe.

Another term often used with fuzzy sets is the **height**, which is the maximum membership grade of an element. For our TALL set, the maximum membership grade is 1. If an element in a fuzzy set attains the maximum possible grade, then the set is called **normalized**. Usually the membership grades are defined in the closed interval

[0,1] and so the maximum possible membership grade is 1. However, the grades may be defined in other intervals and so the membership grade may not necessarily be 1.

An arbitrary fuzzy subset of the universe over the **continuum** is written in the form of an integral. The term *continuum* refers to the set of real numbers. The integral represents the union of the fuzzy singletons, $\mu(x) / x$. For example, we could define

$$\text{TALL} = \int_X \mu_{\text{TALL}}(x)/x$$

$$= \int_5^8 \mu_{\text{TALL}}(x)/x$$

$$= \int_5^6 \frac{(x-5)^2}{2}/x + \int_6^7 \left[1 - \frac{(x-7)^2}{2}\right]/x + \int_7^8 1/x$$

using an S-function for TALL. In this formula, the "+" signs separating the integrals stand for union, as in Boolean logic notation, rather than arithmetic addition.

There are different types of fuzzy sets. The elementary **type 1 fuzzy subset**, F, of a universe, X, is defined as follows.

$$\mu_F \colon X \rightarrow [0,1]$$

That is, a type 1 fuzzy subset is simply defined by giving numeric values for its membership function in the closed interval of real numbers from 0 to 1. For example

$$\text{TALL} = .125/5.5 + .5/6 + .875/6.5 + 1/7 + 1/7.5 + 1/8$$

is a type 1 set because its membership grades are all real numbers in [0,1]. Likewise, from equation (1)

$$\mu_{\text{TALL}}(x) = S(x; \ 5, \ 6, \ 7)$$

is a type 1 fuzzy subset.

In general, a **type N fuzzy subset** is defined by a mapping for μ_F from a universe to the set of fuzzy subsets of type N − 1. For example, a **type 2 fuzzy subset** is defined in terms of a type 1 subset. For heights, a type 2 fuzzy set can be

$$\mu_{\text{TALL}}(5) = \text{LESS THAN AVERAGE}$$
$$\mu_{\text{TALL}}(6) = \text{AVERAGE}$$
$$\mu_{\text{TALL}}(7) = \text{GREATER THAN AVERAGE}$$

where LESS THAN AVERAGE, AVERAGE, and GREATER THAN AVERAGE are all fuzzy subsets of type 1. These might be defined as the following fuzzy subsets.

$$\mu_{\text{LESS THAN AVERAGE}}(x) \quad = 1 - S(x;\ 4.5,\ 5,\ 5.5)$$
$$\mu_{\text{AVERAGE}}(x) \quad = \Pi\ (x;\ 1,\ 5.5)$$
$$\mu_{\text{GREATER THAN AVERAGE}}(x) \quad = S(x;\ 5.5,\ 6,\ 6.5)$$

Fuzzy Set Operations

An ordinary crisp set is a special case of a fuzzy set with membership function $\{0,1\}$. All the definitions, proofs and theorems of fuzzy sets must be compatible in the limit as the fuzziness goes to 0 and the fuzzy sets become crisp sets. The theory of fuzzy sets thus has a wider range of applications than crisp sets and so can deal with situations involving subjective opinions. The basic idea of fuzzy sets is to specify fuzzy real world concepts such as TALL by a set of fuzzy elements rather than demanding a sharp binary threshold. Following is a summary of some fuzzy set operators in a universe X.

• **set equality**

$$A = B$$

$$\mu_A(x) = \mu_B(x) \qquad \text{for all } x \in X$$

• **set complement**

$$A'$$

$$\mu_{A'}(x) = 1 - \mu_A(x) \quad \text{for all } x \in X$$

Figure 5-12 illustrates the fuzzy complement of a set. This definition of complementation is justified by Bellman and Giertz (Bellman 1973).

• **set containment**

$$A \subseteq B$$

Fuzzy set A is contained in B or is a **subset** of B if and only if

$$\mu_A(x) \leq \mu_B(x) \qquad \text{for all } x \in X$$

Fuzzy set A is a **proper subset** of B if A is a subset of B and the two are unequal.

$$\mu_A(x) \leq \mu_B(x) \text{ and } \mu_A(x) < \mu_B(x) \text{ for at least one } x \in X$$

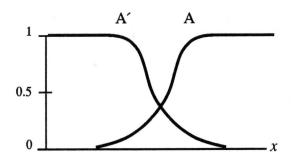

Figure 5-12
Fuzzy Complement

- **set union**

  A ∪ B

  $$\mu_{A \cup B}(x) = \vee(\mu_A(x), \mu_B(x)) \quad \text{for all } x \in X$$

where the **join operator**, ∨, means the maximum of the arguments.

- **set intersection**

  A ∩ B

  $$\mu_{A \cap B}(x) = \wedge(\mu_A(x), \mu_B(x)) \quad \text{for all } x \in X.$$

where the **meet operator**, ∧, means the minimum of the arguments.

You have already encountered the join and meet operators when discussing the application of fuzzy logic in combining antecedents in PROSPECTOR in Section 4.13, in the subsection "Combining Evidence by Fuzzy Logic." The justification for using the max and min functions for join and meet is given in (Bellman 1973).

With these definitions, the standard laws for crisp sets of commutativity, associativity, and so forth, hold for fuzzy sets with the exception of the Laws of the Excluded Middle and Contradiction. Thus, it is possible that for a fuzzy set A

$$A \cup A' \neq U \text{ and } A \cap A' \neq \emptyset$$

where ∅ is the empty set and U is the universe. Since fuzzy sets may have no definite boundary, the only constraint on intersection is that

$$A \cap A' = \min(\mu_A(x), \mu_{A'}(x)) \leq 0.5$$

if $\mu(x)$ is defined in the closed range [0,1] and $\mu_{A'}(x) = 1 - \mu_A(x)$.
  Likewise the only constraint on union is

$$A \cup A' = \max(\mu_A(x), \mu_{A'}(x)) \geq 0.5$$

Because fuzzy sets A and A' may overlap, they may not cover the universe completely.
  If the Laws of the Excluded Middle and Contradiction is defined to hold for fuzzy sets, then idempotentcy and distribution may not be satisfied. For idempotentcy, this is

$$A \cup A \neq A \qquad A \cap A \neq A$$

Because of the fuzzy nature of sets, it appears more reasonable to accept that the Laws of Excluded Middle and Contradiction do not hold so that idempotentcy will be satisfied.

• **set product**

  A B

  $$\mu_{AB}(x) = \mu_A(x)\,\mu_B(x)$$

• **power of a set**

  A^N

  $$\mu_{A^N}(x) = (\mu_A(x))^N$$

• **probabilistic sum**

  $A \mathbin{\hat{+}} B$

  $$\mu_{A\hat{+}B}(x) = \mu_A(x) + \mu_B(x) - \mu_A(x)\,\mu_B(x)$$

  $$= 1 - (1 - \mu_A(x))(1 - \mu_B(x))$$

where the "+" and "–" are ordinary arithmetic operators.

• **bounded sum or bold union**

  $A \oplus B$

  $$\mu_{A\oplus B}(x) = \wedge(1, (\mu_A(x) + \mu_B(x)))$$

where the $\wedge$ is the min function and "+" is the arithmetic operator.

- **bounded product** or **bold intersection**

$$A \odot B$$

$$\mu_{A \odot B}(x) = \vee(0, (\mu_A(x) + \mu_B(x) - 1))$$

where the $\vee$ is the max function and "+" is the arithmetic operator. The bounded sum and product operators do not satisfy idempotentcy, distributivity and absorption, but do satisfy commutativity, associativity, de Morgan's laws, $A \oplus \mathcal{U} = \mathcal{U}$, $A \odot \emptyset = \emptyset$, and the Laws of Excluded Middle and Contradiction (see Appendix C for a summary).

- **bounded difference**

$$A \mid - \mid B$$

$$\mu_{A \mid - \mid B}(x) = \vee(0, (\mu_A(x) - \mu_B(x)))$$

where the "−" separating μ_A and μ_B is the arithmetic minus operator. $A \mid - \mid B$ represents those elements which are more in A than B. The complement can be written in terms of the universe set, $\mathcal{U}$, and bounded difference as

$$A' = \mathcal{U} \mid - \mid A$$

- **concentration**

$$CON(A)$$

$$\mu_{CON(A)}(x) = (\mu_A(x))^2$$

The CON operation concentrates fuzzy elements by reducing the membership grade more of elements that have smaller membership grades. Figure 5-13 illustrates the CON operation. This operation and the following ones of DIL, NORM, and INT have no counterpart in ordinary set operations. The CON operator can be used to roughly approximate the effect of the linguistic modifier *Very*. That is, for some fuzzy set F

$$\text{Very } F = F^2$$

For the example of the TALL set,

$$\text{TALL} = .125/5 + .5/6 + .875/6.5 + 1/7 + 1/7.5 + 1/8$$

then

$$\text{Very TALL} = .016/5 + .25/6 + .76/6.5 + 1/7 + 1/7.5 + 1/8$$

Notice how the membership grades have decreased for all except those of grade 1. The net effect is to make the Very TALL fuzzy set include fewer small grades.

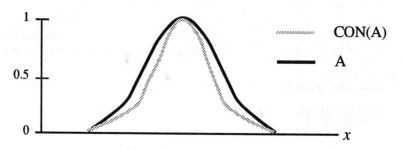

Figure 5-13
Concentration of a Fuzzy Set

• **dilation**

DIL(A)

$$\mu_{\text{DIL}(A)}(x) = (\mu_A(x))^{0.5}$$

The DIL operation dilates fuzzy elements by increasing the membership grade more of elements with smaller membership grades. Figure 5-14 illustrates DIL. Notice that it performs the inverse operation to concentration for these choices of powers 2 and 0.5.

$$A = \text{DIL}(\text{CON}(A)) = \text{CON}(\text{DIL}(A))$$

The dilation operator is roughly approximated by the linguistic modifier *More Or Less*. Thus for any fuzzy set F

$$\text{More Or Less } F = F^{0.5} = \text{DIL}(F)$$

Figure 5-14
Dilation of a Fuzzy Set

- **intensification**

INT (A)

$$\mu_{INT(A)}(x) = \begin{cases} 2\ (\mu_A(x))^2 & \text{for } 0 \le \mu_A(x) \le 0.5 \\ 1 - 2(1 - \mu_A(x))^2 & \text{for } 0.5 < \mu_A(x) \le 1 \end{cases}$$

The INT operation is like contrast intensification of a picture. As illustrated in Figure 5-15, the intensification raises the membership grade of those elements within the crossover points and reduces the membership grade of those outside the crossover points. As an electronic analogy, consider the crossover points as defining the bandwidth of a signal. Intensification amplifies the signal within the bandwidth while reducing the "noise" outside the bandwidth. Intensification thus increases the contrast in grade between those elements within the crossover points compared to those outside the crossover points.

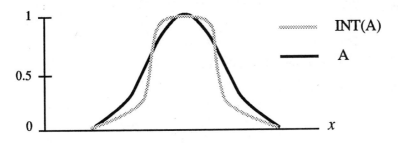

Figure 5-15
Intensification of a Fuzzy Set

• **normalization**

NORM(A)

$$\mu_{\text{NORM}(A)}(x) = \mu_A(x)/\max\{\mu_A(x)\}$$

where the max function returns the maximum membership grade for all elements x. If the maximum grade is < 1, then all membership grades will be increased. If the max = 1, then the membership grades are unchanged.

Fuzzy Relations

An important concept that can also be modeled by fuzzy sets is that of a **relation**. The intuitive idea of a relation is that of some association between elements. Some examples of relations are

```
Bob and Ellis are friends
Los Angeles and New York are very far apart
1, 2, 3, and 4 are much less than 100
1, 2, and 3 are small numbers
apples and oranges are sort of round fruits
```

where the italicized words are fuzzy.

The **Cartesian product** of N crisp sets is defined as the crisp set whose elements are ordered N-tuples $(x_1, x_2, x_3, ... x_N)$, where each x_i is an element of its crisp set X_i. For the two sets A and B

```
A × B = {(a,b) | a ∈ A and b ∈ B}
```

Defining

```
A = {chocolate, strawberry}
B = {pie, milk, candy}
```

then the Cartesian product is

```
A × B = {(chocolate, pie), (chocolate, milk),
         (chocolate, candy), (strawberry, pie),
         (strawberry, milk), (strawberry, candy)}
```

Notice that B × A is generally unequal to A × B if A and B have different elements. That is, generally (a,b) ≠ (b,a). A × B is said to define a **binary variable**, (a,b).

A relation, R, is a subset of the Cartesian product. For example, the relation that R = LIKES PIE could be defined as a subset of A × B by

```
R = {(chocolate, pie), (strawberry, pie)}
```

while the relation R = LIKES SWEETS could be defined as

```
R = {(chocolate, pie), (chocolate, candy),
     (strawberry, pie), (strawberry, candy)}
```

A relation is also sometimes called a **mapping** because it associates elements from one domain to another. In $A \times B$, the relation is a mapping from $A \rightarrow B$, where the $\rightarrow$ means a mapping in this context. Chocolate in A is mapped or associated with pie and candy in B, and likewise for strawberry.

If X and Y are universe sets, then

```
R = { μ_R(x,y)/(x,y) | (x,y) ⊆ X × Y}
```

is a fuzzy relation on $X \times Y$.

A fuzzy relation is fundamentally a fuzzy subset in the Cartesian product universe. Another definition of fuzzy sets is useful when dealing with fuzzy graphs (Zimmerman 85).

The **fuzzy relation** for N sets is defined as an extension of the crisp relation to include the membership grade. That is

```
R = {μ_R(x_1, x_2, ... x_N)/(x_1, x_2, ... x_N)
     | x_i ∈ X_i, i = 1, .. N)}
```

which associates the membership grade of each N-tuple. For the binary relation of the pie example, another definition could be

```
R = {.9/(chocolate, pie),.2/(strawberry,pie)}
```

as the fuzzy relation to indicate that a person is much more fond of chocolate pie than strawberry pie.

A convenient way of representing a relation is by a matrix. For the relation LIKES SWEETS,

$$
M_R = \begin{array}{cc} & \begin{array}{cc} \text{pie} & \text{candy} \end{array} \\ \begin{array}{c} \text{chocolate} \\ \text{strawberry} \end{array} & \left[\begin{array}{cc} 0.9 & 0.7 \\ 0.2 & 0.1 \end{array} \right] \end{array}
$$

where M_R is the matrix representation of the fuzzy relation. Notice that for crisp sets, M_R would consist of only zeroes and ones expressing whether you totally like or totally dislike the ordered pairs (flavor, sweet). (This is probably the best proof that the world is truly fuzzy rather than crisp.)

The **composition** of relations is the net effect of applying one relation after another. For the case of two binary relations P and Q, the composition of their relations is the binary relation R.

$$R(A,C) = Q(A,B) \ o \ P(B,C)$$

where

R(A,C) is a relation between A and C
Q(A,B) is a relation between A and B
P(B,C) is a relation between B and C
A, B, and C are sets

and o is the **composition operator**. The relation of R is the same as applying P first followed by Q. In terms of membership grades

$$R = \{\mu_R(a,c)/(a,c) \ | \ a \in A, \ c \in C\}$$

where μ_R is defined as follows.

$$\mu_R(a,c) = \bigvee_{b \in B} [\mu_Q(a,b) \wedge \mu_P(b,c)]$$

$$= \max_{b \in B} [\min \ (\mu_Q(a,b), \mu_P(b,c))]$$

This composition is commonly defined by the **max-min matrix product** or simply **max-min**.

The max and min functions can be used in place of addition and multiplication for matrix operations. As an example, define

$$Q = \begin{bmatrix} 0.1 & 0.2 \\ 0.3 & 0.4 \end{bmatrix} \qquad P = \begin{bmatrix} 0.1 & 0.3 & 0.5 \\ 0.2 & 0.0 & 0.4 \end{bmatrix}$$

then the composition, R, is

$$R = Q \ o \ P = \begin{bmatrix} 0.1 & 0.2 \\ 0.3 & 0.4 \end{bmatrix} o \begin{bmatrix} 0.1 & 0.3 & 0.5 \\ 0.2 & 0.0 & 0.4 \end{bmatrix}$$

$$R = Q \circ P = \begin{bmatrix} \max(0.1,0.2) & \max(0.1,0.0) & \max(0.1,0.2) \\ \max(0.1,0.2) & \max(0.3,0.0) & \max(0.3,0.4) \end{bmatrix}$$

$$= \begin{bmatrix} 0.2 & 0.1 & 0.2 \\ 0.2 & 0.3 & 0.4 \end{bmatrix}$$

Other common relational operator definitions are the **max-product** and **relational join** (Klir 88). Fuzzy relations have important applications to approximate reasoning, as shown later.

The **projection** of a relation is another useful fuzzy set concept. Basically, the projection eliminates specified elements. Before giving the formal definition, let's look at a simple example. Table 5-10 shows the projections of the previous relation for R, where the rows and columns have been given identifiers of x_i and y_i for convenience.

	y_1	y_2	y_3	*1st Projection*	
x_1	0.2	0.1	0.2	0.2	
x_2	0.2	0.3	0.4	0.4	
2nd Projection	0.2	0.3	0.4	0.4	*Total Projection*

Table 5-10
A Relation and Its Projections

Notice that the column labeled *1st Projection* contains the maximum membership grade for the row. Likewise the row labeled *2nd Projection* contains the maximum membership grade of each column. The cell of value 0.4 at the lower right labeled *Total Projection* is the maximum membership grade of the total relation.

The relation for R can be written in terms of the x_i and y_i as the following

$$R = .2/x_1, y_1 + .1/x_1, y_2 + .2/x_1, y_3 + \\ .2/x_2, y_1 + .3/x_2, y_2 + .4/x_2, y_3$$

The 1st Projection is denoted by R_1 and is obtained by dropping all except the first point, x_i, of the Cartesian pair, x_i, y_j, where the leftmost element is defined as first.

$$R_1 = .2/x_1 + .1/x_1 + .2/x_1 + .2/x_2 + .3/x_2 + .4/x_2$$

$$R_1 = .2/x_1 + .4/x_2$$

Notice that the equation for R_1 has been reduced after the projection because the "+" represents the union operator and so only the maximum fuzzy element is kept.

Likewise the 2nd Projection drops the second point, y_j, of each Cartesian pair.

$$R_2 = .2/y_1 + .1/y_2 + .2/y_3 + .2/y_1 + .3/y_2 + .4/y_3$$

which reduces to the following, upon applying the union operator.

$$R_2 = .2/y_1 + .3/y_2 + .4/y_3$$

In the general case of a relation involving N Cartesian points, drop all components of the N-tuple except those points on which the projection is to be made. For example, if the relation is over N points, then R_{136} would drop all points except the first, third, and sixth.

For a relation over the universe $X \times Y$,

$$R = \{\mu_R(x,y)/(x,y)\} \text{ for all } (x,y) \in X \times Y$$

the 1st Projection is defined as

$$\texttt{proj}(R;X) = R_1$$

where

$$R_1 = \{\max_y \ \mu_R(x,y)/x \mid (x,y) \in X \times Y\}$$

and the max is taken over all y. Likewise

$$\texttt{proj}(R;Y) = R_2$$

where

$$R_2 = \{\max_x \ \mu_R(x,y)/y \mid (x,y) \in X \times Y\}$$

where the max is taken over all x values for R_2.

 The **cylindrical extension** of the projection relation is defined as the largest fuzzy relation that is compatible with a projection. For the previous example

$$\overline{R_1} = \begin{bmatrix} 0.2 & 0.2 & 0.2 \\ 0.4 & 0.4 & 0.4 \end{bmatrix}$$

$$\overline{R_2} = \begin{bmatrix} 0.2 & 0.3 & 0.4 \\ 0.2 & 0.3 & 0.4 \end{bmatrix}$$

where a bar over a projection symbolizes the cylindrical extension of the projection.

The composition can be defined in terms of projections and cylindrical extensions (Zadeh 75). For the binary relation R defined on the universe set $U_1 \times U_2$, and S defined on $U_2 \times U_3$, the composition is

```
R o S = proj ( R̄ ∩ S̄ ; U₁ × U₃)
```

Linguistic Variables

One very important application of fuzzy sets is in **computational linguistics**. The goal is to calculate with natural language statements analogous to the way that logic calculates with logic statements. Fuzzy sets and **linguistic variables** can be used to quantify the meaning of natural language, which can then be manipulated. A linguistic variable is assigned values which are expressions such as words, phrases, or sentences in a natural or artificial language. Table 5-11 shows some linguistic variables and typical values that might be assigned to them.

Linguistic Variable	Typical Values
height	dwarf, short, average, tall, giant
number	almost none, several, few, many
stage of life	infant, toddler, child, teenager, adult
color	red, blue, green, yellow, orange
light	dim, faint, normal, bright, intense
dessert	pie, cake, ice cream, baked alaska

Table 5-11
Typical Values

Although, it's possible to define values such as the color red corresponding to these linguistic values, they are very much subjective in nature. For example, the color red corresponds to a range in frequencies that the eye perceives as red, not just a single frequency. Other problems are colors such as aquamarine. Is it blue or green?

Linguistic variables are commonly used in heuristic rules. However, the variables may be implied, as illustrated in the first two rules of Table 5-12.

IF the TV is too dim THEN turn up the brightness
IF it's too hot THEN add some cold
IF the pressure is too high THEN open the relief valve
IF interest rates are going up THEN buy bonds
IF interest rates are going down THEN buy stocks

Table 5-12
Some Heuristic Rules Involving Implied Linguistic Variables

The implied linguistic variables are Picture Quality and Water Temperature.

Some linguistic variables like Picture Quality may be labels of fuzzy sets of order 2. For example, the values of Picture Quality could be

```
color, tint, brightness, noise, consistency
```

where each of these values may be linguistic variables which can take on values that are fuzzy sets. Thus, linguistic variables may be arranged in a hierarchy corresponding to their fuzzy set order. Eventually, a fuzzy set of order 1 is reached, such as TALL or BRIGHTNESS, which is defined as a mapping into the closed interval [0,1], and so the linguistic value becomes a numeric range.

The **term-set**, T(L), of a linguistic variable, L, is the set of values it may take. For example,

```
T(PIE) = CHOCOLATE + APPLE + STRAWBERRY + PECAN
```

where each of the terms in T(PIE) is a label of a fuzzy set. These sets may be the union of other sets consisting of subsets. For example,

```
CHOCOLATE = SEMI-SWEET CHOCOLATE + MILK CHOCOLATE +
            DUTCH CHOCOLATE + DARK CHOCOLATE + ...
```

Another definition for the CHOCOLATE fuzzy set may involve **hedges** to modify the meaning of a set. For example, a CHOCOLATE fuzzy set of one type of chocolate could be defined as follows.

```
CHOCOLATE = Very CHOCOLATE + Very Very CHOCOLATE +
            More Or Less CHOCOLATE +
            Slightly CHOCOLATE +
            Plus CHOCOLATE + Not Very CHOCOLATE + ...
```

Standard hedges can be defined in terms of some fuzzy set operators and a fuzzy set, F, as shown in Table 5-13.

Hedge	Operator Definition
Very F	$CON(F) = F^2$
More Or Less F	$DIL(F) = F^{0.5}$
Plus F	$F^{1.25}$
Not F	$1 - F$
Not Very F	$1 - CON(F)$
Slightly F	INT [NORM (PLUS F And NOT (VERY F))]

Table 5-13
Some Linguistic Hedges and Operators

As shown by the "Not Very F" hedge, other compound hedges can be made by combining operators. Notice that the "And" in the "Slightly" hedge is the fuzzy set operator for intersection, ∩, acting on the fuzzy sets Plus F and Not (Very F).

The hierarchy of the linguistic variable Appetite is illustrated in Figure 5-16. The LIGHT and HEAVY fuzzy sets are assumed to be S-functions while the MODERATE set is taken as a Π-function.

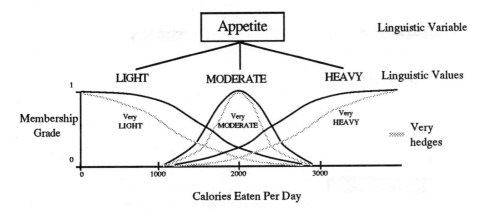

Figure 5-16
The Linguistic Variable Appetite and Its Values

Notice that there is overlap of the fuzzy sets such as LIGHT and MODERATE and even LIGHT and HEAVY. In classical crisp sets, there would be no overlap since all these sets would be disjoint. That is, a LIGHT appetite could not be a MODERATE or HEAVY appetite. However, in fuzzy sets, there are usually not (unless defined) sharp boundaries between sets.

The hedged sets are shown as dashed curves within the borders of the fuzzy sets. The hedges, such as *Very*, act as modifiers to the linguistic values to yield the fuzzy sets Very LIGHT, Very MODERATE, and Very HEAVY.

A linguistic variable must have a valid syntax and semantics, which can be specified by fuzzy sets or rules. A **syntactic rule** defines the well-formed expressions in T(L). For example, the term-set

```
T(Age) = {OLD, Very OLD, Very Very OLD, ...}
```

can be generated recursively using the following syntactic rule (Zadeh 73).

$$T^{i+1} = \{OLD\} \cup \{Very\ T^i\}$$

For example,

$$T^0 = \emptyset \quad \text{(the null set)}$$

$$T^1 = \{OLD\}$$

$$T^2 = \{OLD, \; Very \; OLD\}$$

$$T^3 = \{OLD, \; Very \; OLD, \; Very \; Very \; OLD\}$$

The **semantic rule** associated with T(L) defines the **meaning** of a term, L_i, in L, by a fuzzy set. For example, the semantic rule for Very OLD could be defined as

$$Very \; OLD = \mu_{OLD}^2$$

where the membership function could be defined as the S-function following.

$$\mu_{OLD}(X) = S(x; \; 60, \; 70, \; 80)$$

A **primary term** is a term such as YOUNG, OLD, CHOCOLATE, STRAWBERRY and so on, whose meaning must be defined before a hedge. Hedges modify the meaning of the primary terms to yield other terms in a term-set, such as Very YOUNG, Very OLD, Very CHOCOLATE, Slightly CHOCOLATE, and so forth. The meaning of the hedged fuzzy sets is determined by applying the appropriate fuzzy set operators. For example,

$$\mu_{Very \; CHOCOLATE} = \mu_{CHOCOLATE}^2$$

$$\mu_{Not \; CHOCOLATE} = 1 - \mu_{CHOCOLATE}$$

$$\mu_{More \; Or \; Less \; CHOCOLATE} = \mu_{CHOCOLATE}^{0.5}$$

$$\mu_{Not \; Very \; CHOCOLATE} = 1 - \mu_{Very \; CHOCOLATE}$$

Just as conventional language grammars can be defined by BNF notation (see Section 2.2), so too can a **fuzzy grammar**. In fact, the grammar described in Section 2.2 used a fuzzy modifier "heavy", as in

$$<adjective> \rightarrow heavy$$

to generate the **fuzzy production**

```
an eater was the heavy man
```

In this production, *heavy* is a hedge on the fuzzy set *man*. At first, you may not think *man* is a fuzzy set. However, when does a boy become a man? In some cultures a boy becomes a man at 12 or after a religious ceremony. Some governments define a man at 18 or 21. Newspaper articles appear to have a policy of referring to a male aged 17 to 19 as a man if he is accused of committing a crime, but refer to a 17 to 19 year-old as a youth if he has done something commendable. Males in the Armed Forces are sometimes referred to as boys and sometimes as men, especially in political speeches.

A fuzzy grammar can be specified in BNF notation by adding nonterminals such as

```
<Range Phrase> ::= <Hedged Primary> TO
                        <Hedged Primary>
<Hedged Primary> ::= <Hedge> <Primary> | <Primary>
<Hedge> ::= Very | More Or Less | A Little
<Primary> ::= SHORT | MEDIUM | TALL
```

to generate productions such as

```
Very SHORT TO Very TALL
A Little TALL TO Very SHORT
More Or Less MEDIUM TO TALL
```

A novel application of the linguistic variable concept is the fuzzy car built by Sugeno at the Tokyo Institute of Technology (Zadeh 88). The Sugeno car uses a control system based on fuzzy logic that allows autonomous operation on a rectangular track. The car can park itself at a specified space and also learn from examples. Linguistic variables are used in rules that control the car's movement. Many other types of fuzzy logic control systems have also been built to control devices and industrial processes such as a cement kiln to manufacture cement (Larsen 81).

Extension Principle

The **extension principle** is a very important concept in fuzzy theory. This principle defines how to extend the domain of a given crisp function to include fuzzy sets. By using the extension principle, any ordinary or crisp function from mathematics, science, engineering, business, and so forth can be extended to work in a fuzzy domain with fuzzy sets. This principle makes fuzzy sets applicable to all fields.

Let *f* be an ordinary function which maps from a universe X to Y. If F is a fuzzy subset of X such that

$$F = \int_X \mu_F(x)/x$$

then the extension principle defines the image of the fuzzy set F under a mapping function $f(x)$ as

$$f(F) \;=\; \int_X \mu_F(x)\,/\,f(x)$$

For example, let $f(x)$ be defined as a crisp function which squares its arguments.

$$f(x) \;=\; x^2$$

The extension principle states how to implement a squaring function of fuzzy sets.

$$f(F) \;=\; \int_X \mu_F(x)\,/\,f(x) \;=\; \int_X \mu_F(x)\,/\,x^2$$

For example, define the universes X and Y as the closed real interval [0,1000], and the fuzzy set

$$F \;=\; .3/15 \;+\; .8/20 \;+\; 1/30$$

then the extension principle defines the mapping f(F) as

$$f(F) \;=\; \int_X \mu_F(x)\,/\,f(x) \;=\; .3/f(15) \;+\; .8/f(20) \;+\; 1/f(30)$$

$$f(F) \;=\; .3/225 \;+\; .8/400 \;+\; 1/900$$

Fuzzy Logic

Just as classical logic forms the basis of conventional expert systems, fuzzy logic forms the basis of **fuzzy expert systems.** Besides dealing with uncertainty, fuzzy expert systems are also capable of modeling **commonsense reasoning**, which is very difficult for conventional systems.

A basic limitation of classical logic is its restriction to the two values of true and false. As we discussed in Chapters 2 and 3, this restriction has advantages and disadvantages. The main advantage is that systems based on two-valued logic are easy to model deductively and so the inferences can be exact. The main disadvantage is that very little in the real world is really two-valued. The real world is an analog—not a digital world.

The limitations of two-valued logic have been known since the time of Aristotle. Although he first formulated the syllogistic rules of inference and the Law of the

Excluded Middle, he recognized that propositions about future events were neither actually true or actually false until they occurred.

A number of different logic theories based on multiple values of truth have been formulated, such as those of Lukasiewicz, Bochvar, Kleene, Heyting, and Reichenbach. Some common types are those based on three values of truth representing TRUE, FALSE, and UNKNOWN. These **trivalent** or **three-valued logics** commonly represent the three truth values of TRUE, FALSE, and UNKNOWN by 1, 0, and 1/2 respectively.

Several generalized logics of N truth values, where N is an arbitrary integer number greater than or equal to two, have been developed. Lukasiewicz developed the first N-valued logic in the 1930's. In an N-valued logic, the set T_N of truth values are assumed evenly divided over the closed interval [0,1].

$$T_N = \left\{ \frac{i}{N-1} \right\} \text{ for } 0 \le i < N$$

For example,

$$T_2 = \{0, 1\} \qquad T_3 = \{0, 1/2, 1\}$$

Some **Lukasiewicz logic operators** for N-valued logic, where $N \ge 2$, are defined in Table 5-14. As shown in Problem 5-13, these reduce to the standard logic values for $N = 2$. Notice that the minus, min and max operators are the same as in fuzzy logic.

$$
\begin{array}{ll}
x' & = 1 - x \\
x \wedge y & = \min(x, y) \\
x \vee y & = \max(x, y) \\
x \to y & = \min(1, 1 + y - x)
\end{array}
$$

Table 5-14
Primitive Lukasiewicz N-valued Logic Operators

Each N-valued Lukasiewicz logic or **L-logic**, is written as L_N, where N is the number of truth values. L_2 is the classical two-valued logic, while at the other extreme of $N = \infty$, the L_∞ defines an **infinite-valued logic** with truth values in the set T_∞. While T_∞ is defined on rational numbers, an alternative infinite-valued-logic can be defined on the continuum, which is the set of all real numbers. The term *infinite-valued--logic* is commonly taken for this alternative logic where the truth values are the real numbers in [0,1], and this logic is called L_1.

However, L_1 is *not* the same as the **unary logic** with $N = 1$. Unary logic is not a Lukasiewicz logic at all since **L-logics** are only defined for $N \ge 2$. The 1 in L_1 is actually an abbreviation for $\aleph_1$ (read "aleph 1"), the cardinality of the real numbers. $\aleph_1$ is not a finite, but a **transfinite number**. This theory was first developed by Cantor as a way of computing with infinite numbers. Instead of one infinite number,

Cantor defined different orders of infinity. For example, the smallest transfinite number is $\aleph_0$, which is the cardinality of the natural numbers. $\aleph_1$ is a higher order infinity than $\aleph_0$ since there are infinitely many real numbers for each natural number.

Fuzzy logic may be considered an extension of multivalued logic. However, the goals and applications of fuzzy logic are different because fuzzy logic is the logic of **approximate reasoning** rather than exact multivalued reasoning. Essentially, approximate or **fuzzy reasoning** is the inference of a possibly imprecise conclusion from a set of possibly imprecise premises. People are very familiar with approximate reasoning since it is the most common type of reasoning done in the real world, and is the basis of many heuristic rules. Some examples of heuristic rules of approximate reasoning are the following.

```
IF the TV picture is rolling vertically
THEN adjust the vertical control

IF the TV picture is too dim
THEN turn up the brightness control

IF the red color in the TV picture looks too green
THEN then turn down the tint control

IF you're getting too fat from eating banana splits
and pies and ice cream and cake
THEN reduce the number of bananas
```

Approximate reasoning is concerned with reasoning that is neither exact, nor totally inexact such as a pure guess. Approximate reasoning is particularly concerned with reasoning about natural language statements and the inferences that follow. Fuzzy logic is related to approximate reasoning in the same way that two-valued logic is related to precise reasoning. An example of precise or exact reasoning is deduction and theorem proving, as discussed in Chapter 3.

There are many different possible types of possible fuzzy set theory, fuzzy logic, and approximate reasoning. The type of fuzzy logic discussed from now on is Zadeh's theory of approximate reasoning, which uses a fuzzy logic whose base is Lukasiewicz L_1 logic. In this fuzzy logic, truth values are linguistic variables that are ultimately represented by fuzzy sets.

Fuzzy logic operators based on the Lukasiewicz operators of Table 5-14 are defined in Table 5-15. $x(A)$ is a numeric truth value in the range [0,1] representing the truth of the proposition "x is A", which can be interpreted as the membership grade $\mu_A(x)$.

As an example of fuzzy logic operators, assume a fuzzy set called TRUE defined as

$$\text{TRUE} = .1/.1 + .3/.5 + 1/.8$$

Using the operators of Table 5-15 gives

```
FALSE = 1 - TRUE

      = (1 - .1)/.1 + (1 - .3)/.5 + (1 - 1)/.8

      = .9/.1 + .7/.5
```

Using the CON operator for the hedge Very gives

```
Very TRUE = .01/.1 + .09/.5 + 1/.8

Very FALSE = .81/.1 + .49/.5
```

$x(A')$	$= x(NOT\ A)$	$= 1 - \mu_A(x)$
$x(A) \wedge x(B)$	$= x(A\ AND\ B)$	$= \min(\mu_A(x), \mu_B(x))$
$x(A) \vee x(B)$	$= x(A\ OR\ B)$	$= \max(\mu_A(x), \mu_B(x))$
$x(A) \rightarrow x(B)$	$= x(A \rightarrow B)$	$= x((\sim A) \vee B) = \max[(1 - \mu_A(x)), \mu_B(x)]$

Table 5-15
Some Fuzzy Logic Operators

Fuzzy Rules

As a simple example of fuzzy set operators, consider the problem of pattern recognition. The patterns might represent objects examined for quality control such as manufactured parts or fresh picked fruit. Other types of important pattern recognition problems are medical images, seismic data from mineral and oil exploration, and others.

Table 5-16 shows some hypothetical data representing the membership grade in fuzzy sets of missile, fighter, and airliner corresponding to some images. These images might be produced from a laser TV system at long range and contain uncertainty due to target motion and orientation, noise, and so forth.

The union of the fuzzy sets for each image represents the total uncertainty in the target identification. Figure 5-17 illustrates the fuzzy set unions for the ten target images of Table 5-16. Of course, in a real situation, there would be many other possible images than these ten depending on the system resolution and distance to the target. Besides uncertainty in the system hardware, there is also uncertainty in the primitive fuzzy sets for missile, fighter, and airliner. The membership grades are assigned in a subjective way based on a knowledge of typical missile, fighter, and airliner configurations. In a real situation, there are many types of each of these primitive sets.

Image	Membership Grade		
	Missile	Fighter	Airliner
1	1.0	0.0	0.0
2	0.9	0.0	0.1
3	0.4	0.3	0.2
4	0.2	0.3	0.5
5	0.1	0.2	0.7
6	0.1	0.6	0.4
7	0.0	0.7	0.2
8	0.0	0.0	1.0
9	0.0	0.8	0.2
10	0.0	1.0	0.0

Table 5-16
Membership Grades for Images

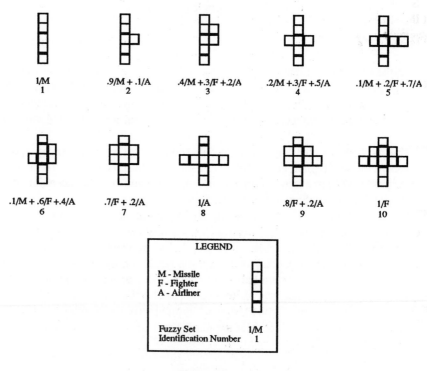

Figure 5-17
Fuzzy Sets for Aircraft Identification

The fuzzy set unions shown in Figure 5-17 can be considered as representing rules such as

```
IF E THEN H
```

where E is the observed image and H is the fuzzy set union. For example

```
IF IMAGE4 THEN TARGET (.2/M + .3/F + .5/A)
```

where the expression in parenthesis is the fuzzy set union of the target. Alternately, the rule could be expressed

```
IF IMAGE4 THEN TARGET4
```

where

```
TARGET4 = .2/M + .3/F + .5/A
```

Suppose that there is additional time to make another observation of the target and that IMAGE6 is observed. This corresponds to a rule

```
IF IMAGE6 THEN TARGET6
```

where

```
TARGET6 = .1/M + .6/F + .4/A
```

The total elements that have been measured for the target are

```
TARGET = TARGET4 + TARGET6
```

where the "+" denotes set union. Thus,

```
TARGET = .2/M + .3/F + .5/A + .1/M + .6/F + .4/A
```

```
TARGET = .2/M + .6/F + .5/A
```

where only the maximum membership grades for each element are retained in the TARGET fuzzy set.

If the element with maximum grade is interpreted as the most likely target, then the target is most likely a fighter since it has the highest membership grade of 0.6. However, if the airliner membership grade was also 0.6, then all we could say is that the target is equally likely to be a fighter or an airliner.

In general, given N observations and rules

```
IF E₁ THEN H₁
IF E₂ THEN H₂
        .
        .
        .
IF Eₙ THEN Hₙ
```

where all the H_i bear on some common hypothesis H, then the union of the hypotheses determines the membership grade of H. That is

$$\mu_H = \max(\mu_{H_1}, \ \mu_{H_2}, \ \ldots \ \mu_{H_N})$$

Notice that this result differs from the Certainty Factors and Dempster-Shafer theories. The μ_H of the hypothesis H is called the **truth value** of H.

It is also a reasonable assumption that the truth of a hypothesis can be no greater than the truth of its evidence. In terms of rules, the truth of the consequent can be no greater than the truth of its antecedent. Thus

$$\mu_H = \max(\mu_{H_1}, \ \mu_{H_2}, \ \ldots \ \mu_{H_N})$$

$$= \max[\min(\mu_{E_1}), \ \min(\mu_{E_2}), \ \ldots \ \min(\mu_{E_N}))$$

where each E_i may be some fuzzy expression. For example, E_1 might be defined as

$$E_1 = E_A \ \text{AND} \ (E_B \ \text{OR NOT} \ E_C)$$

and the fuzzy logic operators are used to evaluate the expression. That is,

$$\mu_{E_1} = \min(\mu_{E_A}, \max(\mu_{E_B}, 1 - \mu_{E_C}))$$

The combined membership grade of the antecedent is called the **truth value of the antecedent**. This is analogous to the partial evidence of the antecedent in PROSPECTOR rules. In fact, recall that the PROSPECTOR antecedent evidence was combined using fuzzy logic on an *ad hoc* basis. Now you can see that this combination is justified by the fuzzy theory compositional rule of inference.

Max-Min Composition

The equation for H above is the fuzzy logic **max-min compositional rule of inference**. In a simple case of two items of evidence per rule,

```
IF E₁₁ AND E₁₂ THEN H₁
IF E₂₁ AND E₂₂ THEN H₂
```

> .
> .

```
IF E_{N1}   AND E_{N2} THEN H_N
```

and so the max-min compositional inference rule is

$$\mu_{H} = \max[\min(\mu_{E11}, \mu_{E12}), \min(\mu_{E21}, \mu_{E22}), \ldots \min(\mu_{EN1}, \mu_{EN2})]$$

with similar extensions for additional evidence E_{13}, E_{14}, and so on.

As another example of the compositional rule of inference, let's see how it is used with a relation. Define the fuzzy relation $R(x,y) = $ APPROXIMATELY EQUAL on the binary relation of people's weights in the range 120-160 of Table 5-17.

	y				
x	120	130	140	150	160
120	1.0	0.7	0.4	0.2	0.0
130	0.7	1.0	0.6	0.5	0.2
140	0.4	0.6	1.0	0.8	0.5
150	0.2	0.5	0.8	1.0	0.8
160	0.0	0.2	0.5	0.8	1.0

Table 5-17
The Relation APPROXIMATELY EQUAL Defined on Weights

In constructing this table, the membership grades were defined so that the difference from the mean of two values is a decrease of 0.075 / %. For example, if the x and y values are 150 and 130, then the average is 140. The absolute difference of 150 and 130 from the average is 10/140 = 7.1%. This value is multiplied by the constant factor of -.075 / % to yield -0.5. Thus, the final membership grade for 150, 130 is 1−.5 = 0.5 and this is the table entry. An alternate and computationally simpler definition would be to define any change of 10 as a fixed decrease in the membership grade, such as .3. However, this alternate definition does not yield reasonable results for small weights such as 10 and 20, which would be APPROXIMATELY EQUAL to grade 0.7.

Notice how the relation $R(x,y)$ acts as a **fuzzy restriction** on any two values x and y which have a non-zero membership grade $R(x,y)$. A fuzzy relation acts as an **elastic constraint** by allowing a range of membership grades rather than demanding the rigid constraint of crisp relations. In fact the term APPROXIMATELY EQUAL could not even be defined in non-fuzzy logic. The rigid constraint of crisp relations would demand that values be either exactly equal or not. That is, either x exactly equals y or it does not.

As an example of a fuzzy restriction, consider the proposition, p, as follows.

```
p = X is F
```

where F is some fuzzy set which acts as a fuzzy restriction on the linguistic variable named X. The following are some examples of fuzzy propositions of the form above.

```
John is tall
Sue is over 21
The concrete mix is too thick
Target is friendly
x is a number approximately equal to 100
The pie is fruit
```

In the last example, a fuzzy set could be defined as

```
FRUIT = 1/apples + 1/oranges
```

to indicate the type of elements that are considered fruit. Notice that in fuzzy theory, you *can* add apples and oranges in a meaningful way.

Let's now define a fuzzy restriction $R_1(x)$. For example, the fuzzy set HEAVY could be defined as

```
R₁(x) = HEAVY = .6/140 + .8/150 + 1/160
```

The compositional rule of inference defines the fuzzy restriction on y values as

```
R₃(y) = R₁(x) o R₂(x,y)
```

where the composition operator, o, is the max-min operation

```
max min(μ₁(x),μ₂(x,y))
 x
```

Another way of viewing $R_3(y)$ is interpreting it as the solution of the relational equations

```
R₁(x)
R₂(x,y)
```

for $R_3(y)$. That is, given the fuzzy restriction of x and the fuzzy restriction on x and y, a fuzzy restriction on y can be deduced. Deductions like this comprise the **calculus of fuzzy restrictions**, which is the basis of approximate reasoning.

Using these definitions, $R_3(y)$ can be calculated as follows.

```
R₃(y) = R₁(x) o R₂(x,y)
```

$$R_3(y) = [\ 0.0 \quad 0.0 \quad 0.6 \quad 0.8 \quad 1.0\ ]\ o$$

$$\begin{bmatrix} 1.0 & 0.7 & 0.4 & 0.2 & 0.0 \\ 0.7 & 1.0 & 0.6 & 0.5 & 0.2 \\ 0.4 & 0.6 & 1.0 & 0.8 & 0.5 \\ 0.2 & 0.5 & 0.8 & 1.0 & 0.8 \\ 0.0 & 0.2 & 0.5 & 0.8 & 1.0 \end{bmatrix}$$

where $R_1(x)$ is represented as a row vector. The nonzero elements of $R_3(y)$ are calculated as follows.

$$R_3(120) = \max \min[(.6,.4),(.8,.2)]$$

$$= \max(.4,.2) = .4$$

$$R_3(130) = \max \min[(.6,.6),(.8,.5),(1,.2)]$$

$$= \max(.6,.5,.2) = .6$$

$$R_3(140) = \max \min[(.6,1),(.8,.8),(1,.5)]$$

$$= \max(.6,.8,.5) = .8$$

$$R_3(150) = \max \min[(.6,.8),(.8,1),(1,.8)]$$

$$= \max(.6,.8,.8) = .8$$

$$R_3(160) = \max \min[(.6,.5),(.8,.8),(1,1)]$$

$$= \max(.5,.8,1) = 1$$

and so if $R_1(x)$ is HEAVY, then

$$R_3(y) = .4/120 + .6/130 + .8/140 + .8/150 + 1/160$$

which has the rough linguistic approximation: $R_3(y)$ is MORE OR LESS HEAVY.

The relation $R_3(y)$ is a rough linguistic approximation since the DIL operation of $\mu^{0.5}$ acting on HEAVY actually yields

$$DIL(HEAVY) = .8/140 + .9/150 + 1/160$$

and the terms for 120 and 130 are missing. However, the elements with large membership grades of $\mu \geq .8$ are represented well and this justifies the claim that MORE OR LESS HEAVY is a rough approximation. Thus, the compositional inference by max-min has shown the fuzzy linguistic relation

MORE OR LESS HEAVY = HEAVY o APPROXIMATELY EQUAL

Note that these relations depend on the fuzzy set definitions and the linguistic labels of the sets. Thus the above relation is not true in an absolute sense since it depends on the definitions of the fuzzy sets, relations, and labels. However, once these basic definitions are made, fuzzy theory provides a mechanism for manipulating these expressions in a formal and consistent way. This is very important since the linguistic manipulation and meanings of terms are then on a sound theoretical basis and do not depend on an *ad hoc* or intuitive understanding by a person.

Maximum and Moments Methods

The choice of the element with the maximum membership grade is called the **maximum method** for deciding the truth of rule consequents. An alternate method called the **moments method** assigns the truth of rule consequents in a way that is analogous to calculating the first moment of inertia of an object. The basic idea of the moments method is to consider the consequents of all rules in a decision rather than just the one maximum. As mentioned before, even the maximum method may lead to ambiguity if the consequents of multiple rules all have the same maximum value.

As a simple example of the moments method, let's first consider the following set of fuzzy production rules for making concrete.

```
R1:   IF MIX IS TOO WET
      THEN ADD SAND AND COARSE AGGREGATE

R2:   IF MIX IS WORKABLE
      THEN LEAVE ALONE

R3:   IF MIX IS TOO STIFF
      THEN DECREASE SAND AND COARSE AGGREGATE
```

Concrete consists of cement, water, sand, and coarse aggregate such as small rocks, mixed in proper proportions. The **mix** is a trial amount of the concrete mixture which is made to determine the optimum proportions for the desired application. General guidelines for the proportions are available depending on the desired concrete strength. However, there is variability due to the local materials used, aggregate sizes, environmental conditions, and other factors. It's a good idea to do a mix before starting a $10,000,000 building.

One common method of determining if the mix is correct or workable is the **slump test**. A trial batch of concrete is put into a cone and the cone is removed. The distance that the mix slumps after cone removal indicates the condition of the material. Concrete designed for ordinary slabs and beams should have a minimum and maximum slump of 4 and 8 inches respectively (Adams 79). The fuzzy sets of Figure 5-18 illustrate possible definitions for the fuzzy concrete mix production rules antecedents. These fuzzy sets also may be defined in a table or as S-functions and $\prod$-functions.

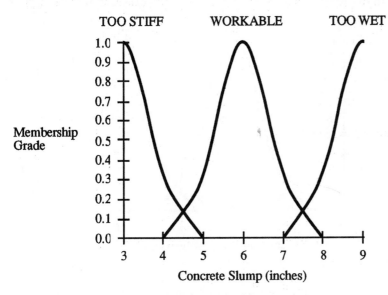

Figure 5-18
Fuzzy Production Rule Antecedents for Concrete Mixture Process Control

The fuzzy sets used for the fuzzy rule consequents are defined in Figure 5-19. As with the antecedents, there is overlap between these fuzzy consequent actions to provide a workable mix. Note that the limits of -20 and 20% for the change in sand and coarse aggregates are defined arbitrarily. Like the fuzzy set antecedents, the consequents may also be defined by S-functions and $\prod$-functions.

As an example of how this fuzzy production rule set works, assume that the concrete slump is 6 inches. From Figure 5-18, the membership grade or antecedent truth value for each rule is the following

$\mu_{TOO\ STIFF}(6) = 0$
$\mu_{WORKABLE}(6) = 1$
$\mu_{TOO\ WET}(6) = 0$

and so the only rule whose antecedent is satisfied is R_2. This rule is activated and fires with the resulting fuzzy consequent LEAVE ALONE.

Applying the compositional rule of inference gives

$$\mu_{\text{LEAVE ALONE}} = \max[\min(\mu_{\text{WORKABLE}}(6)] = \max[\min(1)] = 1$$

and from Figure 5-19, this translates into a 0% change in the sand and coarse aggregate.

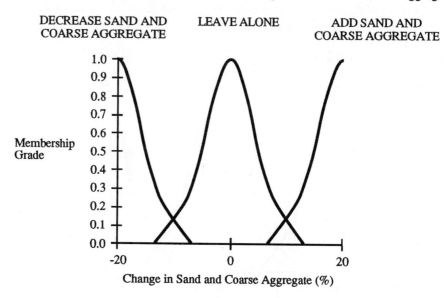

Figure 5-19
Fuzzy Production Rule Consequents for Concrete Mixture Process Control

Now suppose that the slump is 4.8 inches. From Figure 5-18,

$\mu_{\text{TOO STIFF}}(4.8) = .05$
$\mu_{\text{WORKABLE}}(4.8) = .2$
$\mu_{\text{TOO WET}}(4.8) = 0$

Rules R_1 and R_2 have antecedents which are partially satisfied analogous to the partial evidence satisfaction of probabilistic PROSPECTOR rule antecedents. Since there is some nonzero truth that the mix is too stiff or workable, then both rules R_1 and R_2 will become activated and fire. Notice that in a fuzzy production system, unless there is a threshold on antecedent truth, every rule will fire with a nonzero antecedent truth. Setting a threshold may be desirable to prevent inefficiencies due to many rules with low truth values from becoming activated and firing. Recall that in the MYCIN system, the minimum certainty level of a rule to fire must be greater than 0.2 to improve the expert system's efficiency. A similar threshold on the antecedent truth value of fuzzy sets can be defined.

For the slump of 4.8 inches, there are two rules which become activated. Applying the max-min composition rule gives

$$\mu_{\text{DECREASE SAND AND COARSE AGGREGATE}} = \texttt{max} \ [\texttt{min}(\mu_{\text{TOO STIFF}}(4.8)] = .05$$

$$\mu_{\text{LEAVE ALONE}} = \texttt{max} \ [\texttt{min}(\mu_{\text{WORKABLE}}(4.8)] = .2$$

As you can see, for a single antecedent term, the max and min functions are unnecessary.

Since there are now two rules with nonzero consequents, we must decide on a control action. The maximum method will simply pick the rule with the largest membership grade. In this case, the LEAVE ALONE action is chosen since its grade is .2 compared to .05 of the other rule.

The moments method basically calculates the **center of gravity** of the fuzzy consequent rules. The term *center of gravity* comes from Physics where it represents the point where, if all the mass of an object were concentrated, the point mass would act the same under the influence of an external force. The definition of the center of gravity, also called the **first moment of inertia**, I, is

$$I = \frac{\int m(x) \ x \ d(x)}{\int m(x) \ d(x)}$$

where the integral sign denotes ordinary integration.

Figure 5-20 shows the fuzzy sets for the two rules R_2 and R_3. Notice that the fuzzy sets are truncated at the truth values of their antecedents. This reflects the compositional rule of inference. The truncation is done because, intuitively, it makes sense that the truth value of a consequent cannot exceed that of its antecedent.

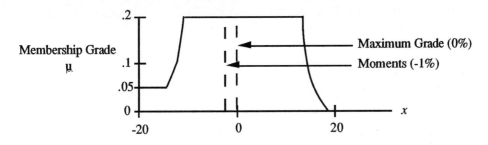

Figure 5-20
Maximum and Moments Methods for the Concrete Process Control Fuzzy Rules

The moment of the consequents is calculated as

$$I = \frac{\int \mu(x) \; x \; d(x)}{\int \mu(x) \; d(x)} \qquad \text{for continuous elements}$$

or

$$I = \frac{\sum_i \mu_i x}{\sum_i \mu_i} \qquad \text{for discrete elements}$$

and is about -1% for Figure 5-20. While this is very close to 0% obtained from the maximum method, the difference may become significant for fuzzy sets that are defined with a considerable amount of overlap. Both the maximum and moments methods have been used in a fuzzy controller for aircraft control (Larkin 85). In this controller, the maximum method calculated the arithmetic mean of all the maxima of the fuzzy consequents. Thus, if there were multiple elements with the same maximum value, one crisp control value would still be calculated.

Besides the maximum and moments methods other approaches have been used to solve the **defuzzification problem** of translating a membership grade into a crisp control value, or a linguistic approximation describing the control variable. However, it is difficult to describe a set of values—the fuzzy set—by a single number or a linguistic phrase.

Possibility and Probability

The term **possibility** has a specific meaning in fuzzy theory. Essentially, possibility refers to allowed values. For example, suppose a proposition is defined regarding the throw of two dice in a universe U of their sum, as follows.

```
p = X is an integer in U

U = {2,3,4,5,6,7,8,9,10,11,12}
```

In fuzzy terminology, for any integer i,

```
Poss {X = i} = 1    for 2 ≤ i ≤ 12
Poss (X = i} = 0    otherwise
```

where **Poss** $(X = i)$ is short for "The possibility that X may assume the value i." (Zadeh 81). The possibility of the dice showing a value from 2 to 12 is very different from the probability of a value *i*. That is, the **possibility distribution** is not the same as a **probability distribution**. The probability distribution of the dice is the frequency of expected occurrence of the **random variable** X, the sum. For example, a 7 can occur due to 1+6, 2+5, and 3+4. So the probability of rolling a 7 is

$$\frac{2 \cdot 3}{36} = \frac{1}{6}$$

while the probability of rolling a 2 is

$$\frac{1}{36}$$

In contrast, the possibility distribution is a constant value of 1 for fair dice for all integers from 2 to 12. A proposition *p* is said to *induce a possibility distribution*, Π_x. That is, given a fuzzy proposition, *p*, based on a fuzzy set F and a linguistic variable X

```
p = X is F
```

The proposition is said to be in **canonical form** when expressed this way, where the term *canonical* means a standard form. The fuzzy set, F, is a **fuzzy predicate** in contrast to the predicates of ordinary logic. F can also be a fuzzy relation. The possibility distribution induced by *p* is equal to F, and is defined by the following **possibility assignment equation.**

$$\Pi_x = F$$

which means that for all values *x* in the universe, $\mathcal{U}$

```
Poss (X = x} = μ_F(x)    x ∈ U
```

As an example, given the proposition

```
p = John is tall
```

a linguistic variable, Height, can be defined with a value, John. The canonical form

```
X is F
```

is represented in terms of the variable Height by

```
Height(John) is TALL
```

and so

$$\text{Poss } \{\text{Height(John)} = x\} = \mu_{\text{TALL}}(x)$$

The proposition, *p*, can be written as a possibility distribution as follows.

$$\text{John is tall} \rightarrow \Pi_{\text{Height(John)}} = \text{TALL}$$

where the arrow symbol means "translates into", Height is a linguistic variable, and TALL is a fuzzy set. Note that John is not a linguistic variable.

Although a fuzzy set can be assigned to a possibility distribution, as in $\Pi_X = F$, the two are not really the same. As an example to illustrate the difference, consider the fuzzy set defined for a roll of dice as follows.

$$\text{ROLL(1)} = 1/3 + 1/4$$

This set is defined to mean that a specific roll of the dice, Roll1, gave a 3 on one die and a 4 on the other. In contrast, the possibility distribution,

$$\Pi_{\text{ROLL(1)}} = 1/3 + 1/4$$

means that the roll gave a 3 *or* a 4, where the "or" is the exclusive-or representing the uncertainty in our knowledge of the roll. There is a possibility of unity that it is a 3 and a possibility of unity that it is a 4. In the fuzzy set, it is certain that the dice values were 3 *and* 4. The possibility distribution means that the dice are fair with regard to whether a 3 or a 4 can occur. The fuzzy set tells what values showed after a roll.

As another example, consider the proposition that "Hans ate X eggs for breakfast" where X is any value in the universe, $X = \{1, 2, ...8\}$ (Zadeh 78).

X	1	2	3	4	5	6	7	8
$\Pi_{\text{ATE (Hans)}}(X)$	1.0	1.0	1.0	1.0	0.8	0.6	0.4	0.2
P(X)	0.1	0.8	0.1	0.0	0.0	0.0	0.0	0.0

The possibility distribution $\Pi_{\text{ATE (Hans)}}(X)$ is interpreted as how easily Hans can eat X eggs. The probability distribution, P(X), is determined empirically by asking Hans if you can join him for breakfast for a year to conduct a scientific study.

An important point to realize is that possibility is *nonstatistical* while probability is *statistical*. For example, although Hans can eat 8 eggs, the empirical study shows that over the period of observation, he has never eaten more than 3 (and kept them down). In this sense, possibility is capability or capacity. A high degree of possibility does not necessarily mean a high degree of probability. That is, there may be no correlation between possibility and probability.

The fuzzy extension to ordinary probability is **fuzzy probability**, which describes probabilities that are only known imprecisely (Zadeh 84b). Some examples of fuzzy probabilities are the **fuzzy qualifiers** *Very Likely*, *Unlikely*, *Not Very Likely*, and so forth. An example of a fuzzy proposition with a fuzzy probability is the following.

```
the battery is BAD is Very Likely
```

Translation Rules

Fuzzy probability is incorporated into the fuzzy logic called **FL** based on Lukasiewicz's L_1 logic (Zadeh 79). One main component of FL is a group of **translation rules** which specify how modified or composite propositions are generated from their elementary propositions.

The translation rules are divided in four categories.

- *Type I* : **modification rules**, such as

```
X is very large
John is much taller than Mike
```

- *Type II* : **composition rules**, such as

   conditional composition
```
If X is TALL then Y is SHORT
```

   conjunctive composition
```
X is TALL and Y is SHORT
```

   disjunctive composition
```
X is TALL or Y is SHORT
```

   conditional and conjunctive composition
```
If X is TALL then Y is SHORT else Y is Rather
SHORT
```

- *Type III* : **quantification rules**, such as

```
Most desserts are WONDERFUL

Too Much nutritious food is FATTENING
```

- *Type IV* : **qualification rules**, such as

truth qualification

```
chocolate pie is DELICIOUS is Very True
```

probability qualification

```
chocolate pie is served SOON is Very Likely
```

possibility qualification

```
chocolate pie is BAD for you is Impossible
```

The qualification rules are those pertaining to fuzzy probabilities. The quantification rules deal with fuzzy quantifiers such as *Most*, which is not capable of being defined using the classical universal and existential quantifiers.

The translation of a Type I rule is represented by

$$X \text{ is } F \rightarrow \prod_x = F$$

with translated proposition

$$X \text{ is } mF \rightarrow \prod_x = F^+$$

where m is a modifier such as *Not, Very, More Or Less*, and so on. F^+ represents the modification of F by m. Some default definitions for m and F^+ are shown in Table 5-18. These are defined the same as the linguistic hedges discussed previously. Other definitions for m and F^+ may also be used.

m	F^+
Not	$F' = \int [1 - \mu_F(x)]/x$
Very	$F^2 = \int \mu_F^2(x)/x$
More Or Less	$\sqrt{F} = \int \sqrt{\mu_F(x)} /x$

Table 5-18
Values of Translation Parameters for Some Type I Rules
(Note that all the integrals are over the universe)

As an example, defining TALL,

```
TALL = .2/5 + .6/6 + 1/7
```

then the translations are as follows.

```
John is not tall → .8/5 + .4/6 + 0/7
John is very tall → .04/5 + .36/6 + 1/7
John is more or less tall → .45/5 + .77/6 + 1/7
```

The variable X does not have to be a unary variable. Instead, X may be a binary or N-ary relation in general. For example, a proposition such as "Y and Z are F" is subsumed by "X is F". Defining CLOSE as a fuzzy binary relation in $U \times U$

```
CLOSE = 1/(1,1) + .5/(1,2) + .5/(2,1)
```

then

```
X and Y are close → Π(x,y) = CLOSE
```

```
X and Y are very close → Π(x,y)
        = CLOSE²
        = 1/(1,1) + .25/(1,2) + .25/(2,1)
```

An example of a type II rule is

```
IF X is F then Y is G → Π(x,y) = F̄´ ⊕ Ḡ
```

where $\bar{F}$ and $\bar{G}$ are the cylindrical extensions of F and G in their universes.

```
F̄ = F × V      Ḡ = U × G
```

and ⊕ is the bounded sum. For this rule

$$\mu_{\bar{F}´ \oplus \bar{G}}(x,y) = 1 \wedge [1 - \mu_F(x) + \mu_G(y)]$$

and the min function is ∧. This definition is consistent with implication in L_1 logic while other definitions may not (Zadeh 79). As an example of a Type II rule, define

```
U = V = {4, 5, 6, 7}
```

```
F = TALL = .2/5 + .6/6 + 1/7
```

```
G = SHORT = 1/4 + .2/5
```

```
IF X is tall then Y is short → Π(x,y)
```

```
    = 1/(5,4) + 1/(5,5) + 1/(6,4) +
      .6/(6,5) + 1/(7,4) + .2/(7,5)
```

where the membership grade of an element such as (5, 4) is calculated as follows.

$$\mu_{\overline{F} \cdot \oplus \overline{G}} (5,4) = 1 \wedge [1 - .2 + 1] = 1 \wedge [1.8] = 1$$

Uncertainty in Fuzzy Expert Systems

When fuzzy probabilities are used in expert systems, there is a difference compared to ordinary probabilistic inference (Zadeh 83). Consider the canonical fuzzy rule

```
If X is F then Y is G (with probability ß)
```

This rule can be written as a conditional probability

```
P(Y is G | X is F) = ß
```

A conventional expert system using classical probability theory would then assume

```
P(Y is not G | X is F) = 1 - ß
```

However, this is not correct in fuzzy theory if F is a fuzzy set. The valid fuzzy result is weaker

```
P(Y is not G | X is F) + P(Y is G | X is F) ≥ 1
```

because it only sets a lower limit on the probabilities, which may be fuzzy numbers. In general, for fuzzy systems

$P(H \mid E)$ is not necessarily equal to $1 - P(H' \mid E)$

In fuzzy expert systems, there may be fuzziness in three areas.
(1) antecedents and/or consequents of rules such as

```
If X is F then Y is G
If X is F then Y is G with CF = α
```

where CF is the certainty factor and α is a numeric value such as 0.5.

(2) partial match between the antecedent and facts which match the antecedent patterns. In nonfuzzy expert systems, a rule does not become activated unless the patterns match the facts exactly. However, in a fuzzy expert system, everything is a matter of degree and all rules may be activated to some extent unless a threshold is set.

(3) fuzzy quantifiers such as *Most*, and fuzzy qualifiers such as *Very Likely, Quite True, Definitely Possible*, and so forth.

Propositions often contain implicit and/or explicit fuzzy quantifiers. As an example, consider the **disposition**

```
d = desserts are WONDERFUL
```

The term *disposition* means a proposition that is usually true, with canonical form

```
Usually(X is R)
```

where *Usually* is an implied fuzzy quantifier and R is a **constraining relation** acting on the constrained variable X to limit the values it may take. Many heuristic rules that people know about the real world are dispositions. In fact, **commonsense knowledge** is basically a collection of dispositions about the real world.

The disposition may be translated into the explicit propositional forms

```
p = Usually desserts are wonderful
p = Most desserts are wonderful
```

which may be expressed as a heuristic rule

```
r = If x is a dessert
      then it is likely that x is wonderful
```

Some rules of inference in fuzzy systems are the following

• **entailment principle**

```
X is F
F ⊂ G
X is G
```

• **dispositional entailment**: limiting case where *Usually* becomes *Always*

```
Usually (X is F)
F ⊂ G
Usually (X is G)
```

• **compositional rule**

```
X is F
(X,Y) is R
Y is F o R
```

where R is a binary relation over the binary variable (X,Y) and

$$\mu_{F \circ R}(y) = \sup_{x} [\mu_F(x) \wedge \mu_R(x,y)]$$

and the **supremum**, symbolized by **sup**, is the **least upper bound**. Generally the supremum is the same as the max function. The difference arises in cases where there is no maximum value such as the real number interval of numbers less than 0. Since there is no maximum real number less than 0, the supremum is used to take 0 as the least upper bound.

- **generalized modus ponens**

```
X is F
Y is G if X is H
Y is F o (H´ ⊕ G)
```

where H´ is the fuzzy negation of H, and the bounded sum is defined

$$\mu_{H' \oplus G}(x,y) = 1 \wedge [1 - \mu_H(x) + \mu_G(y)]$$

The generalized *modus ponens* does not require that the antecedent "X is H" be identical with the premise "X is F". Notice that this is very different from classical logic which requires that they match exactly. The generalized *modus ponens* is actually a special case of the compositional rule of inference. Unlike conventional expert systems in which *modus ponens* is the basic rule of inference, the compositional rule of inference is the basic rule in fuzzy expert systems.

Expert systems using approximate reasoning use one of two different methods. One method is truth value restriction and the second is compositional inference (Whalen 85). In Whalen's survey of eleven fuzzy expert systems, nearly all used compositional inference.

5.6 THE STATE OF UNCERTAINTY

There is no clear consensus as to the best method of dealing with uncertainty, although a number of techniques have been studied such as classical Bayesian, **convex set Bayesian**, Dempster-Shafer, **Kyburg**, and the possibility theory of fuzzy logic (Thompson 85). In the convex set approach to Bayes theory, the belief state is not a single function of the classical Bayes method. Instead, the belief state is characterized by a set of **convex functions**. This means that any function can be represented as a linear combination of two other functions.

Since the Dempster-Shafer theory was first introduced as a generalization of classical probability, there have been rebuttals. For example, Kyburg's paper claims that Dempster-Shafer theory is not a generalization of classical probability, but is actually the other way around. Kyburg believes that Dempster-Shafer theory is included in classical probability and that the Dempster-Shafer intervals are included in the convex set Bayes approach (Kyburg 87). The Dempster-Shafer theory also seems to have difficulties in dealing with beliefs that are close to zero. Very different results are obtained when beliefs are zero compared to when the beliefs are very small (Dubois 85). Another problem with the Dempster-Shafer theory is the exponential explosion in the number of computations as the possible answers to a diagnostic problem increase.

Although the Gordon and Shortliffe approximation avoids the exponential explosion, it may produce poor results in the case of highly conflicting evidence. An alternative approach that is not an approximation and gives good results for hierarchical evidence without the combinatorial explosion has been given (Shafer 87). A number of other papers have attempted to overcome the exponential explosion problem by different generalizations to Dempster-Shafer theory (Liu 86) (Yen 86) (Lee 87).

The major benefit of all this work has been a re-examination of the foundations of probability theory and widespread interest in methods of dealing with uncertainty.

5.7 SUMMARY

In this chapter, non-probabilistic theories of uncertainty were discussed. Certainty factors, Dempster-Shafer theory, and fuzzy theory are all ways of dealing with uncertainty in expert systems. Certainty factors are simple to implement and have been used successfully in expert systems such as MYCIN where the inference chains are short. However, the theory of certainty factors is an *ad hoc* theory that does not appear to be generally valid for longer inference chains.

Dempster-Shafer theory has a rigorous foundation and holds promise for expert systems. However, at the present time, there does not seem to be any clear concensus on how to apply it for general use in expert systems.

Fuzzy theory is the most general theory of uncertainty that has been formulated. It has wide applicability because of the extension principle. Since the first classic paper by Zadeh in 1965, fuzzy theory has been applied to many fields.

PROBLEMS

5-1.   Given that evidence E_2 adds to the original evidence E_1, show that

$$P(D_i \mid E_1 \cap E_2) = \frac{P(E_2 \mid D_i \cap E_1)\ P(D_i \mid E_1)}{\sum_j P(E_2 \mid D_j \cap E_1)\ P(D_j \mid E_1)}$$

Hint: use the results of Problem 4-8 (b).

5-2.   Prove that

$$CF(H, E) + CF(H', E) = 0$$

5-3.   Given rules

```
IF E₁ AND E₂ AND E₃
THEN H        (CF₁)

IF E₄ OR E₅
THEN H        (CF₂)
```

where

$$CF_1(E_1,e) = 1 \qquad CF_1(E_2,e) = 0.5 \qquad CF_1(E_3,e) = 0.3$$
$$CF_2(E_4,e) = 0.7 \qquad CF_2(E_5,e) = 0.2$$
$$CF_1(H,E) = 0.5 \qquad CF_2(H,E) = 0.9$$

   a)   Draw a tree illustrating how these rules support H.
   b)   Calculate the certainty factors $CF_1(H,e)$ and $CF_2(H,e)$.
   c)   Calculate $CF_{COMBINE}$ $[CF_1(H,e),CF_2(H,e)]$

5-4.   a)   In Figure 5-7 (c) assuming

```
m(X) = 0.2
m(Y) = 0.3
m(Z) = 0.5
```

find the evidential intervals of X, Y and Z using Dempster-Shafer theory.
   b)   In Figure 5-7 (d) assuming

```
m(X) = 0.4
m(Y) = 0.6
```

find the evidential intervals for

```
X
X ∩ Y
Y
X ∩ Y´
X´ ∩ Y
```

5-5.   Given the rules

```
Rule 1: IF E THEN H
Rule 2: IF E THEN H´
```

and assuming

$\Theta = \{H, \ H'\}$
$m_1(H) \ = 0.5 \quad m_1(\Theta) \ = 0.5$ for Rule 1
$m_2(H') = 0.3 \quad m_2(\Theta) \ = 0.7$ for Rule 2

  a) Write the Dempster-Shafer table showing the combination of evidence and calculate the combined belief functions.
  b) Calculate the plausibilities.
  c) Calculate the evidential intervals.
  d) Calculate the dubieties.
  e) Calculate the ignorances.

5-6.   Based on reports from different types of sensors, the following table gives the degrees of belief in the aircraft environment of airliner (H), bomber (B), and fighter (F).

Focal elements	Sensor 1 (m_1)	Sensor 2 (m_2)
Θ	0.15	0.2
A,B	0.3	0.1
A,F	0.1	0.05
B,F	0.1	0.1
A	0.05	0.3
B	0.2	0.05
F	0.1	0.2

  a) Calculate the initial belief functions, plausibility, evidential intervals, dubieties, and ignorances.
  b) Calculate these same parameters after the evidence is combined.

5-7.   A policeman stops a motorist for speeding. Due to errors in the policeman's radar gun and the motorist's speedometer, the belief functions are as follows.

Policeman	Motorist
$m_1(57) = 0.3$	$m_2(56) = 0.2$
$m_1(56) = 0.5$	$m_2(55) = 0.6$
$m_1(55) = 0.2$	$m_2(54) = 0.2$

  a) Calculate the belief functions, plausibility, evidential intervals, dubieties and ignorance of each person.
  b) Calculate these parameters after combining the evidences.
  c) Explain why you believe the motorist was or was not speeding based on the parameters.

5-8.   Given the fuzzy sets

$$A = .1/1 + .2/2 + .3/3 \qquad B = .2/1 + .3/2 + .4/3$$

calculate/explain the following

    a) Are the sets equal? Explain.
    b) Set complement
    c) Set union
    d) Set intersection
    e) Does the Law of Excluded Middle hold for each set? Explain.
    f) Set product
    g) Second power of each set
    h) Probabilistic sum
    i) Bounded sum
    j) Bounded product
    k) Bounded difference
    l) Concentration
    m) Dilation
    n) Intensification
    o) Normalization

5-9.   Given the fuzzy sets

$$Q = \begin{bmatrix} 0.2 & 0.3 \\ 0.4 & 1.0 \end{bmatrix} \quad \text{defined on } U_1 \times U_2$$

$$P = \begin{bmatrix} 0.1 & 0.5 & 0.3 \\ 0.2 & 0.0 & 0.4 \end{bmatrix} \quad \text{defined on } U_2 \times U_3$$

    a) Calculate the first, second, and total projections for each set.
    b) Calculate the cylindrical extensions of each set.
    c) Show that

$$Q \circ P = \text{proj}(\overline{Q} \cap \overline{P} \, ; \, U_1 \times U_3)$$

5-10.   Consider the linguistic variable Person as a fuzzy set of order 3.

    a) Define Person as three fuzzy sets of order 2.
    b) Define each of the order 2 sets in terms of three fuzzy sets of order 1.
    c) Define three of the fuzzy order 1 sets in terms of S- and/or $\prod$-functions.

5-11.   a)   Define five linguistic values for the linguistic variable Uncertainty.

         b)   Draw appropriate functions for these values, and explain your choice.

         c)   Draw the fuzzy sets for

```
Not TRUE
More Or Less TRUE
Sort Of TRUE
Pretty TRUE
Rather TRUE
Slightly TRUE
```

         assuming TRUE is a S-function. What are the limits of TRUE? Explain.

5-12.   a)   Define at least six values for the linguistic variable Water Temperature.

         b)   Draw the appropriate functions for the fuzzy set values on one graph.

         c)   Give three hedged fuzzy set functions based on FREEZING.

5-13.   (a) Show by truth table for $N = 2$ and $N = 3$, the values of the primitive L-logic operators of Table 5-14. (b) derive $x \leftrightarrow y$ in terms of the absolute values of x, y.

5-14.   Given numeric truth values

$$x(A) = .2/.1 + .6/.3 + 1/.9$$
$$x(B) = .1/.1 + .3/.5 + 1/.9$$

calculate the fuzzy logic truth of the following

         a)   NOT A

         b)   A AND B

         c)   A OR B

         d) $A \rightarrow B$

         e) $B \rightarrow A$

5-15.   Define a fuzzy grammar using hedged primaries and range phrases to generate productions such as

```
IF PRESSURE IS HIGH
THEN TURN VALVE LOWER

IF PRESSURE IS VERY HIGH
THEN TURN VALVE MUCH LOWER

IF PRESSURE IS VERY VERY HIGH
THEN TURN VALVE MUCH MUCH LOWER
```

```
IF PRESSURE IS LOW TO MEDIUM
THEN TURN VALVE HIGHER
```

Assume (1) that the primaries for PRESSURE are only LOW and HIGH, (2) the range phrases involving TO only occur in the antecedent, and (3) the primaries for VALVE in the conclusion are only LOWER and HIGHER.

BIBLIOGRAPHY

(Adams 79). J.T. Adams, *The Complete Concrete, Masonry and Brick Handbook*, Arco Publishing, p. 1059, p. 1979.

(Adams 85). J. Barclay Adams, "Probabilistic Reasoning and Certainty Factors," in *Rule-based Expert Systems*, Addison Wesley, pp. 263-271, 1985.

(Bellman 73). R.E. Bellman and M. Giertz, "On the Analytic Formalism of the Theory of Fuzzy Sets," *Information Science*, **5**, pp. 149-156, 1973.

(Bogler 87). Philip L. Bogler, "Shafer-Dempster Reasoning with Applications to Multisensor Target Identification Systems," *IEEE Tran. on Systems, Man, and Cybernetics*, **SMC-17**, (6), pp. 968-977, Nov/Dec 1987.

(Carnap 50). R. Carnap, "The Two Concepts of Probability," in *Logical Foundations of Probability*, pp. 19-51, University of Chicago Press, 1950.

(Dempster 67). A. P. Dempster, "Upper and Lower Probabilities Induced by Multivalued Mappings," *Annals of Math. Stat.*, **38**, pp. 325-329, 1967.

(Dubois 85). Didier Dubois and Henri Prade, "Combination and Propagation of Uncertainty with Belief Functions," *IJCAI '85*, pp. 111-113, 1985.

(Garvey 81). T.D. Garvey, J.D. Lowrance, and M.A. Fischler, "An Inference Technique for Integrating Knowledge from Disparate Sources," *Proc. 7th IJCAI*, pp. 319-325, 1981.

(Gordon 85). Jean Gordon and Edward H. Shortliffe. "The Dempster-Shafer Theory of Evidence." in *Rule-based Expert Systems*, ed. Bruce Buchanan and Edward Shortliffe, pp. 272-292, 1985.

(Kandel 82). Abraham Kandel, *Fuzzy Techniques in Pattern Recognition*, John Wiley & Sons, 1982.

(Klir 88). George J. Klir and Tina A. Folger, *Fuzzy Sets, Uncertainty, and Information*, Prentice-Hall, pp. 75-77, 1988.

(Kyburg 87). Henry E. Kyburg, Jr., "Bayesian and Non-Bayesian Evidential Updating," *Artificial Intelligence*, **31**, (3), pp. 271-293, 1987.

(Larkin 85). L. I. Larkin, "A Fuzzy Logic Controller for Aircraft Flight Control," in *Industrial Applications of Fuzzy Control*, ed. M. Sugeno, North-Holland, pp. 87-103, 1985

(Larsen 81). P. Martin Larsen, "Industrial Applications of Fuzzy Logic Control," in *Fuzzy Reasoning and Its Applications*, ed. E.H. Mamdani and B.R. Gaines, Academic Press, pp. 335-342, 1981.

(Lee 87). Sunggu Lee and Kang G. Shin, "Uncertain Inference Using Belief Functions," *Proceedings The Third Conference on Artificial Intelligence Applications*, pp. 238-243, 1987.

(Liu 86). Gerald Shao-Hung Liu, "Causal and Plausible Reasoning in Expert Systems," *AAAI-86*, pp. 220-225, 1986.

(Lowrance 82). J.D. Lowrance and T.D. Garvey, "Evidential Reasoning: A Developing Concept," *Proc. Int. Conf. on Cybernetics and Society*, pp. 6-9, 1982.

(Maiers 85). J. Maiers and Y. S. Sherif, "Applications of Fuzzy Set Theory," *IEEE Transactions on Systems, Man, and Cybernetics*, **SMC-15**, (1), pp. 175-189, Jan./Feb. 1985.

(Shafer 76). Glenn Shafer, *A Mathematical Theory of Evidence*, Princeton University Press, 1976.

(Shafer 87). Glenn Shafer and Roger Logan, "Implementing Dempster's Rule for Hierarchical Evidence," *Artificial Intelligence*, **33**, (3), pp. 271-298, Nov. 1987.

(Shortliffe 85). Edward H. Shortliffe and Bruce G. Buchanan. "A Model of Inexact Reasoning in Medicine," in *Rule-based Expert Systems*, Addison-Wesley, pp. 233-262, 1985.

(Strat 84). Thomas M. Strat, "Continuous Belief Functions for Evidential Reasoning," *Proceedings of the National Conference on AI*, pp. 308-313, 1984.

(Wesley 86). Leonard P. Wesley, "Evidential Knowledge-based Computer Vision," *Optical Eng.*, **25**, (3), pp. 363-379, 1986.

(Whalen 85). Thomas Whalen and Brian Schott, "Alternative Logics for Approximate Reasoning in Expert Systems: A Comparative Study," *Int. J. of Man-Machine Studies*, **22**, pp. 327-346, 1985.

(Yen 86). John Yen, "A Reasoning Model Based on an Extended Dempster-Shafer Theory," *AAAI-86*, pp. 125-131, 1986.

(Zadeh 65). Lotfi A. Zadeh, "Fuzzy Sets," *Information and Control*, pp. 338-353, 1965.

(Zadeh 73). Lotfi A. Zadeh, "The Concept of a Linguistic Variable and Its Application to Approximate Reasoning," *Memorandum ERL-M 411*, University of California at Berkeley, p. 83, October 1973.

(Zadeh 75). Lotfi A. Zadeh, "Calculus of Fuzzy Restrictions," *Fuzzy Sets and Their Applications to Cognitive and Decision Processes*, Academic Press, p. 36, 1975.

(Zadeh 78). Lotfi A. Zadeh, "Fuzzy Sets as a Basis for a Theory of Possibility," *Fuzzy Sets and Systems*, **1**, pp. 3-28, 1978.

(Zadeh 79). Lotfi A. Zadeh, "A Theory of Approximate Reasoning," *Machine Intelligence*, **9**, ed. J. E. Hayes, Donald Michie, and L. I. Mikulich, pp. 149-194, 1979.

(Zadeh 81). Lotfi A. Zadeh, "PRUF - A Meaning Representation Language for Natural Languages," *Fuzzy Reasoning and Its Applications*, ed. E. H. Mamdani and B. R. Gaines, Academic Press, pp. 1-66, 1981.

(Zadeh 83). Lotfi A. Zadeh, "The Role of Fuzzy Logic in the Management of Uncertainty in Expert Systems," *Fuzzy Sets and Systems*, **11**, pp 199-227, 1983.

(Zadeh 84a). Lotfi A. Zadeh, "Review of Books: A Mathematical Theory of Evidence," *The AI Magazine*, pp. 81-83, Fall 1984.

(Zadeh 84b). Lotfi A. Zadeh, "Fuzzy Probabilities," *Information Processing & Management*, **20**, (3), pp. 363-372, 1984.

(Zadeh 88). Lotfi A. Zadeh, "Fuzzy Logic," *IEEE Computer*, pp. 83-93, April 1988.

(Zimmerman 85). H. J. Zimmerman, *Fuzzy Set Theory and Its Applications*, Kluwer-Nijhoff Publishing, pp. 62-63, 1985.

CHAPTER 6 THE DESIGN OF EXPERT SYSTEMS

6.1 INTRODUCTION

In the previous chapters, we have discussed the general concepts and theory of expert systems. This chapter presents general guidelines for building practical expert systems designed for real-world applications, not research prototypes. A **software engineering methodology** is described so that an expert system can be a quality product developed in a cost-effective and timely manner.

6.2 SELECTING THE APPROPRIATE PROBLEM

Before you can build an expert system, you must select an appropriate problem, as discussed in Section 1.6. Like any software project, there are a number of general considerations that should be made before a large commitment of people, resources and time to a proposed expert system. These general considerations are typical of project management concerns in conventional programs, but must be customized for the special requirements of expert systems. A very high-level management view of expert system development is shown in Figure 6-1. The three general stages shown on the left have some more specific considerations shown on the right of the figure. These more specific considerations will be discussed as questions and answers to serve as guidelines for expert system projects.

Selecting the Appropriate Paradigm

Why are we building an expert system?

This is probably the most important question to be asked of *any* project. While Chapter 1, Section 2 described the general advantages of expert systems, only management authorizes the system and technical personnel implement the need. In particular, the answer to this question must eventually be given to the owners or stockholders funding development. Before starting, there should be a clear identification of the problem, expert, and users.

Payoff

What is the payoff?

This question is related to the first question. However this question is more pragmatic by asking for a specific return on investment of people, resources, and time, and money. The payoff may be in money, increased efficiency, or any of the other advantages of expert systems described in Chapter 1. It is also important to remember that if no one uses the system, there will be no payoff. Because expert systems is a new technology, it is more difficult and risky to answer this question compared to conventional programming.

Figure 6-1
Project Management Tasks

Tools

What tools are available to build the system?

There are many expert system tools available today with advantages and disadvantages. Appendix D summarizes the characteristics of some tools. However, this should only be taken as a guide since software tools develop so rapidly. Generally, you can count on a substantial enhancement every year in each tool and a major revision every two to three years.

These enhancements are not limited to the software tools. Many of the state-of-the-art tools that only ran on $50,000 LISP machines in the mid-1980's were later rewritten to run on microcomputers or custom microprocessors. This greatly reduced the cost of hardware to run the tools. Your best guide is to examine current literature and talk to people who have built expert systems.

Cost

How much will it cost?

The cost of building an expert system depends on the people, resources, and time devoted to its construction. Besides the hardware and software required to run an expert system tool, there may also be considerable cost in training. If your personnel have little or no experience with a tool, it can be costly to train them. For example, training on a state-of-the-art expert system tool may cost $2500/week per person.

6.3 STAGES IN THE DEVELOPMENT OF AN EXPERT SYSTEM

How will the system be developed?

To a large extent, the development of an expert system will depend on the resources provided. However, like any other project, the development will also depend on the how the development process is organized and managed.

Project Management

Project management is expected to provide the following. In fact, project management has been the subject of an expert system approach (Sathi 86).

* *Activity Management*

    * planning
        - define activities
        - specify priority of activities
        - resource requirements
        - milestones
        - durations
        - responsibilities

    * scheduling
        - assign starting and ending times
        - resolve conflicts in scheduling tasks of equal priority

    * chronicling
        - monitor project performance

    * analysis
        - analyze plans, schedules, and chronicled activities

- *Product Configuration Management*

    - product management   - manage the different versions of the product

    - change management   - manage change proposals and impact evaluations
                                   - assign personnel to make changes
                                   - install new product versions

- *Resource Management*

    - forecast needs for resources

    - acquire resources

    - assign responsibilities for optimum use of resources

    - provide critical resources to minimize bottlenecks

For the development of an expert system, the activities are those tasks required to build the system. Figure 6-2 shows a high-level view of the activities required to produce a system in terms of the stages that a system goes through.

The Delivery Problem

How will the system be delivered?

While it is convenient and can minimize development time to use a state-of-the-art workstation, it is often too costly to deliver the system on these workstations. For example, a workstation that has $100,000 worth of hardware and software is rather expensive to be used by a thousand field offices of a company. In addition, annual maintenance fees can further increase the cost substantially.

Depending on the number of expert systems to be deployed, the **delivery problem** of the developed systems may be a major factor in development. The delivery problem should be considered in the earliest stage of development (Freedman 86).

Ideally, the delivered expert systems should be capable of running on standard hardware. However, some expert system tools require a special LISP microprocessor board which will substantially increase the cost.

In many cases, the expert system must be integrated with other existing programs. Consideration should be given to the communication and coordination of the expert system input/output with these programs. It may also be desirable to call the expert system as a procedure from a conventional programming language and the system should support this.

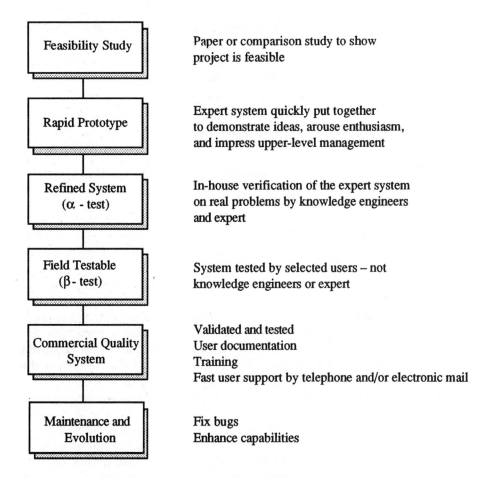

Feasibility Study	Paper or comparison study to show project is feasible
Rapid Prototype	Expert system quickly put together to demonstrate ideas, arouse enthusiasm, and impress upper-level management
Refined System (α - test)	In-house verification of the expert system on real problems by knowledge engineers and expert
Field Testable (β - test)	System tested by selected users – not knowledge engineers or expert
Commercial Quality System	Validated and tested User documentation Training Fast user support by telephone and/or electronic mail
Maintenance and Evolution	Fix bugs Enhance capabilities

Figure 6-2
General Stages in the Development of an Expert System

Maintenance and Evolution

How will the system be maintained and evolve?

The maintenance and evolution of an expert system is more of an open-ended activity than with conventional programs. Because expert systems are not based on algorithms, their performance is dependent on knowledge. As new knowledge is acquired and old knowledge modified, the performance of the system improves.

In a commercial quality product, there must be a systematic and efficient way to collect bug reports from the users. While the collection and repair of bug reports is not a high priority in research-grade systems, it is a high priority in commercial quality systems. Good maintenance can only be done if bug reports are acquired.

The enhancement of an expert system after delivery is also more of a concern in a commercial quality system. The developers of a commercial system want it to be a financial success. This means listening to what the users want and are willing to pay for in improvements. In a very real sense, a commercial expert system may never really be finished—it only keeps getting better.

6.4   ERRORS IN DEVELOPMENT STAGES

The potential major errors of expert system development can be classified by the most likely stage in which they occur, as illustrated in Figure 6-3. These errors include the following.

• **expert's knowledge errors.** The expert is the **knowledge source** of the expert system. If the expert's knowledge is erroneous, the results may be propagated through the entire development process. As mentioned in Chapter 1, a side-benefit of building an expert system is the potential detection of erroneous knowledge when the expert's knowledge is made explicit.

For **mission critical** projects in which human life and property are at risk, it may be necessary to set up formal procedures to certify an expert's knowledge. One approach that NASA has successfully used for space flight is **Flight Technique Panels** which regularly review problem solutions and the analysis techniques used to develop the solutions (Culbert 87). The panels consist of system users, independent domain experts, system developers, and managers to insure coverage all areas affecting development.

The advantage of a panel approach is that the expert's knowledge is placed under close scrutiny at the beginning of the development process when erroneous knowledge is easier to correct. The longer that erroneous knowledge is undetected, the more expensive it is to correct. If the expert's knowledge is not initially verified, the ultimate test is the validation of the expert system. The final validation of the expert system demonstrates whether the system satisfies requirements, especially correctness and completeness of solutions.

The disadvantage of a panel approach is primarily the cost involved. However, this cost may be offset by the greater efficiency of the development process.

• **semantic errors.** An error of semantics occurs when the meaning of knowledge is not properly communicated. As a very simple example, suppose an expert says "You can extinguish a fire with water" and the knowledge engineer interprets this as "All fires can be extinguished by water." Semantic errors occur if the knowledge engineer misinterprets the expert's answers, or the expert misinterprets the knowledge engineers question, or both.

• **syntax errors**. These are simple errors that occur when the incorrect form of a rule or fact is entered. The expert system tools should flag these errors and an appropriate message issued. Other errors that occur in the knowledge-base building phase are due to knowledge source errors that were not detected in the previous stages.

• **inference engine errors**. Just as with any other piece of software, the inference engine may have bugs. By the time that an expert system tool is released for general use, all of the common bugs should be fixed. However, there may be bugs that only show up in rare circumstances such as having 159 rules on the agenda. Some bugs may be very subtle and only show up in certain pattern matching operations.

In general, inference engine bugs may show up in pattern matching, conflict resolution, and execution of the actions. These bugs may be very difficult to detect if they are not consistent. If the expert system tool is used for mission critical applications, you should determine how the tool was validated.

The simplest method of checking for tool errors is the classic method of asking other users and the tool vendor. The tool vendor should be willing to supply a list of customers, bug reports, and fixes, and how long the tool has been in use. A user's group is an excellent source of information.

• **inference chain errors**. These errors may be caused by erroneous knowledge, semantic errors, inference engine bugs, incorrect specification of rule priorities, and unplanned interactions between rules. More complex inference chain errors are due to uncertainty of rules and evidence, the propagation of uncertainty in the inference chain and nonmonoticity.

The choice of a method for dealing with uncertainty does not automatically resolve all issues dealing with uncertainty. For example, before choosing simple Bayesian inference, you should check to see if the assumption of conditional independence is warranted.

• **limits of ignorance errors**. A problem which is common to all development stages is specifying the limits of ignorance of the system. As mentioned in Chapter 1, human experts know the extent of their knowledge and their performance degrades (hopefully) gracefully at the boundaries of their ignorance. Human experts should be honest enough to admit more uncertainty in their conclusions near the boundaries. However, unless an expert system is specifically programmed to admit uncertainty, it may continue to supply answers even if the inference chain and evidence is very weak.

6.5 SOFTWARE ENGINEERING AND EXPERT SYSTEMS

In the previous sections, we have discussed the general considerations in using the expert system paradigm. Now let's examine the stages of expert system development from the more technical perspective of the knowledge engineer who actually builds the system.

Since expert systems have moved out of the research stage, there is a real need to deliver quality software up to the standards of conventional software. The accepted methodology for developing quality software for commercial, industrial, and governmental standards is software engineering.

It is important to follow good standards in the development of a product or the product will probably not be of good quality. Expert systems should now be considered a product just as any other software product such as a word processor, payroll program, computer game, and so forth.

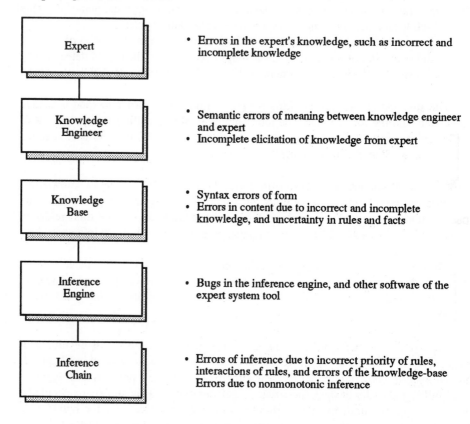

Figure 6-3
Major Errors in Expert Systems and Some Causes

However, there is a significant difference of **mission** between expert systems and typical consumer products such as word processors and video games. The term *mission* refers to the overall purpose of a project or a technology. Expert systems technology generally have a serious mission of supplying expertise in high-performance and possibly hazardous situations where human life and property are at stake. These are the mission critical applications mentioned in the previous section.

Mission critical applications are very different from the more relaxed mission of word processors and video games to increase efficiency and provide recreation. No human's life may depend on a bug in a word processor or video game (or at least it shouldn't).

Expert systems are high performance systems that must be of high quality or they will be prone to bugs. Software engineering provides methodologies for building quality software, as illustrated in Figure 6-4.

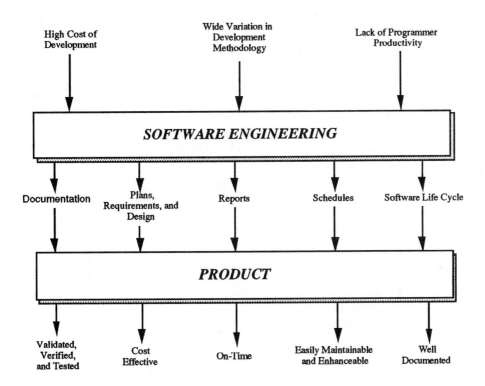

Figure 6-4
The Software Engineering Methodology

Quality is a difficult term to describe in a general sense because it means different things to different people. One way of defining **quality** is as the required or desirable attributes of an object determined on some scale. The term *object* is used here to mean any software or hardware, such as a software product. The attributes and their values are called **metrics** because they are used as measures of an object. For example, the measured reliability of a disk drive is a metric of its quality. One measure of this attribute is the **mean time between failures** (MTBF) of the drive. A reliable drive might have a MTBF of 1000 hours of use between crashes, while an unreliable drive might have a MTBF of 100 hours.

Table 6-1 gives a checklist of some metrics that may be used in assessing the quality of an expert system. These metrics should only be taken as a guide since a specific expert system may have more or less of these. However, the important concept is to have a required list of metrics that can be used in describing quality.

```
Correct outputs given correct input
Complete output given correct input
Consistent output given the same input again
Reliable so that it does not crash (often) due to bugs
Usable for people and preferably user-friendly
Maintainable
Enhanceable
Validated to prove it satisfies the user's needs and requests
Tested to prove correctness and completeness
Cost-effective
Reusable code for other applications
Portable to other hardware/software environments
Interfaceable with other software
Understandable code
Accurate
Precise
Graceful degradation at the boundaries of knowledge
Embedded capability with other languages
Verified knowledge-base
Explanation facility
```

Table 6-1
Some Software Quality Metrics for Expert Systems

A list of metrics allows you to more easily prioritize metrics since many may be in conflict with others. For example, increasing the testing of an expert system to assure its correctness will increase the cost. Deciding when testing ends is generally a complex decision involving the factors of schedules, cost, and requirements. Ideally all three of these requirements should be satisfied. In practice, some may be judged more important than others and the constraints of satisfying all factors will be weakened.

6.6 THE EXPERT SYSTEM LIFE CYCLE

One of the key methods of software engineering is the **life cycle**. The software life cycle is the period of time that starts with the initial concept of the software and ends with its retirement from use. Rather than thinking of development and maintenance separately, the life cycle concept provides a continuity that connects all stages. Planning for maintenance and evolution early in the life cycle reduces the cost of these stages later.

Maintenance Costs

For conventional software, maintenance typically accounts for about 60 - 80% of all software costs and is usually two to four times the original development cost. Although there is little information about maintenance of expert systems because they are so new, the figures will probably be worse for expert systems. If conventional programs with known algorithms require so much maintenance, then expert systems will probably require more maintenance because they are based on much knowledge that is heuristic and experiential. Expert systems that do a lot of inference under uncertainty should be even more susceptible to high maintenance and evolution costs.

Waterfall Model

A number of different life cycle models have been developed for conventional software. The classic waterfall model was the original life cycle model and is illustrated in Figure 6-5 (Boehm 84). This model is very familiar to programmers of conventional software. In the waterfall model each stage ends with a verification and validation (V & V) activity to minimize any problems in that stage. Also, notice that the arrows go back and forth only one stage at a time. This represents the iterative development between two adjacent stages in order to minimize the cost compared to the higher cost of iterating development over several stages.

Another term for life cycle is **process model** because it is concerned with the two fundamental issues of software development.

(1) What should be done next?
(2) How long should the next stage be performed?

The process model is actually a **metamethodology** because it determines the order and duration that the common software methods are applied. The common software development methods (or methodologies) show

- specific methods to accomplish a stage such as
  - planning
  - requirements
  - knowledge acquisition
  - testing

- representation of stage products
  - documentation

- code
- diagrams

Code-and-Fix Model

A number of process models have been used for software development. The earliest "model" is the infamous **code-and-fix model** in which some code is written and then fixed when it doesn't work right (Boehm 88). This is usually the method of choice for new programming students both in conventional programming and expert systems.

By 1970, the deficiencies in the code-and-fix approach were so obvious that the waterfall model was developed to provide a systematic methodology that was especially useful for large projects. However, there were difficulties with the waterfall model because it assumed that all the information necessary for a stage was known. In practice, it was often not possible to write the complete requirements until a prototype had been built. This led to the **"do it twice"** concept in which a prototype was built, the requirements determined, and then the final system was built.

Incremental Model

The **incremental waterfall model** is a refinement of the waterfall and of the standard top-down approach. The basic idea of incremental development is to develop software in increments of functional capability. The incremental model has been used very successfully in large conventional software projects. The incremental model is also useful for expert systems development in which the addition of rules increases the capabilities of the system from assistant, to colleague, and finally expert level. Thus, in an expert system, the **major increments** are from assistant to colleague and from colleague to experts. The **minor increments** correspond to increments of expertise within each level that offer some significant increase. A **micro increment** is the change in expertise by adding or refining an individual rule.

The primary advantage of the incremental model is that the increases in functional capability are easier to test, verify, and validate than the products of individual stages in the waterfall model. Each functional increment can be tested, verified, and validated immediately with the expert rather than trying to do the entire validation at the end. This decreases the cost of incorporating corrections in the system. In essence, the incremental model is similar to a continuous rapid prototype that extends over the entire development. Rather than just a rapid prototype of the initial stages to determine requirements in the "do it twice" approach, the evolving prototype *is* the system.

Spiral Model

One way of visualizing the incremental model is an adaptation of the conventional **spiral model**, as shown in Figure 6-6. Each circuit of the spiral adds some functional capability to the system. The ending point label "Delivered System" is actually not the end of the spiral. Instead a new spiral begins with maintenance and evolution of the system. The spiral can be further refined to specify more precisely the general stages of Knowledge Acquisition, Coding, Evaluation, and Planning.

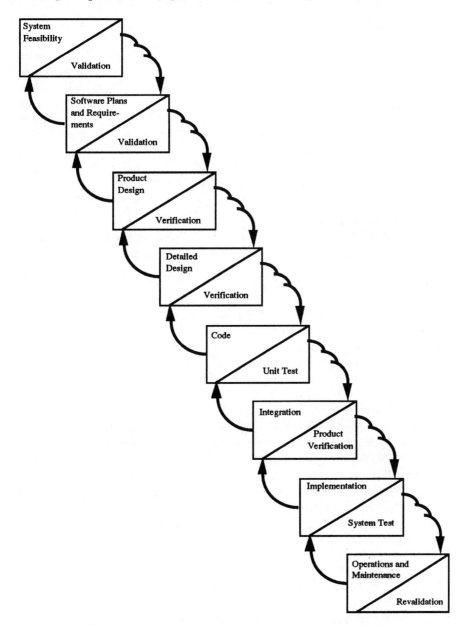

Figure 6-5
The Waterfall Model of the Software Life Cycle

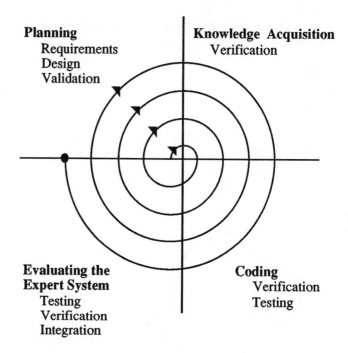

Figure 6-6
A Spiral Model of Expert System Development

6.7 A DETAILED LIFE CYCLE MODEL

A life cycle model that has been successfully used in a number of expert system projects is the **Linear Model** illustrated in Figure 6-7, adapted from Bochsler (Bochsler 88). This life cycle consists of a number of stages from Planning to System Evaluation and describes the development of the system to some point at which its functional capabilities will be evaluated. After this, the life cycle repeats this same sequence from Planning to System Evaluation until the system is delivered for routine use. The life cycle is then used for subsequent maintenance and evolution of the system. Although not explicitly shown, verification and validation proceed in parallel with the stages. Rather than just fixing up some bugs, it is important to follow through with the same sequence of stages to maintain the quality of the expert system. Skipping stages, even to fix one little bug, impairs the entire quality.

This life cycle shown may be considered one circuit of the spiral model. Each stage consists of **tasks**. Not all tasks may be necessary for a stage, especially once the system goes into maintenance and evolution. Instead the tasks are meant to serve as a composite of all tasks for the entire life cycle from initial concept to software retirement. The tasks will also depend on the exact type of application being built and so should only be considered as a guide, rather than absolute requirements that must be performed for each stage to be completed.

This life cycle model will be discussed in detail to illustrate the many factors that should be considered for a large, quality expert system. For small, research type prototypes that are not intended for general use, not all tasks or even stages are necessary. However, it is amazing how much software that is developed for personal or research use gets released to associates and then into general use.

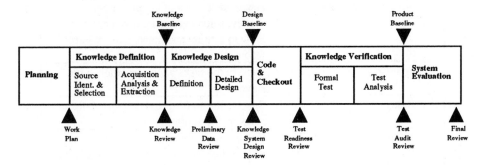

Figure 6-7
The Linear Model of Expert System Development Life Cycle

Planning

The purpose of the Planning Stage is to produce a formal **work plan** for the expert system development. The work plan is a set of documents that will be used to guide and evaluate development. Table 6-2 illustrates the tasks in this stage.

The feasibility assessment is the most important task in the life cycle. The assessment must answer the questions of whether the project is worthwhile and the related question of whether an expert system is the appropriate paradigm. The answers to these two questions determine if the project should proceed using an expert systems approach. Many factors are involved in feasibility assessment. As discussed in Section 6.1, these factors include selection of an appropriate expert system domain, cost, payoff, and others.

Knowledge Definition

The object of the **knowledge definition stage** is to define the knowledge requirements of the expert system. The Knowledge Definition Stage consists of two main tasks, as follows

- Knowledge source identification and selection
- Knowledge acquisition, analysis, and extraction

Each of these major tasks is composed of other tasks. Table 6-3 describes the tasks involved in source identification and selection.

Task	Objective
Feasibility assessment	Determine if it is worthwhile to build the system and if so, whether expert system technology should be used.
Resource management	Assess resources of people, time, money, software, and hardware required. How to acquire and manage the required resources.
Task phasing	Specify the tasks and their order in the stages.
Schedules	Specify the starting and delivery dates of tasks in the stages.
Preliminary functional layout	Defines *what* the system should accomplish by specifying the high-level functions of the system.This task specifies the purpose of the system.
High-level requirements	Describes in high-level terms *how* the functions of the system will be accomplished.

Table 6-2
Planning Stage Tasks

Task	Objective
Source identification	Who and what are the knowledge sources, without regard to availability.
Source importance	Prioritized list of knowledge sources in order of importance to development.
Source availability	List of knowledge sources ranked in order of availability. Books and other documents are generally much more available than human experts.
Source selection	Select the knowledge sources based on importance and availability.

Table 6-3
Knowledge Source Identification And Selection Tasks

Acquisition, analysis, and extraction tasks are described in Table 6-4.

Task	Objective
Acquisition strategy	Specify how knowledge will be acquired by methods for interviewing experts, reading documents, rule induction, repertory grids, and so forth.
Knowledge element identification	Pick out the specific knowledge from sources that will be useful in this iteration of the life cycle.
Knowledge classification system	Classify and organize the knowledge to aid in knowledge verification and understanding by developers. Use hierarchical groups whenever possible.
Detailed functional layout	Specify the functional capabilities of the system in detail. This level is at a more technical level while the preliminary functional layout was at a managerial level.
Preliminary control flow	Describe general phases that the expert system will execute. Phases correspond to logical groups of rules which are activated/deactivated in groups to control execution flow.
Preliminary user's manual	Describes system from user's viewpoint. An often ignored, but essential part of the system. It is absolutely important to involve users as soon as possible for feedback. If they don't use the system, it's worthless.
Requirements specifications	Define exactly what the system is supposed to do. The expert system will be validated using these requirements.
Knowledge baseline	Baseline knowledge for the system. Any changes must now be done by a formal change request. The high level knowledge is now adequate for the next stage of knowledge design.

Table 6-4
Knowledge Acquisition, Analysis, And Extraction Tasks

The main objective of the **knowledge acquisition task**, the **knowledge analysis task**, and the **knowledge extraction task** is to produce and verify the knowledge required by the system. By the time that the knowledge is baselined, it should be correct and suitable for the next stage of knowledge design. In addition to the customary method of interviewing experts, other techniques such as **repertory grids** or **personal construct theory** may be used to perform automated knowledge acquisition (Boose 84).

Knowledge Design

The objective of the **knowledge design stage** is to produce the detailed design for an expert system. There are two main tasks that comprise this stage.

• Knowledge definition
• Detailed design

Table 6-5 describes the tasks associated with knowledge definition.

Task	Objective
Knowledge representation	Specify how knowledge will be represented, such as rules, frames, or logic. Dependent upon what the expert system tool will support.
Detailed control structure	Specify three general control structures. (1) If the system is embedded in procedural code, how it will be called. (2) control of related groups of rules within an executing system. (3) metalevel control structures for rules.
Internal fact structure	Specify the internal structure of facts in a consistent manner to aid in understanding and good style.
Preliminary user interface	Specify a preliminary user interface. Get feedback from users about the interface.
Initial test plan	Specify how code will be tested. Define test data, test drivers, and how test results will be analyzed.

Table 6-5
Knowledge Definition Tasks

The internal fact structures described in Table 6-5 are discussed in much more detail in the chapters on CLIPS. The basic idea of specifying fact structures is to adapt good style. For example, a fact such as

    10

is not very meaningful by itself. What does the 10 represent? If additional information is included with the fact such as

```
price 10
```

or better still

```
gold price 10
```

then the gold price is meaningful. Notice that this form of the fact is in conventional object-attribute-value form and so is convenient for people to read and understand.

In some expert system languages, the fields may have **strong typing** so that only certain values are allowed. If a rule tries to specify a value that is not allowed, the inference engine flags this as an error.

The **detailed design stage** of knowledge is shown in Table 6-6.

Task	Objective
Design structure	Specify how knowledge is logically organized in the knowledge-base and what is in the knowledge-base.
Implementation strategy	Specify how the system is to be implemented.
Detailed user interface	Specify the detailed user interface after receiving user feedback from the preliminary user interface design.
Design specifications and report	Document the design.
Detailed test plan	Specify exactly how the code will be tested and verified.

Table 6-6
Detailed Design Of Knowledge Tasks

The product of the detailed design stage is the baselined design document from which coding can proceed. The baselined design document undergoes a knowledge system design review as a final check before coding begins.

Code and Checkout

The **code and checkout stage** begins the actual implementation of the code. Table 6-7 describes the tasks of this stage. The code and checkout stage terminates with the **test readiness review** which determines if the expert system is ready for the next stage of knowledge verification.

Task	Objective
Coding	Implement coding.
Tests	Test code using test data, test drivers, and test analysis procedures.
Source listings	Produce commented, documented source code.
User manual	Produce working user's manual so experts and users can provide feedback on system.
Installation/operations guide	Document installation/operation of system for users.
System description document	Document overall expert system functionality, limitations, and problems.

Table 6-7
Code And Checkout Tasks

Knowledge Verification

The **knowledge verification stage** has the objective of determining the correctness, completeness, and consistency of the system. This stage is divided into two main tasks

- Formal tests
- Test analysis

Table 6-8 describes the **formal test task** of the knowledge verification stage.

Task	Objective
Test procedures	Implement formal test procedures.
Test reports	Document test results.

Table 6-8
Formal Test Tasks Of The Knowledge Verification Stage

The **test analysis tasks** are shown in table 6-9.

Task	Objective
Results Evaluations	Analyze test results.
Recommendations	Document recommendations and conclusions of tests.

Table 6-9
Test Analysis Tasks

The test analysis looks for the following major problems

* incorrect answers
* incomplete answers
* inconsistent answers

and determines if the problem lies in rules, inference chains, uncertainty, or some combination of these three factors. If the problem cannot be pinned down to the expert system, then it is necessary to analyze the expert system tool software for bugs.

System Evaluation

The final stage in the development life cycle is the **system evaluation stage**. The purpose of this stage is to summarize what has been learned with recommendations for improvements and corrections. The tasks for this stage are shown in table 6-10.

Task	Objective
Results Evaluation	Summarize the results of testing and verification.
Recommendations	Recommend any changes to the system.
Validation	Validate that the system is correct with respect to user needs and requirements.
Interim or final report	If the system is complete, then issue final report. If not, issue an interim report.

Table 6-10
System Evaluation Stage Tasks

Since an expert system is usually built up in iterations, the report from the System Evaluation Stage will usually be an interim report describing the increased functionality of the system as new knowledge is added. However, the new system capability must be verified by itself and also as part of the previous knowledge in the system. That is, the system verification must also be performed in conjunction with all the system knowledge, not just the new knowledge. The expert system should also be validated each time at this stage rather than waiting for the final iteration. Automated systems for validation of knowledge-bases are also being investigated (Stachowitz 87).

6.8   SUMMARY

In this chapter, we discussed a software engineering approach to the construction of expert systems. Now that expert systems technology is being used for solving real-world problems, expert systems *must* be quality products.

A number of factors must be considered in the design of an expert system such as problem selection, cost, and payoff. Both the managerial and technical aspects must be considered in building a successful system.

One very useful concept of software engineering is the life cycle. The life cycle views software development as a series of stages from initial concept to retirement of the software. By consistently following a life cycle, it is possible to build quality software. Several different life cycle models were discussed for expert systems and one was shown in detail.

PROBLEMS

6-1.   Consider a simple knowledge-based system for diagnosing problems in an automobile. Describe this proposed system for each stage of the Linear model. (It is not necessary to do this in terms of each task). Assume there are many people working on the project and consider the coordination of their efforts. Explain any assumptions you make.

6-2.   Write a report on an automated tool for knowledge base validation such as EVA (Stachowitz 87). List all the problems it can detect, and its limitations.

6-3.   Explain any changes or differences in the linear model for a large project development with many developers vs. a small project with only one person.

BIBLIOGRAPHY

(Bochsler 86). Daniel C. Bochsler, "Software Engineering Techniques Used to Develop An Expert System for Automating Space Vehicle Rendezvous," *Proceedings of ROBEX '86*, Instrument Society of America, pp. 87-95, 1986.

(Bochsler 88). Daniel C. Bochsler, "A Project Management Approach to Expert System Applications," *ISA 88*, pp. 1458-1466, 1988.

(Boehm 84). Barry W. Boehm, "Software Life Cycle Factors," in *Handbook of Software Engineering*, ed. by C.R. Vick and C.V. Ramamoorthy, Van Nostrand Reinhold Co., pp. 494-518, 1984.

(Boehm 88). Barry W. Boehm, "A Spiral Model of Software Development and Enhancement," *IEEE Computer*, pp. 61-72, May 1988.

(Boose 84). John H. Boose, "Personal Construct Theory and the Transfer of Human Expertise," *AAAI 84*, pp. 27-33, 1984.

(Charette 86). Robert N. Charette, *Software Engineering Environments Concepts and Technology*, McGraw-Hill, 1986.

(Culbert 87). Chris Culbert, Gary Riley, and Robert T. Savely, "Approaches to the Verification of Rule-based Expert Systems," NASA Conference Publication 2491, *First Annual Workshop on Space Operations Automation and Robotics (SOAR 87)*, NASA, Houston, Texas, pp. 191-196, 1987.

(Freedman 86). Roy S. Freedman and Robert P. Frail, "OPGEN: The Evolution of an Expert System for Process Planning," *The AI Magazine*, pp. 58-70, Winter 1986.

(Sathi 86). Arvind Sathi, Thomas E. Morton, and Steven F. Roth, "Callisto: An Intelligent Project Management System," *The AI Magazine*, pp. 34-52, Winter 1986.

(Stachowitz 87). R.A. Stachowitz, et. al., "Building Validation Tools for Knowledge-based Systems," *First Annual Workshop on Space Operations Automation and Robotics (SOAR 87)*, NASA, Houston, Texas, pp. 209-216, 1987.

CHAPTER 7 INTRODUCTION TO CLIPS

7.1 INTRODUCTION

This chapter begins the introduction of the practical concepts necessary to build an expert system. The previous chapters have discussed the background, history, definitions, terminology, concepts, tools, and applications of expert systems. In short, they have provided an understanding of what expert systems are and what they can do. This theoretical framework of concepts and algorithms is essential in building expert systems. However, there are many practical aspects to building expert systems which must be learned by doing. Building an expert system is much like writing a program in a procedural language. Knowing how an algorithm works is not equivalent to being able to write a procedural program to perform that algorithm. Similarly, capturing an expert's knowledge is not equivalent to building an expert system. For this reason, practical experience using an expert system tool is invaluable in learning about expert systems.

The expert system language that will be used to demonstrate various concepts in the rest of the book is CLIPS. This chapter describes the basic components of an expert system (as discussed in Chapter 1) that are found within CLIPS. The basic elements of CLIPS are:

1. **fact-list**: global memory for data
2. **knowledge-base**: contains all the rules
3. **inference engine**: controls overall execution

These three components of CLIPS will provide the emphasis of this chapter. The first component, facts, will be covered in detail. Adding, removing, browsing, and tracing facts will be discussed. Following this will be a discussion on how the rules of a CLIPS program interact with facts to make a program execute. Finally, the interaction of multiple rules will be demonstrated.

To provide the basis for many examples throughout this chapter, a hypothetical expert system that monitors the activities of an industrial plant will be used. This expert system will monitor and respond to a range of possible emergencies. One such emergency would be a fire. Another would be a flood.

7.2 CLIPS

CLIPS is a forward chaining rule-based language that has inferencing and representation capabilities similar to those of OPS5. Syntactically, CLIPS very closely resembles a subset of ART. ART, however, is a multi-paradigm tool which provides forward and backward chaining, hypothetical reasoning, a schema representation language, and object-oriented programming among other features. CLIPS provides only the forward chaining capabilities of ART. Backward chaining, hypothetical reasoning, a schema representation language and object-oriented programming are not provided in CLIPS.

CLIPS was designed at NASA/Johnson Space Center with the specific purposes of providing high portability, low cost, and easy integration with external systems. CLIPS was written using the C programming language to facilitate these objectives. CLIPS is an acronym for C Language Integrated Production System. The C Language portion of the acronym can be somewhat misleading, however, since there is also an ADA version of CLIPS.

Because of its high portability, CLIPS has been installed on a wide variety of computers ranging from PCs to CRAY supercomputers. The majority of examples shown in this and the following chapters should work on any computer on which CLIPS has been installed. It is recommended, however, that CLIPS users have some knowledge of the operating system of the computer on which CLIPS is being used. For example, the method for specifying files tends to vary from one operating system to another. When commands may vary depending upon the machine or operating system, this will be noted.

7.3 NOTATION

This chapter and the following chapters will use the same notation for describing the syntax of various commands and constructs that are introduced. This notation consists of three different types of text which are to be entered.

The first type of notation is for words and characters that are to be entered exactly as shown. Anything that is not enclosed by the symbol pairs < >, [ ], or { }, should be entered exactly as shown. For example, consider the syntax description shown following.

```
(example)
```

This syntax description means that *(example)* should be entered as shown. To be exact, the character '(' should be entered first, followed by the character 'e', then 'x', 'a', 'm', 'p', 'l', 'e' and finally the character ')'.

Brackets, [ ], indicate that the contents of the brackets are optional. For example, the syntax description

```
(example [1])
```

indicates that the 1 found within the brackets is optional. So the following entry would be consistent with the syntax

```
(example)
```

as would this entry

```
(example 1)
```

The less than and greater than symbols, < > indicate that a replacement is to be made with the value specified by the words found within the < >. For example, finding the following within a syntax description

```
<integer>
```

indicates that a substitution should be made with an actual integer value. Following the previous examples, the syntax description

```
(example <integer>)
```

could be replaced with

```
(example 1)
```

or

```
(example 5)
```

or

```
(example -20)
```

or many more entries which contained the characters "(example ", followed by an integer, followed by the character ')'. It is important to note that spaces shown in the syntax description should also be included in the entry.

Another notation is indicated by the symbol pair << >> enclosing a description. This indicates that the description can be replaced with zero or more occurrences of the value specified. Spaces should be placed after each occurrence of a value. For example, the syntax description

```
<<integer>>
```

could be replaced with

```
1
```

or

```
1 2
```

or

```
    1  2  3
```

or with any number of integers, or with nothing at all.

A description enclosed by three less than and three greater than symbols indicates that one or more of the values specified by the description should by used in place of the syntax description. Note that for this notation, the syntax description

```
    <<<integer>>>
```

is equivalent to the syntax description

```
    <integer> <<integer>>
```

Braces, { }, indicate that one and only one of the items contained within the braces should be used in place of this syntax description. The items within the braces are separated by commas. For example, the syntax description

```
    {all,none,some}
```

could be replaced with

```
    all
```

or

```
    none
```

or

```
    some
```

7.4 FIELDS

As a knowledge base is constructed, CLIPS is required to read input from the keyboard and files to execute commands and load programs. As CLIPS reads characters from the keyboard or files, it groups them together into **tokens**. Tokens represent groups of characters that have special meaning to CLIPS. Some tokens such as left and right parentheses consist of only one character.

The group of tokens known as **fields** are of particular importance. There are three types of fields. A **word** is one type of field that starts with a printable ASCII character and is followed by zero or more characters with certain exceptions. A word may not begin with any of the following characters or groups of characters

```
<    |    &    $    ?    +    -    (    )    ;
```

In addition, a word may not contain any of the following characters

```
<    |    &    (    )    ;
```

These characters have special meaning to CLIPS, and so act as **delimiters** to indicate the end of a word.

Examples of valid words are the following.

```
emergency
fire
emergency-fire
activate_sprinkler_system
notify-fire-department
shut-down-electrical-junction-387
!?#$^*
```

Notice how the underscore and dash characters are used to tie words together to make them a single field. The last word shown demonstrates that words can have unusual characters placed within them.

CLIPS will preserve the uppercase and lowercase letters it finds in tokens. CLIPS is said to be **case-sensitive** because it distinguishes between uppercase and lowercase letters. For example, the following word fields are considered by CLIPS to be different

```
fire
FIRE
Fire
```

The second type of field is the **string**. A string must begin and end with double quotes. The quotes are part of the field. There can be zero or more characters of any kind between the double quotes including characters normally used by CLIPS as delimiters. The following shows some definitions of strings.

```
"Activate the sprinkler system."
"Shut down electrical junction 387."
"!?#$^"
"<-;()  +-"
```

Spaces normally act as delimiters in CLIPS to separate fields (such as words) and other tokens. Additional spaces used between tokens are discarded. Spaces included as part of a string, however, are preserved. For example, the following strings are considered by CLIPS to be four distinct strings.

```
"fire"
"fire "
" fire"
" fire "
```

If the surrounding double quotes were removed, CLIPS would consider each of the lines to contain the same word since spaces other than those used as delimiters would be ignored.

Since double quotes are used to delimit strings, it is not possible to directly place a double quote within a string. For example, the following line

```
""fire""
```

would be interpreted by CLIPS as the three separate tokens shown following

```
""
fire
""
```

since double quotes act as delimiters.

Within a string, double quotes can be included by using the backslash operator, \. For example, the line

```
"\"fire\""
```

will be interpreted by CLIPS as the string field

```
""fire""
```

Only a single field is created because the backslash character prevents the following double quotes from acting as a delimiter. The backslash character itself may be placed within a string by using two backslashes in succession. For example, the line

```
"\\fire\\"
```

will be interpreted by CLIPS as the string field

```
"\fire\"
```

The third type of field is the **numeric field** or simply **number**, which represents a floating point number. All numbers in CLIPS, including integer values, are stored as floating point numbers. A numeric field consists of three parts: the sign, the value, and the exponent. The sign and the exponent are optional. The sign is either + or -. The value contains one or more digits with a single optional decimal point contained with the digits. The exponent consists of the letter e or E followed by an optional + or - followed by one or more digits.

The following are all examples of valid CLIPS numbers

```
1
1.5
.7
+3
-1
65
3.5e10
```

7.5 FACTS

In order to solve a problem, a CLIPS program must have data or information with which it can reason. A "chunk" of information in CLIPS is called a **fact**. A fact consists of one or more fields enclosed in matching left and right parentheses. The following are all examples of facts

```
(single-field)
(two fields)
(speed 38 mph)
(cost 78 dollars 23 cents)
(name "John Doe")
```

Although CLIPS will accept any combination of fields as a fact, good programming style dictates that a method be used to insure that facts are represented in a meaningful manner. For example, consider the following sets of facts

```
(fire)
(flood)
(Tuesday)
(Wednesday)

(emergency-fire)
(emergency-flood)
(day-Tuesday)
(day-Wednesday)

(emergency fire)
```

```
(emergency flood)
(day Tuesday)
(day Wednesday)
```

In the first set of facts, the facts (fire) and (flood) could be used to indicate the presence of these occurrences, as the facts (Tuesday) and (Wednesday) could be used to indicate days of the week. Notice that the facts (fire) and (flood) are related by both being types of emergencies and the facts (Tuesday) and (Wednesday) are both days of the week. However, any relationship between the facts (fire) and (flood) and between the facts (Tuesday) and (Wednesday) can only be inferred. No explicit statement indicates a relationship between the facts (fire) and (flood) exists any more than a relationship between the facts (fire) and (Tuesday) exists.

The second set of facts goes a step further and implies a relationship between facts by using similar components as the first part of each word. Each fact, however, only contains a single field. Since fields are treated as indivisible items, a rule will not be able to access the prefix part of the field. These facts, then, while being recognized by a person as being similar, cannot be recognized by a rule as being similar.

The third set of facts explicitly declares the relationship between fire and flood and between Tuesday and Wednesday. The first field of the facts, emergency and day, is used to describe the relationship of the following fields. When used this way, the first field is called a **relation name**. The remaining fields of the fact are then used for specific values. In this case, fire and flood are types of emergencies, and Tuesday and Wednesday are days. The use of a relation name explicitly states the relationship between fire and flood and the relationship between Tuesday and Wednesday.

7.6   FACT TEMPLATES

Groups of facts having the same relation can be described for purposes of documentation by using a **template**. A template for a fact shows the relation name followed by one or more general items or specific items. For example, the template for the *emergency* facts is

```
(emergency <type>)
```

where the symbol <type> indicates a general item that could be replaced by a specific item such as fire or flood. More than one template can be used to indicate variations on a set of facts. For instance, the following facts

```
(action activate sprinkler-system)
(action activate fire-alarm)
(action notify fire-department)
(action shutdown-electrical-power)
```

could be represented with the following three templates

```
(action activate <device>)
(action notify <group>)
(action <specific-action>)
```

More than one field can be represented with a template. The fact

```
(computer-components cpu disk-drive terminal)
```

could be described with the template

```
(computer-components <<component-list>>)
```

where <<component-list>> represents zero or more fields. The template could be slightly modified to represent more than one component list. For example, these facts

```
(components computer cpu disk-drive terminal)
(components car tires engine body gas-tank)
```

are described by this template

```
(components <item> <<component-list>>)
```

Templates are convenient for documenting facts and the expected fields that are found in them. They are not accepted by CLIPS as commands and should only be used for documenting CLIPS code.

7.7 ENTERING AND EXITING CLIPS

CLIPS can be entered by issuing the appropriate run command for the machine on which CLIPS has been installed. The CLIPS prompt should appear as follows.

```
CLIPS>
```

At this point, commands can be entered directly to CLIPS. This mode, in which direct commands can be entered, is called the **top-level**.

The normal mode of leaving CLIPS is with the **exit** command. The syntax of this command is

```
(exit)
```

Notice that the word *exit* is enclosed within matching parentheses. Many rule-based languages draw their origins from LISP which uses parentheses as delimiters. Since CLIPS is based on a language that was originally developed using LISP machines, it retains these delimiters. The word *exit* without enclosing parentheses has quite a different meaning than the word *exit* with enclosing parentheses. The parentheses around *exit* indicate that *exit* is a command to be executed and not just the word *exit*. We'll see later that parentheses serve as important delimiters for commands.

For now, it is only important to remember that each CLIPS command must having a matching number of left and right parentheses and that the parentheses are properly balanced.

The final step in executing a CLIPS command after the command has been entered with properly balanced parentheses is to press the carriage return key. The carriage return key may also be pressed before or after any token has been entered. Pressing the carriage return key after entering the characters 'ex', but before entering the characters 'it' would create two tokens: a token for the word *ex* and a token for the word *it*.

The following command sequence demonstrates a sample session of entering CLIPS and then immediately exiting. The example shown is for an IBM PC™ using MS-DOS in which the CLIPS executable is stored on a disk in drive A and the current drive is also A. The name of the CLIPS executable is assumed to be CLIPS. Output displayed by MS-DOS or CLIPS is shown in regular type. All input that must be typed by you is shown in bold. The carriage return key is indicated by the character ↵. CLIPS is case sensitive, so it is important to type upper and lower case letters exactly as they appear.

```
A>CLIPS↵
          CLIPS (V4.20 4/29/88)
CLIPS> (exit) ↵
A>
```

7.8 ADDING AND REMOVING FACTS

The group of all facts known to CLIPS is stored in the fact-list. Facts representing information can be added and removed from the fact-list. New facts can be added to the fact-list using the **assert** command. The syntax of the *assert* command is

```
(assert <<<fact>>>)
```

As an example, let's consider a hypothetical expert system that monitors the activities of an industrial plant. This expert system will monitor and respond to a range of possible emergencies. One such emergency would be a fire. A fact representing that a fire emergency exists could be added to the fact-list by using the following command

```
CLIPS>  (assert  (emergency  fire))↵
CLIPS>
```

The **facts** command can be used to display the facts in the fact-list. The basic syntax of the *facts* command is

```
(facts)
```

For example,

```
CLIPS>  (facts)↵
f-1   (emergency fire)
CLIPS>
```

The term "f-1" is the **fact identifier** assigned to the fact by CLIPS. Every fact that is inserted into the fact-list is assigned a unique fact identifier starting with the letter f and followed by an integer called the **fact-index**.

CLIPS does not accept duplicate entries of a fact. Therefore, attempting to place a second (emergency fire) fact into the fact-list will have no result. Of course, other facts that do not duplicate existing facts can be easily added to the fact-list. For example,

```
CLIPS>  (assert  (emergency  flood))↵
CLIPS>  (facts)↵
f-1   (emergency fire)
f-2   (emergency flood)
CLIPS>
```

As the syntax of the *assert* command indicates, more than one fact can be asserted using a single *assert* command. For example, the command

```
CLIPS>  (assert (emergency  fire)↵
                 (emergency  flood))↵
CLIPS>
```

will assert two facts into the fact-list.

An important point to realize is that identifiers in the fact-list are not necessarily sequential. Just as facts can be added to the fact-list, there is also a way to remove facts. As facts are removed from the fact-list, the deleted fact identifiers will be missing in the fact-list. So the fact-identifiers may not be strictly sequential as a CLIPS program executes.

Since large numbers of facts can be contained in the fact-list, it is often useful to be able view only a portion of the fact-list. This can be accomplished using additional arguments for the *facts* command. The complete syntax for the *facts* command is

```
(facts [<start> [<end> [<maximum>]]])
```

where <start>, <end>, and <maximum> are positive integers. Notice that the syntax of the *facts* command allows from zero to three arguments. It no arguments are specified, all facts are displayed. If the <start> argument is specified, all facts with fact-indexes greater than or equal to <start> are displayed. If <start> and <end> are specified, all facts with fact-indexes greater than or equal to <start> and less than or equal to <end> are displayed. Finally, if <maximum> is specified along with <start> and <end>, no more than <maximum> facts will be displayed.

Just as facts can be added to the fact-list, they can also be removed. Removing facts from the fact-list is called **retraction** and is done with the **retract** command. The syntax of the *retract* command is

```
(retract <<<fact-index>>>)
```

The fact indexes of one or more facts to be retracted are included as the arguments of the *retract* command. For example, suppose the fact-list is

```
f-1    (emergency fire)
f-3    (emergency flood)
f-4    (action activate-sprinkler-system)
```

The command

```
(retract 3)
```

would remove the fact (emergency flood). Similarly, the command

```
(retract 1)
```

will retract the fact with identifier f-1 which is (emergency fire) and the command

```
(retract 4)
```

will retract the fact (action activate-sprinkler-system). Notice that to retract a fact , the fact-index and not the position of the fact in the fact-list must be specified. Attempting to retract a non-existent fact will produce the following error message

```
Fact <fact-index> does not exist
```

For example,

```
CLIPS>  (retract 4) ↵
CLIPS>  (retract 4) ↵
```

```
Fact 4 does not exist
CLIPS>
```

A single *retract* command can be used to retract multiple facts at once. For example, the command

```
(retract 3 1 4)
```

will retract all three facts.

7.9 THE COMPONENTS OF A RULE

In order to accomplish useful work, an expert system must have rules as well as facts. Now that fact assertions and retractions have been discussed, it's possible to see how rules work.

Rules can be typed directly into CLIPS or they can be loaded in from a file of rules created by an editor. For information on how to use the editor of CLIPS, refer to Appendix F. Care must be taken when using a word processor to be sure that it does not introduce document formatting characters into the source code since such characters will not be accepted by CLIPS. For example, the non-document mode should be used with Wordstar™ on an IBM PC, and the SAVE AS... with text only option should be used on a Macintosh™ with MacWrite™.

Initially, the examples shown will be rules entered directly into CLIPS from the top-level. The pseudocode for one of the possible rules in the industrial plant monitoring expert system is shown following

```
IF the emergency is a fire
THEN the action is to activate the sprinkler system
```

Shown following is the rule expressed in CLIPS syntax. The rule can be entered by typing it in after the CLIPS prompt.

```
(defrule fire-emergency "An example rule"
    (emergency fire)
    =>
    (assert (action activate-sprinkler-system)))
```

If the rule is entered correctly as shown, then the CLIPS prompt reappears. Otherwise, an error message, most likely indicating a misspelled keyword or misplaced parenthesis, will appear.

Shown following is the same rule with comments added to match the parts of the rule. Comments begin with a semicolon and continue until a carriage return. Comments are ignored by CLIPS and will be discussed in greater detail later.

```
; Rule header
(defrule fire-emergency "An example rule"
  ; Patterns
  (emergency fire)
  ; THEN arrow
  =>
  ; Actions
  (assert (action activate-sprinkler-system)))
```

The general format of a rule is

```
(defrule <rule name> [<optional comment>]
   <<patterns>>   ; Left-Hand Side (LHS) of the rule
   =>
   <<actions>>)   ; Right-Hand Side (RHS) of the rule
```

The entire rule must be surrounded by parentheses. Each of the patterns and actions of the rule must be surrounded by parentheses. A rule may have multiple patterns and actions. The parentheses surrounding patterns and actions must be properly balanced if they are nested. In the *fire-emergency* rule, there is one pattern and one action.

The header of the rule consists of three parts. The rule must start with a **defrule** keyword. Following defrule must be the name of the rule. The name can be any valid CLIPS word. If a rule is entered with a rule name that is the same as an existing rule, then the new rule replaces the old rule. In this rule, the rule name is *fire-emergency*. Next is an optional comment within double quotes. For this rule, the comment is "An example rule". The comment is normally used to describe the purpose of the rule or any other information the programmer desires. Unlike comments beginning with a semicolon, the comment following the rule name is not ignored and can be displayed along with the rest of the rule (using the *pprule* command introduced in Section 7.11).

After the rule header are zero or more **patterns** or conditional elements. Each pattern consists of one or more fields. In the *fire-emergency* rule, the pattern is (emergency fire). The fields are *emergency* and *fire*. CLIPS attempts to match the patterns of rules against facts in the fact-list. If all the patterns of a rule match facts, the rule is **activated** and put on the **agenda**, the collection of activated rules. There may be zero or more rules in the agenda. If a rule has no patterns, then the special pattern (initial-fact) will be added as a pattern for the rule. The reason for using this pattern will become clear when the *reset* command is discussed later.

The symbol => that follows the patterns in a rule is called an **arrow**. It is formed by typing the equal sign followed by the greater than sign. The arrow is a symbol representing the beginning of the THEN part of an IF-THEN rule. The part of the rule before the arrow is called the left-hand side (**LHS**) and the part after the arrow is called the right-hand side (**RHS**).

The last part of a rule is the list of actions that will be executed when the rule **fires**. A rule may have no actions. This is not particularly useful, but it can be done.

In our example, the one action is to assert the fact (action activate-sprinkler-system). The term fires means that CLIPS executes the actions of a rule from the agenda. A program normally ceases execution when there are no rules on the agenda. When there are multiple rules on the agenda, CLIPS automatically determines which is the appropriate rule to fire. CLIPS orders the rules on the agenda in terms of increasing priority and fires the rule with the highest priority, called **salience**. Salience will be discussed in more detail in Chapter 9.

7.10 THE AGENDA AND EXECUTION

A CLIPS program can be made to run with the **run** command. The syntax of the *run* command is

```
(run [<limit>])
```

where the optional argument <limit> is the maximum number of rules to be fired. If <limit> is not included or <limit> is -1, then rules will be fired until no rules are left on the agenda. Otherwise, execution of rules will cease after <limit> number of rules have fired.

When a CLIPS program is run, the rule with the highest salience on the agenda is fired. If there is only one rule on the agenda, that rule will fire. Since the conditional element of the *fire-emergency* rule is satisfied by the fact (emergency fire), the *fire-emergency* rule should fire when the program is run.

If the *run* command is attempted when the *fire-emergency* rule has been entered after the fact (emergency fire), then the *fire-emergency* rule does not fire. The reason CLIPS does not fire the rule has to do with the way CLIPS is designed. The design of CLIPS is such that rules only see facts that have been entered *after* the rules. Thus newly entered rules will not "see" the facts that are currently on the fact-list. Only new facts that are entered will be seen by the rule. This means that a rule can only be activated by facts that are asserted after the rule is entered.

Activating the Rule

To activate the *fire-emergency* rule, the fact (emergency fire) must be asserted after the rule has been entered. At first thought, this seems trivial since the fact (emergency fire) just needs to be asserted. However, if the (emergency fire) fact is already in the fact-list, asserting a new (emergency fire) fact will have no effect. In order to re-assert this fact, the original version of the fact must be retracted. Once this is done, a new (emergency fire) fact can be asserted since no duplication will occur. This new version of the fact will have a different fact-index from the original and the *fire-emergency* rule will be placed on the agenda.

The list of rules on the agenda can be displayed with the **agenda** command. The syntax of the *agenda* command is

```
(agenda)
```

If no activations are on the agenda, the CLIPS prompt will reappear after the *agenda* command is issued. If the *fire-emergeny* rule had been activated by the (emergency fire) fact with a fact index of 2, an *agenda* command would produce the following output

```
CLIPS> (agenda)↵
0    fire-emergency   f-2
CLIPS>
```

The 0 indicates the salience of the rule on the agenda. After the salience comes the name of the rule followed by the fact identifiers that match the rule. In this case, there is only one fact identifier, f-2.

Rules and Refraction

With the *fire-emergency* rule on the agenda, the *run* command will now cause the rule to fire and produce the following output

```
CLIPS> (run)↵
1 rules fired
Run time is 0.0167 seconds
CLIPS>
```

The message "1 rules fired" is an information message generated by the run command indicating the number of rules that were fired. The message following that indicates the amount of time taken to fire the rules. The timing message may not appear on all machines on which CLIPS runs, since some machines do not have internal clocks. The fact (action activate-sprinkler-system) will be added to the fact-list as the action of the rule.

An interesting question occurs at this point. What if the *run* command is issued again? There is a rule and there is a fact which satisfies the rule and so the rule should fire again. However, a *run* command attempted now will produce no results. Checking the agenda will verify that no rules are fired because there were no rules on the agenda.

The rule didn't fire again because of the way that CLIPS is designed. CLIPS was programmed with a characteristic of a nerve cell (**neuron**). After a neuron transmits a nerve impulse (fires), no amount of stimulation will make it fire for some time. This phenomenon is called **refraction** and is very important in expert systems.

Without refraction, expert systems would always be caught in trivial loops. That is, as soon as a rule fired, it would keep on firing on that same fact over and over again. In the real world, the stimulus that caused the firing would eventually disappear. For example, the fire would eventually be put out by the sprinkler system or burn out by itself. However, in the computer world, once a fact is entered in the fact-list, it stays there until explicitly removed.

If necessary, the rule be made to fire again by retracting the fact (emergency fire) and asserting it again. Basically, CLIPS remembers the fact identifiers that triggered a rule into firing and will not activate that rule again with the exact same combination of fact identifiers. Identical sets of fact identifiers must match one-for-one in both order and fact indices. In Chapter 8, examples will shown how a single fact can match a pattern in more than one way. In this case, several activations with the same set of fact identifiers for a single rule can be placed on the agenda, one for each distinct match.

7.11 COMMANDS USED WITH RULES

Displaying the Rules in the Knowledge Base

The **rules** command is used to display the current list of rules maintained by CLIPS. Its syntax is

```
(rules)
```

For example,

```
CLIPS> (rules)
fire-emergency
CLIPS>
```

The **pprule** (pretty print rule) command is used to display the text representation of a rule. Its syntax is

```
(pprule <rule-name>)
```

Its single argument specifies the name of the rule to be displayed. For example,

```
CLIPS> (pprule fire-emergency)
(defrule fire-emergency "An example rule"
   (emergency fire)
   =>
   (assert (action activate-sprinkler-system)))
CLIPS>
```

CLIPS puts different parts of the rule on different lines for the sake of readability. The patterns before the arrow are still considered the LHS and the actions after the arrow are still the RHS of the rule.

Loading Rules from a File

A file of rules made with a text editor can be loaded into CLIPS using the **load** command. The syntax of the *load* command is

```
(load <file-name>)
```

where <file-name> is a string containing the name of the file to be loaded.

Assuming that the fire-emergency rule was stored in a file called fire.clp on drive B of an IBM PC, then the following command would load the rule into CLIPS

```
(load "B:fire.clp")
```

Of course, the specification of a file name will be machine dependent and so this example should be taken only as a guide. A problem that may occur in loading is due to the backslash character used on some operating systems as a directory path separator. Since CLIPS interprets the backslash as an escape character, two backslashes must be used to create a single backslash in a string. For example, normally a pathname might be written as

```
B:\usr\clips\fire.clp
```

To preserve the backslash characters, however, the pathname would have to be written as shown in the following command

```
(load "B:\\usr\\clips\\fire.clp")
```

Rules do not have to all be kept in a single file. They can be stored in more than one file and loaded using several load commands.

Saving Rules to a File

CLIPS also provides the opposite of the *load* command. The **save** command allows the set of rules stored in CLIPS to be saved to a disk file. The syntax of the *save* command is

```
(save <file-name>)
```

For example, the following command will save the *fire-emergency* rule to a file called fire.clp on drive B

```
(save "B:fire.clp")
```

The *save* command will save all the rules in CLIPS to the specified file. It is not possible to save specified rules to a file. The *save* and *load* commands also save and load deffacts (which will be discussed shortly). Normally, if an editor is used to create and modify the rules, there is no need to use the *save* command since the rules will be saved while using the editor. Sometimes, however, it is convenient to enter rules directly at the CLIPS prompt and then save the rules to a file.

7.12   COMMENTING RULES

It's a good idea to include comments in a CLIPS program. Sometimes, rules can be difficult to understand and comments can be used to explain to the reader what the rule is doing. Comments are also used for good documentation of programs and will be very helpful in lengthy programs.

A comment in CLIPS is any text that begins with a semicolon and ends with a carriage return. The following is an example of comments in the fire program.

```
;***********************************
;*                                 *
;* Programmer: G. D. Riley         *
;*                                 *
;* Title    : The Fire Program     *
;*                                 *
;* Date     : 10/31/88             *
;*                                 *
;***********************************

; Facts used in this program use the
; following templates

; (emergency <type-of-emergency>)
; (action <action-to-be-performed>)

; The purpose of this rule is to activate
; the sprinkler system if there is a fire

(defrule fire-emergency "An example rule" ; IF
    ; there is a fire emergency
    (emergency fire)
    =>                                      ; THEN
    ; activate the sprinkler system
    (assert (action activate-the-sprinkler-system)))
```

Loading this rule into CLIPS and then pretty printing it with the *pprule* command will demonstrate that every comment starting with a semicolon is eliminated in the CLIPS program. The only comment that is retained is the one in quotes after the rule name. That is, CLIPS will ignore the semicolon comments as it's loading the program.

7.13 THE PRINTOUT COMMAND

Besides asserting facts in the RHS of rules, the RHS can also be used to print out information using the **printout** command. The syntax of the *printout* command is

```
(printout <logical-name> <<print-items>>)
```

where <logical-name> indicates the output destination of the *printout* command and <<<print-items>>> are the zero or more items to be printed by this command.

The following rule demonstrates the use of the *printout* command

```
(defrule fire-emergency
   (emergency fire)
   =>
   (printout t "Activate the sprinkler system"
              crlf))
```

It is very important to include the letter **t** following the *printout* command as this argument indicates the destination of the output. This destination is also referred to as a **logical name**. In this case, the logical name *t* tells CLIPS to send the output to the **standard output device** of the computer. Generally, the standard output device is the terminal. However, this may be redefined so that the standard output device is some other device such as a modem or printer. In Chapter 10, the concept of logical names will be fully introduced and the *printout* command will be used for disk I/O.

The arguments following the logical name are items to be printed by the *printout* command. The string

```
"Activate the sprinkler system"
```

will be printed at the terminal without the enclosing quotes. The word **crlf** is treated specially by the *printout* command. It forces a carriage return/line feed. This is useful in improving the appearance of output by formatting it on different lines.

7.14   USING MULTIPLE RULES

Until now, only the simplest type of program consisting of just one rule has been shown. However, expert systems consisting of only one rule are not too useful. Practical expert systems may consist of hundreds or thousands of rules. In addition to the *fire-emergency* rule, the expert system monitoring the industrial plant might also include a rule for emergencies in which flooding has occurred. The expanded set of rules now looks like

```
(defrule fire-emergency
   (emergency fire)
   =>
   (printout t "Activate the sprinkler system"
             crlf))

(defrule flood-emergency
   (emergency flood)
   =>
   (printout t "Shut down electrical equipment"
             crlf))
```

Once these rules have been entered into CLIPS, asserting the fact (emergency fire) and then issuing a *run* command will produce the output "Activate the sprinkler system". Asserting the fact (emergency flood) and issuing a *run* command will produce the output "Shut down the electrical equipment."

Capturing the Real World in a Rule

As long as the fires and floods are the only two emergencies which must be handled, then the rules above would be sufficient. However, the real world is not quite that simple. For instance, not all fires can be extinguished using water. Some fires may require chemical extinguishers. What should be done if a fire produces poisonous gas or an explosion may occur? Should an off-site fire department be notified in addition to the on-site firemen? Does it matter which floor of the building the fire is on? Activating the water sprinklers on the second floor might cause water damage to both the first and second floors. Electrical power to equipment might have to be shut off on both floors. A fire on the first floor may only require that power be shut off to equipment on the first floor. If the building is flooded, are there watertight doors that can be shut to prevent damage? What should be done in case a plant break-in is detected? If all of these situations are included as rules, have all possibilities now been covered?

Unfortunately, the answer is no. In the real world, things don't always operate perfectly. Capturing all pertinent knowledge in an expert system can be quite difficult. In the best case, it may be possible to recognize most major emergencies and to provide rules to allow the expert system to recognize when it doesn't recognize an emergency.

Rules with Multiple Patterns

Most real-world heuristics are too complicated to be expressed as a rule with just a single pattern. For example, activating the sprinkler system for any type of fire might not only be wrong—it could be dangerous. Fires involving ordinary combustibles such as paper, wood, and cloth (class A fires) can be extinguished using water or water-based extinguishers. However, fires involving flammable and combustible liquids, greases, and similar materials (class B fires) must be extinguished using a different method such as a carbon-dioxide extinguisher.

Rules with more than one pattern could be used to express these conditions. The first pattern would determine that a fire emergency exists. The second pattern would determine whether the fire was a class A fire or a class B fire. In addition, more rules could be used to determine whether a specific burning material constituted either a class A or B fire. Two rules for class A and B fire emergencies are shown as follows

```
(defrule class-A-fire-emergency
   (emergency fire)
   (fire-class A)
   =>
   (printout t "Activate sprinkler system" crlf))

(defrule class-B-fire-emergency
   (emergency fire)
   (fire-class B)
   =>
   (printout t "Use carbon dioxide extinguisher"
               crlf))
```

Both rules have two patterns. Both patterns in each of the rules must be satisfied by facts in the fact-list for the rule to fire. Entering both rules and then asserting the facts (emergency fire) and (fire-class A) will cause the *class-A-fire-emergency* rule to be placed on the agenda. Running the system would then produce the output "Activate sprinkler system".

Any number of patterns can be placed in a rule. The important point to realize is that the rule is placed on the agenda only if *all* the patterns are satisfied by facts. This type of restriction is called a **logical AND**. Because the patterns are of the logical AND type, the rule will not fire if only one of the patterns is satisfied. All the facts must be present before the LHS of a rule is satisfied and the rule is placed on the agenda.

7.15   THE DEFFACTS CONSTRUCT

It is often very convenient to be able to automatically assert a set of facts instead of typing in the same assertions from the top-level. This is particularly true for facts which are known to be true before running a program (i.e., the initial knowledge). Running test cases to debug a program is another instance in which it is useful to automatically assert a group of facts. Groups of facts which represent initial knowledge can be defined using the define facts keyword, **deffacts**. For example, the following deffacts statement provides initial information about the type of emergency

```
(deffacts status "Some facts about the emergency"
    (emergency fire)
    (fire-class A))
```

The general format of a deffacts is

```
(deffacts <deffacts name> [<optional comment>]
    <<facts>>)
```

Following the deffacts keyword is the required name of this deffacts statement. Any valid symbolic field can be used as the name. In this case, the name chosen was *status*. Following the name is an optional comment in double quotes. Like the optional comment of a rule, this comment will be retained with the deffacts after it's been loaded by CLIPS. After the name or comment are the facts that will be asserted in the fact-list by this deffacts statement.

The facts in a deffacts statement are asserted using the CLIPS **reset** command. The syntax of the *reset* command is

```
(reset)
```

Assuming that the *status* deffacts had been entered, the following dialog shows how the *reset* command adds the facts to the fact-list

```
CLIPS> (reset)↵
CLIPS> (facts)↵
f-0     (initial-fact)
f-1     (emergency fire)
f-2     (fire-class A)
CLIPS>
```

The output shows the facts from the deffacts statement and a new fact generated by the reset command called **initial-fact**. Upon startup, CLIPS automatically defines a deffacts statement with the following format

```
(deffacts initial-fact
    (initial-fact))
```

Thus, even if you have not defined any deffacts statements, a reset will assert the fact (initial-fact). The fact-identifier of the initial-fact is always f-0. The utility of (initial-fact) lies in starting the execution of a program. A CLIPS program will not start running unless there are rules whose LHS are satisfied by facts. The *reset* command asserts a default startup fact as well as asserting the facts in deffacts statements. As stated previously, a rule without any patterns has the pattern (initial-fact) added to its LHS. Thus any rule without LHS patterns will be placed on the agenda when a reset is performed.

The *reset* command is the key method for starting or restarting an expert system in CLIPS. The *reset* command removes all activated rules from the agenda and all facts from the fact-list. It then asserts the facts from existing deffacts statements. Normally, this will cause the fact (initial-fact) to be asserted, since this is a fact found in the *initial-facts* deffacts provided for you by CLIPS.

There are some additional commands that are useful with deffacts. For example, **list-deffacts** will list the names of deffacts that are currently loaded in CLIPS. Another useful command is **ppdeffact** that prints the facts stored in a deffacts. The syntax of these two commands are

```
(list-deffacts)
(ppdeffact <deffacts-name>)
```

For example

```
CLIPS> (list-deffacts)↵
initial-fact
status
CLIPS> (ppdeffact status)↵
(deffacts status "Some facts about the emergency"
    (emergency fire)
    (fire-class A))
CLIPS>
```

7.16 REMOVING DEFFACTS AND RULES

Deffacts statements can be removed from CLIPS by using the **undeffacts** command. The syntax of this command is

```
(undeffacts <deffacts-name>)
```

For example, to remove the *status* deffacts, the command

```
(undeffacts status)
```

would be used. A reset now would only add the fact (initial-fact). The *undeffacts status* command has erased the status deffacts from memory. To regain a deffacts statement after an undeffacts command, the deffacts statement must be re-entered.

Even the *initial-fact* deffacts can be remove using undeffacts command as shown following.

```
(undeffacts initial-fact)
```

Now, whenever a *reset* command is performed, the initial-fact will not appear.

CLIPS also allows rules to be selectively removed by using the **excise** command. The syntax of the *excise* command is

```
(excise <rule-name>)
```

For example, to get rid of the *fire-emergency* rule, the following command with the name of the rule as an argument would be used.

```
(excise fire-emergency)
```

The **clear** command can be used to remove all information contained in the CLIPS environment. It restores the original state of CLIPS just as if it has just been started up. The syntax of the *clear* command is

```
(clear)
```

The *clear* command causes all of the facts in the fact-list to be removed as well as removing all rule and deffacts currently contained in CLIPS.

7.17 THE WATCH COMMAND

The **watch** command is useful for debugging programs. The syntax of this command is

```
(watch {facts,rules,activations,all})
```

Facts, rules, and activations may be watched in any combination to provide the appropriate amount of debugging information. The *watch* command can be used more than once to watch more than one feature of CLIPS execution. The word *all* can be used to enable all of the watch features (facts, rules, and activations).

If facts are being watched, CLIPS will automatically print a message indicating that an update has been made to the fact-list whenever facts are asserted or retracted. The following command dialog illustrates the use of this debugging command.

```
CLIPS> (reset)↵
CLIPS> (watch facts)↵
CLIPS> (assert (emergency fire))↵
==> f-1    (emergency fire)
CLIPS> (assert (emergency flood))↵
==> f-2    (emergency flood)
CLIPS> (retract 2)
<== f-2    (emergency flood)
```

If activations are being watched, CLIPS will automatically print a message whenever an activation has been added to or removed from the agenda. If rules are being watched, CLIPS will print a message whenever a rule is fired. Note that watching activations will not cause a message to be displayed when a rule is fired.

In addition, if the rules are being watched while loading a program, CLIPS will display a message such as

```
Compiling rule: cut-power-to-electrical-fire +j+j+j
```

As the rules are being loaded, CLIPS is compiling the source code. The "+j+j+j" string at the end of the message is some information from CLIPS about the internal structure of the compiled rules. This information will be useful to know for tuning a program and will be discussed in Chapter 11 which deals with efficiency.

The effects of a *watch* command may be turned off by using the corresponding **unwatch** command. The syntax of the *unwatch* command is

```
(unwatch {facts,rules,activations,all})
```

7.18 THE MATCHES COMMAND

CLIPS has a debugging command called **matches** which indicates which patterns in a rule match facts. This capability is useful for debugging cases in which a rule appears to have all of its patterns satisfied, but is nonetheless not activated. Those patterns which do not match prevent the rule from becoming activated. One common reason that a pattern won't match a fact is misspelling an element either in the pattern or the assertion of the fact. The syntax of the *matches* command is

```
(matches <rule-name>)
```

The argument of the *matches* command is the name of the rule to be checked for matches. The following rule will be used to demonstrate the *matches* command.

```
; Class C Fires involve energized electrical
; equipment. Remove the power to such a fire
; if possible.

(defrule cut-power-to-electrical-fire
    ; Emergency is a fire
    (emergency fire)
    ; Fire involves energized electrical equipment
    (fire-class C)
    ; Power can be safely removed
    (power can-be-safely-removed)
    =>
    (printout t "Remove power from the fire" crlf))
```

The following command sequence shows how the *matches* command is used. Notice that the *watch facts* command is used to provide immediate feedback when facts are asserted.

```
CLIPS> (watch facts)↵
CLIPS> (assert (emergency fire))↵
=> f-1      (emergency fire)
CLIPS> (matches cut-power-to-electrical-fire)↵
Matches for Pattern 1
  f-1
Matches for Pattern 2
  None
Matches for Pattern 3
  None
Partial matches for patterns 1 - 2
  None
Activations
  None
```

The *matches* command considers the patterns to be ordered sequentially as follows.

```
(defrule cut-power-to-electrical-fire
    (emergency fire)                      ;Pattern 1
    (fire-class C)                        ;Pattern 2
    (power can-be-safely-removed)         ;Pattern 3
    =>
    (printout t "Remove power from the fire" crlf))
```

The fact with fact-identifier f-1 matches the first pattern in the rule and is so reported by the *matches* command. Given that a rule has N patterns, the term **partial matches** refers to any set of matches of the first N-1 patterns with facts. That is, the partial matches begin with the first pattern in a rule and end with any pattern up to but not including the last (N'th) pattern. As soon as one partial match can't be made, CLIPS does not check any further. For example, a rule with four patterns would have partial matches of the first and second patterns, and also the first, second and third patterns. If all N patterns match, the rule will be activated.

The following commands continue this example

```
CLIPS> (assert (fire-class C))↵
=> f-2    (fire-class C)
CLIPS> (matches  cut-power-to-electrical-fire)↵
Matches for Pattern 1
 f-1
Matches for Pattern 2
 f-2
Matches for Pattern 3
 None
Partial matches for patterns 1 - 2
 f-1  f-2
Activations
 None
```

Notice that with the second fact asserted, there is now a partial match for patterns 1 and 2. Of course, if the fact (power can-be-safely-removed) had been asserted instead of (fire-class C), there would have been no partial match for patterns 1 - 2.

This next command sequence asserts the final fact to match the third pattern in the rule.

```
CLIPS> (assert (power  can-be-safely-removed))↵
=> f-3    (power can-be-safely-removed)
CLIPS> (matches  cut-power-to-electrical-fire)↵
Matches for Pattern 1
 f-1
Matches for Pattern 2
 f-2
Matches for Pattern 3
 f-3
Partial matches for patterns 1 - 2
 f-1  f-2
Activations
 f-1  f-2  f-3
```

With the addition of the third and final pattern, the Activations information shows the fact-identifiers which cause an activation of the rule.

7.19 THE SET-BREAK COMMAND

CLIPS has a debugging command called **set-break** which allows execution to be halted before any rule from a specified group of rules is fired. A rule which halts execution before being fired is called a **breakpoint**. The syntax of the set-break command is

```
(set-break <rule-name>)
```

where <rule-name> is the name of a rule to make a breakpoint. As an example, consider the following rules

```
(defrule first
   =>
   (assert (fire second)))

(defrule second
   (fire second)
   =>
   (assert (fire third)))

(defrule third
   (fire third)
   =>)
```

The following command dialog shows execution of the rules without any breakpoints set.

```
CLIPS> (watch all)↵
CLIPS> (reset)↵
==> f-0      (initial-fact)
==> Activation 0      first: f-0
CLIPS> (run)↵
FIRE     1 first: f-0
==> f-1      (fire second)
==> Activation 0      second: f-1
FIRE     2 second: f-1
==> f-2      (fire third)
==> Activation 0      third: f-2
FIRE     3 third: f-2
```

```
3 rules fired
CLIPS>
```

All three rules fire in succession when the *run* command is issued. The following command dialog demonstrates the use of the *set-break* command to halt execution.

```
CLIPS> (set-break  second) ↵
CLIPS> (set-break  third) ↵
CLIPS> (watch all) ↵
CLIPS> (reset) ↵
<== Activation 0       first: f-0
==> f-0       (initial-fact)
==> Activation 0       first: f-0
CLIPS> (run) ↵
FIRE    1 first: f-0
==> f-1       (fire second)
==> Activation 0        second: f-1
Breaking on rule second
1 rules fired
CLIPS> (run) ↵
FIRE    1 second: f-1
==> f-2       (fire third)
==> Activation 0       third: f-2
Breaking on rule third
1 rules fired
CLIPS> (run) ↵
FIRE    1 third: f-2
1 rules fired
CLIPS>
```

In this case, execution halts before the rules *second* and *third* are allowed to fire. Notice that at least one rule must be fired by the *run* command before a breakpoint will stop execution. For example, after the rule *second* has halted execution, it does not halt execution again when the *run* command is given.

The **show-breaks** command can be used to list all breakpoints. Its syntax is

```
(show-breaks)
```

The **remove-break** command can be used to remove breakpoints. Its syntax is

```
(remove-break [<rule-name>]
```

If <rule-name> is provided as an argument, only the breakpoint for that rule will be removed. Otherwise, all breakpoints will be removed.

7.20 SUMMARY

This chapter introduced the fundamental components of CLIPS. Facts are the first component of a CLIPS system. Facts are made up of fields which are either a word, string, or number. The first field of a fact is normally used to indicate the type of information stored in a fact and is called a relation. Fact templates can be used to document the type of information that is stored in a fact. Commands for adding, removing and displaying facts were discussed. The deffacts construct can be used to specify facts as initial knowledge.

Rules are the second component of a CLIPS system. A rule is divided into a LHS and a RHS. The LHS of a rule can be thought of as the IF portion and the RHS can be thought of as the THEN portion of a rule. Rules can have multiple patterns and actions. Commands are available for displaying the list of rules and the text of an individual rule.

The third component of CLIPS is the inference engine. Rules that have their patterns satisfied by facts produce an activation which is placed on the agenda. Refraction prevents rules from constantly being activated by old facts.

Fact assertions and retractions, rule firings, and activations can be traced by using the *watch* command. The *matches* command will display the facts that have matched the patterns of a rule as well as the list of partial matches for a rule. The *set-break* command allows execution to be halted before a rule is fired. The *printout* command can be used to output information from the RHS of a rule. The *clear* command is used to re-initialize the state of the CLIPS environment.

PROBLEMS AND PROGRAMS

7-1.   Convert the following sentences to facts in a deffacts statement. For each group of related facts, build a fact template which describes a more general relationship.

```
The father of John is Tom.
The mother of John is Susan.
The parents of John are Tom and Susan.
Tom is a father.
Susan is a mother.
John is a son.
Tom is a male.
Susan is a female.
John is a male.
```

7-2.   Describe a fact template for a fact containing information about a set. The fact template should include information about the name or description of the set, the list of elements in the set and whether it is a subset of another set. Represent the following sets as facts using the format specified by your fact templates.

```
A = { 1, 2, 3 }
B = { 1, 2, 3, 4, 5 }
C = { red, green, yellow, blue }
D = { CPU, memory, I/O, address bus,
      data bus, video display }
```

7-3.   A sparsely populated array is an array that contains relatively few non-zero elements. It is more efficiently represented as a linked list or tree. How might a sparsely populated array be represented using facts? Describe the templates used for the facts to represent the array. What are the possible disadvantages of representing an array using facts as opposed to using an array data structure in a procedural language?

7-4.   Convert the general net representing airline routes as shown in Figure 2-4 (a) to a series of facts in a deffacts statement. Use a single template to describe the facts.

7-5.   Convert the semantic net representing a family as shown in Figure 2-4 (b) as a series of facts in a deffacts statement. Use several templates to describe the facts produced.

7-6.   How might facts be used to represent Object-Attribute-Value triplets and Attribute-Value pairs? Give examples for the sentences in Problem 7-1.

7-7.   Convert the semantic net shown in Figure 2-5 to a series of facts in a deffacts statement. Use several templates to describe the facts. For example, the IS-A links and AKO links should be relation names and each should have its own template.

7-8.   Convert the binary decision tree representing animal classification information of Figure 3-3 to a series of facts in a deffacts statement. Show how the links between the nodes can be represented. Do the leafs of the tree require a different representation than the other nodes of the tree?

7-9.   Explain the output from the *matches* command for the following command sequence.

```
CLIPS> (assert (b))
CLIPS> (defrule matcher (a) (b) (c) =>)
CLIPS> (assert (a) (c))
CLIPS> (matches matcher)
```

7-10.   Convert the decision tree shown in Figure 3-3 to a series of CLIPS rules. Create patterns to match facts using the template (question <query-string> <answer>). For example, if the answer to the question represented by the root node in the tree was no, the fact representing this information would be (question "Is it very big?" no).

What information that was contained in the decision tree is now lost by representing the tree as rules in this manner?

7-11.   Plants require many different types of nutrients for proper growth. Three of the most important plant nutrients that are provided by fertilizer are nitrogen, phosphorus, and potassium. A deficiency in one of these nutrients will produce various symptoms. Translate the following heuristics below to rules which determine nutrient deficiency. Assume that the plant is normally green.

```
A plant with stunted growth may have a nitrogen
    deficiency.
A plant that is pale yellow in color may have a
    nitrogen deficiency.
A plant that has reddish-brown leaf edges may have a
    nitrogen deficiency.
A plant with stunted root growth may have a
    phosphorus deficiency.
A plant with a spindly stalk may have a phosphorus
    deficiency.
A plant that is purplish in color may have a
    phosphorus deficiency.
A plant that has delayed in maturing may have a
    phosphorus deficiency.
A plant with leaf edges that appear scorched may have
    a potassium deficiency.
A plant with weakened stems may have a potassium
    deficiency.
A plant with shriveled seeds or fruits may have a
    potassium deficiency.
```

Include comments which define the templates used for the facts in the rules. The input to the program should be made by asserting symptoms as facts. The output should indicate which nutrient deficiencies exist by printing to the terminal. Implement a method so that multiple printouts for a single deficiency caused by more than one symptom are avoided. Test your program with the following inputs:

```
The plant has stunted root growth.
The plant is purplish in color.
```

7-12.   Fires are classified according to their principal burning material. Translate the following information to rules for determining fire class.

```
Type A fires involve ordinary combustibles such as
    paper, wood, and cloth.
```

Type B fires involve flammable and combustible
   liquids, greases, and similar materials.
Type C fires involve energized electrical equipment.
Type D fires involve combustible metals such as
   magnesium, sodium, potassium, titanium, and
   zirconium.

The type of extinguisher that should be used on a fire depends upon the fire class. Translate the following information to rules.

Class A fires should be extinguished with
   heat-absorbing or combustion-retarding
   extinguishers such as water or water based liquids
   and dry chemicals.
Class B fires should be extinguished by excluding
   air, inhibiting the release of combustible vapors,
   or interrupting the combustion chain reaction.
   Extinguishers include dry chemicals, carbon
   dioxide, foam, and bromotrifluoromethane.
Class C fires should be extinguished with a
   non-conducting agent to prevent shock. If
   possible the power should be cut. Extinguishers
   include dry chemicals, carbon dioxide, and
   bromotrifluoromethane.
Class D fires should be extinguished with smothering
   and heat-absorbing chemicals that do not react
   with the burning metals. Such chemicals include
   trimethoxyboroxine and screened graphitized coke.

Include comments which define the templates used for the facts in the rules. The input to the program should be made by asserting the type of burning material as a fact. The output should indicate which extinguishers may be used on the fire and other actions that should be taken such as cutting off the power. Show that your program works for a material from each of the fire classes.

CHAPTER 8   PATTERN MATCHING

8.1   INTRODUCTION

The type of rules shown in Chapter 7 illustrate simple pattern matching of patterns to facts. This chapter will introduce several concepts which provide very powerful capabilities for matching and manipulating facts. The first concept will be the use of variables in pattern matching. Secondly, field constraints will be discussed and the use of functions in CLIPS will then be introduced and basic arithmetic will be covered.

8.2   VARIABLES

Just as with other programming languages, CLIPS has **variables** available to store values. Variables in CLIPS are always written in the syntax of a question mark followed by a symbolic field name. Variable names follow the syntax of a word with the exception that they must begin with a character. For good programming style, variables should be given meaningful names. Some examples of variables are as follows.

```
?speed
?sensor
?value
?noun
?color
```

Spaces should not be used between the question mark and symbolic field name. As will be discussed later, a question mark by itself has its own use.

Before a variable can be used, it must be assigned a value. The following rule shows a case in which the variable ?x is used in a printout command without having been assigned a value.

```
(defrule test
   (initial-fact)
   =>
   (printout t ?x crlf))
```

In the above example, notice how initial-fact is used to trigger the rule. This is convenient since (initial-fact) can be asserted by simply using the *reset* command. In fact, for this rule, it is not necessary to place the (initial-fact) pattern on the LHS, since a rule with no patterns automatically has the (initial-fact) pattern added to its LHS.

When the rule is entered, CLIPS will respond with the error message

```
Undefined variable x referenced on rhs of rule
```

CLIPS gives an error message because it cannot find a value which has been bound to ?x. The terms **bound** and **bind** are used to describe the assignment of a value to a variable.

One common use of variables is to bind a value on the LHS and then assert the bound variable on the RHS. The following rule demonstrates this use

```
(defrule grandfather
   (is-a-grandfather ?name)
   =>
   (assert (is-a-man ?name)))
```

If the fact (is-a-grandfather Jack) is asserted and the program is run, the grandfather rule will assert the fact (is-a-man Jack) because the variable ?name was bound to Jack.

Of course, a variable can be used more than once as the following rule shows

```
(defrule grandfather
   (is-a-grandfather ?name)
   =>
   (assert (is-a-father ?name)
           (is-a-man ?name)))
```

If the fact (is-a-grandfather Jack) is asserted and the rule is fired, the facts (is-a-father Jack) and (is-a-man Jack) will be placed in the fact-list since the variable ?name is used twice.

Variables are also commonly used in printing output, as in

```
(defrule grandfather
   (is-a-grandfather ?name)
   =>
   (printout t ?name " is a grandfather" crlf))
```

If the fact (is-a-grandfather Jack) is asserted and the rule is executed, the following output would be produced

```
Jack is a grandfather
```

8.3   FACT ADDRESSES AND RETRACTION

Retraction is very useful in expert systems and is usually done on the RHS rather than in the top-level. Before a fact can be retracted, it must be specified to CLIPS. To retract a fact from a rule, the **fact-address** must first be bound to a variable on the LHS.

There is a big difference between binding a variable to the contents of a fact and binding a variable to the fact-address. In the examples of patterns previously used, such as (is-a-grandfather ?name), a variable was bound to the value of a field. That is, ?name was bound to Jack. However, if the fact whose contents are (is-a-grandfather Jack) is to be removed, then CLIPS must know the address of the fact to be retracted.

The address of the fact is specified using the **left arrow** operator, "<-". This operator is made by typing a "<" symbol followed by a "-".

Shown following is an example of fact retraction from a rule

```
(defrule modify-grandfather-fact
   ?old-fact <- (is-a-grandfather Jack)
   =>
   (retract ?old-fact)
   (assert (has-a-grandchild Jack)
           (is-a-man Jack)))
```

If the fact (is-a-grandfather Jack) is asserted and the rule is executed, then the fact (is-a-grandfather Jack) will be retracted from the fact-list and the two facts (has-a-grandchild Jack) and (is-a-man Jack) will be asserted into the fact-list. The pattern in the rule assigns the address of (is-a-grandfather Jack) to the variable ?old-fact. The *retract* command then removes the fact (is-a-grandfather Jack) whose address was assigned to ?old-fact.

Variables can be used to pick up a fact value at the same time as an address. For example

```
(defrule modify-grandfather-fact
   ?old-fact <- (is-a-grandfather ?name)
   =>
   (retract ?old-fact)
   (assert (has-a-grandchild ?name)
           (is-a-man ?name)))
```

The above rule will fire when ?name is assigned to any field. For example, if the facts (is-a-grandfather Brian), (is-a-grandfather Steve), and (is-a-grandfather Gary) are asserted into the fact-list, the rule will produce an activation for each of the three facts.

The *assert* command can be used with *retract* command to produce some interesting effects. The following rule demonstrates a simple looping effect. It can be activated by asserting the fact (loop-fact).

```
(defrule simple-loop
   ?old-fact <- (loop-fact)
   =>
   (printout t "Looping" crlf)
   (retract ?old-fact)
   (assert (loop-fact)))
```

The program executes an infinite loop since it asserts a new (loop-fact) after retracting the fact bound to ?old-fact. Note that to make a new (loop-fact) the individual fields must be asserted. CLIPS is not designed to allow assertions of entire facts with statements like (assert (?old-fact)). After the new (loop-fact) is asserted, the rule then fires on the new (loop-fact).

The only way to stop an infinite loop like this is by interrupting CLIPS using a Control-C or other appropriate interrupt command for the computer on which CLIPS is running. In extreme cases on personal computers it may be necessary to reboot and then restart CLIPS.

The program will not produce an infinite loop if the *retract* command is removed since the attempted assertions would then be duplicates of the fact already in memory.

8.4 MULTIPLE USE OF VARIABLES

The *modify-grandfather-fact* rule can only be activated by a fact with two fields. A fact matching the template

```
(is-a-grandfather <grandfather> <grandchild>)
```

such as (is-a-grandfather Jack John), will not match the rule because it contains three fields. In order to match against a template containing the name of both the grandfather and the grandchild, the rule must be modified to match against three fields. One approach to modify the rule might be to use two variables called ?name to match the two name fields in (is-a-grandfather Jack John).

```
(defrule modify-grandfather-fact
   ?old-fact <- (is-a-grandfather ?name ?name)
   =>
   (retract ?old-fact)
   (assert (has-a-grandchild ?name ?name)
           (is-a-man ?name)))
```

However, this rule won't fire on (is-a-grandfather Jack John) because the pattern (is-a-grandfather ?name ?name) specifies that the two fields must be the same since the same variable ?name is used for both fields.

The way to bind both names is to use two different variables, as follows

```
(defrule modify-grandfather-fact
   ?old-fact <- (is-a-grandfather ?grandfather
                                  ?grandchild)
   =>
   (retract ?old-fact)
   (assert (has-a-grandchild ?grandfather
```

```
                                ?grandchild)
            (is-a-man ?grandfather)))
```

This rule will become activated when the fact (is-a-grandfather Jack John) is asserted.

This rule will also fire if Jack has a grandchild named after him. That is, the fact (is-a-grandfather Jack Jack) will also cause the rule to become activated. Different variables are allowed to have the same values.

Notice that the pattern (is-a-grandfather ?grandfather ?grandchild) matched any two symbolic fields for the variables while (is-a-grandfather ?name ?name) required that the two fields bound to the variables were the same.

Variables that are used in multiple patterns have an important and useful property. The first time that a variable is bound to a value, it retains that value within the rule. The following rule and deffacts demonstrate this principle. Notice that the same variable, ?father, is used in both patterns of the *determine-grandfather* rule.

```
(defrule determine-grandfather
    (the-father-of ?grandchild is ?father)        pattern
    (the-father-of ?father is ?grandfather)       pattern
    =>
    (printout t "The grandfather of " ?grandchild
               " is " ?grandfather crlf))


(deffacts father-of-relations
    (the-father-of Jill is John)
    (the-father-of Bob is John)
    (the-father-of John is Jack)
    (the-father-of Bill is Fred)
    (the-father-of Sally is Fred)
    (the-father-of Fred is Gene)
```

When CLIPS is reset and the facts from the deffacts construct are asserted, the first pattern will match all six facts. The variable ?father will be bound to the names John, John, Jack, Fred, Fred, and Gene respectively for each of the six facts. When CLIPS — in pattern 1 tries to match the second pattern of the rule, only the facts with a second field bound to one of these values will be able to match. Of the six facts, only the fact (the-father-of John is Jack) and (the-father-of Fred is Gene) will be able to match the second pattern for facts which matched the first pattern.

8.5 SINGLE FIELD WILDCARDS

Rather than having to specify a specific field of a fact to trigger a rule, a general pattern can be specified by using a **wildcard**. For example, suppose a database of information exists about the eye and hair color of a group of people. Each fact in the database is specified by the following template

```
(person <name> <eye-color> <hair-color>)
```

and the database could be the described by the deffacts

```
(deffacts persons
    (person John brown black)
    (person Jill blue blond)
    (person Jack green brown)
    (person Jane brown brown)
    (person Fred green red))
```

where, for example, the fact (person John brown black) indicates that John has brown eyes and black hair. Rules can be written to search the fact-list for people meeting certain specifications. One such specification could be to write a rule which finds all people who have brown hair. For this specification, the color of the person's eyes is unimportant.

This type of situation in which only part of the fact is needed to determine a match is very common. To solve this problem, a wildcard can be used for the fields that are unimportant.

The simplest form of wildcard is called a **single-field wildcard** and is shown by a question mark, "?". A single-field wildcard stands for one field. The following rule shows how a wildcard can be used with the previous deffacts to find all people with brown hair.

```
(defrule find-brown-haired-people
    (person ?name ? brown)
    =>
    (printout t ?name " has brown hair" crlf))
```

The pattern includes a wildcard to indicate that the color of the person's eyes is not important. So long as the hair color of the person is brown, the rule will be satisfied and fire.

Notice now the importance of not including a space between the question mark and the symbolic name of a variable. Doing this to the pattern

```
(person ?name ? brown)
```

would produce the pattern

```
(person ? name ? brown)
```

which is completely different. The first pattern would match a fact with four fields. The first field of the fact would be the word *person* and the fourth field of the fact would be the word *brown*. The second pattern would match a fact with five fields whose first field was the word *person*, third field was the word *name*, and fifth field was the word *brown*.

Suppose it is desired to match against a fact with the following template

```
(person <name> <eye-color> <hair-color>
        <nationality>)
```

to find all persons with brown hair. Since this template has an additional field, an additional wildcard must be added to the previous pattern. Thus the pattern

```
(person ?name ? brown ?)
```

would have to be used. The important point to remember is that each field of the pattern must match to a field in the fact.

8.6 BLOCKS WORLD *skipped*

As an example to demonstrate variables bindings, a program to move blocks in a simple blocks world will be built. This type of program is analogous to the classic blocks world program in which the knowledge domain is restricted to blocks [Firebaugh 88]. An example like this is a good example of planning and might be applied to automated manufacturing where a robot arm is manipulating parts.

The only thing of interest in blocks world are blocks. A single block may be stacked upon another block. The goal of a complex blocks world program would be to rearrange the stacks of block into a goal configuration with the minimum number of moves. For this example, a number of simplifying restrictions will be made. The first of these restrictions is that only one primary goal is allowed and this goal can only be to move one block on top of another block. With this restriction, it is rather trivial to determine the optimal moves to achieve the goal. If the goal is to move block x on top of block y, then move all blocks (if any) on top of block x to the floor and all blocks (if any) on top of block y to the floor and then move block x on top of block y.

The second restriction will be that any goal must not have already been achieved. That is, the goal cannot be to move block x on top of block y if block x is already on top of block y. This is a rather simple condition to check, however, the appropriate syntax to test for this condition is not introduced until Chapter 9.

To begin to solve this problem, it will be useful to set up a configuration of blocks which can be used for testing the program. Figure 8-1 shows the configuration that will be used. There are two stacks in this configuration. The first stack has block A on top of block B on top of block C. The second stack has block D on top of block E on top of block F.

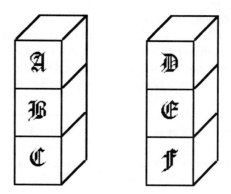

Figure 8-1

To determine which type of rules would be useful in solving the problem, a step by step completion of a blocks world goal would be useful. What steps must be taken to move block C on top of block E? The easiest solution for this problem would be to directly move block C on top of block E. This rule, however, could only be applied if both block C and block E had no blocks on top of them. The pseudo code for this rule would be

```
RULE MOVE-DIRECTLY
IF    The goal is to move block ?upper on top of
         block ?lower and
      block ?upper is the top block in its stack and
      block ?lower is the top block in its stack,
THEN Move block ?upper on top of block ?lower.
```

The *move-directly* rule cannot be used in this case, however, since blocks A and B are on top of block C, and block D is on top of block E. In order to allow the *move-directly* rule to move block C on top of block E, blocks A, B, and D must be moved to the floor. The blocks are moved to the floor since this is the easiest step to take to get them out of the way. The simple blocks world does not require that the blocks be restacked and only a single primary goal is allowed, so there is no need to stack blocks when they are moved out of the way. This rule can be expressed as two pseudocode rules: one rule to clear blocks off the block to be moved and one rule to clear blocks off the block to be stacked on.

```
RULE CLEAR-UPPER-BLOCK
IF    The goal is to move block ?x and
      block ?x is not the top block in its stack and
      block ?above is on top of block ?x,
THEN The goal is to move block ?above to the floor
```

```
RULE CLEAR-LOWER-BLOCK
IF   The goal is to move another block on top of
        block ?x and
     block ?x is not the top block in its stack and
     block ?above is on top of block ?x,
THEN The goal is to move block ?above to the floor
```

The *clear-upper-block* rule will work to clear the blocks off block C. It will first determine that block B needs to be moved to the floor. In order to move block B to the floor, this same rule will determine that block A needs to be moved to the floor. Similarly, the *clear-lower-block* rule will determine that block D needs to be moved to the floor in order to move something on top of block E.

Now there are goals to move blocks A, B, and D to the floor. Blocks A and D can be moved directly to the floor. If written properly, the *move-directly* rule might be able to handle moving blocks on top of the floor as well as other blocks. However, since the floor is really not a block, it may be necessary to treat the floor differently. The following pseudocode rule will handle the special case of moving a block to the floor

```
RULE MOVE-TO-FLOOR
IF   The goal is to move block ?upper on top of the
        floor and
     block ?upper is the top block in its stack,
THEN Move block ?upper on top of the floor.
```

The *move-to-floor* rule can now move blocks A and D to the floor. Once block A is moved to the floor, the *move-to-floor* rule can be activated to move block B to the floor. With blocks A, B, and D on the floor, blocks C and E are now the top blocks in their stacks and it is possible to use the *move-directly* rule to move block C on top of block E.

Now that the rules have been written using pseudocode, the facts to be used by the rules should be determined. The types of facts needed cannot always be determined without some prototyping. In this case, however, the pseudocode rules point out several types of facts that will be needed. For example, the information about which blocks are on top of other blocks is crucial. This information could be described with the following template

```
(on-top-of <upper-block> <lower-block>)
```

and the facts described by this template would be

```
(on-top-of A B)
(on-top-of B C)
(on-top-of D E)
(on-top-of E F)
```

Since it is also important to know which block is at the top of a stack and which block is at the bottom of a stack, it would be useful to include the facts

```
(on-top-of nothing A)
(on-top-of C floor)
(on-top-of nothing D)
(on-top-of F floor)
```

The words *nothing* and *floor* have special meaning in these facts. The facts (on-top-of nothing A) and (on-top-of nothing D) indicate that A and D are the top blocks in their stacks. Similarly, the facts (on-top-of C floor) and (on-top-of F floor) indicate that blocks A and F are the bottom blocks in their stacks. Including these facts, however, does not necessarily solve the problem of determining the top and bottom blocks in a stack. If the rules are not written correctly, the words *floor* and *nothing* might be mistaken as the names of blocks. Facts that indicate the name of the blocks might be useful. The following template

```
(block <name>)
```

can be used to identify the blocks from the special words *nothing* and *floor*. The facts described by this template would be

```
(block A)
(block B)
(block C)
(block D)
(block E)
(block F)
```

Finally, a fact is needed to describe the block moving goals that are being processed. These goals could be described with the template

```
(move-goal <block> on-top-of <target-destination>)
```

and the initial goal using this template would be

```
(move-goal C on-top-of E)
```

Note that the word *on-top-of* has been included in the template. This word serves no other purpose in the template and fact other than providing increased readability. The target destination in the move goal could also be the floor.

With the facts and templates now defined, the initial configuration of the blocks world can be described by the following deffacts.

```
(deffacts initial-state
   (block A)
   (block B)
   (block C)
   (block D)
   (block E)
   (block F)
   (on-top-of nothing A)
   (on-top-of A B)
   (on-top-of B C)
   (on-top-of C floor)
   (on-top-of nothing D)
   (on-top-of D E)
   (on-top-of E F)
   (on-top-of F floor)
   (move-goal C on-top-of E))
```

Notice that information is included in the *on-top-of* facts to indicate which blocks are the top blocks and which blocks are the bottom blocks. The *block* facts help distinguish the blocks from the words *floor* and *nothing*. The goal for the program is to move block C on top of block E.

The *move-directly* rule is written as follows

```
(defrule move-directly
   ?goal <- (move-goal ?block1 on-top-of ?block2)
   (block ?block1)
   (block ?block2)
   (on-top-of nothing ?block1)
   ?stack-1 <- (on-top-of ?block1 ?block3)
   ?stack-2 <- (on-top-of nothing ?block2)
   =>
   (retract ?goal ?stack-1 ?stack-2)
   (assert (on-top-of ?block1 ?block2))
   (assert (on-top-of nothing ?block3))
   (printout t ?block1 " moved on top of " ?block2
              "." crlf))
```

The first three patterns determine that there is a goal to move a block on top of another block. Patterns two and three insure that a goal to move a block onto the floor will not be processed by this rule. The fourth and sixth patterns check that the blocks are the top blocks in their stacks. The fifth pattern matches against information necessary to update the stack from which the moving block is being taken. The actions of the rule update the stack information for the two stacks and prints a message. The block beneath the moved block is now the top block in that stack, and the block being moved is now the top block in the stack to which it was moved.

The *move-to-floor* rule is implemented as follows

```
(defrule move-to-floor
    ?goal <- (move-goal ?block1 on-top-of floor)
    (block ?block1)
    (on-top-of nothing ?block1)
    ?stack <- (on-top-of ?block1 ?block2)
    =>
    (retract ?goal ?stack)
    (assert (on-top-of ?block1 floor))
    (assert (on-top-of nothing ?block2))
    (printout t ?block1 " moved on top of floor."
              crlf))
```

This rule is similar to the *move-directly* rule with the exception that it is not necessary to update some information about the floor since it is not a block.

The *clear-upper-block* rule is implemented as follows

```
(defrule clear-upper-block
    (move-goal ?block1 on-top-of ?)
    (block ?block1)
    (on-top-of ?block2 ?block1)
    (block ?block2)
    =>
    (assert (move-goal ?block2 on-top-of floor)))
```

The *clear-lower-block* rule is implemented as follows

```
(defrule clear-lower-block
    (move-goal ? on-top-of ?block1)
    (block ?block1)
    (on-top-of ?block2 ?block1)
    (block ?block2)
    =>
    (assert (move-goal ?block2 on-top-of floor)))
```

The program is now complete with the *move-directly, move-to-floor, clear-upper-block*, and *clear-lower-block* rules and the *initial-state* deffacts. The following output shows a sample run of this blocks world program.

```
CLIPS> (reset)↵
CLIPS> (run)↵
```

```
A moved on top of floor.
B moved on top of floor.
D moved on top of floor.
C moved on top of E.
7 rules fired
CLIPS>
```

Blocks A and B are first moved to the floor to clear block C. Block D is then moved to the floor to clear block E. Finally, block C can be moved on top of block E to solve the primary goal.

This example has demonstrated building a program using a step by step method. First, pseudorules were written using English-like text. Second, the pseudorules were used to determine the types of facts that would be required. Templates describing the facts were designed, and the initial knowledge for the program was coded using these templates. Finally, the pseudorules were translated to CLIPS rules using the fact templates as a guide for translation.

Typically, the development of an expert system requires a great deal more prototyping and iterative development than was shown in developing this example. It is not always possible to determine the best method for representing facts or the types of rules that will be needed to build an expert system. Following a consistent methodology, however, can aid in the development of an expert system even when a great deal of prototyping and iteration needs to be performed.

8.7 MULTIFIELD WILDCARDS AND VARIABLES

Multifields

Multifield wildcards and variables can be used to match against zero or more fields of a pattern. The **multifield wildcard** is a dollar sign followed by a question mark, "$?", and represents zero or more occurrences of a field. Note that ordinary variables and wildcards match exactly one field. This is a slight, but very important difference. The following rule and deffacts show how multifield wildcards can be used to find all occurrences of facts that represent a list of items, regardless of the size of the list.

```
(defrule find-list
    (list $?)
    =>
    (printout t "Found a list" crlf))

(deffacts different-lists
    (list a)
    (list b d)
    (list a b c)
```

```
(list a c c e)
(list c d b))
```

This program, when run, will fire the *find-list* rule five times since there are five *list* facts.

Wildcards have another important use because they can be attached to a symbolic field to create a variable such as ?x, $?x, ?name, $?name. Single field variables are preceded by a "?", while multifield variables are preceded by a "$?".

As an example of a multifield variable, the following version of the *find-list* rule also prints out the item field(s) of the matching fact because a variable is equated to the item field(s) that match.

```
(defrule find-list
   (list $?items)
   =>
   (printout t "Found a list with items: " $?items
             crlf))
```

When this rule is fired, the items found in the lists will be printed. The multifield wildcard can match any number of fields. No matter how many item fields that a list has, the multifield wildcard will match against all of them.

Multifield variables can also be used to find all lists that contain a particular item field, even if the position of the item field is not known in advance. Suppose we want to find all *list* facts containing the item c. The following facts from the *different-lists* deffacts all contain the item c

```
(list a b c)
(list a c c e)
(list c d b)
```

Notice that the fact (list a c c e) would actually match twice since there are two c's in the item list. This represents a case in which two activations of the same rule are placed on the agenda with the exact same fact identifiers. Normally, CLIPS will not allow this to happen, but in this case, the facts have been matched in different ways because multifield variables were used.

The following rule will match all facts containing the item c and print out the item fields found before and after the item c.

```
(defrule find-item-c
   (list $?before c $?after)
   =>
   (printout t "Items before c: " $?before crlf)
   (printout t "Items after c: " $?after crlf))
```

The pattern matches any *list* facts that have an item c anywhere in them.

Single and multifield wildcards can be combined. For example, the pattern

```
(list ? $? c ?)
```

means that the first and last fields can be anything, and that the field just before the last field must be the word *c*. The pattern also requires that the matching fact must have at least four fields. Table 8-1 shows which of the facts found in the *different-lists* deffacts will match this pattern.

Fact	Matches
(list c)	No
(list c d)	No
(list a c e)	Yes
(list a c d b)	No
(list a d c b)	Yes

Table 8-1
Matches for the Pattern (list ? $? c ?)

Note that the $? can match zero or more occurrences of a field. Matching zero occurrences means that there can be a match with no fields. So a pattern like (list $?items) will match any *list* fact. In contrast, the ? requires a field to match. *needs one*

Although multifield variables can be essential for pattern matching in many cases, their overuse can cause a lot of inefficiency because of increased memory requirements and slower execution. As a general rule of style, $? should only be used when the length of the fields being matched against is not known. The $? should not be used as a convenience to avoid typing several single field wildcards. Chapter 11, which discusses efficiency, has more details on the efficient use of multifield wildcards and variables.

Implementing a Stack   *skipped*

A **stack** is an ordered data structure to which items can be added and removed. Items are added and removed to one "end" of the stack. A new item can be pushed (added) to the stack or the last item added can be popped (removed) from the stack. In a stack, the first value added is the last item to be removed and the last item added is the first item to be removed.

A useful analogy for a stack is a set of cafeteria trays. New trays are added (pushed) on the top of the trays already in the stack. The last trays added to the top of the stack will be the first trays removed (popped).

It is relatively easy to implement a stack capable of performing push and pop operations using multifield variables. First of all, a *stack* fact similar to the *list* facts previously discussed can be used. The following rule will push a value onto the *stack* fact.

```
(defrule push-value
   ?push-value <- (push-value ?value)
   ?stack <- (stack $?rest)
   =>
   (retract ?push-value ?stack)
   (assert (stack ?value $?rest))
   (printout t "Pushing value " ?value crlf))
```

Two rules are necessary to implement the pop action: one for an empty stack and another if the stack has a value to pop.

```
(defrule pop-value-valid
   ?pop-value <- (pop-value)
   ?stack <- (stack ?value $?rest)
   =>
   (retract ?pop-value ?stack)
   (assert (stack $?rest))
   (printout t "Popping value " ?value crlf))

(defrule pop-value-invalid
   ?pop-value <- (pop-value)
   (stack)
   =>
   (retract ?pop-value)
   (printout t "Popping from empty stack" crlf))
```

These rules could easily be changed to push and pop values to named stacks. For example, the patterns

```
   ?push-value <- (push-value ?value)
   ?stack <- (stack $?rest)
```

could be replaced with

```
   ?push-value <- (push-value ?name ?value)
   ?stack <- (stack ?name $?rest)
```

where ?name represents the name of the stack.

Blocks World Revisited   *skipped*

Using multifield variables and wildcards, the blocks world problem can be reimplemented in a much easier fashion. Each stack can be represented by a single fact as shown below. The operations on moving the blocks are very similar to those used in the push/pop example.

```
(deffacts initial-state
    (stack A B C)
    (stack D E F)
    (move-goal C on-top-of E)
    (stack))
```

The empty *stack* fact is included to prevent this fact from being added later, for example, when a stack has one block in it and that block is moved on top of another stack.

The rules for the blocks world program using multifield variables are shown below.

```
(defrule move-directly
    ?goal <- (move-goal ?block1 on-top-of ?block2)
    ?stack-1 <- (stack ?block1 $?rest1)
    ?stack-2 <- (stack ?block2 $?rest2)
    =>
    (retract ?goal ?stack-1 ?stack-2)
    (assert (stack $?rest1))
    (assert (stack ?block1 ?block2 $?rest2))
    (printout t ?block1 " moved on top of "
              ?block2 "." crlf))

(defrule move-to-floor
    ?goal <- (move-goal ?block1 on-top-of floor)
    ?stack-1 <- (stack ?block1 $?rest)
    =>
    (retract ?goal ?stack-1)
    (assert (stack ?block1))
    (assert (stack $?rest))
    (printout t ?block1 " moved on top of floor."
              crlf))

(defrule clear-upper-block
    (move-goal ?block1 on-top-of ?)
    (stack ?top $? ?block1 $?)
    =>
    (assert (move-goal ?top on-top-of floor)))

(defrule clear-lower-block
    (move-goal ? on-top-of ?block1)
    (stack ?top $? ?block1 $?)
```

```
=>
(assert (move-goal ?top on-top-of floor)))
```

8.8   FIELD CONSTRAINTS

The NOT Field Constraint

Chapter 7 demonstrated elementary pattern matching using the industrial plant monitoring system example. In addition to those elementary pattern matching capabilities, CLIPS has more powerful pattern matching operators. These additional pattern matching capabilities will be introduced by reconsidering the problem of determining groups of people with certain hair and eye colors. Suppose, for example, it is necessary to find all people who do not have brown hair. One way to do this is to write rules for each type of hair color. For example, the following rule finds people with black hair.

```
(defrule black-hair-is-not-brown-hair
    (person ?name ? black)
    =>
    (printout t ?name " does not have brown hair"
            crlf))
```

Another rule would cover people having blonde hair.

```
(defrule blonde-hair-is-not-brown-hair
    (person ?name ? blonde)
    =>
    (printout t ?name " does not have brown hair"
            crlf))
```

Yet another rule could be written to find people having red hair. The problem with writing the rules in this manner, however, is that the condition being checked is that the hair is not brown. The previous rules attempt to test this condition in a round-about manner. That is, determine all the hair colors other than brown and write a rule for each one. If all the colors can be specified, then this technique will work. For this example, however, it would be simpler to assume that hair color could be anything (even purple or green).

A way of handling this case is to use a **field constraint** to restrict the values a field may have on the LHS. The field constraint put limits on the values a field may have on the LHS. The field constraint acts like operators on patterns.

One type of field constraint is called a **logical constraint**. There are three types of logical constraints. The first type of logical constraint is called a **N O T**

constraint. Its symbol is the **tilde,** "~". The NOT constraint acts on the one value that immediately follows it. It prevents that value from matching a field of the pattern.

The rule that looks for people without brown hair can be written much more easily using the NOT constraint as shown in the following rule.

```
(defrule person-without-brown-hair
    (person ?name ? ~brown)
    =>
    (printout t ?name " does not have brown hair"
            crlf))
```

By using the NOT constraint, this one rule does the work of many others that required specifying each hair color.

The OR Field Constraint

The second logical constraint is the **OR constraint,** represented by the bar "|". The OR constraint is used to allow one or more possible values to match a field of a pattern.

For example, the following rule finds all people with either black or brown hair using the OR constraint.

```
(defrule black-or-brown-hair
    (person ?name ? brown | black)
    =>
    (printout t ?name " has dark hair" crlf))
```

Asserting the facts (person Joe blue brown) and (person Mark brown black) would place an instantiation for each of the facts on the agenda.

The AND Field Constraint

The third type of logical constraint is the **AND constraint.** The AND constraint is different from the logical AND discussed in Chapter 7. The symbol of the AND constraint is the ampersand, "&". The AND constraint is normally used only with the other constraints since otherwise it's not of much practical use.

One case in which the AND constraint is useful is to place additional constraints with the binding instance of a variable. Suppose, for example, that a rule is triggered by a *person* fact with hair color of brown or black. The pattern to find such a fact can be expressed easily using the OR constraint as shown in the previous example. However, how can the value of the hair color be identified? The solution is to bind a variable to the color that is matched using the AND constraint and then print out the variable. This is a case in which the AND constraint is useful, as shown following.

```
(defrule black-or-brown-hair
   (person ?name ? ?color&brown|black)
   =>
   (printout t ?name " has " ?color " hair" crlf))
```

The variable ?color will be bound to whatever color is matched by the brown|black field.

The AND constraint is also useful with the NOT constraint. For example, the following rule triggers when a person's hair color is not black and not brown.

```
defrule black-or-brown-hair
   (person ?name ? ?color&~brown&~black)
   =>
   (printout t ?name " has " ?color " hair" crlf))
```

[handwritten margin note: ? order of precedence ? ?color = Null?]

The following rule illustrates a case in which the AND constraint is *not* useful.

```
(defrule person-with-black-and-blonde
   (person ?name ? black&blonde)
   =>
   (printout t ?name " has black and blonde hair"
                 crlf))
```

This rule will never be triggered since there is no possible fact whose hair color value is both black and blonde (assuming, of course, that a person's natural hair color can only be one color). The pattern will not match on black, blonde, or even blackblonde.

The following rule illustrates another case where the AND constraint is not very useful.

```
(defrule person-with-black-hair
   (person ?name ? black&~blonde)
   =>
   (printout t ?name " has black hair" crlf))
```

The pattern will match a person whose hair color is black and not blonde. In this case, the rule can be triggered by the fact (person Mark brown black) since black is black and not blonde. However, it's much more efficient to just write the rule as

```
(defrule person-with-black-hair
   (person ?name ? black)
   =>
   (printout t ?name " has black hair" crlf))
```

since hair that is black cannot be blonde anyway.

Combining Field Constraints

Field constraints can be mixed together with variables and other literal values to provide very powerful pattern matching capabilities. Suppose, for example, a rule is needed which determines if two people exist with the following conditions. The first person has either blue or green eyes and does not have black hair. The second person does not have the same color eyes as the first person and has either red hair or the same color hair as the first person. The following rule will match these constraints.

```
(defrule complex-eye-hair-match
    (person ?name1 ?eyes1&blue|green ?hair1&~black)
    (person ?name2&~?name1 ?eyes2&~?eyes1
            ?hair1&red|?hair1)
    =>
    (printout t ?name1 " has " ?eyes1 " eyes and "
              ?hair1 " hair" crlf)
    (printout t ?name2 " has " ?eyes2 " eyes and "
              ?hair2 " hair" crlf))
```

This example is worth studying in some detail. The field ?eyes1&blue|green binds the first person's eye color to the variable ?eyes1 if the eye color value of the fact being matched is either blue or green. The field ?hair1&~black binds the variable ?hair1 if the hair color value of the fact being matched is not black.

The pattern ?name2&~?name1 performs a very useful operation. It binds the name value of the person fact to the variable ?name2 if it is not the same as the value of ?name1. If the names are unique tags, this will insure that both patterns do not match the same fact. For these two patterns, this cannot happen since the eye color of the second person must be different from the eye color of the first person. However, it is a useful technique to understand and has many useful applications. Chapter 12 will show how this same technique can be accomplished using fact addresses to make sure that the facts are different. This will allow the rule to work for people with the same names, but different hair and eye colors.

The pattern field ?eyes2&~?eyes1 performs much the same test as the previous field. The final field, ?hair2&red|?hair1, binds the hair color value of the second person to the variable ?hair2 if the hair color is either red or the same value as the variable ?hair1. Note that a variable must already be bound if it used as part of an OR field constraint.

Variables will be bound only if they are the first condition in a field and only if they occur singly or are tied to the other conditions by an AND field constraint. For example, the following rule

```
(defrule bad-variable-use
   (person ?name ? red|?hair)
   =>
   (printout t ?name " has " ?hair " hair " crlf))
```

will produce an error since ?hair is not bound.

As a final note for combining constraints, keep in mind the combinations of constraints that perform no useful purpose. As shown previously, using the AND constraint to tie together literal constants will always produce a matching failure unless the constants are identical. Similarly, tying together negated literals using the OR constraint will always succeed in a pattern match if the literals are different.

8.9 FUNCTIONS AND EXPRESSIONS

Elementary Math Functions

Besides dealing with symbolic facts, CLIPS can also perform calculations. However, keep in mind that an expert system language like CLIPS is not designed for number-crunching. Although the math functions of CLIPS are very powerful, they are primarily meant for modification of numbers that are being reasoned about by the application program. Other languages such as FORTRAN are better for number-crunching in which little or no reasoning about the numbers is done. CLIPS provides the elementary arithmetic operators as shown in Table 8-2. All arithmetic is done in floating-point and all numbers are stored in floating-point.

Arithmetic Operators	Meaning
+	Addition
-	Subtraction
*	Multiplication
/	Division
**	Exponentiation

Table 8-2 CLIPS Elementary Arithmetic Operators

Numeric expressions are represented in CLIPS according to the style of LISP. In LISP and CLIPS, a numeric expression that would customarily be written as 2 + 3 must be written in **prefix form**, (+ 2 3). The customary way of writing numeric expressions is called **infix form** because the math operators are in between the **operands** or **arguments**. In the prefix form of CLIPS, the operator must go before the operands and parentheses must surround the numeric expression.

It is relatively easy to convert from infix to prefix format. For example, suppose two points are to be checked to see if they have a positive slope. In the customary infix way, this can be written as

```
(y2 - y1) / (x2 - x1)    >    0
```

Note that the greater than symbol, >, is a CLIPS function which will be introduced later. It is used to determine if its first argument is greater than its second argument. In order to write this expression in prefix form, it will be useful to start by thinking of the numerator as (Y) and the denominator as (X). So the expression above can be written as

```
(Y) / (X)    >    0
```

The prefix form for division is then

```
(/ (Y) (X))
```

since in prefix the operator comes before the argument. Now the result of the division must be tested to determine if it is greater than 0. So the prefix form is as follows.

```
(> (/ (Y) (X)) 0))
```

In infix form, Y = y2 - y1. But the prefix form needs to be used, since a prefix expression is being created. So (- y2 y1) will be used for (Y) and (- x2 x1) for (X). Replacing (Y) and (X) by their prefix forms will yield the final expression of whether the two points have a positive slope.

```
(> (/ (- y2 y1) (- x2 x1)) 0)
```

The simplest way to evaluate a numeric expression in CLIPS (as well as any other expression) is to evaluate the expression at the top-level prompt. For example, entering (+ 2 2) at the CLIPS prompt would produce the following output.

```
CLIPS> (+ 2 2)↵
4
CLIPS>
```

The output shows the correct response of 4. In general, any CLIPS expression can be entered at the top level to be evaluated. In fact, many of the commands already discussed such as the *facts* and *agenda* commands are simply functions that, when evaluated, produce output as a side effect. Most functions, such as the addition function, have a **return value**. This return value can be a number, word, string, or even a multifield value. Other functions, such as the *facts* and *agenda* commands have no return value. Functions without a return value typically have what is called a **side effect**. The side effect of the *facts* command is to list the facts in the fact-list.

The other arithmetic functions also work at the top-level. The following output demonstrates the evaluation of some other expressions.

```
CLIPS> (+ 2 3) ↵
5
CLIPS> (- 2 3) ↵
-1
CLIPS> (* 2 3) ↵
6
CLIPS> (/ 2 3) ↵
0.66666669
CLIPS> (** 2 3) ↵
8
CLIPS>
```

Note that the answer for division will probably show a round-off error in the last digit. This result may vary from machine to machine.

Variable Numbers of Arguments

Prefix notation allows variable numbers of arguments to be represented quite simply. Many CLIPS functions accept a variable number of arguments. The arguments in a numeric expression can be extended beyond two for all operators except exponentiation. The same sequence of arithmetic calculations is performed for more than two arguments. The following examples entered at the top level shows how three arguments are used. Evaluation proceeds from left to right.

```
CLIPS> (+ 2 3 4) ↵
9
CLIPS> (- 2 3 4) ↵
-5
CLIPS> (* 2 3 4) ↵
24
CLIPS> (/ 2 3 4) ↵
0.16666667
CLIPS>
```

Once again note that the answer for division may differ slightly depending upon the machine being used.

Precedence and Nesting Expressions

One important fact about CLIPS and LISP calculations is that there is no built-in precedence of arithmetic operations. In other computer languages, multiplication and division rank higher than addition and subtraction and the computer does the higher ranked operations first. However, in LISP and CLIPS, there is no built-in precedence.

Everything is simply evaluated from left to right with parentheses determining precedence.

Mixed calculations can be done in prefix notation. For example, suppose the following infix expression is to be evaluated

```
2 + 3 * 4
```

The customary evaluation is to multiply 3 by 4 and then add the result to 2. However, in CLIPS, the precedence must be explicitly written. The expression could be evaluated by entering the following at the top level

```
CLIPS> (+ 2 (* 3 4))↵
14
CLIPS>
```

In this rule, the expression in the innermost parentheses is evaluated first and so 3 is multiplied by 4. The result is then added to 2. If the desired evaluation is (2 + 3) * 4, where again addition is done first, the top level expression would be

```
CLIPS> (* (+ 2 3) 4)↵
20
CLIPS>
```

Using Expressions Within Asserts

In general, expressions may be freely embedded within other expressions. It would therefore seem natural to use an expression within an assert in the following manner

```
CLIPS> (assert (answer (+ 2 2)))↵
CLIPS>
```

The expected result would be the addition of the fact (answer 4) to the fact-list. Attempting this assertion, however, will produce an error. To understand this error, one must look back to the origin of CLIPS. The syntax of CLIPS is based very closely upon the syntax of ART. ART allows the use of embedded lists within facts. For example, the following facts are all valid ART facts:

```
(tools (hammer wrench pliers))
(names (Paul Tom Harry) (Martha Anne Jane Janet))
(answer (+ 2 2))
```

All of these facts are invalid in CLIPS since they contain embedded lists. Notice the fact (answer (+ 2 2)). Since this is a valid fact with an embedded list, namely (+ 2 2), how does ART specify an expression to be evaluated? The answer is that ART uses an "escape" character to indicate that a list is an expression to be evaluated and not an embedded list. To maintain compatibility, CLIPS uses this same escape character, even though embedded lists are not allowed in CLIPS.

The escape character used to signify an expression to be evaluated is the "=" operator. The operator may also be associated with the words "equal to the value of.". For example, the following command

```
CLIPS> (assert (answer =(+ 2 2))) ↵
CLIPS>
```

will correctly assert the fact (answer 4) because the = operator uses the value of 4 returned by the expression (+ 2 2). Note that the = operator is only used within *assert* commands (and sometimes within patterns as will be shown in Chapter 9), and it should only be used at the beginning of an expression to be evaluated (never within an expression).

8.10   SUMMING VALUES USING RULES

As a simple example of using functions to perform calculations, consider the problem of summing up the area of a group of rectangles. The height and width of the rectangles can be specified using the following template.

```
(rectangle <height> <width>)
```

and the sum of rectangle areas could be specified with the following template.

```
(sum <total-area>)
```

A deffacts containing sample information is

```
(deffacts initial-information
    (rectangle 10 6)
    (rectangle 7 5)
    (rectangle 6 8)
    (rectangle 2 5)
    (sum 0))
```

An initial attempt to produce a rule to sum the rectangle might be as follows:

```
(defrule sum-rectangles
    (rectangle ?height ?width)
    ?sum <- (sum ?total)
    =>
```

```
(retract ?sum)
(assert (sum =(+ ?total (* ?height ?width)))))))
```

This rule, however, will loop endlessly. Retracting the *sum* fact and then reasserting it will produce a loop with a single *rectangle* fact. One solution to solve the problem would be to retract the *rectangle* fact after its area was added to the *sum* fact. This would prevent the rule from firing off the same *rectangle* fact with a different *sum* fact. If the *rectangle* fact needs to be preserved, however, a different approach is required. A temporary fact containing the area to be added to the sum is created for each *rectangle* fact. This temporary fact can then be retracted which prevents an endless loop. The modified program is as follows:

```
(defrule sum-rectangles
   (rectangle ?height ?width)
   =>
   (assert (add-to-sum =(* ?height ?width))))

(defrule sum-areas
   ?sum <- (sum ?total)
   ?new-area <- (add-to-sum ?area)
   =>
   (retract ?sum ?new-area)
   (assert (sum =(+ ?total ?area))))
```

The following output shows how these two rules interact to sum the areas of the rectangles.

```
CLIPS> (watch all) ↵
CLIPS> (reset) ↵
==> f-0      (initial-fact)
==> f-1      (rectangle 10 6)
==> Activation 0      sum-rectangles: f-1
==> f-2      (rectangle 7 5)
==> Activation 0      sum-rectangles: f-2
==> f-3      (rectangle 6 8)
==> Activation 0      sum-rectangles: f-3
==> f-4      (rectangle 2 5)
==> Activation 0      sum-rectangles: f-4
==> f-5      (sum 0)
CLIPS> (run) ↵
FIRE    1 sum-rectangles: f-4
==> f-6      (add-to-sum 10)
==> Activation 0      sum-areas: f-5,f-6
FIRE    2 sum-areas: f-5,f-6
```

```
<== f-5       (sum 0)
<== f-6       (add-to-sum 10)
==> f-7       (sum 10)
FIRE     3 sum-rectangles: f-3
==> f-8       (add-to-sum 48)
==> Activation 0        sum-areas: f-7,f-8
FIRE     4 sum-areas: f-7,f-8
<== f-7       (sum 10)
<== f-8       (add-to-sum 48)
==> f-9       (sum 58)
FIRE     5 sum-rectangles: f-2
==> f-10      (add-to-sum 35)
==> Activation 0        sum-areas: f-9,f-10
FIRE     6 sum-areas: f-9,f-10
<== f-9       (sum 58)
<== f-10      (add-to-sum 35)
==> f-11      (sum 93)
FIRE     7 sum-rectangles: f-1
==> f-12      (add-to-sum 60)
==> Activation 0        sum-areas: f-11,f-12
FIRE     8 sum-areas: f-11,f-12
<== f-11      (sum 93)
<== f-12      (add-to-sum 60)
==> f-13      (sum 153)
8 rules fired
CLIPS>
```

The *sum-rectangles* rule is activated four times when the *rectangle* facts are asserted as a result of the *reset* command. Each time the *sum-rectangles* rule is fired, it asserts a fact which activates the *sum-areas* rule. The *sum-areas* rules adds the area to the running total and removes the *add-to-sum* fact. Since the *sum-rectangles* rule does not pattern match against the *sum* fact, it is not reactivated when a new *sum* fact is asserted.

8.11 THE BIND FUNCTION

Quite often it is useful to store a value in a temporary variable to avoid recalculation. Avoiding recalculation can often be crucial when functions produce side effects. The **bind** function can be used to bind the value of a variable to the value of an expression. The syntax of the *bind* function is

```
(bind <variable> <value>)
```

The bound variable, <variable>, can be either a multifield variable or a single field variable. The new value, <value>, should either be a single field value or an expression. If <value> is an expression, its return value should be a single field value for a single field variable. A multifield variable can accept either a single field or a multifield return value. For example, the *sum-areas* rule could printout the total sum and the area being added to it for each rectangle.

```
(defrule sum-areas
    ?sum <- (sum ?total)
    ?new-area <- (add-to-sum ?area)
    =>
    (retract ?sum ?new-area)
    (printout t "Adding " ?area " to " ?total crlf)
    (printout t "New sum is " (+ ?total ?area) crlf)
    (assert (sum =(+ ?total ?area))))
```

Notice that the expression (+ ?total ?area) can be embedded within the *printout* command and that it does not require the = operator. The expression is used twice in the RHS of the rule. Replacing the two separate evaluations with one *bind* function would eliminate unnecessary calculations. The rule rewritten with the *bind* function is

```
(defrule sum-areas
    ?sum <- (sum ?total)
    ?new-area <- (add-to-sum ?area)
    =>
    (retract ?sum ?new-area)
    (printout t "Adding " ?area " to " ?total crlf)
    (bind ?new-total (+ ?total ?area))
    (printout t "New sum is " ?new-total crlf)
    (assert (sum ?new-total)))
```

In addition to creating new variables for use on the RHS of a rule, the *bind* function can also be used to rebind the value of a variable used in the LHS of a rule.

8.12 USING FUNCTIONS ON THE RHS

Commands that are entered at the top-level prompt and actions performed from the RHS of a rule are all CLIPS functions. Commands have been used to describe functions that are primarily entered at the top-level prompt and actions are used to describe functions that are primarily used on the RHS of a rule. In general, any function which can be entered as a command at the top-level can also be used on the RHS of a rule as an action and vice-versa. The only major exception are the defrule and deffacts constructs which cannot be used on the RHS of a rule. The following is an example of a rule which displays the facts in the fact-list as its RHS action.

```
(defrule print-facts
   =>
   (facts))
```

Note that some commands such as *reset*, *run*, *clear*, and *excise* are dangerous to use on the RHS because they may modify the current state of an executing rule. For example, a rule may be deleted in the process of executing the actions on its RHS, and so the results are unpredictable.

8.13   SUMMARY

In this chapter, the concept of variables was introduced. The use of variables for retrieving information from facts was discussed as well as the use of variables for pattern matching on the LHS of a rule. Variables can be used to store the fact addresses of patterns on the LHS of a rule so that the fact bound to the pattern can be retracted on the RHS of the rule. Single field wildcards can be used in place of variables when the field to be matched against can be anything and its value is not needed later in the LHS or RHS of the rule. Multifield variables and wildcards allow more than one field in a pattern to be matched against.

Field constraints allow the negation and combination of more than one constraint for a given field. The NOT field constraint is used to prevent matching against certain values. The AND field constraint is used to guarantee that all of a series of matching conditions are true. The OR field constraint is used to guarantee that at least one of a series of matching conditions are true.

Functions can be entered into the CLIPS top level command loop or used on the LHS or RHS of a rule. Many functions, such as some of the arithmetic functions, can have a variable number of arguments. Function calls can be nested within other function calls. The bind command allows variables to be bound on the RHS of a rule.

PROBLEMS AND PROGRAMS

8-1.   Given the following fact templates for facts describing a family tree

```
(father-of <father> <child>)
(mother-of <mother> <child>)
(male <person>)
(female <person>)
(wife-of <wife> <husband>)
(husband-of <husband> <wife>)
```

write rules which will infer the following relations

a) Uncle, aunt
b) Cousin
c) Grandparent
d) Grandfather, grandmother
e) Sister, brother
f) Ancestor

8-2.   An industrial plant has ten sensors with id numbers 1 through 10. Each sensor has either good or bad status. Build a template for representing the sensors and write one or more rules which will print a warning message if three or more sensors have bad status. Test your rules with sensors 3 and 5 bad, sensors 2, 8 and 9 bad, and sensors 1, 3, 5 and 10 bad. What must be done to prevent the warning message from being displayed multiple times?

8-3.   Given facts which describe the hair and eye color of a person as shown by the following fact template

```
(person <name> <eye-color> <hair-color>)
```

and a fact describing a hair or eye color being sought as shown by the following fact template

```
(looking-for <eye-color> <hair-color>)
```

write one or more rules which will

a) Print a message indicating that a person has either the same eye color or same hair color that is being sought.
b) Print a message indicating that a person has both the same eye color and hair color being sought.

8-4.   Rewrite the stack rules found in Section 8.7 to work with named stacks.

8-5.   In a stack, the first value added is the last value to be removed and the last value added is the first value to be remove. A queue works in the opposite manner. The first value added is the first value removed and the last value added is the last value removed. Write rules which will add and remove values to a queue. Assume that only one queue exists.

8-6.   Write one or more rules which will generate all of the permutations of a base fact and print them out. For example, the fact

```
(base-fact red green blue)
```

should generate the output

```
Permutation is red green blue
Permutation is red blue green
Permutation is green red blue
Permutation is green blue red
Permutation is blue red green
Permutation is blue green red
```

8-7.   Given sets represented using the following fact template

```
(set <name> <<elements>>)
```

write one or more rules which will

    a) Compute the union of two sets given a fact of the format (find-union <set-1> <set-2>).

    b) Compute the intersection of two sets given a fact of the format (find-intersection <set-1> <set-2>).

Note that when computing the union and intersection, duplicate elements should not be allowed to appear in the union or intersection of the sets.

8-8.   Given a series of facts describing shapes with the following templates

```
(square <id-name> <side-length>)
(rectangle <id-name> <width> <length>)
(circle <id-name> <radius>)
(triangle <id-name> <base-length> <height>)
```

write one or more rules which will compute the sum of

    a) The area of the shapes.

    b) The perimeter of the shapes.

Test the output of the rules with the following deffacts

```
(deffacts test-8-8
   (square A 3)
   (square B 5)
   (rectangle C 5 7)
   (circle D 2)
```

```
(circle E 6)
(triangle F 3 4))
```

8-9.   Given information about the name, eye color, hair color, and nationality of a person from a group in the following format

```
(person <name> <eye-color> <hair-color>
        <nationality>)
```

write one rule which will identify

   a)   Anyone with blue or green eyes who has brown hair and is from France.
   b)   Anyone who does not have blue eyes or black hair and does not have the same color hair and eyes.
   c)   Two people. The first having brown or blue eyes, not having blond hair, and a German nationality. The second having green eyes and the same hair color as the first person. The second person's eyes may be brown if the first person's hair is brown.

8-10.   Convert the following infix expressions to prefix expressions.

   a)   (3 + 4) * (5 + 6) + 7
   b)   (5 * (5 + 6 + 7)) - ((3 * (4 / 9) + 2) / 8)
   c)   6 - 9 * 8 / 3 + 4 - (8 - 2 - 3) * 6 / 7

8-11.   Write rules which will take a finite state machine from its present state to its next state given a fact of the form

```
(input <value>)
```

The state machine and its arcs should be represented as facts. The input fact should be retracted when the machine goes to its next state. Test your rules and fact representations on the finite state machines shown in Figures 3-5 and 3-6.

8-12.   Write a set of rules for classifying syllogisms by mood and figure. For example, the syllogism

```
No M is P
Some M is not S
∴ Some S is P
```

is of type EOI-3. The input for the rules should be facts representing the major and minor premises and the conclusion. The output should a printed statement of the mood and figure.

8-13.   Create rules for implementing the decision procedure for determining if a syllogism is valid. Test your program on the syllogism from Problem 8-12.

BIBLIOGRAPHY

Morris W. Firebaugh, *Artificial Intelligence: A Knowledge-Based Approach*, boyd & fraser Pub. Co., pp. 224 - 226, 1988.

CHAPTER 9 CONTROL TECHNIQUES

9.1 INTRODUCTION

This chapter introduces various techniques for controlling the execution of rules. Groups of rules are used to build more powerful and complex programs than have been shown in previous chapters. Techniques for input, comparing values, and generating loops will be demonstrated. Rule salience is introduced as a method for prioritizing rules, and techniques for specifying control knowledge using rules is demonstrated. Finally, logical pattern operators are introduced. These operators allow a single rule to perform the function of several rules and provide the capability to allow matching against the absence of facts.

9.2 THE GAME OF STICKS

A simple two player game called Sticks will be used as an example in this chapter to demonstrate various techniques of control in a rule-based language. The object of Sticks is to avoid being forced to take the last stick in a pile of sticks. Each player may take 1, 2, or 3 sticks on their turn. The trick (or heuristic) to winning this game can be found by noticing that you can force your opponent to lose if it is their turn and there are 2, 3, or 4 sticks remaining. Thus a player who has 5 sticks remaining on their move has lost. To force the other player to 5 sticks, always leave a number of sticks equal to a multiple of 4 plus 1 at the end of your turn. At the end of your turn, force the pile to 5, 9, 13, etc. sticks. If you move first and the pile is set to one of the "losing" numbers, then you cannot win unless your opponent makes a mistake. If you move first and the pile is not set to a "losing" number, then you can always win.

9.3 INPUT TECHNIQUES

Before beginning to play Sticks, the program must determine some information. The program will play against a human opponent, so it must be determined who will get the first move. In addition, the starting size of the pile must be determined. This information could be placed in a deffacts construct. However, it is quite simple to ask the program's opponent for it by input from the keyboard. CLIPS allows information to be read from the keyboard using the **read** function. The basic syntax of the *read* function requires no arguments. The following example shows how the *read* function is used to input data.

```
(deffacts initial-phase
    (phase choose-player))
```

```
(defrule player-select
   (phase choose-player)
   =>
   (printout t "Who moves first (Computer: c "
              "Human: h)? ")
   (assert (player-select =(read))))

(defrule good-player-choice
   ?phase <- (phase choose-player)
   ?choice <- (player-select ?player&c | h)
   =>
   (retract ?phase ?choice)
   (assert (player-move ?player)))
```

Both rules use the pattern (phase choose-player) to indicate their applicability only when a specific fact is in the fact-list. This type of pattern is called a **control pattern** because it is specifically used to control when the rule is applicable. A **control fact** is used to trigger a control pattern. Since the control pattern for these rules contains only literal fields, the control fact must match the pattern exactly. In this case, the control fact to trigger these rules must be the fact (phase choose-player). This control fact will be useful for error correction when the input received by the read function does not match the expected values of "c" or "h" for "computer" and "human". By retracting and re-asserting the control fact, the *player-select* rule can be retriggered.

The following output shows how the *player-select* and *good-player-choice* rules work to determine who should move first.

```
CLIPS>  (watch facts)↵
CLIPS>  (reset)↵
==> f-0      (initial-fact)
==> f-1      (phase choose-player)
CLIPS>  (run)↵
Who moves first (Computer: c Human: h)? c↵
==> f-2      (player-select c)
<== f-1      (phase choose-player)
<== f-2      (player-select c)
==> f-3      (player-move c)
2 rules fired
CLIPS>
```

Notice that the *read* function requires a carriage return before it will read the token entered. The *read* function can only be used to input a single field at a time. All extra characters entered after the first field up to the carriage return are discarded. For example, if the *player-select* rule tried to read both the first player and the number of sticks in the pile with the following input,

```
c 15↵
```

only the first field, "c", will be read. To read all of the input, both fields must be enclosed within double quotes. Of course, once the input is within double quotes, it is a single literal field. The individual fields "c" and 15 cannot be easily accessed.

The read function allows fields that are not words, strings, or numbers, such as parentheses, to be entered. Such fields are placed within double quotes and treated as strings. The following command line dialog demonstrates this capability

```
CLIPS> (read) ↵
( ↵
"("
CLIPS>
```

Other input functions are also available, including a function which allows an entire line of data to be read as a string. In addition, information can also be written to and read from a file. These capabilities will be discussed in greater detail in Chapter 10.

The preceding rules work properly if the correct response of "c" or "h" is entered, but if an incorrect response is entered no error checking is performed. There are many situations in which an input request should be repeated to correct faulty input. One way of programming an input request loop is shown in the following example. The following rules use the control fact (phase choose-player) to indicate that a player selection needs to be made.

```
(deffacts initial-phase
   (phase choose-player))

(defrule player-select
   (phase choose-player)
   =>
   (printout t "Who moves first (Computer: c "
             "Human: h)? ")
   (assert (player-select =(read))))

(defrule good-player-choice
   ?phase <- (phase choose-player)
   ?choice <- (player-select ?player&c | h)
   =>
   (retract ?phase ?choice)
   (assert (player-move ?player)))

(defrule bad-player-choice
   ?phase <- (phase choose-player)
   ?choice <- (player-select ?player&~c&~h)
```

```
=>
(retract ?phase ?choice)
(assert (phase choose-player))
(printout t "Choose c or h." crlf))
```

Once again, note the use of the control pattern (phase choose-player). It provides the basic control for the input loop and also prevents this group of rules from firing during other phases of execution in the program.

Notice how the two rules, *player-select* and *bad-player-choice*, work together in that each rule supplies the facts necessary to activate the other. If the response to the player question is incorrect, the *bad-player-choice* rule will retract the control fact (phase choose-player) and then reassert it causing the *player-select* rule to be reactivated.

9.4 PREDICATE FUNCTIONS

A **predicate function** is defined to be any function which is intended to return a value of either true or false. CLIPS treats the value of zero as being false and *any* other value as true. Predicate functions may either be **predefined functions** or **user-defined functions**. Predefined functions are those functions already provided by CLIPS. User-defined functions or **external functions** are functions other than predefined functions that are written in C or another language and linked with CLIPS. Table 9-1 lists the predefined **logical predicate functions** provided by CLIPS.

Function Name	Purpose
not	boolean not function
and	boolean and function
or	boolean or function

Table 9-1
Logical Predicate Functions

The syntax of these functions is shown following

```
(and <<<predicate-function>>>)
(or  <<<predicate-function>>>)
(not <predicate-function>)
```

Table 9-2 lists the predefined **comparison predicate functions** provided by CLIPS.

Function Name	Purpose
eq	equal (any)
neq	not equal (any)
=	equal (numeric)
!=	not equal (numeric)
>=	greater than or equal
>	greater than
<=	less than or equal
<	less than

Table 9-2
Comparison Predicate Functions

The syntax of these functions is shown following

```
(eq  <any-value> <any-value>)
(neq <any-value> <any-value>)
(=   <numeric-value> <numeric-value>)
(!=  <numeric-value> <numeric-value>)
(>=  <numeric-value> <numeric-value>)
(>   <numeric-value> <numeric-value>)
(<=  <numeric-value> <numeric-value>)
(<   <numeric-value> <numeric-value>)
```

All of the comparison functions except the *eq* and *neq* functions will give an error message if given a non-numeric value as an argument. The *eq* and *neq* functions should be used for comparing values which may be non-numeric.

Table 9-3 lists the predefined **type predicate functions** provided by CLIPS.

Function Name	Purpose
numberp	argument is number
stringp	argument is string
wordp	argument is word
integerp	argument is an integer
evenp	argument is even
oddp	argument is odd

Table 9-3
Type Predicate Functions

The type predicate functions can be used to determine the type of a field. The syntax of these functions is shown following.

```
(numberp  <value>)
(stringp  <value>)
(wordp    <value>)
(integerp <value>)
(evenp    <value>)
(oddp     <value>)
```

9.5   TEST PATTERNS

There are many cases in which it is useful to repeat a calculation or other information processing. The common way of doing this is by setting up a loop. In the previous example, a loop was set up to repeat until the user responded correctly to a question. But there are also many situations in which a loop needs to terminate automatically as the result of the evaluation of an arbitrary expression.

The **test pattern** provides a very powerful way to evaluate expressions on the LHS of the rule. Instead of pattern matching against a fact in the fact-list, the test pattern evaluates an expression. The outermost function of the expression must be a predicate function. If the expression evaluates to true, the test pattern is satisfied. If the expression evaluates to false, the test pattern is not satisfied. A rule will be triggered only if all its test patterns are satisfied, along with other patterns. The syntax of the test pattern is shown following.

```
(test <predicate-function>)
```

As an example, suppose that it is the human player's turn. If only one stick remains in the pile, the human player has lost. If there is more than one stick, the human player should be asked how many sticks are to be removed from the pile. The rule which asks the human player how many sticks should be removed from the pile needs to check that there is more than one stick remaining in the pile. The > comparison predicate function can be used to express this constraint as shown in the following test pattern

```
(test (> ?size 1))
```

where ?size is the number of sticks remaining in the pile.

Once the human player has stated the number of sticks to be removed, the response needs to be checked to insure that it is valid. The number of sticks taken must be an integer and must be greater than or equal to one and less than or equal to three. A player cannot take more sticks than are in the pile and must be forced to take the last stick. The *and* logical predicate function can be used to express all of these constraints as shown in the following test pattern

```
(test (and (integerp ?choice)
           (>= ?choice 1)
           (<= ?choice 3)
           (< ?choice ?size)))
```

where ?choice would contain the number of sticks to be taken and ?size is the number of sticks remaining in the pile.

Likewise, an invalid number of sticks to take would be a value that is not an integer, less than one or greater than three, or greater than or equal to the number of sticks remaining. This can be expressed using the *or* logical function as shown in the following test pattern

```
(test (or  (not (integerp ?choice))
           (< ?choice 1)
           (> ?choice 3)
           (>= ?choice ?size)))
```

where ?choice would contain the number of sticks to be taken and ?size is the number of sticks remaining in the pile.

The following rules use the preceding test patterns to check that the human player has taken a valid number of sticks. The *pile-size* facts used in these rules stores the information about the number of sticks remaining in the pile.

```
(defrule get-human-move
    (player-move h)
    (pile-size ?size)
    ; Human player only has a choice when there is
    ; more than one stick remaining in the pile
    (test (> ?size 1))
    =>
    (printout t
            "How many sticks do you wish to take? ")
    (assert (human-takes =(read))))

(defrule good-human-move
    ?whose-turn <- (player-move h)
    (pile-size ?size)
    ?number-taken <- (human-takes ?choice)
    (test (and (integerp ?choice)
               (>= ?choice 1)
               (<= ?choice 3)
               (< ?choice ?size)))
    =>
    (retract ?whose-turn ?number-taken)
```

```
                    (printout t "Human made a valid move" crlf))

(defrule bad-human-move
    ?whose-turn <- (player-move h)
    (pile-size ?size)
    ?number-taken <- (human-takes ?choice)
    (test (or   (not (integerp ?choice))
                (< ?choice 1)
                (> ?choice 3)
                (>= ?choice ?size)))
    =>
    (printout t "Human made an invalid move" crlf)
    (retract ?whose-turn ?number-taken)
    (assert (player-move h)))
```

This program will end when a valid choice for the number of sticks taken has been entered. Once again, a control fact is used to retrigger a rule to allow invalid responses to be reentered. The *bad-human-move* rule will reassert the control fact (player-move h) to reactivate the *get-human-move* rule. The human player can then reenter the number of sticks to be taken from the pile.

9.6 THE PREDICATE FIELD CONSTRAINT

The **predicate field constraint**, ":", is useful for performing tests directly within patterns. In many ways it is similar to performing a test directly after a pattern, although in some cases, as will be discussed in Chapter 11, it is more efficient to use the predicate field constraint than it is to use a test pattern. The predicate field constraint can be used just like a literal field constraint. It can stand by itself in a field or be used as one part of a more complex field using the NOT, AND, and OR field constraints. The predicate field constraint is always followed by a function for evaluation. As with a test pattern, this function should be a predicate function.

As an example, the *get-human-move* rule in the previous section used the following two patterns to check that the pile contained at least one stick.

```
    (pile-size ?size)
    (test (> ?size 1))
```

These two pattern could be replaced with the single pattern

```
    (pile-size ?size&:(> ?size 1))
```

The predicate field constraint can be used in a pattern field by itself. However, there are few situations in which this is useful. Typically a variable is bound and then tested using the predicate field constraint. When reading a pattern it is useful to think of the predicate field constraint as meaning *such that*. For example, the pattern field shown previously

```
?size&:(> ?size 1)
```

could be read as "bind ?size such that ?size is greater than 1".

One application of the predicate field constraint is error checking of data. For example, the following rule checks that a data item is numeric before adding it to a running total

```
(defrule add-sum
    (data-item ?value&:(numberp ?value))
    ?old-total <- (total ?total)
    =>
    (retract ?old-total)
    (assert (total =(+ ?total ?value))))
```

The second field of the first pattern can be read as "bind ?value such that ?value is a number." The following two rules both perform the same kind of error checking. They demonstrate the use of the NOT and OR field constraints with the predicate field constraint.

```
(defrule found-symbol-1
    (data-item ?item&:(stringp ?item)|:(wordp ?item))
    =>
    (printout t "Found symbol or word " ?item crlf))

(defrule found-symbol-2
    (data-item ?item&~:(numberp ?item))
    =>
    (printout t "Found symbol or word " ?item crlf))
```

The rule *found-symbol-1* checks that a data item is either a string or a word by using the *stringp* and *wordp* type predicate functions. The rule *found-symbol-2* performs the same check, but uses the *numberp* type predicate function and then negates the return value.

9.7 THE EQUALITY FIELD CONSTRAINT

The **equality field constraint**, "=", allows the return value of a function to be used for comparison inside a pattern. The equality field constraint can be used in conjunction with the NOT, AND, and OR field constraints as well as the predicate field constraint.

Like the predicate field constraint, the equality field constraint must be followed by a function. However, the function does not have to be a predicate function. The only restriction is that the function must have a single field return value. The following rule shows how the equality constraint can be used in the Sticks program to determine the number of sticks that the computer player should remove from the pile.

```
(deffacts take-sticks-information
    (computer-take 1 sticks-if-remainder 1)
    (computer-take 1 sticks-if-remainder 2)
    (computer-take 2 sticks-if-remainder 3)
    (computer-take 3 sticks-if-remainder 0))

(defrule computer-move
    ?whose-turn <- (player-move c)
    ?pile <- (pile-size ?size)
    (test (> ?size 1))
    (computer-take ?number sticks-if-remainder
                =(mod ?size 4))
    =>
    (retract ?whose-turn ?pile)
    (assert (pile-size =(- ?size ?number)))
    (assert (player-move h)))
```

The *computer-move* rule determines the appropriate number of sticks for the computer to take on its turn. The first pattern insures that the rule is applicable only when it is the computer's move. The second and third patterns check to see that the remaining number of sticks is greater than one. If there had only been one remaining stick, then the computer would be forced to take it and lose. The final pattern works in conjunction with the *take-sticks-information* deffacts to determine the appropriate number of sticks to take. The **mod** function, short for modulus, returns the integer remainder of its first argument divided by its second. When reading a pattern it is useful to think of the equality field constraint as meaning *is equal to*. For example, the pattern field shown above

```
=(mod ?size 4)
```

could be read as "The field is equal to ?size modulus 4".

The computer will try to take enough sticks to set the remainder to one when the total number of sticks is divided by four. If the remainder is one when the computer has begun its move, then it has lost unless its opponent makes a mistake. It only takes one stick in this case to make the game last longer (hoping that the human player will make a mistake). In all other cases, the computer can take the appropriate number of sticks to cause its opponent to lose.

To demonstrate how the equality field constraint works in more detail, let's consider a specific example. Assume that the pile size is 7 and that it is the computer's move. The first two patterns of the *computer-move* rule will be satisfied with the last pattern remaining. The function expression (mod ?size 4) will have the value of 7 substituted for ?size leaving the expression (mod 7 4) which evaluates to 3. The *computer-move* rule now "appears" as follows

```
(defrule computer-move
   ?whose-turn <- (player-move c)
   ?pile <- (pile-size ?size)
   (test (> ?size 1))
   (computer-take ?number sticks-if-remainder 3)
   =>
   (retract ?whose-turn ?pile)
   (assert (pile-size =(- ?size ?number)))
   (assert (player-move h)))
```

The fourth pattern will match the *computer-take* fact with 3 in the fourth field. For this case, the computer will take two sticks leaving a pile size of 5. After the human player's next move, the computer can force a loss.

As another example of the equality field constraint, suppose a rule has the following patterns.

```
(data length ?y)
(data width ?x)
(test (or (= (?x (+ 5 ?y)) (= ?x (- 12 ?y)))))
```

The second and third patterns can be read as "?x is equal to 5 + ?y or ?x is equal to 12 - ?y". So if the facts

```
(data length 4)
(data width 9)
```

are asserted then ?y will be bound to 4, and ?x will be bound to 9. Note that this application of "=" in the test pattern is completely different from the use of the "=" as the equality field constraint in the computer-move rule. In the computer-move rule, the "=" substitutes a return value into a pattern. This is called **pattern substitution**. In the test pattern above, the "=" is used as a predicate comparison function. So the symbol "=" can be used in two different ways.

The two patterns

```
(data width ?x)
(test (or (= (?x (+ 5 ?y)) (= ?x (- 12 ?y)))))
```

can be expressed as a single pattern using the equality field constraint, as shown following

```
(data width ?x&=(+ 5 ?y)|=(- 12 ?y))
```

The field

```
?x&=(+ 5 ?y)|=(- 12 ?y)
```

can be read as "bind ?x such that ?x is equal to ?y plus 5 or ?x is equal to 12 minus ?y".

9.8   THE STICKS PROGRAM

All of the basic techniques needed for completing the Sticks program have been discussed. The complete listing of the Sticks program in shown in Appendix G. A sample run of the program after it has been loaded is shown following

```
CLIPS> (reset) ↵
CLIPS> (run) ↵
Who moves first (Computer: c Human: h)? c↵
How many sticks in the pile? 15↵
Computer takes 2 stick(s).
13 stick(s) left in the pile.
How many sticks do you wish to take? 3↵
10 stick(s) left in the pile.
Computer takes 1 stick(s).
9 stick(s) left in the pile.
How many sticks do you wish to take? 2↵
7 stick(s) left in the pile.
Computer takes 2 stick(s).
5 stick(s) left in the pile.
How many sticks do you wish to take? 1↵
4 stick(s) left in the pile.
Computer takes 3 stick(s).
1 stick(s) left in the pile.
You must take the last stick!
You lose!
15 rules fired
CLIPS>
```

9.9 SALIENCE

Up to this point, control facts have been used to indirectly control the execution of programs. CLIPS provides a direct way of control through **salience**. Normally, the agenda acts like a stack. That is, the most recent activation placed on the agenda is the first to fire. Salience allows more important rules to stay at the top of the agenda regardless of when the rules were added to the agenda. Lower salience rules are pushed onto the agenda below higher salience rules.

CLIPS has a keyword called salience which is used to set the priority of rules. The salience is set using a numeric value ranging from the smallest value of -10,000 to the highest of 10,000. If a rule has no salience explicitly assigned by the programmer, then CLIPS assumes a salience of 0. Notice that a salience of 0 is midway between the largest and smallest salience values. A salience of 0 does not mean that the rule has no salience but rather that it has an intermediate priority level. A newly activated rule is placed on the agenda before all rules with an equal or lesser salience and below all rules with a greater salience.

One use of salience is to force rules to fire in a sequential fashion. Consider the following set of rules in which no salience values are declared.

```
(defrule fire-first
   (priority first)
   =>
   (printout t "Print first" crlf))

(defrule fire-second
   (priority second)
   =>
   (printout t "Print second" crlf))

(defrule fire-third
   (priority third)
   =>
   (printout t "Print third" crlf))
```

The order in which the rules fire is dependent upon the order in which the facts that satisfy the LHS's of the rules are asserted. For example, if the rules are entered, then the following commands will produce the output shown below.

```
CLIPS> (reset) ↵
CLIPS> (assert (priority first)) ↵
CLIPS> (assert (priority second)) ↵
CLIPS> (assert (priority third)) ↵
CLIPS> (run) ↵
Print third
```

```
Print second
Print first
3 rules fired
CLIPS>
```

Notice the order of output statements. First "Print third" is printed, then "Print second", and finally "Print first". The reason this occurs is that the activated rules are placed on the agenda, which acts like a stack (last on is first off). The first fact (priority first) activates the rule *fire-first*. When the second fact is asserted, it activates the rule *fire-second*, which is stacked on top of the activation for rule *fire-first*. Finally, the third fact is asserted and its activated rule, *fire-third*, is stacked on top of the activation for rule *fire-second*.

In CLIPS, rules of equal salience which are activated by different patterns are prioritized based on the stack order of facts. Rules are fired from the agenda from the top of the stack down. So rule *fire-third* is fired first because it's on the top of the stack, then rule *fire-second* and finally rule *fire-first*. If the order in which the facts are asserted is reversed, then the order in which the rules are fired will also be reversed. This is shown by the following output.

```
CLIPS> (reset).┘
CLIPS> (assert (priority third)).┘
CLIPS> (assert (priority second)).┘
CLIPS> (assert (priority first)).┘
CLIPS> (run).┘
Print first
Print second
Print third
3 rules fired
CLIPS>
```

One important point is that if two or more rules having the same salience are all activated by the same fact, there is no guarantee of which order that the rules will be placed on the agenda.

Salience can be used to force the rules to fire in the order *fire-first*, *fire-second*, and then *fire-third*, no matter what order the activating facts are asserted. This can be accomplished by declaring salience values as shown following

```
(defrule fire-first
   (declare (salience 30))
   (priority first)
   =>
   (printout t "Print first" crlf))
```

```
(defrule fire-second
   (declare (salience 20))
   (priority second)
   =>
   (printout t "Print second" crlf))

(defrule fire-third
   (declare (salience 10))
   (priority third)
   =>
   (printout t "Print third" crlf))
```

Regardless of the order in which the priority facts are asserted, the agenda will always be ordered the same. Performing the *agenda* command after asserting the priority facts would produce the following output.

```
30   fire-first    f-1
20   fire-second   f-2
10   fire-third    f-3
```

Notice how the salience values have rearranged the priority of rules in the agenda. When the program is run, the order of rule firing will always be *fire-first*, *fire-second*, and then *fire-third*.

9.10 PHASES AND CONTROL FACTS

The purest concept of a rule-based expert system is one in which the rules act opportunistically whenever they are applicable. Most expert systems, however, have some procedural aspect to them. The Sticks program, for example, had different rules which were applicable depending upon whether it was the human or computer's move. The control for this program was handled by facts which indicated whose turn it was. These control facts allow information about the control structure of the program to be embedded into the rules of domain knowledge. However, doing this has a drawback. The knowledge about the control of the rules is intermixed with the knowledge about how to play the game. This is not a major drawback in the case of the Sticks program, because it is a small program. However, for larger programs involving hundreds or thousands of rules, the intermixing of domain knowledge and control knowledge make development and maintenance a major problem.

As an example, consider the problem of performing **fault detection, isolation and recovery** of a a system such as an electronic device. Using an electronic device as an example, fault detection is the process of recognizing that the electronic device is not working properly. Isolation is the process of determining the components of the device that have caused the fault. Recovery is the process of determining the steps necessary to correct the fault, if possible. Typically for this type of problem, the expert system will have rules to determine if a fault has occurred, other rules will isolate the cause of the fault, and still other rules will determine how to recover from the fault. The cycle will then loop back. Figure 9-1 shows an example of control flow in this type of system.

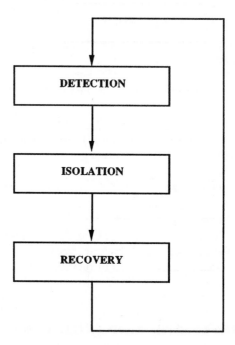

Figure 9-1

Different Phases for Fault Detection, Isolation, and Recovery Problem

Implementing the flow of control in this system can be attempted in at least three ways. The first would be to embed the control knowledge directly into the rules. For instance, the detection rules would include rules indicating when the isolation phase should be entered. Each group of rules would be given a pattern indicating in which phase it would be applicable. This technique has two drawbacks. First, as already mentioned, control knowledge is being embedded into the domain knowledge rules which makes them more difficult to understand. Second, it is not always very easy to determine when a phase is completed. This generally requires writing a rule which is applicable only when all the other rules have fired.

The second approach is to use salience to organize the rules as shown in Figure 9-2. This approach also has two major drawbacks. First, control knowledge is still being embedded into the rules using salience. Second, this approach does not guarantee the correct order of execution. Detection rules will always fire before isolation rules.

However, when the isolation rules begin firing they might cause a detection rule to become activated and immediately fire because of its higher salience.

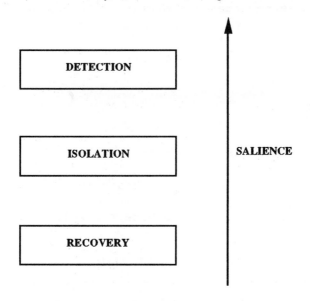

Figure 9-2
Assignment of Salience for Different Phases

A better approach in controlling the flow of execution is to separate the control knowledge from the domain knowledge as shown in Figure 9-3. Using this approach, each rule is given a control pattern which indicates its applicable phase. Control rules are then written to transfer control between the different phases as shown below.

```
(defrule detection-to-isolation
    (declare (salience -10))
    ?phase <- (phase detection)
    =>
    (retract ?phase)
    (assert (phase isolation)))

(defrule isolation-to-recovery
    (declare (salience -10))
    ?phase <- (phase isolation)
    =>
    (retract ?phase)
    (assert (phase recovery)))
```

```
(defrule recovery-to-detection
   (declare (salience -10))
   ?phase <- (phase recovery)
   =>
   (retract ?phase)
   (assert (phase detection)))
```

Each of the rules for a particular phase is then given a control pattern which checks that appropriate control fact is present for the rule to be applicable. For example, a recovery rule might look like the following.

```
(defrule find-fault-location-and-recovery
   (phase recovery)
   (recovery-solution switch-device ?replacement on)
   =>
   (printout t "Switch device " ?replacement " on "
             crlf))
```

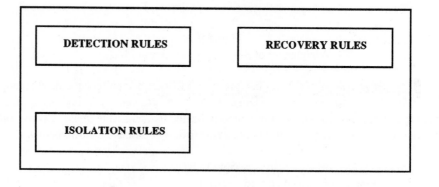

Figure 9-3
Separation of Expert Knowledge from Control Knowledge

A **salience hierarchy** is a description of the salience values used by an expert system. Each level in a salience hierarchy corresponds to a specific set of rules that are all given the same salience. If the rules for detection, isolation and recovery are given a default salience of zero, then the salience hierarchy is shown in Figure 9-4. Notice that while the fact (phase detection) is in the fact-list, the *detection-to-isolation* rule will be on the agenda. However, since it has a lower salience than the detection rules, it will not fire until all of the detection rules have had an opportunity to fire. The following output shows a sample run of the three previous control rules

```
CLIPS> (assert (phase detection))↵
CLIPS> (watch rules)↵
CLIPS> (run 10)↵
FIRE     1 detection-to-isolation: f-1
FIRE     2 isolation-to-recovery: f-2
FIRE     3 recovery-to-detection: f-3
FIRE     4 detection-to-isolation: f-4
FIRE     5 isolation-to-recovery: f-5
FIRE     6 recovery-to-detection: f-6
FIRE     7 detection-to-isolation: f-7
FIRE     8 isolation-to-recovery: f-8
FIRE     9 recovery-to-detection: f-9
FIRE    10 detection-to-isolation: f-10
rule firing limit reached
10 rules fired
CLIPS>
```

Notice that the control rules just keep firing in sequence since there are no domain knowledge rules to be applied during any of the phases. If there were domain knowledge rules for any of these phases, then the domain knowledge rules would be applied for activated rules during their appropriate phase.

The previous control rules could be more generically written with a deffacts construct and a single rule as shown following.

```
(deffacts control-information
    (phase detection)
    (phase-after detection isolation)
    (phase-after isolation recovery)
    (phase-after recovery detection))

(defrule change-phase
    (declare (salience -10))
    ?phase <- (phase ?current-phase)
    (phase-after ?current-phase ?next-phase)
    =>
```

```
(retract ?phase)
(assert (phase ?next-phase)))
```

or it could be written using a sequence of phases to be cycled through as shown following.

```
(deffacts control-information
    (phase detection)
    (phase-sequence isolation recovery detection))

(defrule change-phase
    (declare (salience -10))
    ?current-phase <- (phase ?current-phase)
    (phase-sequence ?next-phase $?other-phases)
    =>
    (retract ?current-phase)
    (assert (phase ?next-phase))
    (assert (phase-sequence $?other-phases
                           ?next-phase)))
```

Figure 9-4
Salience Hierarchy using Expert and Control Rules

Additional levels can easily be added to the salience hierarchy. Figure 9-5 shows a hierarchy with two additional levels. The constraint rules represent rules that detect illegal or unproductive states that may occur in the expert system. For example, an expert system scheduling people to various tasks may produce a schedule that violates a constraint. Instead of allowing the lower salience rules to continue working on the schedule, the constraint rules will immediately remove violations in the schedule. As another example, the user may enter in response to a series of questions a series of legal values that result in an illegal value being generated. The constraint rules could be used to detect such violations.

The query rules shown in the diagram represent rules that ask the user particular questions to aid the expert system in determining an answer. These rules have lower salience than the expert rules because it is undesirable to ask the user a question that can be determined by the expert rules. Thus, the query rules are only fired when no more information can be derived by the expert rules.

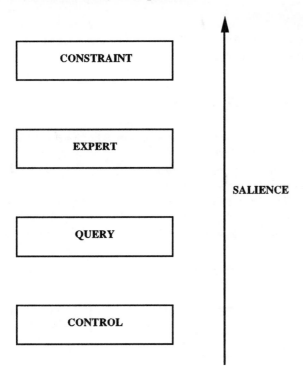

Figure 9-5
Four Level Salience Hierarchy

9.11 MISUSE OF SALIENCE

Although salience is a powerful tool for controlling execution, it can be easily abused. In particular, people who are just learning rule-based programming tend to overuse salience because it gives them explicit control of execution. It is more like the procedural programming they are used to, in which statements execute sequentially.

Overuse of salience results in a poorly coded program. The main advantage of a rule-based program is that the programmer does not have to worry about controlling execution. A well-designed rule-based program has a natural mode of execution that permits the inference engine to guide rule firings in an optimum manner. Salience interferes with the normal operation of the inference engine by increasing the priority of certain rules. While salience is very useful at times, it should not be overused.

In general, *any* salience value used in a rule should correspond to a level in the salience hierarchy of the expert system. The range of salience values from -10,000 to 10,000 is somewhat misleading. Rarely should more than seven salience values ever be required for coding an expert system and most well-coded expert systems need no more than three or four salience values. Using salience as a "quick fix" to get rules to fire in the proper order should be avoided. Chapter 11 contains some suggestions on ways to avoid overusing salience in rules.

9.12 THE PATTERN LOGICAL OR

So far all the rules shown have an **implicit logical AND** between the patterns. That is, a rule will not be triggered unless all of the patterns are true. However, CLIPS also provides the capability of specifying an **explicit logical AND** condition and also an **explicit logical OR** condition on the LHS.

As an example of a logical OR, consider the following rules for use by the industrial plant monitoring system (as discussed in Chapter 7) which are first written without a logical OR. Then you will see how to rewrite them with a logical OR.

```
(defrule shut-off-electricity-1
   (emergency flood)
   =>
   (printout t "Shut off the electricity" crlf))

(defrule shut-off-electricity-2
   (fire-class C)
   =>
   (printout t "Shut off the electricity" crlf))

(defrule shut-off-electricity-3
   (sprinkler-systems active)
   =>
   (printout t "Shut off the electricity" crlf))
```

Rather than writing three separate rules, they can all be combined into the following rule, using a logical OR.

```
(defrule shut-off-electricity
   (or  (emergency flood)
        (fire-class C)
        (sprinkler-systems active))
   =>
```

```
(printout t "Shut off the electricity" crlf))
```

The group of patterns enclosed within the logical OR element is called a **logic block**. The one rule using the logical OR is equivalent to the previous three rules. Asserting the three facts matching the patterns of this rule would cause the rule to be triggered three times, once for each of the facts.

Other patterns can be included outside the logical OR block and will be part of the implicit logical AND. For example, the following rule

```
(defrule shut-off-electricity
    (electrical-power on)
    (or  (emergency flood)
         (fire-class C)
         (sprinkler-systems active))
    =>
    (printout t "Shut off the electricity" crlf))
```

is equivalent to the three rules shown following.

```
(defrule shut-off-electricity-1
    (electrical-power on)
    (emergency flood)
    =>
    (printout t "Shut off the electricity" crlf))

(defrule shut-off-electricity-2
    (electrical-power on)
    (fire-class C)
    =>
    (printout t "Shut off the electricity" crlf))

(defrule shut-off-electricity-3
    (electrical-power on)
    (sprinkler-systems active)
    =>
    (printout t "Shut off the electricity" crlf))
```

As can be seen, the logical OR is similar to a true logical OR. In a true logical OR, the rule *shut-off-electricity* would only be triggered once if one or more conditions are true. However, in the logical OR of CLIPS, the *shut-off-electricity* rule will be triggered for each OR pattern that is true, since the one rule using the logical OR is equivalent to three rules.

Since multiple triggerings of a logical OR will occur with multiple facts, a natural question is how to prevent the problem of more than one triggering. For example, multiple printouts of "Shut off the electricity" appearing for multiple facts are unnecessary. After all, the power only needs to be shut off once, regardless of the number of reasons to shut it off.

Perhaps the most appropriate manner to prevent the other rules from firing is to change the rule to update the fact-list indicating that the electricity has been shut off. The modified rule is shown following.

```
(defrule shut-off-electricity
   ?power <- (electrical-power on)
   (or   (emergency flood)
         (fire-class C)
         (sprinkler-systems active))
   =>
   (retract ?power)
   (assert (electrical-power off))
   (printout t "Shut off the electricity" crlf))
```

The rule now only fires once because the fact containing information about the electrical power is retracted when the rule fires. This will remove other activations of the rule made by the other patterns. If it is also necessary to remove the supporting reason for shutting off the power from the fact-list, then the rule would have to be written as follows.

```
(defrule shut-off-electricity
   ?power <- (electrical-power on)
   (or   ?reason <- (emergency flood)
         ?reason <- (fire-class C)
         ?reason <- (sprinkler-systems active))
   =>
   (retract ?power ?reason)
   (assert (electrical-power off))
   (printout t "Shut off the electricity" crlf))
```

Notice that all patterns within the logical OR are bound to the same variable, ?reason. At first, this may appear to be an error since the same variables are normally not assigned to patterns of an ordinary rule. But a rule using a logical OR is different. Since a logical OR will produce multiple rules, the above rule is equivalent to the following three rules.

```
(defrule shut-off-electricity-1
   ?power <- (electrical-power on)
   ?reason <- (emergency flood)
   =>
   (retract ?power ?reason)
```

```
      (assert (electrical-power off))
      (printout t "Shut off the electricity" crlf))

   (defrule shut-off-electricity-2
      ?power <- (electrical-power on)
      ?reason <- (fire-class C)
      =>
      (retract ?power ?reason)
      (assert (electrical-power off))
      (printout t "Shut off the electricity" crlf))

   (defrule shut-off-electricity-3
      ?power <- (electrical-power on)
      ?reason <- (sprinkler-systems active)
      =>
      (retract ?power ?reason)
      (assert (electrical-power off))
      (printout t "Shut off the electricity" crlf))
```

By looking at the three rules, if can be seen that the same variable name was necessary to match the (retract ?power ?reason) action. For example, suppose separate names had been assigned to the patterns such as ?reason1, ?reason2, and ?reason3 and then a (retract ?power ?reason1 ?reason2 ?reason3) action was used.

```
   (defrule shut-off-electricity
      ?power <- (electrical-power on)
      (or  ?reason1 <- (emergency flood)
           ?reason2 <- (fire-class C)
           ?reason3 <- (sprinkler-systems active))
      =>
      (retract ?power ?reason1 ?reason2 ?reason3)
      (assert (electrical-power off))
      (printout t "Shut off the electricity" crlf))
```

The (retract ?power ?reason1 ?reason2 ?reason3) action would be in error because two out of three variables would not be defined in the equivalent rules.

9.13 THE PATTERN LOGICAL AND

The logical AND is opposite in concept to the logical OR. Instead of any patterns triggering a rule, the logical AND requires that all of the patterns be matched to facts. Normally there is an implicit logical AND for the patterns of a rule. A rule such as

```
(defrule electrical-fire
   (emergency fire)
   (fire-class C)
   =>
   (printout t "Shut off the electricity" crlf))
```

could also be written with an explicit logical AND as

```
(defrule electrical-fire
   (and (emergency fire)
        (fire-class C))
   =>
   (printout t "Shut off the electricity" crlf))
```

Of course, there is no advantage to writing a rule with an explicit logical AND. It's easier to use the implicit logical AND of patterns if it is not necessary to specify a logical AND. The logical AND is provided so that it can be used with the other logical functions to make more complex patterns. For example, it can be used with a logical OR to require groups of multiple conditions to be true, as shown in the following example.

```
(defrule shut-off-electricity
   ?power <- (electrical-power on)
   (or   (emergency flood)
         (and (emergency fire)
              (fire-class C))
         (sprinkler-systems active))
   =>
   (retract ?power)
   (assert (electrical-power off))
   (printout t "Shut off the electricity" crlf))
```

So the rule *shut-off-electricity* is equivalent to the three following rules,

```
(defrule shut-off-electricity-1
   ?power <- (electrical-power on)
   (emergency flood)
   =>
   (retract ?power)
   (assert (electrical-power off))
   (printout t "Shut off the electricity" crlf))

(defrule shut-off-electricity-2
   ?power <- (electrical-power on)
```

```
(emergency fire)
(fire-class C)
=>
(retract ?power)
(assert (electrical-power off))
(printout t "Shut off the electricity" crlf))

(defrule shut-off-electricity-3
   ?power <- (electrical-power on)
   (sprinkler-systems active)
   =>
   (retract ?power)
   (assert (electrical-power off))
   (printout t "Shut off the electricity" crlf))
```

9.14 THE PATTERN LOGICAL NOT

Sometimes it is useful to be able to pattern match against the absence of a particular fact in the fact-list. CLIPS allows the specification of the absence of a fact as a pattern on the LHS using the logical **NOT**. As a simple example, the monitoring expert system might have two rules for reporting its status.

```
If the monitoring status is to be reported and
there is an emergency being handled
then report the type of the emergency

If the monitoring status is to be reported and
there is no emergency being handled
then report that no emergency is being handled
```

The logical NOT can be conveniently applied to the simple rules above as follows.

```
(defrule report-emergency
   (report-status)
   (emergency ?type)
   =>
   (printout t "Handling " ?type " emergency" crlf))

(defrule no-emergency
   (report-status)
   (not (emergency ?))
   =>
   (printout t "No emergency being handled" crlf))
```

Notice that these two rules are mutually exclusive. That is, they cannot both be on the agenda at the same time because the second pattern in both rules cannot be satisfied simultaneously.

Variables can also be used within a negated pattern to produce some interesting effects. Consider the following rule which looks for the largest number out of a group of facts representing numbers.

```
(defrule largest-number
    (number ?x)
    (not (number ?y&:(> ?y ?x)))
    =>
    (printout t "Largest number is " ?x crlf))
```

The first pattern will bind to all of the *number* facts, however, the second pattern will not allow the rule to become activated for any but the fact with the largest value for ?x.

Note that variables first bound within a logical NOT are limited in scope to that logical NOT. For example, the following rule

```
(defrule demonstrate-not-1
    (pair ?x ?y)
    (pair ?y ?z)
    (not (triplet ?x ?x ?z))
    =>)
```

will be activated if the fact-list is

```
f-1    (pair 3 4)
f-2    (pair 4 5)
f-3    (triplet 4 4 6)
```

The first pattern will match f-1, the second pattern will match f-2, and the third pattern will look for instances of the fact (triplet 3 3 5) which does not exist and so this pattern will also match.

If the third pattern is move to the front as shown following, however, the rule will not match using the same set of facts.

```
(defrule symmetric-pair-2
    (not (triplet ?x ?x ?y))
    (pair ?x ?y)
    (pair ?y ?z)
    =>)
```

The first pattern will be matched by f-3 thus failing to satisfy the logical NOT. Thus the placement of a NOTed pattern within a rule can be very important.

Variables that were previously bound in another pattern without a logical NOT can be freely used within a NOTed pattern. However, variables that are first bound within a NOTed pattern cannot be used outside of that pattern. These variables are bound only for the purpose of determining if any fact matches the pattern. If no fact matches the pattern, there is no real binding and so the variable cannot be used outside of the pattern.

Since variables cannot be used outside the logical NOT, it follows that the *find-largest-number* rule cannot be rewritten using a test as shown below.

```
(defrule largest-number
    (number ?x)
    (not (number ?y))
    (test (> ?y ?x))
    =>
    (printout t "Largest number is " ?x crlf))
```

Finally, a logical NOT can only be used to negate a single pattern. Multiple patterns, the logical AND, and the logical OR cannot be used with a logical NOT.

9.15   SUMMARY

In this chapter, various concepts for controlling the flow of execution were introduced. The read function was used to demonstrate how a simple control loop for input could be created using control facts that were retracted and then asserted again. Test patterns along with predicate functions can be used on the LHS of a rule to provide more powerful pattern matching capabilities. In addition, test patterns can be used to maintain a control loop. The predicate field constraint allows test expressions to be placed directly within a pattern. The equality field constraint is used to compare a field to a value returned by a function. The Sticks program demonstrates several of these control techniques.

Salience provides a mechanism for even more complex control structures. Salience can be used to prioritize rules such that the activated rule with the highest salience is fired first. Salience can be combined with control facts in order to separate expert knowledge from control knowledge.

Logical pattern operators can be used to express several rules as a single rule. The logical AND and OR can be arbitrarily nested to express complex conditions needed to satisfy a rule. The logical NOT allows pattern matching against the absence of a fact. Care must be exercised with the logical NOT since variables that are first bound within a NOTed pattern have their scope limited to that pattern.

PROBLEMS AND PROGRAMS

9-1.   Add rules to the Sticks program which will ask if the human player wishes to play again after the game has finished. Do not use salience.

9-2.   Modify the Sticks program such that the control rules are separated from the rules of playing the game. Use salience to give the control rules a lower priority.

9-3.   Modify the Sticks program to allow two human players to play the game in addition to the computer playing against a human.

9-4.   Rewrite the following rules as a single rule using logical pattern operators.

```
(defrule rule-1
   (fact-a)
   (fact-d)
   =>)

(defrule rule-2
   (fact-b)
   (fact-c)
   (fact-e)
   (fact-f)
   =>)

(defrule rule-3
   (fact-a)
   (fact-e)
   (fact-f)
   =>)

(defrule rule-4
   (fact-b)
   (fact-c)
   (fact-d)
   =>)
```

9-5   Determine if the variable x is referenced properly for each of the following rules. Explain your answer.

a)
```
(defrule example-1
   (not (fact ?x))
   (test (> ?x 4))
```

```
   =>)
```

b)
```
(defrule example-2
   (not (fact ?x&:(> ?x 4)))
   =>)
```

c)
```
(defrule example-3
   (not (fact ?x))
   (fact ?y&:(> ?y ?x)))
   =>)
```

d)
```
(defrule example-4
   (not (fact ?x))
   (fact ?x&:(> ?x 4)))
   =>)
```

9-6.   Since logical pattern operators cannot be placed inside of a logical pattern NOT operator, show how the following rule can be expressed as a group of valid CLIPS rules.

```
(defrule invalid-pattern-operator-rule
   (not (and (a ?x)
             (b ?x)))
   =>
   (assert (c)))
```

Hint: Using salience, it can be done with four rules.

9-7.   Add a rule to the blocks world program found in Section 8.6 which would remove a move goal if it has already been satisfied.

9-8.   Rewrite the blocks world program found in Section 8.6 so that it can rearrange the blocks from any initial state of stacked blocks to any goal state of stacked blocks. For example, if the initial state of the blocks was

```
(stack A B C)
(stack D E F)
```

One possible goal state might be

```
(stack D C B)
```

```
(stack A)
(stack F E)
```

9-9.   Write a program using the logical AND, OR, and NOT's for the AND/OR tree of getting to work shown in Figure 3-10. Test it for all branches.

9-10.   Implement a finite state machine driver using rules. Given the current state and the next input, the rules should determine the transition to the next state. Implement the rules such that the knowledge about the states and transitions are stored as facts. Make sure that an error state is entered for any invalid input. Test your rules as follows.

a) Implement the finite state machine shown in Figure 3-5. Use only deffacts constructs in addition to the rules written above.

b) Implement the finite state machine shown in Figure 3-6. Use only deffacts constructs in addition to the rules written above.

CHAPTER 10 CLIPS FUNCTIONS

10.1 INTRODUCTION

This chapter introduces a variety of functions for performing useful actions in CLIPS. Functions for controlling flow of execution of actions on the RHS of a rule will be introduced. File I/O and the concept of reading from and writing to sources other than the keyboard and terminal will be discussed. Additionally, useful math, string, multifield, and other utility commands will be demonstrated.

10.2 FLOW OF CONTROL FUNCTIONS

CLIPS provides some functions for controlling the flow of execution of actions on the RHS of a rule. Two of these functions are the **while** and **if** that are also found as control structures in modern high-level languages such as Ada, Pascal, and C. In addition, the **halt** function allows the execution of rules to be stopped from the RHS of a rule.

The If Function

The syntax of the *if* function is

```
(if <predicate-function>
   then
   <<<actions>>>
   [else
   <<<actions>>>])
```

where <predicate-function> is a predicate function to be evaluated and <<<actions>>> represent one or more function calls. Notice that the else clause is optional.

When an *if* function is evaluated, the condition represented by <predicate-function> is first evaluated to determine whether the actions of the *then* clause or the *else* clause are executed. If the condition evaluates to true, the actions in the *then* clause of the function are executed. If the condition evaluates to false, the actions in the *else* clause are executed. If the *else* clause has not been included, then no action is taken upon a false condition. Once the *if* function completes execution, CLIPS continues with the next action, if any, on the RHS.

The *if* function can be useful for checking values on the RHS of a rule instead of having other rules perform a test. For example, the following rule could be used to determine whether a program should continue.

```
(defrule continue-check
   ?phase <- (phase check-continue)
```

```
=>
(retract ?phase)
(printout t "Continue? " crlf)
(bind ?answer (read))
(if (or (eq ?answer y) (eq ?answer yes))
   then (assert (phase continue))
   else (assert (phase halt))))
```

Notice that the *if* function is used to convert the user's yes/no response to a fact indicating the type of action to be taken. In this case the action is to either continue or halt.

The While Function

The syntax of the *while* function is

```
(while <predicate-function> [do]
   <<<actions>>>)
```

where <predicate-function> is a predicate function to be evaluated and <<<actions>>> represent one or more functions. The actions of the *while* function comprise the **body** of the loop. The keyword **do** is optional.

The part of the while function represented by <predicate-function> represents a condition that is tested before the actions in the body are executed. If the while-condition is true, the actions in the body will be executed. If the while-condition is false, execution continues with the next statement after the *while* function, if any. The condition of the *while* function will be checked each time the body is executed to determine if the body should be executed again.

The *while* function can be used with the *if* function to implement input error checking on the RHS of a rule. The following modification to the rule *continue-check* uses the *while* function to continue looping until an appropriate answer is received.

```
(defrule continue-check
   ?phase <- (phase check-continue)
   =>
   (retract ?phase)
   (printout t "Continue? " crlf)
   (bind ?answer (read))
   (while (and (neq ?answer yes) (neq ?answer no)) do
      (printout t "Continue? " crlf)
      (bind ?answer (read)))
   (if (eq ?answer yes)
      then (assert (phase continue))
      else (assert (phase halt))))
```

CLIPS is designed to be an efficient rule-based language. The *if* and *while* procedural functions are intended for judicious use only. Writing a lengthy procedural program on the RHS of a rule defeats the entire purpose of using a rule-based language. In general, the *if* and *while* functions should be used for performing simple tests and loops on the RHS of a rule. Complex nesting of *if* and *while* functions on the RHS of a rule should be avoided.

The Halt Function

The *halt* function can be used on the RHS of a rule to stop the execution of rules on the agenda. It requires no arguments. When called, no further actions will be executed from the RHS of the rule being fired and control will return to the top-level prompt. The agenda will contain any remaining rules that were activated when the *halt* function was called.

As an example, the *continue-check* rule could replace the action

```
(assert (phase halt))
```

with the following action

```
(halt)
```

which would stop the execution of rules.

The *halt* function is particularly useful for halting execution when the intent to restart execution later using the *run* command. Consider the following modification to the *continue-check* rule

```
(defrule continue-check
    ?phase <- (phase check-continue)
    =>
    (retract ?phase)
    (printout t "Continue? " crlf)
    (bind ?answer (read))
    (while (and (neq ?answer yes) (neq ?answer no)) do
        (printout t "Continue? " crlf)
        (bind ?answer (read)))
    (assert (phase continue))
    (if (neq ?answer yes)
        then (halt)))
```

Notice that the rule asserts the fact (phase continue) regardless of the user's response to the continue question. Asserting this fact will place the appropriate rules on the agenda to continue execution. However, if the reply to the continue question was not yes, execution will be stopped by the *halt* function. The user could then examine the rules and facts, later restarting execution where it had left off by issuing a *run* command.

10.3   FILE I/O FUNCTIONS AND LOGICAL NAMES

The Open Function

In addition to keyboard input and terminal output, CLIPS can also read from and write to files. Before a file can be accessed for reading or writing, it must be opened using the **open** function. The number of files that can be open simultaneously is dependent on your operating system and hardware.

The syntax of the *open* function is

```
(open <file-name> <file-ID> [<file-access>])
```

As an example,

```
(open "input.dat" data "r")
```

The first argument of open, <file-name>, is a string representing the name of the file on your computer. Generally, this will be the physical file name known to the operating system. For the example shown, the file-name is "input.dat".

The second argument, <file-ID>, is the **logical name** under which CLIPS knows the file. The logical name is a global name by which CLIPS can access the file from any rule or the top-level prompt. Although the logical name could be the same as the file-name, it is good idea to use a different name to avoid confusion. For the example shown, the logical name *data* was used to refer to the file "input.dat". Other meaningful names, such as input or file-data, could have been used.

One advantage of using a logical name is that a different file name can easily be substituted without making major changes to the program. Since the file name is only used in the *open* function and is later referred to by its logical name, only the *open* function need be changed to read from a different file.

The third argument, <file-access>, is a string representing one of the four possible modes of file access. Table 10-1 list the file access modes.

Mode	Action
"r"	read access only
"w"	write access only
"r+"	read and write access
"a"	append access only

Table 10-1
File Access Modes

If <file-access> is not included as an argument, the default value of "r" will be used. Some access modes may not be meaningful to certain operating systems. Most operating systems will support read access (for inputting data) and write access (for outputting data). Read and write access and append access (for appending output data to the end of a file) may not always be available.

It is important to remember that the consequences of opening a file may vary from one machine to another. For example, operating systems which do not support multiple file versions, such as MS-DOS on an IBM PC or UNIX, will replace an existing file if that file is opened using write access. In contrast, VMS on a VAX will create a new version of a file if it already exists and is opened using write access.

The *open* function acts as a predicate function. It returns true if a file was successfully opened, otherwise false is returned. The return value can be used to perform error checking. For example, if the user supplies the name of a file that does not exist and an attempt is made to open the file using read access, the *open* function will return a value of false. The rule that opens the file could detect this and perform the appropriate actions to prompt the user for another file name.

The Close Function

Once access is no longer needed to a file, it should be closed. Unless a file is closed, there is no guarantee that the information written to it will be saved. Also, the longer a file is open, the greater is the chance of a power loss or other malfunction which would prevent the information from being saved.

The general form of the **close** function is

```
(close [<file-ID>])
```

where the optional argument <file-ID> specifies the logical name of the file to be closed. If <file-ID> is not specified, all open files will be closed. As an example,

```
(close data)
```

will close the file known to CLIPS by the logical file-name *data*. The statements

```
(close input)
(close output)
```

will close the files associated with the logical names *input* and *output*. Note that separate statements are necessary to close specific files.

When using files, it is important to remember that each opened file should eventually be closed with the *close* function. In particular, if a command is not issued to close a file, the data written to it may be lost. CLIPS will not prompt you to close an open file. The only safeguard built into CLIPS for closing files that have been inadvertently left open is that all open files will be closed when an *exit* command is issued.

However, a problem arises if CLIPS is terminated with an interrupt control character such as Control C. Depending on the operating system, the data written to open files may not be saved. That's why it's always a good idea to exit CLIPS with an *exit* command rather than an interrupt. A graceful exit will usually save any data in files inadvertently left open. As another safeguard, you can always include a rule with a very low salience which closes all open files. The salience of this rule should be made low enough that all other rules in the system fire before it does.

Reading and Writing to a File

In all the examples so far, all input has been read from the keyboard and all output has been sent to the terminal. However, the use of logical names allow input and output to and from other sources. In Chapter 7, the *printout* function used the logical name *t* to send output to the screen. Other logical names can be used with the *printout* function to send output to destinations other than the screen.

When used as a logical name for an output function, the logical name *t* writes output to the standard output device which is usually the terminal. Similarly, when used as the logical name for an input function, the logical name *t* reads input from the **standard input device** which is normally the keyboard. For example, the *read* function introduced in Chapter 9 defaults to reading from the standard input device if it is given no arguments. The general format of the read function is

```
(read [<logical-name>])
```

As an example of using logical names with the *read* and *printout* functions, let's simulate monitoring the oil pressure of an oil pump. Values will be read in from a file indicating the oil pressure of the pump, then the values will be analyzed, and the analysis will be written to the terminal as well as a **trace file**. The trace file will keep a record of all important information that has been written to the terminal.

The first step in solving this problem is to open the input and output files. The following rule will do this

```
(defrule open-files
   =>
   (open "oil.dat" oil "r")
   (open "trace.txt" trace "w")
   (assert (phase read-oil-pressure)))
```

The input data is stored in the file "oil.dat" and tracing information will be sent to the output file "trace.txt". The logical name *oil* is now associated with the file "oil.dat" and the logical name *trace* is now associated with the file "trace.txt". Note that the "r" option did not have to used for opening the "oil.dat" file since this is the default. The fact (read-oil-pressure) will be used to create a loop for reading the oil pressure values. The rule used for reading the value is shown following

```
(defrule read-data
    ?phase <- (phase read-oil-pressure)
    =>
    (retract ?phase)
    (bind ?value (read oil))
    (if (eq ?value EOF)
        then (assert (phase close-files))
        else (assert (oil-value ?value)))))
```

Notice that the *read* function uses an additional argument to specify the logical name from which input is to be read. In this case, the logical name *oil* tells the *read* function to access the file "oil.dat" for input. After a value is read from the file, it is compared against the **EOF** symbolic field. CLIPS returns this value for input functions when an attempt is made to read past the end of the file. In this case, if the EOF field is returned, the *read-data* rule asserts a fact indicating that the files should be closed. Otherwise, it asserts the oil pressure value that was read from the file.

If the end of the file was reached, then the following rule will close both the input file "oil.dat" and the output file "trace.txt" that were opened by the *open-files* rule.

```
(defrule close-files
    ?phase <- (phase close-files)
    =>
    (retract ?phase)
    (close oil)
    (close trace))
```

The following two rules analyze the oil pressure value asserted by the *read-data* rule. For simplicity, we will assume that a value greater than or equal to 60 is good and any value less than 60 is bad. The first pattern of the rule *good-oil-value* checks for an oil value greater than or equal to 60, while the first pattern of the rule *bad-oil-value* checks for an oil value less than 60.

```
(defrule good-oil-value
    ?data <- (oil-value ?pressure&:(>= ?pressure 60))
    =>
    (retract ?data)
    (printout t "Oil pressure of " ?pressure
                " is good " crlf)
    (printout trace ?pressure " good " crlf)
    (assert (read-oil-pressure)))
```

```
(defrule bad-oil-value
   ?data <- (oil-value ?pressure&:(< ?pressure 60))
   =>
   (retract ?data)
   (printout t "Oil pressure of " ?pressure
              " is bad " crlf)
   (printout trace ?pressure " bad " crlf)
   (assert (read-oil-pressure)))
```

Notice that each rule has two *printout* actions. One *printout* action uses the logical name *t* to send output to the terminal. The other *printout* action uses the logical name *trace* to send the output to the trace file "trace.txt". Both rules then assert the *read-oil-pressure* fact which sends the program through another input loop. This will continue until the end of file is reached for the "oil.dat" file.

If the following values are stored in the "oil.dat" file,

```
71
64
60
56
58
61
```

then the following output represents a sample run of the program

```
CLIPS>  (watch rules).↵
CLIPS>  (reset).↵
CLIPS>  (run).↵
FIRE     1 open-files: f-0
FIRE     2 read-data: f-1
FIRE     3 good-oil-value: f-2
Oil pressure of 71 is good
FIRE     4 read-data: f-3
FIRE     5 good-oil-value: f-4
Oil pressure of 64 is good
FIRE     6 read-data: f-5
FIRE     7 good-oil-value: f-6
Oil pressure of 60 is good
FIRE     8 read-data: f-7
FIRE     9 bad-oil-value: f-8
Oil pressure of 56 is bad
FIRE    10 read-data: f-9
FIRE    11 bad-oil-value: f-10
Oil pressure of 58 is bad
```

```
FIRE    12 read-data: f-112
FIRE    13 good-oil-value: f-12
Oil pressure of 61 is good
FIRE    14 read-data: f-13
FIRE    15 close-files: f-14
CLIPS>
```

After running this program, the file "trace.txt" should contain the following information

```
71 good
64 good
60 good
56 bad
58 bad
61 good
```

which indicates that the tracing information has been properly written to the trace file.

10.4   OTHER I/O FUNCTIONS

The Format Function

There are many times when it is desirable to format output from a CLIPS program, such as arranging data in tables. While the *printout* function is useful, there is a function specifically designed for formatting, called **format**, which provides a wide variety of formatting styles. The syntax of the *format* function is

```
(format <logical-name> <control-string>
        <<parameters>>)
```

The *format* function has several parts. The <logical-name> is the logical name where the output is sent. The default standard output device can be specified with the logical name *t*. Next comes a **control string** which must be contained within double quotes. The control string consists of **format flags** which indicate how the parameters to the *format* function should be printed. Following the control string is a list of parameters. The number of format flags in the control string will determine how many parameters should be specified.

An example of a *format* statement in CLIPS is shown by the following command which prints the integer forms of two numbers reserving 15 spaces for each number. Note that there are no spaces between the "%" signs.

```
CLIPS> (format  t  "Integer%n%15d%15d%n"  5.25
10)
Integer
                    5               10
CLIPS>
```

Format flags always begin with a "%" sign. Ordinary strings such as "Integer" can also be put in the control string and will be printed in the output. Some format flags do not format parameters. In this example, the "%n" is used to put a carriage return/linefeed in the output. For this example, the *format* function has printed the integer form of its parameters: 5.25 and 10. Besides constants, the *format* function can also evaluate and print expressions used as arguments. Notice in the output that the number 5.25 was printed in its integer form of 5 since the fractional part of a number is not allowed in an integer format.

Note that there is no space between the "Integer" and the control flag "%n". Although it would help readability to put a space in between, CLIPS would also print the space since that is a valid character. Another flag format is the "%15d". The "15" specifies in how many columns the parameter is to be printed in. After the "15" is the part of the format flag which specifies how the output is to be displayed, such as "d" for an integer specification. The general specification of a format flag is

%-M.Nx

where "-" is optional and means to **left justify**. The default is to **right justify**.

M   specifies the field width in columns. At least M characters will be output. Spaces are normally used to pad the output to make up the M columns unless M starts with a 0, in which case zeroes are used. If the output exceeds M columns, then the format function will expand the field as needed.

N   is an optional specification of the number of digits past the decimal point that will be printed. The default is six digits past the decimal point for floating-point numbers.

x   specifies the display format specification. Table 10-2 gives the display format specifications.

Shown following are some top-level *format* commands to illustrate output formats. The text Float, Exponential, General, Octal, and Hexadecimal in the control strings of the *format* function examples are not required keywords. They were just chosen as headings for the output in these examples.

```
CLIPS> (format  t  "Float%n%15f%15f%15f%n"  1  5.25
10)↵
Float
        1.000000        5.250000        10.000000
CLIPS> (format  t  "Exponential%n%15e%15e%n"  5.25
10)↵
Exponential
  5.250000e+000  1.000000e+001
CLIPS> (format  t  "General%n%15g%15g%n"  5.25
10)↵
General
           5.25             10
CLIPS> (format  t  "Octal%n%15o%15o%n"  5.25  10)↵
Octal
              5             12
CLIPS> (format  t  "Hexadecimal%n%15x%15x%n"  5.25
10)↵
Hexadecimal
              5              a
CLIPS> (format  t  "String%n%15s%15s%n"  "efg"
hij)↵
String
            efg            hij
```

Character	Meaning
d	Integer
f	Floating-point
e	Exponential (in power-of-ten format)
g	General (numeric).Display in whatever format is shorter.
o	Octal. Unsigned number (N specifier not applicable)
x	Hexadecimal. Unsigned number (N specifier not applicable)
s	String. Quoted strings will be stripped of quotes.
n	Carriage return/linefeed
%	The "%" character itself

Table 10-2
Display Format Specifications

The Readline Function

The **readline** function can be used to read an entire line of input. Its syntax is

```
(readline [<logical-name>])
```

As with the *read* function, the logical name is optional. If no logical name is provided or the logical name *t* is used, input will be read from the standard input device. The *readline* function will return as a string the next line of input from the input source associated with the logical name up to and including the carriage return. The following rule illustrates the use of the *readline* function.

```
(defrule get-name
   =>
   (printout t "What is your name? ")
   (assert (name =(readline))))
```

The following command dialog illustrates the use of the *readline* function in the *get-name* rule.

```
CLIPS> (reset)↵
CLIPS> (watch facts)↵
CLIPS> (run)↵
What is your name? John Smith↵
==> f-1       (name "John Smith")
1 rules fired
CLIPS>
```

The *readline* function will return the word *EOF* if the end of file has been reached. This will only occur when the logical name used by readline is associated with a file.

Loading and Saving Facts

It is often useful to be able to load facts from a file or save facts to a file. The **load-facts** and **save-facts** functions provide these capabilities. The syntax of these two functions is

```
(load-facts <file-name>)
(save-facts <file-name>)
```

The *load-facts* function will load in a group of facts stored in the file specified by <file-name>. The facts in the file should be in the standard format of a fact. That is, each fact should begin with a left parenthesis, have one or more fields after the left parenthesis, and end with a right parenthesis. For example, if the file "facts.dat" contained the following

```
(data 34)
(data 89)
(data 64)
(data 34)
```

then the command

```
(load-facts "facts.dat")
```

would load the facts contained in this file.

The *save-facts* function can be used to save all of the facts in the fact-list to the file specified by <file-name>. The facts are stored in the format required by the *load-facts* function. If you only want to save certain facts, then it is necessary to write rules which will match against the facts to be saved and store them in a file in the format required by the *load-facts* function. The following rules illustrate how the *data* facts shown above could be selectively saved to a file.

```
(defrule start-save-data
   ?phase <- (phase start-save)
   =>
   (retract ?phase)
   (printout t "Save data in which file? ")
   (bind ?file-name (readline))
   (if (open ?file-name save-file "w")
       then
       (assert (phase write-data))
       else
       (printout t "Unable to open file" crlf)))

(defrule save-data-info
   (phase write-data)
   (data $?rest)
   =>
   (printout save-file "(data " $?rest ")" crlf))

(defrule finish-save-data
   (declare (salience -1))
   ?phase <- (phase write-data)
   =>
   (retract ?phase)
   (close save-file))
```

The rule *start-save-data* is activated by the control fact (phase start-save). It prompts for a file name in which the *data* facts should be stored and then opens the file. If it is able to open the file, it asserts the fact (phase write-data) to indicate that the *data* facts should be written out to the file. The rule *save-data-info* will be activated once for every *data* fact in the fact-list. It writes each *data* fact to the file in the format expected by the *load-facts* function. The rule *finish-save-data* closes the file once all the facts have been saved. It is given a lower salience than the *save-data-info* rule to allow all of the facts to be written to the file before it is closed. If rules had been included to perform switching from one phase to the next phase, the *finish-save-data* rule could have been placed in the phase following the *write-data* phase and the salience value of -1 would not have been required for the rule.

10.5 STRING FUNCTIONS

CLIPS provides several functions for manipulating strings. These functions are **str_assert**, **str_cat**, **str-index**, and **sub-string**. The syntax of these functions is shown following.

```
(str_assert <string>)
(str_cat <<items>>)
(str-index <string-1> <string-2>)
(sub-string <integer-1> <integer-2> <string>)
```

The Str_assert Function

The *str_assert* function takes a string as argument and breaks it up into fields which are asserted as a fact. For example, the top-level command

```
(str_assert "data-values 1 5 6")
```

would cause the assertion of the fact

```
(data-values 1 5 6)
```

Notice that there are no double quotes around the asserted fact. The fact consists of four fields while the original string was one field.

Spaces, carriage returns, or tabs within a string are used as delimiters by the *str_assert* function in determining where to create fields. A quoted string may be included by using the "\" as an escape character. For example,

```
(str_assert "data-values green \"red blue\" black")
```

would cause the fact

```
(data-values green "red blue" black)
```

to be asserted.

The Str_cat Function

The *str_cat* function constructs a single quoted string from one or more individual items. The items can be words, numbers, strings, bound variables or functions which return a word, string, or numbers. For example, the following top-level command would produce the output shown

```
CLIPS> (str_cat "data-" 9 ".txt")↵
"data-9.txt"
CLIPS>
```

Notice that the fields are all run together. If it is necessary to have a space between the words in the fact, a space should be entered between the double quotes as shown following.

```
CLIPS> (str_cat colors " " red " " green " "
blue)↵
"colors red green blue"
CLIPS>
```

The Str-index Function

The *str-index* function returns the position of the first string within the second string. If the string is not found, then zero is returned. For example,

```
CLIPS> (str-index "red" "blueredgreen")↵
5
CLIPS> (str-index "red" "bluegreen")↵
0
CLIPS>
```

The Sub-string Function

The *sub-string* function returns a portion of a string. It requires three arguments. The first two arguments are the beginning and ending indices of the substring. The third argument is the string from which the substring is to be taken. For example,

```
CLIPS> (sub-string 3 5 "a string")↵
"str"
CLIPS>
```

10.6   MULTIFIELD FUNCTIONS

CLIPS provides a number of functions that are useful with multifield variables. These functions are **mv-append, mv-delete, length, nth, member, subset, mv-subseq, str-explode,** and **str-implode**. The syntax is as follows.

```
(mv-append <<items>>)
(mv-delete <field-index> <multifield value>)
(length <multifield value>)
(nth <field-index> <multifield value>)
(member <field> <multifield value>)
(subset <multifield value-1>
        <multifield value-2>)
(mv-subseq <field-index-1> <field-index-2>
           <multifield value>)
(str-explode <string>)
(str-implode <multifield value>)
```

The Mv-append and Mv-delete Functions

The *mv-append* function constructs a single multifield value from individual items. The items can be words, numbers, strings, bound single or multifield variables or functions which return a word, string, numbers, or multifields. The *mv-delete* function deletes an indexed field from a multifield value. For example,

```
CLIPS> (mv-append a b 9 "red")↵
a b 9 "red"
CLIPS> (mv-delete 3 (mv-append a b 9 "red"))↵
a b "red"
CLIPS>
```

If no arguments are passed to *mv-append*, a multifield value of length zero is created. A multifield value of length zero is referred to as **null**, which literally means "nothing." Only a multifield variable can be bound to null. Notice that *mv-append* is used to generate a multifield value for the *mv-delete* function. Since variables cannot be used at the top-level, there is no other way to generate a multifield constant.

The Length Function

The *length* function returns the number of fields in a multifield value. For example,

```
CLIPS> (length (mv-append a b 9 "red"))↵
4
CLIPS>
```

The Nth Function

The *nth* function returns the field of the multifield specified by the first argument. If the field does not exist, the value **nil** is returned. For example,

```
CLIPS> (nth 2 (mv-append a b 9 "red"))↵
b
CLIPS> (nth 5 (mv-append a b 9 "red"))↵
nil
CLIPS>
```

The Member Function

The *member* function determines if a specific field is contained within a multifield value. If the field is found, an index to the field is returned, otherwise zero is returned. For example,

```
CLIPS> (member 9 (mv-append a b 9 "red"))↵
3
CLIPS> (member 5 (mv-append a b 9 "red"))↵
0
CLIPS>
```

The Subset Function

The *subset* function determines if one multifield value is a subset of another multifield value. A set such as (a b c) is considered a subset of (c b a), (b a c), and so forth. A null multifield value is a subset of *everything*, including itself. The value 1 is returned if the first argument is a subset of the second argument, otherwise the value 0 is returned. For example,

```
CLIPS> (subset (mv-append a b c)
               (mv-append c b a))↵
1
CLIPS> (subset (mv-append a b b c)
               (mv-append b c a))↵
1
CLIPS> (subset (mv-append a d c)
               (mv-append c a))↵
0
CLIPS>
```

The Mv-subseq Function

The *mv-subseq* function returns a portion of a multifield value. It requires three arguments. The first two arguments are the beginning and ending indices of the subsequence. The third argument is the multifield value from which the subsequence is to be taken. For example,

```
CLIPS> (mv-subseq 2 4 (mv-append a b c d e))↵
b c d
CLIPS>
```

The Str-explode Function

The *str-explode* function converts a string to a multifield value. For example,

```
CLIPS> (str-explode "a b c d e")↵
a b c d e
CLIPS>
```

The Str-implode Function

Conversely, the *str-implode* function converts a multifield value to a string. For example,

```
CLIPS> (str-implode (mv-append a b c d e))↵
"a b c d e"
CLIPS>
```

10.7   EXTENDED MATH FUNCTIONS

In addition to the standard CLIPS math functions of +, -, * and /, there are a large number of additional mathematical functions provided by the CLIPS extended math package. The extended math functions are normally provided with CLIPS, but may be excluded from some CLIPS systems to conserve memory.

Trigonometric Functions

Table 10-3 show the list of trigonometric functions provided by the extended math package. Each of the trigonometric functions expects a single argument. Where applicable, each trigonometric function expects its argument to be in radians.

Function Name	Purpose
cos	cosine
sin	sine
tan	tangent
sec	secant
csc	cosecant
cot	cotangent
acos	arccosine
asin	arcsine
atan	arctangent
asec	arcsecant
acsc	arccosecant
acot	arccotangent
cosh	hyperbolic cosine
sinh	hyperbolic sine
tanh	hyperbolic tangent
sech	hyperbolic secant
csch	hyperbolic cosecant
coth	hyperbolic cotangent
acosh	hyperbolic arccosine
asinh	hyperbolic arcsine
atanh	hyperbolic arctangent
asech	hyperbolic arcsecant
acsch	hyperbolic arccosecant
acoth	hyperbolic arccotangent

Table 10-3
Trigonometric Functions

The function **pi** can be used to obtain the value of π in radians. It requires no arguments. For example,

```
CLIPS> (pi)↵
3.14159274
CLIPS> (cos (pi))↵
-1
CLIPS>
```

Conversion Functions

The functions **deg-rad**, **rad-deg**, **deg-grad**, and **grad-deg** are provided for converting between degrees, radians and gradients. The syntax of these functions is as follows

```
(deg-rad <argument-in-degrees>)
(rad-deg <argument-in-radians>)
(deg-grad <argument-in-degrees>)
(grad-deg <argument-in-gradients>)
```

The *deg-rad* function converts its argument from degrees to radians. The *rad-deg* function converts its argument from radians to degrees. The *deg-grad* function converts its argument from degrees to gradients. The *grad-deg* function converts its argument from gradients to degrees.

Min and Max Functions

The **min** and **max** functions can be used to find the minimum and maximum value from a group of numeric values. The syntax of these functions is

```
(min <<numbers>>)
(max <<numbers>>)
```

Both functions expects one or more numeric arguments. The *min* function will return the smallest value of all its arguments and the *max* function will return the largest value of all its arguments. For example

```
CLIPS> (min 3 1 8 5)↵
1
CLIPS> (max 3 1 8 5)↵
8
CLIPS>
```

Logarithm Functions

The functions **log, log10,** and **exp** are useful for performing mathematical operations with logarithms. The syntax of these functions is

```
(log <number>)
(log10 <number>)
(exp <number>)
```

Each function takes a single numeric argument. The *log* function returns the logarithm base e of its argument. The *log10* function returns the logarithm base 10 of its argument. The *exp* function returns e^n where n is the argument passed to the function.

Predicate Functions

The functions *evenp*, *oddp*, and *integerp* are provided as part of the extended math package. These functions were introduced in Chapter 9 and are listed in Table 9-3 which shows a list of CLIPS type predicate functions.

Miscellaneous Functions

Several other miscellaneous functions are provided by the extended math package. They are **sqrt**, **trunc**, **abs**, **mod**, and ******. The syntax of these functions is

```
(sqrt <number>)
(trunc <number>)
(abs <number>)
(mod <number> <number>)
(** <number> <number>)
```

The *sqrt* function returns the square root of its argument. The *trunc* function truncates its argument so that it is the floating point equivalent of an integer value. The *abs* function returns the absolute value of its argument. The *mod* function returns the remainder that results from dividing its first argument by its second argument (the first argument modulus the second argument). The ** function returns the value of its first argument raised to the power of its second argument. For example,

```
CLIPS> (sqrt 9) ↵
3
CLIPS> (trunc 11.3) ↵
11
CLIPS> (abs -5) ↵
5
CLIPS> (mod 9 2) ↵
1
CLIPS> (** 3 2) ↵
9
CLIPS>
```

10.8   UTILITY COMMANDS

The System Command

The **system** command allows the execution of operating system commands from within CLIPS. The syntax of the system command is

```
(system <<single-field arguments>>)
```

For example, the following rule will give a directory listing for a specified directory on a machine using the UNIX operating system.

```
(defrule list-directory
    (list-directory ?directory)
    =>
    (system "ls " ?directory))
```

For this example, the first argument to the *system* command, "ls ", is the UNIX command for listing a directory. Notice that a space is included after the characters "ls". The *system* command simply appends all its arguments together as strings before allowing the operating system to process the command. Any spaces needed for the operating system command must be included as part of an argument in the *system* command call.

The effects of the *system* command may vary from one operating system to another. Not all operating systems provide the functionality for implementing the *system* command, so you cannot rely on this command being available in CLIPS.

The Batch Command

The **batch** command allows commands and responses that would normally have to be entered at the top-level prompt to be read directly from a file. The syntax of the *batch* command is

```
(batch <file-name>)
```

For example, suppose the following dialog shows the commands and responses which must be entered to run a CLIPS program. Remember that the bold face letters indicate keys entered by you.

```
CLIPS> (load "rules1.clp")↵
CLIPS> (load "rules2.clp")↵
CLIPS> (load "rules3.clp")↵
CLIPS> (reset)↵
CLIPS> (run)↵
How many iterations? 10↵
Starting value? 1↵
End value? 20↵
Completed
CLIPS>
```

The commands and responses needed to run the program could be stored in a file as shown following.

```
(load "rules1.clp") ↵
(load "rules2.clp") ↵
(load "rules3.clp") ↵
(reset) ↵
(run) ↵
10↵
1↵
20↵
```

If the file with the commands and responses was named "commands.bat", the following dialog shows how the *batch* command can be used. Notice again that the bold face letters indicate keys entered by you.

```
CLIPS> (batch "commands.bat") ↵
CLIPS> (load "rules1.clp") ↵
CLIPS> (load "rules2.clp") ↵
CLIPS> (load "rules3.clp") ↵
CLIPS> (reset) ↵
CLIPS> (run) ↵
How many iterations? 10↵
Starting value? 1↵
End value? 20↵
Completed
CLIPS>
```

Once all the commands and responses have been read from a batch file, keyboard interaction at the top-level prompt is returned to normal.

When run under operating systems that support command line arguments for executables (such as UNIX), CLIPS can automatically execute commands from a batch file upon startup. Assuming that the CLIPS executable can be executed by typing "clips", the syntax for executing a batch file upon startup is

```
clips -f <file-name>
```

If an *exit* command is processed in the startup batch file, control will be returned to the operating system. Otherwise, CLIPS will enter its interactive state displaying the top-level prompt "CLIPS>". Unlike the *batch* command, only commands can be processed from a startup batch file. Responses to input functions cannot be stored in a startup batch file. Furthermore, the CLIPS prompt and the command being executed will not be displayed until CLIPS enters its interactive state.

The Dribble-on and Dribble-off Commands

The **dribble-on** command can be used to store a record of all output to the terminal and all input from the keyboard. The syntax of the *dribble-on* command is

```
(dribble-on "<file-name>")
```

Once the dribble-on command has been executed, all output sent to the terminal and all input entered at the keyboard will be echoed to the file specified by <file-name> as well as to the terminal.

The effects of the *dribble-on* command can be turned off with the **dribble-off** command. The syntax of the *dribble-off* command is

```
(dribble-off)
```

10.9 THE GENSYM FUNCTION

CLIPS has a function called **gensym** which returns a unique word every time it's called. The general form of the value returned by the *gensym* function is shown following.

```
gen<number>
```

where <number> is a suffix numeral supplied by CLIPS each time the *gensym* function is called. The numbers used by the *gensym* function always start at 1 when CLIPS is first started and increment by 1 each time the *gensym* function is called until CLIPS is exited. The following command sequence demonstrates the use of the *gensym* function.

```
CLIPS> (gensym) ↵
gen1
CLIPS> (gensym) ↵
gen2
CLIPS> (gensym) ↵
gen3
CLIPS>
```

The **setgen** function can be used to reset the gensym count or to set it to a specific value. The *setgen* function takes a single argument, the starting number to be appended to the word "gen". For example,

```
CLIPS> (setgen 10) ↵
CLIPS> (gensym) ↵
gen10
```

```
CLIPS>  (gensym) ↵
gen11
CLIPS>  (setgen 3) ↵
CLIPS>  (gensym) ↵
gen3
CLIPS>
```

The usefulness of the gensym function will be demonstrated in Chapter 12 using an example that demonstrates how uncertainty can be represented in CLIPS.

10.10 SUMMARY

This chapter introduced a wide variety of functions. CLIPS provides functions for manipulating strings and multifield values. A number of math functions are provided by the CLIPS extended math package.

The *if* and *while* functions can be used for flow of control on the RHS of a rule. The *halt* function can be used to halt the execution of rules. Overuse of these functions on the RHS is poor programming style.

The *open* and *close* functions can be used to open and close files. Opened files are associated with a logical name. Logical names can be used in most functions that perform input and output to more than one type of physical device. Both the *printout* and *read* functions used logical names. The *printout* function can output to the terminal and files. The *read* function can input from the keyboard and files. The *format* and *readline* functions also accept logical names. The *format* function allows more control over the appearance of output. The *readline* function can be used to read an entire line of data. The *save-facts* and *load-facts* functions can be used to save facts to a file and load facts from a file.

The *system* command allows operating system commands to be executed from within CLIPS. The *batch* commands allows a series of commands and responses stored in a file to replace normal keyboard input. The *dribble-on* and *dribble-off* commands allow a record of terminal output to be stored in a file. The *gensym* function can be used to generate unique words.

PROBLEMS AND PROGRAMS

10-1.   Modify the oil pump program in Section 10.3 to ask for the name of the input and output files. Check to see if the files can be opened. If they cannot, prompt the user for another file name.

10-2.   Rewrite the following rule into one or more rules that do not use the if and while functions. Verify that your rules perform the same actions by comparing the output and final fact-list of your rules with the following rule.

```
(defrule continue-check
   ?phase <- (phase check-continue)
   =>
   (retract ?phase)
   (printout t "Continue? " crlf)
   (bind ?answer (read))
   (while (and (neq ?answer yes) (neq ?answer no)) do
      (printout t "Continue? " crlf)
      (bind ?answer (read)))
   (if (eq ?answer yes)
      then (assert (phase continue))
      else (assert (phase halt)))))
```

10-3.   Write a program that saves a specified group of facts. The facts to be save should be specified with a fact using the following template

```
(save-relations <file-name> <<relation-names>>)
```

where <file-name> indicates the file in which the facts should be stored and <<relation-names>> are the relation names of the facts to be saved. Only those facts beginning with one of the relation names should be saved. Verify your program using the following deffacts construct.

```
(deffacts test-data
   (save-relations "facts.sav" data numbers)
   (numbers 10 20 30)
   (words a b c)
   (data a b 34 c 34)
   (numbers 23 22)
   (words x y z)
   (strings "abc" "def" "ghi")
   (data a b c d 34)
   (data a b))
```

10-4.   Write a program which will read a data file containing a list of people's names and ages and create a new file containing the list of people's names and ages sorted in ascending order by age. The program should prompt for both the input and output files. For example, the following input file

```
John Carter 34
Mary Jane Campbell 25
Bill Smith 37
Janis Page 22
```

should create the following output file

```
Janis Page 22
Mary Jane Campbell 25
John Carter 34
Bill Smith 37
```

CHAPTER 11 EFFICIENCY IN RULE-BASED LANGUAGES

11.1 INTRODUCTION

This chapter provides many techniques for increasing the efficiency of a rule-based expert system which uses the Rete Pattern Matching Algorithm. The reasons for needing an efficient pattern matching algorithm are discussed before the Rete Algorithm is explained. Several techniques for writing rules more efficiently are discussed.

11.2 THE RETE PATTERN MATCHING ALGORITHM

Rule-based languages such as CLIPS, ART, OPS5, and OPS83 use a very efficient algorithm for matching facts against the patterns in rules to determine which rules have their conditions satisfied. This algorithm is called the **Rete Pattern Matching Algorithm**. Writing efficient CLIPS rules does not require an understanding of the Rete Algorithm. However, an understanding of the underlying algorithm used in CLIPS and other rule-based languages makes it easier to understand why writing rules one way is more efficient than writing them another way.

    To understand why the Rete Algorithm is efficient, it will be helpful to look at the problem of matching facts to rules in general and examine other algorithms which are not as efficient. Figure 11-1 shows the problem addressed by the Rete Algorithm.

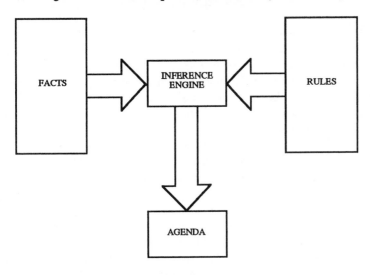

Figure 11-1
Pattern Matching: Rules and Facts

If the matching process only has to occur once, then the solution to the problem is straightforward. The inference engine can examine each rule and then search the set of facts to determine if the rule's patterns have been satisfied. If the rule's patterns are satisfied, then the rule can be placed on the agenda. Figure 11-2 shows this approach of having the rules look for the facts needed to match their conditions.

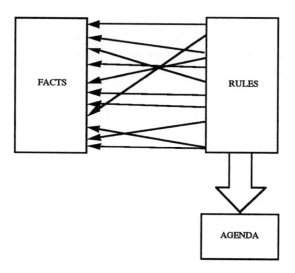

Figure 11-2
Rules Searching for Facts

In rule-based languages, however, the matching process takes place repeatedly. Normally, the fact-list will be modified during each cycle of execution. New facts may be added to the fact-list or old facts may be removed from the fact-list. These changes may cause previously unsatisfied patterns to be satisfied or previously satisfied patterns to become unsatisfied. The problem of matching now becomes an ongoing process. During each cycle, as facts are added and removed, the set of rules that are satisfied must be maintained and updated.

Having the inference engine check each rule to direct the search for facts after each cycle of execution provides a very simple and straightforward technique for solving this problem. The primary disadvantage of such a technique is that it can be very slow. Most rule-based expert systems exhibit a property called **temporal redundancy**. Typically, the actions of a rule will only change a few facts in the fact-list. That is, the facts in the expert system change slowly over time. Each cycle of execution may see only a small percentage of facts either added or removed and so only a small percentage of rules are typically affected by the changes in the fact-list. Thus having the rules drive the search for needed facts requires a lot of unnecessary computation since most of the rules are likely to find the same facts in the current cycle as found in the last cycle. The inefficiency of this approach is shown in Figure 11-3. The shaded area represents the changes that have been made to the fact-list. Unnecessary recomputation could be avoided by remembering what has already matched from cycle to cycle and computing only the changes necessary for the newly added or removed facts as shown in Figure 11-4. It is the rules that remain static and the facts that change. Thus the facts should find the rules and not the other way around.

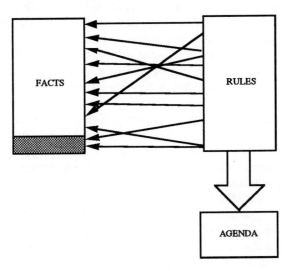

Figure 11-3
Unnecessary Computations when Rules Search for Facts

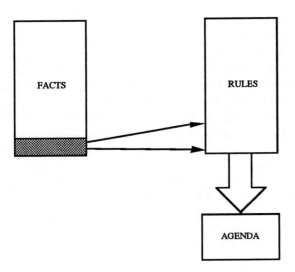

Figure 11-4
Facts Searching for Rules

The Rete Pattern Matching algorithm is designed to take advantage of the temporal redundancy exhibited by rule-based expert systems. It does this by saving the state of the matching process from cycle to cycle and recomputing the changes in this state only for the changes that occur in the fact-list. That is, if a set of patterns finds two of three required facts in one cycle, a check does not have to be made in the next cycle for the two facts that have already been found. Only the third fact is of interest. The state of the matching process is updated only as facts are added and removed. If the number of facts added and removed is small compared to the total number of facts and patterns, then the process of matching will proceed quickly. As a worst case, if all the facts were to be changed, then the matching process would work as if all the facts were compared against all of the patterns.

If only updates to the fact-list are processed, then each rule must remember what has already matched it. That is, if a new fact has matched the third pattern of a rule, then information about the matches for the first two patterns must be available to finish the matching process. This type of state information indicating the facts that have matched previous patterns in a rule is called a **partial match**. A partial match for a rule is any set of facts which satisfy the rule's patterns beginning with the first pattern of the rule and ending with any pattern up to and including the rule's last pattern. Thus, a rule with three patterns would have partial matches for the first pattern, the first and second patterns, and the first, second, and third patterns. A partial match of all of the patterns of a rule will also be an activation. The other type of state information saved is called a **pattern match**. A pattern match occurs when a fact has satisfied a single pattern in any rule without regard to variables in other patterns that may restrict the matching process.

The primary disadvantage of the Rete Pattern Matching Algorithm is that it is very memory intensive. Simply comparing all of the facts to all of the patterns requires no memory. Saving the state of the system using pattern matches and partial matches, however, can consume considerable amounts of memory. In general, this tradeoff of memory for speed is worthwhile. It is important to note that the Rete Algorithm does not perform a simple search in attempting to match facts against rules. Since memory is used to save both pattern matches and partial matches for the rules, a poorly written rule can not only run slowly, but it can use up considerable amounts of memory. Like errors in procedural languages such as a recursive loop that never bottoms out or nested loops that have a combinatorial number of iterations, this is a commonly made error in rule-based programming.

The Rete Algorithm also improves the efficiency of rule-based systems by taking advantage of **structural similarity** in the rules. Structural similarity refers to the fact that many rules often contain similar patterns or groups of patterns. The Rete Algorithm takes advantage of this feature to increase efficiency by pooling common components together so that they do not have to be computed more than once.

11.3 THE PATTERN NETWORK

The problem of matching facts to rules can be divided into two steps. First, when facts are added and removed, it must be determined which patterns have been matched. This step determines the pattern matches. Second, comparison of variable bindings across patterns must be checked. This step determines the partial matches for a group of patterns.

The process of determining which facts have matched which patterns is performed in the **pattern network**. All matching that does not involve comparison against variables bound in other patterns can be performed in the pattern network. The pattern network is structured like a tree where the nodes connected to the root of the tree represent the first fields of all the patterns, the nodes connected to those nodes represent the second fields of all of the patterns, and so on. The leaves of the tree then represent the end of a pattern. The nodes in the pattern network are called **one-input nodes** because they only receive information from the node above them. Nodes in the pattern network are sometimes referred to as **pattern nodes**. The leaf nodes are also referred to as **terminal nodes**. Each pattern node contains an expression to be evaluated to determine if a field of a fact has matched a field of a pattern. For example, the fact

```
(data 27)
```

would be represented by two nodes. The first node corresponding to the first field of the fact would contain the matching expression

```
The first field is equal to the constant data
```

and the second node corresponding to the second field of the fact would contain the matching expression

```
The second field is equal to the constant 27
```

Matching specifications include all of the information for matching a single field. Several tests can be performed together. For example, the pattern

```
(data ~red&~green)
```

would contain the following matching specification for the second field

```
The second field is not equal to the constant red and
                   is not equal to the constant green
```

Normally, variable bindings are not checked in the pattern network, unless the variable is used more than once in the pattern. For example, the pattern

```
(data ?x ?y ?x)
```

would use the match specification for checking against the constant *data* for the first field. The second and third fields should always match against the second and third fields of a fact (provided, that is, that the fact has a second and third field). So the match expressions for the second and third fields would simply indicate respectively that

```
The second field matches
```

and

```
The third field matches
```

However, the fourth field must have the same value as the second field, so the match expression for the fourth field would be

```
The fourth field is equal to the second field
```

Expressions containing variables that are all found within the pattern can be checked within the pattern network. For example, the second field in the pattern

```
(data ?x&:(> ?x ?y))
```

would have the match specification

```
The second field matches
```

because the variable ?y is not contained within the pattern. However, the second field in the pattern

```
(data ?x&:(> ?x 4))
```

would have the match specification

```
The second field is greater than the constant 4
```

since the only variable found in the expression, ?x, is also contained within the pattern.

As stated previously, the pattern network is arranged hierarchically with the pattern nodes corresponding to the first fields of the patterns at the top. When a fact is asserted, the pattern nodes for the first fields in the pattern network are checked. Any pattern node whose matching expression is satisfied will activate the pattern nodes directly below it. This process continues until a terminal node in the pattern network has been reached. The terminal nodes in the pattern network represent the end of a pattern and a successful pattern match. Each terminal node has an **alpha memory** associated with it. The alpha memory is also referred to as the **right memory**. The alpha memory contains the set of all facts that have matched the pattern associated with the terminal node. In other words, the alpha memory stores the set of pattern matches for a particular pattern.

The pattern network takes advantage of structural similarity by sharing common pattern nodes among patterns. Since the pattern nodes are stored hierarchically, two patterns can share their first N pattern nodes if the match specifications for their first N fields are identical. For example, the patterns

```
(data red green)
(data red blue)
```

can share common pattern nodes for their first two fields. Notice that it is the match expressions that must be identical, and not necessarily the pattern field. For example, the patterns

```
(data ?x ?y)
(data ?y ?x)
```

have identical match expressions for all three fields, even though the variables in the second and third field are switched from one pattern to the next.

Figure 11-5 shows the pattern network generated by the following rules.

```
(defrule Rete-rule-1
(match red green)
(data ?x ?x)
(data ?y green)
=>)

(defrule Rete-rule-2
    (match ?x red)
(data ~green ?x)
(data ?x ?x)
=>)
```

The use of multifield variables complicates the pattern matching process because these variables throw off the strict correspondence between levels in the pattern network and fields in the fact. That is, if a multifield variable is the second field of a pattern, then the third field of the pattern does not necessarily match against the third field of the fact being matched. Matching against multifield variables requires that extra information about the number of fields that have matched against a multifield variable be kept in the pattern matching process.

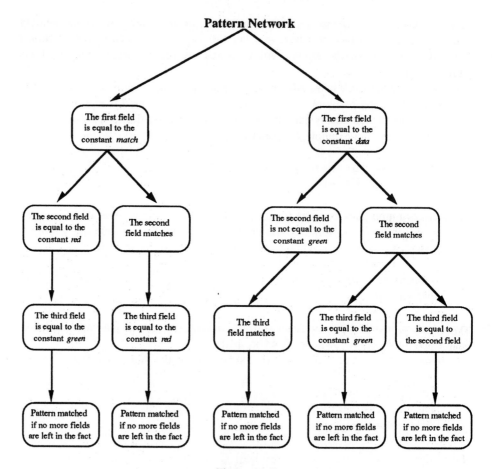

Figure 11-5
Pattern Network for Two Rules

11.4 THE JOIN NETWORK

Once it has been determined which patterns have been matched by facts, comparison of variable bindings across patterns must be checked to insure that variables used in more than one pattern have consistent values. This comparison is performed in the **join network**. Each terminal node in the pattern network acts as an input to a **join**, or **two-input node**, in the join network. Each join contains a matching expression for the matches of the alpha memory that is associated with its terminal node and for the set of partial matches that have matched previous patterns. The partial matches for previous patterns are stored in the **beta memory**, or **left memory**, of the join. A rule with N patterns would then have N-1 joins (although CLIPS actually uses N joins to simplify the Rete algorithm since this allows each join to be entered by only one pattern).

The first join compares the first two patterns and the remaining joins compare an additional pattern to the partial matches of the previous join. For example, given the rule *Rete-rule-2* used in the previous example

```
(defrule Rete-rule-2
(match ?x red)
(data ~green ?x)
(data ?x ?x)
=>)
```

the first join would contain the match expression

```
The value of the second field of the fact
    bound to the first pattern is equal to
the value of the third field of the fact
    bound to the second pattern.
```

The second join would receive as input the set of partial matches from the first join. It would contain the match expression

```
The value of the second field of the fact
    bound to the third pattern is equal to
the value of the third field of the fact
    bound to the second pattern.
```

Notice that the variable ?x in the third pattern could have its value compared to the variable ?x in the first pattern instead of variable ?x in the second pattern. The second occurrence of ?x in the third pattern does not have to be checked in the join network, since it can be checked in the pattern network. The pattern and join networks for rule *Rete-rule-2* are shown in Figure 11-6.

The join network takes advantage of structural similarity by sharing joins between rules. Joins in the join network can be shared by two rules if they have identical patterns and join comparisons for two or more patterns starting with their first pattern. For example, the following rules

```
(defrule sharing-1
   (match ?x red)
   (data ~green ?x)
   (data ?x ?x)
   (other ?z)
   =>)
```

```
(defrule sharing-2
   (match ?y red)
   (data ~green ?y)
   (data ?y ?y)
   (other ?y)
   =>)
```

could share all of their patterns in the pattern network and share their first three patterns in the join network. The fourth pattern cannot be shared in the join network because the match expressions for the two rules are different. The match expression for the fourth pattern of rule *sharing-1* does not have to perform any comparisons because the variable ?z is not used in other patterns. However, the match expression for the fourth pattern of rule *sharing-2* must compare the variable ?y to the variable ?y in another pattern to insure that the variable bindings are consistent. Notice again that the variable names do not have to be identical to take advantage of structural similarity. All that matters is that the match expressions are identical.

CLIPS provides useful information about join sharing if the *watch rules* command has been issued. For example, the following commands illustrate how information about sharing is displayed. Assume that rules *sharing-1* and and *sharing-2* are in the file "rules.clp".

```
CLIPS> (watch rules)↵
CLIPS> (load "rules.clp")↵
Compiling rule: sharing-1 +j+j+j+j
Compiling rule: sharing-2 =j=j=j+j
CLIPS>
```

The +j in the output indicates that a join is being added, whereas =j indicates that a join in being shared. Thus when rule *sharing-1* is added four new joins are created. When rule *sharing-2* is added, it shares its first three joins with rule *sharing-1* and creates a new join for its last pattern. Notice that CLIPS has used four joins to represent the rule as opposed to the three joins that would normally be required.

11.5 THE IMPORTANCE OF PATTERN ORDER

Programmers new to rule-based languages often have misconceptions about the importance of ordering the patterns in rules correctly for both speed and memory efficiency. Since the Rete Algorithm saves the state from one cycle to the next, it is very important to make sure that rules do not generate large numbers of partial matches. For example, consider the following simple program.

Pattern Network

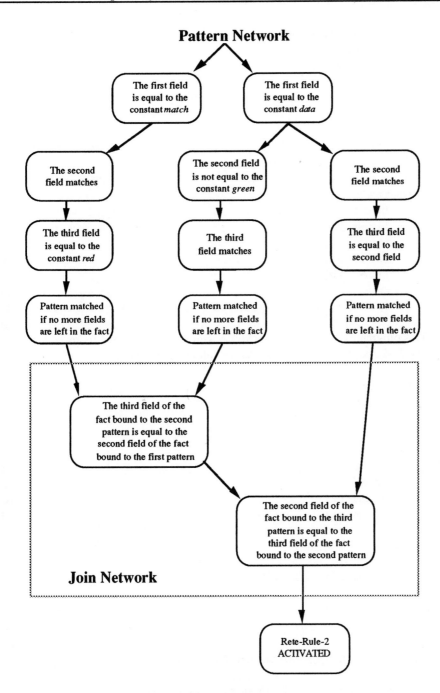

Figure 11-6
Pattern and Join Networks for Rule Rete-Rule-2

```
(deffacts information
   (match a c e g)
   (item a)
   (item b)
   (item c)
   (item d)
   (item e)
   (item f)
   (item g))

(defrule match-1
   (match ?x ?y ?z ?w)
   (item ?x)
   (item ?y)
   (item ?z)
   (item ?w)
   =>
   (assert (found-match ?x ?y ?z ?w)))
```

This program will reset very quickly. A *watch facts* command followed by a *reset* command will verify this. Now consider the following program.

```
(deffacts information
   (match a c e g)
   (item a)
   (item b)
   (item c)
   (item d)
   (item e)
   (item f)
   (item g))

(defrule match-2
   (item ?x)
   (item ?y)
   (item ?z)
   (item ?w)
   (match ?x ?y ?z ?w)
   =>
   (assert (found-match ?x ?y ?z ?w)))
```

A *watch facts* command followed by a *reset* command for this program will demonstrate a considerably slower reset time. As the reset is performed, the first few facts in the deffacts construct will be asserted quickly. However, subsequent facts will require an increasingly longer time to be asserted. Rules *match-1* and *match-2* each have the same patterns, but rule *match-2* requires much longer to reset than rule *match-1*. In fact, rule *match-2* may may cause CLIPS to run out of memory on some computers. An even greater difference in speed can be demonstrated by adding more item facts to the information deffacts.

Counting for Rule match-1

Counting the pattern matches and partial matches for rule *match-1* provides useful information. Instead of using the entire fact in listing the pattern matches and partial matches, the fact ids will be used in place of the fact. In addition, partial matches will be enclosed in braces. So given the fact ids as follows:

```
f-1 (match a c e g)
f-2 (item a)
f-3 (item b)
f-4 (item c)
f-5 (item d)
f-6 (item e)
f-7 (item f)
f-8 (item g)
```

Rule *match-1* has the following pattern matches:

```
Pattern 1: f-1
Pattern 2: f-2, f-3, f-4, f-5, f-6, f-7, f-8
Pattern 3: f-2, f-3, f-4, f-5, f-6, f-7, f-8
Pattern 4: f-2, f-3, f-4, f-5, f-6, f-7, f-8
Pattern 5: f-2, f-3, f-4, f-5, f-6, f-7, f-8
```

Rule *match-1* has the following partial matches:

```
Pattern  1:    [f-1]
Patterns 1-2:  [f-1,f-2]
Pattern  1-3:  [f-1,f-2,f-4]
Pattern  1-4:  [f-1,f-2,f-4,f-6]
Pattern  1-5:  [f-1,f-2,f-4,f-6,f-8]
```

In total, rule *match-1* has a total of 29 pattern matches and 5 partial matches.

Counting for Rule match-2

Now the pattern matches and partial matches for rule *match-2* will be examined. Rule *match-2* has the following pattern matches:

```
Pattern 1: f-2,  f-3,  f-4,  f-5,  f-6,  f-7,  f-8
Pattern 2: f-2,  f-3,  f-4,  f-5,  f-6,  f-7,  f-8
Pattern 3: f-2,  f-3,  f-4,  f-5,  f-6,  f-7,  f-8
Pattern 4: f-2,  f-3,  f-4,  f-5,  f-6,  f-7,  f-8
Pattern 5: f-1
```

Rules *match-1* and *match-2* have the same number of pattern matches. Now consider just the partial matches for pattern 1:

```
[f-2],[f-3],[f-4],[f-5],[f-6],[f-7],[f-8]
```

Pattern 1 has 7 partial matches. This is no surprise, however, since the partial matches for the first pattern will be the same as the pattern matches for the first pattern. The partial matches for patterns 1 and 2 however are quite numerous.

```
[f-2,f-2],[f-2,f-3],[f-2,f-4],[f-2,f-5],
          [f-2,f-6],[f-2,f-7],[f-2,f-8],
[f-3,f-2],[f-3,f-3],[f-3,f-4],[f-3,f-5],
          [f-3,f-6],[f-3,f-7],[f-3,f-8],
[f-4,f-2],[f-4,f-3],[f-4,f-4],[f-4,f-5],
          [f-4,f-6],[f-4,f-7],[f-4,f-8],
[f-5,f-2],[f-5,f-3],[f-5,f-4],[f-5,f-5],
          [f-5,f-6],[f-5,f-7],[f-5,f-8],
[f-6,f-2],[f-6,f-3],[f-6,f-4],[f-6,f-5],
          [f-6,f-6],[f-6,f-7],[f-6,f-8],
[f-7,f-2],[f-7,f-3],[f-7,f-4],[f-7,f-5],
          [f-7,f-6],[f-7,f-7],[f-7,f-8],
[f-8,f-2],[f-8,f-3],[f-8,f-4],[f-8,f-5],
          [f-8,f-6],[f-8,f-7],[f-8,f-8]
```

In all there are a total of 49 partial matches for patterns 1 and 2 (7 pattern matches for pattern 1 multiplied by 7 pattern matches for pattern 2). Space will quickly limit the partial matches that can be listed for the other patterns since there will be 343 partial matches for pattern 1 through 3 and 2401 partial matches for patterns 1 through 4. Just as for rule *match-1*, only one partial match exists for patterns 1 through 5.

```
[f-2,f-4,f-6,f-8,f-1]
```

Notice that while the number of pattern matches and activations are the same for rules *match-1* and *match-2*, rule *match-1* has only 5 partial matches, while rule *match-2* has 2801 partial matches. This difference in partial matches would continue to grow as more item facts are added. The fact (item h) will create no new partial matches for rule *match-1*, however, it will create 1880 new partial matches for rule *match-2*. This example demonstrates that the number of partial matches created can drastically affect the performance of a program. An efficient set of rules should attempt to minimize not only the creation of new partial matches, but the deletion of old partial matches. In effect, an attempt should be made to minimize the change of state of the system from one cycle to the next. Specific techniques for minimizing the change of state will be discussed later in this chapter.

Watching the Changing State

The matches command provides one useful way of examining partial matches for a rule. Another way to watch partial matches is to consider them as being partial activations of a rule. If rule *match-1* is considered as several separate rules each trying to compute partial matches, then the *watch activations* command can be used to see the partial matches as they are generated. The rule *match-1* can be split into several rules as follows

```
(defrule match-1-pm-1
        "Partial matches for pattern 1"
   (match ?x ?y ?z ?w)
   =>)

(defrule match-1-pm-1-to-2
        "Partial matches for patterns 1 and 2"
   (match ?x ?y ?z ?w)
   (item ?x)
   =>)

(defrule match-1-pm-1-to-3
        "Partial matches for patterns 1 to 3"
   (match ?x ?y ?z ?w)
   (item ?x)
   (item ?y)
   =>)

(defrule match-1-pm-1-to-4
        "Partial matches for patterns 1 to 4"
   (match ?x ?y ?z ?w)
   (item ?x)
   (item ?y)
   (item ?z)
   =>)

(defrule match-1 "Activations for the match rule"
   (match ?x ?y ?z ?w)
   (item ?x)
```

```
(item ?y)
(item ?z)
(item ?w)
=>
(assert (found-match ?x ?y ?z ?w)))
```

If the preceding rules and the *information* deffacts are loaded, the following command dialog shows how the partial matches can be watched as they are created.

```
CLIPS>  (watch activations).⌐
CLIPS>  (watch facts).⌐
CLIPS>  (reset).⌐
==> f-0      (initial-fact)
==> f-1      (match a c e g)
==> Activation 0       match-1-pm-1:   f-1
==> f-2      (item a)
==> Activation 0       match-1-pm-1-to-2:   f-1   f-2
==> f-3      (item b)
==> f-4      (item c)
==> Activation 0       match-1-pm-1-to-3:   f-1   f-2
f-4
==> f-5      (item d)
==> f-6      (item e)
==> Activation 0       match-1-pm-1-to-4:   f-1   f-2
f-4  f-6
==> f-7      (item f)
==> f-8      (item g)
==> Activation 0       match-1:   f-1   f-2   f-4   f-6
f-8
CLIPS>
```

Using this same technique for rule *matches-2* would produce hundreds of partial activations. It should be clear, by now, that the LHS of a rule cannot be considered as a whole for the purpose of efficiency. Each LHS of a rule should be considered as several separate rules each producing a set of partial matches for the rule as a whole. Writing an efficient rule becomes a matter of not just limiting the total number of activations for a rule, but a matter of limiting the partial matches for each of the separate subrules which make up the LHS of the rule.

11.6   ORDERING PATTERNS FOR EFFICIENCY

There are several guidelines that should be kept in mind when ordering patterns to limit the number of partial matches that are made. Finding the best way to order patterns can be difficult, because some guidelines may conflict with others. In general, the guidelines for ordering are used to avoid gross inefficiencies that may appear in a rule-based system. Fine-tuning of an expert system, however, can require considerable trial and error in reordering patterns to determine what changes make the system run faster. Often, trying a completely different approach rather than attempting the fine-tuning of patterns may yield much better results.

Most Specific Patterns Go First

The most specific pattern should be placed toward the front of the LHS of a rule. A specific pattern will generally have the fewest number of matching facts in the fact-list and will have the largest number of variable bindings which constrain other patterns. The pattern (match ?x ?y ?z ?w) shown in rules *match-1* and *match-2* is very specific because it constrains the facts allowed to generate partial matches for the other four patterns of the rule.

Patterns Matching Volatile Facts Go Last

Patterns matching against facts that are frequently added and removed from the fact-list should be placed towards the end of the LHS of a rule. This causes the smallest number of changes in the partial matches for the rule. It is important to note that patterns matching volatile facts are very often the most specific patterns in the rule. This can create a dilemma in trying to arrange the patterns of the rule for greatest efficiency. For example, it is generally advantageous to place control facts as the beginning pattern of a rule. If the control fact is not present, no partial matches will be generated for the rule. However, if control facts are being asserted and retracted quite frequently, and a larger number of partial matches are constantly being recomputed, then it can be more efficient to place the control fact towards the end of a rule.

Patterns Matching the Fewest Facts Go First

Placing patterns that will match very few facts in the fact-list near the front of the rule will reduce the number of partial matches that can be generated. Once again, use of this guideline may conflict with other guidelines. A pattern matching that matches very few facts is not necessarily the most specific pattern or the facts matched by the pattern might be volatile.

11.7 MULTIFIELD VARIABLES AND EFFICIENCY

Multifield wildcards and multifield variables provide very powerful pattern matching capabilities. When used improperly, however, they can lead to inefficiency. Two rules should be applied to the use of multifield wildcards and variables. First, they should not be used unless needed. Second, when used care should be taken to limit the number of multifield wildcards and variables used in a single pattern.

Multifield wildcards and variables are not needed when the exact number of fields to be matched is known. If this is the case, then single field wildcards or variables can be used in place of the multifield wildcards or variables. Use of unnecessary multifield wildcards can be tempting when much of the information in a fact is not needed, or rules are being converted to CLIPS from languages such as OPS5 which allows a notational shorthand for accessing fields. Consider the conversion of the following OPS5 statements:

```
(literalize object name mass x-position y-position)

(p find-large-mass
   (object ^mass { <m> > 10000 })
   -->
   (write Large object found with mass <m> (crlf)))
```

The *literalize* statement allows a shorthand for accessing the fields within a fact. Thus the pattern in the rule *find-large-mass* is checking that the field in the *object* fact associated with the keyword *mass* is greater than 10000. A conversion to a CLIPS rule might include adding the keywords to act as positional operators in the fact. The fact would look like

```
(object name obj-1 mass 20000
        x-position 10 y-position 20)
```

and the rule to match it would be

```
(defrule find-large-mass
   (object $? mass ?m&:(> ?m 10000) $?)
   =>
   (printout t "Large object found with mass " ?m
                crlf))
```

This technique will work under most situations, however, it is not very efficient. The multifield wildcards will work to find all possible combinations of matches. For this example, Table 11-1 shows all the possible combinations that are attempted for the first multifield wildcard.

The matching process will fail for all the match attempts except attempt 3. The multifield does not have some magic property which automatically positions the match at the appropriate keyword. It is designed and intended to be used under situations in which all possible combinations are desired. Consider also what might happen if the name of the object was mass as in the following fact:

```
(object name mass mass 20000
        x-position 10 y-position 20)
```

The rule *find-large-mass* would have two activations. One activation would bind the variable ?mass to the word *mass*, the other activation would bind the variable ?mass to the correct value of 20000.

Match Attempt	Fields Matched
1	
2	name
3	name obj-1
4	name obj-1 mass
5	name obj-1 mass 20000
6	name obj-1 mass 20000 x-position
7	name obj-1 mass 20000 x-position 10
8	name obj-1 mass 20000 x-position 10 y-position
9	name obj-1 mass 20000 x-position 10 y-position 20

Table 11-1
Matching Attempts for a Multifield Wildcard

The preferred translation of the rule denotes the attributes by position and not by keyword. Thus the attribute *name* is in the second field, the attribute *mass* is in the third field, and so on. A guideline to follow is that multifield wildcards and variables should not be used when they can be replaced with an equivalent number of single field wildcards or variables.

```
(object obj-1 20000 10 20)

(defrule find-large-mass
   (object ? ?m&:(> ?m 10000) ? ?)
   =>
   (printout t "Large object found with mass " ?m
             crlf))
```

As another example, the following rule demonstrates that multifield wildcards and variables can be useful, but are also quite expensive:

```
(defrule produce-twoplets
   (list $?b $?m $?e)
   =>
   (assert (front $?b))
```

```
(assert (middle $?m))
(assert (back $?e)))
```

Given a fact such as (list a 4 z 2), this rule will produce facts representing the front part, the middle part, and the back part of the list. The lengths of the various parts will vary from zero to the length of the list. This rule is easy to state using multifield variables, however it is an extremely expensive pattern matching operation. Table 11-2 shows all of the matches that are attempted. This table shows that multifield wildcards and variables can perform a great deal of work as part of the pattern matching process.

Match Attempt	Fields Matched by $?b	Fields Matched by $?m	Fields Matched by $?e
1			a 4 z 2
2		a	4 z 2
3		a 4	z 2
4		a 4 z	2
5		a 4 z 2	
6	a		4 z 2
7	a	4	z 2
8	a	4 z	2
9	a	4 z 2	
10	a 4	z	2
11	a 4	z 2	
12	a 4 z		2
13	a 4 z	2	
14	a 4 z 2		

Table 11-2
Matching Attempts for Three Multifield Variables

11.8   PERFORM TESTS AS SOON AS POSSIBLE

Any test patterns within a rule should be placed as close to the top of the rule as possible. For example, the following rule tests to find three distinct points.

```
(defrule three-distinct-points
    ?point-1 <- (point ?x1 ?y1)
    ?point-2 <- (point ?x2 ?y2)
    ?point-3 <- (point ?x3 ?y3)
    (test (and (neq ?point-1 ?point-2)
               (neq ?point-2 ?point-3)
               (neq ?point-1 ?point-3)))
```

```
=>
(assert (distinct-points ?x1 ?y1 ?x2 ?y2
                         ?x3 ?y3)))
```

The test condition which tests that the fact address?point-1 is not the same as the fact-address ?point-2 can be placed immediately after the second pattern. Placing the test pattern at this point will reduce the number of partial matches that are created.

```
(defrule three-distinct-points
   ?point-1 <- (point ?x1 ?y1)
   ?point-2 <- (point ?x2 ?y2)
   (test (neq ?point-1 ?point-2))
   ?point-3 <- (point ?x3 ?y3)
   (test (and (neq ?point-2 ?point-3)
              (neq ?point-1 ?point-3)))
   =>
   (assert (distinct-points ?x1 ?y1 ?x2 ?y2
                            ?x3 ?y3)))
```

Test patterns on the LHS of a rule are always evaluated when partial matches are being generated. Expressions used with the predicate or equality field constraint may be evaluated during the pattern matching process if certain conditions are met. Expression evaluation during the pattern matching process yields greater efficiency. An expression used by the predicate or equality field constraints will be evaluated during the pattern matching process if all variables referenced in the expression can be found within the enclosing pattern.

The expression in the following rule will be evaluated during the generation of partial matches because it is within a test pattern.

```
(defrule points-share-common-x-or-y-value
   (point ?x1 ?y1)
   (point ?x2 ?y2)
   (test (or (= ?x1 ?x2) (= ?y1 ?y2)))
   =>
   (assert (common-x-or-y-value ?x1 ?y1 ?x2 ?y2)))
```

Placing the expression within the pattern does not cause evaluation during pattern matching because the variables ?x1 and ?y1 are not contained within the second pattern.

```
(defrule points-share-common-x-or-y-value
   (point ?x1 ?y1)
   (point ?x2 ?y2&:(or (= ?x1 ?x2) (= ?y1 ?y2)))
   =>
   (assert (common-x-or-y-value ?x1 ?y1 ?x2 ?y2)))
```

Once again, the expression in the following rule will be evaluated during the generation of partial matches because it is within a test pattern.

```
(defrule point-not-on-x-y-diagonals ""
    (point ?x1 ?y1)
    (test (and (!= ?x1 ?y1) (!= ?x1 (- ?y1))))
    =>
    (assert (non-diagonal-point ?x1 ?y1)))
```

This time, however, placing the expression within the pattern does allow it to be eval-uated during pattern matching because the two variables ?x1 and ?y1 are both contained within the enclosing pattern of the expression.

```
(defrule point-not-on-x-y-diagonals
    (point ?x1 ?y1&:(and (!= ?x1 ?y1)
                         (!= ?x1 (- ?y1))))
    =>
    (assert (non-diagonal-point ?x1 ?y1)))
```

11.9   USE BUILT-IN PATTERN MATCHING PRIMITIVES

The built-in pattern matching primitives are always more efficient than an equivalent expression. For example, a rule such as

```
(defrule primary-color
    (color ?x&:(or (eq ?x red)
                   (eq ?x green)
                   (eq ?x blue)))
    =>
    (assert (primary-color ?x)))
```

should not be used when pattern matching primitives can be used to accomplish the same tests as shown here.

```
(defrule primary-color
    (color ?x&red|green|blue)
    =>
    (assert (primary-color ?x)))
```

11.10 SALIENCE AND EFFICIENCY

Salience should primarily be used as a mechanism for determining the order in which rules fire. This means that, in general, a rule that is placed on the agenda is eventually fired. Salience should not be used as a method for selecting a single rule from a group of rules when patterns can be used to express the criteria for selection. Consider, for example, a very simple set of rules which suggest which square to mark in a tic-tac-toe game. The rules are listed in the order that they should be applied.

```
If the middle square is open, then take it.
If a corner square is open, then take it.
If a side square is open, then take it.
```

If the *choose-move* fact indicates the a move should be taken and the *open-square* facts indicate whether a middle, corner, or side square is open, then the following rules will select the appropriate move.

```
(defrule pick-middle
    (declare (salience 10))
    ?phase <- (choose-move)
    (open-square middle)
    =>
    (retract ?phase)
    (assert (move move-to-middle)))

(defrule pick-corner
    (declare (salience 5))
    ?phase <- (choose-move)
    (open-square corner)
    =>
    (retract ?phase)
    (assert (move move-to-corner)))

(defrule pick-side
    ?phase <- (choose-move)
    (open-square side)
    =>
    (retract ?phase)
    (assert (move move-to-side)))
```

Notice that if a middle, corner, and side square are all available, all three rules will be placed on the agenda. When rule *pick-middle* is fired, the retraction of the control fact will remove the other rules from the agenda. All three rules are thus very closely interrelated. It is not possible to understand the intent of each of these rules without seeing all the rules together. This violates a basic concept of rule-based programming. As much as possible, a rule should represent a completely expressed heuristic. In this case, salience is used to express an implicit relationship among these rules that could be explicitly stated with additional patterns in the rules. The rules can be rewritten without salience as follows.

```
(defrule pick-middle
   ?phase <- (choose-move)
   (open-square middle)
   =>
   (retract ?phase)
   (assert (move move-to-middle)))

(defrule pick-corner
   ?phase <- (choose-move)
   (open-square corner)
   (not (open-square middle))
   =>
   (retract ?phase)
   (assert (move move-to-corner)))

(defrule pick-side
   ?phase <- (choose-move)
   (open-square side)
   (not (open-square corner))
   (not (open-square middle))
   =>
   (retract ?phase)
   (assert (move move-to-side)))
```

Adding the additional patterns to the rules explicitly states the conditions under which the rules are applicable. The tight interaction between the rules is removed allowing the rules to act opportunistically. Rewriting the rules also demonstrates that the original heuristics could have been expressed more clearly.

```
If the middle square is open, then take it.
If a corner square is open, and
   the middle square is not open, then take it.
If a side square is open, and
   the middle square is not open, and
   a corner square is not open, then take it
```

As stated in Chapter 9, salience should primarily be used to aid controlling the flow of execution. For this purpose, few programs if any should ever require more than five salience values.

11.11   GENERAL RULES VS. SPECIFIC RULES

It is not always obvious whether many specific rules will perform more efficiently than fewer more general rules. Specific rules tend to isolate much of the pattern matching process in the pattern network, reducing the amount of work in the join network. General rules often provide more opportunity for sharing in the pattern and join networks. A single rule can also be more maintainable than a larger group of specific rules. General rules, however, need to be written carefully. Since they tend to perform the work of several rules, it is much easier to write an inefficient general rule than a inefficient specific rule. To illustrate the differences of the two techniques, consider the following four rules which will update a fact containing the grid coordinates of an object which can move north, south, east, or west. The location fact contains the x and y coordinates of the object. A move north increases the value of the y coordinate. A move east increases the value of the x coordinate.

```
(defrule move-north
   (move north)
   ?old-location <- (location ?x ?y)
   =>
   (retract ?old-location)
   (assert (location ?x =(+ ?y 1))))

(defrule move-south
   (move south)
   ?old-location <- (location ?x ?y)
   =>
   (retract ?old-location)
   (assert (location ?x =(- ?y 1))))

(defrule move-east
   (move east)
   ?old-location <- (location ?x ?y)
   =>
   (retract ?old-location)
   (assert (location =(+ ?x 1) ?y)))

(defrule move-west
   (move west)
   ?old-location <- (location ?x ?y)
```

```
         =>
         (retract ?old-location)
         (assert (location =(- ?x 1) ?y)))
```

The four previous rules can be replaced with a single, more general, rule and a deffacts statement:

```
    (deffacts direction-information
        (direction north  0  1)
        (direction south  0 -1)
        (direction east   1  0)
        (direction west  -1  0))

    (defrule move-direction
        (move ?dir)
        (direction ?dir ?dx ?dy)
        ?old-location <- (location ?x ?y)
        =>
        (retract ?old-location)
        (assert (location =(+ ?x ?dx) =(+ ?y ?dy))))
```

where ?dx and ?dy are the delta x and delta y values which need to be added to the x and y values of the old location to obtain the x and y values for the new location.

This new rule requires more work in creating partial matches to determine the delta x and delta y to add to the current location. However, it provides a level of abstraction which makes it very simple to add more directions. To move northeast, southeast, northwest, and southwest would require the addition of four new specific rules. The general example only requires the addition of four new facts in the deffacts statement as shown following.

```
    (deffacts direction-information
        (direction north     0  1)
        (direction south     0 -1)
        (direction east      1  0)
        (direction west     -1  0)
        (direction northeast  1  1)
        (direction southeast  1 -1)
        (direction northwest -1  1)
        (direction southwest -1 -1))
```

11.12   SIMPLE RULES VS. COMPLEX RULES

Rule-based languages allow many problems to be expressed in a very simple, yet elegant manner. Although not specifically designed for algorithmic or computational problems, CLIPS can be easily used to find the largest number of a group of numbers. The following rule and associated deffacts will assert a group of sample numbers which will be used as test data by the rule which finds the largest number.

```
(deffacts max-num
    (loop-max 100))

(defrule loop-assert
    (loop-max ?n)
    =>
    (bind ?i 1)
    (while (<= ?i ?n) do
        (assert (number ?i))
        (bind ?i (+ ?i 1)))))
```

The simplest way of finding the largest number was demonstrated in Chapter 9. As shown below, one rule can be used to find the largest number.

```
(defrule largest-number
    (number ?number1)
    (not (number ?number2&:(> ?number2 ?number1)))
    =>
    (printout t "Largest number is " ?number1 crlf))
```

This rule, while simple, is not the fastest method for finding the largest number. If N represents the number of facts with the *number* relation, then both the first and second pattern will have a number of pattern matches equal to N. Even though there will only be one partial match for the first two patterns, N-squared comparisons will have to be performed to find that partial match. Increasing the value of the *loop-max* fact to values of 200, 300, 400, etc. will demonstrate that the time to run the problem is proportional to the square of N.

This type of comparison is extremely inefficient because as each number is added, it is compared to *all* of the other numbers to determine if it is the largest number. For example, if the facts representing the numbers 2 through 200 have already been asserted and the fact representing the number 1 is asserted, then 199 comparisons will be made to determine if 1 is the largest number. The fact (number 1) will match the first pattern, so it will be compared to the 99 facts matching the second pattern to determine if it is the largest. The first comparison will fail (because any of the numbers between 2 and 100 will be larger), but the remaining numbers will still be compared. Similarly, the fact (number 1) will match the second pattern so it will be compared to the 100 facts matching the first pattern (which now includes the (number 1) fact as well.

The key to speeding up the program is to prevent the unnecessary comparisons from occurring. This can be accomplished by using an additional fact to keep track of the largest number and comparing the *number* facts with it. The following rules show how this is done.

```
(defrule try-number
   (number ?n)
   =>
   (assert (try-number ?n)))

(defrule largest-unknown
   ?attempt <- (try-number ?n)
   (not (largest ?))
   =>
   (retract ?attempt)
   (assert (largest ?n)))

(defrule largest-smaller
   ?old-largest <- (largest ?n1)
   ?attempt <- (try-number ?n2&:(> ?n2 ?n1))
   =>
   (retract ?old-largest ?attempt)
   (assert (largest ?n2)))

(defrule largest-bigger
   (largest ?n1)
   ?attempt <- (try-number ?n2&:(<= ?n2 ?n1))
   =>
   (retract ?attempt))

(defrule print-largest
   (declare (salience -1))
   (largest ?number)
   =>
   (printout t "Largest number is " ?number crlf))
```

Running this program for *max-loop* values of 100, 200, 300, 400, etc. will demonstrate that the time to run this program is proportional to N. This is even more interesting considering that the first program will fire only 2 rules while the second program will fire approximately 2N rules. The second group of rules demonstrate that a rule should not only try to limit the number of partial matches it has, but it should also limit the number of comparisons needed for determining the partial matches. As demonstrated by the first rule, if the first pattern has N pattern matches and the second pattern has N matches, then the rule will make N-squared comparisons in determining the partial matches for the first two patterns. Even if no partial matches are generated, the computational time spent will be roughly equivalent to having generated N-squared partial matches. The second group of rules limits the number of comparisons that will be made to N. Since only one *largest* fact exists at a time, the largest number of partial matches that could be generated for the rules would be N, which limits the maximum computational time to that of generating N partial matches.

This example demonstrates two important concepts. First, the easiest way to code a problem in a rule-based language is not necessarily the best. Second, the number of comparisons performed can often be reduced by using temporary facts to store data. The *largest* fact is used in this problem to store the value for later comparison so that all the *number* facts do not have to be searched when comparing.

11.13 SUMMARY

This chapter has demonstrated the importance of matching facts against rules in an efficient manner. The Rete Algorithm was introduced as an efficient algorithm for this matching process. The Rete Algorithm works efficiently because it takes advantage of the temporal redundancy and structural similarity exhibited by rule-based expert systems.

Rules are converted into data structures in a rule network. This network consists of a pattern network and a join network. The pattern network matches facts against patterns and the join network insures that variable bindings across pattern are consistent. The importance of ordering patterns correctly was demonstrated with a rule that produced large numbers of partial matches when its patterns were poorly ordered. A technique for viewing the generation of partial matches by splitting rules into multiple rules was demonstrated. The general rules for ordering patterns by placing the most specific patterns and patterns matching the fewest facts first in the LHS and placing the most volatile patterns last in the LHS was discussed.

Other topics of efficiency such as the use of multifield variables, the positioning of test patterns, the use of built-in pattern matching primitives, and the misuse of salience were also discussed. Finally, the tradeoffs associated with writing general vs. specific rules and simple vs. complex rules were shown.

PROBLEMS AND PROGRAMS

11-1. List the pattern node expressions generated for the fields of the following patterns.

a) (altitude 100)
b) (altitude ?x&:(> ?x 100))

c)   (data ~red ~green)
d)   (color bluelwhite)

11-2.   Draw the pattern network for the following group of patterns.

```
(data red green blue)
(data ~red)
(item ? ?y ?x&:(> ?x ?y))
(item red blue|yellow)
(data red ?x)
```

11-3.   Draw the pattern and join network for the following rules. List the expressions evaluated at each node.

```
(defrule rule1
  (phase testing)
  (data ?x ?y)
  (data ?y ?x&:(> ?x ?y))
  =>)
```

```
(defrule rule2
  (phase testing)
  (data ?x ?y)
  (data ?y&~red ?x&~green)
  =>)
```

11-4.   Rewrite the following rule to make it more efficient.

```
(defrule bad-rule
  (items ?x1 ?x2 ?x3)
  (items ?y1 ?y2 ?y3)
  (items ?z1 ?z2 ?z3)
  (test (and (or (eq ?z1 green)
                 (eq ?z1 red))
             (eq ?y3 ?z2)
             (> ?x2 ?x1)
             (< ?x3 ?x1)
             (neq ?z3 ?x1)))
  =>)
```

11-5.   Figure 11-7 shows a fault network for a hypothetical piece of equipment. The arrows indicate the direction in which faults will be propagated. For example, if component A has a fault, then components B and C will also have faults. The following rules will propagate faults throughout the network.

```
(defrule propagate-device-A-fault
  (fault device-A)
  =>
  (assert (fault device-B))
  (assert (fault device-C)))

(defrule propagate-device-C-fault
  (fault device-C)
  =>
  (assert (fault device-D))
  (assert (fault device-E)))

(defrule propagate-device-E-fault
  (fault device-E)
  =>
  (assert (fault device-F)))
```

Rewrite these three rules as one general rule and a deffacts statement that will propagate the faults as these three rules do. Explain the changes that must be made for each of these approaches when a new device is added to the fault network.

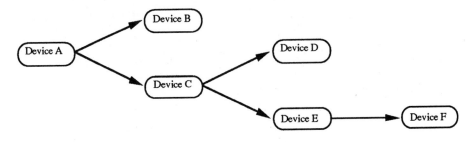

Figure 11-7
A Fault Network for a Hypothetical Machine

11-6.   List the pattern matches and partial matches created for the following rule

```
(defrule generate-matches
  (number ?x)
  (number ?y&:(> ?y ?x))
  (number ?z&:(> ?z ?y))
  (number ?w&:(> ?w ?z))
  =>)
```

when the following facts are asserted.

```
f-1    (number 1)
f-2    (number 2)
f-3    (number 3)
f-4    (number 4)
f-5    (number 5)
```

BIBLIOGRAPHY

Lee Brownston, *et al.*, *Programming Expert Systems in OPS5: An Introduction to Rule-Based Programming*, Addison-Wesley, 1985.

Charles L. Forgy, "Rete: A Fast Algorithm for the Many Pattern/Many Object Pattern Match Problem," *Artificial Intelligence*, **19,** pp 17-37, 1985.

Charles L. Forgy, "On the Efficient Implementation of Production Systems," Ph.D. Thesis, Carnegie-Mellon University, 1979.

CHAPTER 12 EXPERT SYSTEM DESIGN EXAMPLES

12.1 INTRODUCTION

This chapter provides several examples of CLIPS programs. The first example demonstrates how uncertainty can be represented in CLIPS. The next two examples demonstrate how other knowledge representation paradigms can be emulated using CLIPS. The second example shows how decision trees can be represented in CLIPS and the third example shows how backward chaining rules can be represented in CLIPS. The forth and final example builds the framework of a simple monitoring expert system that monitors a group of sensors.

12.2 CERTAINTY FACTORS AND CLIPS

CLIPS has no built-in capabilities for handling uncertainty. However, it is possible to incorporate uncertainty into CLIPS by placing information dealing with uncertainty directly into facts and rules. As an example, the MYCIN uncertainty mechanism will be emulated using CLIPS. This section will demonstrate how the following MYCIN rule can be rewritten in CLIPS.

```
IF
     The stain of the organism is gramneg AND
     The morphology of the organism is rod AND
     The patient is a compromised host
THEN
     There is suggestive evidence (0.6) that the
         identity of the organism is pseudomonas
```

MYCIN represents factual information as Object-Attribute-Value triples. These OAV triples can be represented in CLIPS using the following fact template.

```
(<object> <attribute> <value>)
```

Using this template, some of the facts required by the IF portion of the preceding MYCIN rule would be

```
(organism stain gramneg)
(organism morphology rod)
(patient is-a compromised-host)
```

MYCIN also associates a certainty factor (CF) with each fact which represents a degree of belief in the fact. The certainty factor ranges from -1 to 1 where -1 means the fact is known to be false, 1 means the fact is known to be true, and 0 means no information is known about the fact (complete uncertainty).

Since CLIPS does not handle certainty factors automatically, this information must also be maintained. To do this, an additional field in each fact will be used to represent the certainty factor. The OAV template for each fact now becomes

```
(<object> <attribute> <value> <certainty-factor>)
```

and the examples facts might be

```
(organism stain gramneg 0.3)
(organism morphology rod 0.7)
(patient is-a compromised-host 0.8)
```

One further modification must be made to the OAV template. MYCIN allows the same OAV triple to be derived by separate rules. The OAV triples are then combined to produce a single OAV triple that combines the certainty factors of the two OAV triples. The current OAV template will allow two identical OAV triples to be asserted only if the two have different certainty factors. In order to allow identical OAV triples to be asserted with the same certainty factors, a fifth field will be added to the OAV template to tag each fact uniquely. A unique tag will be generated for each fact using the *gensym* function. The final OAV fact template is now

```
(<object> <attribute> <value>
          <certainty-factor> <tag>)
```

and the examples facts using this template might be

```
(organism stain gramneg 0.3 gen1)
(organism morphology rod 0.7 gen2)
(organism morphology rod 0.5 gen3)
(patient is-a compromised-host 0.8 gen4)
(patient is-a compromised-host 0.8 gen5)
```

As stated, MYCIN will combines two identical OAV triples into a single OAV triple with a combined certainty. If the certainty factors of the two facts (represented by CF_1 and CF_2) are both greater than or equal to zero, MYCIN uses the following formula to compute the new certainty factor

```
New Certainty = (CF₁ + CF₂) - (CF₁ * CF₂)
```

For example, assume that the following facts are in the fact-list.

```
(organism morphology rod 0.7 gen2)
(organism morphology rod 0.5 gen3)
```

Let C_1 be 0.7 and C_2 be 0.5, then the new certainty for the combination of the two facts is computed as following

```
New Certainty = (0.7 + 0.5) - (0.7 * 0.5)
              = 1.2 - 0.35
              = 0.85
```

and the new fact to replace the two original facts would then be

```
(organism morphology rod 0.85 gen6)
```

Since CLIPS does not automatically handle certainty factors for facts, it follows that it also does not automatically combine two OAV triples derived from different rules. The combination of OAV triples can be easily handled by a rule which searches the fact-list for identical OAV triples to be combined. The following rule demonstrates how this can be accomplished when the certainty factors of both OAV triples are greater than zero.

```
(defrule combine-certainties-both-positive
    ?fact1 <- (?object ?attribute ?value
                        ?C1&:(>= ?C1 0) ?)
    ?fact2 <- (?object ?attribute ?value
                        ?C2&:(>= ?C1 0) ?)
    (test (neq ?fact1 ?fact2))
    =>
    (retract ?fact1 ?fact2)
    (bind ?C3 (- (+ ?C1 ?C2) (* ?C1 ?C2)))
    (assert (?object ?attribute ?value
                     ?C3 =(gensym))))
```

Notice that the fact identifiers ?fact1 and ?fact2 are compared to each other in the test pattern. This is to insure that the rule does not match using the exact same fact for the first two patterns. The functions eq and neq are able to compare fact addresses. In addition to the *retract* command, these are the only places that fact identifiers may be used. Alternately, instead of comparing the fact addresses, the tags for each fact could also be compared for inequality.

The next step in implementing certainty factors is to link the certainty factors of the facts which match the LHS of the rule to the certainty factors of the facts asserted by the RHS of the rule. In MYCIN, the certainty factor associated with the LHS of a rule is derived using the following formulas

```
CF (P₁ or P₂) = max { CF (P₁), CF (P₂) }
CF (P₁ and P₂) = min { CF (P₁), CF (P₂) }
CF (not P) = - CF (P)
```

where P, P_1, and P_2 represent patterns of the LHS. Additionally, if the certainty factor of the LHS is less than 0.2, the rule is considered to be inapplicable and will not be fired.

The certainty factor of a fact asserted from the RHS of a rule is derived by multiplying the certainty factor of the assertion by the certainty factor of the LHS of the rule. The following CLIPS rule translation of the MYCIN rule introduced at the beginning of this section demonstrates the computation of LHS and RHS certainty factors.

```
(defrule MYCIN-to-CLIPS-translation
    (organism stain gramneg ?C1 ?)
    (organism morphology rod ?C2 ?)
    (patient is-a compromised-host ?C3 ?)
    (test (> (min ?C1 ?C2 ?C3) 0.2))
    =>
    (bind ?C4 (* (min ?C1 ?C2 ?C3) 0.6))
    (assert (organism identity pseudomonas
                      ?C4 =(gensym))))
```

Two more steps are required for completing the MYCIN certainty factor emulation. First, the *combine-certainties-both-positive* rule only handles one case of certainty factor combination. The remaining combination cases are

$$\text{New Certainty} = (CF_1 + CF_2) + (CF_1 * CF_2)$$

$$\text{if} \quad CF_1 \leq 0 \text{ and } CF_2 \leq 0$$

$$\text{New Certainty} = \frac{CF_1 + CF_2}{1 - \min \{ |CF_1|, |CF_2| \}}$$

$$\text{if} \quad -1 < CF_1 * CF_2 < 0$$

Finally, the rules which combine the certainty factors should be given a higher salience than the other rules. It will normally be desirable to combine certainty values as soon as possible. The certainty combination rules would most likely be placed in the salience hierarchy at the highest level in an expert system using this certainty factor technique.

12.3   DECISION TREES

This section will provide algorithms for traversing several types of decision trees and show how a decision tree that learns can be represented in CLIPS. Decision trees, as discussed in Chapter 3, provide a useful paradigm for solving certain types of classification problems. Problems suitable for decision trees are typified by two primary characteristics. First, they provide the answer to a problem from a predetermined set of possible answers. Taxonomy and diagnosis problems generally meet this requirement. For example, a taxonomy problem might require the identification of a gem from the set of all known gems. A diagnosis problem might require the selection of a possible remedy from a set of remedies or the selection of the cause of a failure from a set of possible causes. Because the answer set must be predetermined, decision trees do not work well for scheduling, planning, or synthesis problems. In general, decision trees will not work well for problems which must generate solutions in addition to selecting them. The second characteristic of decision trees is the manner in which they derive a solution by reducing the set of possible solutions with a series of decisions or questions that prune the search space of the decision tree.

A decision tree is composed of nodes and branches. Nodes represent locations in the tree. These locations can either be decision nodes or answer nodes. Branches represent connections between nodes. Branches connect parent nodes to child nodes when moving from top to bottom and connect child nodes to parent nodes when moving from bottom to top. The node at the top of the tree which has no parent is called the root node. Note that in a tree, every node has only one parent, with the exception of the root node, which has none. Nodes with no children are called leaves.

The leaf nodes of a decision tree represent each of the possible solutions that can be derived from the tree. These nodes will be referred to as answer nodes. All other nodes in the tree will be referred to as decision nodes. Each decision node represents a question or decision which when answered or decided determines the appropriate branch of the decision tree to follow. In simple decision trees this question could be a yes/no question such as "Is the animal warm blooded?" The left branch of the node would represent the path to follow if the question is answered yes and the right branch of the node would represent the path to follow if the question is answered no. In general, a decision node may use any criteria to select which branch to follow as the selection process yields a single branch to follow. Thus, decision nodes may select a branch corresponding to a set or range of values, a series of cases, or functions mapping from the state at the decision node to the branches of the decision node. Sophisticated decision nodes might even allow backtracking or probabilistic reasoning.

To illustrate the operation of a decision tree, consider the following heuristics for selecting the appropriate color wine to serve with a meal.

```
IF the main course is red meat
THEN serve red wine
```

```
IF the main course is poultry and it is turkey
THEN serve red wine

IF the main course is poultry and it is not turkey
THEN serve white wine

IF the main course is fish
THEN serve white wine.
```

The representation of the wine heuristics as a binary decision tree is shown in Figure 12-1. The decision nodes assume that each question can only be answered with a yes or no response. A default answer node containing the answer "The best color is unknown" has been added to the set of heuristics in the event that the main course is neither red meat, poultry, nor fish. The procedure for traversing the tree to reach an answer node is quite simple. The inferencing process is started by setting the current location in the decision tree to the root node. If the current location is a decision node, then the question associated with the decision node must be answered in some manner (typically by the person consulting the decision tree). If the answer to the question is yes, then the current location is set to the child node connected to the yes branch of the current location (the left branch). If the answer to the question is no, then the current location is set to the child node connect to the no branch of the current location (the right branch). If at any point an answer node becomes the current location, then the value of the answer node is the answer derived through consultation with the decision tree. Otherwise the procedure for handling a decision node is repeated until an answer node is finally reached. The pseudocode for this algorithm is as follows:

```
procedure Solve_Binary_Tree
    Set the current location in the tree
        to the root node.
    while the current location is a decision node do
        Ask the question at the current node.
        If the reply to the question is yes
            Set the current node to the yes branch.
        else
            Set the current node to the no branch.
        end if
    end do
    Return the answer at the current node.
end procedure
```

Decision Trees with Multiple Branches

Decision trees that allow only binary branches from a decision node make it difficult to represent a decision that allows for a set of responses or a series of cases. The binary

decision tree constructed for the wine example provides a good example of this inefficiency. In the event that the main course is fish, three decisions must be made before it
can be determined that the best color is white. That is, the questions, "Is the main
course red meat?", "Is the main course poultry?", and "Is the main course fish?" must
all be asked. A much more direct question that would allow the decision node to be
expressed succinctly is "What is the main course?". A decision node capable of handling this question must allow multiple branches given a series of possible decisions
(in this case red meat, poultry, fish, and other). Figure 12-2 shows the modified decision tree show of Figure 12-1 that now allows multiple branches. A simple modification in the *Solve_Binary_Tree* algorithm allows multiple branches to be used and is
shown as follows:

```
procedure Solve_Tree
    Set the current location in the tree
        to the root node.
    while the current location is a decision node do
        Ask the question at the current node until an
            answer in the set of valid choices for this
            node has been provided.
        Set the current node to the child node of the
            branch associated with the choice selected.
    end do
    Return the answer at the current node.
end procedure
```

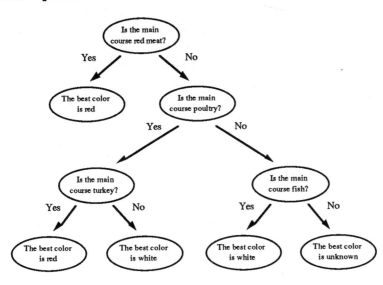

Figure 12-1
Binary Decision Tree

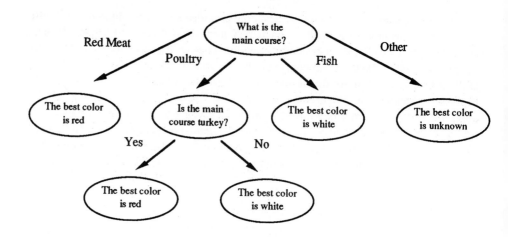

Figure 12-2
Decision Tree with Multiple Branches

Decision Trees that Learn

Occasionally it is useful to add new knowledge to a decision tree as it is learned. A commonly used example that demonstrates this technique is an animal identification decision tree. This decision tree asks a series of questions to determine the identity of an animal. Once the decision tree has reached an answer, it asks if it is the correct answer. If it is the correct answer, then nothing more is done. If the answer is incorrect, however, the decision tree is modified to accommodate the correct answer. The answer node is replaced with a decision node that contains a question that will differentiate between the old answer that was at the node and the answer that was not correctly guessed. Figure 12-3 shows a decision tree that will classify an animal by characteristics. The decision tree is somewhat naive (having knowledge of only three animals) and is in need of learning. An example guessing session with the tree might proceed as follows:

```
Is the animal warm-blooded? (yes or no) yes⏎
Does the animal purr? (yes or no) no⏎
I guess it is a dog
Am I correct? (yes or no) no⏎
What is the animal? bird⏎
What question when answered yes will distinguish
a bird from a dog? Does the animal fly?⏎
Now I can guess bird
Try again? (yes or no) no⏎
```

The session can continue on and on with the decision tree learning more and more information. Figure 12-4 shows the representation of the decision tree after the session shown above. One drawback to learning in this manner is that the decision tree may not end up being very hierarchically structured or very efficient in guessing the appropriate animal. An efficient decision tree should have the number of branches from root to answer nodes to be approximately the same for all paths.

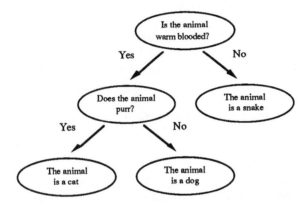

Figure 12-3
Animal Identification Decision Tree

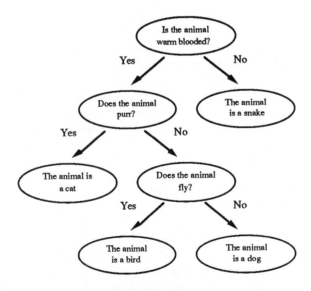

Figure 12-4
Animal Identification Decision Tree after Learning Bird

The pseudocode to modify the *Solve_Tree* algorithm to incorporate learning is shown below:

```
procedure Solve_Tree_and_Learn

    Set the current location in the tree
        to the root node

    while the current location is a decision node do
        Ask the question at the current node.
        if the reply to the question is yes
            Set the current node to the yes branch.
        else
            Set the current node to the no branch.
        end if
    end do


    Ask if the answer at the current node is correct.
    if the answer is correct
        Return the correct answer.
    else
        Determine the correct answer.
        Determine a question which when answered yes
            will distinguish the answer at the current
            node from the correct answer.
        Replace the answer node with a decision node
            that has as its no branch the current answer
            node and as its yes branch an answer node
            with the correct answer. The decision node's
            question should be the question which
            distinguishes the two answer nodes.
    end if
end  procedure
```

A Rule-based Decision Tree Program

The first step in determining how a learning decision tree can be implemented in CLIPS is to decide how the knowledge should be represented. Since the decision tree must learn, it will probably be worthwhile to represent the decision tree as facts instead of rules. Facts can easily be added and removed to update the decision tree as it learns. A set of CLIPS rules can be used to traverse the decision tree by implementing the *Solve_Tree_and_Learn* algorithm using a rule-based approach.

Each node of the decision tree will be represented by a fact. Since the answer nodes and decision nodes hold different types of information, it will be necessary to use different templates for the different nodes. An answer node will use the following template

```
(node <name> answer <value>)
```

where <name> is the unique name for the node and <value> represents the answer stored in the node. Notice that the word *answer* is used to indicate an answer node.

A decision node will use the following template

```
(node <name> decision <question>
      <yes-node> <no-node>)
```

where <name> is the unique name for the node, <question> is the question that is asked when this node is traversed, <yes-node> is the node to proceed to if the question is answered affirmatively, and <no-node> is the node to proceed to if the question is answered negatively. Notice that the word *decision* is used to indicate a decision node.

Because the animal program will learn, it will be necessary to store information about what has been learned from one run of the program to the next. Since the decision tree will be structured as a collection of facts, it will be useful to store them in a file in the *load-facts* command format and assert them using the *load-facts* command when the program begins and save them using the *save-facts* command when the program finishes. For this program, the facts will be stored in a file called "animal.dat". If Figure 12-3 is used for the initial decision tree then the file "animal.dat" should contain the following text. Notice that the root node has been labeled as such and each of the other nodes has been given a unique name.

```
(node root  decision "Is the animal warm-blooded?"
            node1 node2)
(node node1 decision "Does the animal purr?"
            node3 node4)
(node node2 answer snake)
(node node3 answer cat)
(node node4 answer dog)
```

Now the rules to traverse the decision tree must be written. The following rule will initialize the learning decision tree program.

```
(defrule initialize
   (not (node root $?))
   =>
   (load-facts "animal.dat")
   (assert (current-node root)))
```

This *initialize* rule will fire if the root node is not present in the fact-list. Notice the use of the multifield variable in the pattern condition. The root node may be either an answer node or a decision node. The multifield variable allows either type of node to match the pattern. The actions of the *initialize* rule load the decision tree representation into the fact-list and assert a fact indicating that the current node of interest is the root node.

The next rule executes the actions needed at a decision node.

```
(defrule do-decision-node
    ?node <- (current-node ?name)
    (node ?name decision ?question
         ?yes-branch ?no-branch)
    =>
    (retract ?node)
    (format t "%s (yes or no) " ?question)
    (bind ?answer (read))
    (if (eq ?answer yes)
       then (assert (current-node ?yes-branch))
       else (assert (current-node ?no-branch))))
```

The second pattern matches against the current node only if it is a decision node. The *current-node* fact is retracted and and then updated with a new assertion that is dependent upon the answer to the question.

The next rule handles the actions needed at an answer node.

```
(defrule do-answer-node
    ?node <- (current-node ?name)
    (node ?name answer ?value)
    =>
    (printout t "I guess it is a " ?value crlf)
    (printout t "Am I correct? (yes or no) ")
    (bind ?answer (read))
    (if (eq ?answer yes)
       then (assert (ask-try-again))
            (retract ?node)
       else (assert (replace-answer-node))))
```

Again, the second pattern matches against the current node only if it is an answer node. If the value of the answer node is verified to be the correct answer, then the *ask-try-again* fact is asserted to indicate the user should be asked to continue. The *current-node* fact is also retracted since it is no longer of use. If the answer is wrong, then learning will occur and the *replace-answer-node* fact is asserted.

The following rule is used to determine if the user wishes to continue.

```
(defrule try-again
   ?phase <- (ask-try-again)
   =>
   (retract ?phase)
   (printout t "Try again? (yes or no) ")
   (bind ?answer (read))
   (if (eq ?answer yes)
       then (assert (current-node root))
       else (save-facts "animal.dat")))
```

If the "Try again?" question is answered yes, the current-node fact will be reset to the root node. Otherwise the facts representing the decision tree are saved to the "animal.dat" file using the *save-facts* command. Notice that the *ask-play-again* control fact has been retracted before the facts are saved to prevent unnecessary facts being added to the file.

Finally, if the answer was wrong the following rule will add a new decision node allowing the decision tree to learn.

```
(defrule replace-answer-node
   ?phase <- (replace-answer-node)
   ?node <- (current-node ?ptr)
   ?data <- (node ?ptr answer ?value)
   =>
   (retract ?phase ?node ?data)
   ; Determine what the guess should have been
   (printout t "What is the animal? ")
   (bind ?new-animal (read))
   ; Get the question for the guess
   (printout t "What question when answered yes ")
   (printout t "will distinguish " crlf "a ")
   (printout t ?new-animal " from a " ?value "? ")
   (bind ?question (readline))
   (printout t "Now I can guess " ?new-animal crlf)
   ; Create the new learned nodes
   (bind ?newnode1 (gensym))
   (bind ?newnode2 (gensym))
   (assert (node ?newnode1 answer ?new-animal))
   (assert (node ?newnode2 answer ?value))
   (assert (node ?ptr decision ?question
                               ?newnode1 ?newnode2))
   ; Determine if the player wants to try again
   (assert (ask-try-again)))
```

The *replace-answer node* rule retracts the *node* fact representing the incorrect answer that was given. It then asks for the correct identification of the animal and for a question which will distinguish this animal from the animal that the decision tree had identified as the correct answer. A decision node and two answer nodes are created to replace the old answer node with the newly learned information. The *gensym* function is used to provide a unique tag for each of the two new answer nodes. The *ask-try-again* fact is then asserted to determine if another run of the program should be made.

A Step-by-Step Trace of the Decision Tree Program

The behavior of the decision tree program can be observed by watching its execution. Assuming that decision tree rules have been loaded and the file "animal.dat" containing the facts representing the initial decision tree has been created, the following dialog shows the state of the system after a *reset* command has been performed.

```
CLIPS>  (watch all)↵
CLIPS>  (reset)↵
==> Activation 0      initialize:
==> f-0      (initial-fact)
CLIPS>  (agenda)↵
0      initialize:
CLIPS>
```

The *initialize* rule has been activated by the absence of the *root node* fact. Allowing the *initialize* rule to fire will load in the decision tree.

```
CLIPS>  (run 1)↵
FIRE    1 initialize:
==> f-1      (node root decision "Is the animal warm-
blooded?" node1 node2)
==> f-2      (node node1 decision "Does the animal
purr?" node3 node4)
==> f-3      (node node2 answer snake)
==> f-4      (node node3 answer cat)
==> f-5      (node node4 answer dog)
==> f-6      (current-node root)
==> Activation 0      do-decision-node: f-6,f-1
rule firing limit reached
1 rules fired
CLIPS>  (agenda)↵
0      do-decision-node: f-6,f-1
CLIPS>
```

The *initialize* rule uses the load-fact function to load in the decision tree. The *current-node* fact is set to the *root node* fact. Since the root node is a decision node, the *do-decision-node* rule is activated. Allowing this rule to fire produces the following dialog.

```
CLIPS> (run 1)↵
FIRE    1 do-decision-node: f-6,f-1
<== f-6      (current-node root)
Is the animal warm-blooded? (yes or no) yes↵
==> f-7      (current-node node1)
==> Activation 0      do-decision-node: f-7,f-2
rule firing limit reached
1 rules fired
CLIPS> (agenda)↵
0       do-decision-node: f-7,f-2
CLIPS>
```

The question associated with the root decision node is "Is the animal warm blooded?". Since the reply to the question if yes, the left node of the decision node which is node1 is made the current node. Since node1 is also a decision node, the rule *do-decision-node* is activated again. Allowing this rule to fire again produces the following dialog.

```
CLIPS> (run 1)↵
FIRE    1 do-decision-node: f-7,f-2
<== f-7      (current-node node1)
Does the animal purr? (yes or no) no↵
==> f-8      (current-node node4)
==> Activation 0      do-answer-node: f-8,f-5
rule firing limit reached
1 rules fired
CLIPS> (agenda)↵
0       do-answer-node: f-8,f-5
CLIPS>
```

The question associated with the node1 decision node is "Does the animal purr?" Since the reply to the question if no, the right node of the decision node which is node4 is made the current node. Since node4 is an answer node, the rule *do-answer-node* is activated. Allowing this rule to fire produces the following dialog.

```
CLIPS> (run 1)↵
FIRE    1 do-answer-node: f-8,f-5
I guess it is a dog
Am I correct? (yes or no) no↵
```

```
==> f-9      (replace-answer-node)
==> Activation 0        replace-answer-node: f-9,f-8,f-
5
rule firing limit reached
1 rules fired
CLIPS> (agenda) ↵
0       replace-answer-node: f-9,f-8,f-5
CLIPS>
```

The guess associated with this answer node is dog. Since the guess is incorrect, the *replace-answer-node* rule is activated to determine the correct answer. Allowing this rule to fire produces the following dialog.

```
CLIPS> (run 1) ↵
FIRE    1 replace-answer-node: f-9,f-8,f-5
<== f-9      (replace-answer-node)
<== f-8      (current-node node4)
<== f-5      (node node4 answer dog)
What is the animal? bird↵
What question when answered yes will distinguish
a bird from a dog? Does the animal fly?↵
Now I can guess bird
==> f-10     (node gen9 answer bird)
==> f-11     (node gen10 answer dog)
==> f-12     (node node4 decision "Does the animal
fly?" gen9 gen10)
==> f-13     (ask-try-again)
==> Activation 0        try-again: f-13
rule firing limit reached
1 rules fired
CLIPS> (agenda)
0       try-again: f-13
CLIPS>
```

First, the control fact (replace-answer-node), the *current-node* fact, and the *node* fact associated with the *current-node* fact are retracted. The correct guess is then determined along with the question that will determine the correct guess. The facts with indices 10, 11, and 12 are then added which represent respectively the two new answer nodes and one new decision node. Finally, the *ask-try-again* control fact is asserted to determine if another identification is to be made. Allowing the *try-again* rule to fire produces the following dialog.

```
CLIPS> (run 1) ↵
FIRE    1 try-again: f-13
```

```
<== f-13     (ask-try-again)
Try again? (yes or no) no⏎
rule firing limit reached
1 rules fired
CLIPS> (agenda)⏎
CLIPS>
```

The *ask-try-again* control fact is retracted. The user is asked if another identification is to be made. Since the reply is no, the only action taken is to save the decision tree back to the "animal.dat" file. After this session, the final form of the "animal.dat" file is shown following.

```
(initial-fact)
(node root decision "Is the animal warm-blooded?"
node1 node2)
(node node1 decision "Does the animal purr?" node3
node4)
(node node2 answer snake)
(node node3 answer cat)
(node gen9 answer bird)
(node gen10 answer dog)
(node node4 decision "Does the animal fly?" gen9
gen10)
```

The node4 answer node has been replaced with a decision node that refers to two new answer nodes. Notice also that the initial-fact has been saved in this file. This additional fact will have no effect when the decision tree is loaded by the *initialize* rule, since it will already be in the fact-list.

12.4 BACKWARD CHAINING

CLIPS does not directly implement backward chaining as part of its inference engine. However, backward chaining; can be emulated using forward chaining CLIPS rules. This section will demonstrate how a simple backward chaining system can be built in CLIPS. It should be noted, however, that CLIPS is designed to be used as a forward chaining language. If a backward chaining approach is most suitable for solving a problem, then a language that directly implements backward chaining within its inference engine, such as PROLOG, should be used.

The CLIPS backward chaining system will be built with the following capabilities and limitations.

- Facts will be represented as Attribute-Value pairs.
- Backward chaining will be started with the assertion of a single goal attribute.

- Only the equality of an attribute to a specific value will be tested as a condition in the antecedent of a rule.
- The only action of the antecedent of a rule will be to assign the value of a single attribute.
- If the value of a goal attribute cannot be determined using rules, the backward chainer will ask for the value of the attribute to be supplied. Attributes cannot be assigned an unknown value.
- An attribute may only have a single value. Hypothetical reasoning about different attribute values from different rules will not be supported.
- Uncertainty will not be represented.

An Algorithm for the Backward Chainer

Before writing a backward chaining inference engine using CLIPS, it will be useful to consider a procedural algorithm before attempting a rule-based approach. The following pseudo-code procedure can be used to determine the value of a goal attribute using a backward chaining approach with the capabilities and limitations discussed previously.

```
procedure Solve_Goal(goal)
    goal: the current goal to be solved

    if value of the goal attribute is known
       Return the value of the goal attribute.
    end if

    for each rule whose consequent is the goal
    attribute do
       call Attempt_Rule with the rule
       if Attempt_Rule succeeded then
          Assign the goal attribute the value
          indicated by the consequent of the rule.
          Return the value of the goal attribute.
       end if
    end do

    Ask the user for the value of the goal attribute.
    Set the goal attribute to the value supplied
    by the user.
    Return the value of the goal attribute.

end procedure
```

Procedure *Solve_Goal* is passed a goal attribute as an argument. This procedure will determine the value of the goal attribute and return it. Procedure *Solve_Goal* first checks if the value of the goal attribute is already known. The value may have already been assigned as the consequent of another rule or supplied by the user of the backward chainer. If the value is indeed known, it is returned.

If the attribute value is not known, procedure *Solve_Goal* will attempt to determine the value by finding a rule which assigns the attribute a value as its consequent. Procedure *Solve_Goal* will attempt each rule that assigns a value to the goal attribute as its consequent until one of the rules succeeds. Procedure *Attempt_Rule* (which will be discussed in more detail shortly) is given each of the rules with the desired goal attribute to attempt. If the antecedent of the attempted rule is satisfied, the rule will succeed, otherwise it will fail. If the rule succeeds, the attribute value in the consequent of the rule is assigned to the goal attribute and this value is returned by procedure *Solve_Goal*. If the rule does not succeed, then the next rule which assigns a value to the goal attribute as its consequent is attempted.

If none of the rules succeed, then the user must be queried to determine the value of the goal attribute. The value supplied by the user is returned by procedure *Solve_Goal*.

Procedure *Attempt_Rule* is used to determine if the antecedent of a rule is satisfied. If the antecedent is satisfied, the consequent can be used to assign the value of a goal attribute. The pseudocode for this procedure is shown following.

```
procedure Attempt_Rule(rule)
    rule: rule to be attempted to solve goal

    for each condition in the antecedent
    of the rule do
        call Solve_Goal with condition attribute
        if the value returned by solve_goal is not
        equal to the value required by the condition
        then
            Return unsuccessful.
        end if
    end for

    Return successful

end procedure
```

Procedure *Attempt_Rule* will start at the first condition of a rule and attempt to prove it before attempting the subsequent conditions of the rule. In order to determine if a condition is satisfied, procedure *Attempt_Rule* must know the value of the attribute being tested in the condition. To determine the value, procedure *Solve_Goal* is called recursively. If the value returned by procedure *Solve_Goal* is not equal to the value required by the condition, then procedure *Attempt_Rule* exits with the return value of unsuccessful (remember that only equality is being tested in conditions). Otherwise the next condition of the rule is tested. If all conditions of the rule are satisfied, procedure *Attempt_Rule* exits with the return value of successful.

Representing Backward Chaining Rules in CLIPS

Once again, the first step in solving this problem is determining how the knowledge should be represented. Since CLIPS does not automatically perform backward chaining, it will be quite useful to represent backward chaining rules as facts so that the antecedents and consequents can be examined by rules which will act as a backward chaining inference engine. A template for representing backward chaining rules is shown following

```
(if <conditions> then <goal-attribute> is <value>)
```

where <conditions> is either

```
<attribute> is <value>
```

or

```
<attribute> is <value> and <conditions>
```

As an example of representing rules using this template, consider the decision tree shown in Figure 12-2. This tree can easily be converted to rules using AV pairs as described by the template. The pseudocode for the converted rules is shown following

```
IF main-course is red-meat
THEN best-color is red

IF main-course is poultry and
   meal-is-turkey is yes
THEN best-color is red

IF main-course is poultry and
   meal-is-turkey is no
THEN best-color is white

IF main-course is fish
THEN best-color is white
```

The attributes used in the rules are *main-course*, *meal-is-turkey*, and *best-color*. The *main-course* attribute corresponds to the answer determined by the decision tree question "What is the main course?". *The meal-is-turkey* attribute corresponds to the answer determined by the question "Is the main course turkey?". Notice that the branch of the decision tree which determines that the best color is unknown is not represented as a rule, since one of the limitations of our backward chainer is that unknown values are not represented. If the main course is not one of the ones which produce an answer, the user in this case will be asked the value of the *best-color* attribute.

The following deffacts show how the wine rules can be represented using the backward chaining rule template.

```
(deffacts wine-rules
   (if main-course is red-meat
    then best-color is red)
   (if main-course is fish
    then best-color is white)
   (if main-course is poultry and
       meal-is-turkey is yes
    then best-color is red)
   (if main-course is poultry and
       meal-is-turkey is no
    then best-color is white))
```

This representation provides a great deal of flexibility when manipulating the backward chaining rules. For example, if the attribute *main-course* is determined to have the value *poultry*, the facts

```
(if main-course is red-meat
 then best-color is red)
```

and

```
(if main-course is fish
 then best-color is white)
```

can be removed from the fact-list to indicate that these rules are not applicable, and the facts

```
(if main-course is poultry and
    meal-is-turkey is yes
 then best-color is red)
```

and

```
(if main-course is poultry and
    meal-is-turkey is no
 then best-color is white)
```

can be respectively modified to the facts

```
(if meal-is-turkey is yes
   then best-color is red)
```

and

```
(if meal-is-turkey is no
   then best-color is white)
```

to indicate that first condition of these two rules has been satisfied.

As backward chaining proceeds, goals will be generated to determine the value of attributes. A fact will be needed to represent information about goal attributes. The template for representing a goal attribute will be

```
(goal <attribute>)
```

Initially, the goal attribute is *best-color*. This can be represented using a deffacts as shown following.

```
(deffacts initial-goal
   (goal best-color))
```

When values for attributes are determined, it will be necessary to store these values. Values for known attributes will be stored using the following template.

```
(attribute <attribute-name> <value>)
```

The CLIPS Backward Chaining Inference Engine

The backward chaining inference engine can be implemented with two sets of rules. The first group will generate goals for attributes and ask the user to supply attribute values when these values cannot be determined by rules. The second group of rules will perform update operations. Update operations include modifying rules when their conditions have been satisfied and removing goals when they have been satisfied. The first set of rules are shown following.

```
(defrule attempt-rule
   (goal ?name)
   (not (attribute ?name ?))
   (if ?variable $? then ?name ? ?)
   =>
   (assert (goal ?variable)))
```

```
(defrule ask-attribute-value
   ?goal <- (goal ?name)
   (not (attribute ?name ?))
   (not (if $? then ?name ? ?))
   =>
   (retract ?goal)
   (printout t "What is the value of " ?name "? ")
   (assert (attribute ?name =(read))))
```

The *attempt-rule* rule searches for rules thats antecedent will supply the attribute value for a goal attribute. The first pattern matches against a goal attribute fact. The second pattern checks to see that the value of the goal attribute has not already been determined. The third pattern searches for all rules whose antecedent assigns a value to the goal attribute. For each rule found, the RHS of the *attempt-rule* rule will assert a goal to determine the value of the attribute tested by the first condition of the rule.

The *ask-attribute-value* rule is quite similar to the *attempt-rule* rule. Its first two patterns are identical. Its third pattern, however, checks that there are no remaining rules which can be used to determine the value of the goal attribute. In this case, the user is asked to supply the value of the attribute. A fact representing the attribute's value is asserted and the *goal* fact for the attribute is retracted.

The next four rules are used to update the backward chaining rules and goals which are represented as facts. These rules are given a salience of 100, so that updates will occur before any attempts are made to generate new goals or ask the user for attribute values.

```
(defrule goal-satisfied
   (declare (salience 100))
   ?goal <- (goal ?name)
   (attribute ?name ?)
   =>
   (retract ?goal))

(defrule rule-satisfied
   (declare (salience 100))
   (attribute ?name ?v-value)
   ?rule <- (if ?name ? ?v-value
               then ?goal ? ?g-value)
   =>
   (retract ?rule)
   (assert (attribute ?goal ?g-value)))

(defrule remove-rule-no-match
   (declare (salience 100))
   (attribute ?name ?value)
```

```
    ?rule <- (if ?name ? ~?value $?)
    =>
    (retract ?rule))

(defrule modify-rule-match
   (declare (salience 100))
   (attribute ?name ?value)
   ?rule <- (if ?name ? ?value and $?rest-if
              then ?goal is ?goal-value)
   =>
   (retract ?rule)
   (assert (if $?rest-if then ?goal is ?goal-value)))
```

The *goal-satisfied* rule removes any goals for which the attribute value has been determined.

The *rule-satisfied* rule searches for any rules that have a single remaining condition. If an attribute exists that satisfies this remaining condition, then the attribute value of the consequent of the rule is added to the fact-list.

The *remove-rule-no-match* rule searches for rules with one or more conditions thats first condition conflicts with a value assigned to an attribute. If this is the case, then the rule is removed from fact-list since it is not applicable.

The *modify-rule-match* rule searches for rules with more than one condition whose first condition is satisfied by a value assigned to an attribute. If such a rule is found, the first condition is removed from the rule to leave the the remaining conditions which must be tested.

Notice that the rules which perform backward chaining will also perform forward chaining. That is, if the antecedents of a rule are satisfied by attributes determined in the pursuit of other goals unrelated to the consequent of the rule, the consequent of the rule will be added.

A Step-by-Step Trace of the Backward Chainer

The behavior of the CLIPS backward chaining inference engine implemented using rules can be observed by watching its execution. Assuming that the *wine-rules* and *initial-goal* deffacts along with the backward chaining inference engine rules have been loaded, the initial state of the system after a *reset* command is shown below.

```
CLIPS> (reset) ↵
CLIPS> (facts) ↵
f-0     (initial-fact)
f-1     (if main-course is red-meat then best-color
is red)
f-2     (if main-course is fish then best-color is
white)
```

```
f-3       (if main-course is poultry and meal-is-turkey
is yes then best-color is red)
f-4       (if main-course is poultry and meal-is-turkey
is no then best-color is white)
f-5       (goal best-color)
CLIPS>  (agenda) ↵
0       attempt-rule: f-5,,f-1
0       attempt-rule: f-5,,f-2
0       attempt-rule: f-5,,f-3
0       attempt-rule: f-5,,f-4
CLIPS>
```

Notice that the agenda contains four activations of the *attempt-rule* rule. The starting goal is to determine the value of the *best-color* attribute as specified by fact f-5. Since the consequent of rule facts f-1, f-2, f-3, and f-4 each assign a value to the *best-color* attribute, each of these rules should be attempted to satisfy the *best-color* attribute goal.

The next step in execution is to fire the first activation of the *attempt-rule* rule. All watch features are activated before the rule is fired.

```
CLIPS>  (watch all) ↵
CLIPS>  (run 1) ↵
FIRE    1 attempt-rule: f-5,,f-1
==> f-6      (goal main-course)
==> Activation 0      ask-attribute-value: f-6,,
rule firing limit reached
1 rules fired
CLIPS>  (agenda) ↵
0       ask-attribute-value: f-6,,
0       attempt-rule: f-5,,f-2
0       attempt-rule: f-5,,f-3
0       attempt-rule: f-5,,f-4
CLIPS>
```

The attempt-rule rule fires based in part upon fact f-1 which represents the backward chaining rule shown following.

```
IF main-course is red-meat
THEN best-color is red
```

Before this rule can be applied to assign the value of the *best-color* attribute, the conditions in its antecedents must be satisfied. The first condition requires the value of the attribute main-course. Since this attribute is unknown, a goal is created for it. This goal is represented by fact f-6. Since there are no rules which assign the value of the *main-course* attribute, the rule *ask-attribute-value* rule is activated to determine its value.

Proceeding with execution, the *ask-attribute-value* rule fires to determine the value of the attribute *main-course*.

```
CLIPS>  (run 1)↵
FIRE    1 ask-attribute-value: f-6,,
<== f-6      (goal main-course)
What is the value of main-course? poultry↵
==> f-7      (attribute main-course poultry)
==> Activation 100    modify-rule-match: f-7,f-4
==> Activation 100    modify-rule-match: f-7,f-3
==> Activation 100    remove-rule-no-match: f-7,f-2
==> Activation 100    remove-rule-no-match: f-7,f-1
rule firing limit reached
1 rules fired
CLIPS>  (agenda)↵
100     remove-rule-no-match: f-7,f-1
100     remove-rule-no-match: f-7,f-2
100     modify-rule-match: f-7,f-3
100     modify-rule-match: f-7,f-4
0       attempt-rule: f-5,,f-2
0       attempt-rule: f-5,,f-3
0       attempt-rule: f-5,,f-4
CLIPS>
```

Since the user is being asked to supply the value of the *main-course* attribute, the goal for this attribute f-6 is removed. The value supplied by the user is asserted as the *attribute* fact f-7. The assertion of this fact causes four new activations to be placed on the agenda. The rules represented by facts f-3 and f-4 each require as their first condition that the *main-course* attribute is *poultry*. Since the value of the *main-course* attribute is *poultry*, both of these facts must be modified to represent that their first condition has been satisfied. Thus both facts cause activations of the *modify-rule-match* rule. The rules represented by facts f-1 and f-2 both require as their first condition that the *main-course* attribute is something other than *poultry*. Thus both of these facts representing rules are no longer applicable. The rule *remove-rule-no-match* is activated to cause both of them to be removed.

Allowing the two *remove-rule-no-match* activations to fire produces the following output.

```
CLIPS>  (run 2)↵
FIRE    1 remove-rule-no-match: f-7,f-1
<== f-1      (if main-course is red-meat then best-
color is red)
```

```
FIRE     2 remove-rule-no-match: f-7,f-2
<== f-2      (if main-course is fish then best-color
is white)
<== Activation 0      attempt-rule: f-5,,f-2
rule firing limit reached
2 rules fired
CLIPS> (agenda) ⏎
100     modify-rule-match: f-7,f-3
100     modify-rule-match: f-7,f-4
0       attempt-rule: f-5,,f-3
0       attempt-rule: f-5,,f-4
CLIPS>
```

The facts f-1 and f-2 are removed from the fact-list indicating that the rules represented by these facts are no longer applicable. The *attempt-rule* activations for these facts are removed from the agenda when the facts are removed.

Moving now to the execution of the two *modify-rule-match* activations produces the following output.

```
CLIPS>(run 2) ⏎
FIRE     1 modify-rule-match: f-7,f-3
<== f-3      (if main-course is poultry and meal-is-
turkey is yes then best-color is red)
<== Activation 0      attempt-rule: f-5,,f-3
==> f-8      (if meal-is-turkey is yes then best-color
is red)
==> Activation 0      attempt-rule: f-5,,f-8
FIRE     2 modify-rule-match: f-7,f-4
<== f-4      (if main-course is poultry and meal-is-
turkey is no then best-color is white)
<== Activation 0      attempt-rule: f-5,,f-4
==> f-9      (if meal-is-turkey is no then best-color
is white)
==> Activation 0      attempt-rule: f-5,,f-9
rule firing limit reached
2 rules fired
CLIPS> (agenda) ⏎
0       attempt-rule: f-5,,f-9
0       attempt-rule: f-5,,f-8
CLIPS>
```

The first firing of the *modify-rule-match* rule is based in part upon fact f-3 which represents the backward chaining rule shown following

```
IF main-course is poultry and
   meal-is-turkey is yes
THEN best-color is red
```

The actions of the *modify-match-rule* rule modify this backward chaining rule as shown following.

```
IF meal-is-turkey is yes
THEN best-color is red
```

The new fact representing the modified rule is f-8. This new fact represents the conditions of the initial rule which remain after the first condition has been satisfied. This new fact causes another activation of the *attempt-rule* rule which replaces the activation that was removed when the rule was modified. This new activation will assert a new goal to determine the value of the meal-is-turkey so that the consequent of the rule can be applied to assign the value of the best-color attribute.

The second firing of the modify-rule-match rule is similar to the first firing. The fact representing the rule

```
IF main-course is poultry and
   meal-is-turkey is no
THEN best-color is white
```

is modified to the following rule

```
IF meal-is-turkey is no
THEN best-color is white
```

which is represented by fact f-9. Similarly, this new fact causes an activation of the attempt-rule rule to replace the activation lost when the fact representing the rule was retracted.

Allowing the first attempt-rule activation to fire produces the following output.

```
CLIPS> (run 1) ↵
FIRE    1 attempt-rule: f-5,,f-9
==> f-10    (goal meal-is-turkey)
==> Activation 0      ask-attribute-value: f-10,,
rule firing limit reached
1 rules fired
CLIPS> (agenda) ↵
0      ask-attribute-value: f-10,,
0      attempt-rule: f-5,,f-8
CLIPS>
```

The fact f-10 is asserted representing a goal to determine the value of the *meal-is-turkey* attribute. Since no rule assigns the value of this attribute, the *ask-attribute-value* rule is activated to determine the value.

Allowing the *ask-attribute-value* rule to fire produces the following output.

```
CLIPS> (run 1)↵
FIRE    1 ask-attribute-value: f-10,,
<== f-10    (goal meal-is-turkey)
What is the value of meal-is-turkey? yes↵
==> f-11    (attribute meal-is-turkey yes)
==> Activation 100    remove-rule-no-match: f-11,f-9
==> Activation 100    rule-satisfied: f-11,f-8
rule firing limit reached
1 rules fired
CLIPS>
```

An *attribute* fact representing the value of the *meal-is-turkey* attribute is asserted as a result of this rule firing. The *goal* fact to determine the value of this attribute is removed as well. The new *attribute* fact causes two activations. The first activation is for the *remove-rule-no-match* rule. Since fact f-9's first condition is inconsistent with the value of the new attribute, this fact needs to be removed since the rule represented by the fact is no longer applicable. The second activation is for the *rule-satisfied* rule. Since fact f-8's remaining condition is satisfied by the new *attribute* fact, the consequent of this fact can be applied.

The remaining rule left to fire finishes the backward chaining process.

```
CLIPS> (run)↵
FIRE    1 rule-satisfied: f-11,f-8
<== f-8    (if meal-is-turkey is yes then best-color
is red)
<== Activation 0    attempt-rule: f-5,,f-8
==> f-12    (attribute best-color red)
==> Activation 100    goal-satisfied: f-5,f-12
FIRE    2 goal-satisfied: f-5,f-12
<== f-5    (goal best-color)
FIRE    3 remove-rule-no-match: f-11,f-9
<== f-9    (if meal-is-turkey is no then best-color
is white)
3 rules fired
CLIPS> (agenda)↵
CLIPS> (facts)↵
f-0    (initial-fact)
f-7    (attribute main-course poultry)
f-11    (attribute meal-is-turkey yes)
```

```
f-12      (attribute best-color red)
CLIPS>
```

The rule *rule-satisfied* is fired to assign the value of the *best-color* attribute as part of the consequent of the rule represented by fact f-8. The *attribute* fact asserted by this rule satisfies the remaining *goal* fact in the fact-list. The rule *goal-satisfied* is activated and then fired to remove the remaining *goal* fact. Finally, the update rule *remove-rule-no-match* fires to remove a fact representing an inapplicable rule.

The *agenda* command shows that there are no rules remaining to fire. The *facts* command shows the attributes that have been assigned values. Fact f-12 shows that the initial goal attribute *best-color* was assigned the value *red*.

12.5 A MONITORING PROBLEM

This section presents the step-by-step development of a CLIPS program as the solution of a simple problem. The development steps include the initial description of the problem, assumptions made about the nature of the problem, and the initial definitions for representation of problem knowledge, followed by an incremental buildup of the rules to solve the problem.

Problem Statement

The problem to be solved in this section is an example of a simple monitoring system. Monitoring problems tend to be well suited for forward-chaining rule-based languages because of their data-driven nature. Typically a set of input or sensor values are read during each program cycle. Inferencing occurs until all possible conclusions which can be derived from the input data are reached. This is consistent with a data-driven approach in which reasoning occurs from data to the conclusions that can be derived from the data.

For this example, the type of monitoring to be performed will be very generic in nature. A hypothetical processing plant will contain several devices which have to be monitored. Some devices will be dependent upon other devices for their operation. Each device will have one or more sensors attached to it which can provide numeric readings indicating the general health of the device. Each sensor will have an average expected value (AEV) associated with it, as well as low guard line (LGL), low red line (LRL), high guard line (HGL), and high red line (HRL) values. A reading between the low and high guard line will be considered as normal. A reading above the high guard line but below the high red line or below the low guard line but above the low red line will be considered acceptable, although it is an indication that the device may soon become unhealthy. A reading above the high red line or below the low red line will indicate an unhealthy device. An unhealthy device should be shut down. Any device in the guard region should have warnings issued for it. In addition, any device which appears to be heading toward a guard region should have periodic warnings issued. Table 12-1 summarizes the actions to be taken for a given sensor value.

Sensor Value	Action
Less than or equal to low red line	Shut down device
Greater than low red line and less than or equal to low guard line	Issue warning
Greater than low guard line and less than high guard line	None
Greater than or equal to high guard line and less than high red line	Issue warning
Greater than or equal to high red line	Shut down device

Table 12-1
Actions For Sensor Values

The monitoring program should be able to read in sensor data, evaluate the sensor readings and determine trends, and issue warnings and shut down devices based upon sensor evaluations and trends. Sample output from the monitoring program might look as follows:

```
Cycle 20 - System status has not changed
Cycle 40 - System status has not changed
Cycle 47 - Detecting an increasing trend for sensor 2
Cycle 53 - Detecting an increasing trend for sensor 2
Cycle 60 - Sensor 2 exceeds high guard Line
Cycle 61 - Sensor 2 exceeds high guard Line
Cycle 62 - Sensor 2 exceeds high guard Line
Cycle 63 - Sensor 2 exceeds high red line:
           Sensor taken offline
Cycle 83 - System status has not changed
Cycle 91 - Detecting decreasing trend for sensor 5
```

For this example, Figure 12-5 shows the connections between the devices and sensors to be monitored. Table 12-2 lists the attributes of each of the sensors.

Part of the solution of this problem involves taking the general description of the problem and determining specific details which must be resolved in order for the solution of the problem to be implemented. Typically this process would include iterative consultation with experts knowledgeable about the problem domain, but not necessarily able to completely specify the task intended to be captured by an expert system. Prototypes of the problem would be developed which point out missing details in the problem specification. These details would be determined through consultations with the experts and another prototype would be developed which may reveal further missing details in the problem specification. Eventually, the problem specification is completely captured through this iterative development programming philosophy.

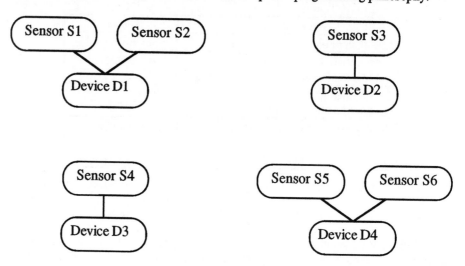

Figure 12-5
Devices and Sensors in Monitored System

Sensor	LRL	LGL	AEV	HGL	HRL
S1	60	70	100	120	130
S2	20	40	120	160	180
S3	60	70	100	120	130
S4	60	70	100	120	130
S5	65	70	100	120	125
S6	110	115	120	125	130

Table 12-2
Sensor Attributes

For this problem, many specification details remain unanswered. How will the various information about the sensors and devices be represented? How general or specific should the facts and rules be made? How will the sensor data be retrieved? What constitutes a trend for a sensor? What actions are to be taken when the monitor detects unhealthy devices?

The Details Necessary to Begin

One of the major problems encountered in building an expert system is that the problem, more often than not, is poorly specified. The idea is to emulate an expert, but no one except the expert is sufficiently knowledgeable to specify the details. Typically, the expected behavior of the system is known, but the manner in which this behavior is to be generated is not known. An expert may have difficulty in communicating the exact steps that are taken in coming to a solution. Because of the iterative development techniques that the expert system paradigm naturally supports, it is relatively easy to build expert systems that solve problems that are poorly specified. However, this does not mean the expert systems can solve problems that have never been solved before, or that problems that are not understood can be solved.

Several problem specifications are necessary before an expert system for this monitoring example can be built. First of all, the expected behavior of the expert system should be specified. The initial information that expert system is to start with and the information that the expert system is to produce should be decided upon before the expert system is built. This does not mean that this specification cannot change. Development of the program may indicate that scope of the problem should be narrowed or could perhaps be widened and this would affect the initial inputs and final outputs. Some assumptions must be made and initial details about how the expert system should perform its tasks must be decided. Again, these types of decisions are not permanent. Experts can very often demonstrate how they go about solving a problem, but often cannot easily formulate the rules they use to do so. In describing the rules they use, experts may often leave out details that are obvious to them or forget special exceptions.

The monitoring problem requires many initial decisions to be made. The first of these is in implementation. Should the solution be specifically geared to the exact details of the problem specification or should it incorporate enough generality to allow it to be easily upgraded or modified? Specific rules could be written for each of the devices to be monitored or a general rule could be written to monitor all of the devices. For this problem, writing general rules appears to be more appropriate because the devices and sensors to be modeled have no individually unique specific details. This type of generality should allow the easy addition of more devices and sensors. Details about the flow of control for the system are also missing. For this problem, a simple monitoring cycle will be used. Each monitoring cycle will have three phases. During the first phase values will be read from the sensors. During the second phase an analysis will be made of the sensor values. During the third phase, any appropriate actions will be taken. Assumptions must also be made about how the sensor data is to be retrieved. Will it be read directly from sensors? Will it be necessary to handle the simulation of sensor data? Will sensor data always be available when requested? Is the sensor data reliable or is it subject to error? The last major assumption involves trend analysis. The problem specification states that increasing and decreasing trends in sensor values should be detected. What constitutes such a trend? Under normal prototyping situations, the experts could be interviewed to determine this information, but for the purposes of this problem assumptions will be made to fill in details.

All of these questions point out gaps that may be encountered in a poorly defined problem. During development a list of assumptions, questions, and possible inconsistencies relating to the problem specification should be maintained. In the iterative development of the program, this list should be the focal point of discussion in interviews with experts to assure that the problem specification matches the expert's view of how the problem is to be solved. The beginnings of this list for the monitoring problem follows:

- Sensor data is always available upon request and is always reliable.
- Sensor values should be able to be read directly from sensors. Simulated sensor values should also be supported.
- Increasing and decreasing trends should be considered as an increase or decrease of a specified value over a specified period of time.
- Sensor values will not be monitored for a machine that has been shut down.
- The problem will be split into three phases: reading of sensor values, analysis of sensor values, and appropriate actions.

In addition to listing details of problem specification, details of problem implementation must also be decided. These details include how to represent the available information, flow of control, and testing of the expert system.

Knowledge Definitions

Once again, we start solving the problem by determining how the knowledge should be represented. A good start for this problem is to encode the knowledge contained in Figure 12-5 and Table 12-2. The following template will be used to describe each of the devices

```
(device <name> <status>)
```

where <name> is the id of the device and <status> indicates whether the device is on or off. Using Figure 12-5 and assuming the all devices are initially turned on, the following deffacts describes the initial state of the devices

```
(deffacts device-information
    (device D1 on)
    (device D2 on)
    (device D3 on)
    (device D4 on))
```

Figure 12-5 also indicates which sensors are associated with which devices. The following template will be used to represent this relation

```
(sensor <name> <associated-device>)
```

where <name> is the name of the sensor and <associated-device> is the device with which the sensor is associated. The following deffacts can be used to describe the sensors in Figure 12-5.

```
(deffacts sensor-information
   (sensor S1 D1)
   (sensor S2 D1)
   (sensor S3 D2)
   (sensor S4 D3)
   (sensor S5 D4)
   (sensor S6 D4))
```

The information for each sensor contained in Table 12-2 will be represented by the following template

```
(ranges <name> <LRL> <LGL> <AEV> <HGL> <HRL>)
```

where <name> represents the id of a sensor and <LRL>, <LGL>, <AEV>, <HGL>, and <HRL> represent respectively the low red line, low guard line, expected average value, high guard line, and high red line. Table 12-2 can now be represented with the following deffacts.

```
(deffacts guard-and-red-line-information
   (ranges S1   60   70 100 120 130)
   (ranges S2   20   40 120 160 180)
   (ranges S3   60   70 100 120 130)
   (ranges S4   60   70 100 120 130)
   (ranges S5   65   70 100 120 125)
   (ranges S6 110 115 120 125 130))
```

Since the monitoring system will be cyclic, a fact will be needed to represent the current cycle. The first cycle can be started at 1 and be incremented by 1 with each new cycle. The template for this information would be

```
(cycle <number>)
```

where number is the value of the current cycle. In addition, since sensor values might be read from more than one source (e.g. one source for simulation and another for actual operation), it will be useful to have a fact indicating the sensor data source. This fact can be represented with the following template

```
(data-source <source>)
```

where <source> is a name representing the source from which data is read. Potential sources could be the sensors, a simulator, a text file, a set of facts, or user input.

A deffacts containing this initial information is shown following.

```
(deffacts cycle-start
   (data-source user)
   (cycle 1))
```

Notice that the user will supply data for the sensors. For this example, entering data from the keyboard will be more convenient than reading data from a file.

Control of Execution

The statement of problem assumptions indicates that there will be three specific phases to the monitoring process. The first phase will read in either user-supplied, simulated, or actual values from the sensors. The second phase will associate guardline and redline conditions for the sensor values and determine any developing trends. Once trends have been established the monitoring system will issue any appropriate warnings, shutdown malfunctioning equipment, and restart equipment that can be brought back online.

Control of the monitoring expert system will be handled using the techniques similar to the ones described in Section 9.10. Control will be handled with the use of control facts to indicated the phase of the expert system. The *phase* facts will use the following template.

```
(phase <current-phase>)
```

where <current-phase> will be one of the values *input, trends,* or *warnings.*

Information about the which phases follow each other will be contained by facts described by the following template.

```
(phase-after <current-phase> <next-phase>)
```

where <next-phase> is the phase to be entered after <current-phase>.

The expert system will start in the input phase and cycle from input to trends to warnings and back to input again. The following deffacts describes this cycle using the templates previously defined.

```
(deffacts startup-phase-information
   (phase-after input trends)
   (phase-after trends warnings)
   (phase-after warnings input)
   (phase input))
```

The rule *CONTROL-Change-Phase* shown following will cycle between the three phases.

```
(defrule CONTROL-Change-Phases
  (declare (salience -10))
  ?phase <- (phase ?current-phase)
  (phase-after ?current-phase ?next-phase)
  =>
  (retract ?phase)
  (assert (phase ?next-phase)))
```

Notice that this rule uses one of the methods demonstrated in Section 9.10 for changing between phases of execution. The rule name for this rule has been prepended with the word *CONTROL* to indicate that this is a rule for controlling execution. Other rules in the system will be prepended with the word *INPUT*, *TRENDS*, or *WARNINGS* to indicated their phase of applicability.

The rule *CONTROL-Change-Phases* will be the only rule in the monitoring system given an explicit salience. All other rules will be given the default salience of 0. The salience hierarchy will be modeled after the hierarchy shown in Figure 9-4.

When to Change Cycles?

As execution of the monitoring system moves from cycle to cycle, the fact representing the current cycle must be updated to contain the current cycle of execution. Many of the rules will be dependent upon this fact. Its information must be updated in a correct and appropriate manner. However, during which phase should the cycle fact be updated? The cycle number should be up to date during the input phase when new sensor values are read, so this phase seems appropriate. However, it is not enough to update the cycle number as the following rule attempts.

```
(defrule INPUT-Update-Current-Cycle
  (phase input)
  ?f <- (cycle ?cycle)
  =>
  (retract ?f)
  (assert (cycle =(+ 1 ?cycle))))
```

This rule will update the current cycle, although a bit too eagerly. Once this rule fires, it will continue to loop endlessly. The problem with the rule is that even though it removes the old *cycle* fact that activated the rule, it updates with a new *cycle* fact that reactivates the rule. Assigning the rule a lower salience will not help; it will merely allow other input rules to fire before this one is fired, but the rule will still continue to loop. Removing the phase fact, however, as the following rule demonstrates would cause the rule to stop looping.

```
(defrule INPUT-Update-Current-Cycle
  (declare (salience -10))
  ?f1 <- (phase input)
  ?f2 <- (cycle ?cycle)
  =>
  (retract ?f1 ?f2)
  (assert (phase trends))
  (assert (cycle =(+ 1 ?cycle))))
```

This rule waits until the end of the input phase (with a salience of -10) before it updates the current cycle and transfers control to the trends phase. Giving the rule a low salience, however, is counterproductive to the desired purpose of the rule. The cycle should be updated at the beginning of input phase rather than at the end, so that during any cycle of execution each phase has the same cycle fact. The rule also directly changes the phase of execution. While this should not necessarily be strictly avoided, the current situation does not warrant this type of departure from the current control strategy.

The behavior that is desired is that given the next cycle of execution in the *input* phase, update to that cycle. In the *warnings* phase, given the current cycle of execution, determine the next cycle of execution. The two rules that produce this behavior are shown following.

```
(defrule INPUT-Process-Next-Cycle
  (phase input)
  ?f <- (next-cycle ?cycle)
  =>
  (retract ?f)
  (assert (cycle ?cycle)))

(defrule WARNINGS-Assert-Next-Cycle
  (phase warnings)
  ?f <- (cycle ?cycle)
  =>
  (retract ?f)
  (assert (next-cycle =(+ 1 ?cycle))))
```

In the *warnings* phase, the rule *WARNINGS-Assert-Next-Cycle* removes the old cycle of execution and asserts a new fact indicating the next cycle of execution. Because this rule has no salience and may opportunistically fire at any time during the *warnings* phase, the assumption is made that the *cycle* fact is not accessed by any other rules during the *warnings* phase. The rule *INPUT-Process-Next-Cycle* removes the *next cycle* fact during the *input* phase and asserts the updated *cycle* fact. Several assumptions are made for this rule. First of all, other rules that are dependent upon the current cycle cannot be activated until this rule has been fired. This implies that a *cycle* fact is not present in the fact-list when the *input* phase is entered. One exception will be made for this assumption for the first cycle of execution during which the current cycle will be explicitly asserted, rather than being asserted by this rule.

Reading the Raw Sensor Values

The next step in building the monitoring system is to read in the sensor values from the sensors. The logical phase to read the values is the *input* phase (by definition). For debugging and testing purposes, it will convenient to be able to read sensor values from several sources. This section will demonstrate how to read values directly from the sensors, from deffacts, from a file, and from the user. The data-source fact described previously is used to indicate the source of data for the monitoring system.

Sensor values read as "raw" data will be stored directly in a fact and processing and analysis of this raw value will be performed in the analysis phase. A template for the raw sensor value is shown following

```
(raw-sensor-value <sensor-id> <raw-value> <cycle>)
```

where <sensor-id> is the id of the sensor for which the value applies, <raw-value> is the raw data value for the sensor, and <cycle> indicates the cycle for which the sensor value was read.

Under actual operating conditions, the values would probably be extracted directly from the sensors, requiring external functions to do this work. Let's assume that the function *get-sensor-value* will return the current sensor value given a argument representing the sensor id for which the value is desired. The rule for directly reading sensor values is shown following

```
(defrule INPUT-Read-Sensor-Values-From-Sensors
   (phase input)
   (data-source sensors)
   (cycle ?time)
   (sensor ?id ?device)
   (device ?device on)
   =>
   (bind ?raw-value (get-sensor-value ?id))
   (assert (raw-sensor-value ?id ?raw-value ?time)))
```

The first pattern of the rule, (phase input), guarantees that the rule will only be active during the input phase. The second pattern of the rule, (data-source sensors), limits the rule to uses only when the data source is from the sensors. The third pattern, (cycle ?time), retrieves the current cycle. The next two patterns, (sensor ?id ?device) and (device ?device ?on), form the major part of the LHS of the rule. The rule will be activated for every sensor fact in the fact-list that has a corresponding device that is on. The RHS of the rule then makes an external function call to the function *get-sensor-value* with the id of the sensor and binds the return value to the variable ?raw-value. This raw sensor value is then asserted into the fact-list in a *raw-sensor-value* fact.

This particular rule might be difficult to use during the actual prototyping of the expert system. One technique for reading the sensor values would be to query the user directly for them. This would allow the maximum flexibility in debugging since the user will be directly queried for each sensor value. The following rule demonstrates how this can be done.

```
(defrule INPUT-Get-Sensor-Value-From-User
   (phase input)
   (data-source user)
   (cycle ?time)
   (sensor ?id ?device)
   (device ?device on)
   =>
   (printout "What is the value for sensor " ?id "? ")
   (bind ?raw-value (read))
   (if (not (numberp ?raw-value)) then (halt))
   (assert (raw-sensor-value ?id ?raw-value ?time)))
```

All of the patterns of rule *INPUT-get-sensor-value-from-user* are identical to the rule *INPUT-Read-Sensor-Values-From-Sensors* with the exception of the third pattern (data-source user). This pattern will limit the rule's activations to scenarios in which the data source is the user. The RHS of the rule is also similar with the exception that the user is queried for the value of the variable ?raw-value. Notice also the *if* expression that follows the binding of the variable ?raw-value. This expression will halt the program if a non-numeric field is returned by the *read* function. This test allows a convenient method for the user to halt execution of the program when sensor values are being entered.

For test cases or to avoid a great deal of user input, it might be more desirable to read data from a "script" rather than actually reading from a sensor or questioning the user for every value. One technique for accomplishing this would store the data in facts which the rules could then access. The following template describes a fact used to store data values

```
(fact-data-for-sensor <sensor-id> <<values>>)
```

where <sensor-id> is the id of the sensor associated with the data values and <<values>> is the actual list of data values for the sensor.

Using this template a deffacts containing test values might look like the following

```
(deffacts sensor-fact-data-values
   (fact-data-for-sensor S1 100 100 110 110 115 120)
   (fact-data-for-sensor S2 110 120 125 130 130 135))
```

```
(fact-data-for-sensor S3 100 120 125 130 130 125)
(fact-data-for-sensor S4 120 120 120 125 130 135)
(fact-data-for-sensor S5 110 120 125 130 135 135)
(fact-data-for-sensor S6 115 120 125 135 130 135))
```

The following rule could be used to access the data values from the *fact-data-for-sensor* facts.

```
(defrule INPUT-Read-Sensor-Values-From-Facts
  (phase input)
  (data-source facts)
  (cycle ?time)
  (sensor ?id ?device)
  (device ?device on)
  ?f <- (fact-data-for-sensor ?id ?raw-value $?rest)
  (not (raw-sensor-value ?id ? ?time))
  =>
  (retract ?f)
  (assert (raw-sensor-value ?id ?raw-value ?time))
  (assert (fact-data-for-sensor ?id $?rest)))
```

This rule is quite similar to the two previous input rules. The last two patterns on the LHS are worth comment. The *fact-data-for-sensor* fact contains the data values to be used for the sensor with the id bound to the variable ?id. The first data value in the fact is bound to the variable ?raw-value and the remaining values are bound to the variable $?rest. The first data value is then asserted as a *raw-sensor-value* fact. The *fact-data-for-sensor* fact is then retracted and reasserted with the just used data value missing. The last pattern in the rule prevents the rule from continuously looping, reading data values in from the *fact-data-for-sensor* fact. This rule will only be activated if there is no *raw-sensor-value* fact for the current cycle for the sensor in question. One final problem remains in that the rule will not fire if the *fact-data-for-sensor* fact has no data values. We now make the assumption that if there are no data values left for a sensor, then the system should be halted. The following rule handles this situation:

```
(defrule INPUT-No-Fact-Data-Values-Left
  (phase input)
  (data-source facts)
  (cycle ?time)
  (sensor ?id ?device)
  (device ?device on)
  (fact-data-for-sensor ?id)
  (not (raw-sensor-value ?id ? ?time))
  =>
  (printout t "No fact data for sensor " ?id crlf)
```

```
(printout t "Halting monitoring system" crlf)
(halt))
```

The final input technique to be discussed involves reading the information from a data file. This is more complicated than the previous examples. Several issues must be handled. The data file must be initially opened and the data must be read sequentially from the file. The previous input techniques were not dependent on reading the data sequentially, but rather could access the new data values for the sensors in any order. It is also not necessarily known how many sensor values have to be read and it is desirable to prevent hardcoding of such information in the rules. To add more complexity, an assumption will be made that sensor data values may be left unspecified in which case they will assume the raw data value of the sensor from the previous cycle.

The first issue which must be handled is to open the data file initially. To indicate that the data file has been opened a fact will be used to act as a flag. The presence of the fact (data-file-open) will indicate that a data file has been opened using the logical name *data-file*. The absence of this fact will indicate the need to open the data file. The following rule will open the data file if it has not already been opened.

```
(defrule INPUT-Open-File-With-Sensor-Values
   (phase input)
   (data-source file)
   (not (data-file-open))
   =>
   (bind ?flag file-closed)
   (while (eq ?flag file-closed)
     (printout "What is the name of the data file?")
     (bind ?file-name (readline))
     (if (open ?file-name data-file "r")
        then (bind ?flag true)))
   (assert (data-file-open)))
```

This rule has three simple conditions: The current phase must be the *input* phase, the data source must be a file, and the data file must not have already been opened. If these conditions have been met, then the RHS of the rule will open a data file thats name is supplied by the operator of the monitoring system. The *while* loop in conjunction with the variable ?flag set up a convenient method for insuring that the file supplied by the operator has been successfully opened. The operator will be repeatedly queried for the name of a source data file as long as the *open* function is unsuccessful in opening the file supplied. Once a file has been successfully opened, the *data-file-open* fact flag will be asserted.

The next decision involves the file format for storing the sensor data. It is desirable to be able to specify only those sensor values that have changed since the last cycle. Therefore, for a given cycle it is not known how many sensor values are to be read. The order in which sensor values are to be read cannot also be necessarily determined beforehand. These assumptions dictate a data format in which the id of the sensor is kept alongside the raw sensor value to be read. Since the number of data values to be read is unknown, the end of data values for a cycle will be indicated by the keyword *end-of-cycle*. The data format will look like the following.

```
S1 430
S2 300
S3 200
S4 500
end-of-cycle
S2 310
S3 215
end-of-cycle
S3 220
S4 490
end-of-cycle
...
```

The first rule needed is one to read all the raw values from the data file for the current cycle. The rule to perform this operation is shown following.

```
(defrule INPUT-Read-Sensor-Values-From-File
   (phase input)
   (data-source file)
   (data-file-open)
   (cycle ?time)
   =>
   (bind ?id (read data-file))
   (if (eq ?id EOF) then (halt))
   (while (neq ?id end-of-cycle)
       (bind ?raw-value (read data-file))
       (if (eq ?raw-value EOF) then (halt))
       (assert (raw-sensor-value ?id ?raw-value ?time))
       (bind ?id (read data-file)
       (if (eq ?id EOF) then (halt)))
     (assert (data-values-read)))
```

This rule reads all of the data values from the data file until the keyword *end-of-cycle* has been reached. If the end of file is reached, then the monitoring system is halted. The *data-values-read* fact that is asserted from the RHS acts as a flag indicating that the data file has been read for this cycle.

The following rule will remove the raw data value fact for any sensor that has been shut off so that reasoning is limited only to those sensors that are on.

```
(defrule INPUT-Remove-Values-For-Inactive-Sensors
  (phase input)
  (data-source file)
  (data-file-open)
  (cycle ?time)
  (sensor ?id ?device)
  (device ?device off)
  ?data <- (raw-data-value ?id ?raw-value ?time)
  =>
  (retract ?data))
```

The following rule generates *raw-data-values* facts for sensors that did not have data values in the data file.

```
(defrule INPUT-No-Data-Values-For-Sensor
  (phase input)
  (data-source file)
  (data-file-open)
  (data-values-read)
  (sensor ?id on)
  (cycle ?time)
  (not (raw-sensor-value ?id ? ?time))
  (sensor-trend ?id ?state ?raw-value ? ?)
  =>
  (if (eq ?state unknown)
    then
    (printout t "HALTING" crlf)
    (printout t "Previous sensor state unknown" crlf)
    (halt))
  (assert (raw-sensor-value ?id ?raw-value ?time)))
```

Notice that (data-values-read) pattern on the LHS of the rule. This pattern prevents this rule from being activated until the data for this cycle has been read from the data file.

The last two patterns on the LHS of the this rule are of particular interest. The second to last pattern looks for sensors that do not have a sensor value. The last pattern matches against a *sensor-trend* fact. This fact will be used to keep tract of trend information for the sensors and will be described in more detail in the next subsection. For now, it is only important to understand the significance of the fields in this pattern that are bound to the variables ?state and ?raw-value. The variable ?state will contain information about the previous state of the sensor (e.g. normal, low-guard-line, high-red-line, etc.). If this value is unknown, no previous information is known about the sensor. If this occurs, the monitoring system will be halted since it will be assumed that all the sensors should be started with some initial value from the data file.

If the sensor does have previous state information, the raw sensor value from the previous cycle stored in the variable ?raw-value will be used as the raw sensor value for this cycle.

Detecting a Trend

The next phase of activity, the *trends* phase, determines the current state of the sensors and calculates trends that may be developing. The current state of the sensor (normal, low or high guard line, or low or high red-line) must be determined from the raw sensor value asserted during the *input* phase. The current state of the sensor will be stored in a fact described by the following template

```
(sensor-state <sensor-id> <state> <raw-value>
               <cycle>)
```

where <sensor-id> is the id of the sensor, <state> corresponds to the state of the sensor (e.g. normal, low guard line, high red line, etc.), <raw-value> is the raw data value for the sensor, and <cycle> is the cycle for which the state information applies.
The following rule determine if a sensor is in the normal state.

```
(defrule TRENDS-Normal-State
   (phase trends)
   (cycle ?time)
   (raw-sensor-value ?sensor ?raw-value ?time)
   (ranges ?sensor ? ?low-guard-line ?
                   ?high-guard-line ?)
   (test (and (> ?raw-value ?low-guard-line)
               (< ?raw-value ?high-guard-line)))
   =>
   (assert (sensor-state ?sensor normal
                          ?raw-value ?time)))
```

The first pattern insures that the rule applies during the correct phase and the second pattern retrieves the current cycle. The third pattern retrieves the raw sensor value for which the state is to be determined. The *input* phase should produce one fact of this type for each sensor that has an associated device that is currently on. The *cycle* fact is actually unnecessary given the current construction of the rules. The variable ?time does not help to constrain the *raw-sensor-value* facts since these facts will all have the same value for ?time. If a history of all raw data were to be kept, however, then the *cycle* fact would be necessary to constrain the *raw-sensor-value* fact to the value generated for this cycle. The valid ranges for the sensor are retrieved by the fourth pattern. The only values of interest for testing a normal state are the low and high guard line ranges. Finally, the test pattern constrains the rule to situations in which the raw sensor value is in the normal state range. The only action of this rule is to assert the derived state of the sensor.

Four more rules are necessary to analyze the remaining four possible states of a sensor. Each of the rules will be similar to the rule *TRENDS-Normal-State* with the exception of the values retrieved from the *ranges* fact and the test used to determine the current state. All five of the state rules could be written as a single rule with an *if* expression on the RHS of the rule to determine the appropriate state of the sensor. This type of coding, however, defeats the purpose of a data driven system. In addition, further modifications involving actions and/or conditions of a subset of the possible states would be made much more difficult by a single unwieldy rule. The remaining four state analysis rules are as follows.

```
(defrule TRENDS-High-Guard-Line-State
  (phase trends)
  (cycle ?time)
  (raw-sensor-value ?sensor ?raw-value ?time)
  (ranges ?sensor ? ? ? ?high-guard-line
                        ?high-red-line)
  (test (and (>= ?raw-value ?high-guard-line)
             (< ?raw-value ?high-red-line)))
  =>
  (assert (sensor-state ?sensor high-guard-line
                        ?raw-value ?time)))

(defrule TRENDS-High-Red-Line-State
  (phase trends)
  (cycle ?time)
  (raw-sensor-value ?sensor ?raw-value ?time)
  (ranges ?sensor ? ? ? ? ?high-red-line)
  (test (> ?raw-value ?high-red-line))
  =>
  (assert (sensor-state ?sensor high-red-line
                        ?raw-value ?time)))

(defrule TRENDS-Low-Guard-Line-State
  (phase trends)
  (cycle ?time)
  (raw-sensor-value ?sensor ?raw-value ?time)
  (ranges ?sensor ?low-redline ?low-guard-line ? ? ?)
  (test (and (> ?raw-value ?low-redline)
             (<= ?raw-value ?low-guard-line)))
  =>
  (assert (sensor-state ?sensor low-guard-line
                        ?raw-value ?time)))
```

```
(defrule TRENDS-Low-Red-Line-State
  (phase trends)
  (cycle ?time)
  (raw-sensor-value ?sensor ?raw-value ?time)
  (ranges ?sensor ?low-red-line ? ? ? ?)
  (test (<= ?raw-value ?low-red-line))
  =>
  (assert (sensor-state ?sensor low-red-line
                        ?raw-value ?time)))
```

The five previous rules determine the state of a sensor for the current cycle. Since detecting trends in the sensors is one of the objectives of the *trends* phase, it will be necessary to maintain information about the past state of a sensor. The following relation will be used to store this information

```
(sensor-trend <sensor-id> <state> <raw-value>
              <start> <end>)
```

where <sensor-id> is the id of the sensor, <state> corresponds to the most current state of the sensor, <raw-value> is the raw data value associated with the state, <start> is the first cycle during which the sensor was in its current state, and <end> is the current cycle.

The rules which update the trend information will depend upon a *sensor-trend* fact existing in the fact-list for each sensor. For this reason, the initial sensor trends will be defined in a deffacts construct. The start state for each sensor will be indicated by the word *unknown* to indicate that the trend information is not yet valid.

```
(deffacts start-trends
  (sensor-trend S1 unknown 0 0 0)
  (sensor-trend S2 unknown 0 0 0)
  (sensor-trend S3 unknown 0 0 0)
  (sensor-trend S4 unknown 0 0 0)
  (sensor-trend S5 unknown 0 0 0)
  (sensor-trend S6 unknown 0 0 0))
```

With this information, two rules may be defined which monitor the trends for a sensor. One rule will monitor a trend that has not changed since the last cycle and the other will monitor a trend that has changed since the last cycle.

```
(defrule TRENDS-State-Has-Not-Changed
  (phase trends)
  (cycle ?time)
  ?trend <- (sensor-trend ?sensor ?state ?
                          ?start-cycle ?end-cycle)
```

```
      (test (= ?end-cycle (- ?time 1)))
      (sensor-state ?sensor ?state ?raw-value ?time)
      =>
      (retract ?trend)
      (assert (sensor-trend ?sensor ?state ?raw-value
                            ?start-cycle ?time)))

  (defrule TRENDS-State-Has-Changed
    (phase trends)
    (cycle ?time)
    ?trend <- (sensor-trend ?sensor ?state ?
                            ?start-cycle ?end-cycle)
    (test (= ?end-cycle (- ?time 1)))
    (sensor-state ?sensor ?new-state&~?state
                  ?raw-value ?time)
    =>
    (retract ?trend)
    (assert (sensor-trend ?sensor ?new-state
                          ?raw-value ?time ?time)))
```

The first two patterns of both rules establish both the correct phase and cycle. The next pattern and accompanying test find the sensor trend fact for the previous cycle. The test pattern should be unnecessary since only one *sensor-tread* fact should exist for each sensor. For the rule *TRENDS-State-Has-Not-Changed*, the next pattern checks that the state from the previous cycle is the same as the state for the current cycle. The conditional pattern ?new-state&~?state in the rule *TRENDS-State-Has-Changed* performs exactly the opposite test, making sure that the state has changed from the last cycle. In both rules, the raw value and the end cycle time are updated. If the state has changed, then the state value and start cycle time must be updated as well.

Cleaning Up

As the rules in the *input* and *trends* phases fire in each cycle, a large number of facts will be generated. The *sensor-state* and *raw-sensor-value* facts will be generated during each cycle of execution and are not specifically removed by any one rule as are the *sensor-trend* facts. Since the current cycle has been updated by the time the *trends* phase has been entered and rules in the *trend* phase do not depend on the previous cycle's *sensor-state* or *raw-sensor-value* facts, these facts can be removed without adverse effect in the *trends* phase.

In addition to the *sensor-state* and *raw-sensor-value* facts, the *data-values-read* fact may be asserted in the *input* phase to act as a flag. If asserted, this fact should also be removed. The following rule will remove all unneeded facts.

```
(defrule TRENDS-Remove-Old-Values-And-Flags
  (phase trends)
  (cycle ?time)
  (or ?f <- (sensor-state ? ? ? ~?time)
      ?f <- (raw-sensor-value ? ? ~?time)
      ?f <- (data-values-read))
  =>
  (retract ?f))
```

The rule *TRENDS-Remove-Old-Values-And-Flags* is quite simple, as are most cleanup rules. The rule removes any *sensor-state* or *raw-sensor-value* facts that have a different cycle time than the current cycle. In addition, the *data-values-read* fact will be removed if it exists. Generally, it is best to keep the amount of information in the fact-list small in order to increase efficiency. However, it is not always possible to cleanup all information. For instance, if a history of raw sensor values needed to be maintained, the old raw value facts could not be retracted.

Issuing Warnings

The final phase of the cycle is the *warnings* phase. Three types of actions must be handled during this phase: sensors that have entered a red line region will have their associated device shut off, sensors that have stayed in the guard line region for a specified number of cycles will have their associated device shut off, and sensors that are in the guard line region that did not have their associated device shut off will have a warning issued.

The following rule shuts off sensors that have entered a red line region.

```
(defrule WARNINGS-Shutdown-In-Red-Region
  (phase warnings)
  (cycle ?time)
  (sensor-trend ?sensor
                ?state&high-red-line | low-red-line
                ? ? ?)
  (sensor ?sensor ?device)
  ?on <- (device ?device on)
  =>
  (printout t "Cycle " ?time " - ")
  (printout t "Sensor " ?sensor " in " ?state crlf)
  (printout t "   Shutting down device " ?device
               crlf)
  (retract ?on)
  (assert (device ?device off)))
```

The state of a sensor is checked using the *sensor-trend* fact. If the sensor is in a red line region, the associated device is turned off. Devices are immediately shut off once one of their sensors enters a red line region, so it makes little sense to check how long a sensor has been in this state.

The rule *WARNINGS-Shutdown-In-Guard-Region* is similar to the previous rule with the difference that the sensor must have been in the guard line region for a period of time. The information for this period will be contained in a fact described by the following template.

```
(trend <sensor-id> <time-duration>)
```

where <sensor-id> is the sensor for which this period applies, and <time-duration> is the minimum number of cycles the a sensor must be in a guard line region for its associated device to be shut down.

The trend information is described by the following deffacts construct. Arbitrary values have been selected for <time-duration> since none were supplied as part of the problem definition. Experts would have normally been consulted at this point to determine exactly how a trend is detected.

```
(deffacts trends-information
    (trend S1 3)
    (trend S2 5)
    (trend S3 4)
    (trend S4 4)
    (trend S5 4)
    (trend S6 2))
```

With the *trend* fact now available, the following rule can be defined which shuts off sensors that have been in a guard line region for a period of time specified by the *trend* fact.

```
(defrule WARNINGS-Shutdown-In-Guard-Region
    (phase warnings)
    (cycle ?time)
    (sensor-trend
        ?sensor
        ?state&high-guard-line | low-guard-line
        ? ?start ?end)
    (trend ?sensor ?length)
    (test (>= (+ (- ?end ?start) 1)  ?length))
    (sensor ?sensor ?device)
    ?on <- (device ?device on)
    =>
    (printout t "Cycle " ?time " - ")
```

```
(printout t "Sensor " ?sensor " in " ?state " ")
(printout t "for " (+ (- ?end ?start) 1) " cycles "
          crlf)
(printout t "   Shutting down device " ?device
          crlf)
(retract ?on)
(assert (device ?device off)))
```

The addition of the *trend* pattern and associated test pattern is the only major difference between this rule and the *WARNINGS-Shutdown-In-Red-Region* rule. These two patterns determine if a sensor has been in a guard region long enough to shut down the device associated with the sensor.

The final rule for the monitoring system will issue a warning for sensors that are in a guard region, but have not been in the region long enough to warrant shutting off their associated device.

```
(defrule WARNINGS-Sensor-In-Guard-Region
   (phase warnings)
   (cycle ?time)
   (sensor-trend
       ?sensor
       ?state&high-guard-line | low-guard-line
       ? ?start ?end)
   (trend ?sensor ?length)
   (test (< (+ (- ?end ?start) 1) ?length))
   =>
   (printout t "Cycle " ?time " - ")
   (printout t "Sensor " ?sensor " in " ?state crlf))
```

This rule acts as the complement of the *WARNINGS-Shutdown-In-Guard-Region* rule. The test pattern has been modified to check that the sensor has been in the guard line region less than the number of cycles required to shut down its associated device. Since the sensor's associated device does not need to be shut down, the patterns to determine the associated device are not included.

This final rule completes the basis of a very simple monitoring system. Additional rules could be added to cover specific situations that should be monitored. In addition, more rules could be added to the system to provide a generic model for handling complex monitoring situations and representing sensor/device relationships.

12.6 SUMMARY

A technique for representing MYCIN style certainty factors in CLIPS was demonstrated in this chapter. Facts were used to represent Object-Attribute-Value triples. Two additional fields in each fact were used to represent the certainty factor of the fact and a unique id tag. Rules can compute certainty values for newly asserted facts on the RHS of a rule by using the certainty values bound in the LHS of the rule. A rule is then used to combine two occurrences of an OAV triple into a single occurrence with a new certainty factor computed from the certainty factors of the original pair.

This chapter demonstrated how decision trees can be represented using the forward chaining paradigm of CLIPS. Algorithms for traversing binary decision trees, multiple-branch decision trees, and learning multiple-branch decision trees were presented. The algorithm for a multiple-branch decision tree that learns was implemented in CLIPS.

CLIPS can also emulate a backward chaining inferencing strategy. A backward chaining inference engine was built using CLIPS rules. This engine was based in part upon an algorithm presented for accomplishing backward chaining in a procedural language. Backward chaining rules were then represented as facts and acted upon by the CLIPS backward chaining inference rules. A step-by-step trace of a sample backward chaining session demonstrated how this paradigm was represented in CLIPS.

The final example in this chapter was a simple monitoring expert system. An initial statement of the monitoring problem was used to begin the process of writing the expert system. Assumptions were made and additional details were added as more rules were added to the monitoring system. The execution of the monitoring system was split into three phases. The *input* phase gathered raw data values for the sensors. Several different methods for supplying data values were demonstrated. The *trends* phase analyzed the raw sensor values and checked for developing trends. Finally, the *warnings* phase issued warnings and performed appropriate actions based upon the analysis of the *trends* phase.

PROBLEMS AND PROGRAMS

12-1. Write CLIPS rules to combine MYCIN certainty factors as shown in Section 12.2 for the following two cases

$$\text{New Certainty} = (CF_1 + CF_2) + (CF_1 * CF_2)$$

$$\text{if} \quad CF_1 \leq 0 \text{ and } CF_2 \leq 0$$

$$\text{New Certainty} = \frac{CF_1 + CF_2}{1 - \min \{ |CF_1| , |CF_2| \}}$$

$$\text{if} \quad -1 < CF_1 * CF_2 < 0$$

12-2. Show how classical probability could be incorporated into CLIPS using the same types of techniques demonstrated in Section 12.2. List possible advantages and disadvantages of using classical probability in rules.

12-3.   Implement the *Solve_Tree_and_Learn* algorithm described in Section 12.3 using a procedural language such as LISP, C, or PASCAL. Test your implementation using the animal identification example.

12-4.   Implement the *Solve_Goal* and *Attempt_Rule* algorithms described in Section 12.4 using a procedural language such as LISP, C, or PASCAL. Test your implementation using the wine example.

12-5.   Modify rule *INPUT-Get-Sensor-Value-From-User* so that it will only allow numeric input from the user. The rule should cause a halt only if the word halt is entered during input.

12-6.   Modify rule *INPUT-Get-Sensor-Value-From-User* and add additional rules if necessary to allow the user to use a carriage return to indicate that the previous value of the sensor should be retained. For example, if the previous values for sensors 1 and 2 were 100 and 120, then the following responses to the questions

```
What is the value for sensor 1? ⏎
What is the value for sensor 2? 130⏎
```

should set the raw data value of sensor 1 to 100 and the raw data value of sensor 2 to 130. The functions *string_assert* and *readline* should be useful for solving this problem as well as the *trends* facts. What assumptions should be made and what actions should be taken if the previous sensor value is unknown?

12-7.   Modify the program so that a device that has been shut off will continue to have its sensors monitored. If all sensors for the device return to a normal state, then the device should be turned back on.

12-8.   The rule *WARNINGS-Sensor-In-Guard-Region* will issue a warning for a sensor even if a rule is on the agenda after it which would shut off its associated device. What change should be made to this rule to prevent it from issuing a warning if another rule in the *trends* phase would turn off its associated device.

12-9.   Add rules to print a message in the *warnings* phase to indicate that a sensor has had normal status for at least n cycles where the number n is specified in a fact. Print the message only every nth cycle.

BIBLIOGRAPHY

Koenradd Lecot and D. Stott Parker, "Control Over Inexact Reasoning," *AI Expert*, pp. 32-43, *Premier Issue*, 1986.

Morris W. Firebaugh, *Artificial Intelligence: A Knowledge-Based Approach*, boyd & fraser Pub. Co., p. 309, 1988.

APPENDIX A SOME USEFUL EQUIVALENCES

$\sim\sim p \equiv p$

$p \rightarrow q \equiv \sim p \vee q \equiv \sim q \rightarrow \sim p$

$\sim(p \wedge q) \equiv \sim p \vee \sim q$
$\sim(p \vee q) \equiv \sim p \wedge \sim q$

$p \wedge (q \vee r) \equiv (p \wedge q) \vee (p \wedge r)$
$p \vee (q \wedge r) \equiv (p \vee q) \wedge (p \vee r)$

$(p \wedge q) \wedge r \equiv p \wedge (q \wedge r)$
$(p \vee q) \vee r \equiv p \vee (q \vee r)$

$p \wedge q \equiv q \wedge p$
$p \vee q \equiv q \vee p$

$\sim(\forall x)\ P(x) \equiv (\exists x)\ \sim P(x)$
$\sim(\exists x)\ P(x) \equiv (\forall x)\ \sim P(x)$

$(\forall x)\ P(x) \wedge (\forall x)\ Q(x) \equiv (\forall x)\ (P(x) \wedge Q(x))$
$(\exists x)\ P(x) \vee (\exists x)\ Q(x) \equiv (\exists x)\ (P(x) \vee Q(x))$

Note: The $\forall$ does not distribute over an $\vee$, and $\exists$ does not distribute over $\wedge$, and so a new dummy variable z, is needed in the following two equivalences.

$$(\forall x)\ P(x) \vee (\forall x)\ Q(x) \equiv (\forall x)\ P(x) \vee (\forall z)\ Q(z)$$
$$\equiv (\forall x)\ (\forall z)\ (P(x) \vee Q(z))$$

$$(\exists x)\ P(x) \wedge (\exists x)\ Q(x) \equiv (\exists x)\ P(x) \wedge (\exists z)\ Q(z)$$
$$\equiv (\exists x)\ (\exists z)\ (P(x) \wedge Q(z))$$

APPENDIX B SOME ELEMENTARY QUANTIFIERS AND THEIR MEANING

Formula	Meaning
$(\forall x)\ (P(x) \rightarrow Q(x))$	For all x, all P are Q
$(\forall x)\ (P(x) \rightarrow {\sim}Q(x))$	For all x, no P are Q
$(\exists x)\ (P(x) \wedge Q(x))$	For some x, x are P and Q
$(\exists x)\ (P(x) \wedge {\sim}Q(x))$	For some x, x are P and not Q
$(\forall x)\ P(x)$	For all x, x is P
$(\exists x)\ P(x)$	Some x is P (or there are P)
${\sim}(\forall x)\ P(x)$	Not all x are P (or some x are P)
$(\forall x)\ {\sim}P(x)$	All x are not P
$(\forall x)\ (\exists y)\ P(x,y)$	For all x, there is a y such that P
$(\exists x)\ {\sim}P(x)$	Some x is not P

APPENDIX C SOME SET PROPERTIES

Commutativity
$$A \cup B = B \cup A$$
$$A \cap B = B \cap A$$

Associativity
$$A \cup (B \cup C) = (A \cup B) \cup C$$
$$A \cap (B \cap C) = (A \cap B) \cap C$$

Idempotence
$$A \cup A = A$$
$$A \cap A = A$$

Distributivity
$$A \cup (B \cap C) = (A \cup B) \cap (A \cup C)$$
$$A \cap (B \cup C) = (A \cap B) \cup (A \cap C)$$

Law of the Excluded Middle
$$A \cup A' = U$$

Law of Contradiction
$$A \cap A' = \emptyset$$

Identity
$$A \cup \emptyset = A$$
$$A \cap U = A$$

Absorption
$$A \cup (A \cap B) = A$$
$$A \cap (A \cup B) = A$$

de Morgan's Laws
$$(A \cap B)' = A' \cup B'$$
$$(A \cup B)' = A' \cap B'$$

Involution
$$(A')' = A$$

Equivalence
$$(A' \cup B) \cap (A \cup B') = (A' \cap B') \cup (A \cap B)$$

Symmetrical Difference
$$(A' \cap B) \cup (A \cap B') = (A' \cup B') \cap (A \cup B)$$

APPENDIX D SOME COMMERCIAL EXPERT SYSTEM TOOLS

A SUBJECTIVE VIEW OF THE IMPORTANCE OF VARIOUS EXPERT SYSTEM TOOL ATTRIBUTES FOR PARTICULAR FUNCTIONAL APPLICATIONS

● VERY ○ SOMEWHAT (blank) LITTLE

	DIAGNOSIS AND CLASSIFICATION	DATA ANALYSIS AND INTERPRETATION	DESIGN AND SYNTHESIS	PREDICTION AND SIMULATION	MONITORING	USE ADVISOR	INTELLIGENT ASSIST.	PLANNING AND SCHEDULING	CONTROL
INFERENCE APPROACH									
BC	●	○	○		○	○	○	○	○
FC & FORWARD REASONING	○	●	●	●	●	●	●	●	●
BC, FC, & FORWARD REASON.	●	●	●	○	●	○	●	●	○
HYPOTHETICAL REASONING	●	●	●	●	●	●	●	●	
OBJECT-ORIENTED	○	○	○	●	○	○	○	○	
BLACKBOARD	●	●	●	○	○	○	●	●	●
INDUCTION	●	○	○		○	○	○		○
OBJECT DESCRIPTION									
FRAMES	●	○	●	○	○	○	○	●	○
FRAMES W/ INHERITANCE	●	○	●	○	○	○	○	●	○
OBJECTS	○	●	○	●	○	○	○	○	●
PARAMETER VALUES PAIRS	○	○	○	●	●	○		○	○
LOGIC	○	○	○	●	●	●	●	●	●
RULES	○	○	●	○	●	●	●	●	●
CERTAINTIES	●	●	○	○	○	○	○	○	○
ACTIONS									
RULES	●	●	●	●	●	●	●	●	●
EXAMPLES	●	○	○	●		○	○	○	○
LOGIC	●	●	●	●	○	○	○	○	○
MESSAGES	●	●	●	●	○	○	○	●	●
PROCEDURES	●	○	●	●	●	○	○	●	●

COMPOSITE VIEW OF COMMERCIAL EXPERT SYSTEM BUILDING TOOLS

SYSTEM	TOOL LANG.	COMPILABLE	LANG/DB HOOKS (COMPUTERS)	1st UNIT COST
ART	L	D, IN	V, Su, S, L, T	65
KEE	L	IN	A, S, L, T, X, O	52† + SIM KIT
KNOWLEDGE CRAFT	L	IN	L, S, T, V, O	50† + SIM
PICON	L, C	Y	L, T	60
S.1	C	Y	370, V, Su, M, O	25, 45
ES ENVIRON/VM OR VMS	PA	IN	370	60
ENVISAGE (ADVISOR)	PA	Y	V, µV	25, 15
KES	C	Y	I, A, V, O, Su, µV	4, 7†, 25†
M.1	C	IN		5
NEXPERT OBJECT	C	IN	I, M, O	3, 5
PERSONAL CONSULTANT +	L	Y	I, TP, T	3
EXSYS 3.0	C	IN	I, V	0.4, 5
EXPERT EDGE	C	Y	I	2.5, 5
ESP FRAME ENGINE	PR	IN	I	0.9
INSIGHT 2 +	PA	Y	I, O	0.5
TIMM	F	R	TP, I, V, O	1.9, 19
RULEMASTER 3.0	C	DT	I, A, Su, V	1, 5, 17.5
KDS 3	A	R	I, TP	1.5
1st CLASS	PA	DT	I, TP	0.5
OPS5+	C	Y	A, Su, I, M, O	1.8, 3

Legend:

● STRONG   ○ FAIR   □ USER PROG.

FR — FORWARD REASONING

C — CONFID. FACTOR   F — FUZZY LOGIC   B — BAYSIAN LOGIC   I — INCOMPLETE INFO

L — LISP   PA — PASCAL   A — ASSEMBLY   F — FORTRAN   PR — PROLOG   O — OTHERS   C — C

@ D — DISCRIM. NET   R — RULES   IN — INCREMENTAL   Y — YES   DT — DECIS. TREE

@@ 370 — IBM 370   M — MACINTOSH   TP — TI PC   s — IBM PCs   L — SYMBOLICS   L — LMI
T — TI EXPLORER   X — XEROX   V — VAX   µV — MICROVAX   Su — SUN   A — APOLLO   O — OTHERS

† — INCLUDES TRAINING

Characteristics of Expert Systems Tools for Microcomputers

Name	AION DEVEL. SYSTEM	EXSYS PROFESSIONAL	FUSION (FIRST CLASS)	GOLDWORKS	GURU	LEVEL 5 1.0	NEXPERT OBJECT	VP EXPERT	KES II (2.4)	PERSONAL CONSULTANT PLUS
Functional Use	On PC: Advisory, help desk, front end to apps. not data intensive but interactive.	Wide range incl. diagnostics and real-time processing	Diagnostics, data analysis	Variety of applications	Variety, including medical and personnel applications	Variety of applications	All types including real-time	Services, individual aids, front ends to other systems.	Variety	Variety
K.B. Representation										
Rules	X	X	Decision trees	X	X	X	X	X	X	X
Certainty Factors	X	X	X	If/Backwrd Chaining	X	X		X	X	X
Frames w/Inheritance	Data Scoping	X		X			X			
Object-oriented	Objects as Data	X		If/Backwrd Chaining			X			
Logic										
Examples								X		
Procedures	X (by calling out)	X (by calling out)	X (by calling out)	X	X	X	X	X	X	
Inference Engine										
Forward Chaining	X	X	X	X	X	Limited	X	Forced	X	X
Backward Chaining	X	X	X	X	X	X	X	X	X	X
Demons	X	X	X	X			X		X	X
Blackboard		X	X				Forced			
Time Modelling		X				On VAX	X			
Truth Maintenance	X	X	X	X	Forced	X	X	X	X	X
Meta Control (Conditional Contrl)			X	X	X			X		
Logic										
Induction	X		Forced	X	X		X	X		
Math Calculations	X	X	X	X	X	X	X	X	X	X
Context (Viewpoints) (Through iteration)			X	X	Forced		X			
Pattern Matching			X	X			X		X	
Developer Interface										
Word Processor	X	X	X	X	X	X	X	X	External Packages	X
KB Editor	X	X	X	X	X	X	X	X	External	X
Menu	Commands		X	X	X	X	X	X	X	
Consistency Checks	X	X	X	X	X		X			
Graphic Rep. of K.B	X		X	X	X	X	X	X	X	X
Inference Tracing	X	X	Capture & Replay	X	X	X	X	X	External	X
Graphics Utilities				X	X		X		External	Special Package
Screen Formatting	X		X	X	X		X		External	X
Graphics Simulation					Business Graphics		X		X	Special Package
Why	X		X	X	X	X	X	X	X	X
How	X		X	X	X	X	X	X	X	X
Expand Explanation	X	X	X	X	X	X	X	X	X	X
Online Help	X	X	X	X	X	X	X	X	X	X
Syntax Help	X	X	X	X	X	X	X	X	X	X

Source: The Spang Robinson Report on Artificial Intelligence, December 1987, vol. 3, no. 12.

(continued)

Name	AION DEVEL. SYSTEM	EXSYS PROFESSIONAL	FUSION (FIRST CLASS)	GOLDWORKS	GURU	LEVEL 5 1.0	NEXPERT OBJECT	VP EXPERT	KES II (2.4)	PERSONAL CONSULTANT PLUS
Software										
Language of Tool	Pascal	C	Pascal,Assembler	GC LISP	C	Pascal	C	C	C	LISP
Compilable	Q2 1988	X	X			X	Incremental		X	X
Other Lang. Require.										
Operating System	DOS, OS2, all IBM MainF but DOS/VSE	MSDOS, UNIX, VMS	MSDOS	MSDOS	MSDOS, VMS	MSDOS, VMS	MSDOS, VMS, OS2 UNIX, MAC OS	DOS	MSDOS, XENIX, UNIX ULTRIX, VMS, MVS	MSDOS/Explorer
Computers Supported										
Symbolics										
Explorer										
Xerox										X
VAX	X	X				X	X		X	
IBM PC	X	X	X	X	X	X	X	X	X	X
IBM PS/2	X	X	X	X	X	Planned	X	X	X	X
Macintosh		This month				Planned	X		X	
Sun		X					X		X	
Apollo							X			
IBM Mainframes	X	Considering				Planned	Planned for 1988		X	
Other									Gould,HP,ATT,SG	TI Prof.
Systems Interface										
Language Hooks	All technically avail.	Any Proced.Lang.	C, Pascal	C,Frtrn,Pascl,Basic	C	Any Proc.Lang.	C,ADA,Cobl,Frtrn		Any Procedrl Lang.	C,Turbo Pascal,etc.
D.B Hooks	dBase, Lotus, RBase	dBase III	dBase,C,Pascal	dBase, Lotus	Own relatnl DB	dBase III	SQL,RDB,dBas,Lts	dBase wks files,ascii	Many inc. dBase, IMS	dBase, Lotus
End User Interface										
Line										
Menu	X	X	X	X	X	X	X		X	X
Graphics	Business	Third Party	X	X	X	X	X	X	External	X
Simulation		Third Party							External	Special Package
Why	X	X	X	X	X	X	X	X	X	X
How	X	X	X	X	X	X	X	X	X	X
Help		X	X		X	X	X	X	X	X
Multiple Solutions		X	X		X	X	X	X	X	X
Examples Saved			X							
What If	Done by Back-up		X		Forced	X	Forced	X	X	X
Company	AION	Exsys	Programs in Motion	Gold Hill Computers	mdbs	Level 5 (IBI)	Neuron Data	Paperback Sftware	Software A&E	Texas Instruments
Bottom Line:	$7000 PC, $70000 Main Frame	$795; $5-8000 for UNIX or VMS	Fusion: $1295, First Class: $495	$7,500	PC: $6500 VAX/VMS:$17000	$685	$5-8000	$124.95	$4-60,000	$2,950
(First Copy Price)										

Source: The Spang Robinson Report on Artificial Intelligence, December 1987, vol. 3, no. 12.

ATTRIBUTES OF THE COMMERCIAL ESBTs

NAME	ART 3.0	KEE 3.0	KNOW-LEDGE CRAFT	PICON	S.1	ES ENVIRON/ VM OR MVS	ENVISAGE	KES	M.1	NEXPERT OBJECT	PERSONAL CONSUL.*	EXSYS 3.0	EXPERT EDGE	ESP FRAME ENGINE	INSIGHT 2+	TIMM	RULE-MASTER	KDS 3	1st CLASS
FUNCTIONAL USES																			
Classification	X	X	X	X	X	X	X	X	X	X	X	X	X	X	X	X	X	X	X
Design	X	X	X		X			X		X		X		X			X	X	
Planning/Scheduling	X	X	X	X						X				X		X	X	X	
Process Control	X	X	X	X						X									
KB REPRESENTATION																			
Rules																			
Structured Rules	X	X	X	X	X	X	X	X	X	Catalogued	X	X	X	X	X		X	X	X
Certainty Factors				X	X	X	X	X	X 1000	2000	X 800	X 5000	X	X	X 2000	X	X	X 16000 from 4000 examples	X
Rule Limit																		X	
Frames w/inherit.	X	X	X	X	No inherit.					X	X			X					
Object-Oriented	X	X	X	X	X									X				X	X
Logic	X	X	X								X					X	X	X	X
Examples																			
Structured Examples	X	X	X		X	X	X	X	X	X	X			X					
Procedures																			
INFERENCE ENGINE																			
Forward Chaining	X (goal rules)	X	X	X	FR X	X	X	X	FR X	X	X	X	X	X	X	X	X	X	X
Backward Chaining	X	X	X	X	X	X	X		X	X	X	X		X	X		X	X	X
Demons	X	X		X															
Blackboard-Like	X	X		X						X			X					X	
Time-Modeling	X	X	X											X					
Truth Maintenance	X	X		X	X	X	X		X	X	X			X					
Meta Control	X	X	X		X														
Logic	X	X	X	X	X	X	X	X	X	X	X	X		X	X	X	X		X
Induction	X	X																	
Math Calculations	X	X	X																
Context (Viewpoints, Worlds)	X	X																	
PATTERN MATCHING																			
Variables	X	X	X	X				X	X	X	Numeric	Numeric	Numeric	Numeric & String	Numeric		X	Numeric	Numeric & Logical
Literals	X	X	X	X	X					X		X							
Sequences	X	X	X	X			X												
Segments	X			X															
Wildcards	X	X	X					X					X						X

ATTRIBUTES OF THE COMMERCIAL ESBTs (continued)

DEVELOPER INTERFACE														
KB Creation														
Word Processor	x		x						x	x	x	x	x	x x
Line Entry	x x	x x	x x				x x	x x	x x	x x	x x	x x	x x	x x
KB Editor	x	x x	x x	x			x	x x	x x	x	x	x	x x	x x
Menu	x	x x	x x				x	x	x x	x				x x
Check for Consistency	x	x	x	x					x	x	x	x		
Graphics Rep of KB	x x		x x	x	x				x		x		x	
Inference Tracing	x x	x x	x x	x •			x	x x	x x	x x	x	x	x x	x
Graphics Utilities to build end-user interface	x x	x x	x x					x x		x	x		x x	
Screen Format Utilities	x x	x	Sim Kit (Extra cost)	Simulation-Craft (Extra cost)	x x		x	x	x	x	x	x	x	x •
Graphics Simulation Capabilities	x x	x			x x				x					x •
Why	x x	x x	x x	x x	x	x x	x x	x x	x x	x x	x x	x	x x	TRACE
How	x x	x x	x x	x	x	x x	x x	x x	x x	x x	x x			
Explanation Expansion	x x	x x	x x	x	x x	x x	x x	x x	x x	x x	x x	x	x x	x x
Online Help	x x	x x	x x		x x	x x	x x	x x	x x	x x	x x		x x	x x
Syntax Help	x x	x x	x x	x x	x x		x	x x	x x	x x	x x		x	x x
Tool Extensible	x	x	x	x x	x						x	x		x
SOFTWARE														
Language of Tool	COMMON-LISP	COMMON-LISP	COMMON-LISP	ZETA-LISP-C	C	PASCAL	PASCAL	C	C	C	C	LISP	C	PASCAL
Compilable	Incremental	Incremental	Incremental	x	x	Incremental	x	x	x	x	Incremental	x	x	x
Other Lang. Req.	COMMON-LISP	COMMON-LISP	COMMON-LISP	LISP	C Compiler	CMS, GDDM, PASCAL/VS VM/CMS or MVS								
Operating Sys.	VMS, UNIX				UNIX VM/CMS VMS	VMS	MSDOS on PC	MSDOS	MSDOS VMS	MSDOS VMS	MSDOS VMS	MSDOS	DOS 3.0 UNIX, VMS	MSDOS
COMPUTERS SUPPORTED														
Symbolics	x x	x x	x x	x										
LMI	x x	x	x								VMS UNIX			
TI Explorer	x	x	x x	x										x
VAX			x x	x										x
XEROX	x	x							x	AT				
IBM PC							x	x	AT	x	x	x	x	x
Macintosh									x				AT	
TI Prof.										x		x		x
APOLLO			x x			x x		x x					x x	
SUN	x	x x	x x			x x		x x					x x	
IBM 370														
Others		x	x		x	x	x	x	x				x	x

ATTRIBUTES OF THE COMMERCIAL ESBTs (continued)

Company	Lang. Hooks	DB Hooks	Screen Cap. (Line / Menu)	Graphics / Simulation	Why / How	Help / Initial Pruning	Multiple Solution / Examples Saved	Mult. & Uncertain User Resp. OK	What If	Cost (1st unit)	Run Time Sys. Cost
Inference	Via Host Computer	Via Host Computer	x / x	x / Sim Kit	x / x	x / x	x /	x	x	$85K	$1-8K
Intellicorp	Via Host Computer	Via Host Computer	x / x	x / Sim Kit	x / x	x / x	x /	x	x	$52K includes training	PC Host + VAX $20K + 0.5K/PC
Carnegie Group	Via Host Mach	Via Host Mach	x / x	x / Simulation Craft	x / x	x /	x / x	x		$50K includes training	None Yet
LMI	Via Host Mach	Via Host Mach	x / x	x / x	x / x	x /	x /	x		$46K	
Teknowledge	C. Others	Via ~	x / x	• / •	x / x	x /	x /	x	x	$25K (1 user mach) / $45K (mult. user)	$9.5K
IBM	x	x	x / x		x / x	x	x /		x	$35K	$25K
Sys. Designers Software	PASCAL, etc.	x			x / x	x	x /	x	x	$25K on VAX / $15K on MicVAX	
S/W Arch. & Engr.	C	x	x / x	•	x / x	x / x	x /	x	x	$4K PC / $7K Wkstns / $25K VAX	10% of Develop Sys.
Teknowledge	x	x	x / x		x / x	x			x	$5K	-$50
Neuron Data	C, PASCAL	DBASE III	x / x	•	x / x	x / x	x /	x	x	$5K PC-AT / $3K MAC	$1K
TI	LISP	DBASE III	x / x	•	x / x	x / x	x / x	x	x	$3K	$75 First Unit
Exsys, CA Intell	x	x	x / x	•	x / x	x / x	x / x	x	x	$395 PC / $5K VAX	One Time Fee
Human Edge	x	x	x / x		x / x	x / x	x / x	x	x	$2500 Adv / $5000 Pro	$50
Exp Sys Inter	Prolog 2	Via ~	x / x		x / x	x	x		x	$895	By Agreement
Level-5-R	x	DBASE II	x /		x / x	x / x	x / x	x	x	$485	Negot.
GRC	x	x	x /		x /	x	x	x	x	$1.9K PC / $1K others	No Fee
Radian	Most	x	x /		x / x	x				$995 PC / $5K Wkst / $17.5K VAX	$100 PC / $500 UNIX/VMS
KDS Dev Sys	PASCAL, BASIC, Reada, Assem. Lang.	x	x /		x / x	x / x	x / x	x		$1495	Based on Quality
Prog. In Motion	ANY	x	x / •		x / x	x	x		x	$495	No Fee

NOTE: • = external programs; FR forward reasoning.

Source: William B. Gevarter "The Nature and Evaluation of Commercial Expert System Building Tools: Revision 1," NASA Technical Memorandum 88331, Rev.1, March 1987.

APPENDIX E CLIPS COMMAND AND FUNCTION SUMMARY

FACT COMMANDS

facts [<start> [<end> [<maximum>]]]	Display the facts in the fact-list
assert <<<fact>>>	Add facts to the fact-list
retract <<<fact-index or fact-address>>>	Remove facts from the fact-list

RULE COMMANDS

rules	Display the list of rules
pprule <rule-name>	Display the text representation of a rule
excise <rule-name>	Remove a rule

DEFFACTS COMMANDS

list-deffacts	Display the list of deffacts
ppdeffact <deffacts-name>	Display the text representation of a deffacts
undeffacts <deffacts-name>	Remove a deffacts

EXECUTION COMMANDS

run [<limit>]	Start execution of rules
agenda	Display the list of activations on the agenda
reset	Reset the knowledge base
clear	Clear the knowledge base
exit	Exit CLIPS

DEBUGGING COMMANDS

watch {facts, rules, activations, all}	Turn debugging options on
unwatch {facts, rules, activations, all}	Turn debugging options off
set-break <rule-name>	Set a breakpoint for a rule
remove-break [<rule-name>]	Remove a breakpoint for a rule
show-breaks	List all breakpoints

matches <rule-name>   List the matches for a rule

FILE COMMANDS

load <file-name>   Load a file of rules and deffacts
                                                              into the knowledge base
save <file-name>   Save rules and deffacts in the
                                                              knowledge base to a file
load-facts <file-name>   Load a group of facts into the
                                                              knowledge base from a file
save-facts <file-name>   Save the facts in the knowledge
                                                              base to a file
dribble-on <file-name>   Opens trace file
dribble-off   Closes trace file
batch <file-name>   Executes commands from a file

I/O COMMANDS

open <file-name> <logical-name> [<file-access>]   Open a file
close [<logical-name>]   Close a file
format <logical-name> <control-string>   Formatted output
  <<parameters>>
readline [<logical-name>]   Read a line of input
read [<logical-name>]   Read a single field
printout <logical-name> <<print-items>>   Simple output

ELEMENTARY MATH FUNCTIONS

+ <numeric-value> <<<numeric-value>>>   Addition
- <numeric-value> <<<numeric-value>>>   Subtraction
* <numeric-value> <<<numeric-value>>>   Multiplication
/ <numeric-value> <<<numeric-value>>>   Division

LOGICAL PREDICATE FUNCTIONS

not <predicate-function>   Boolean not
and <<<predicate-function>>>   Boolean and
or <<<predicate-function>>>   Boolean or

COMPARISON PREDICATE FUNCTIONS

eq <any-value> <any-value>	Equal
neq <any-value> <any-value>	Not equal
= <numeric-value> <numeric-value>	Numeric equal
!= <numeric-value> <numeric-value>	Numeric not equal
>= <numeric-value> <numeric-value>	Greater than or equal
> <numeric-value> <numeric-value>	Greater than
<= <numeric-value> <numeric-value>	Less than or equal
< <numeric-value> <numeric-value>	Less than

TYPE PREDICATE FUNCTIONS

numberp <value>	Tests for numeric value
stringp <value>	Tests for string value
wordp <value>	Tests for word value
integerp <value>	Tests for integer value
evenp <value>	Tests for even value
oddp <value>	Tests for odd value

FLOW OF CONTROL FUNCTIONS

if <predicate-function> then <<<actions> [else <<<actions>>>]	Procedural if
while <predicate-function> [do] <<<actions>>>	Procedural while
halt	Halts execution of rules

STRING FUNCTIONS

str_assert <string>	Assert the fields of a string as a fact
str_cat <<value>>	Create a string from one or more values
str-index <string> <string>	Returns the position of the first string within the second string
sub-string <integer> <integer> <string>	Returns a portion of a string

MULTIFIELD FUNCTIONS

mv-append <<items>>	Create a multifield value from one or more values
mv-delete <field-index> <multifield value>	Deletes a field from a multifield value
length <multifield value>	Number of fields in a multifield value
nth <field-index> <multifield value>	Returns specific field of a multifield value
member <field> <multifield value>	Determines if a value is contained within a multifield value
subset <multifield value-1> <multifield value-1>	Determines if one multifield value is a subset of another multifield value
mv-subseq <field-index-1> <field-index-2> <multifield value>	Returns a portion of a multifield value
str-explode <string>	Creates a multifield value from a string
str-implode <multifield value>	Creates a string from a multifield value

MISCELLANEOUS COMMANDS

bind <variable> <value>	Binds a variable
system <<values>>	Concatenates <values> and executes as a system command
gensym	Returns unique symbol

TRIGONOMETRIC FUNCTIONS

cos	Cosine
sin	Sine
tan	Tangent
sec	Secant
csc	Cosecant
cot	Cotangent
acos	Arccosine
asin	Arcsine
atan	Arctangent
asec	Arcsecant

acsc	Arccosecant
acot	Arccotangent
cosh	Hyperbolic cosine
sinh	Hyperbolic sine
tanh	Hyperbolic tangent
sech	Hyperbolic secant
csch	Hyperbolic cosecant
coth	Hyperbolic cotangent
acosh	Hyperbolic arccosine
asinh	Hyperbolic arcsine
atanh	Hyperbolic arctangent
asech	Hyperbolic arcsecant
acsch	Hyperbolic arccosecant
acoth	Hyperbolic arccotangent
pi	Value of π

CONVERSION FUNCTIONS

deg-rad <numeric-value>	Converts from degrees to radians
rad-deg <numeric-value>	Converts from radians to degrees
deg-grad <numeric-value>	Converts from degrees to gradients
grad-deg <numeric-value>	Converts from gradients to degrees

MISCELLANEOUS MATH FUNCTIONS

min <<<numeric-value>>>	Returns minimum value
max <<<numeric-value>>>	Returns maximum value
log <numeric-value>	Logarithm base e of argument
log10 <numeric-value>	Logarithm base 10 of argument
exp <numeric-value>	Returns $e^{<numeric-value>}$
sqrt <numeric-value>	Square root
trunc <numeric-value>	Truncate
abs <numeric-value>	Absolute value
mod <numeric-value> <numeric-value>	Modulus
** <numeric-value> <numeric-value>	Exponentiation

APPENDIX F THE MICROEMACS EDITOR

This Appendix is a brief introduction to the MicroEMACS Editor of CLIPS. MicroEMACS is a public domain editor which has been integrated with CLIPS and offers additional commands for CLIPS. To call the editor from within CLIPS, just enter the *edit* command at the top-level. The syntax of the *edit* command is

```
(edit [<file-name>])
```

If the optional <file-name> argument is not given, the editor will be entered without any file being loaded. If the <file-name> argument is given, the specified file will be loaded by the editor.

After the *edit* command is given, you will see the MicroEMACS logo appear in a window at the bottom of the screen. This window is used for displaying prompts and information from MicroEMACS. The upper window is used for text entry. The upper window may be split up into further windows, each with a separate buffer for storage of text.

Table F-1 lists several commands of general use.

Keys	Actions
<Ctrl-G>	Cancel any command. Very useful if you change your mind in the middle of a command sequence.
<Ctrl-L>	Refresh the screen.
<Ctrl-C>	Start a new interactive command shell. This command only works under Unix and VMS. Any text on the screen will appear to disappear since you are in a new shell. When you logout of the new shell, you will return to MicroEMACS. Be careful when using this command.
<Ctrl-X>!	Execute a single external command to the operating system.

Table F-1
General Utility Commands

To insert text, just start typing. Use the arrow keys on your terminal to move the cursor. Alternatively, if your terminal does not support arrow keys, other keys can be used. A list of cursor movement keys is shown following in Table F-2.

The Control key is symbolized by a "Ctrl". A dash (-) indicates that another key is to be held down while pressing the Control key. If another key then follows, release the previous. For example, <Ctrl-X-P> means hold down Control, press X, release X, press P, and then release all keys.

The Meta key is the Escape key or the sequence Ctrl-[on some terminals.

The angle brackets around keys indicate that they are to be pressed together and then released. The Repeat Count is a number that specifies how many times the next action is to be done. Press <Ctrl-U> and you will see the default value of Repeat Count equal to 4. To change Repeat Count, just type in the new value. For example, press <Ctrl-U> and then press the "A" key. Four As will be inserted at the cursor position. Do a <Ctrl-U> before every use of a Repeat Count command.

Keys	Actions
<Ctrl-A>	Beginning of line
<Ctrl-B>	Back one character
<Ctrl-E>	End of line
<Ctrl-F>	Forward one character
<Ctrl-N>	Next line
<Ctrl-P>	Previous line
<Ctrl-V>	View the next screen (scroll up one screen)
<Ctrl-X>:	Go to a specific line number.
<Ctrl-X>=	shows current cursor column and line number.
<Ctrl-X-O>	Deletes following blank lines
<Meta>!	Move current line to Repeat Count lines from top of window
<Meta><	Beginning of buffer
<Meta>>	End of buffer
<Meta>F	Forward one word
<Meta>B	Backward one word
<Meta>V	View the previous screen

Table F-2
Cursor Movement Commands

To delete a character, you can use the standard delete key for your terminal, <del>, or the keypresses shown in Table F-3. On some terminals, delete is <Ctrl-H>. Table F-3 shows some simple deletion commands.

Keys	Actions
<Ctrl-D>	Character under cursor
<Ctrl-H>	Previous character (to the left of cursor)
<Ctrl-K>	To end of line from cursor position
<Meta>D	Next word
<Meta><del>	Previous word

Table F-3
Simple Deletion Commands

More extensive operations on multiple lines can be done by defining regions. A region is defined by first setting a mark by holding down the <Meta> key and typing a period. Alternatively, the <Ctrl-@> keys can be pressed.

The mark is made at the current cursor position. The region is then the text between the mark and the current cursor position. So as you move the cursor, the region expands or contracts depending on whether the cursor is moving away or towards the mark. Only one region can be marked at a time. As soon as a new mark is made, the old mark is deleted. Table F-4 shows the commands which affect regions and buffers.

Keys	Actions
<Ctrl-W>	Delete region
<Ctrl-X>K	Delete a buffer (other than the current buffer). To find the names of all buffers, enter <Ctrl-X-B>.
<Meta>W	Copies region into Kill Buffer (does not delete it from current buffer). The Kill Buffer is a buffer into which deleted text is put. The last text put into the Kill Buffer can be retrieved using the <Ctrl-Y> command.

Table F-4
Region and Buffer Deletion Commands

The editor also has some commands for both searching and replacing text as shown in Table F-5. Commands to aid in insertions and for manipulating words and characters are shown in Table F-6. There are also a number of commands to save and load files as shown in Table F-7. Other commands shown in Table F-8 deal with using windows and buffers. The commands shown in Table F-9 let you set up keyboard macros to combine multiple keys.

Keys	Actions
<Ctrl-R>	Reverse search
<Ctrl-S>	Forward search. The <Meta-J> can also be used.
<Ctrl-X>R	Global reverse search and replace
<Ctrl-X>S	Global forward search and replace
<Meta>R	Query reverse search and replace
<Meta>S	Query forward search and replace

Table F-5
Search and Replace Commands

Keys	Actions
<Ctrl-I>	Insert Tab
<Ctrl-J>	Insert CR/LF and indent the next line
<Ctrl-M>	Insert CR/LF
<Ctrl-O>	Insert new line
<Ctrl-Q>	Quote the next character. This allows you to insert special control codes such as backspace or CR in the text. After the <CTRL-Q> should be the special character to be inserted.
<Ctrl-T>	Transpose characters. That is, switch the positions of the character at the cursor with the character on the left.
<Meta-C>	Capitalize first letter of word
<Meta-L>	Make lowercase next word
<Meta-U>	Make uppercase next word

Table F-6
Insertion and Manipulation Commands

Keys	Actions
<Ctrl-Z>	Save current buffer only and exit; Quick save
<Ctrl-X-S>	Save current buffer. The <Meta-Z> can also be used.
<Ctrl-X-W>	Save current buffer with option to change name
<Ctrl-X-C>	Exit without saving buffers
<Ctrl-X-F>	Find file. Load if not already in buffer.
<Ctrl-X-R>	Rename file. Change file name for buffer
<Ctrl-X-V>	Visit a file. Load file in current window.

Table F-7
File Commands

Keys	Actions
<Ctrl-X>1	Display only current window
<Ctrl-X>2	Split the current window
<Ctrl-X>B	Switch to a different buffer
<Ctrl-X>N	Move to next window
<Ctrl-X>P	Move to previous window
<Ctrl-X-N>	Scroll window up by Repeat Count lines
<Ctrl-X-P>	Scroll window down by Repeat Count lines
<Ctrl-X>Z	Enlarge current window by Repeat Count lines
<Ctrl-X-Z>	Reduce current window by Repeat Count lines

Table F-8
Windows and Buffer Commands

Keys	Actions
<Ctrl-X>(	Begin definition of keyboard macro
<Ctrl-X>)	End keyboard macro
<Ctrl-X>E	Execute a keyboard macro

Table F-9
Keyboard Macros Commands

The commands shown in Table F-10 are for convenience in using CLIPS and have been added to the basic MicroEMACS Editor. The commands to compile CLIPS programs are very helpful since you do not need to exit the editor. Once you have typed in the CLIPS source code into the editor, simply issue a <Meta-T> command and it will be compiled and loaded into CLIPS. You can then pause the editor, and return to CLIPS.

Keys	Actions
<Ctrl-X-T>	Compile region and load it into CLIPS
<Meta-T>	Compile the current buffer and load it into CLIPS
<Ctrl-X>Q	Return to CLIPS; do not clear editor
<Ctrl-X-C>	Return to CLIPS; clear editor
<Ctrl-X>M	Finds matching parentheses or { } or [ ]

Table F-10
CLIPS Commands for MicroEMACS

APPENDIX G THE STICKS PROGRAM

```
; **************
; FACT TEMPLATES
; **************

; The phase fact indicates the current action to be
; undertaken before the game can begin

; (phase
;     <action>)        ; Either choose-player or
                       ; select-pile-size

; The player-select fact contains the human's response to
; the "Who moves first?" question.

; (player-select
;     <choice>)        ; Valid responses are c (for computer)
                       ; and h (for human).

; The pile-select fact contains the human's response to
; the "How many sticks in the pile?" question.

; (pile-select
;     <choice>)        ; Valid responses are integers
                       ; greater than zero.

; The pile-size fact contains the current number
; of sticks in the stack.

; (pile-size
;     <sticks>)        ; An integer greater than zero.

; The player-move fact indicates whose turn it is.

; (player-move
;     <player>)        ; Either c (for computer)
                       ; or h (for human).

; The human-takes fact contains the human's response to
; the "How many sticks do you wish to take?" question.
```

```
;  (human-takes
;     <choice>)          ; Valid responses are 1, 2, and 3.

; The computer-take facts indicate how many sticks the
; computer should take based on the remainder when the
; stack size is divided by 4.

; (computer-take
;     <sticks-to-take>          ; Number of sticks to take.
;     sticks-if-remainder
;     <remainder>)              ; Remainder when stack is
;                               ; divided by 4.

; ********
; DEFFACTS
; ********

(deffacts initial-phase
    (phase choose-player))

(deffacts take-sticks-information
    (computer-take 1 sticks-if-remainder 1)
    (computer-take 1 sticks-if-remainder 2)
    (computer-take 2 sticks-if-remainder 3)
    (computer-take 3 sticks-if-remainder 0))

; *****
; RULES
; *****

; RULE player-select
; IF
;    The phase is to choose the first player
; THEN
;    Ask who should move first, and
;    Get the human's response

(defrule player-select
    (phase choose-player)
    =>
    (printout t "Who moves first (Computer: c "
              "Human: h)? ")
    (assert (player-select =(read))))
```

```
; RULE good-player-choice
; IF
;   The phase is to choose the first player, and
;   The human has given a valid response
; THEN
;   Remove unneeded information, and
;   Indicate whose turn it is, and
;   Indicate that the pile size should be chosen

(defrule good-player-choice
   ?phase <- (phase choose-player)
   ?choice <- (player-select ?player&c | h)
   =>
   (retract ?phase ?choice)
   (assert (player-move ?player))
   (assert (phase select-pile-size)))

; RULE bad-player-choice
; IF
;   The phase is to choose the first player, and
;   The human has given a invalid response
; THEN
;   Remove unneeded information, and
;   Indicate that the first player should be chosen again,
;   and Print the valid choices

(defrule bad-player-choice
   ?phase <- (phase choose-player)
   ?choice <- (player-select ?player&~c&~h)
   =>
   (retract ?phase ?choice)
   (assert (phase choose-player))
   (printout t "Choose c or h." crlf))

; RULE pile-select
; IF
;   The phase is to choose the pile size
; THEN
;   Ask what the pile size should be, and
;   Get the human's response
```

```
(defrule pile-select
   (phase select-pile-size)
   =>
   (printout t "How many sticks in the pile? ")
   (assert (pile-select =(read))))
```

```
; RULE good-pile-choice
; IF
;    The phase is to choose the pile size, and
;    The human has given a valid response
; THEN
;    Remove unneeded information, and
;    Store the pile size
```

```
(defrule good-pile-choice
   ?phase <- (phase select-pile-size)
   ?choice <- (pile-select ?size&:(integerp ?size)
                                  &:(> ?size 0))
   =>
   (retract ?phase ?choice)
   (assert (pile-size ?size)))
```

```
; RULE bad-pile-choice
; IF
;    The phase is to choose the pile size, and
;    The human has given a invalid response
; THEN
;    Remove unneeded information, and
;    Indicate that the pile size should be chosen again,
;    and Print the valid choices
```

```
(defrule bad-pile-choice
   ?phase <- (phase select-pile-size)
   ?choice <- (pile-select ?size&~:(integerp ?size)
                                   |:(<= ?size 0))
   =>
   (retract ?phase ?choice)
   (assert (phase select-pile-size))
   (printout t "Choose an integer greater than zero."
             crlf))
```

```
; RULE computer-loses
; IF
;    The pile size is 1, and
;    It is the computer's move
; THEN
;    Print that the computer has lost the game

(defrule computer-loses
    (pile-size 1)
    (player-move c)
    =>
    (printout t "Computer must take the last stick!" crlf)
    (printout t "I lose!" crlf))


; RULE human-loses
; IF
;    The pile size is 1, and
;    It is the human's move
; THEN
;    Print that the human has lost the game

(defrule human-loses
    (pile-size 1)
    (player-move h)
    =>
    (printout t "You must take the last stick!" crlf)
    (printout t "You lose!" crlf))


; RULE get-human-move
; IF
;    The pile size is greater than 1, and
;    It is the human's move
; THEN
;    Ask how many sticks to take, and
;    Get the human's response

(defrule get-human-move
    (pile-size ?size&:(> ?size 1))
    (player-move h)
    =>
    (printout t "How many sticks do you wish to take? ")
    (assert (human-takes =(read))))
```

```
; RULE good-human-move
; IF
;    There is a pile of sticks, and
;    The human has chosen how many sticks to take, and
;    It is the human's move, and
;    The human's choice is valid
; THEN
;    Remove unneeded information, and
;    Compute the new pile size, and
;    Update the pile size, and
;    Print the number of sticks left in the stack, and
;    Trigger the computer player's turn

(defrule good-human-move
    ?pile <- (pile-size ?size)
    ?move <- (human-takes ?choice)
    ?whose-turn <- (player-move h)
    (test (and (integerp ?choice)
               (>= ?choice 1)
               (<= ?choice 3)
               (< ?choice ?size)))
    =>
    (retract ?pile ?move ?whose-turn)
    (bind ?new-size (- ?size ?choice))
    (assert (pile-size ?new-size))
    (printout t ?new-size " stick(s) left in the pile."
              crlf)
    (assert (player-move c)))

; RULE bad-human-move
; IF
;    There is a pile of sticks, and
;    The human has chosen how many sticks to take, and
;    It is the human's move, and
;    The human's choice is invalid
; THEN
;    Print the valid choices, and
;    Remove unneeded information, and
;    Retrigger the human player's move
```

```
(defrule bad-human-move
    (pile-size ?size)
    ?move <- (human-takes ?choice)
    ?whose-turn <- (player-move h)
    (test (or (not (integerp ?choice))
              (< ?choice 1)
              (> ?choice 3)
              (>= ?choice ?size)))
    =>
    (printout t "Number of sticks must be between 1 and 3,"
              crlf
              "and you must be forced to take the last "
              "stick." crlf)
    (retract ?move ?whose-turn)
    (assert (player-move h)))


; RULE computer-move
; IF
;   It is the computers's move, and
;   The pile size is greater than 1, and
;   The computer's response is available
; THEN
;   Remove unneeded information, and
;   Compute the new pile size, and
;   Print the number of sticks left in the stack, and
;   Update the pile size, and
;   Trigger the human players move

(defrule computer-move
    ?whose-turn <- (player-move c)
    ?pile <- (pile-size ?size&:(> ?size 1))
    (computer-take ?number sticks-if-remainder
                   =(mod ?size 4))
    =>
    (retract ?whose-turn ?pile)
    (bind ?new-size (- ?size ?number))
    (printout t "Computer takes " ?number " stick(s)."
              crlf)
    (printout t ?new-size " stick(s) left in the pile."
              crlf)
    (assert (pile-size ?new-size))
    (assert (player-move h)))
```

INDEX

A

a posteriori 63
a posteriori probability 195
a priori 63
a priori probability 190
α-cuts 300
A-KIND-OF 70
abduction 169
abs 493
absolute probability 200
accuracy 187
act 30, 204
action frame 85
actions 29, 435
activated 13, 29, 386
activation function 50
acyclic 108
addition 428
Additive Law 199
adequate 96
affirmative in quality 123
agenda 26, 386, 387, 454
AKO 70
algorithm 37
algorithmic programming 37
alpha memory 506
alternative denial 96
ambiguity 186
ampersand 425
analogy 8, 166
AND constraint 425
AND field constraint 427
angle brackets 67
ANS 48
antecedent 27, 122
APL 40
application operations 40
approximate reasoning 320
arcs 70
ARE 72
arguments 119, 428, 430
arithmetic operators 428
arrow 386
ART 373, 431, 501

artificial neural systems 48
askable nodes 235
assert 382, 431
assertion 139, 236
association 38
associative memory 52
associative nets 70
assuming the antecedent 128
assumption-based truth maintenance 172
atomic 69
atoms 40
attenuation factor 272
Attribute-Value pairs 74, 549
attributes 72
autoepistemic reasoning 173
automated knowledge acquisition 109
automated reasoning systems 87
AV 74
axioms 92, 139

B

back-propagation 50, 53
backtracking 46
backward chaining 28, 208, 549
backward induction 208
bandwidth 298
bar 39, 67
basic assignment 279
basic probability assignment 279
batch 494
Bayes' Theorem 204
Bayesian decision making 205
Bel 284
belief function 284
belief measure 284
beta memory 508
biconditional 93
binary variable 308
bind 408, 434
bivalent logic 292
blocks world 413, 422
body 474